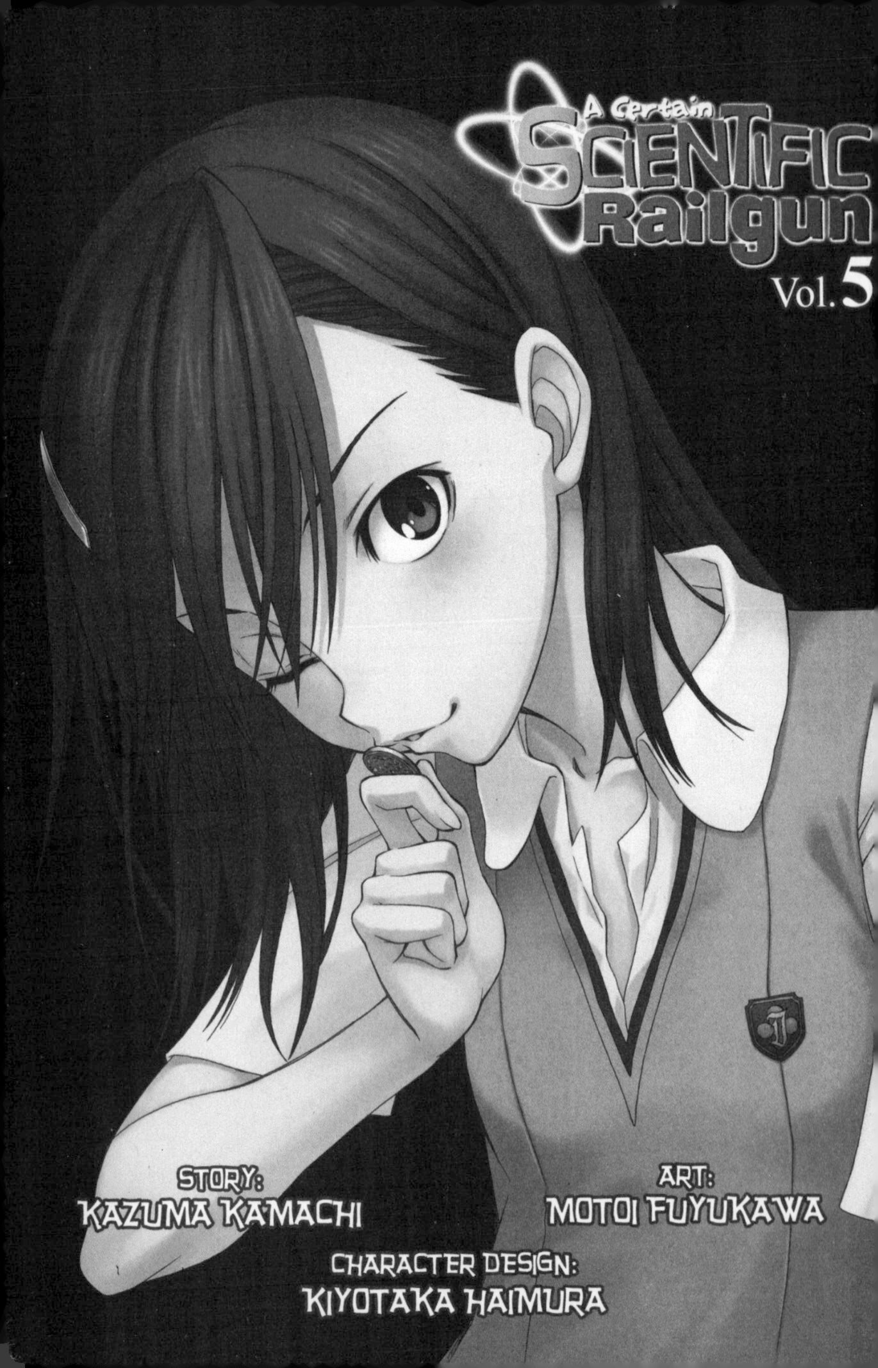
A Certain SCIENTIFIC Railgun
Vol. 5
STORY:
KAZUMA KAMACHI
ART:
MOTOI FUYUKAWA
CHARACTER DESIGN:
KIYOTAKA HAIMURA

A Certain SCIENTIFIC Railgun
VOLUME 5

story by **Kazuma Kamachi**

art by **Motoi Fuyukawa**

Character Design **Kiyotaka Haimura**

STAFF CREDITS

translation	**Nan Rymer**
adaptation	**Janet Houck, Maggie Danger**
lettering	**Roland Amago**
layout	**Bambi Eloriaga-Amago**
cover design	**Nicky Lim**
copy editor	**Shanti Whitesides**
assistant editor	**Alexis Roberts**
editor	**Jason DeAngelis**
publisher	**Seven Seas Entertainment**

A CERTAIN SCIENTIFIC RAILGUN VOL. 5
Copyright © 2010 Kazuma Kamachi / Motoi Fuyukawa
First published in 2010 by ASCII MEDIA WORKS, Tokyo, Japan.
English translation rights arranged with ASCII MEDIA WORKS.

ISBN: 978-1-935934-78-3

Printed in Canada

First Printing: August 2012

10 9 8 7 6 5 4 3 2

Seven Seas

FOLLOW US ONLINE: www.gomanga.com

READING DIRECTIONS

This book reads from *right to left*, Japanese style.
If this is your first time reading manga, you start
reading from the top right panel on each page and
take it from there. If you get lost, just follow the
numbered diagram here. It may seem backwards
at first, but you'll get the hang of it! Have fun!!

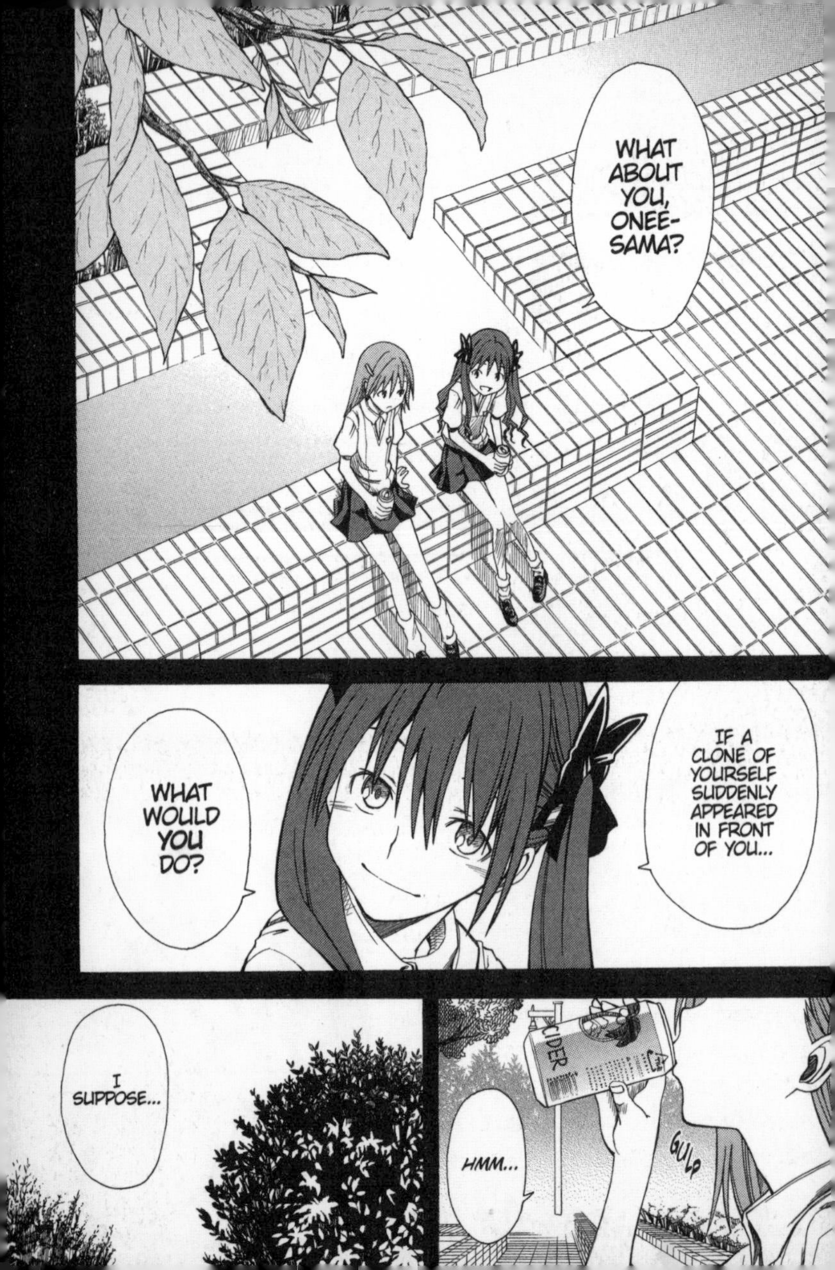
WHAT ABOUT YOU, ONEE-SAMA?
IF A CLONE OF YOURSELF SUDDENLY APPEARED IN FRONT OF YOU...
WHAT WOULD YOU DO?
CIDER
GULP
HMM...
I SUPPOSE...

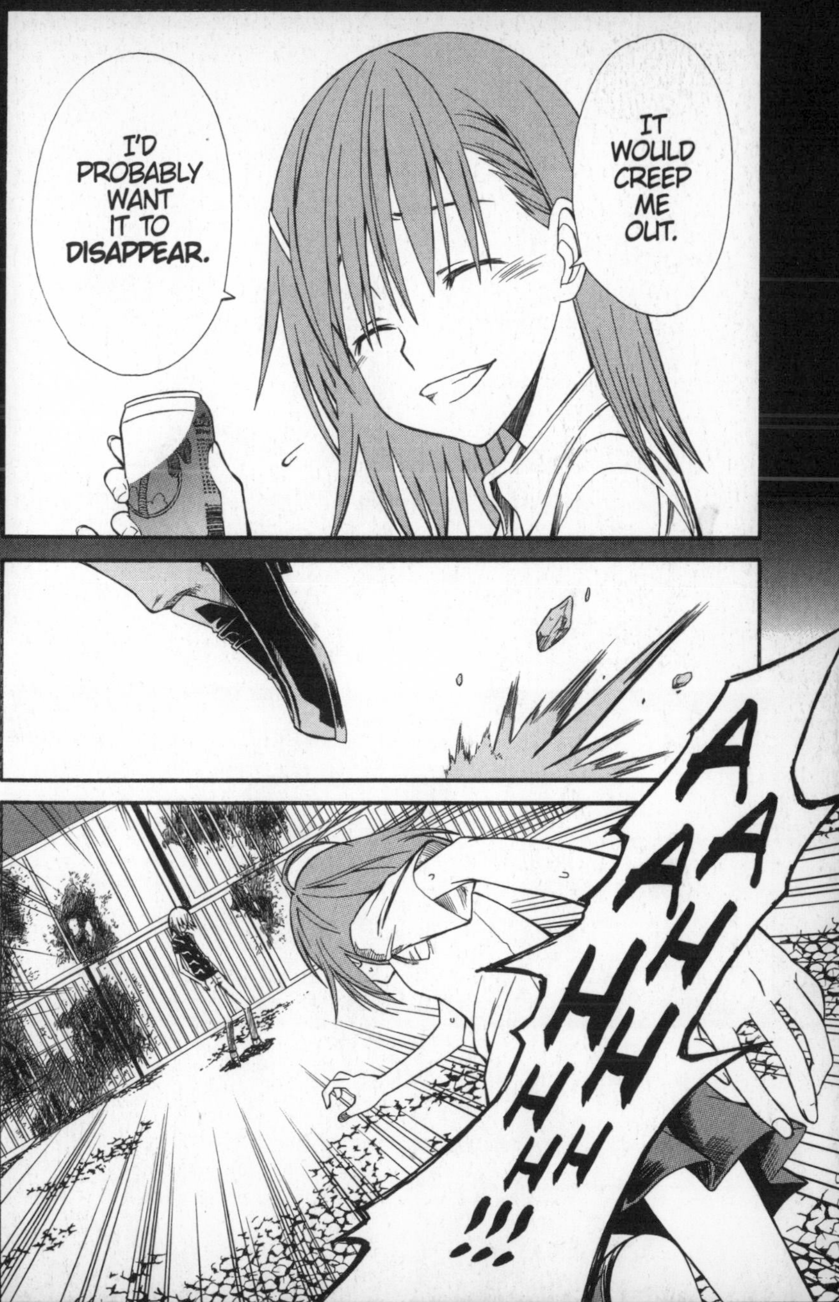
IT WOULD CREEP ME OUT.
I'D PROBABLY WANT IT TO DISAPPEAR.
AAAAHHHHHHHH!!!

[redacted]

CHAPTER 24: AUGUST 15 (4)

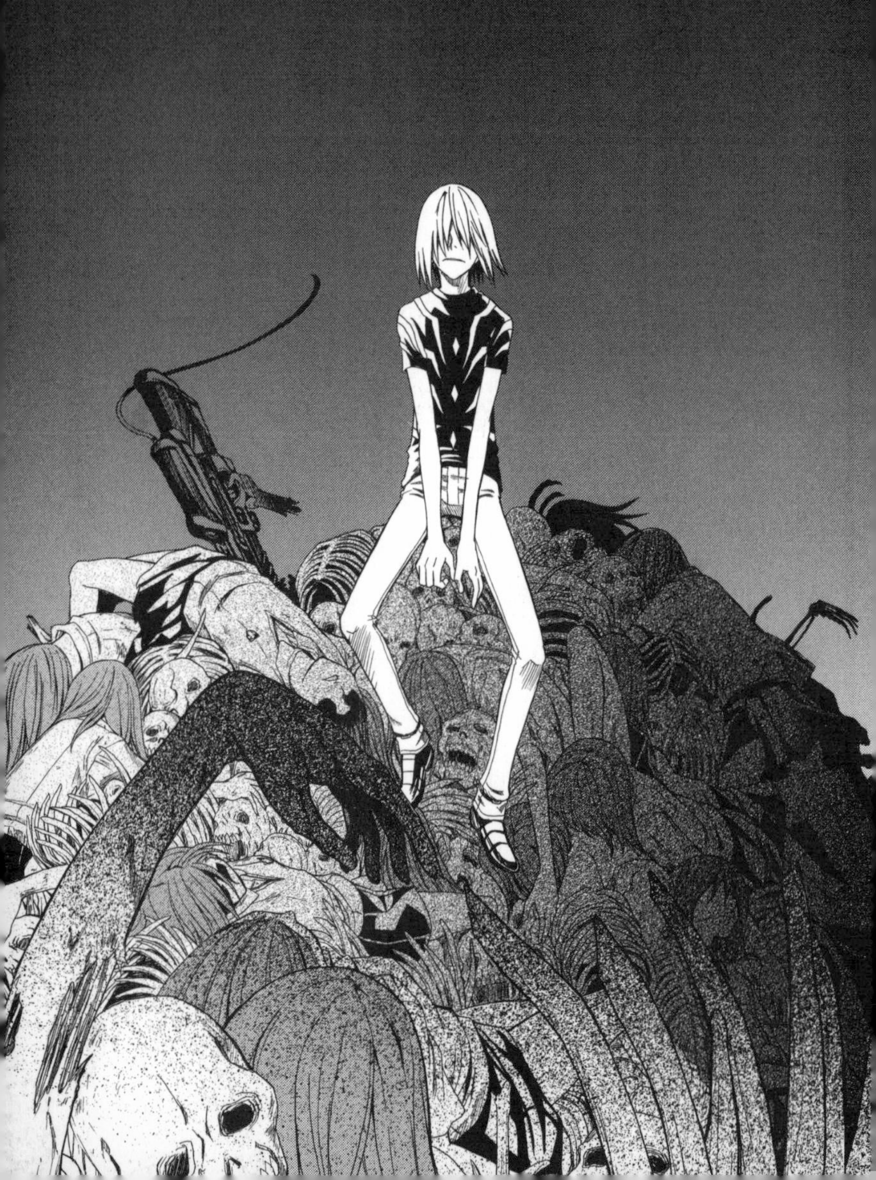

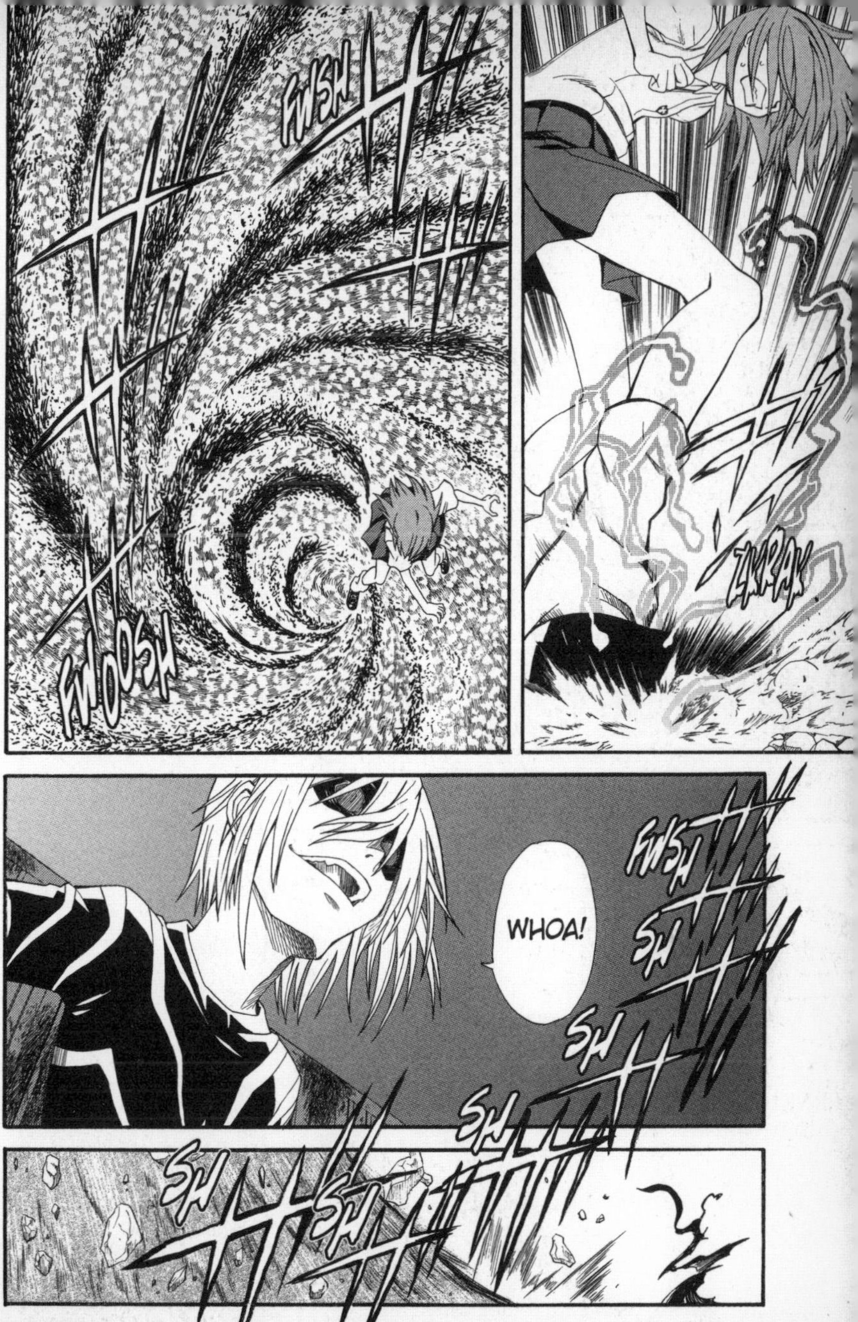
FWSH
FWOOSH
FWSH
SH
SH
WHOA!
SH
SH
SH

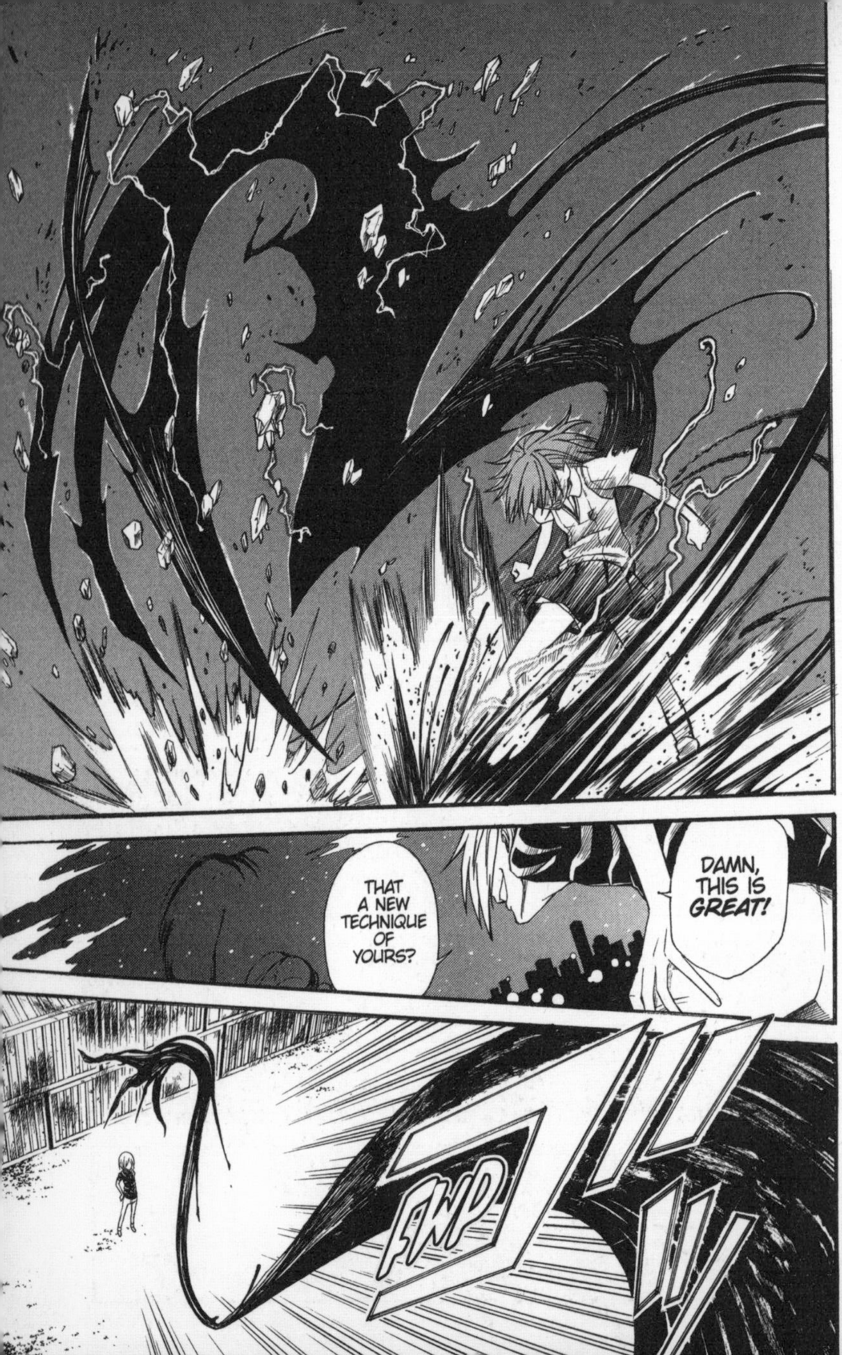
DAMN, THIS IS GREAT!
THAT A NEW TECHNIQUE OF YOURS?
FWP

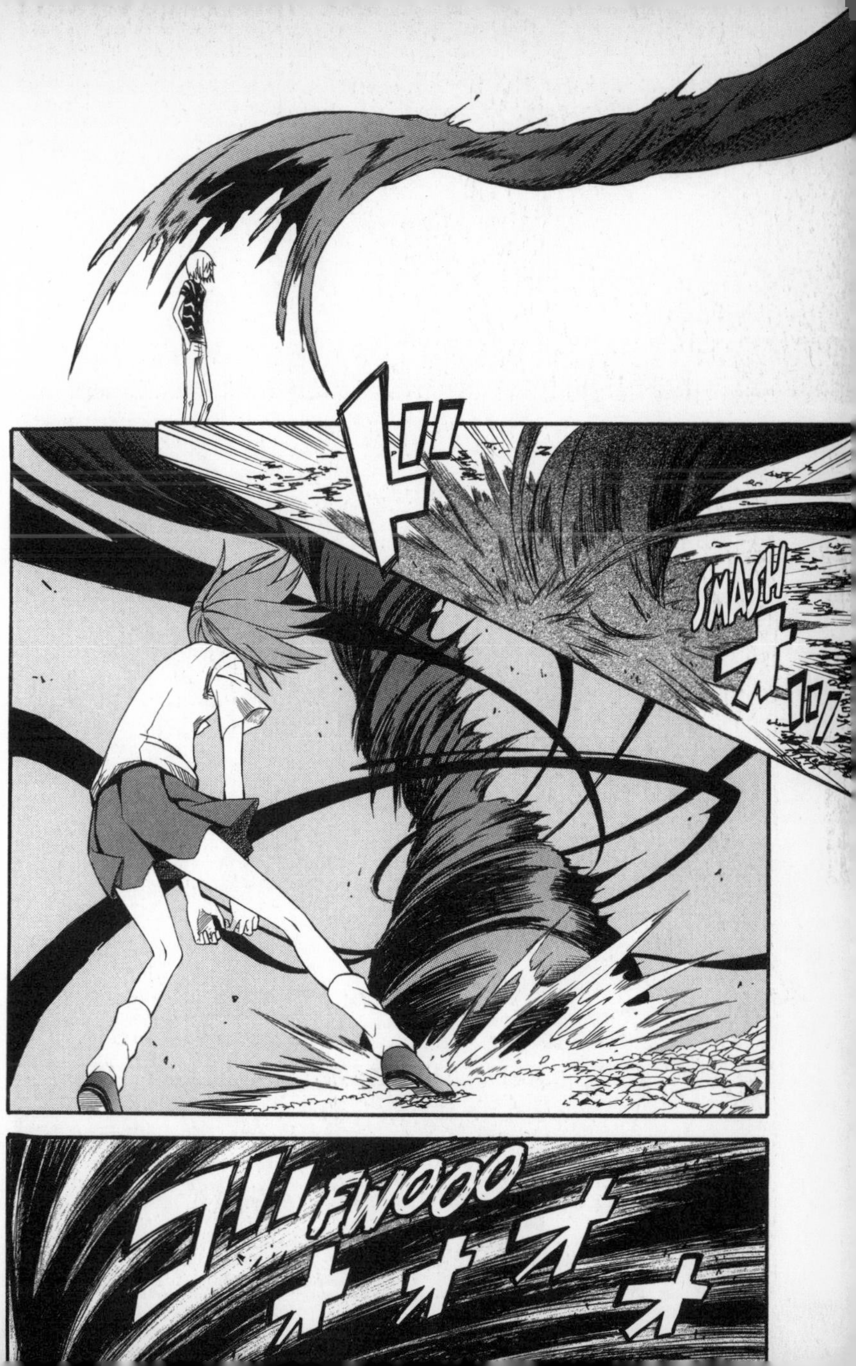
SMASH
FWOOO

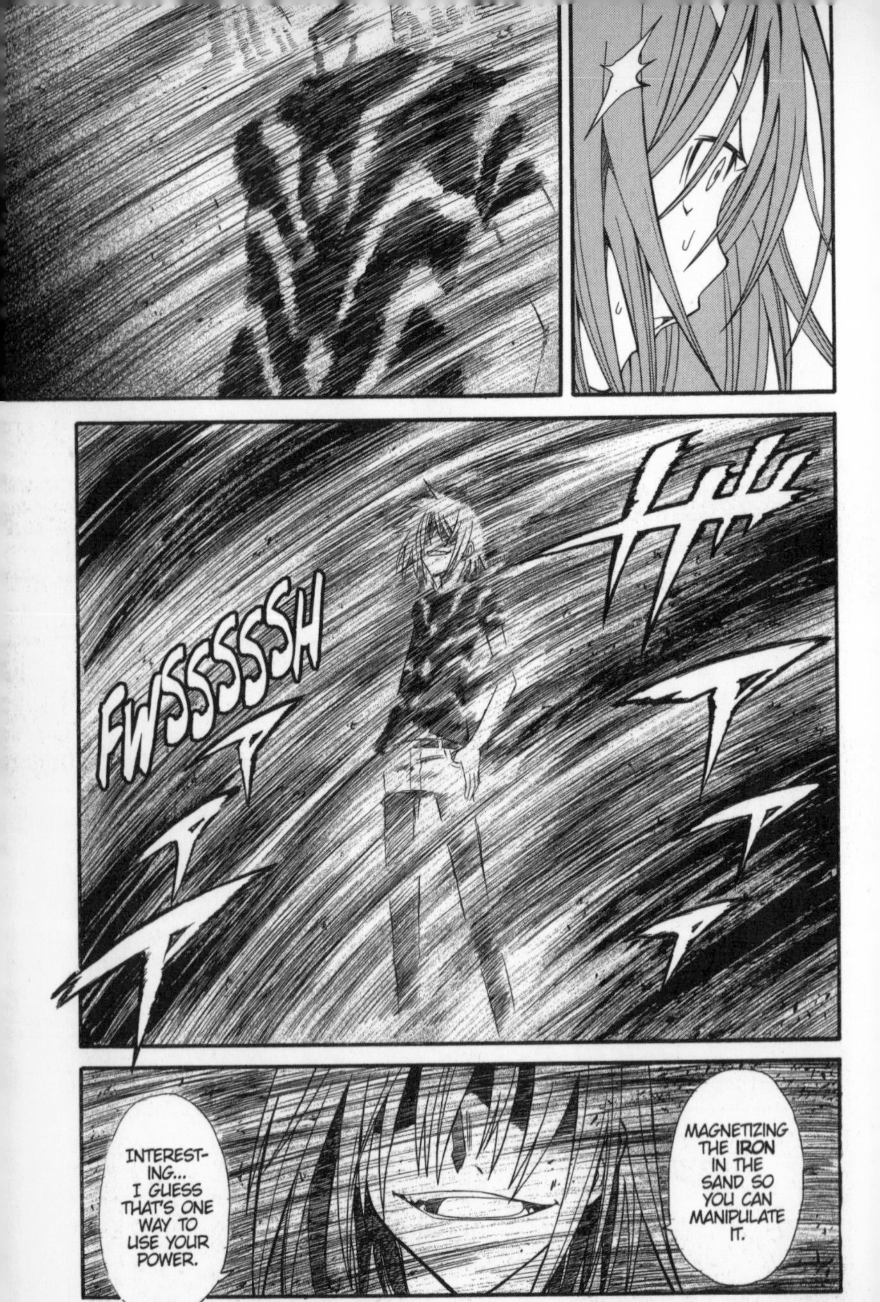
FWSSSSSSH
MAGNETIZING THE IRON IN THE SAND SO YOU CAN MANIPULATE IT.
INTEREST-ING... I GUESS THAT'S ONE WAY TO USE YOUR POWER.

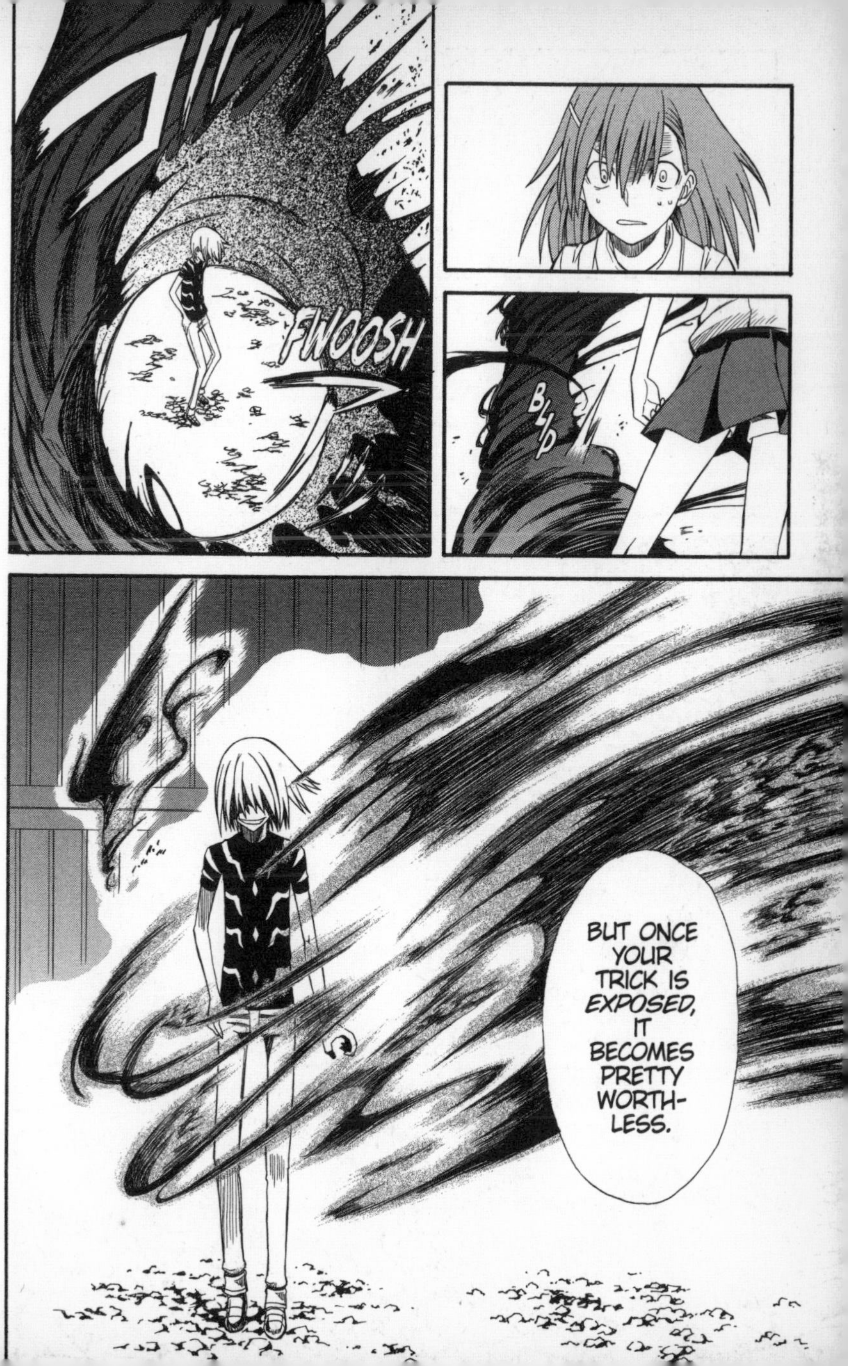
BLIP
FWOOSH
BUT ONCE YOUR TRICK IS *EXPOSED,* IT BECOMES PRETTY WORTH-LESS.

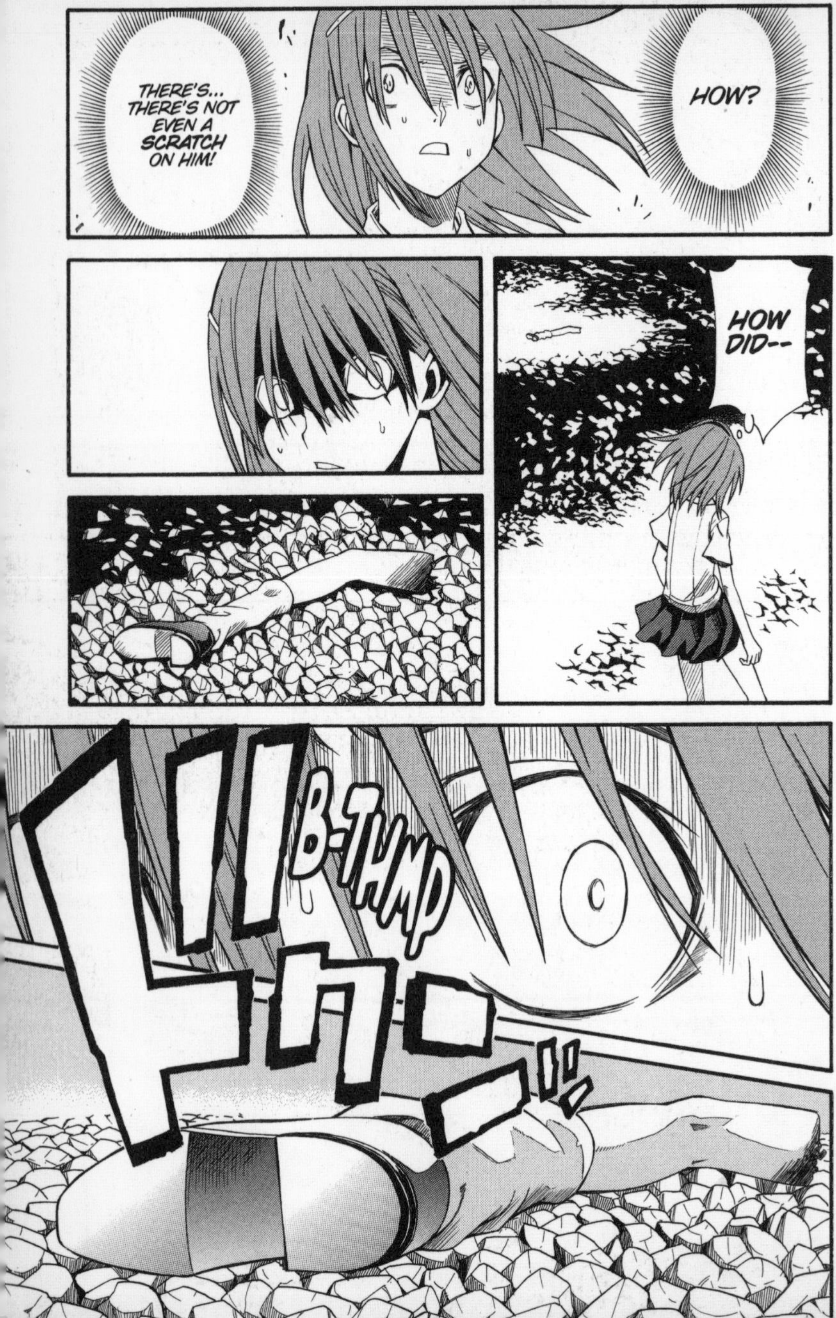
HOW?
THERE'S... THERE'S NOT EVEN A SCRATCH ON HIM!
HOW DID--
B-THUMP

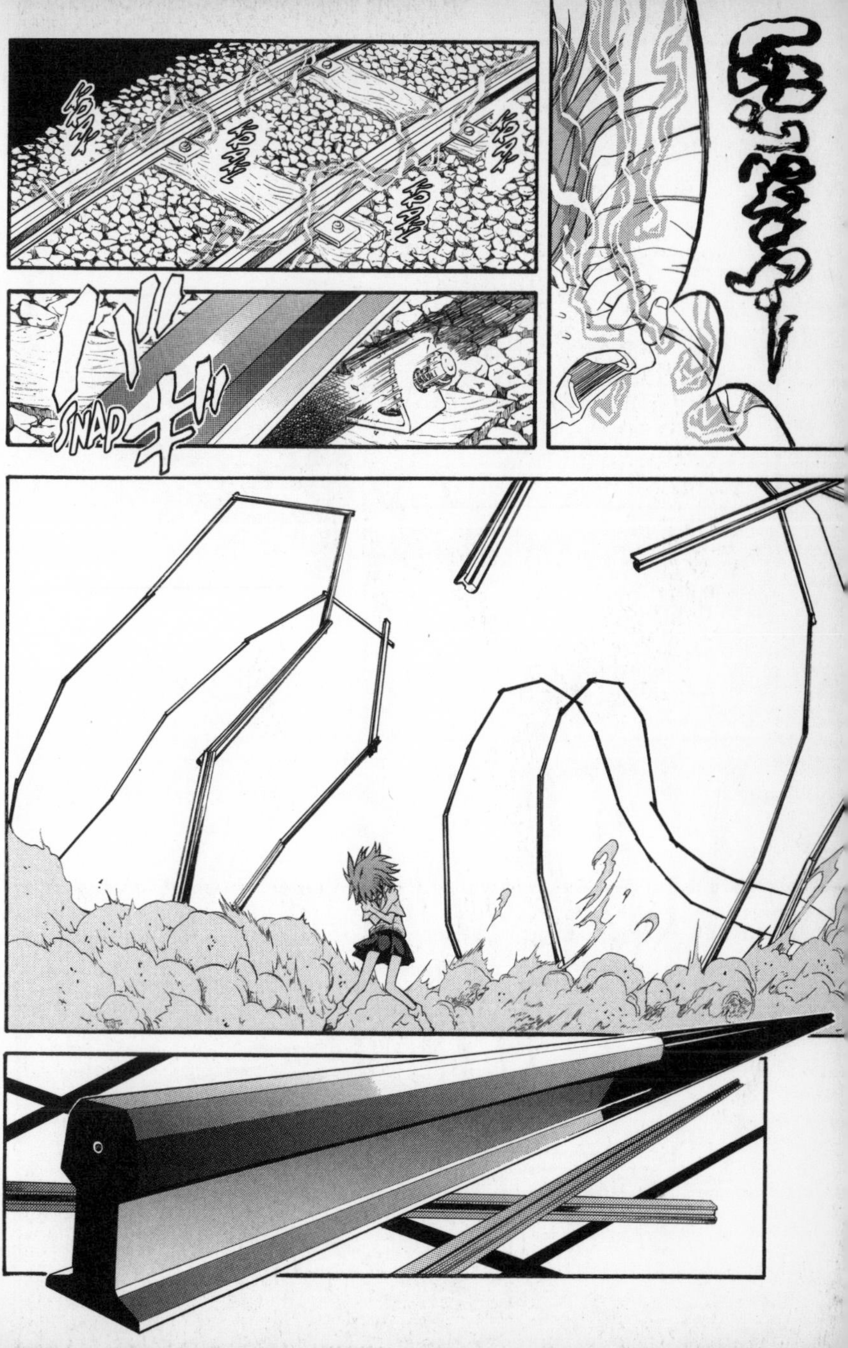
SNAP

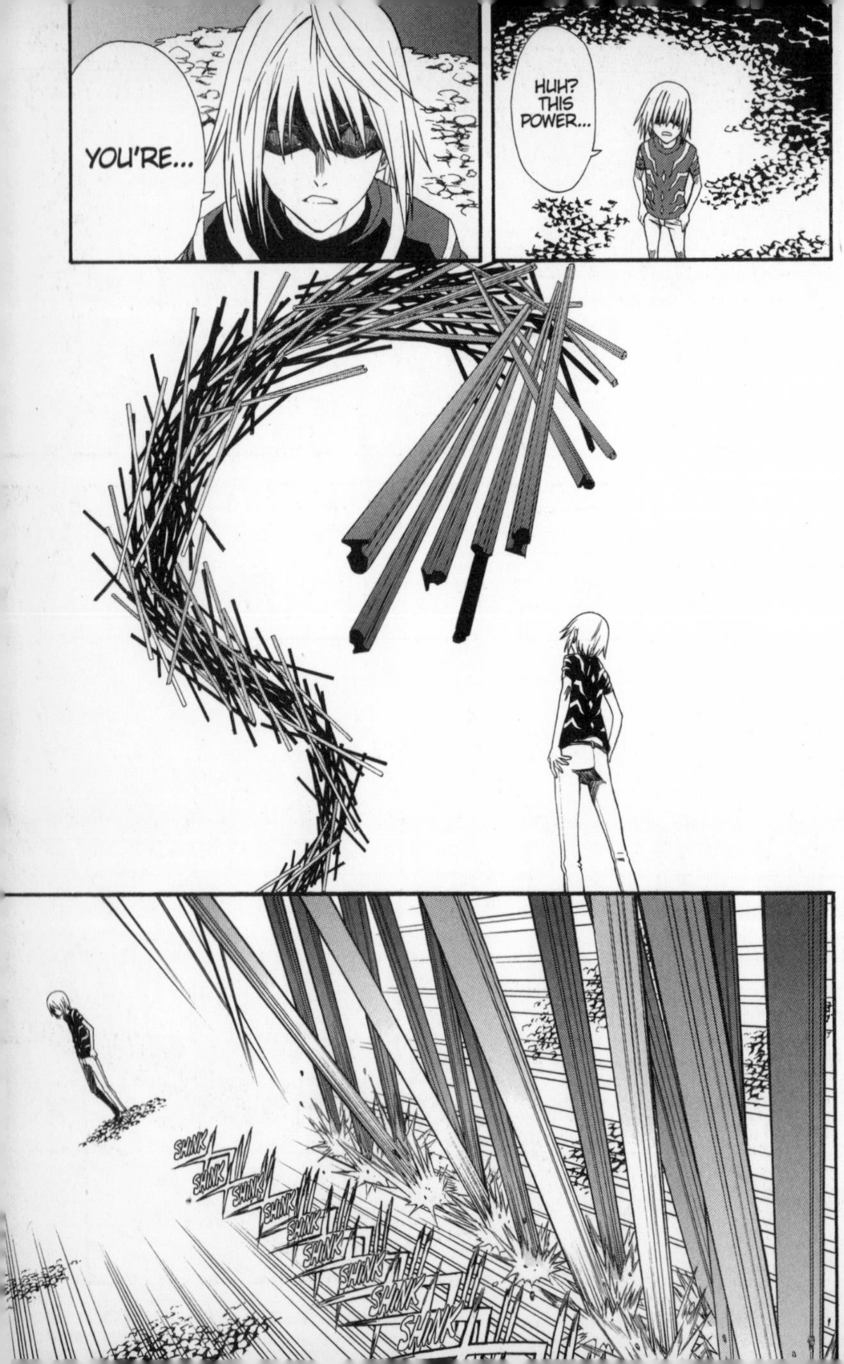
HUH? THIS POWER...
YOU'RE...
SHINK
SHINK
SHINK
SHINK
SHINK
SHINK
SHINK
SHINK
SHINK

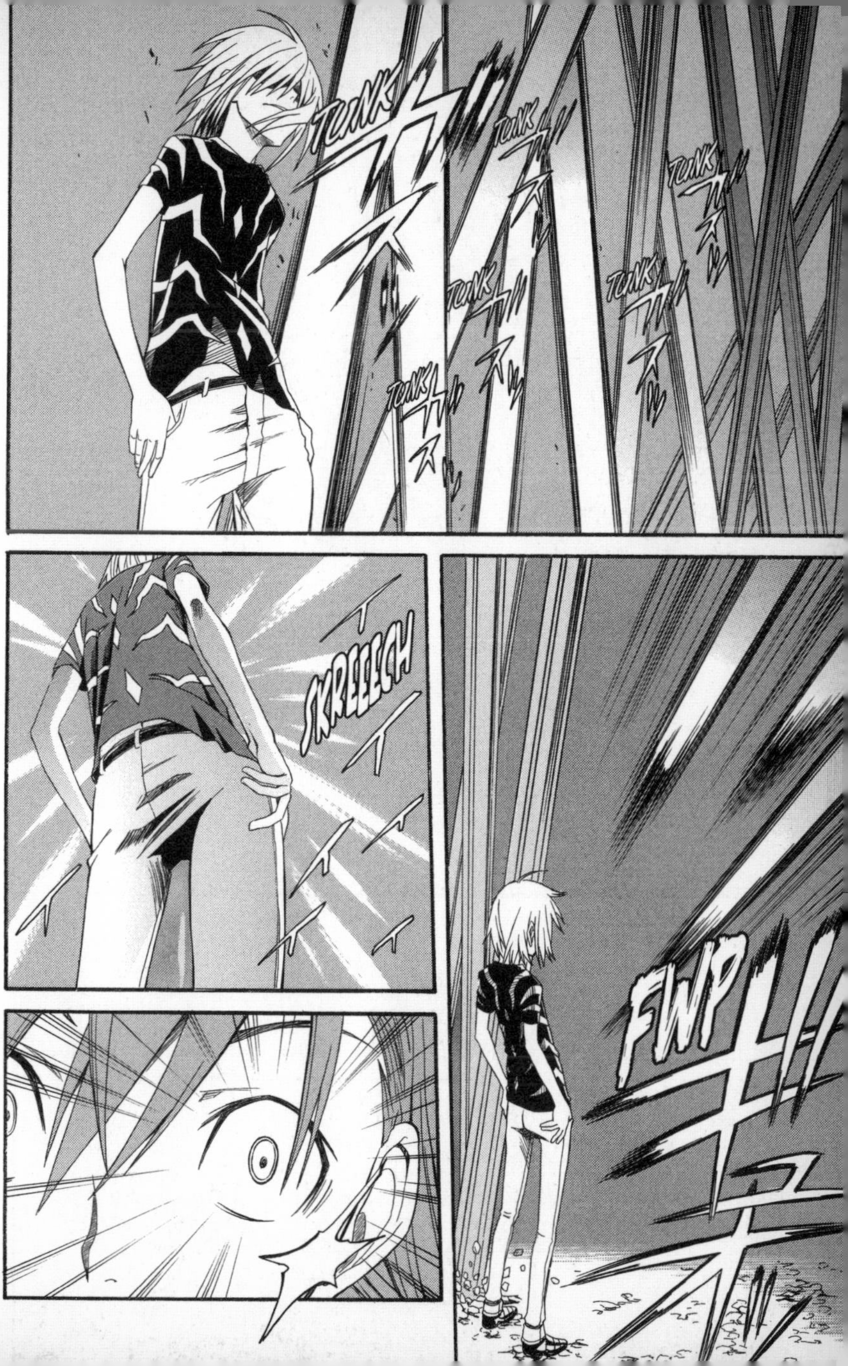
TCINK
TCINK
TCINK
TCINK
TCINK
TCINK
FWP
SKREEECH

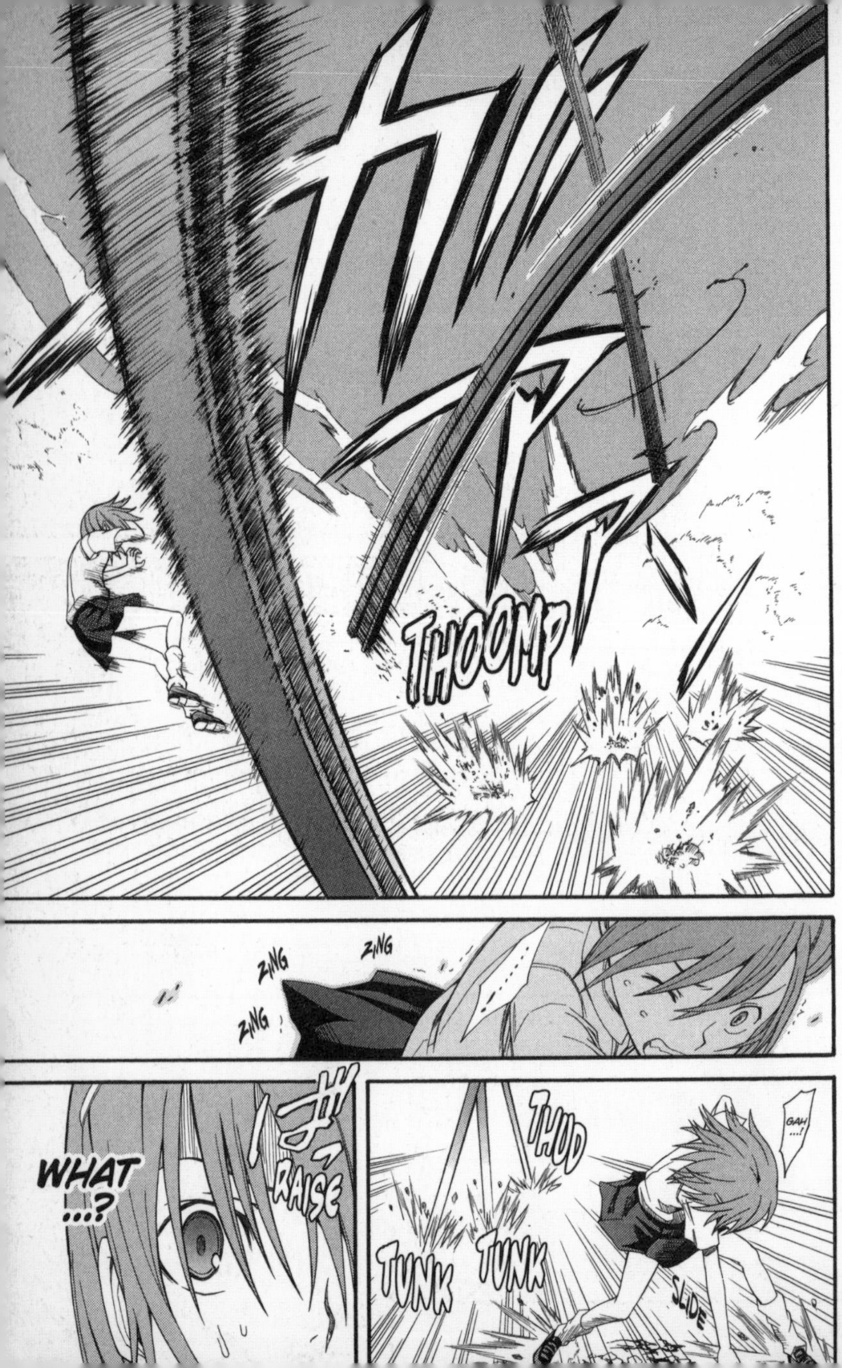
THOOMP
ZING
ZING
ZING
GAH ...!
THUD
TUNK
TUNK
SLIDE
RAISE
WHAT ...?

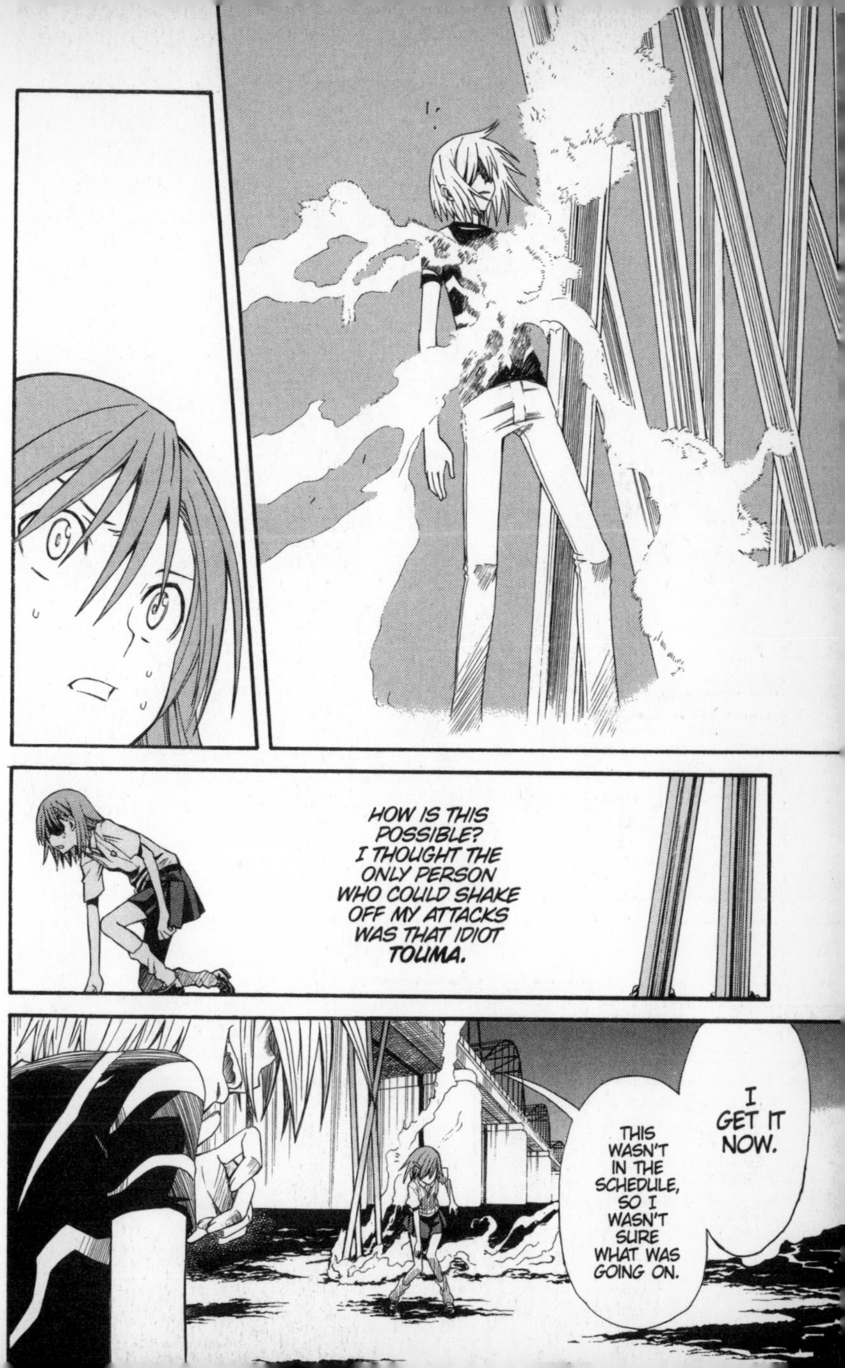
!?
HOW IS THIS POSSIBLE? I THOUGHT THE ONLY PERSON WHO COULD SHAKE OFF MY ATTACKS WAS THAT IDIOT TOUMA.
I GET IT NOW.
THIS WASN'T IN THE SCHEDULE, SO I WASN'T SURE WHAT WAS GOING ON.

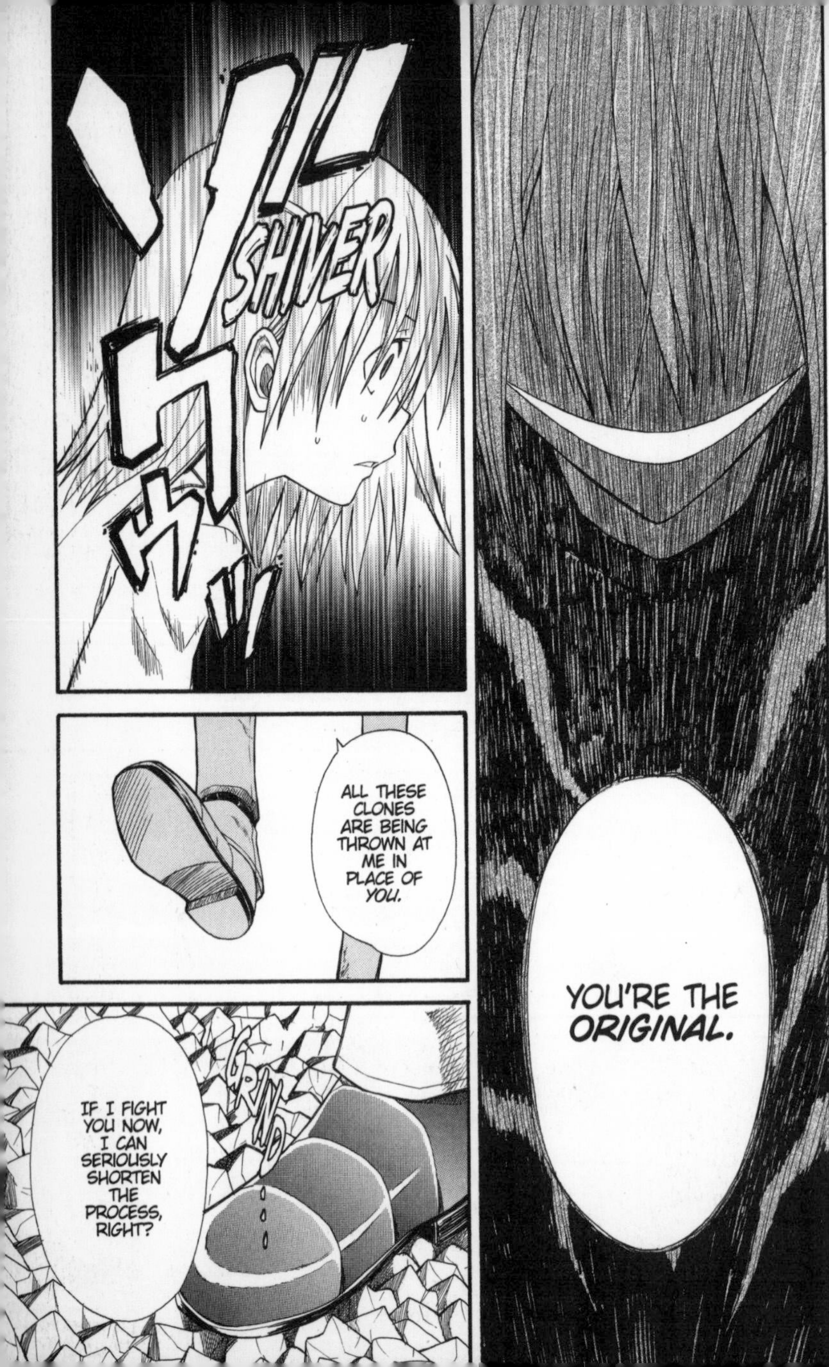

YOU'RE THE ORIGINAL.
SHIVER
ALL THESE CLONES ARE BEING THROWN AT ME IN PLACE OF YOU.
GRIND
IF I FIGHT YOU NOW, I CAN SERIOUSLY SHORTEN THE PROCESS, RIGHT?

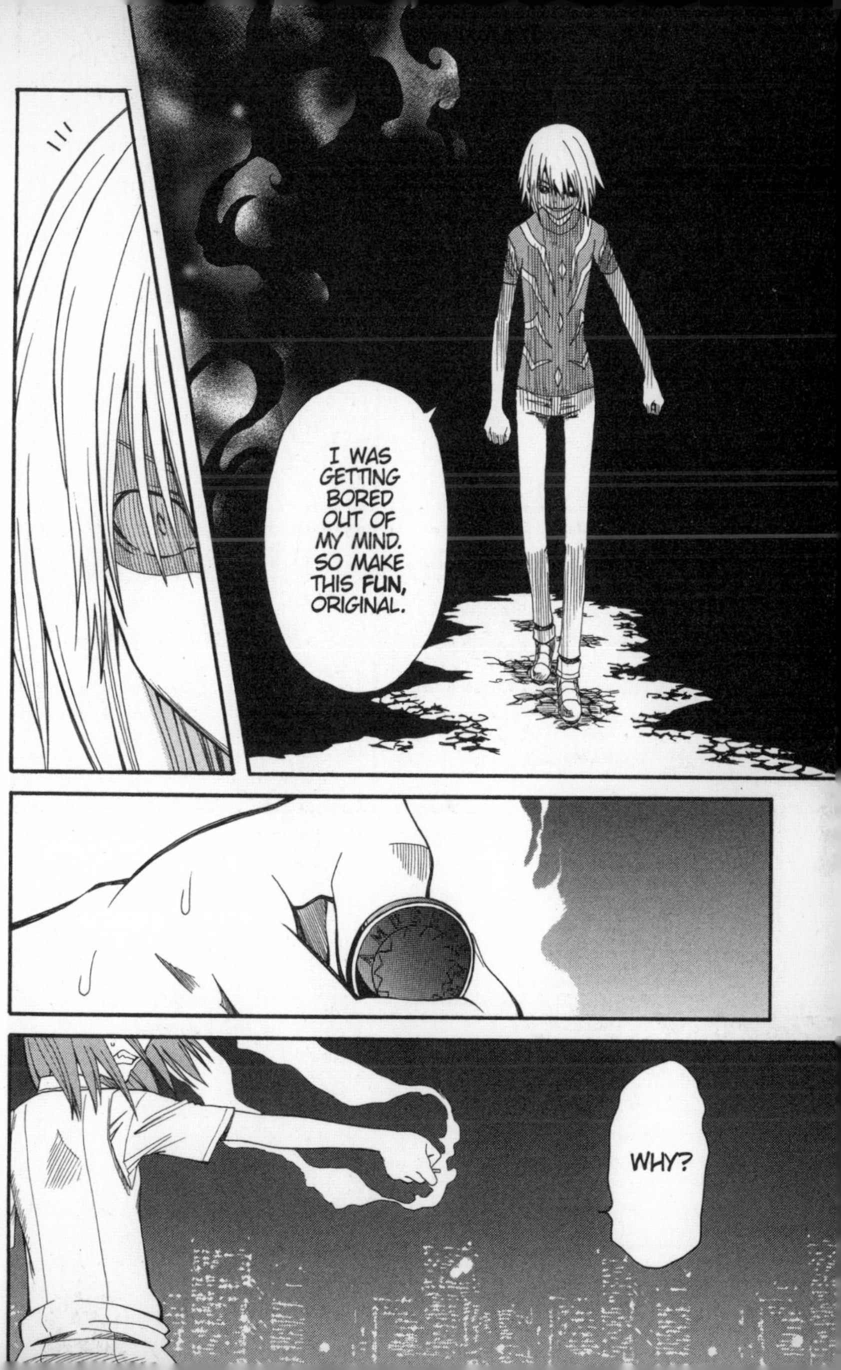
I WAS GETTING BORED OUT OF MY MIND. SO MAKE THIS FUN, ORIGINAL.
WHY?

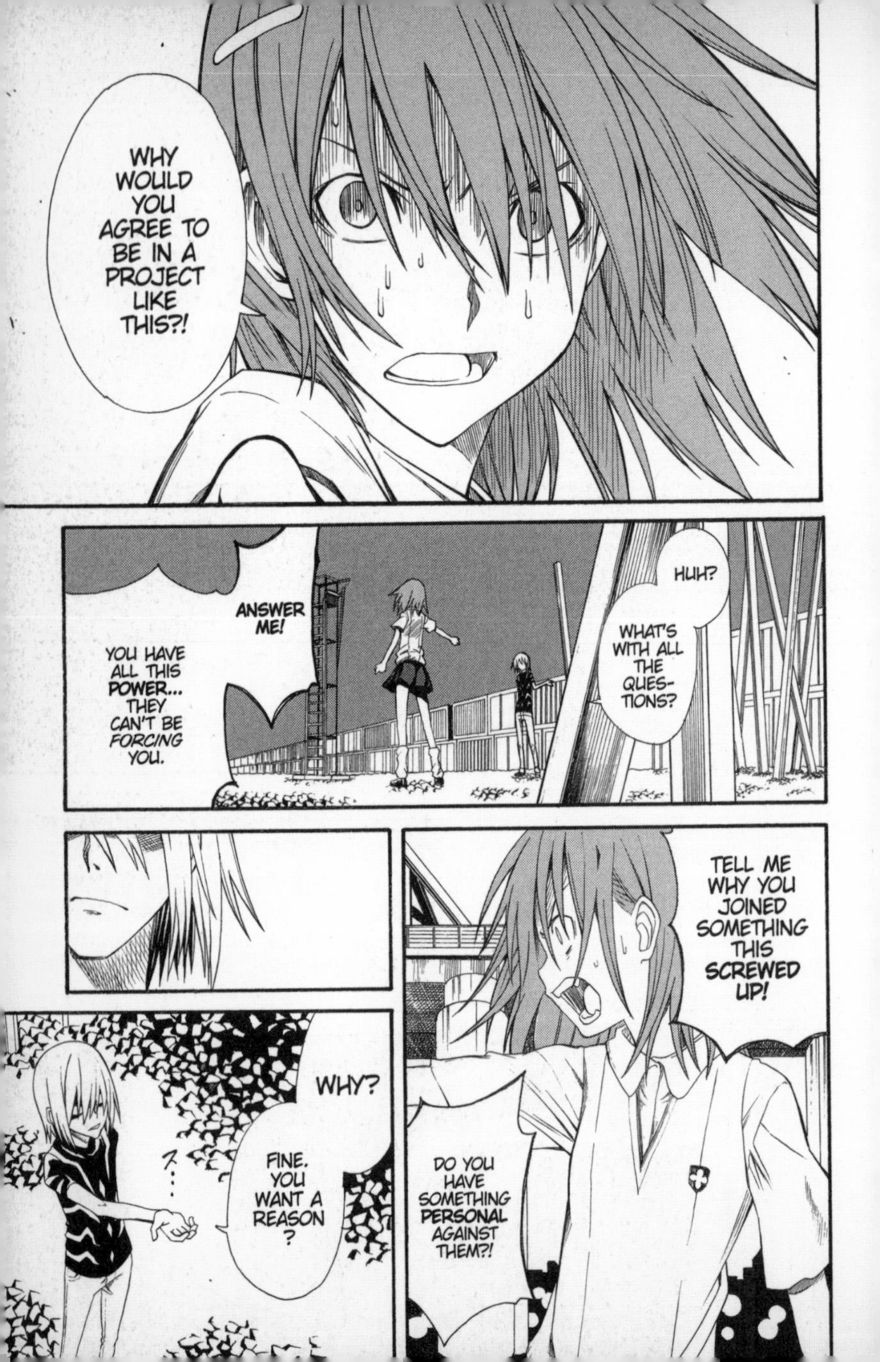
WHY WOULD YOU AGREE TO BE IN A PROJECT LIKE THIS?!
HUH?
WHAT'S WITH ALL THE QUES-TIONS?
ANSWER ME!
YOU HAVE ALL THIS POWER... THEY CAN'T BE *FORCING* YOU.
TELL ME WHY YOU JOINED SOMETHING THIS SCREWED UP!
DO YOU HAVE SOMETHING PERSONAL AGAINST THEM?!
WHY?
FINE. YOU WANT A REASON?
ス…

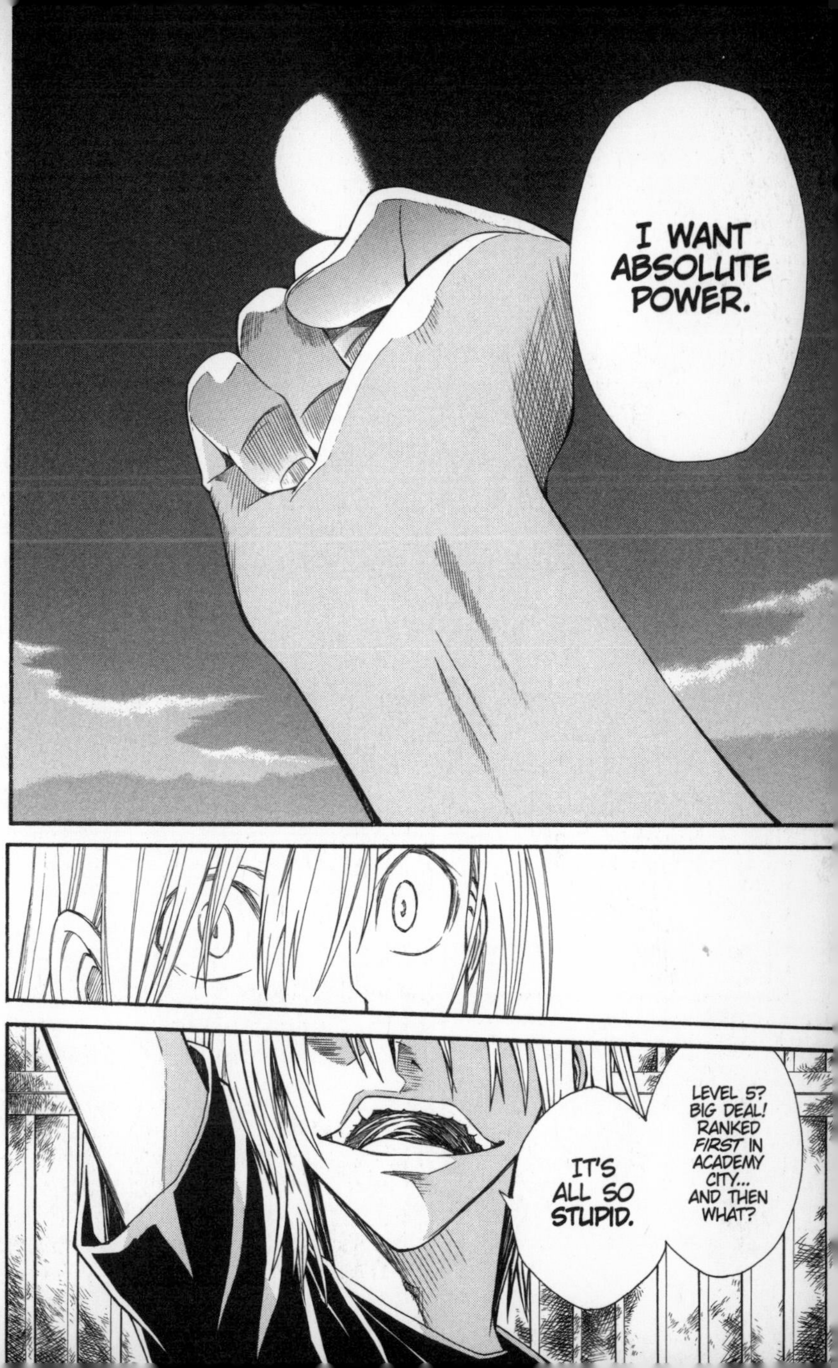
I WANT ABSOLUTE POWER.
LEVEL 5? BIG DEAL! RANKED *FIRST* IN ACADEMY CITY... AND THEN WHAT?
IT'S ALL SO STUPID.

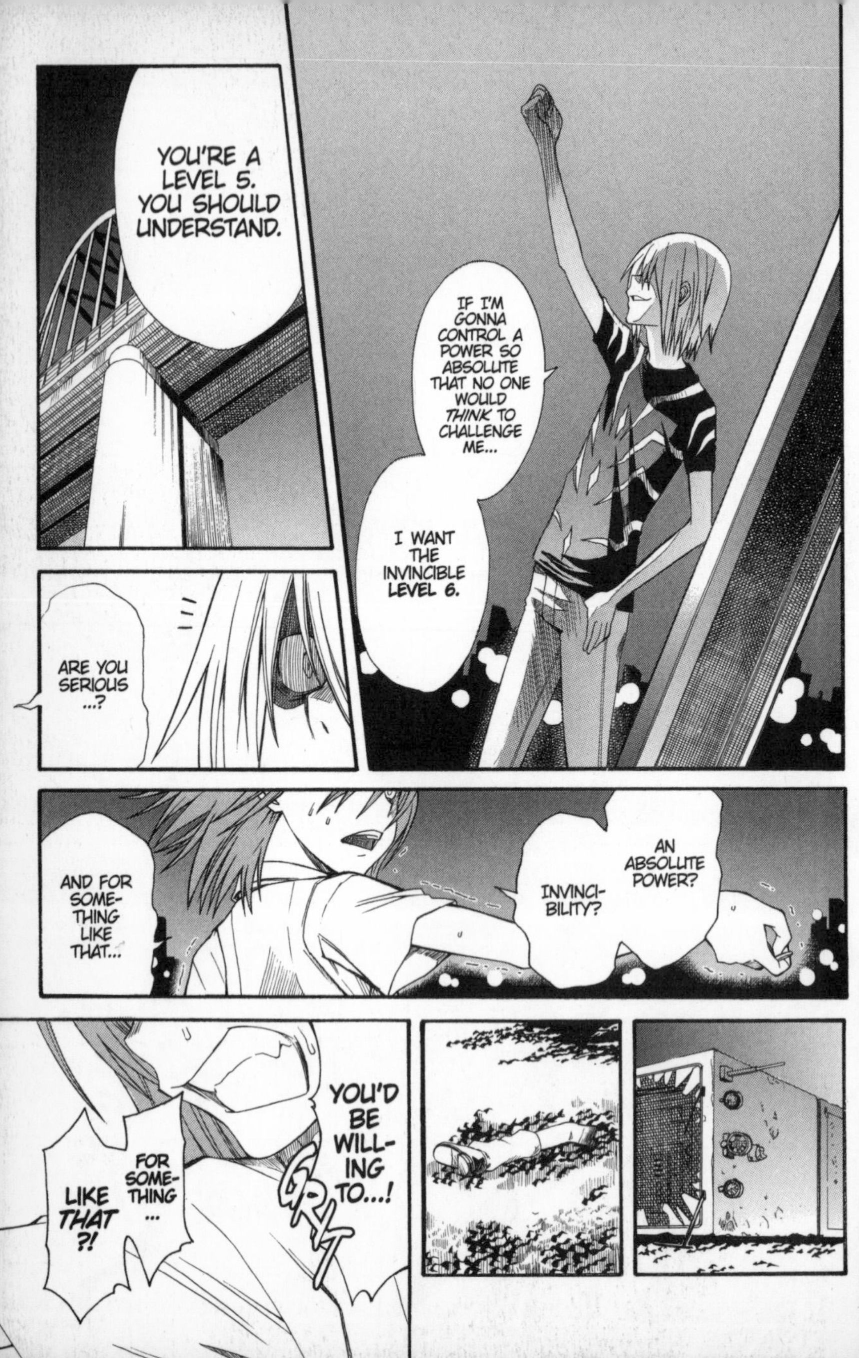
IF I'M GONNA CONTROL A POWER SO ABSOLUTE THAT NO ONE WOULD *THINK* TO CHALLENGE ME...
I WANT THE INVINCIBLE LEVEL 6.
YOU'RE A LEVEL 5. YOU SHOULD UNDERSTAND.
ARE YOU SERIOUS ...?
AN ABSOLUTE POWER?
INVINCI-BILITY?
AND FOR SOME-THING LIKE THAT...
YOU'D BE WILL-ING TO...!
GRK
FOR SOME-THING ...
LIKE *THAT* ?!

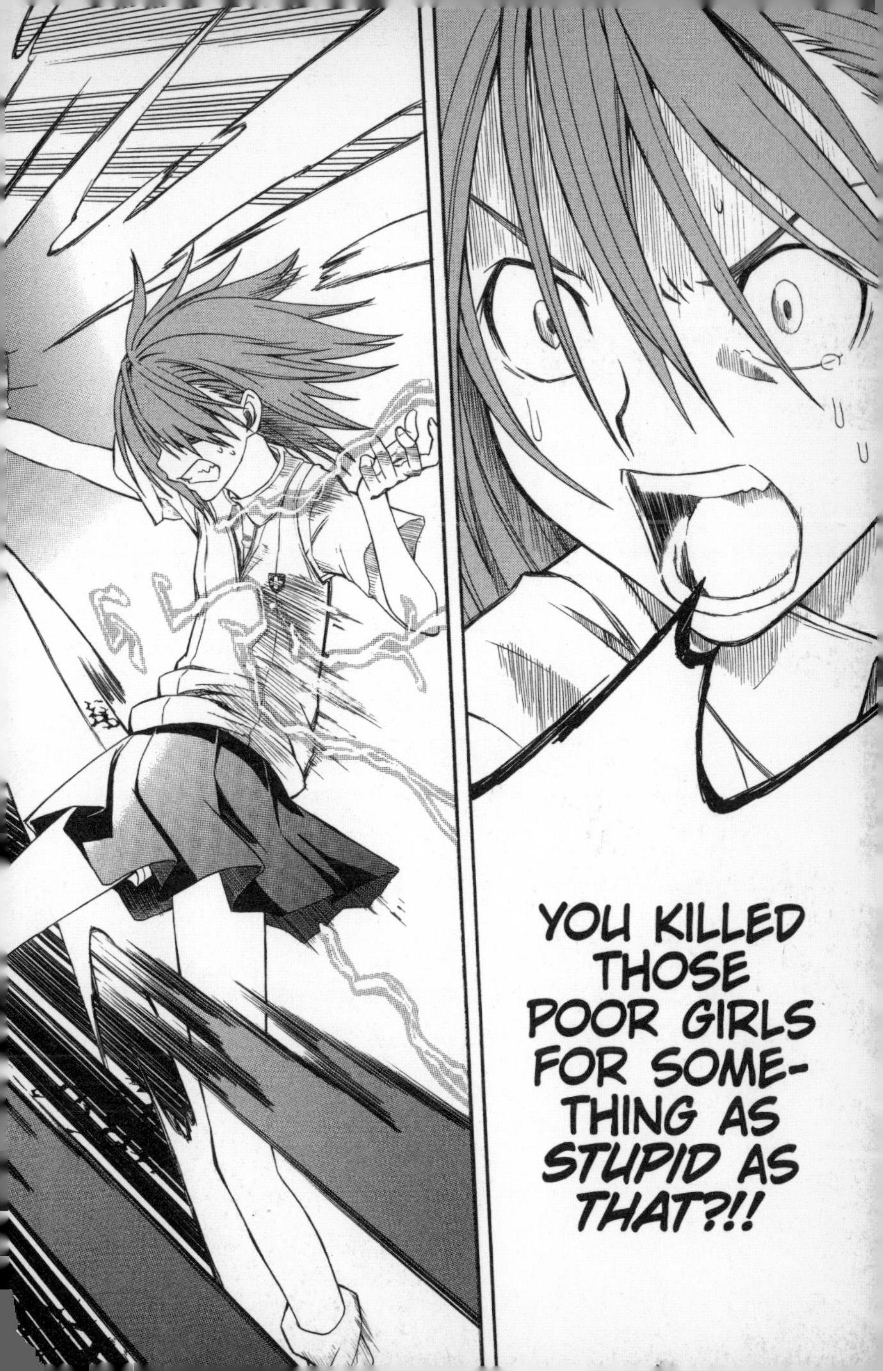
YOU KILLED THOSE POOR GIRLS FOR SOME-THING AS STUPID AS THAT?!!

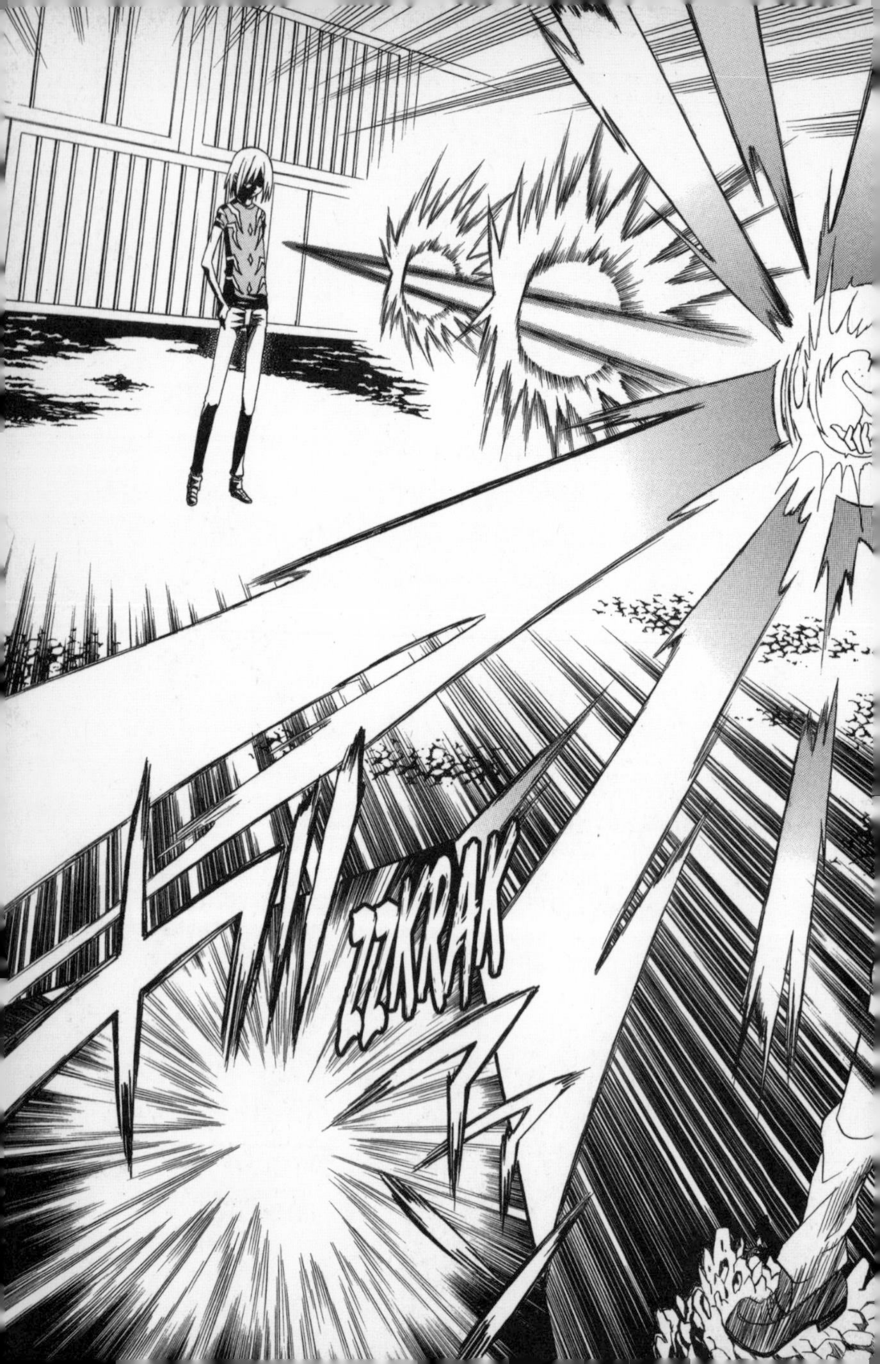
ZZKRAK

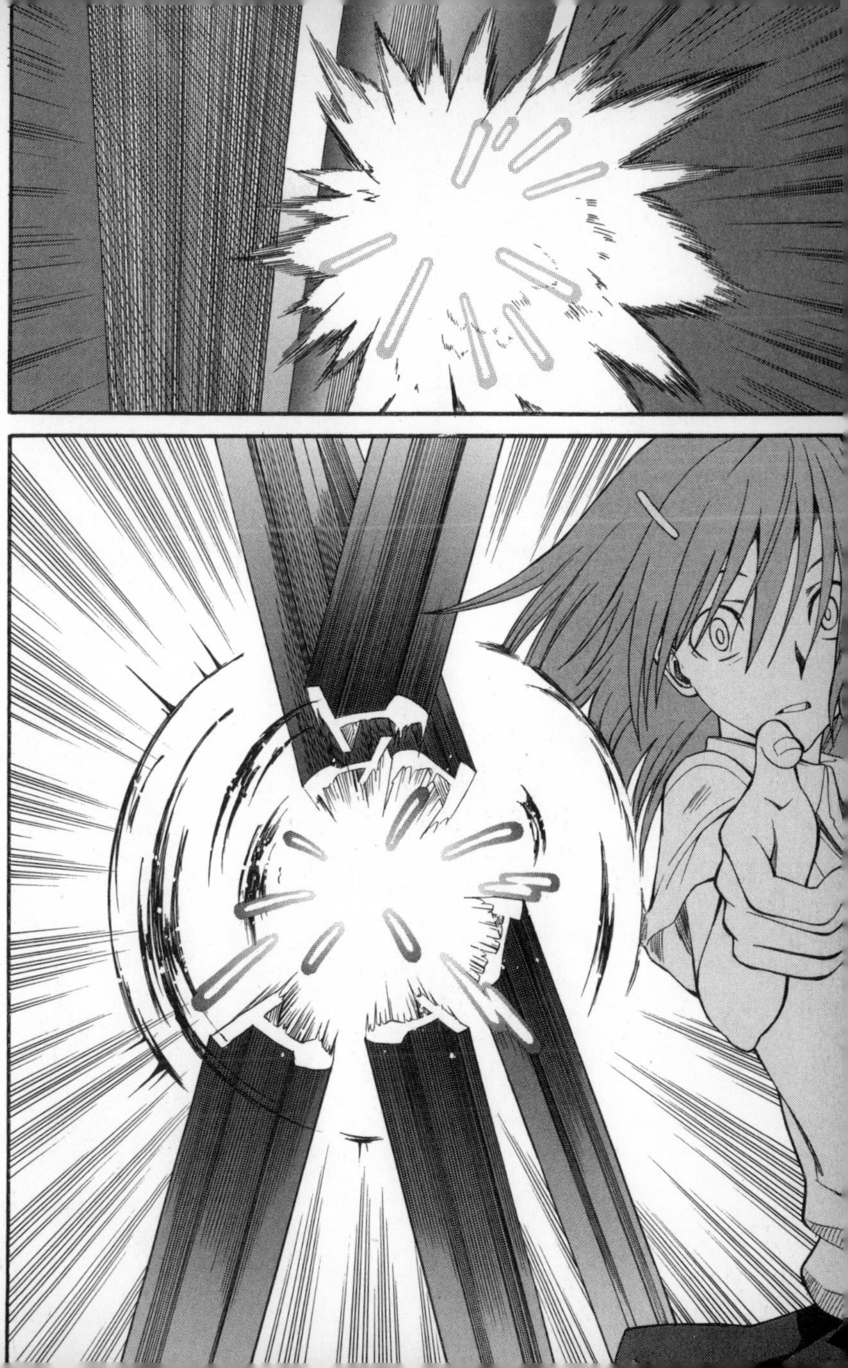

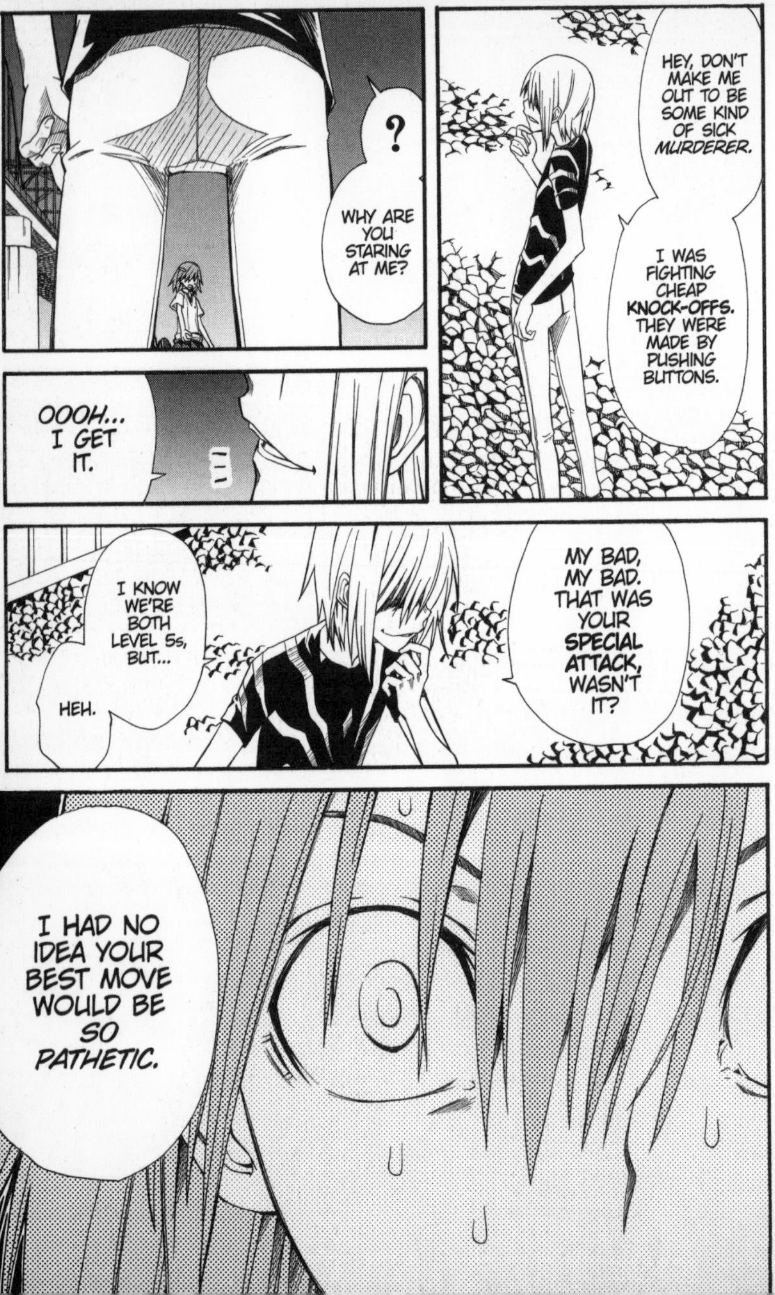

HEY, DON'T MAKE ME OUT TO BE SOME KIND OF SICK MURDERER.
I WAS FIGHTING CHEAP KNOCK-OFFS. THEY WERE MADE BY PUSHING BUTTONS.
?
WHY ARE YOU STARING AT ME?
...
OOOH... I GET IT.
MY BAD, MY BAD. THAT WAS YOUR SPECIAL ATTACK, WASN'T IT?
I KNOW WE'RE BOTH LEVEL 5s, BUT...
HEH.
I HAD NO IDEA YOUR BEST MOVE WOULD BE SO PATHETIC.

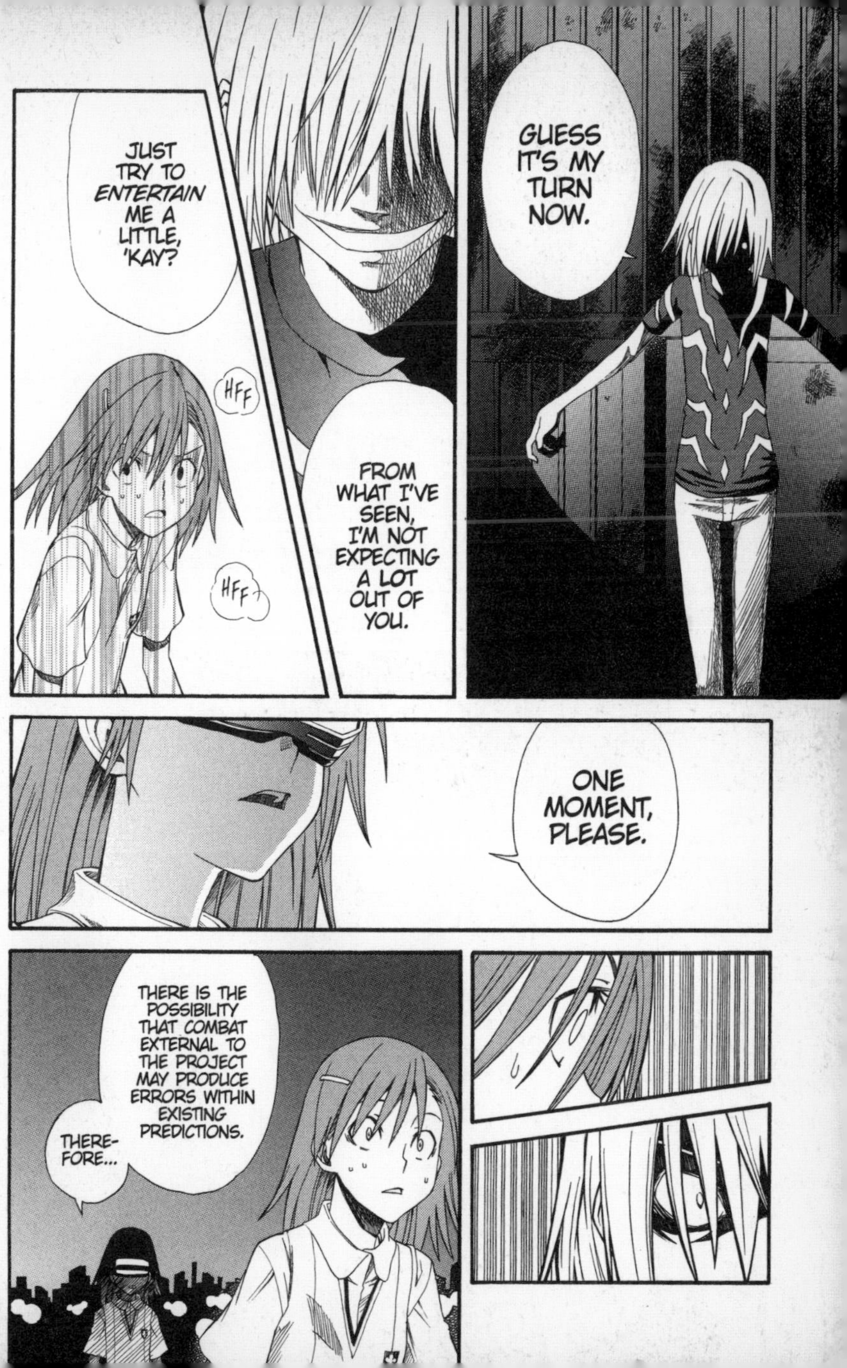
GUESS IT'S MY TURN NOW.
FROM WHAT I'VE SEEN, I'M NOT EXPECTING A LOT OUT OF YOU.
JUST TRY TO *ENTERTAIN* ME A LITTLE, 'KAY?
HFF
HFF
ONE MOMENT, PLEASE.
THERE IS THE POSSIBILITY THAT COMBAT EXTERNAL TO THE PROJECT MAY PRODUCE ERRORS WITHIN EXISTING PREDICTIONS.
THERE-FORE...

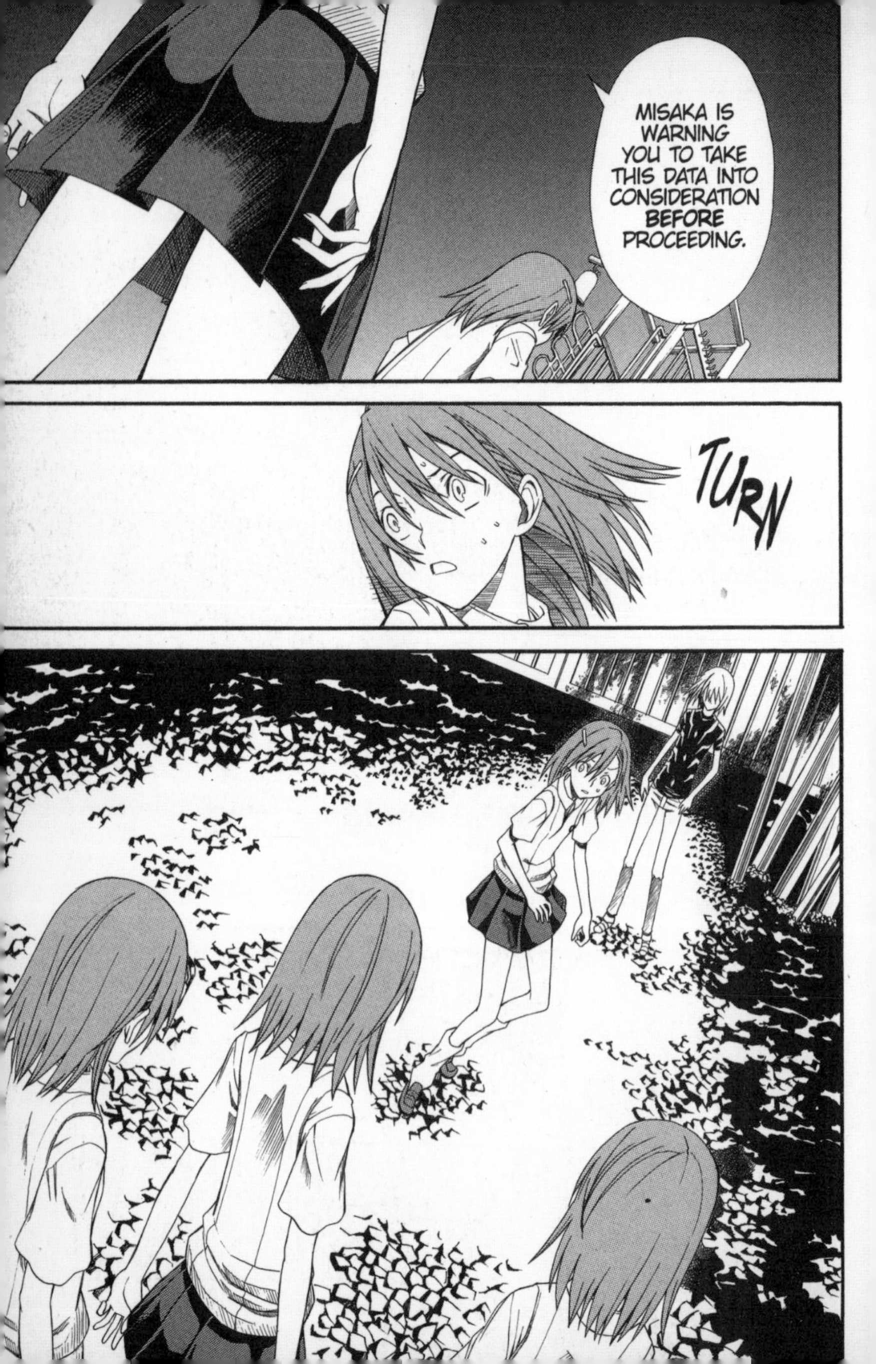
MISAKA IS WARNING YOU TO TAKE THIS DATA INTO CONSIDERATION BEFORE PROCEEDING.
TURN

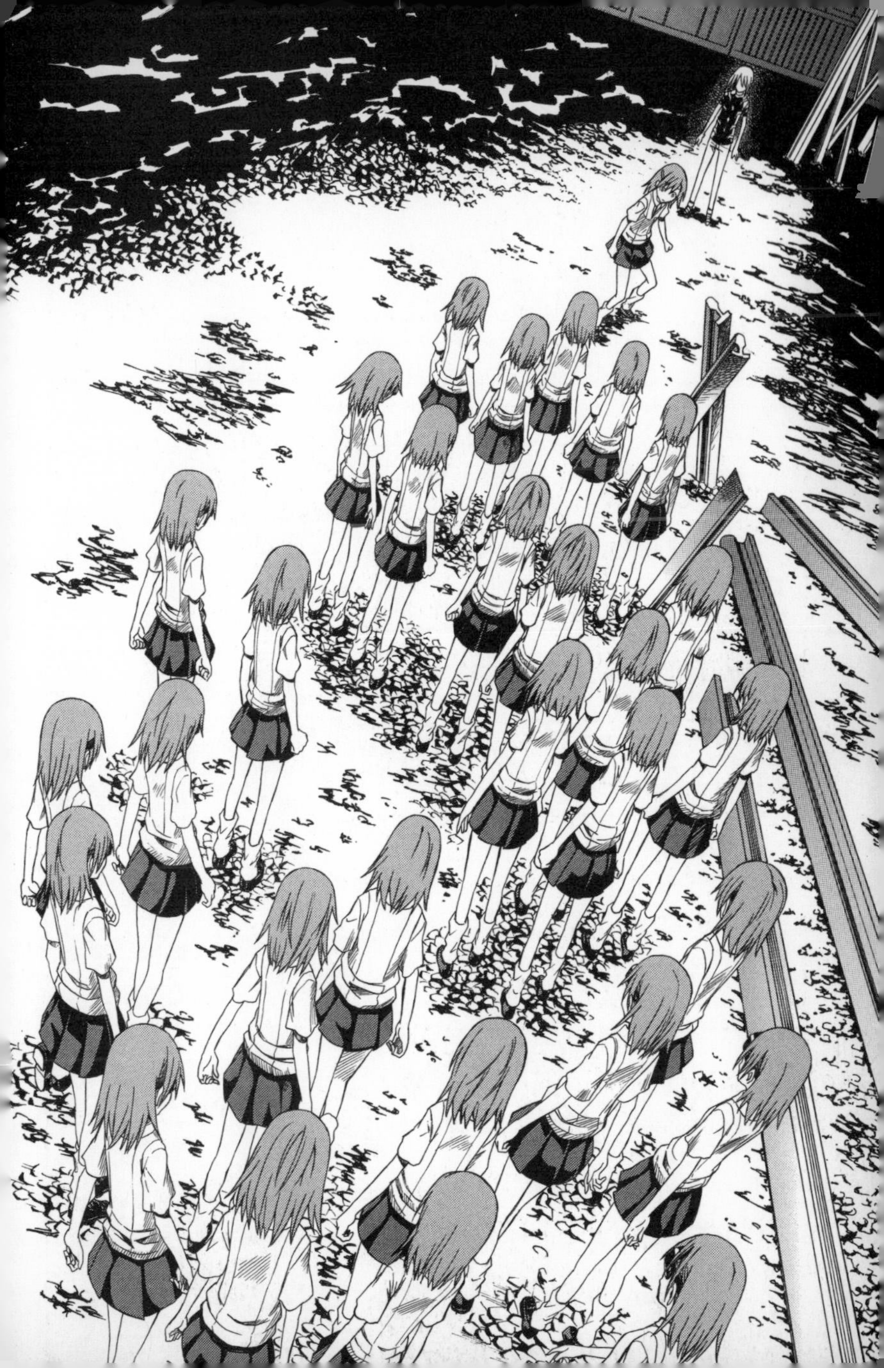

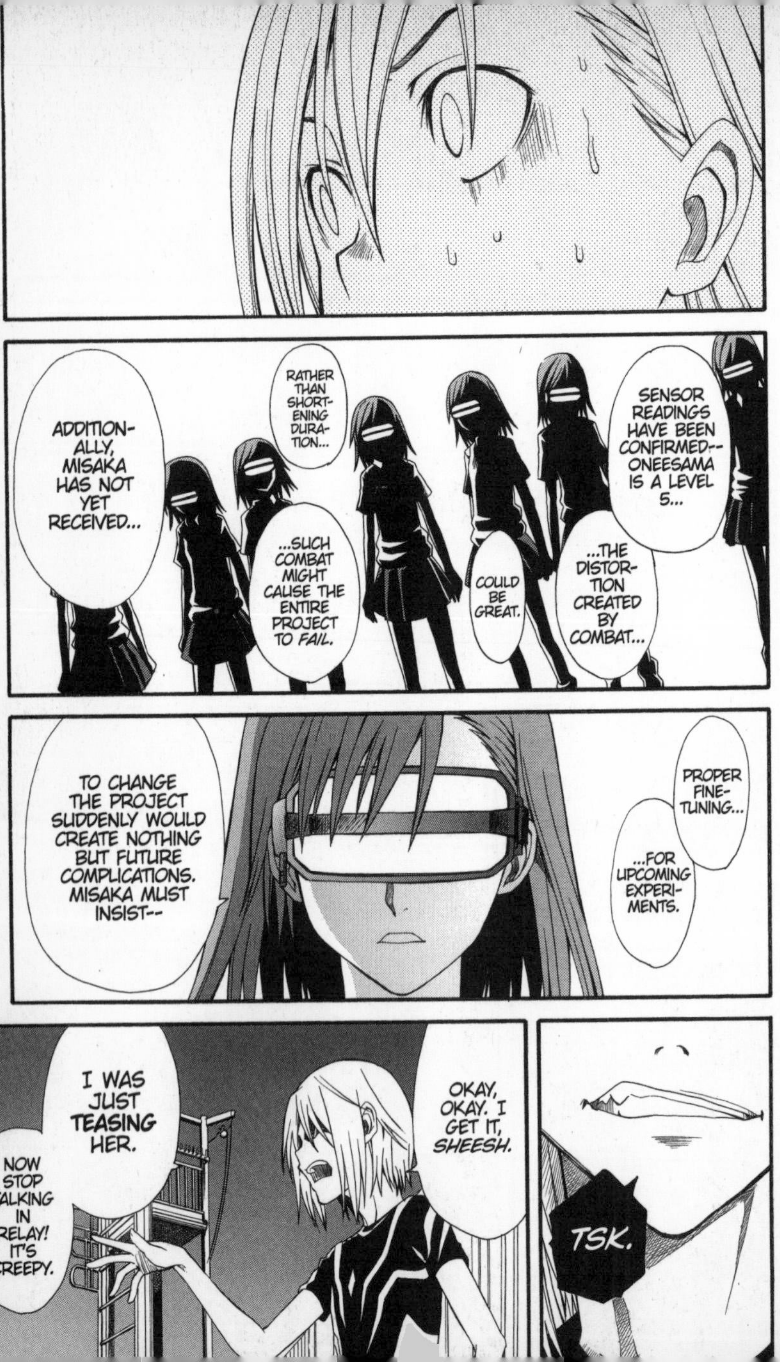
SENSOR READINGS HAVE BEEN CONFIRMED--ONEESAMA IS A LEVEL 5...
...THE DISTORTION CREATED BY COMBAT...
COULD BE GREAT.
RATHER THAN SHORTENING DURATION...
...SUCH COMBAT MIGHT CAUSE THE ENTIRE PROJECT TO *FAIL.*
ADDITIONALLY, MISAKA HAS NOT YET RECEIVED...
PROPER FINE-TUNING...
...FOR UPCOMING EXPERIMENTS.
TO CHANGE THE PROJECT SUDDENLY WOULD CREATE NOTHING BUT FUTURE COMPLICATIONS. MISAKA MUST INSIST--
TSK.
OKAY, OKAY. I GET IT, *SHEESH.*
I WAS JUST **TEASING** HER.
NOW STOP TALKING IN RELAY! IT'S CREEPY.

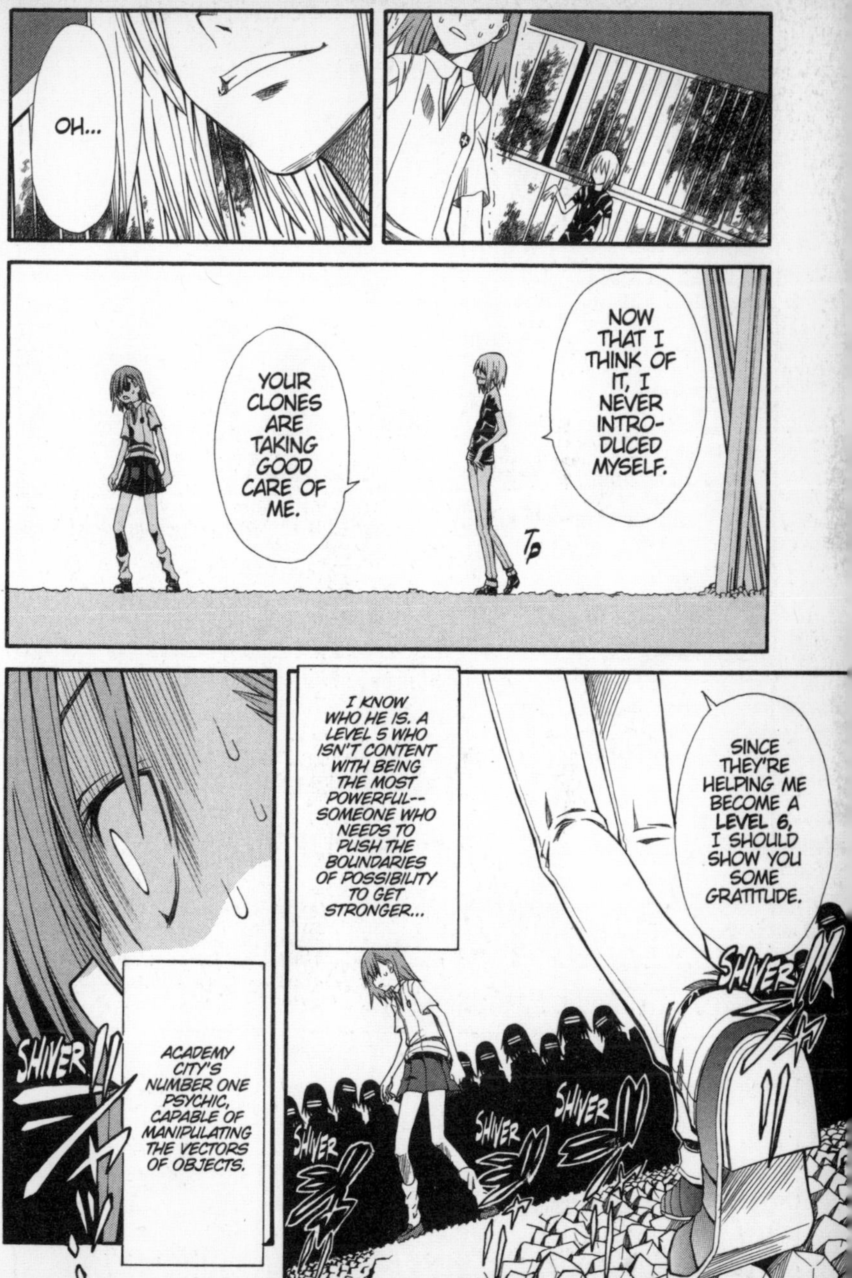
OH...
NOW THAT I THINK OF IT, I NEVER INTRO-DUCED MYSELF.
TP
YOUR CLONES ARE TAKING GOOD CARE OF ME.
SINCE THEY'RE HELPING ME BECOME A LEVEL 6, I SHOULD SHOW YOU SOME GRATITUDE.
I KNOW WHO HE IS. A LEVEL 5 WHO ISN'T CONTENT WITH BEING THE MOST POWERFUL--SOMEONE WHO NEEDS TO PUSH THE BOUNDARIES OF POSSIBILITY TO GET STRONGER...
SHIVER
SHIVER
SHIVER
SHIVER
ACADEMY CITY'S NUMBER ONE PSYCHIC, CAPABLE OF MANIPULATING THE VECTORS OF OBJECTS.
SHIVER

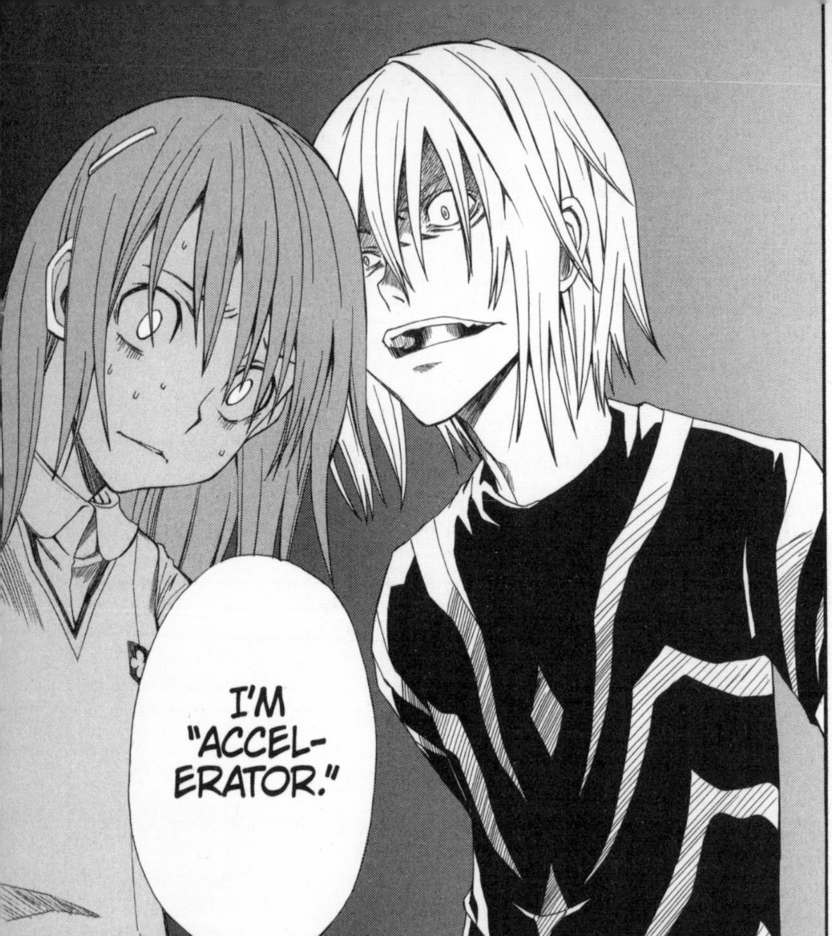
I'M "ACCEL-ERATOR."
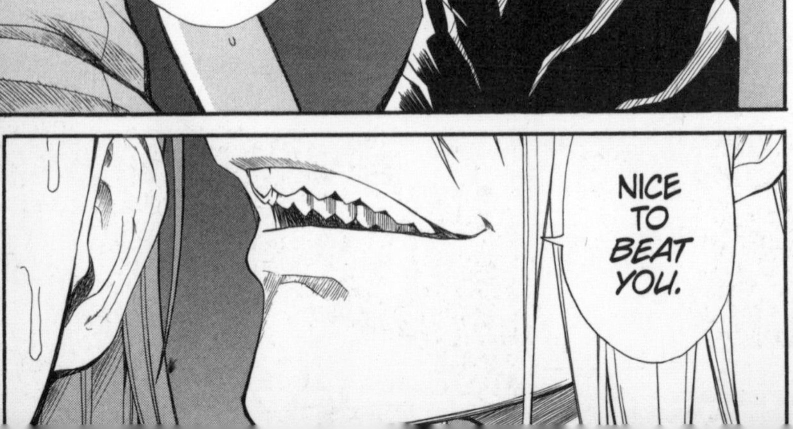
NICE TO BEAT YOU.

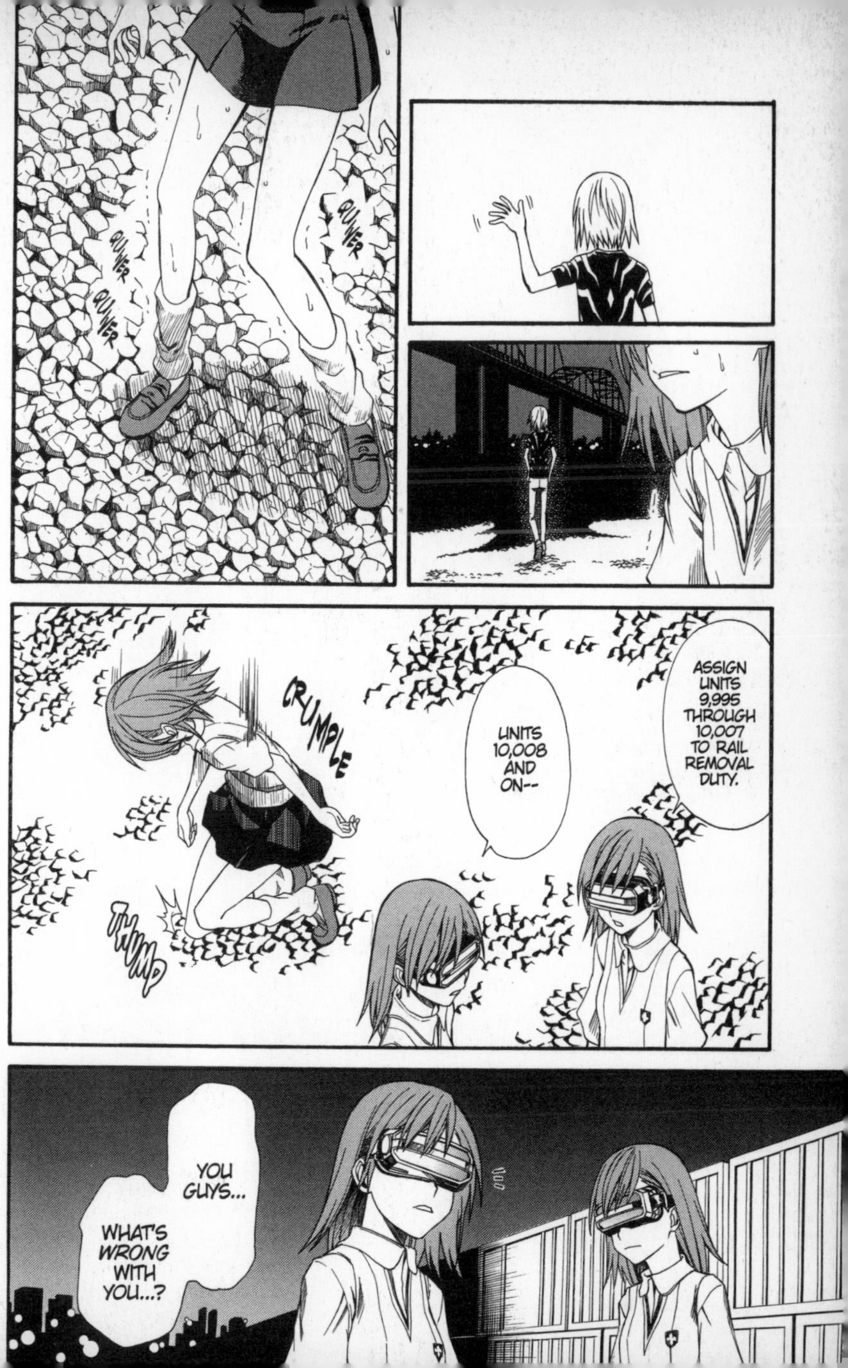
QUIVER
QUIVER
QUIVER
QUIVER
ASSIGN UNITS 9,995 THROUGH 10,007 TO RAIL REMOVAL DUTY.
UNITS 10,008 AND ON--
CRUMPLE
THUMP
YOU GUYS...
WHAT'S WRONG WITH YOU...?

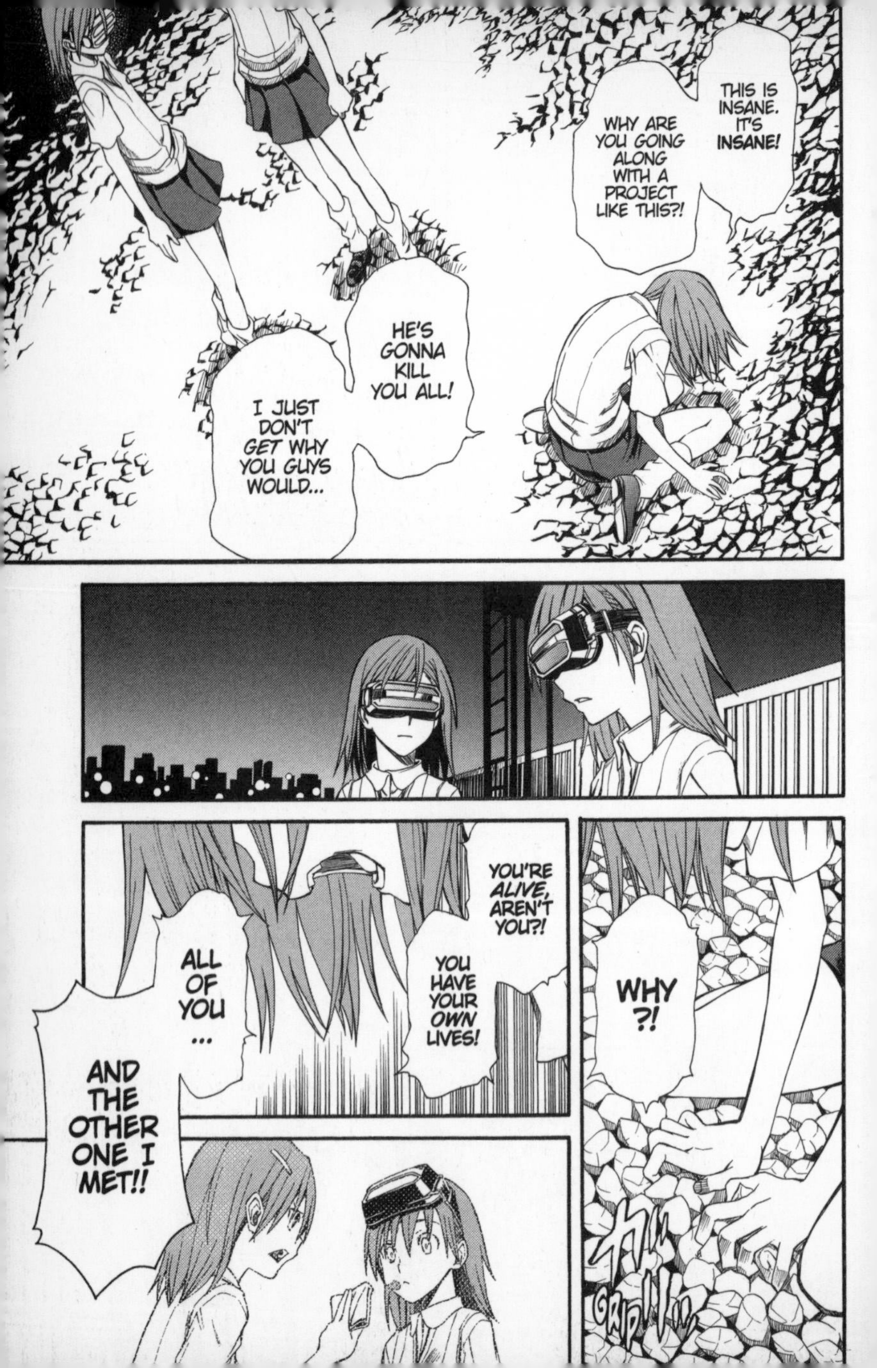
THIS IS INSANE. IT'S INSANE!
WHY ARE YOU GOING ALONG WITH A PROJECT LIKE THIS?!
HE'S GONNA KILL YOU ALL!
I JUST DON'T GET WHY YOU GUYS WOULD...
WHY?!
YOU'RE ALIVE, AREN'T YOU?!
YOU HAVE YOUR OWN LIVES!
ALL OF YOU...
AND THE OTHER ONE I MET!!

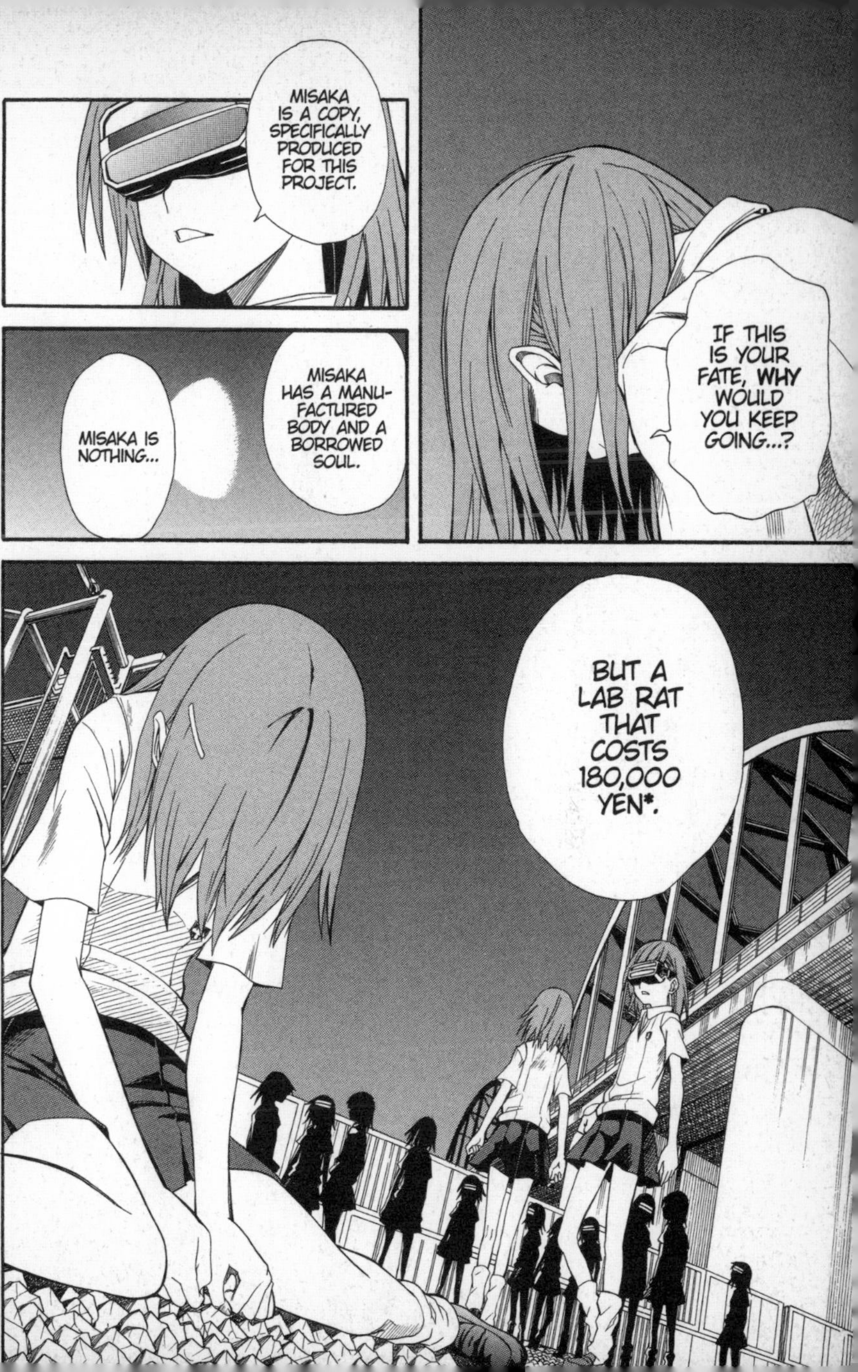
IF THIS IS YOUR FATE, WHY WOULD YOU KEEP GOING...?
MISAKA IS A COPY, SPECIFICALLY PRODUCED FOR THIS PROJECT.
MISAKA HAS A MANUFACTURED BODY AND A BORROWED SOUL.
MISAKA IS NOTHING...
BUT A LAB RAT THAT COSTS 180,000 YEN*.

*Or $2,200 American dollars, £1400 British pound sterling, or €1,650 euros, depending on current foreign exchange rates. Misaka approves of this footnote.

A Certain SCIENTIFIC Railgun

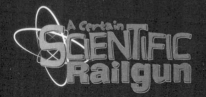

A Certain Ability Overkill

A LEVEL 5 CAPABLE OF MANIPULATING VECTORS.
TNK
TNK
ACCELERATOR AT YOUR LOCAL KAITEN SUSHI BAR*.
SALMON ROE...
LIFT
!!!
RATTLE
RATTLE
VECTOR
SALMON ROE
WHRRRRRRR—!!
SNATCH
WHA...?! EXCUSE ME, SIR!
VECTOR

*An eating establishment that uses a conveyor belt to circulate menu items in front of customers.

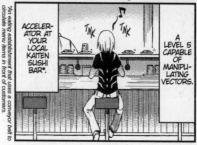

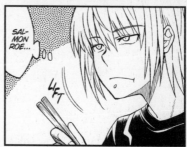

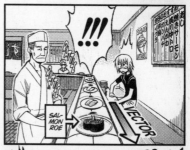

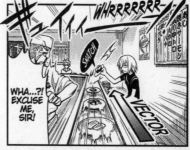

CHAPTER 25: AUGUST 16

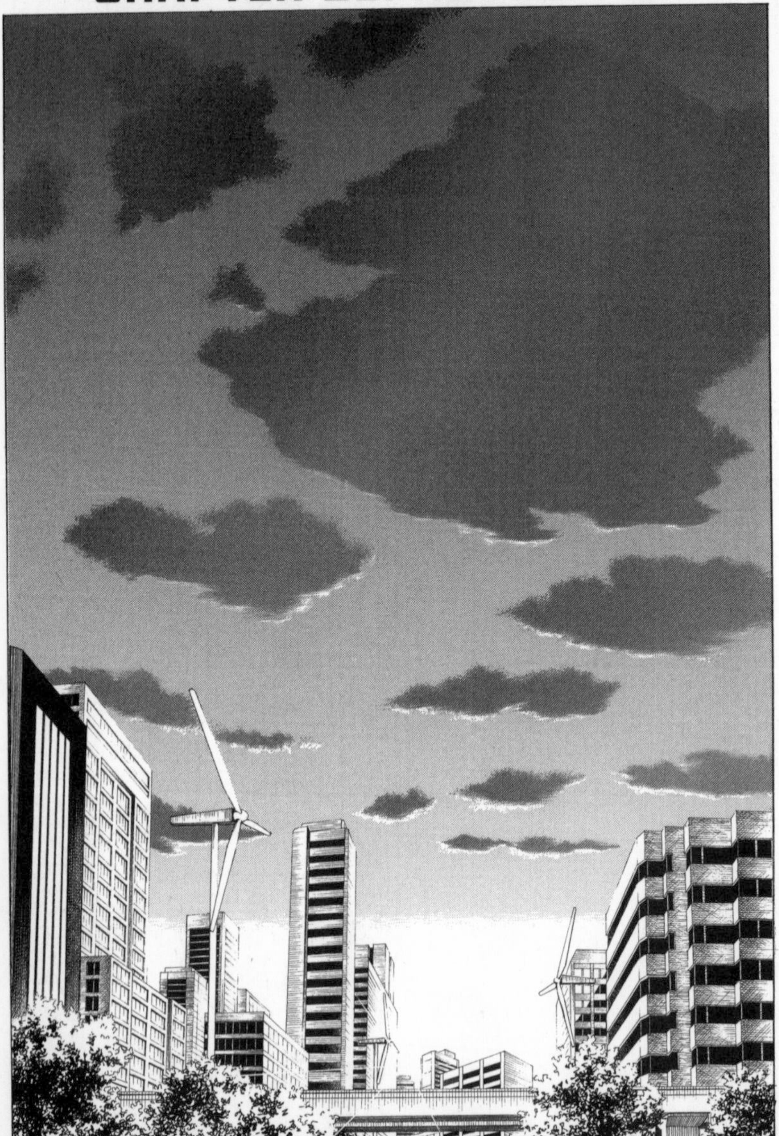

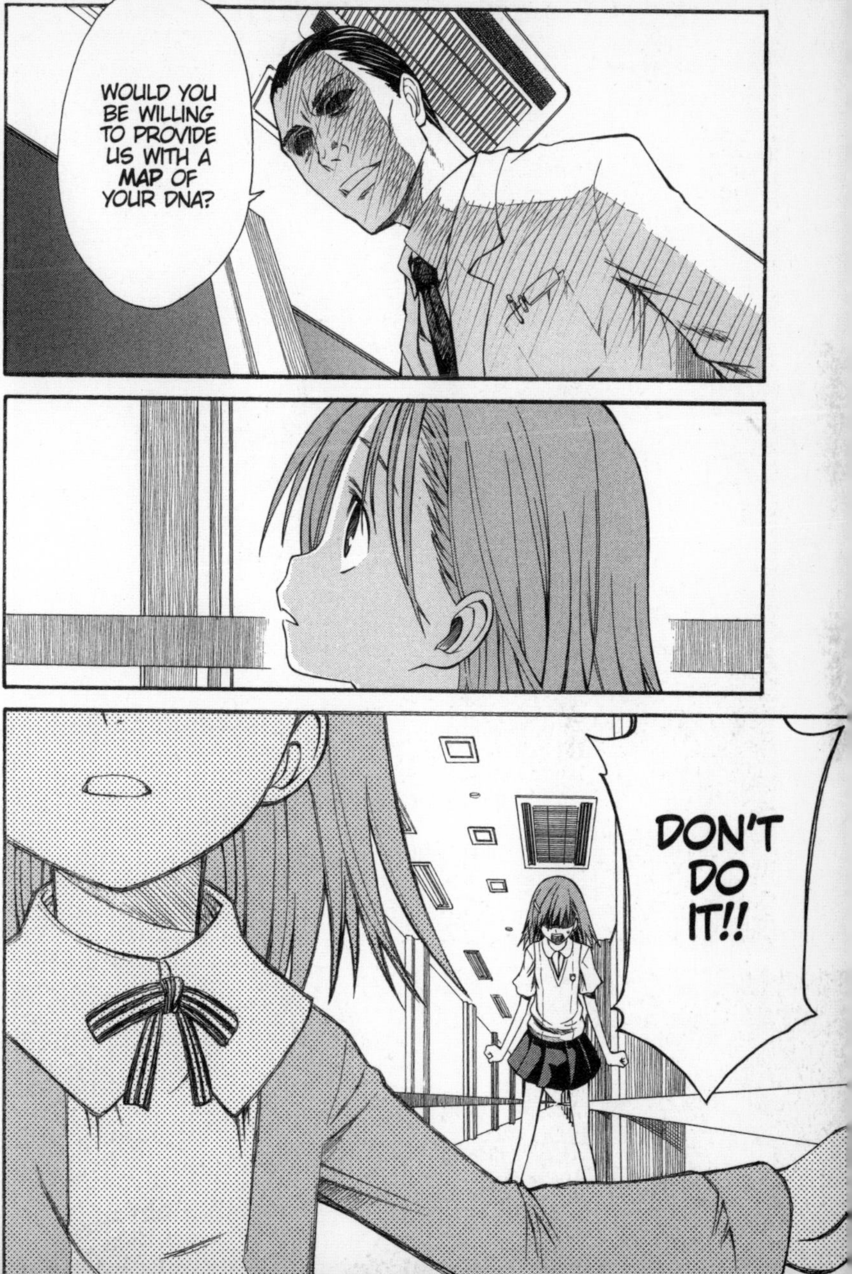
WOULD YOU BE WILLING TO PROVIDE US WITH A MAP OF YOUR DNA?
DON'T DO IT!!

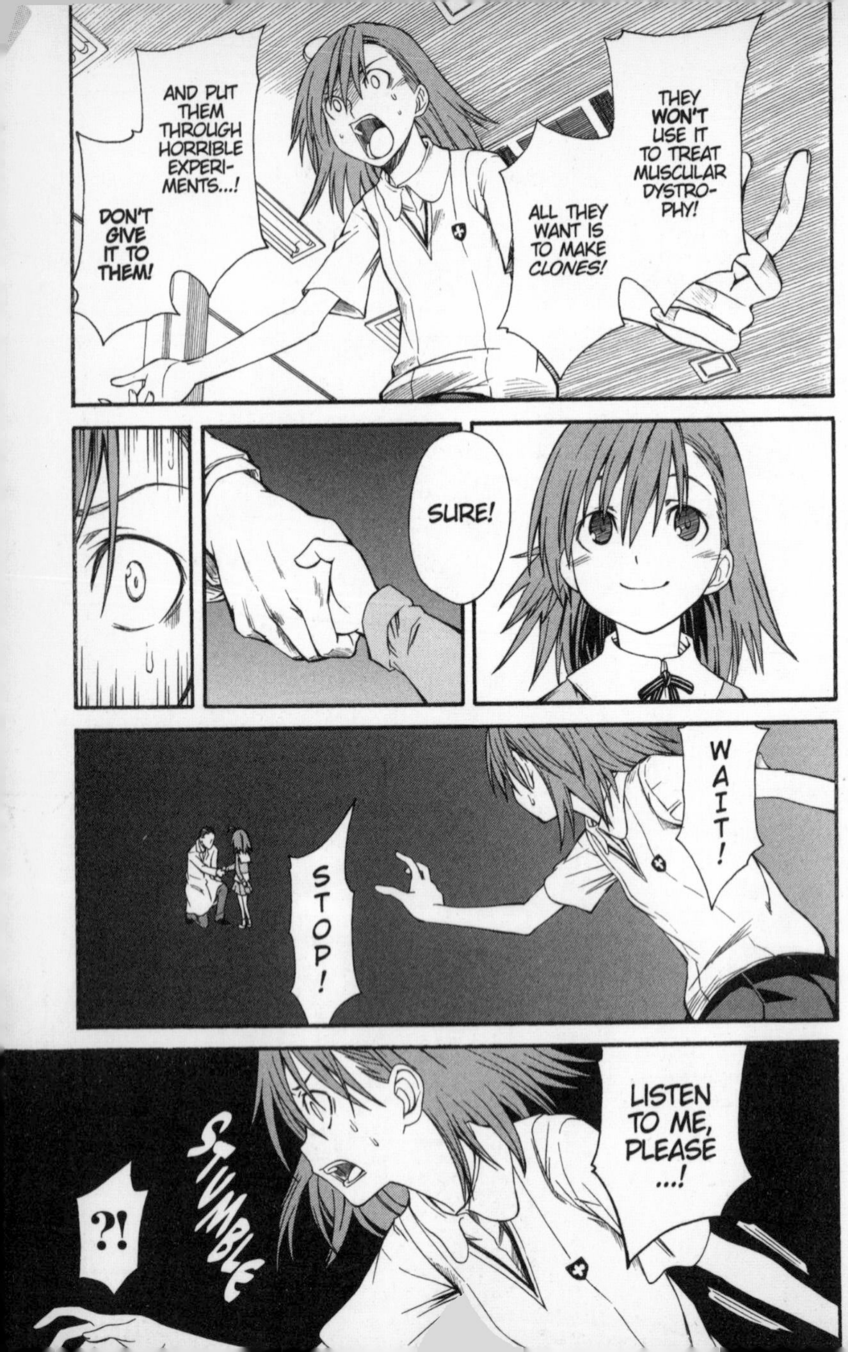
THEY WON'T USE IT TO TREAT MUSCULAR DYSTROPHY!
ALL THEY WANT IS TO MAKE CLONES!
AND PUT THEM THROUGH HORRIBLE EXPERIMENTS...!
DON'T GIVE IT TO THEM!
SURE!
WAIT!
STOP!
LISTEN TO ME, PLEASE ...!
STUMBLE
?!

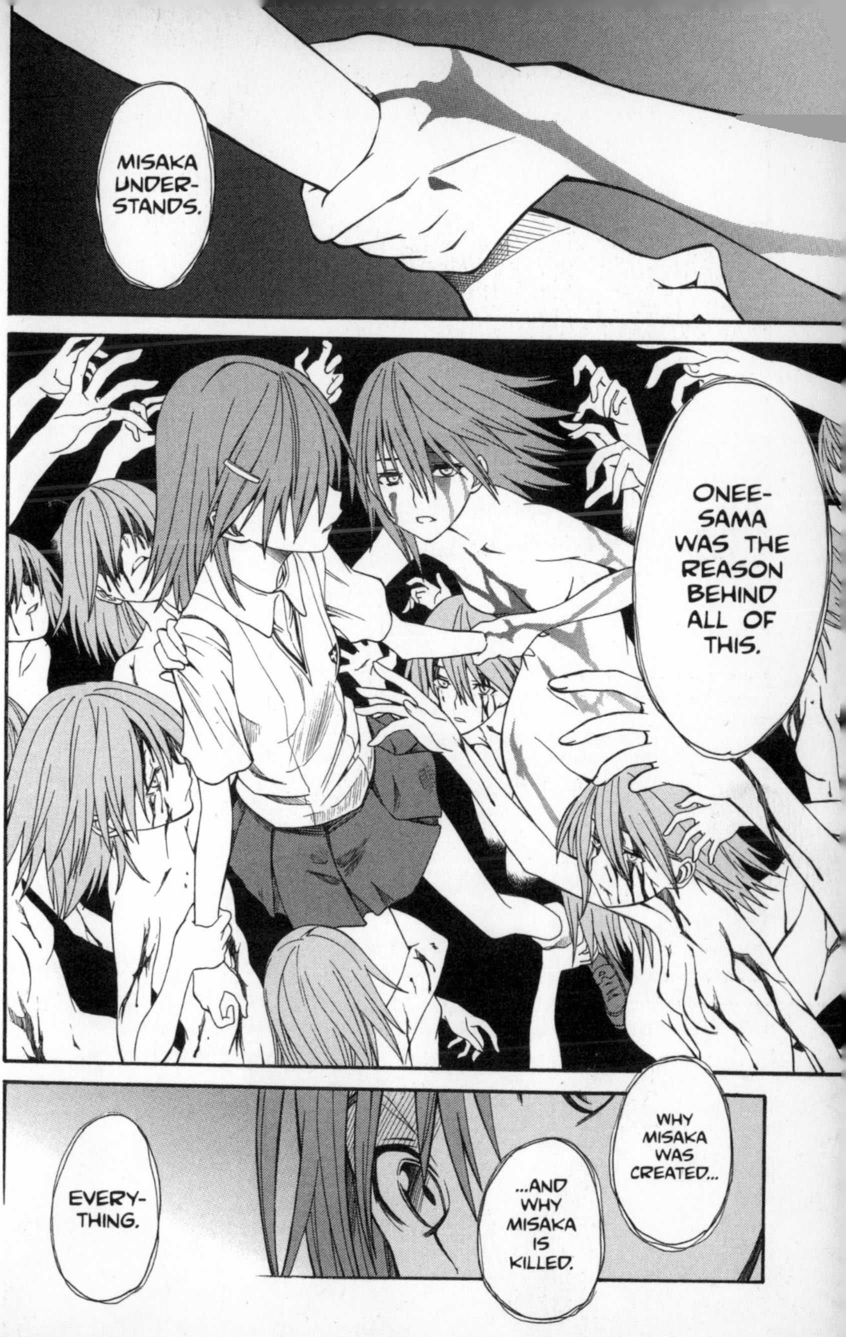
MISAKA UNDER-STANDS.
ONEE-SAMA WAS THE REASON BEHIND ALL OF THIS.
WHY MISAKA WAS CREATED...
...AND WHY MISAKA IS KILLED.
EVERY-THING.

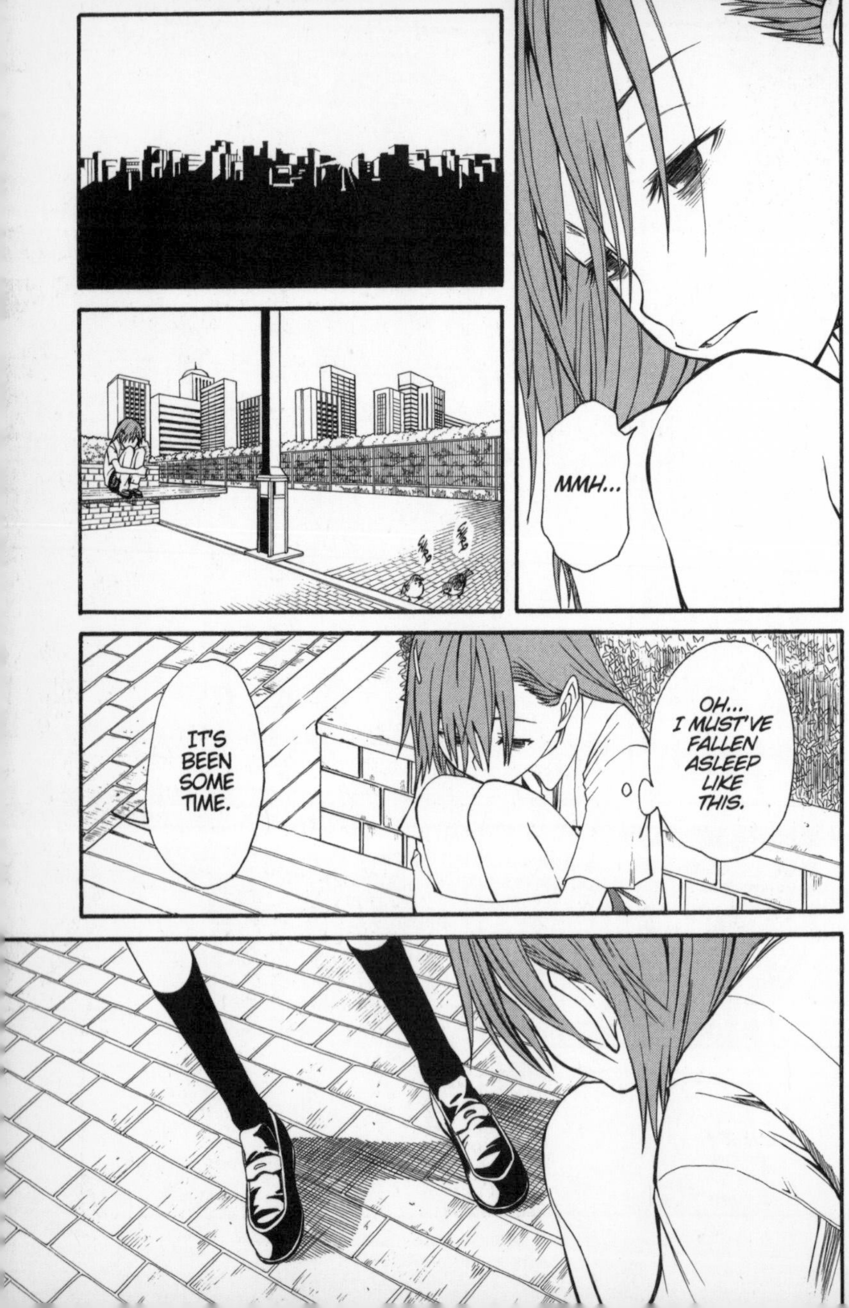
MMH...
OH... I MUST'VE FALLEN ASLEEP LIKE THIS.
IT'S BEEN SOME TIME.

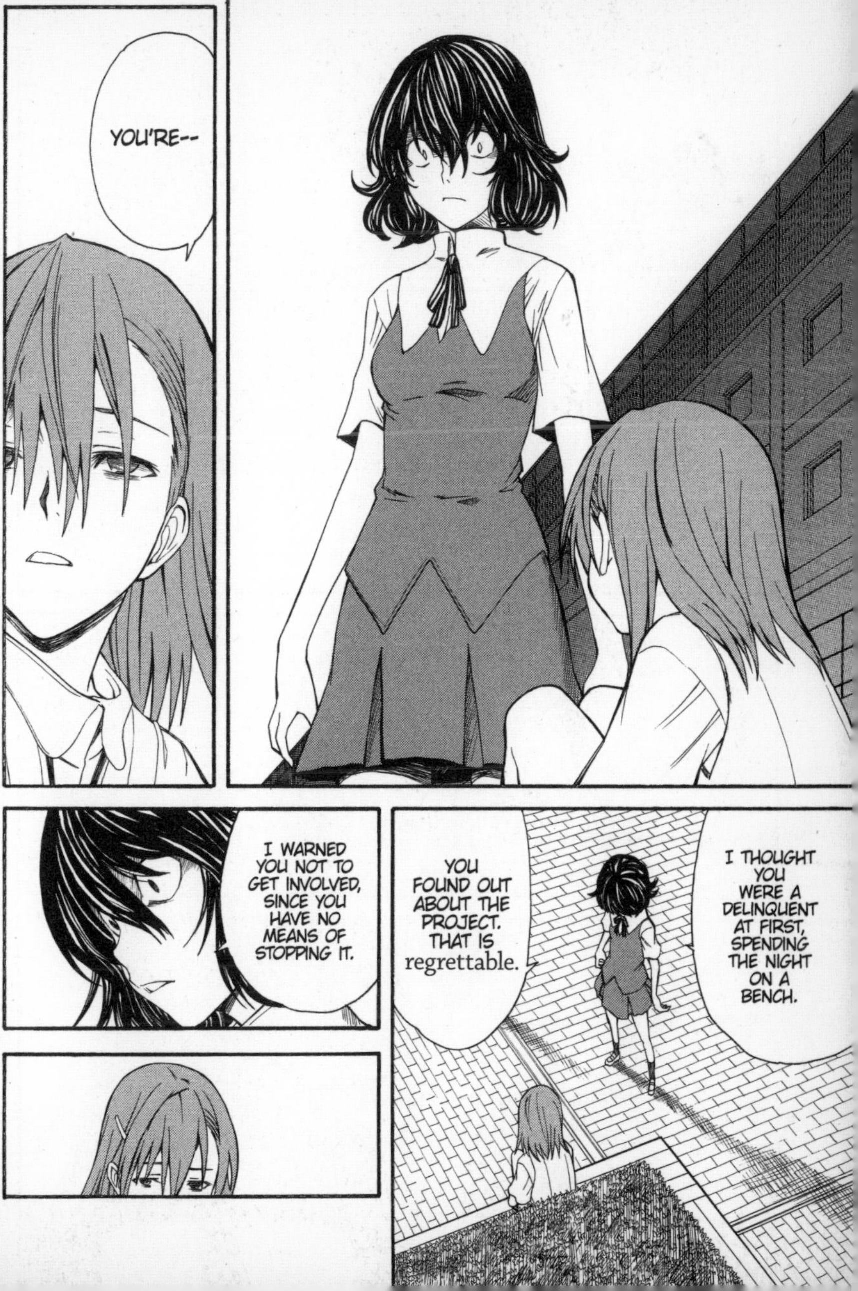
YOU'RE--
I THOUGHT YOU WERE A DELINQUENT AT FIRST, SPENDING THE NIGHT ON A BENCH.
YOU FOUND OUT ABOUT THE PROJECT. THAT IS regrettable.
I WARNED YOU NOT TO GET INVOLVED, SINCE YOU HAVE NO MEANS OF STOPPING IT.

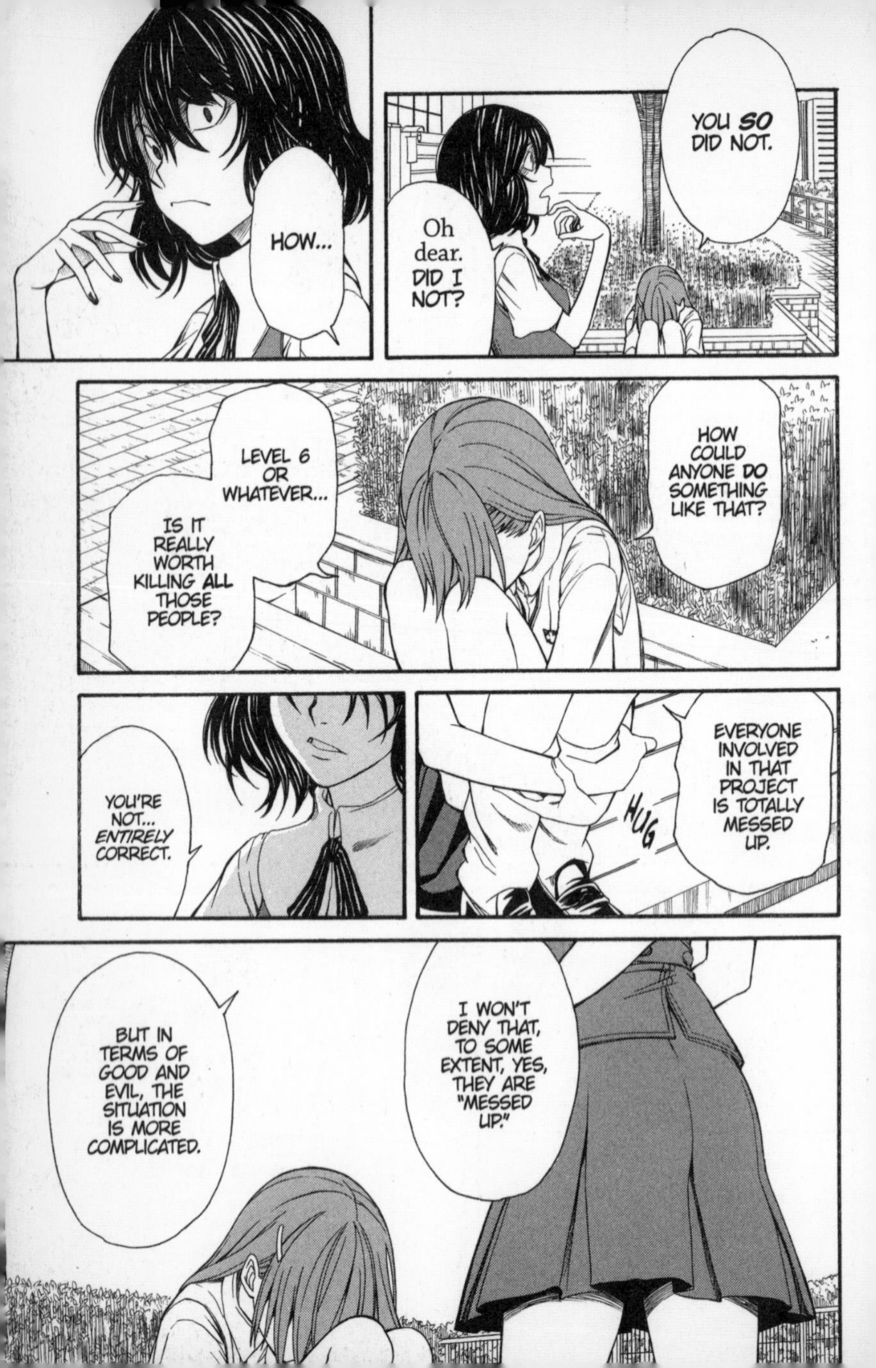
YOU SO DID NOT.
Oh dear. DID I NOT?
HOW...
HOW COULD ANYONE DO SOMETHING LIKE THAT?
LEVEL 6 OR WHATEVER...
IS IT REALLY WORTH KILLING ALL THOSE PEOPLE?
EVERYONE INVOLVED IN THAT PROJECT IS TOTALLY MESSED UP.
HUG
YOU'RE NOT... *ENTIRELY* CORRECT.
I WON'T DENY THAT, TO SOME EXTENT, YES, THEY ARE "MESSED UP."
BUT IN TERMS OF GOOD AND EVIL, THE SITUATION IS MORE COMPLICATED.

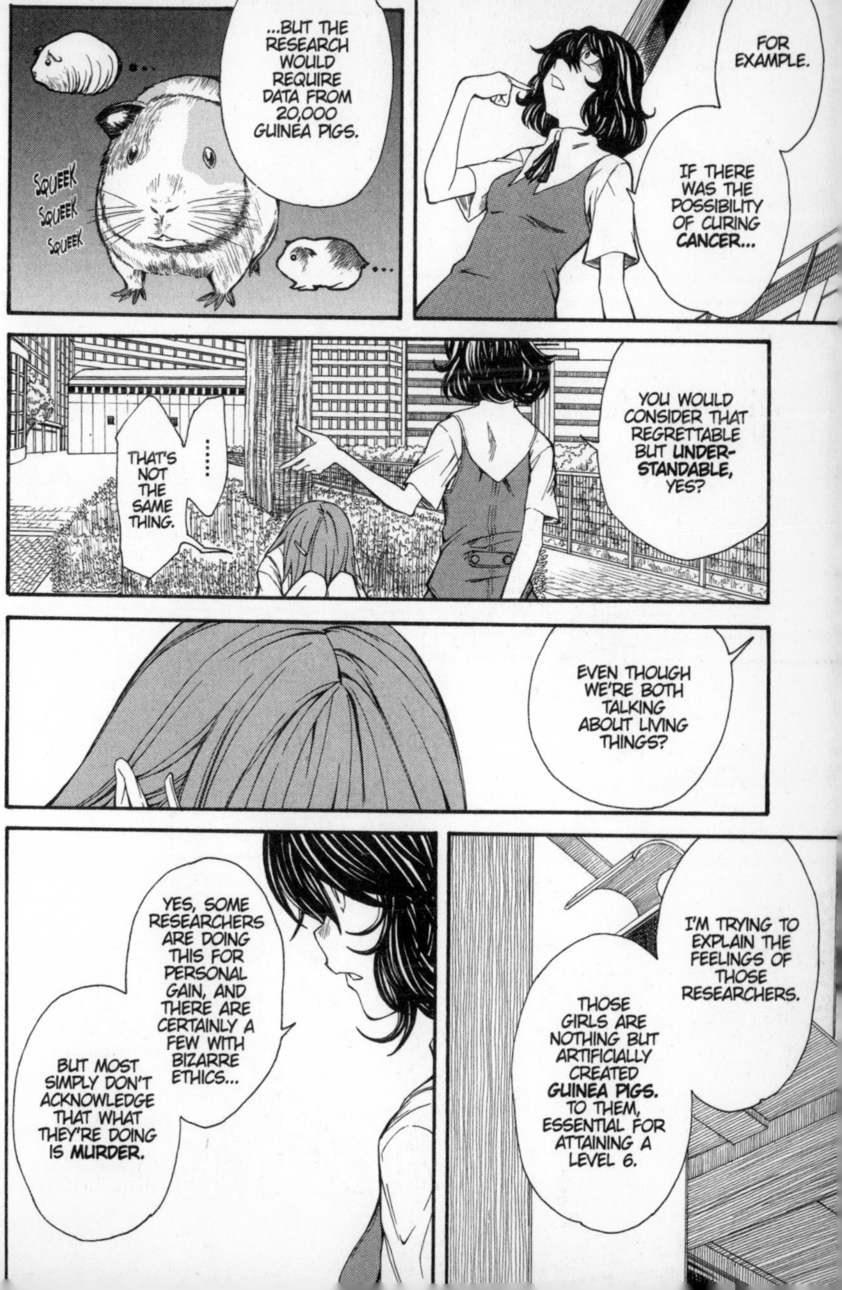
FOR EXAMPLE.
IF THERE WAS THE POSSIBILITY OF CURING CANCER...
...BUT THE RESEARCH WOULD REQUIRE DATA FROM 20,000 GUINEA PIGS.
SQUEEK
SQUEEK
SQUEEK
YOU WOULD CONSIDER THAT REGRETTABLE BUT UNDER-STANDABLE, YES?
......
THAT'S NOT THE SAME THING.
EVEN THOUGH WE'RE BOTH TALKING ABOUT LIVING THINGS?
I'M TRYING TO EXPLAIN THE FEELINGS OF THOSE RESEARCHERS.
THOSE GIRLS ARE NOTHING BUT ARTIFICIALLY CREATED GUINEA PIGS. TO THEM, ESSENTIAL FOR ATTAINING A LEVEL 6.
YES, SOME RESEARCHERS ARE DOING THIS FOR PERSONAL GAIN, AND THERE ARE CERTAINLY A FEW WITH BIZARRE ETHICS...
BUT MOST SIMPLY DON'T ACKNOWLEDGE THAT WHAT THEY'RE DOING IS MURDER.

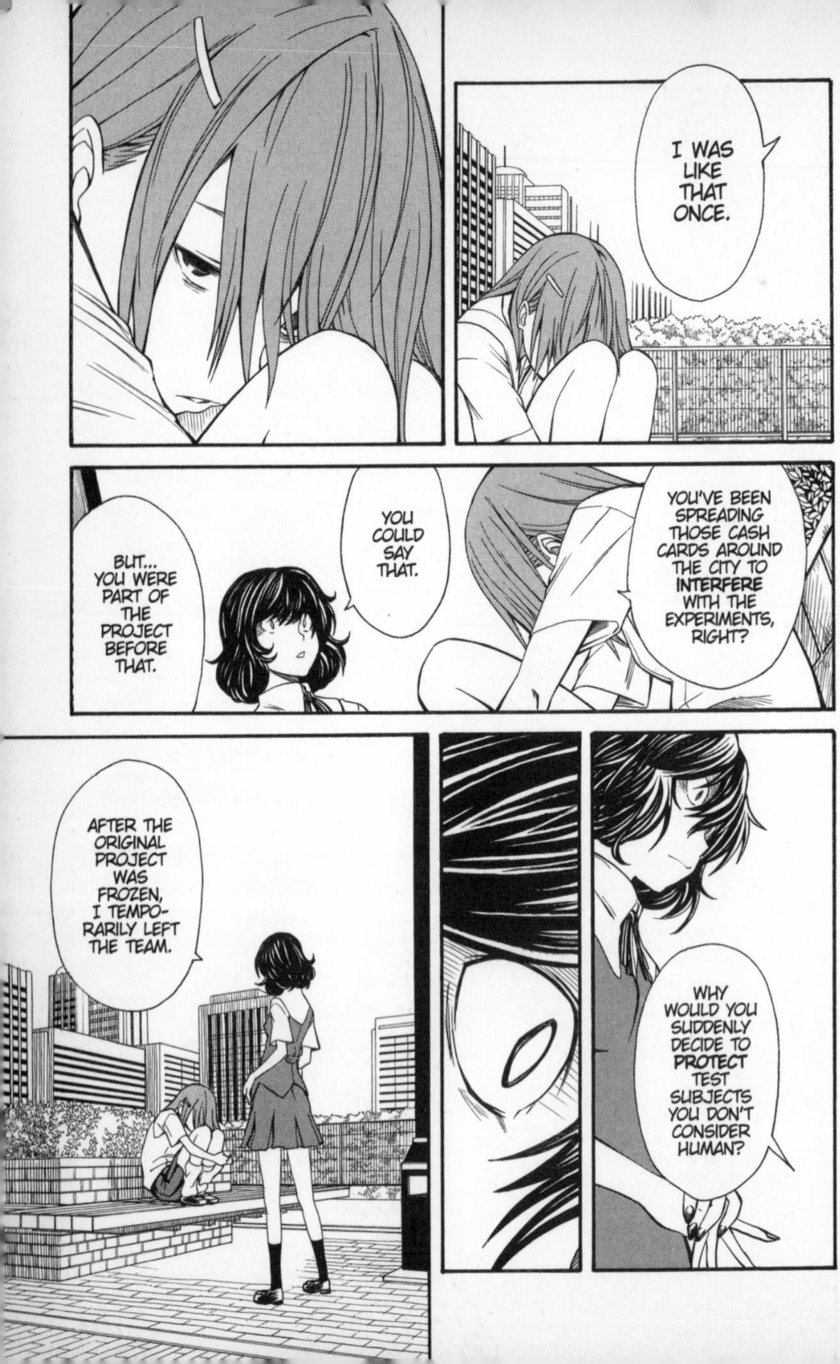
I WAS LIKE THAT ONCE.
YOU'VE BEEN SPREADING THOSE CASH CARDS AROUND THE CITY TO **INTERFERE** WITH THE EXPERIMENTS, RIGHT?
YOU COULD SAY THAT.
BUT... YOU WERE PART OF THE PROJECT BEFORE THAT.
WHY WOULD YOU SUDDENLY DECIDE TO **PROTECT** TEST SUBJECTS YOU DON'T CONSIDER HUMAN?
AFTER THE ORIGINAL PROJECT WAS FROZEN, I TEMPO-RARILY LEFT THE TEAM.

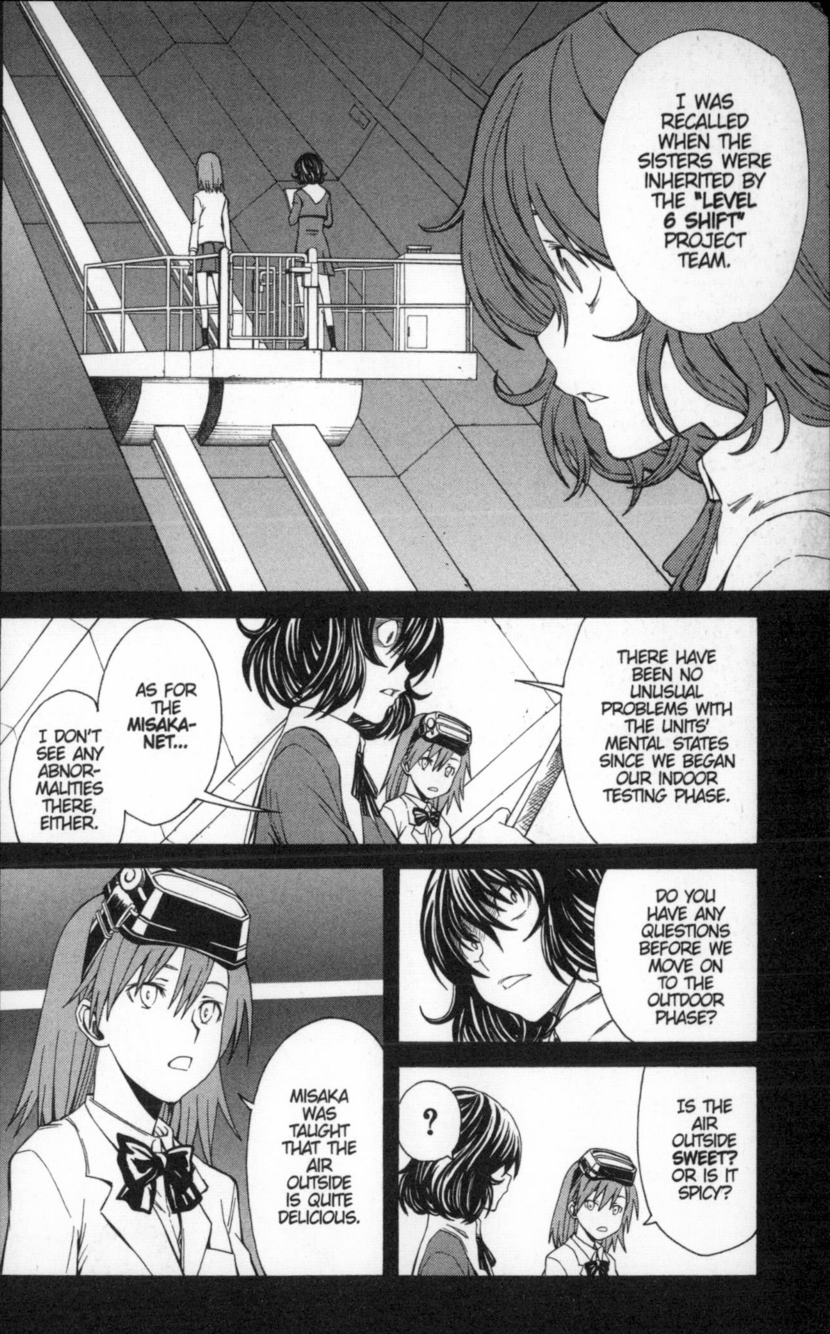
I WAS RECALLED WHEN THE SISTERS WERE INHERITED BY THE "LEVEL 6 SHIFT" PROJECT TEAM.
THERE HAVE BEEN NO UNUSUAL PROBLEMS WITH THE UNITS' MENTAL STATES SINCE WE BEGAN OUR INDOOR TESTING PHASE.
AS FOR THE MISAKA-NET...
I DON'T SEE ANY ABNOR-MALITIES THERE, EITHER.
DO YOU HAVE ANY QUESTIONS BEFORE WE MOVE ON TO THE OUTDOOR PHASE?
IS THE AIR OUTSIDE SWEET? OR IS IT SPICY?
?
MISAKA WAS TAUGHT THAT THE AIR OUTSIDE IS QUITE DELICIOUS.

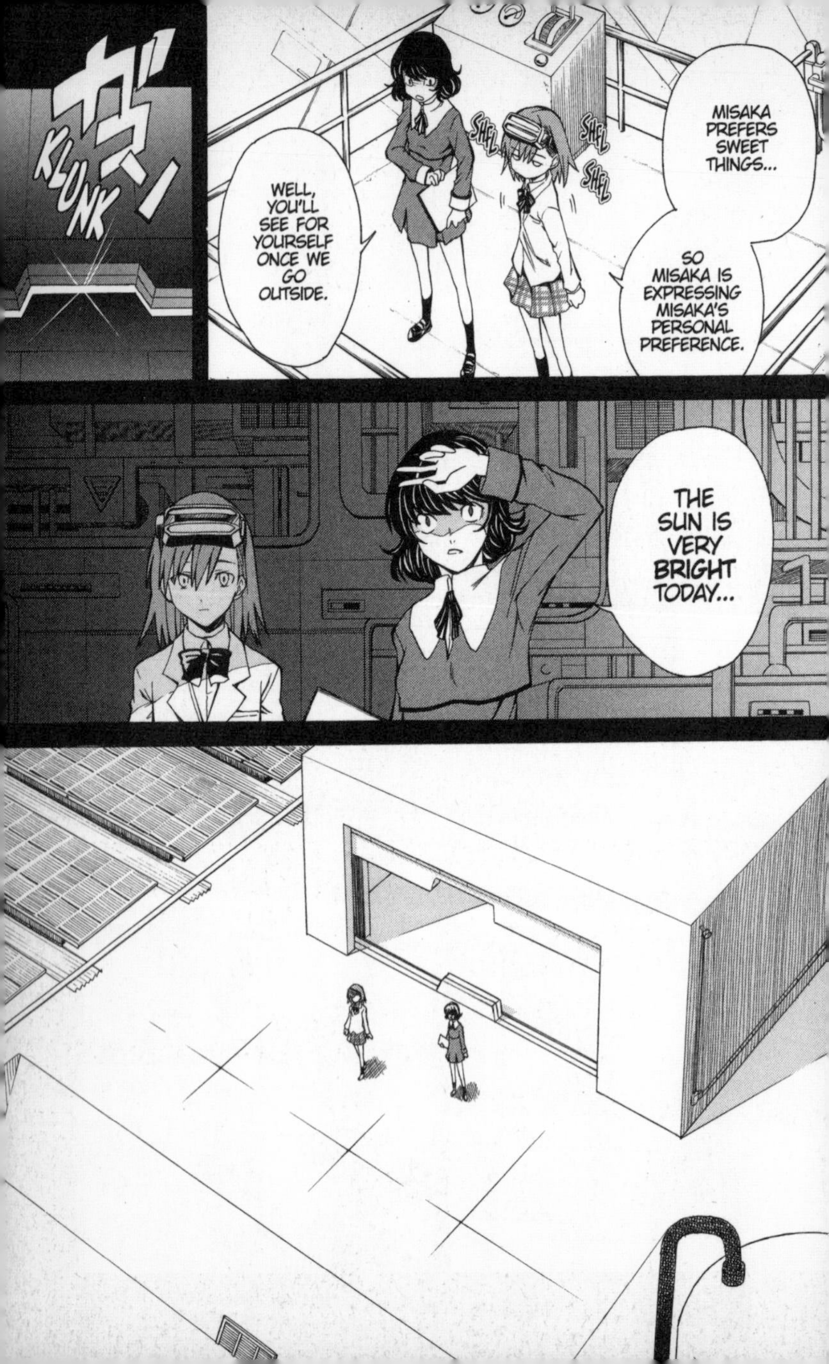
MISAKA PREFERS SWEET THINGS...
SO MISAKA IS EXPRESSING MISAKA'S PERSONAL PREFERENCE.
SHEL SHEL SHEL SHEL
WELL, YOU'LL SEE FOR YOURSELF ONCE WE GO OUTSIDE.
KLUNK
THE SUN IS VERY BRIGHT TODAY...

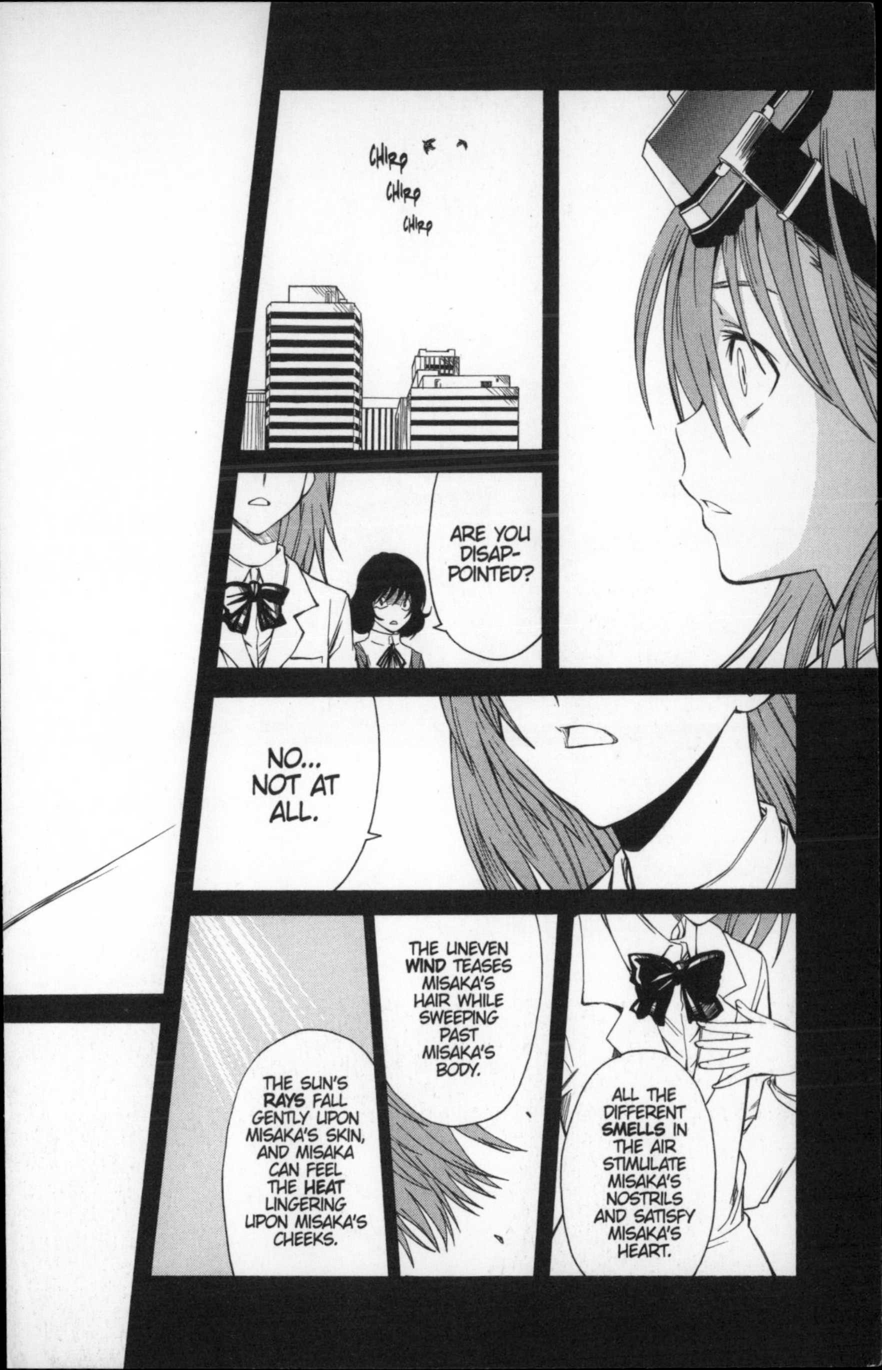
CHIRP
CHIRP
CHIRP
ARE YOU DISAP-POINTED?
NO... NOT AT ALL.
ALL THE DIFFERENT SMELLS IN THE AIR STIMULATE MISAKA'S NOSTRILS AND SATISFY MISAKA'S HEART.
THE UNEVEN WIND TEASES MISAKA'S HAIR WHILE SWEEPING PAST MISAKA'S BODY.
THE SUN'S RAYS FALL GENTLY UPON MISAKA'S SKIN, AND MISAKA CAN FEEL THE HEAT LINGERING UPON MISAKA'S CHEEKS.

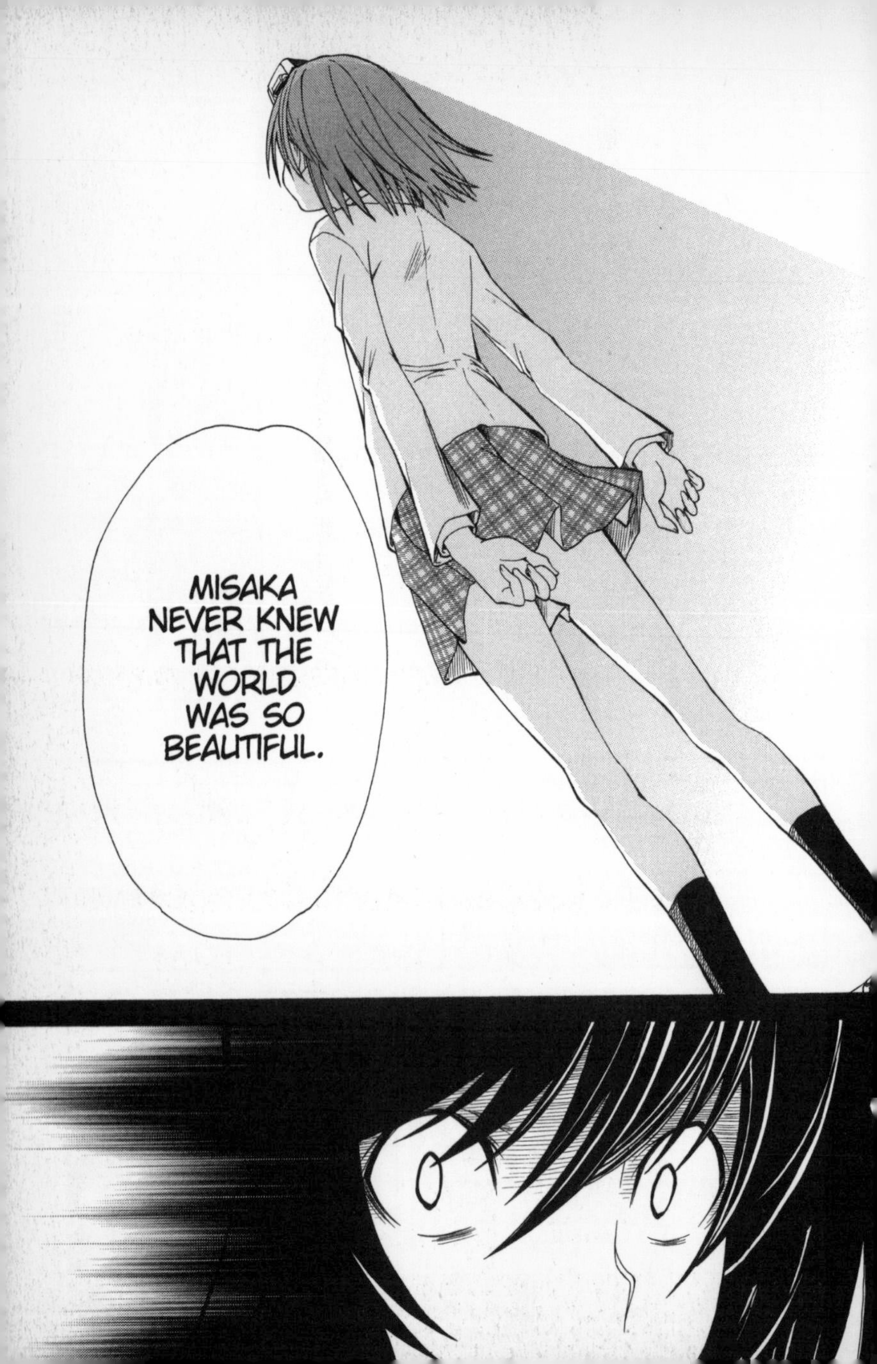
MISAKA NEVER KNEW THAT THE WORLD WAS SO BEAUTIFUL.

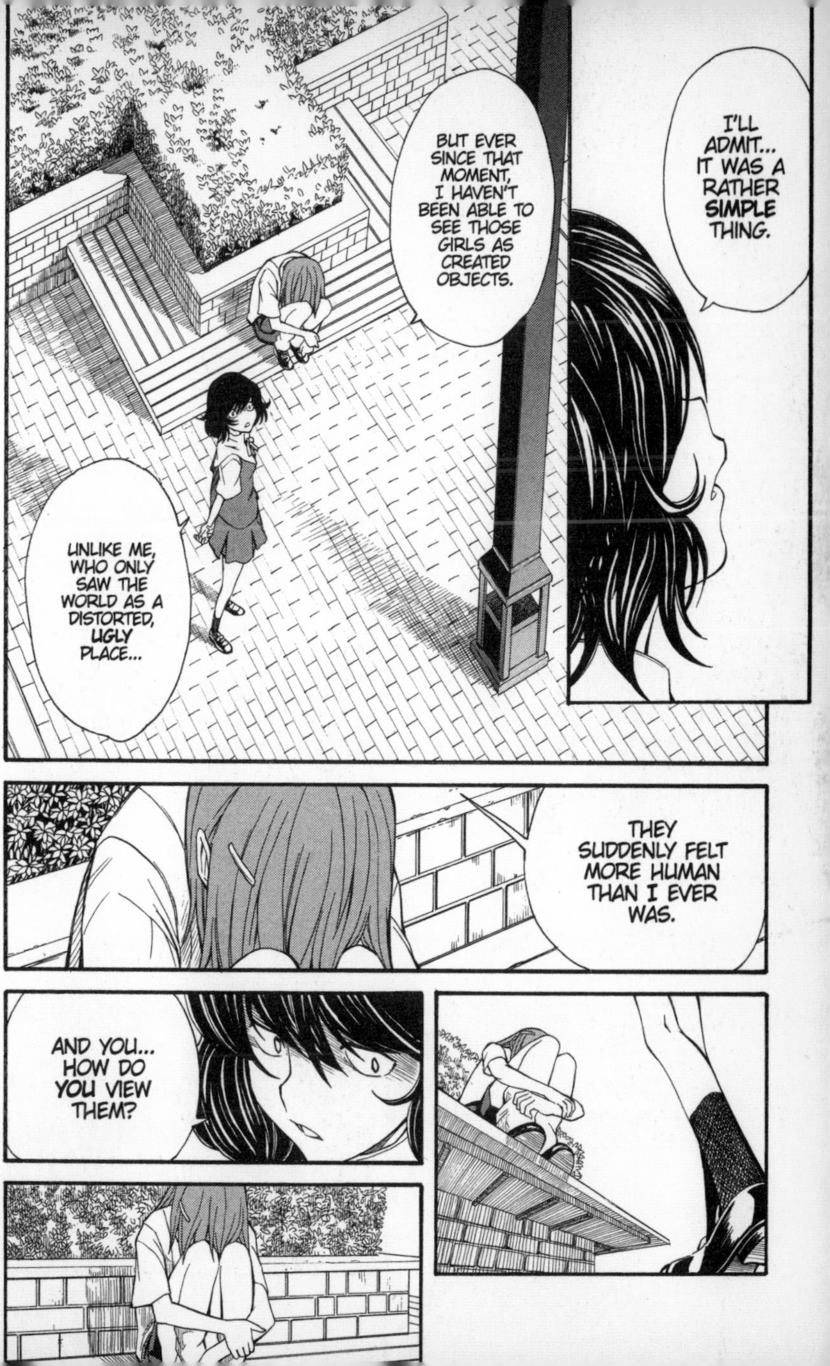
I'LL ADMIT... IT WAS A RATHER SIMPLE THING.
BUT EVER SINCE THAT MOMENT, I HAVEN'T BEEN ABLE TO SEE THOSE GIRLS AS CREATED OBJECTS.
UNLIKE ME, WHO ONLY SAW THE WORLD AS A DISTORTED, UGLY PLACE...
THEY SUDDENLY FELT MORE HUMAN THAN I EVER WAS.
AND YOU... HOW DO YOU VIEW THEM?

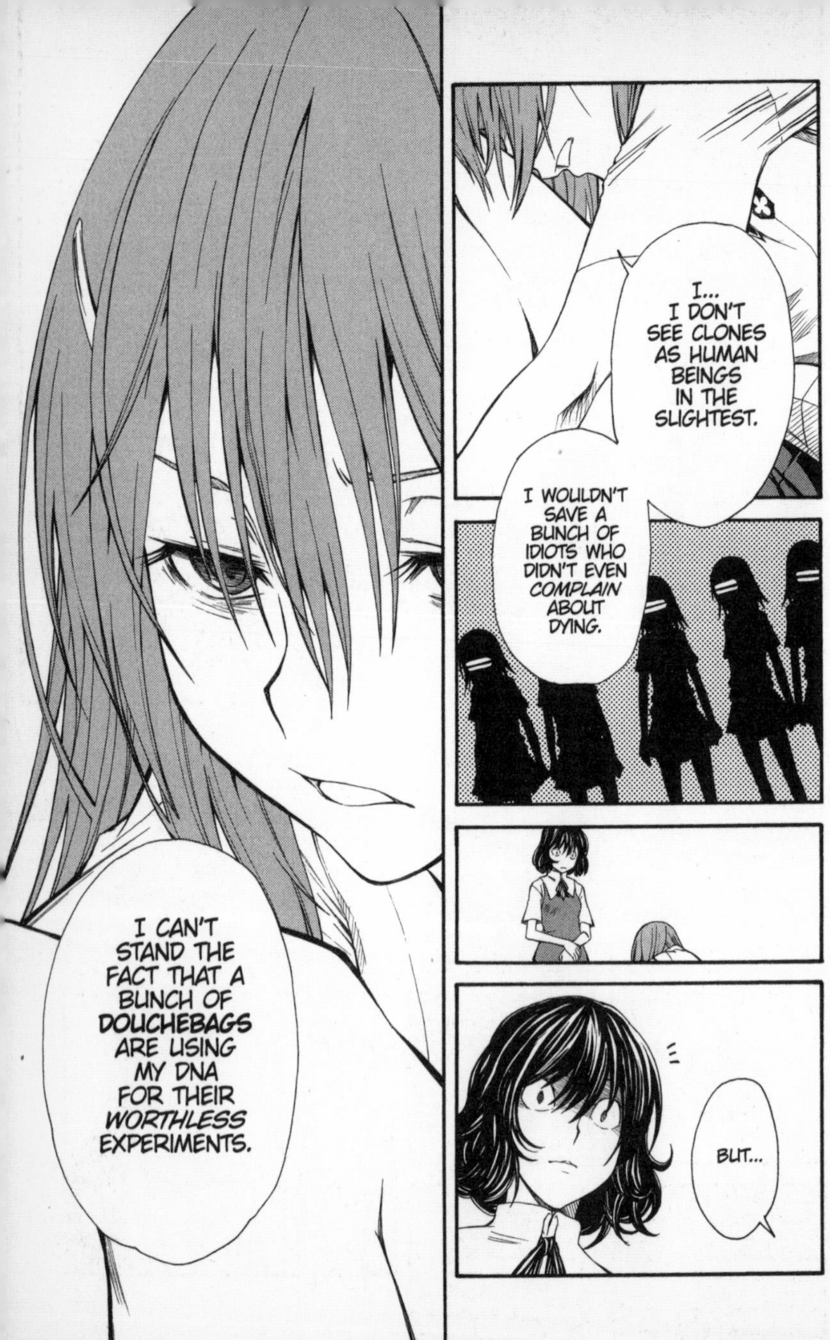
I... I DON'T SEE CLONES AS HUMAN BEINGS IN THE SLIGHTEST.
I WOULDN'T SAVE A BUNCH OF IDIOTS WHO DIDN'T EVEN *COMPLAIN* ABOUT DYING.
BUT...
I CAN'T STAND THE FACT THAT A BUNCH OF **DOUCHEBAGS** ARE USING MY DNA FOR THEIR *WORTHLESS* EXPERIMENTS.

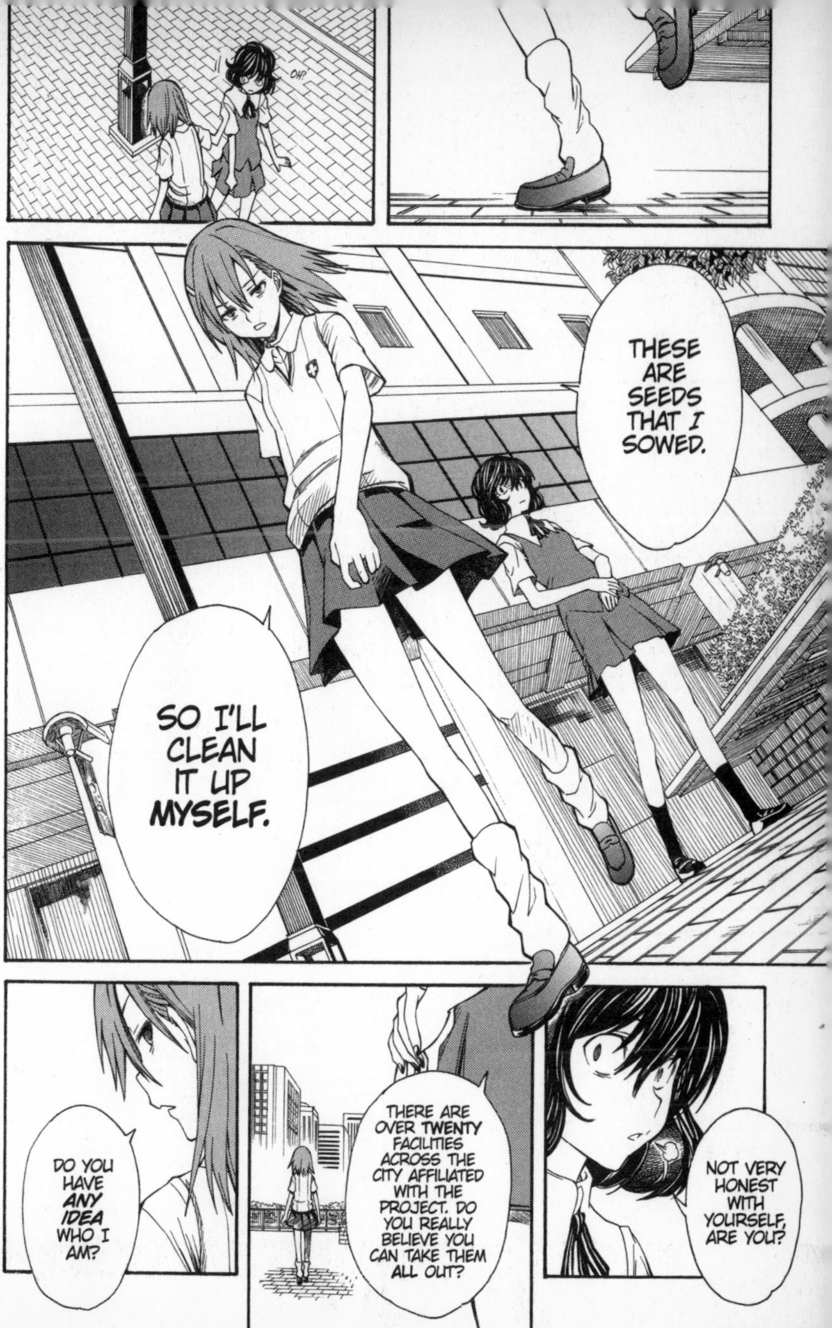
OH?
THESE ARE SEEDS THAT I SOWED.
SO I'LL CLEAN IT UP MYSELF.
NOT VERY HONEST WITH YOURSELF, ARE YOU?
THERE ARE OVER TWENTY FACILITIES ACROSS THE CITY AFFILIATED WITH THE PROJECT. DO YOU REALLY BELIEVE YOU CAN TAKE THEM ALL OUT?
DO YOU HAVE ANY IDEA WHO I AM?

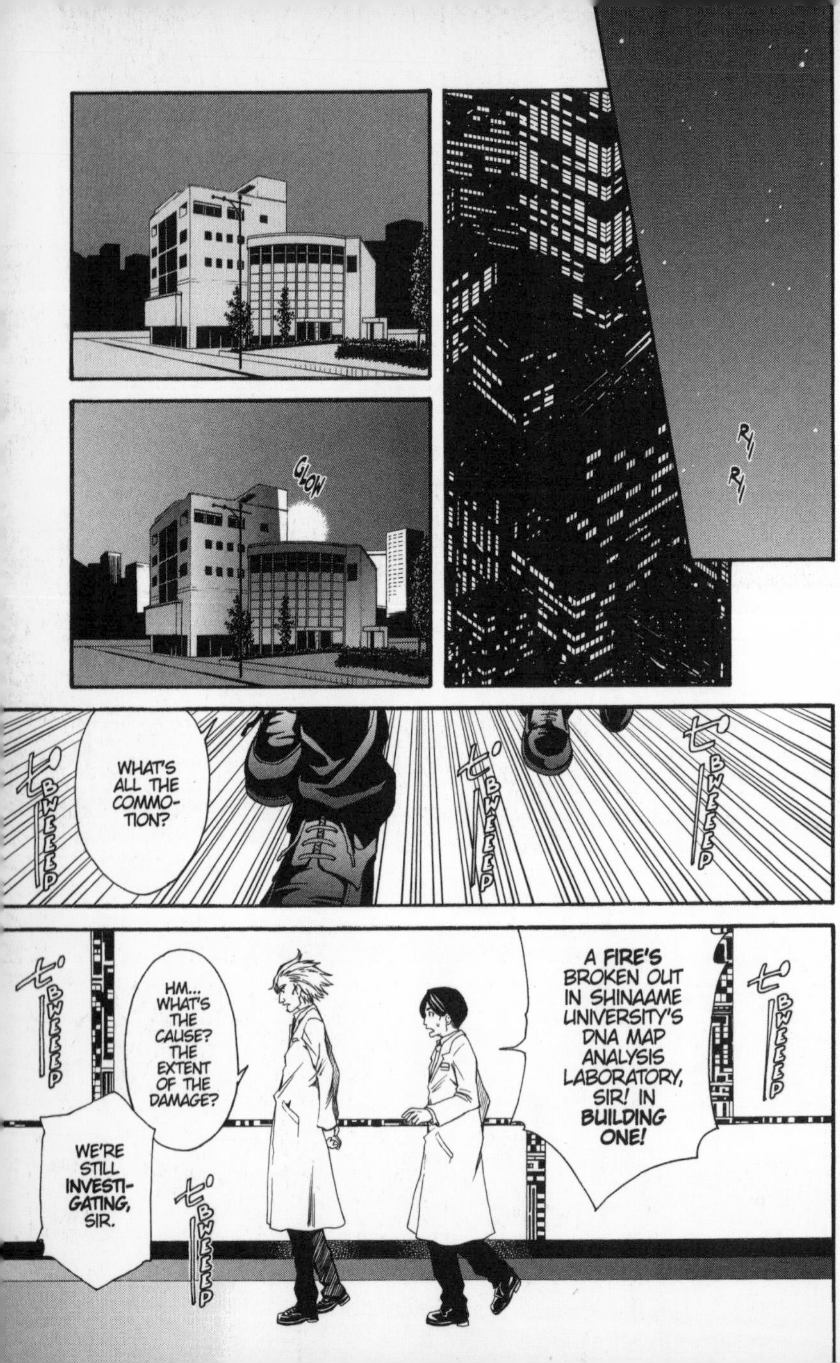
RI RI
GLOW
BWEEEP
BWEEEP
WHAT'S ALL THE COMMOTION?
BWEEEP
BWEEEP
A FIRE'S BROKEN OUT IN SHINAAME UNIVERSITY'S DNA MAP ANALYSIS LABORATORY, SIR! IN BUILDING ONE!
HM... WHAT'S THE CAUSE? THE EXTENT OF THE DAMAGE?
BWEEEP
WE'RE STILL INVESTIGATING, SIR.
BWEEEP

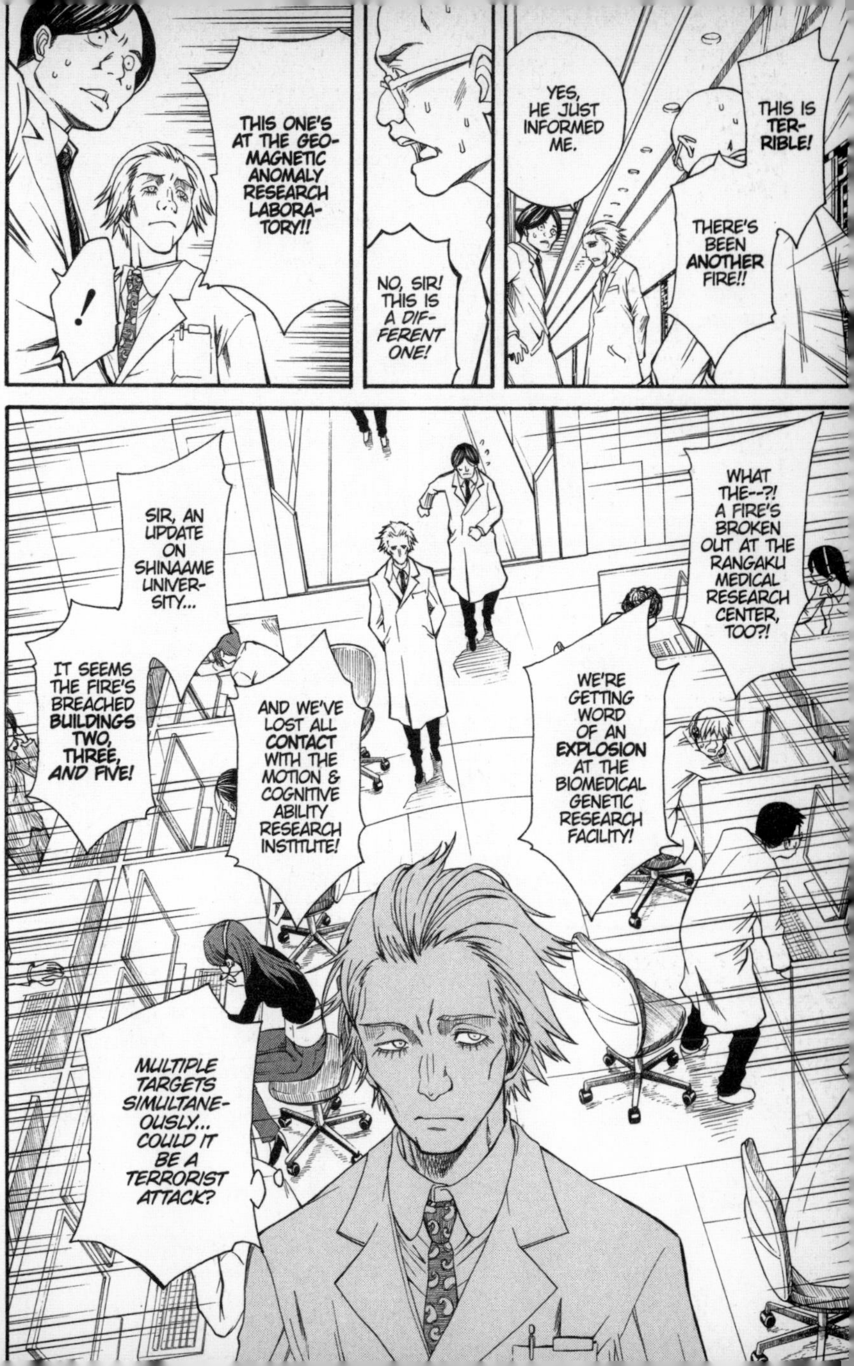
THIS IS TER-RIBLE!
THERE'S BEEN ANOTHER FIRE!!
YES, HE JUST INFORMED ME.
NO, SIR! THIS IS A DIF-FERENT ONE!
THIS ONE'S AT THE GEO-MAGNETIC ANOMALY RESEARCH LABORA-TORY!!
!
WHAT THE--?! A FIRE'S BROKEN OUT AT THE RANGAKU MEDICAL RESEARCH CENTER, TOO?!
SIR, AN UPDATE ON SHINAAME UNIVER-SITY...
WE'RE GETTING WORD OF AN EXPLOSION AT THE BIOMEDICAL GENETIC RESEARCH FACILITY!
AND WE'VE LOST ALL CONTACT WITH THE MOTION & COGNITIVE ABILITY RESEARCH INSTITUTE!
IT SEEMS THE FIRE'S BREACHED BUILDINGS TWO, THREE, AND FIVE!
MULTIPLE TARGETS SIMULTANE-OUSLY... COULD IT BE A TERRORIST ATTACK?

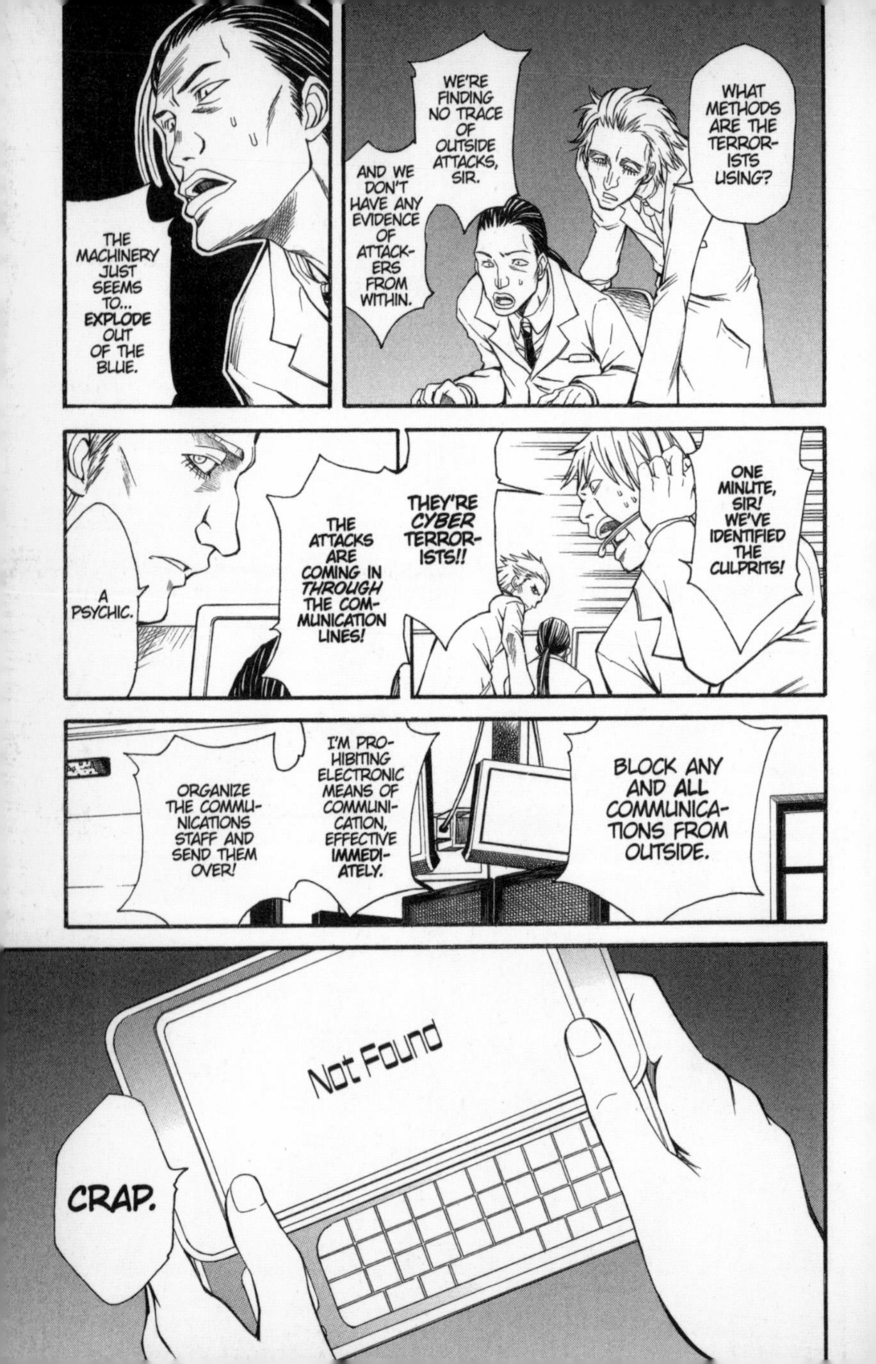

WHAT METHODS ARE THE TERRORISTS USING?
WE'RE FINDING NO TRACE OF OUTSIDE ATTACKS, SIR.
AND WE DON'T HAVE ANY EVIDENCE OF ATTACKERS FROM WITHIN.
THE MACHINERY JUST SEEMS TO... EXPLODE OUT OF THE BLUE.
ONE MINUTE, SIR! WE'VE IDENTIFIED THE CULPRITS!
THEY'RE *CYBER* TERRORISTS!!
THE ATTACKS ARE COMING IN *THROUGH* THE COMMUNICATION LINES!
A PSYCHIC.
BLOCK ANY AND ALL COMMUNICATIONS FROM OUTSIDE.
I'M PROHIBITING ELECTRONIC MEANS OF COMMUNICATION, EFFECTIVE IMMEDIATELY.
ORGANIZE THE COMMUNICATIONS STAFF AND SEND THEM OVER!
Not Found
CRAP.

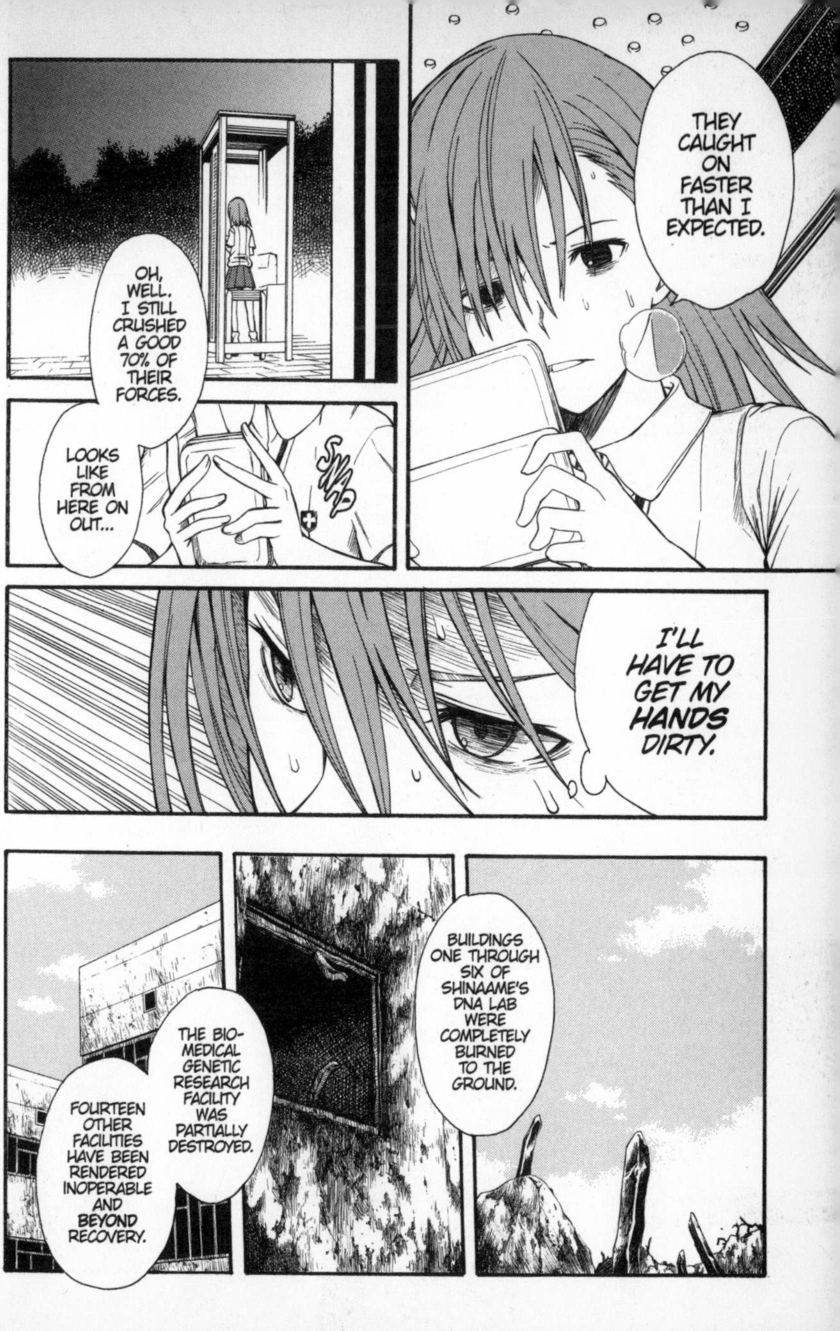
THEY CAUGHT ON FASTER THAN I EXPECTED.
OH, WELL. I STILL CRUSHED A GOOD 70% OF THEIR FORCES.
SNAP
LOOKS LIKE FROM HERE ON OUT...
I'LL HAVE TO GET MY HANDS DIRTY.
BUILDINGS ONE THROUGH SIX OF SHINAAME'S DNA LAB WERE COMPLETELY BURNED TO THE GROUND.
THE BIO-MEDICAL GENETIC RESEARCH FACILITY WAS PARTIALLY DESTROYED.
FOURTEEN OTHER FACILITIES HAVE BEEN RENDERED INOPERABLE AND BEYOND RECOVERY.

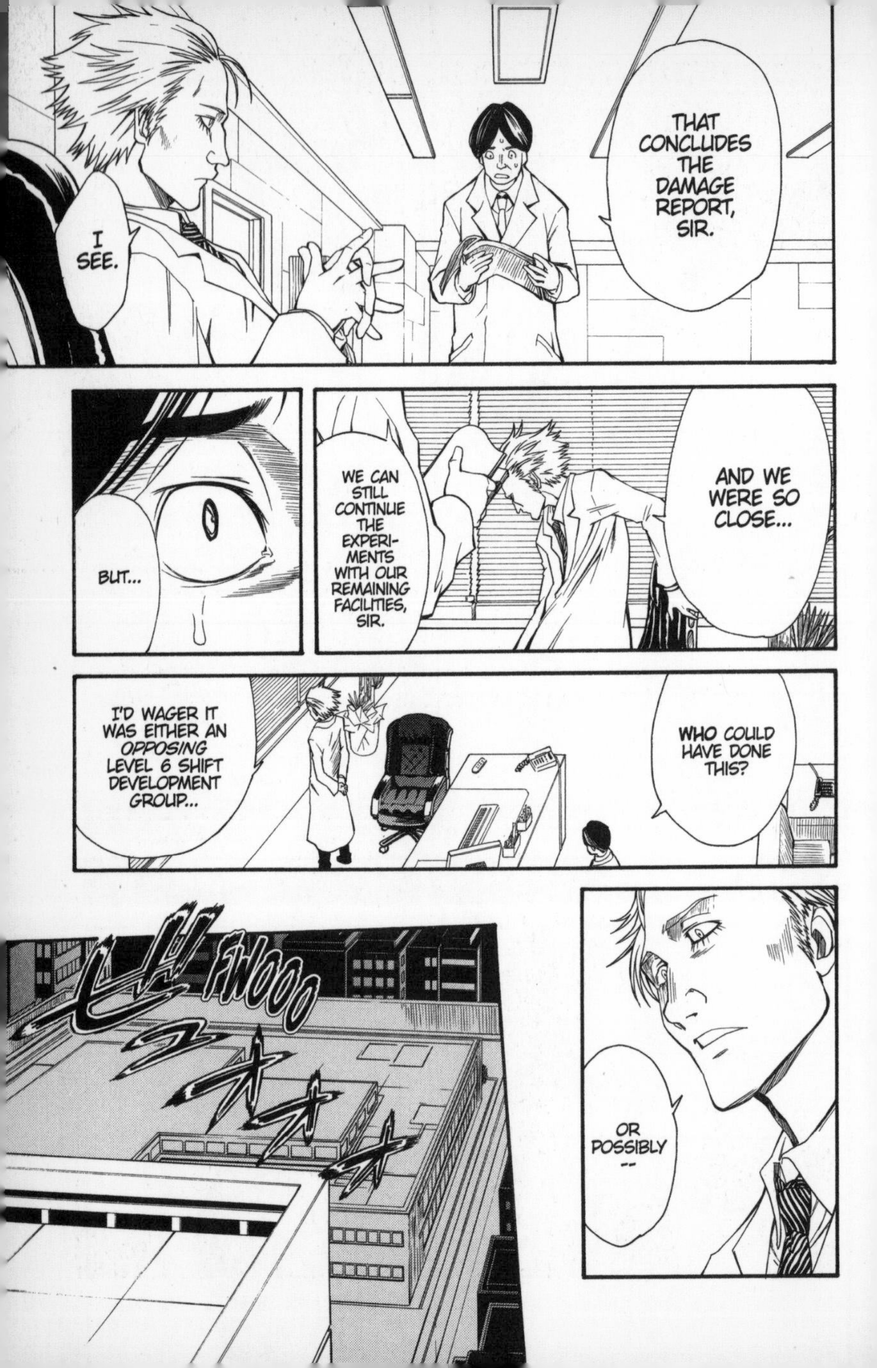
THAT CONCLUDES THE DAMAGE REPORT, SIR.
I SEE.
AND WE WERE SO CLOSE...
WE CAN STILL CONTINUE THE EXPERIMENTS WITH OUR REMAINING FACILITIES, SIR.
BUT...
WHO COULD HAVE DONE THIS?
I'D WAGER IT WAS EITHER AN *OPPOSING* LEVEL 6 SHIFT DEVELOPMENT GROUP...
OR POSSIBLY --
FWOOO

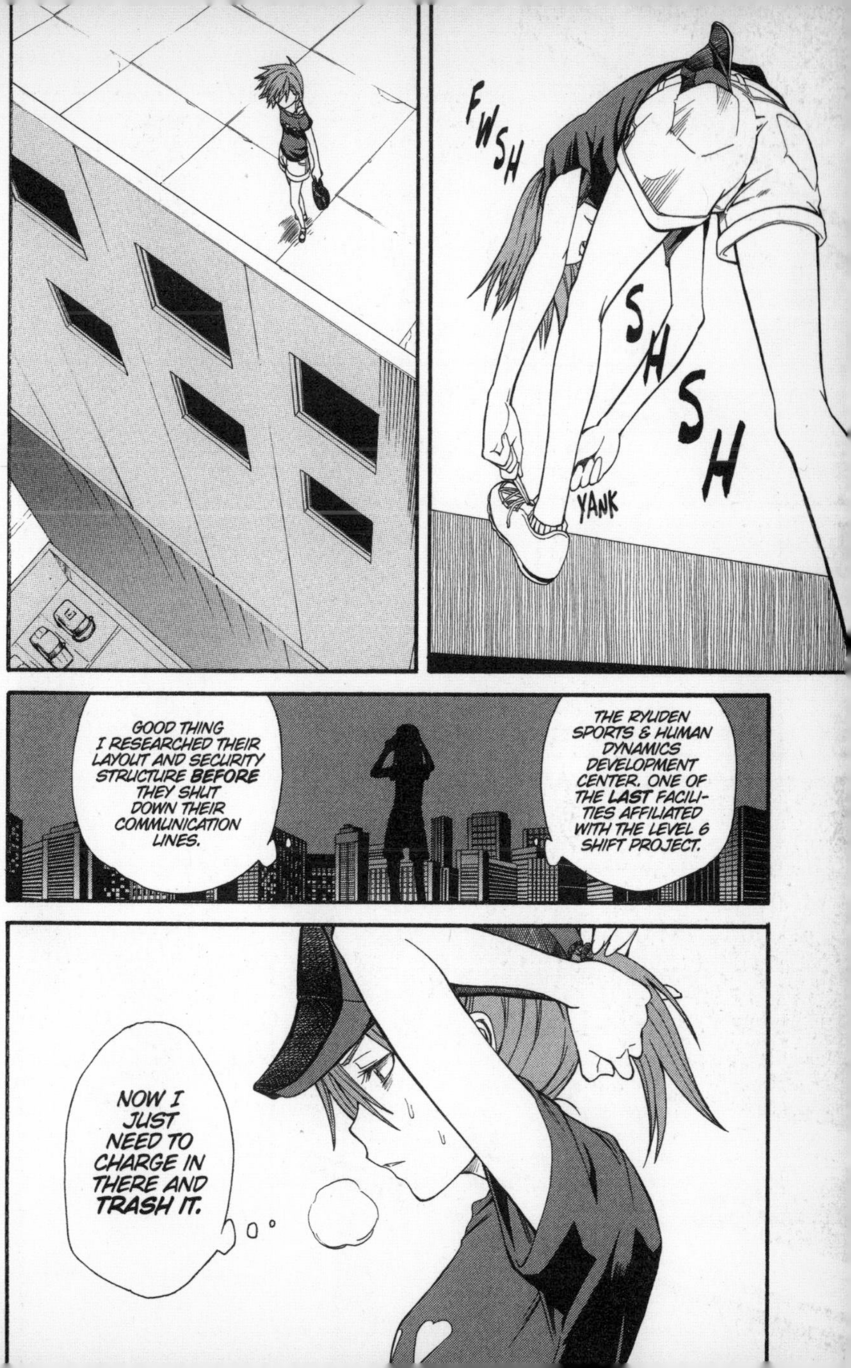
FWSH
SHSH
YANK
THE RYUDEN SPORTS & HUMAN DYNAMICS DEVELOPMENT CENTER. ONE OF THE LAST FACILI-TIES AFFILIATED WITH THE LEVEL 6 SHIFT PROJECT.
GOOD THING I RESEARCHED THEIR LAYOUT AND SECURITY STRUCTURE BEFORE THEY SHUT DOWN THEIR COMMUNICATION LINES.
NOW I JUST NEED TO CHARGE IN THERE AND TRASH IT.

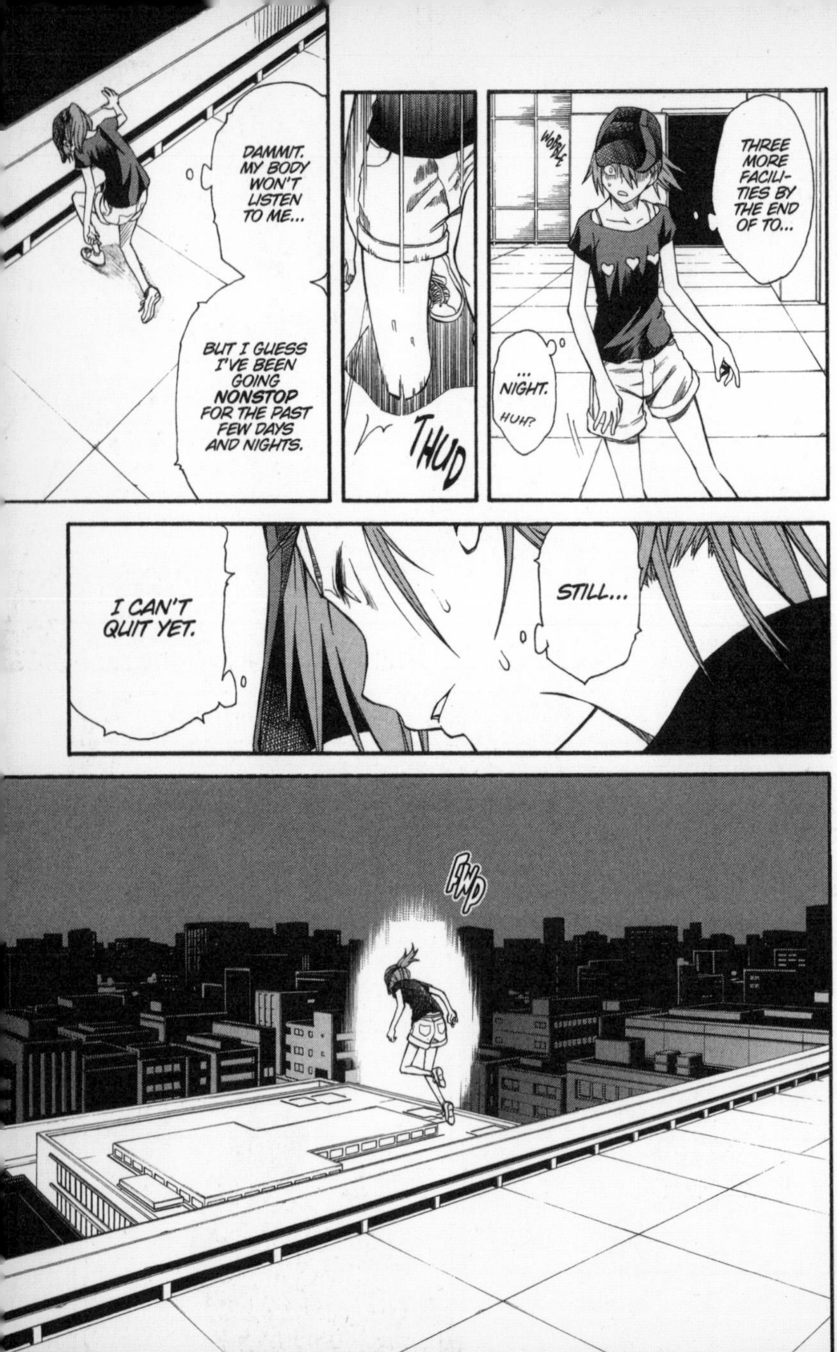
THREE MORE FACILI-TIES BY THE END OF TO...
WOBBLE
...NIGHT.
HUH?
THUD
DAMMIT. MY BODY WON'T LISTEN TO ME...
BUT I GUESS I'VE BEEN GOING **NONSTOP** FOR THE PAST FEW DAYS AND NIGHTS.
STILL...
I CAN'T QUIT YET.
FWP

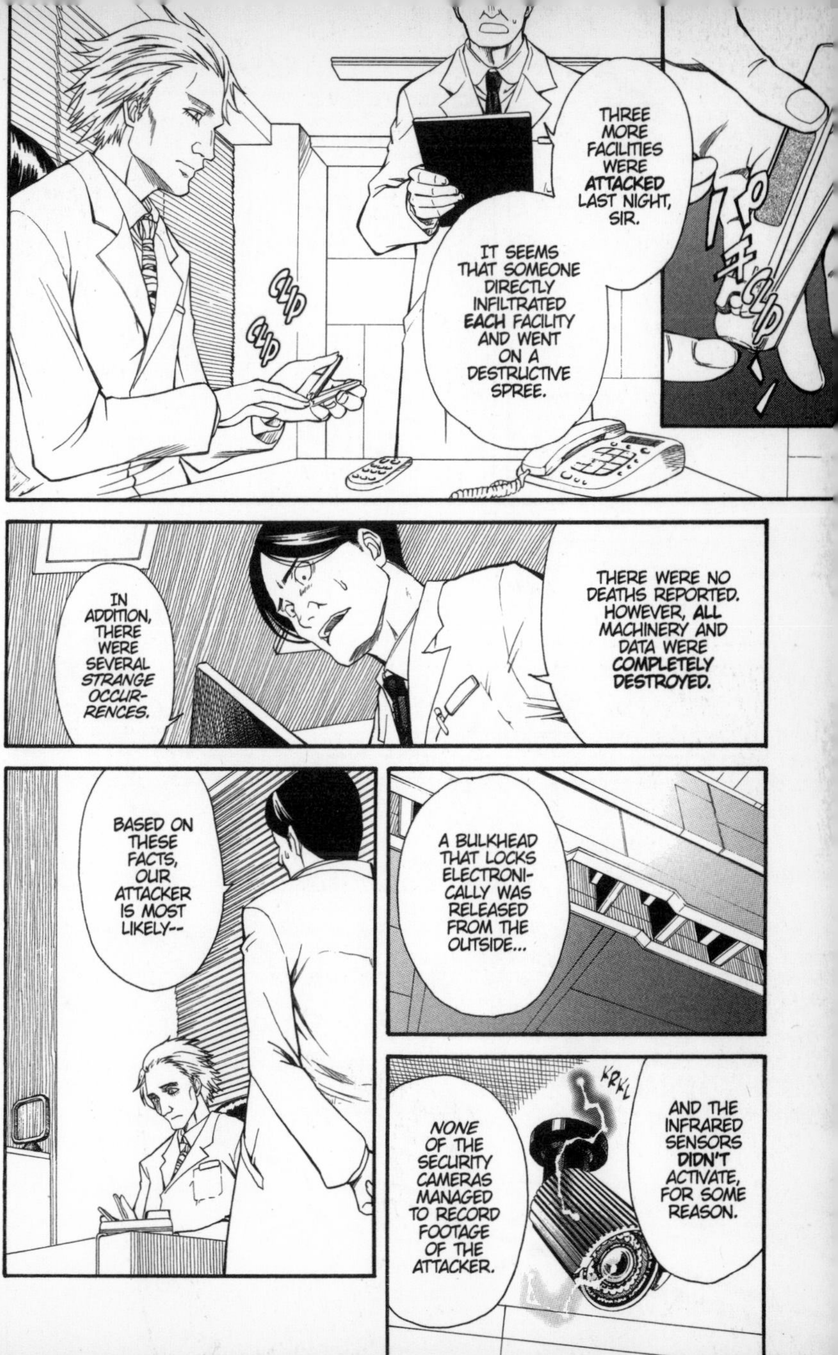
CLIP
CLIP
CLIP
THREE MORE FACILITIES WERE ATTACKED LAST NIGHT, SIR.
IT SEEMS THAT SOMEONE DIRECTLY INFILTRATED EACH FACILITY AND WENT ON A DESTRUCTIVE SPREE.
THERE WERE NO DEATHS REPORTED. HOWEVER, ALL MACHINERY AND DATA WERE COMPLETELY DESTROYED.
IN ADDITION, THERE WERE SEVERAL STRANGE OCCURRENCES.
A BULKHEAD THAT LOCKS ELECTRONICALLY WAS RELEASED FROM THE OUTSIDE...
KRKL
AND THE INFRARED SENSORS DIDN'T ACTIVATE, FOR SOME REASON.
NONE OF THE SECURITY CAMERAS MANAGED TO RECORD FOOTAGE OF THE ATTACKER.
BASED ON THESE FACTS, OUR ATTACKER IS MOST LIKELY--

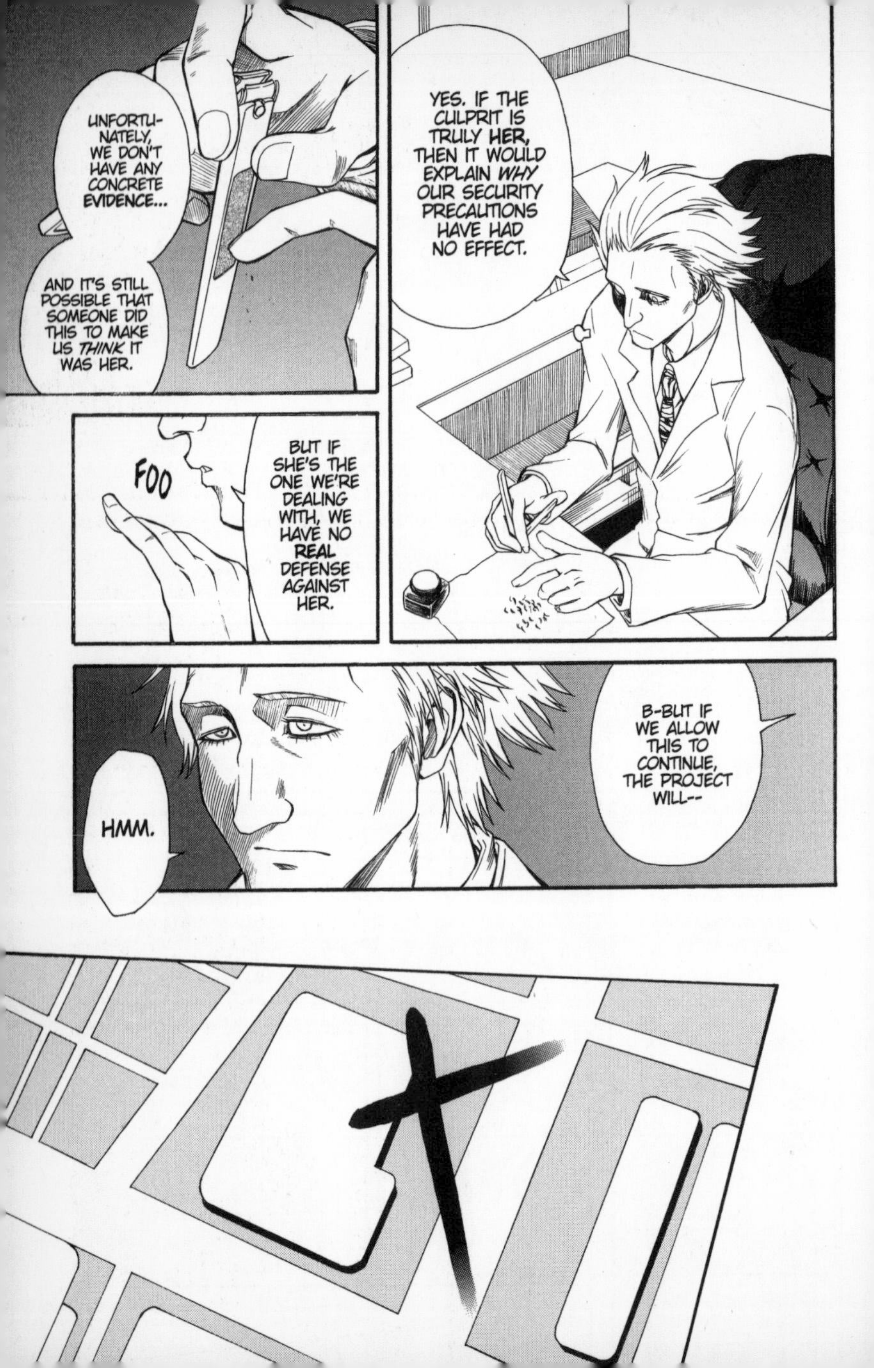
YES. IF THE CULPRIT IS TRULY HER, THEN IT WOULD EXPLAIN WHY OUR SECURITY PRECAUTIONS HAVE HAD NO EFFECT.
UNFORTU-NATELY, WE DON'T HAVE ANY CONCRETE EVIDENCE...
AND IT'S STILL POSSIBLE THAT SOMEONE DID THIS TO MAKE US THINK IT WAS HER.
FOO
BUT IF SHE'S THE ONE WE'RE DEALING WITH, WE HAVE NO REAL DEFENSE AGAINST HER.
B-BUT IF WE ALLOW THIS TO CONTINUE, THE PROJECT WILL--
HMM.

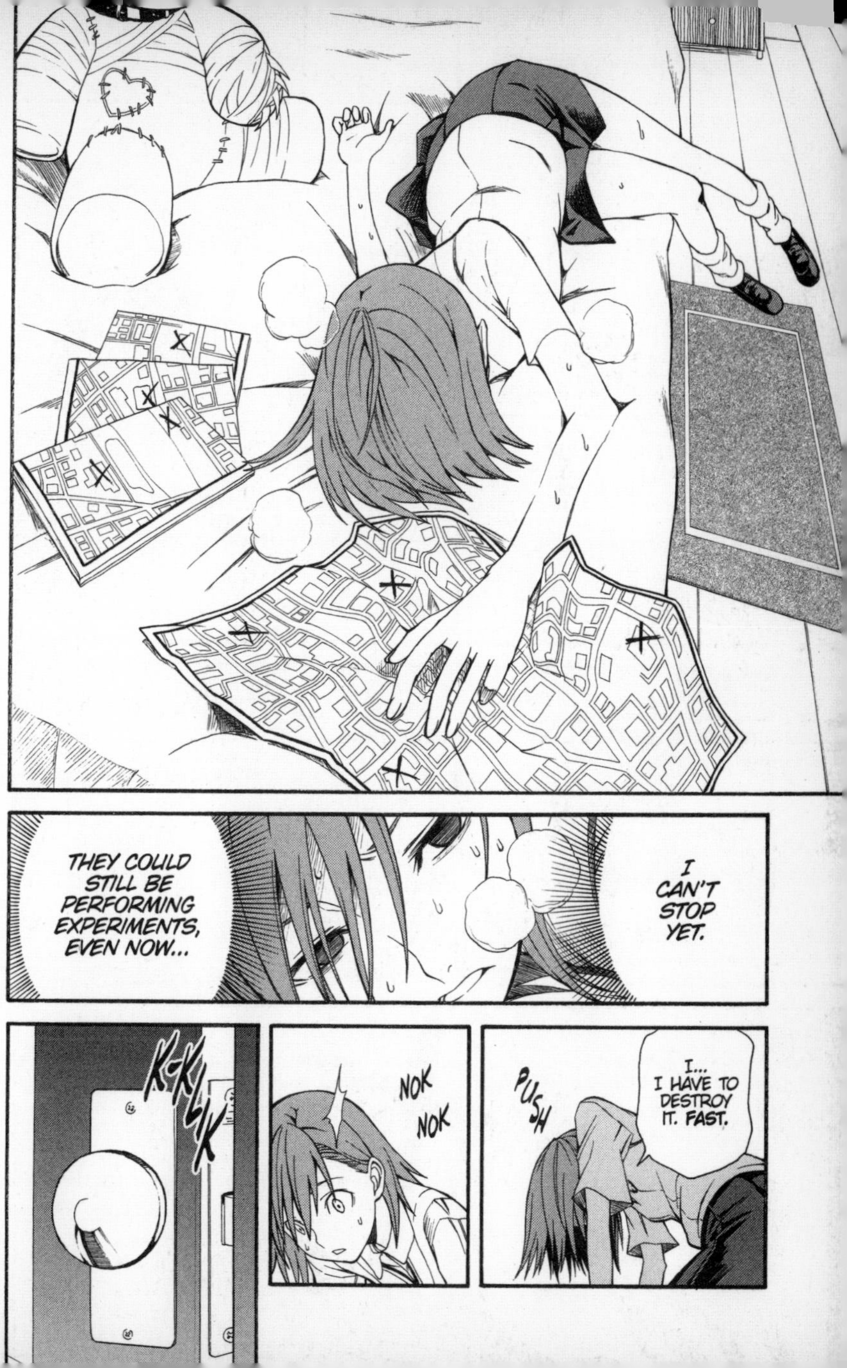
I CAN'T STOP YET.
THEY COULD STILL BE PERFORMING EXPERIMENTS, EVEN NOW...
I... I HAVE TO DESTROY IT. FAST.
PUSH
NOK NOK
K-KLIK

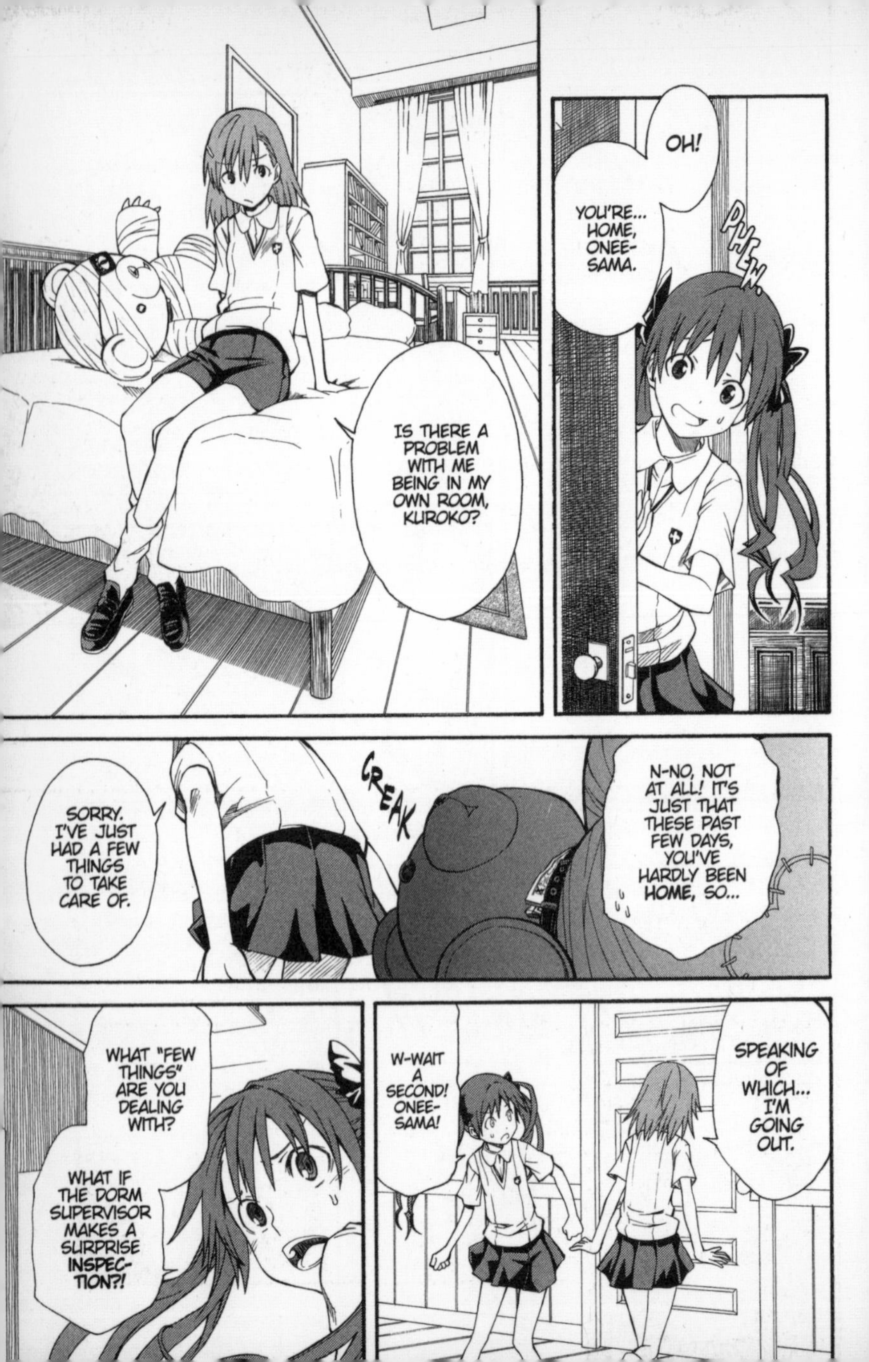
OH!
YOU'RE... HOME, ONEE-SAMA.
PHEW.
IS THERE A PROBLEM WITH ME BEING IN MY OWN ROOM, KUROKO?
N-NO, NOT AT ALL! IT'S JUST THAT THESE PAST FEW DAYS, YOU'VE HARDLY BEEN HOME, SO...
CREAK
SORRY. I'VE JUST HAD A FEW THINGS TO TAKE CARE OF.
SPEAKING OF WHICH... I'M GOING OUT.
W-WAIT A SECOND! ONEE-SAMA!
WHAT "FEW THINGS" ARE YOU DEALING WITH?
WHAT IF THE DORM SUPERVISOR MAKES A SURPRISE INSPECTION?!

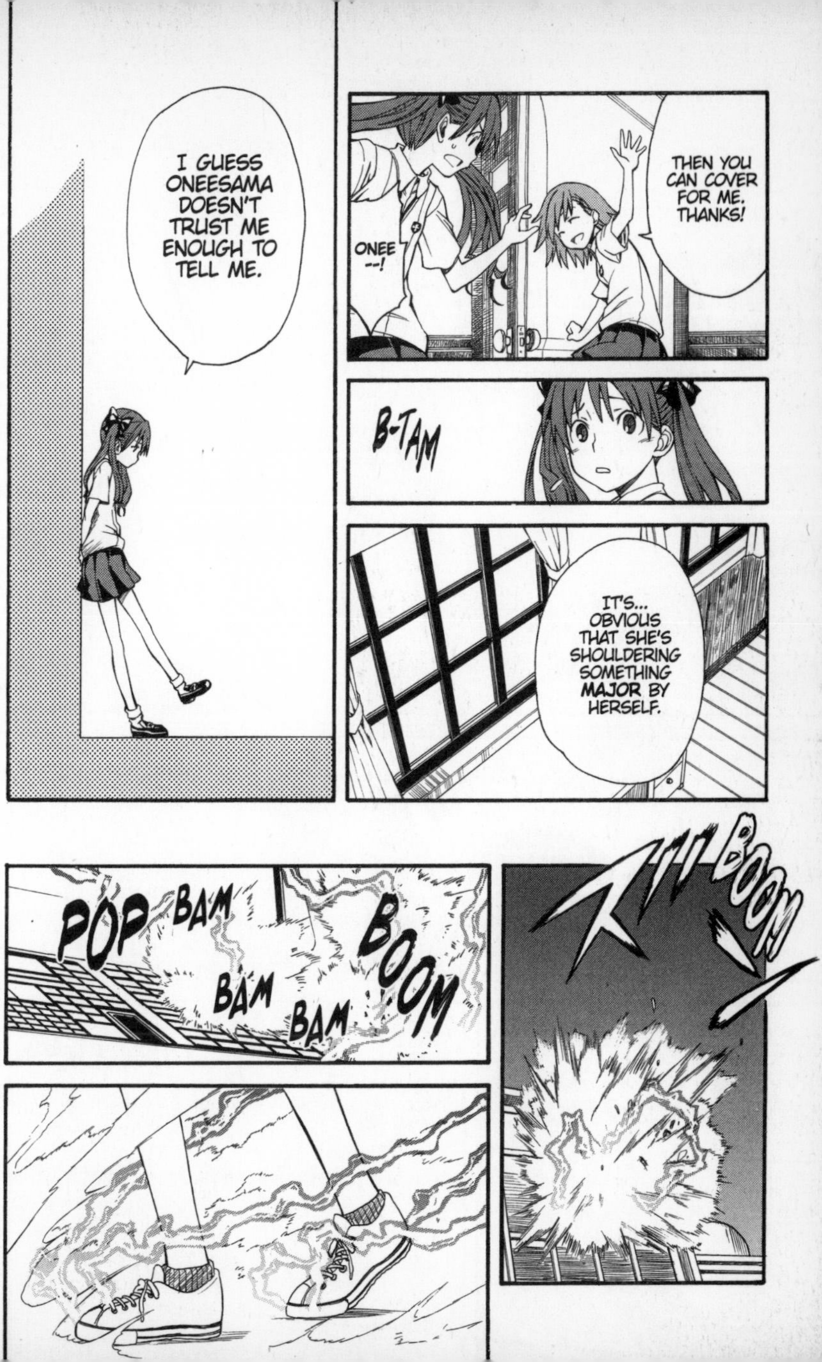
THEN YOU CAN COVER FOR ME. THANKS!
ONEE --!
B-TAM
IT'S... OBVIOUS THAT SHE'S SHOULDERING SOMETHING **MAJOR** BY HERSELF.
I GUESS ONEESAMA DOESN'T TRUST ME ENOUGH TO TELL ME.
BOOM
POP
BAM
BOOM
BAM
BAM

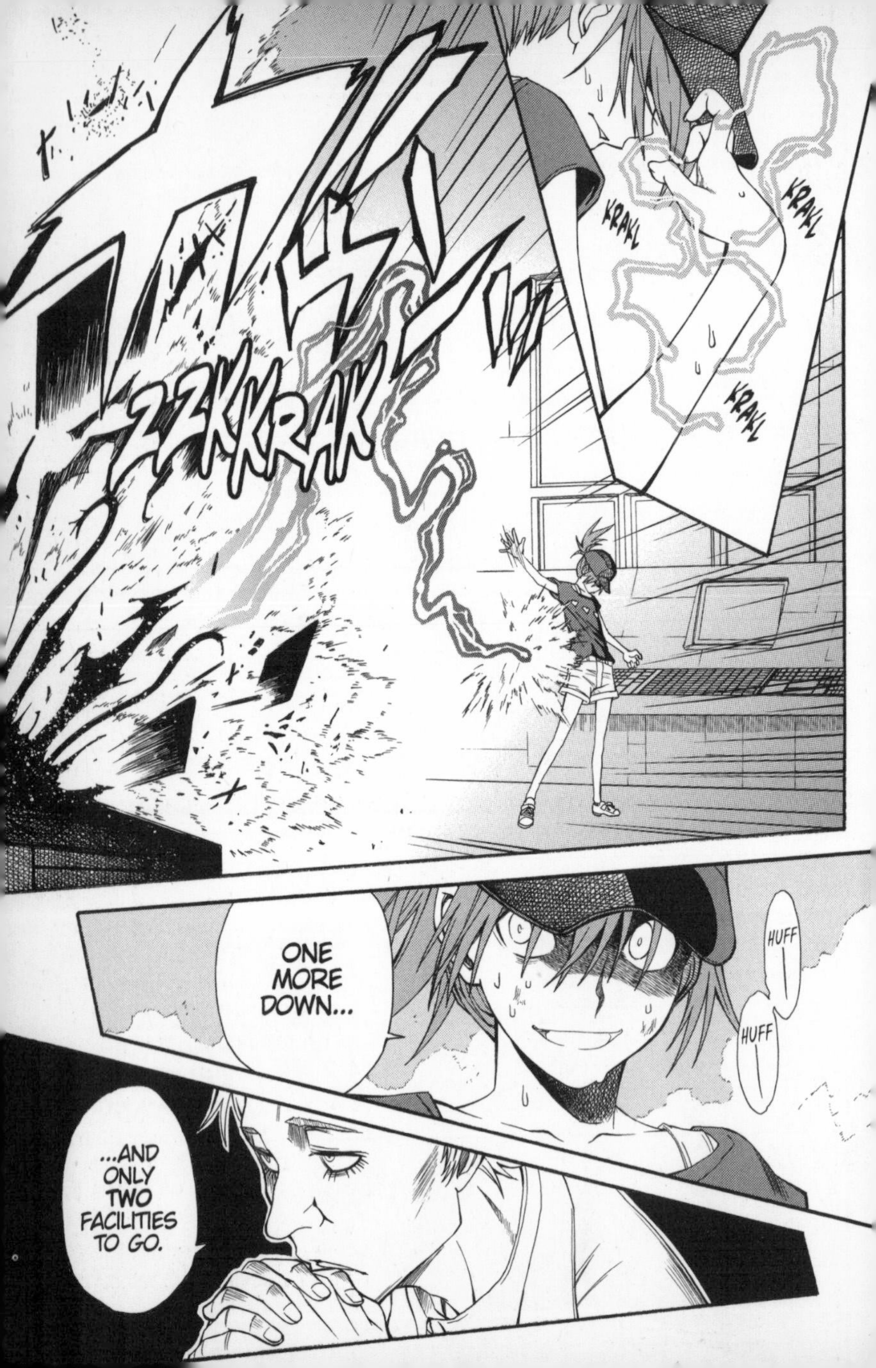
KRAKL
KRAKL
KRAKL
ZZKKRAK
HUFF
HUFF
ONE MORE DOWN...
...AND ONLY TWO FACILITIES TO GO.

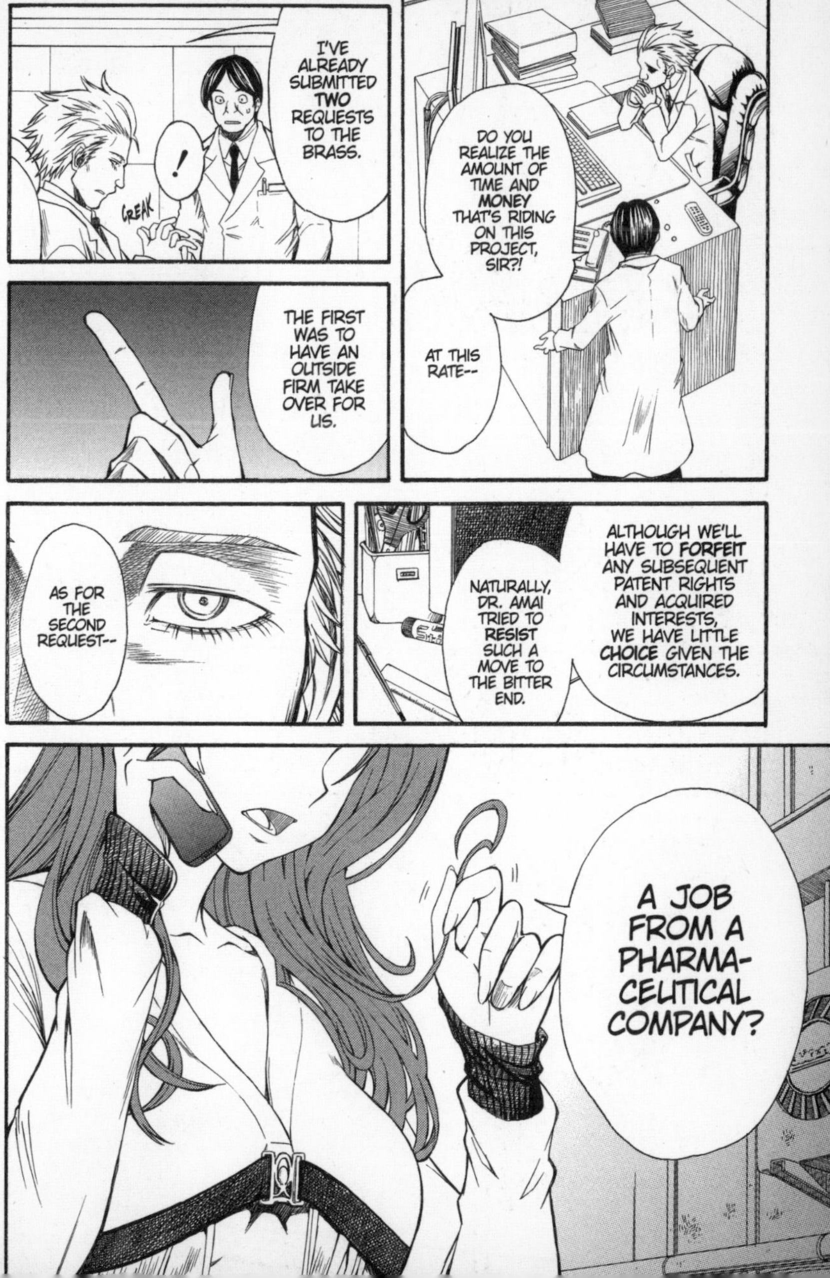
DO YOU REALIZE THE AMOUNT OF TIME AND MONEY THAT'S RIDING ON THIS PROJECT, SIR?!
AT THIS RATE--
I'VE ALREADY SUBMITTED TWO REQUESTS TO THE BRASS.
!
CREAK
THE FIRST WAS TO HAVE AN OUTSIDE FIRM TAKE OVER FOR US.
ALTHOUGH WE'LL HAVE TO FORFEIT ANY SUBSEQUENT PATENT RIGHTS AND ACQUIRED INTERESTS, WE HAVE LITTLE CHOICE GIVEN THE CIRCUMSTANCES.
NATURALLY, DR. AMAI TRIED TO RESIST SUCH A MOVE TO THE BITTER END.
AS FOR THE SECOND REQUEST--
A JOB FROM A PHARMACEUTICAL COMPANY?

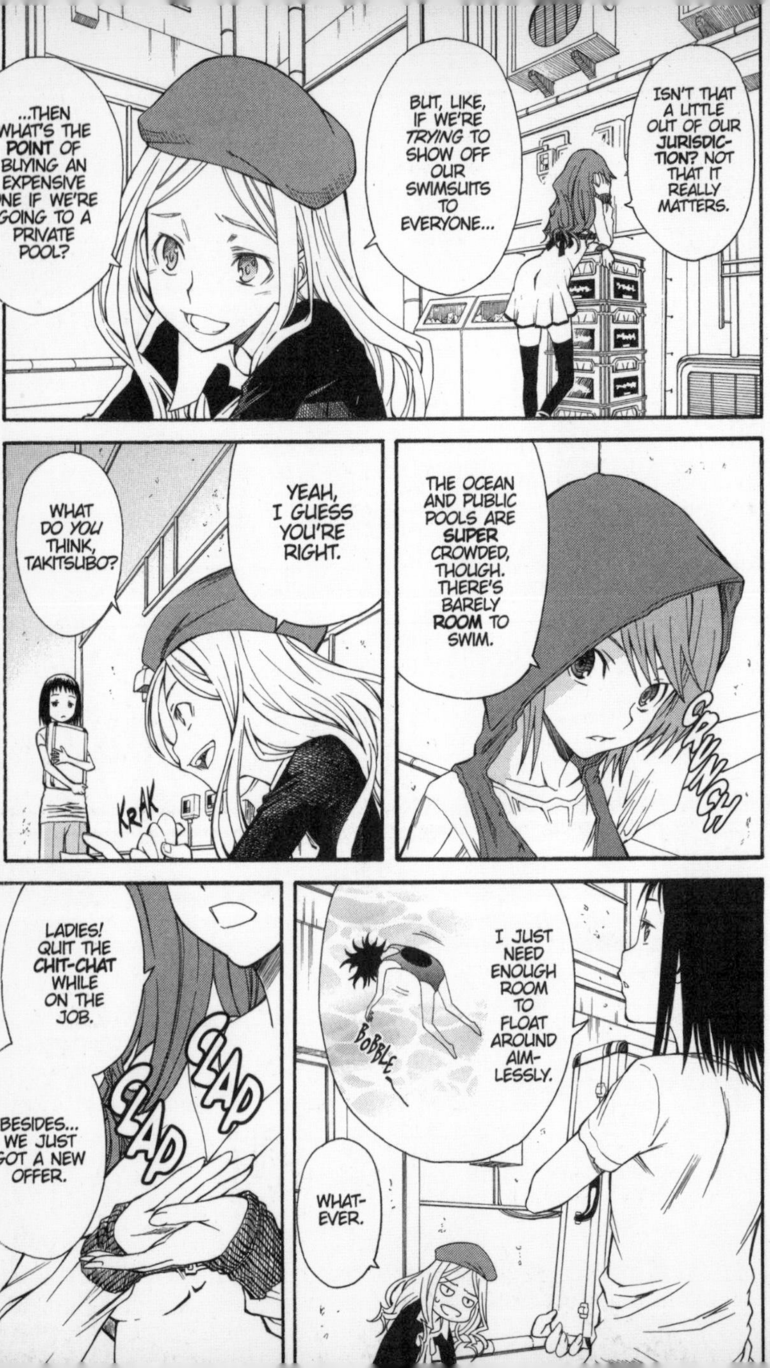

ISN'T THAT A LITTLE OUT OF OUR JURISDICTION? NOT THAT IT REALLY MATTERS.
BUT, LIKE, IF WE'RE *TRYING* TO SHOW OFF OUR SWIMSUITS TO EVERYONE...
...THEN WHAT'S THE **POINT** OF BUYING AN EXPENSIVE ONE IF WE'RE GOING TO A PRIVATE POOL?
THE OCEAN AND PUBLIC POOLS ARE **SUPER** CROWDED, THOUGH. THERE'S BARELY **ROOM** TO SWIM.
CRUNCH
YEAH, I GUESS YOU'RE RIGHT.
WHAT DO *YOU* THINK, TAKITSUBO?
KRAK
I JUST NEED ENOUGH ROOM TO FLOAT AROUND AIM-LESSLY.
BOBBLE
WHAT-EVER.
LADIES! QUIT THE **CHIT-CHAT** WHILE ON THE JOB.
CLAP
CLAP
CLAP
BESIDES... WE JUST GOT A NEW OFFER.

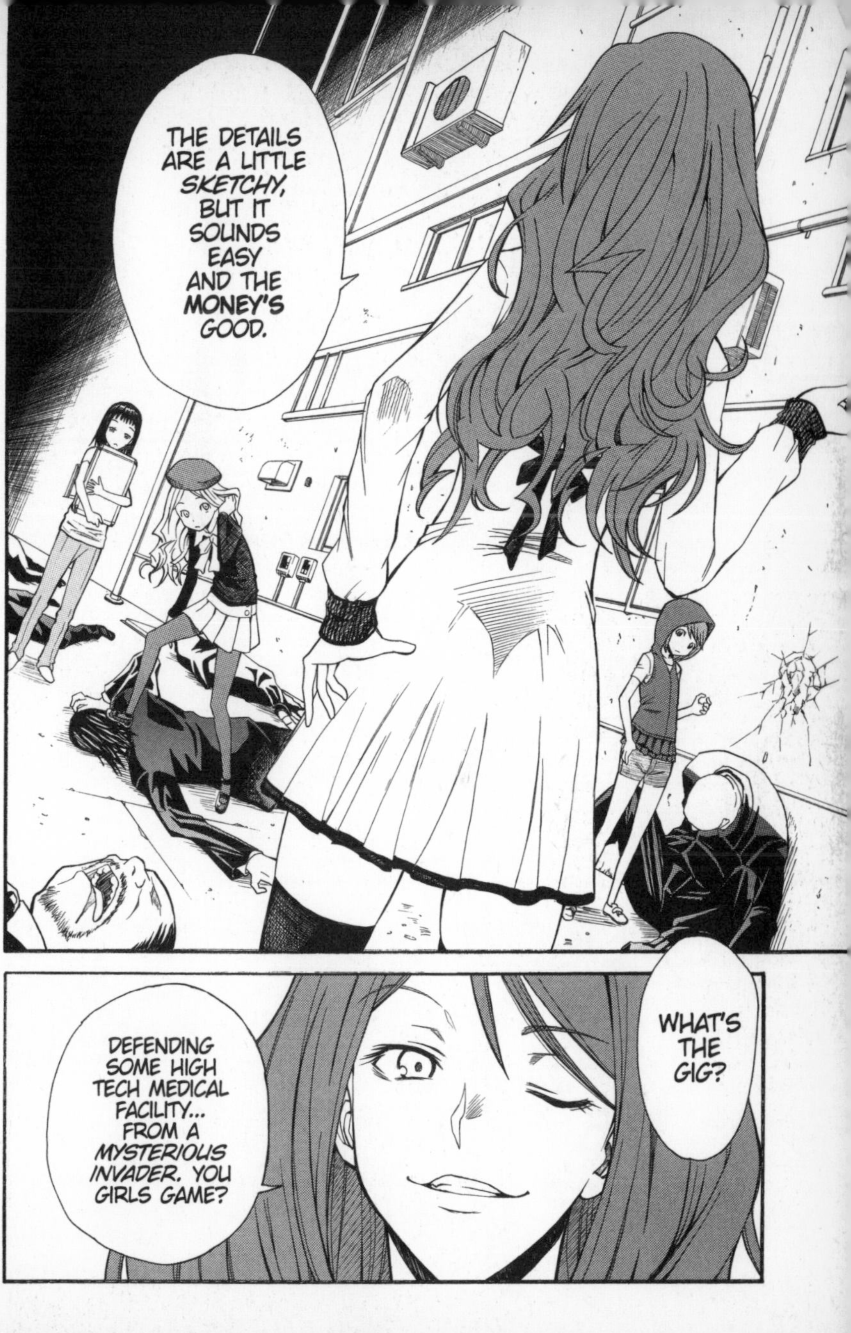
THE DETAILS ARE A LITTLE SKETCHY, BUT IT SOUNDS EASY AND THE MONEY'S GOOD.
WHAT'S THE GIG?
DEFENDING SOME HIGH TECH MEDICAL FACILITY... FROM A MYSTERIOUS INVADER. YOU GIRLS GAME?

CHAPTER 26: AUGUST 19 (1)

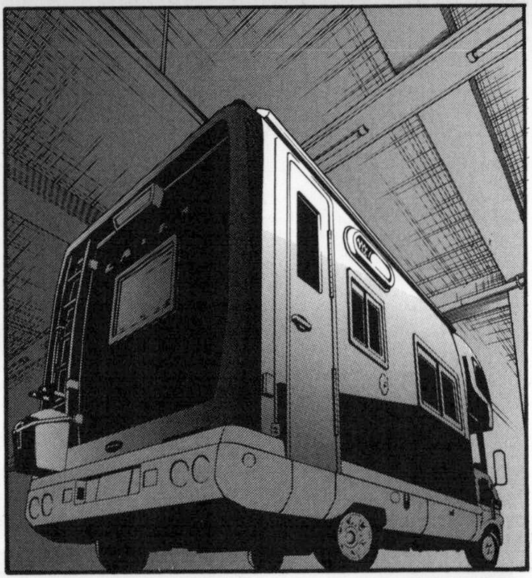

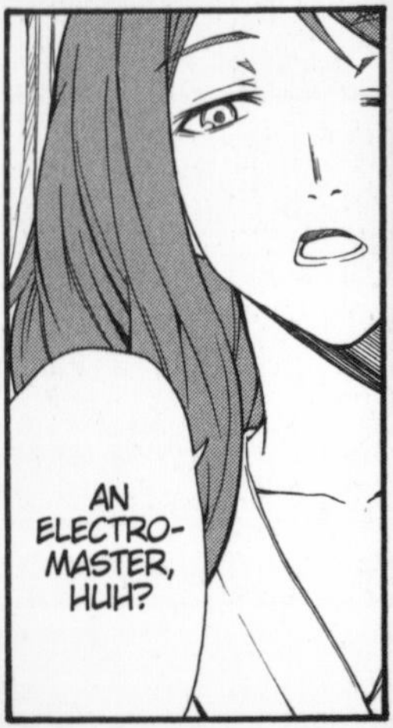
AN ELECTRO-MASTER, HUH?

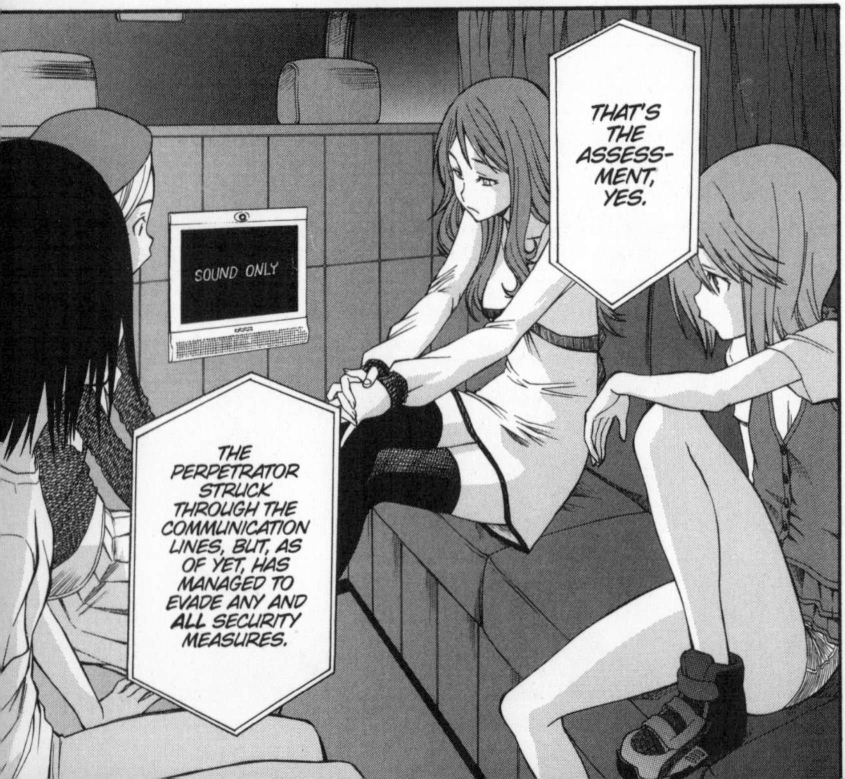
THAT'S THE ASSESS-MENT, YES.
SOUND ONLY
THE PERPETRATOR STRUCK THROUGH THE COMMUNICATION LINES, BUT, AS OF YET, HAS MANAGED TO EVADE ANY AND ALL SECURITY MEASURES.

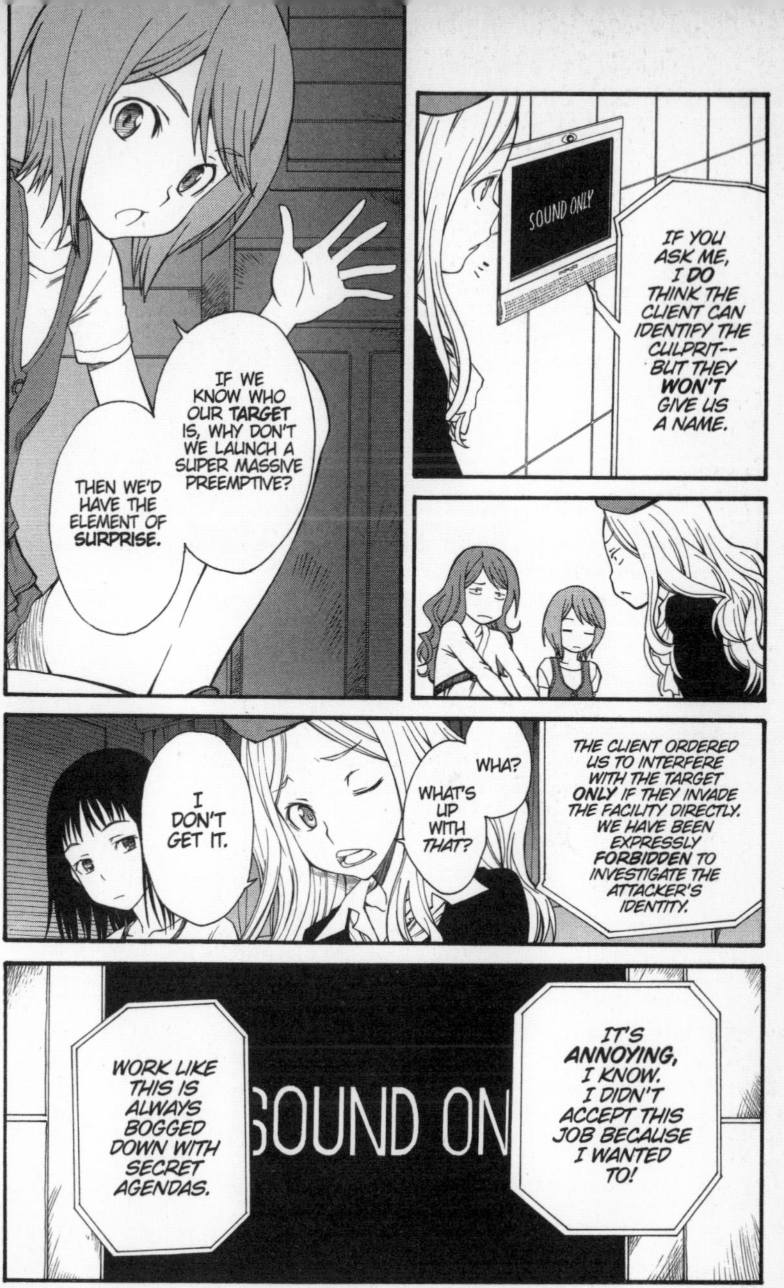
SOUND ONLY
IF YOU ASK ME, I DO THINK THE CLIENT CAN IDENTIFY THE CULPRIT-- BUT THEY WON'T GIVE US A NAME.
IF WE KNOW WHO OUR TARGET IS, WHY DON'T WE LAUNCH A SUPER MASSIVE PREEMPTIVE?
THEN WE'D HAVE THE ELEMENT OF SURPRISE.
THE CLIENT ORDERED US TO INTERFERE WITH THE TARGET ONLY IF THEY INVADE THE FACILITY DIRECTLY. WE HAVE BEEN EXPRESSLY FORBIDDEN TO INVESTIGATE THE ATTACKER'S IDENTITY.
WHA?
WHAT'S UP WITH THAT?
I DON'T GET IT.
IT'S ANNOYING, I KNOW. I DIDN'T ACCEPT THIS JOB BECAUSE I WANTED TO!
SOUND ON
WORK LIKE THIS IS ALWAYS BOGGED DOWN WITH SECRET AGENDAS.

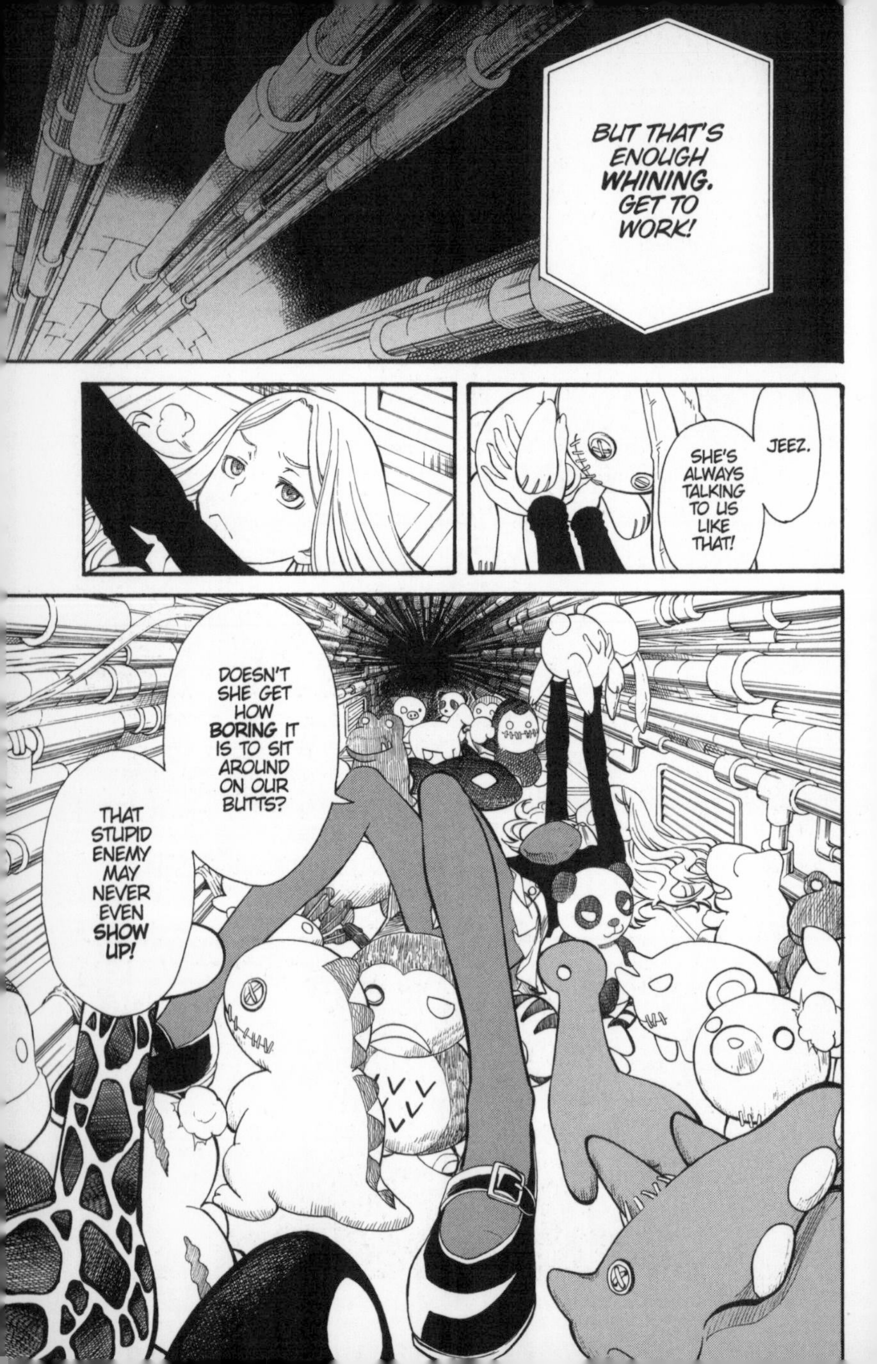
BUT THAT'S ENOUGH WHINING. GET TO WORK!
JEEZ.
SHE'S ALWAYS TALKING TO US LIKE THAT!
DOESN'T SHE GET HOW BORING IT IS TO SIT AROUND ON OUR BUTTS?
THAT STUPID ENEMY MAY NEVER EVEN SHOW UP!

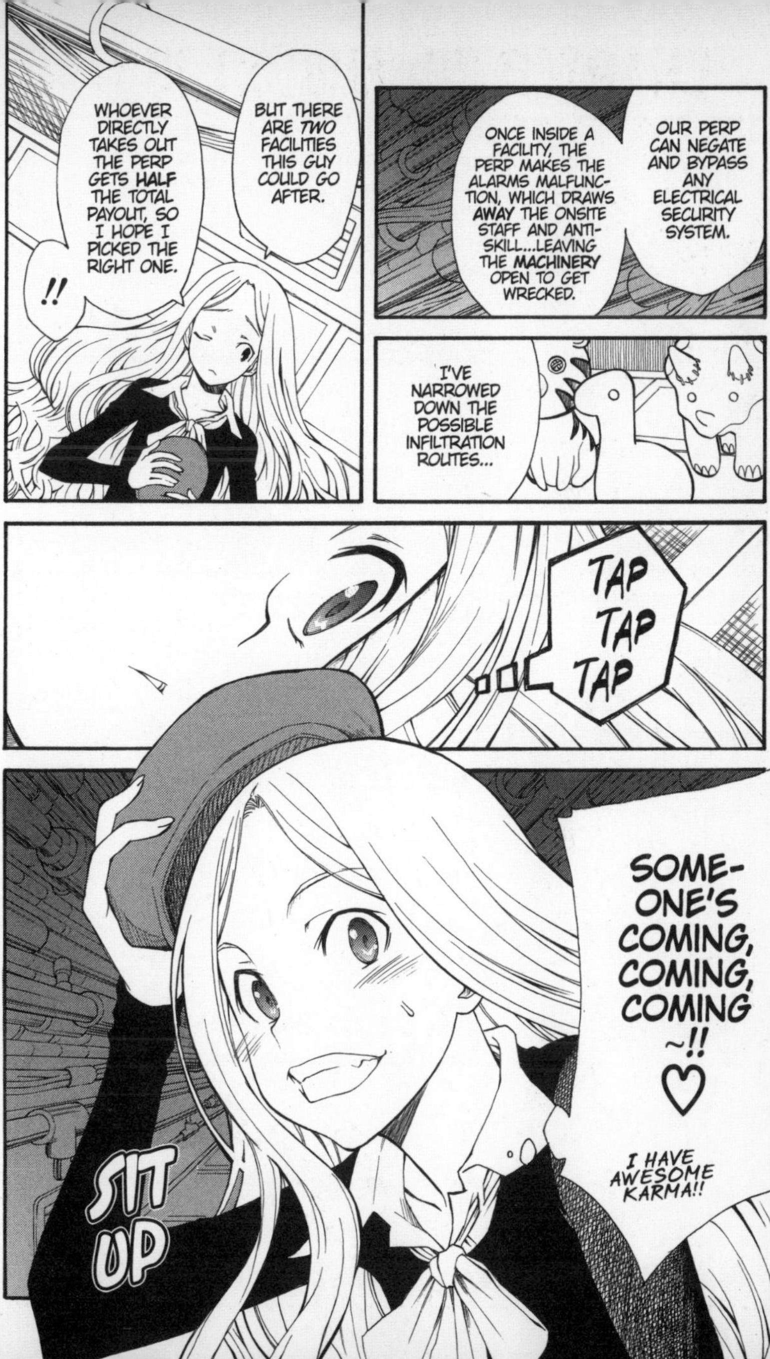
OUR PERP CAN NEGATE AND BYPASS ANY ELECTRICAL SECURITY SYSTEM.
ONCE INSIDE A FACILITY, THE PERP MAKES THE ALARMS MALFUNCTION, WHICH DRAWS AWAY THE ONSITE STAFF AND ANTI-SKILL...LEAVING THE MACHINERY OPEN TO GET WRECKED.
I'VE NARROWED DOWN THE POSSIBLE INFILTRATION ROUTES...
BUT THERE ARE TWO FACILITIES THIS GUY COULD GO AFTER.
WHOEVER DIRECTLY TAKES OUT THE PERP GETS HALF THE TOTAL PAYOUT, SO I HOPE I PICKED THE RIGHT ONE.
!!
TAP TAP TAP
...
SOME-ONE'S COMING, COMING, COMING ~!! ♡
I HAVE AWESOME KARMA!!
SIT UP

CHAPTER 26: AUGUST 19 (1)

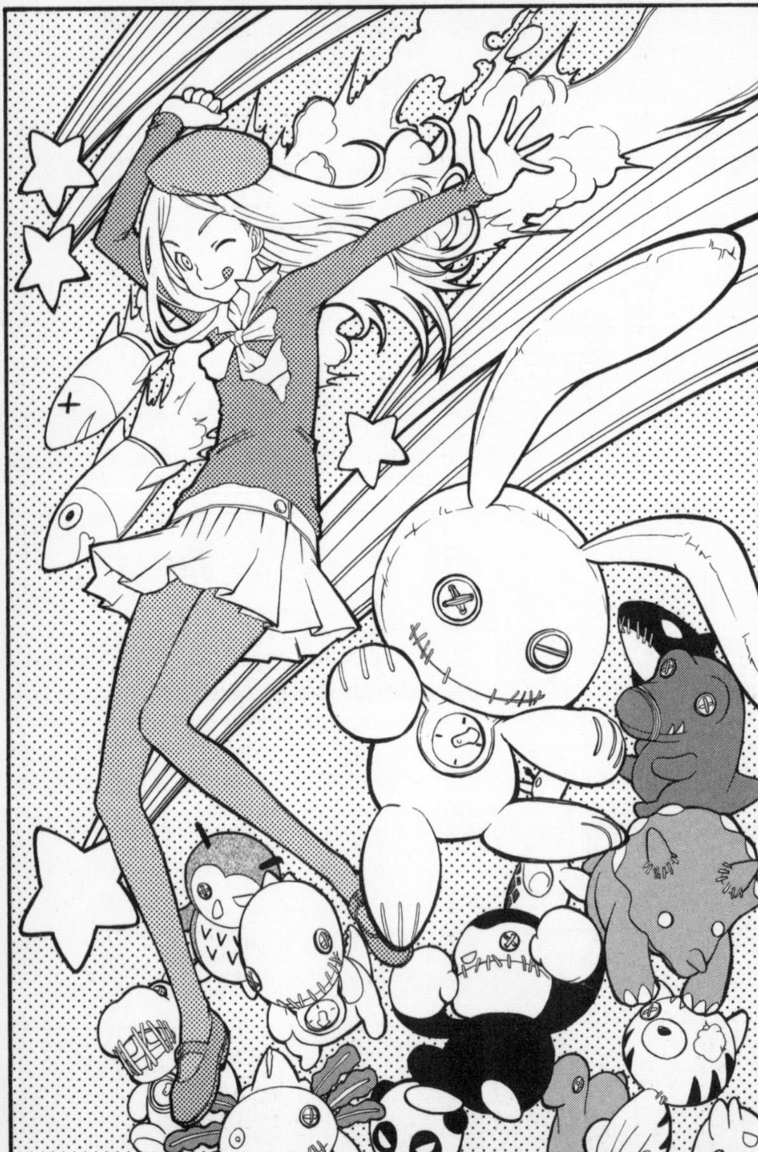

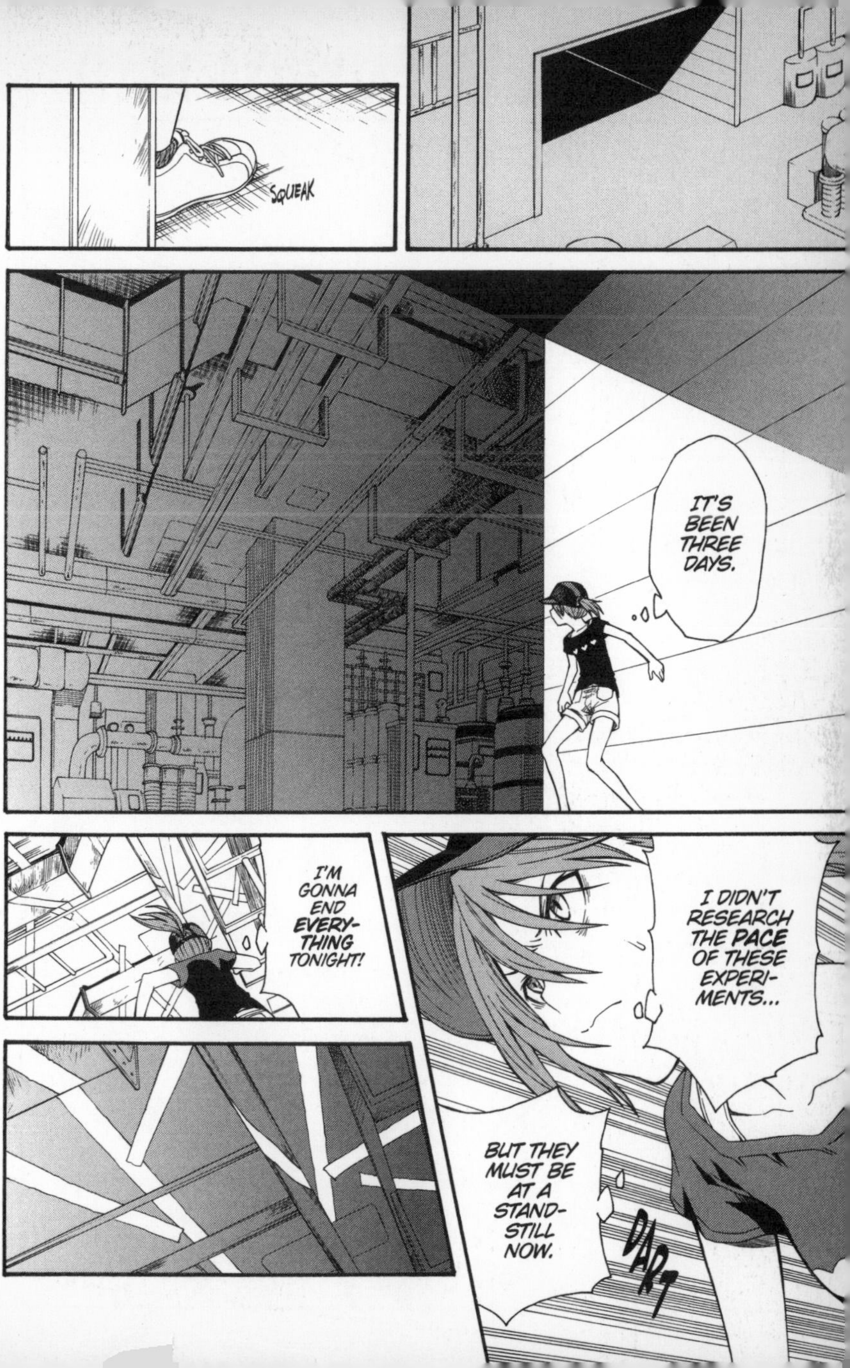
SQUEAK
IT'S BEEN THREE DAYS.
I DIDN'T RESEARCH THE PACE OF THESE EXPERIMENTS...
BUT THEY MUST BE AT A STANDSTILL NOW.
DART
I'M GONNA END EVERYTHING TONIGHT!

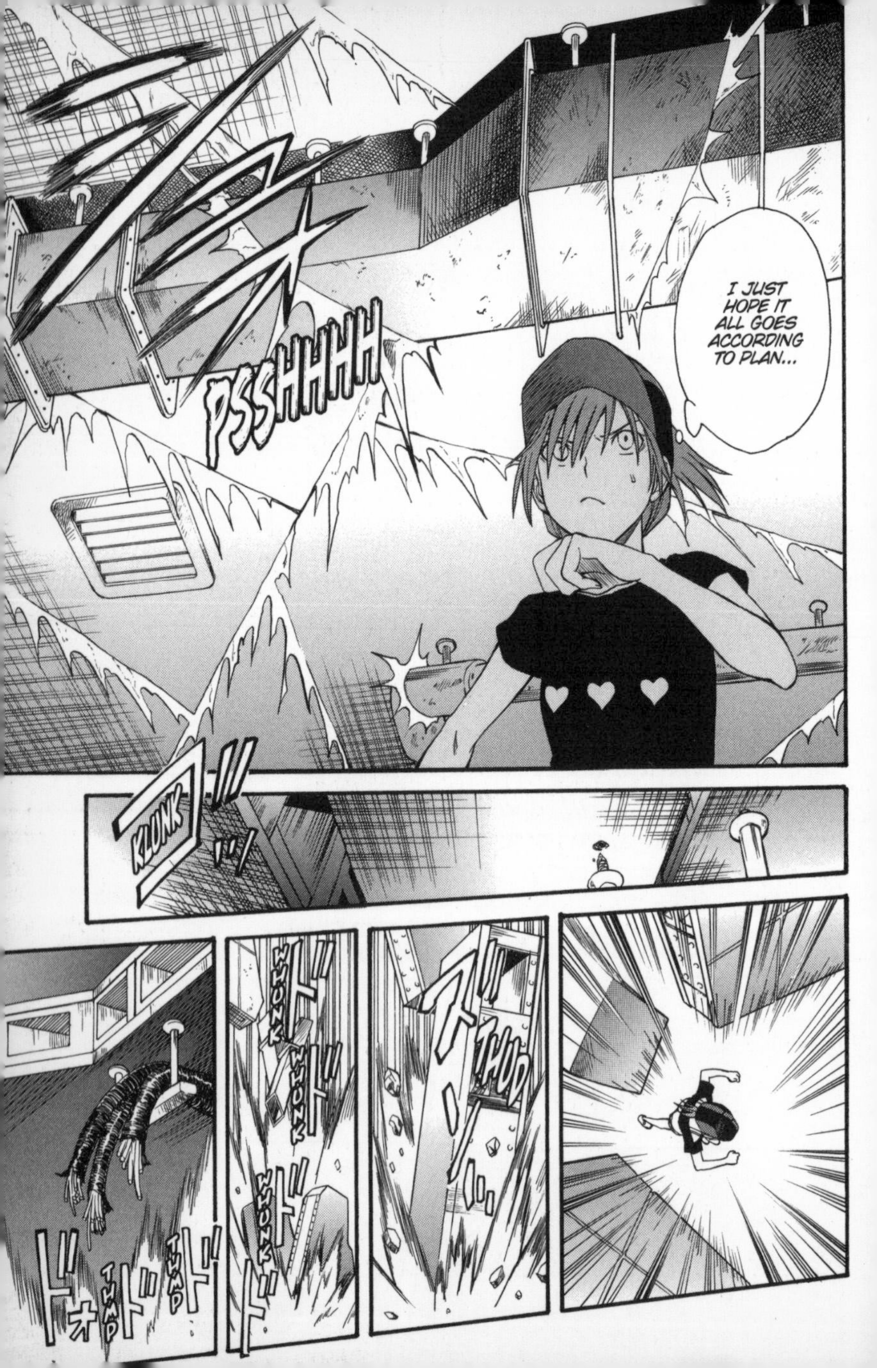
I JUST HOPE IT ALL GOES ACCORDING TO PLAN...
PSSHHHH
KLUNK
THUD
WHUNK
WHUNK
WHUNK
THUMP
THUMP

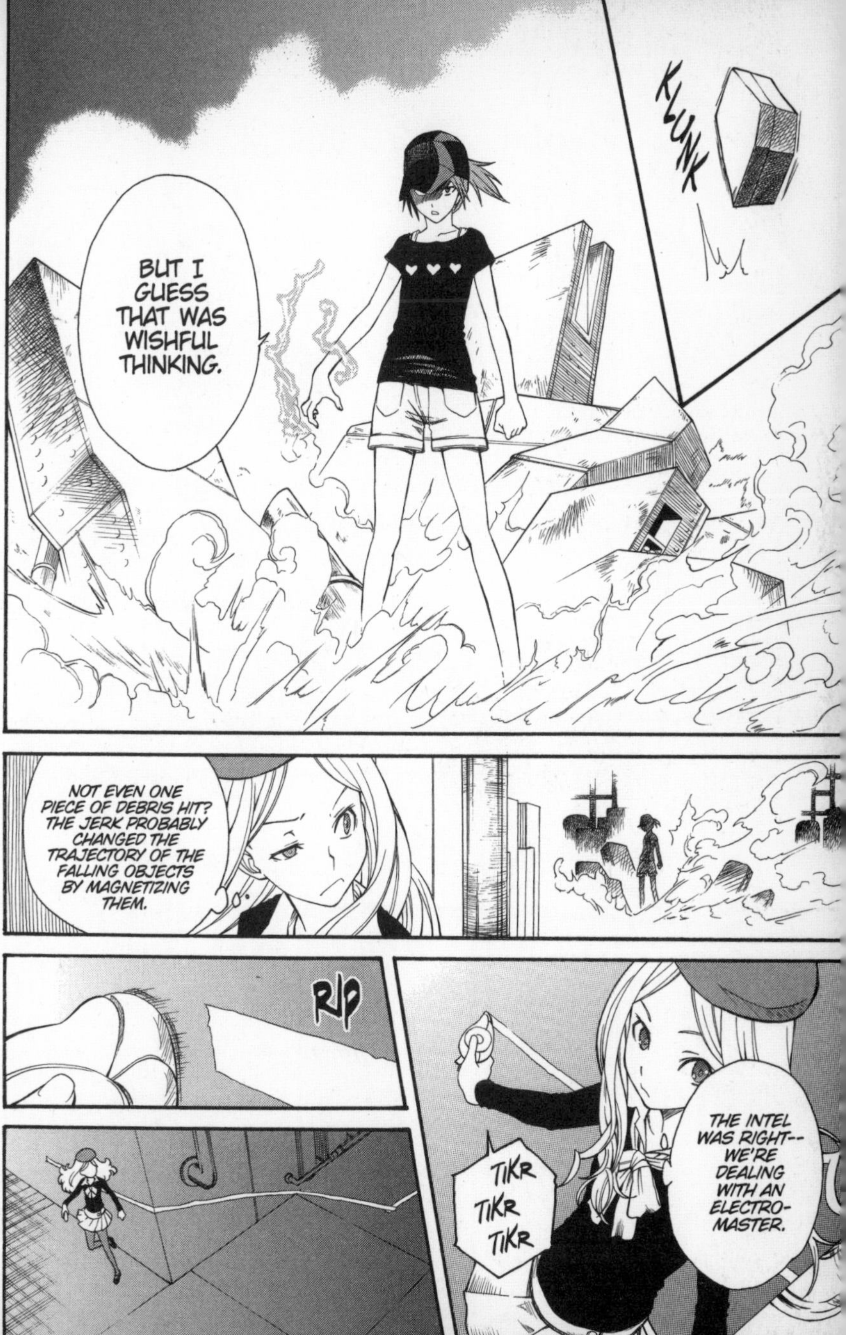
KLUNK
BUT I GUESS THAT WAS WISHFUL THINKING.
NOT EVEN ONE PIECE OF DEBRIS HIT? THE JERK PROBABLY CHANGED THE TRAJECTORY OF THE FALLING OBJECTS BY MAGNETIZING THEM.
THE INTEL WAS RIGHT-- WE'RE DEALING WITH AN ELECTRO-MASTER.
TIKR TIKR TIKR
RIP

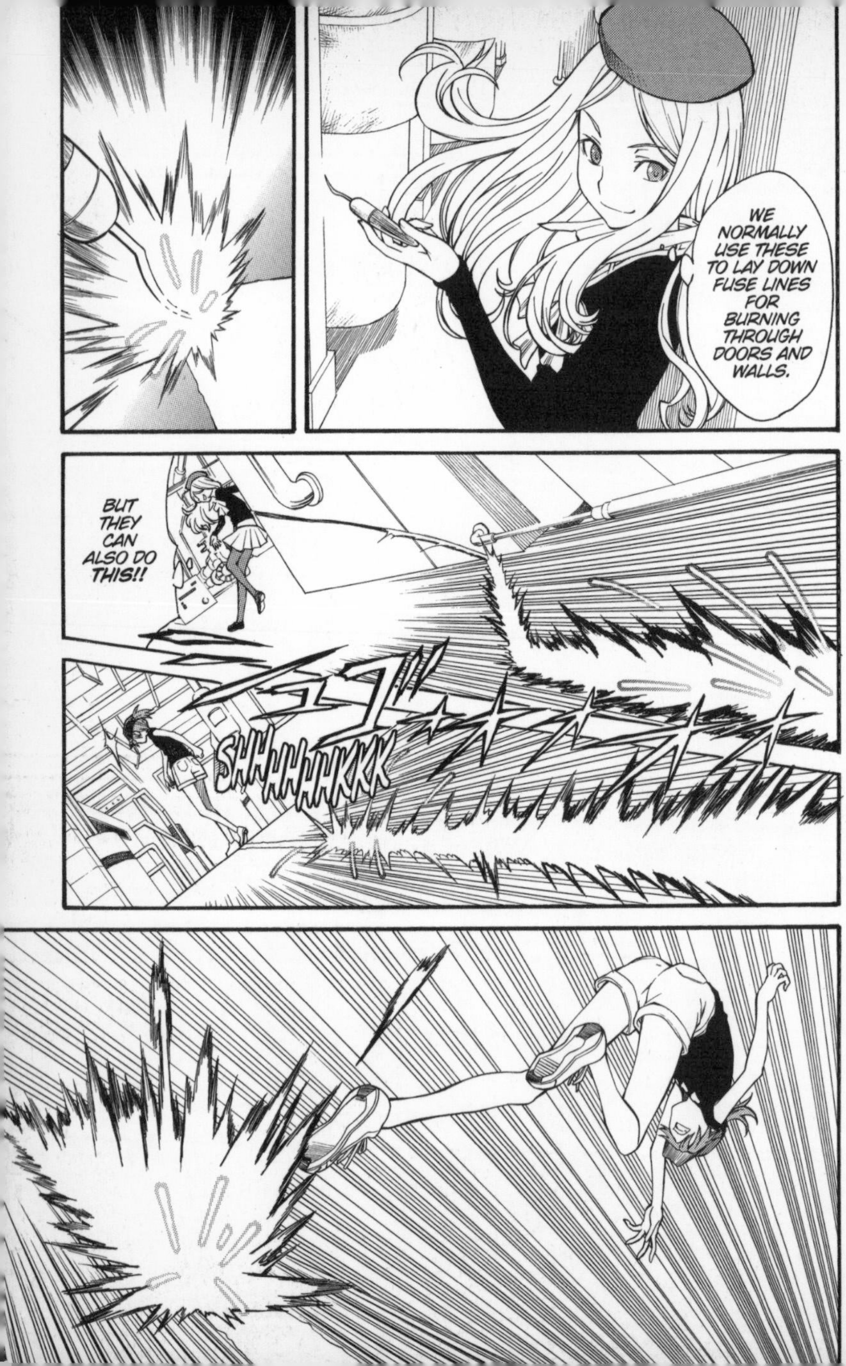
WE NORMALLY USE THESE TO LAY DOWN FUSE LINES FOR BURNING THROUGH DOORS AND WALLS.
BUT THEY CAN ALSO DO THIS!!
SHHHHHKKK

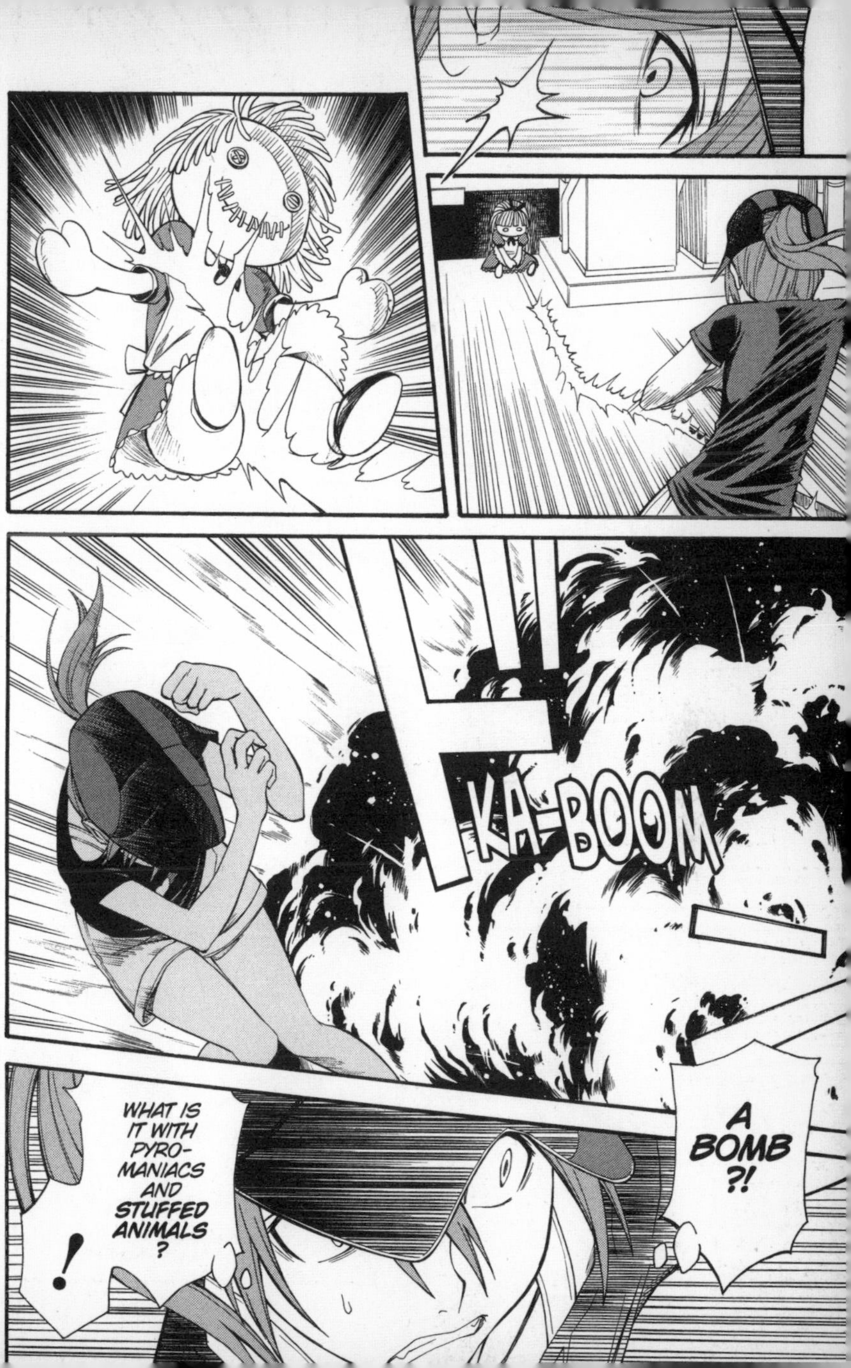

KA-BOOM
A BOMB ?!
WHAT IS IT WITH PYRO-MANIACS AND STUFFED ANIMALS ?
!

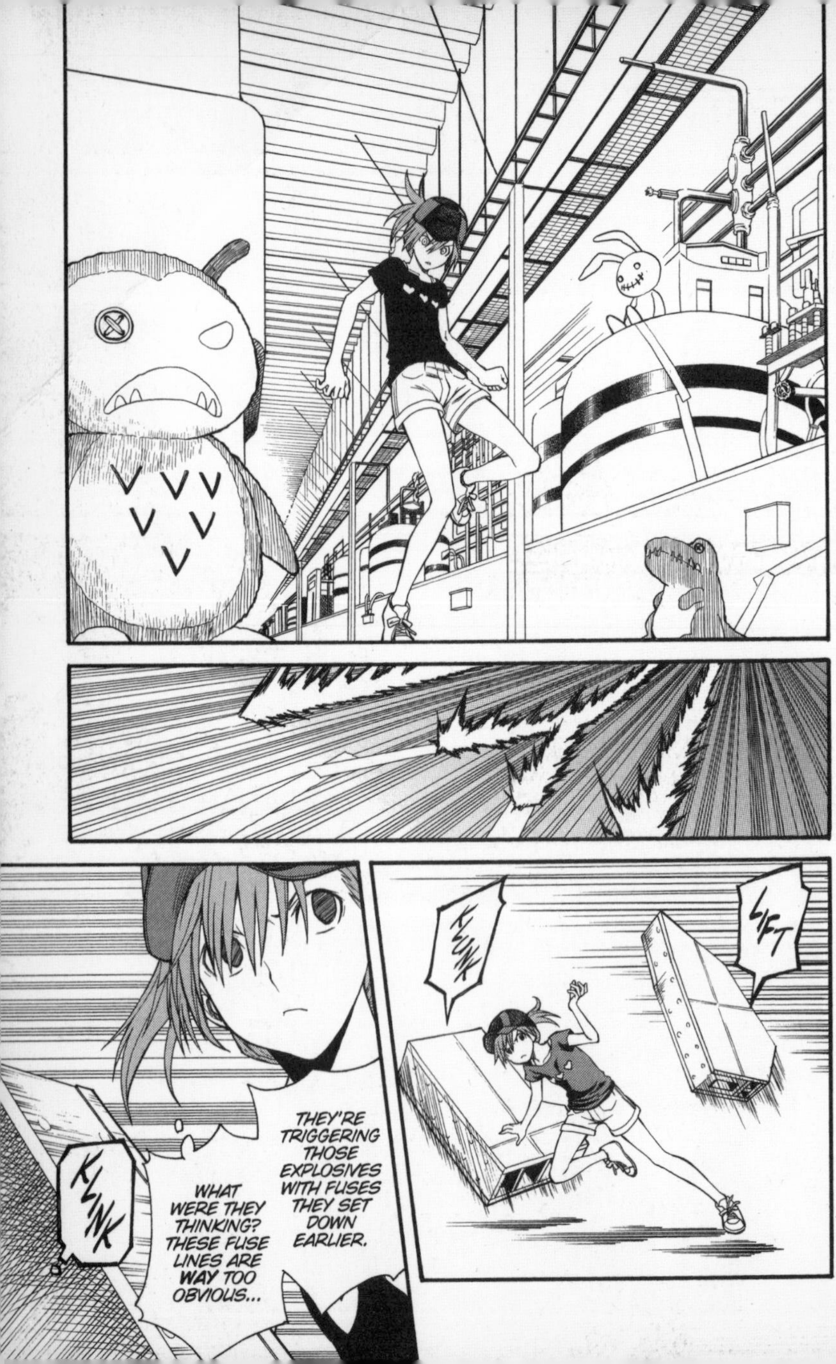
LIFT
KLUNK
THEY'RE TRIGGERING THOSE EXPLOSIVES WITH FUSES THEY SET DOWN EARLIER.
WHAT WERE THEY THINKING? THESE FUSE LINES ARE **WAY** TOO OBVIOUS...
KLINK

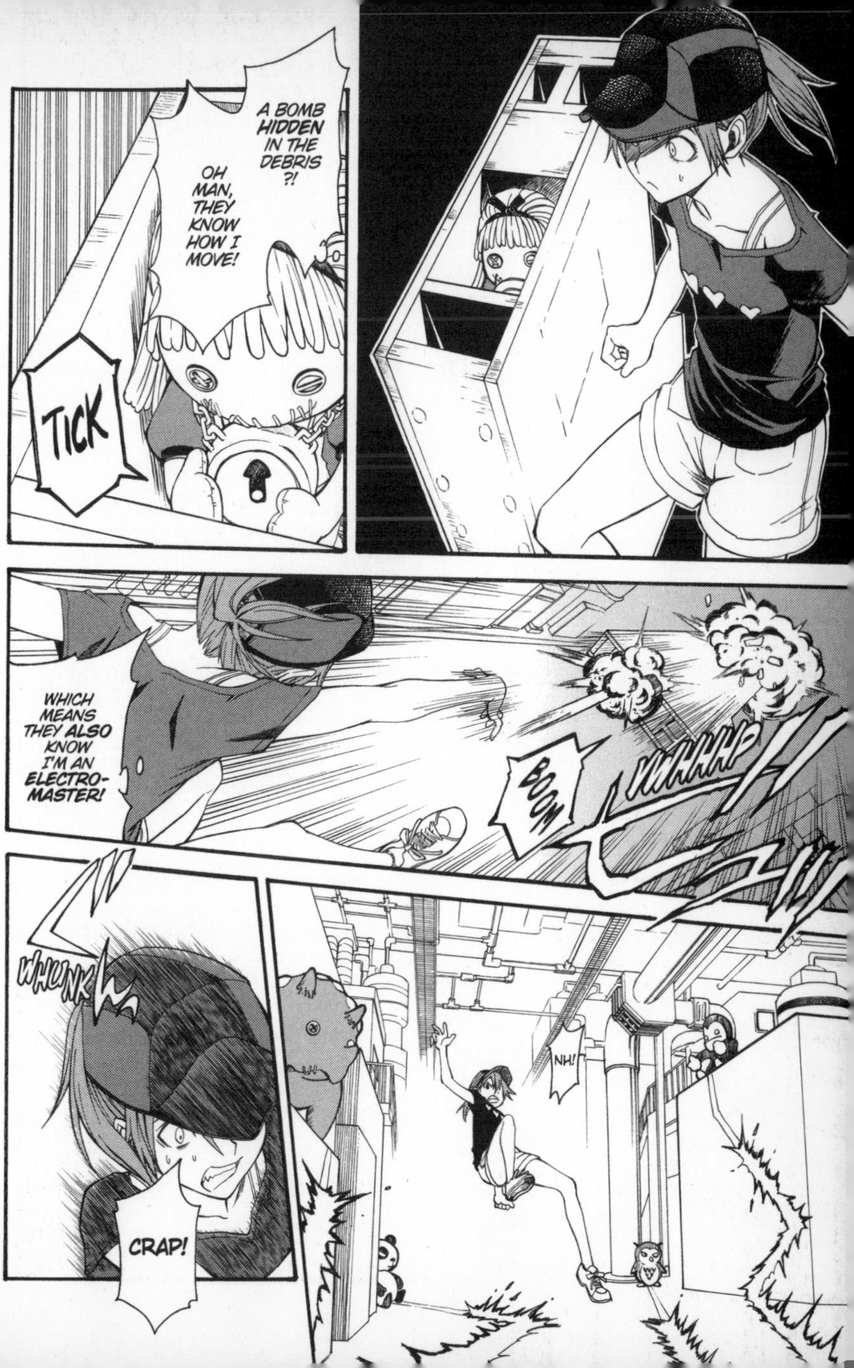
A BOMB HIDDEN IN THE DEBRIS?!
OH MAN, THEY KNOW HOW I MOVE!
TICK
BOOM
WHICH MEANS THEY ALSO KNOW I'M AN ELECTRO-MASTER!
NH!
WHUNK
CRAP!

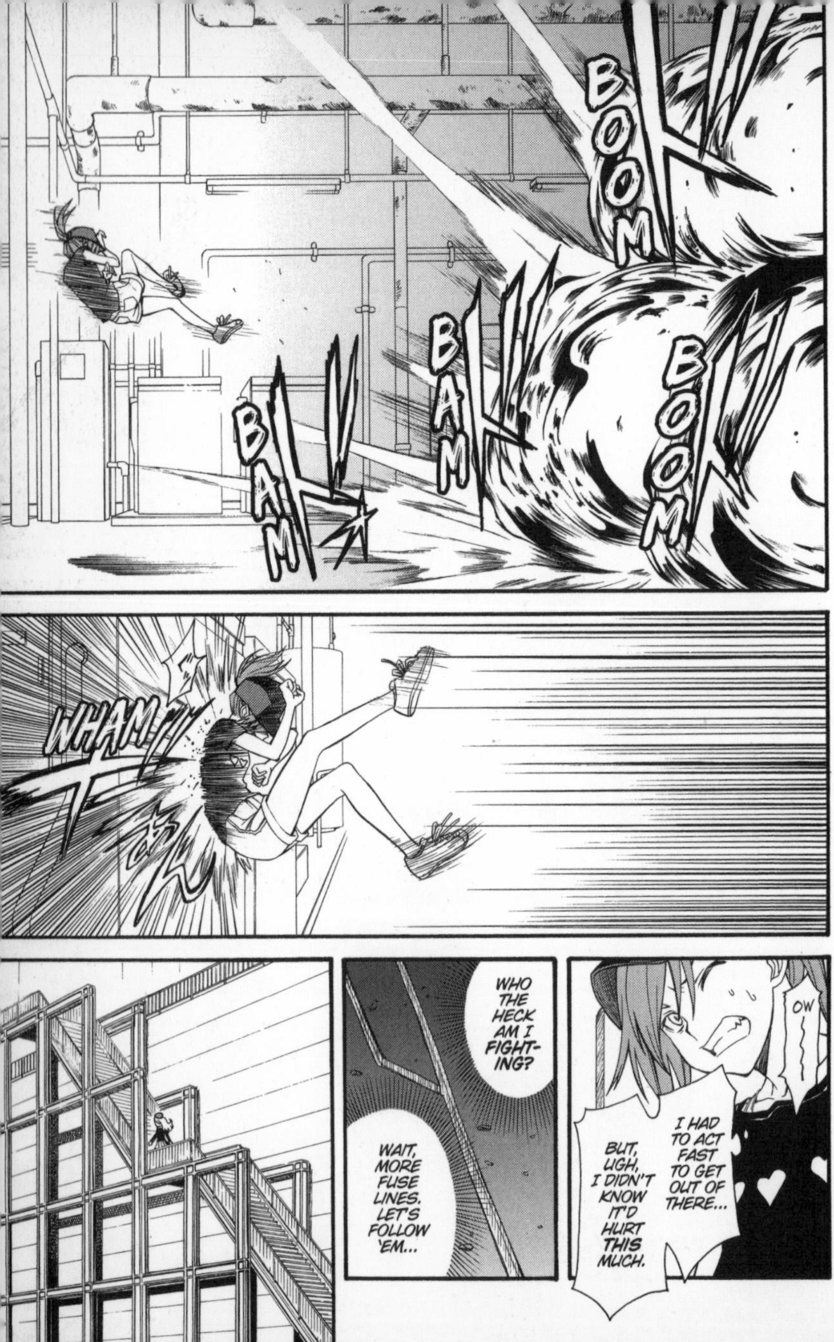
BOOM
BOOM
BAM
BAM
WHAM
OW...
I HAD TO ACT FAST TO GET OUT OF THERE...
BUT, UGH, I DIDN'T KNOW IT'D HURT THIS MUCH.
WHO THE HECK AM I FIGHT-ING?
WAIT, MORE FUSE LINES. LET'S FOLLOW 'EM...

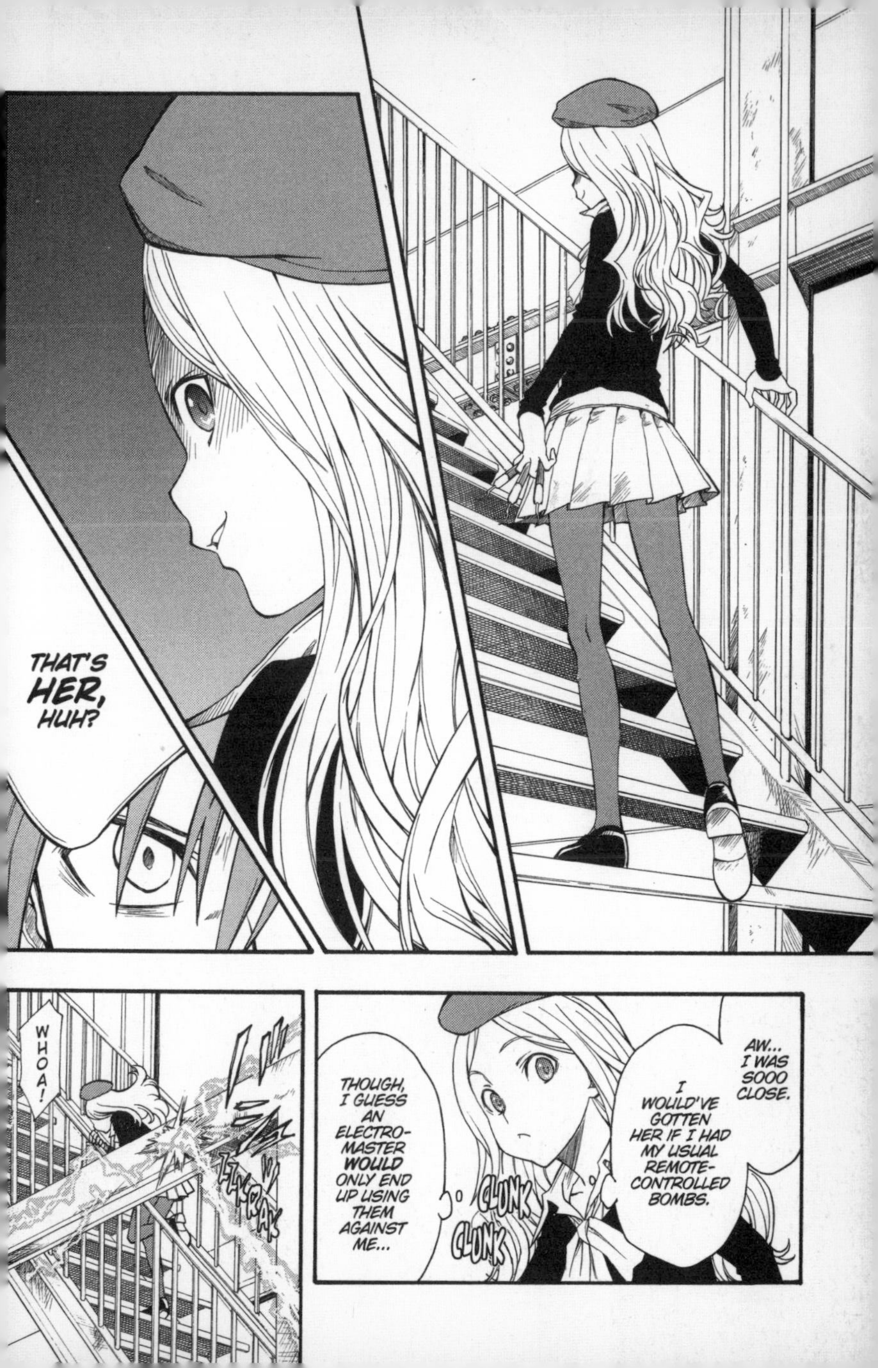
THAT'S HER, HUH?
AW... I WAS SOOO CLOSE.
I WOULD'VE GOTTEN HER IF I HAD MY USUAL REMOTE-CONTROLLED BOMBS.
THOUGH, I GUESS AN ELECTRO-MASTER WOULD ONLY END UP USING THEM AGAINST ME...
CLUNK
CLUNK
WHOA!

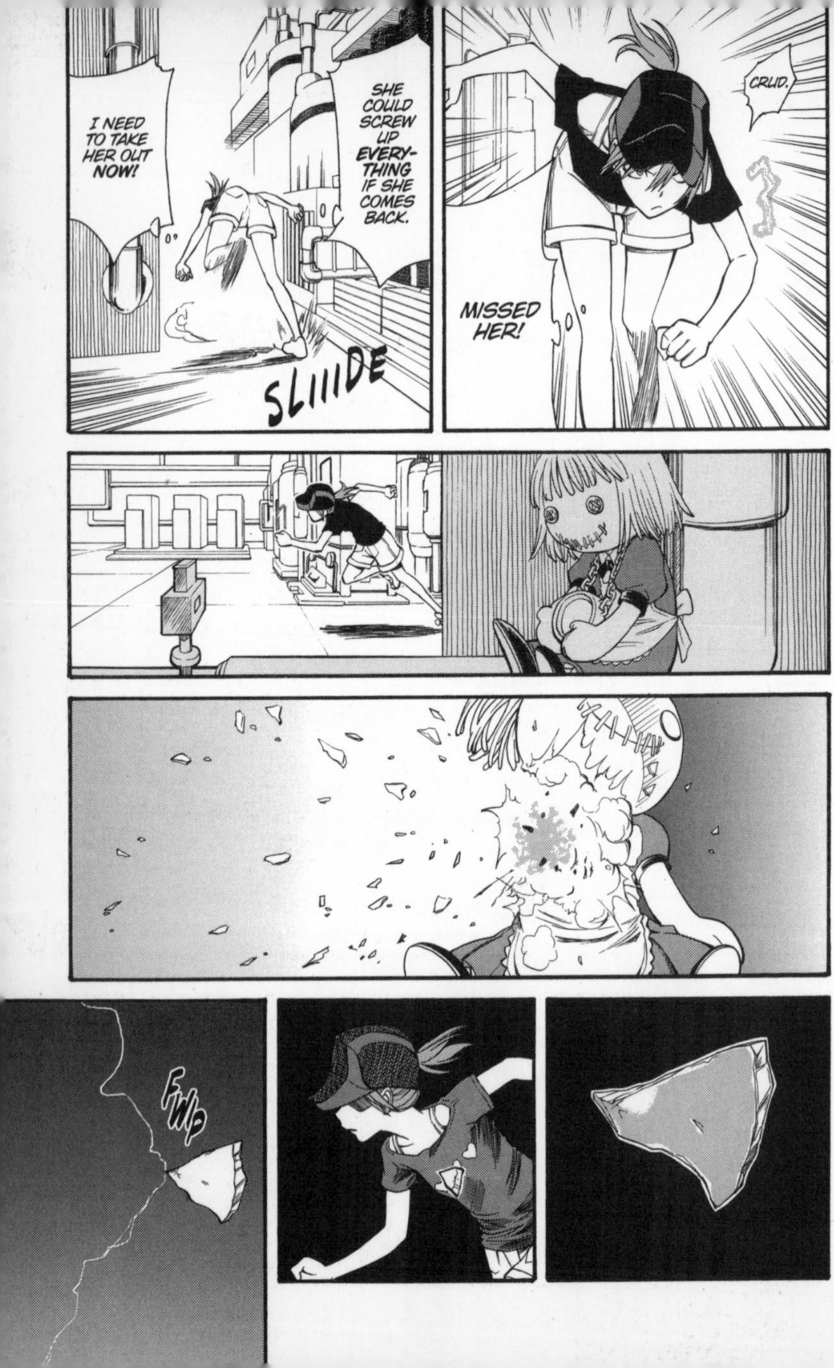

CRUD.
MISSED HER!
SHE COULD SCREW UP EVERY-THING IF SHE COMES BACK.
I NEED TO TAKE HER OUT NOW!
SLIIIDE
Fwip

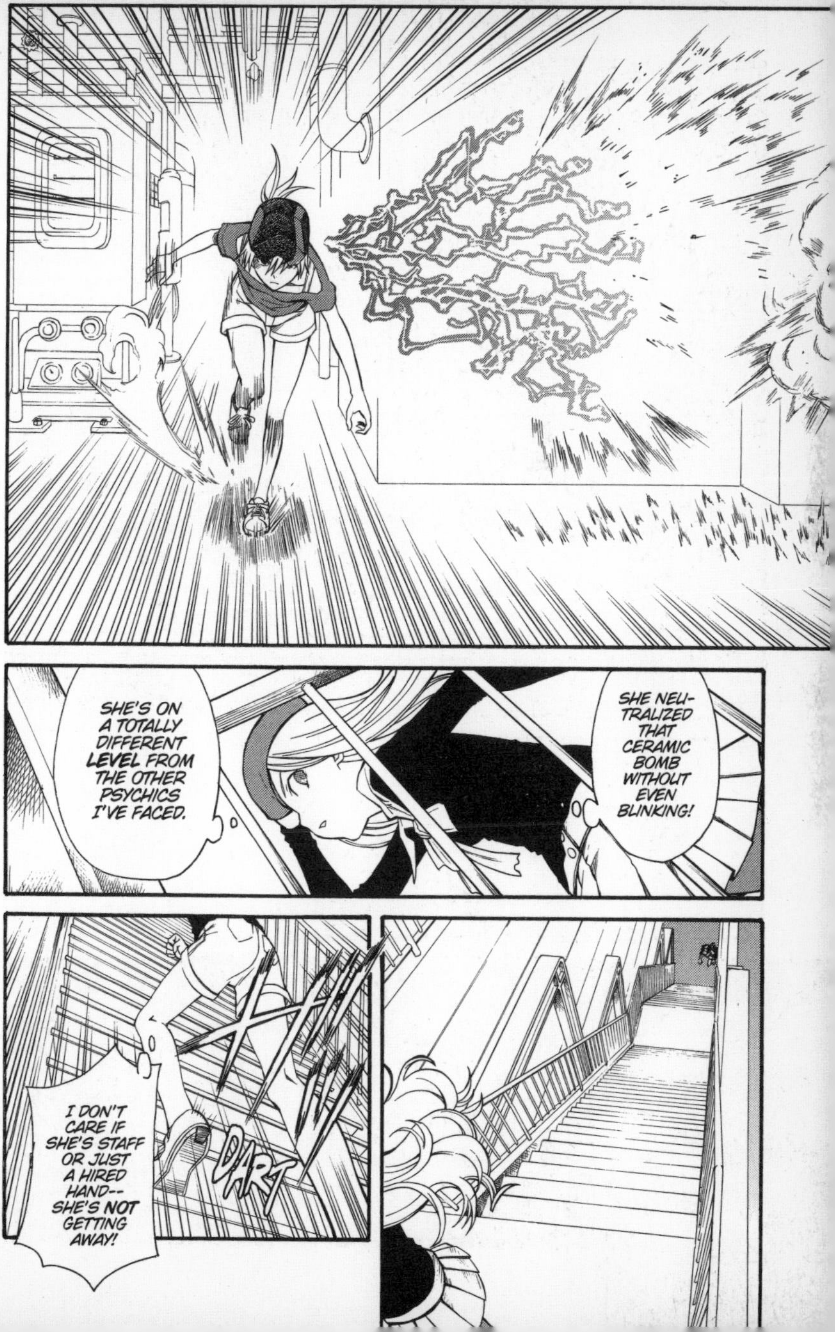
SHE NEU-TRALIZED THAT CERAMIC BOMB WITHOUT EVEN BLINKING!
SHE'S ON A TOTALLY DIFFERENT LEVEL FROM THE OTHER PSYCHICS I'VE FACED.
DART
I DON'T CARE IF SHE'S STAFF OR JUST A HIRED HAND-- SHE'S NOT GETTING AWAY!

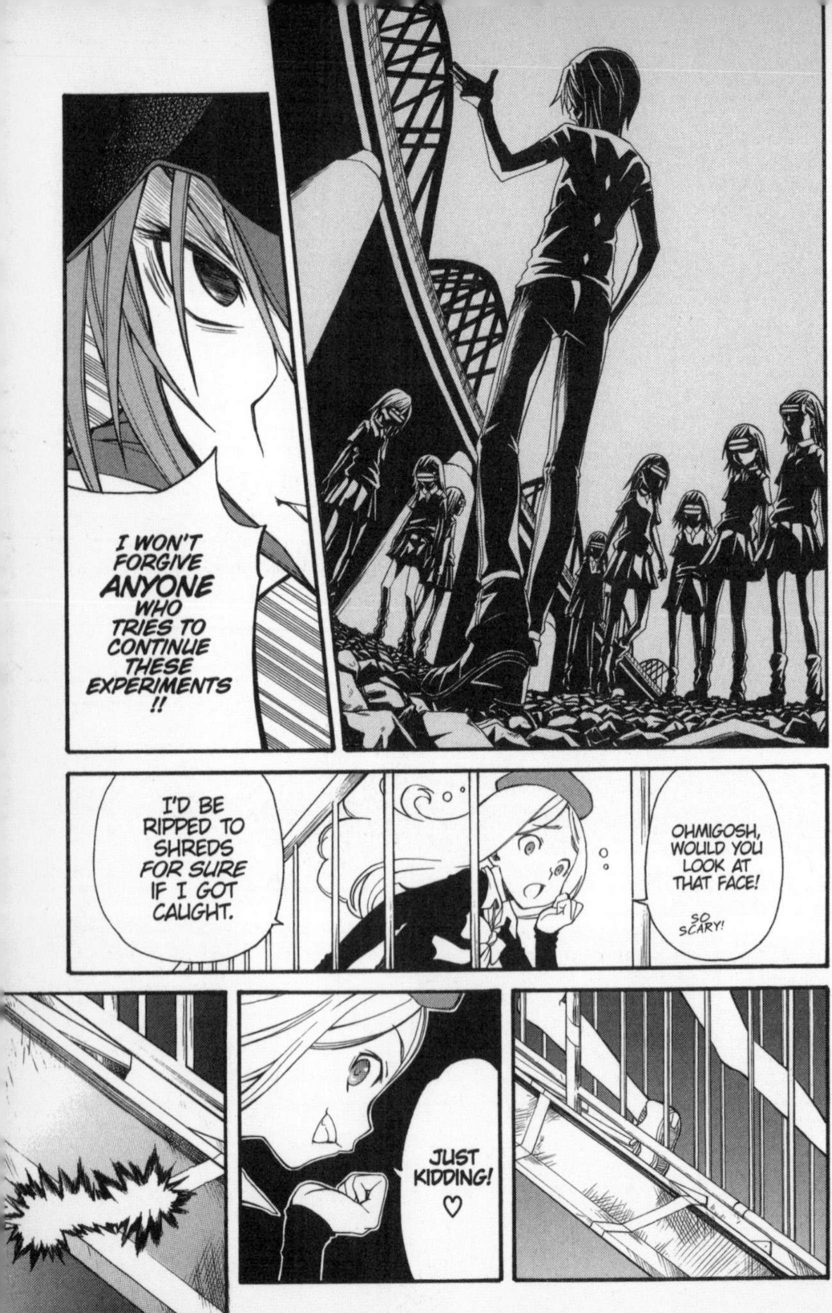
I WON'T FORGIVE ANYONE WHO TRIES TO CONTINUE THESE EXPERIMENTS !!
OHMIGOSH, WOULD YOU LOOK AT THAT FACE!
SO SCARY!
I'D BE RIPPED TO SHREDS FOR SURE IF I GOT CAUGHT.
JUST KIDDING! ♡

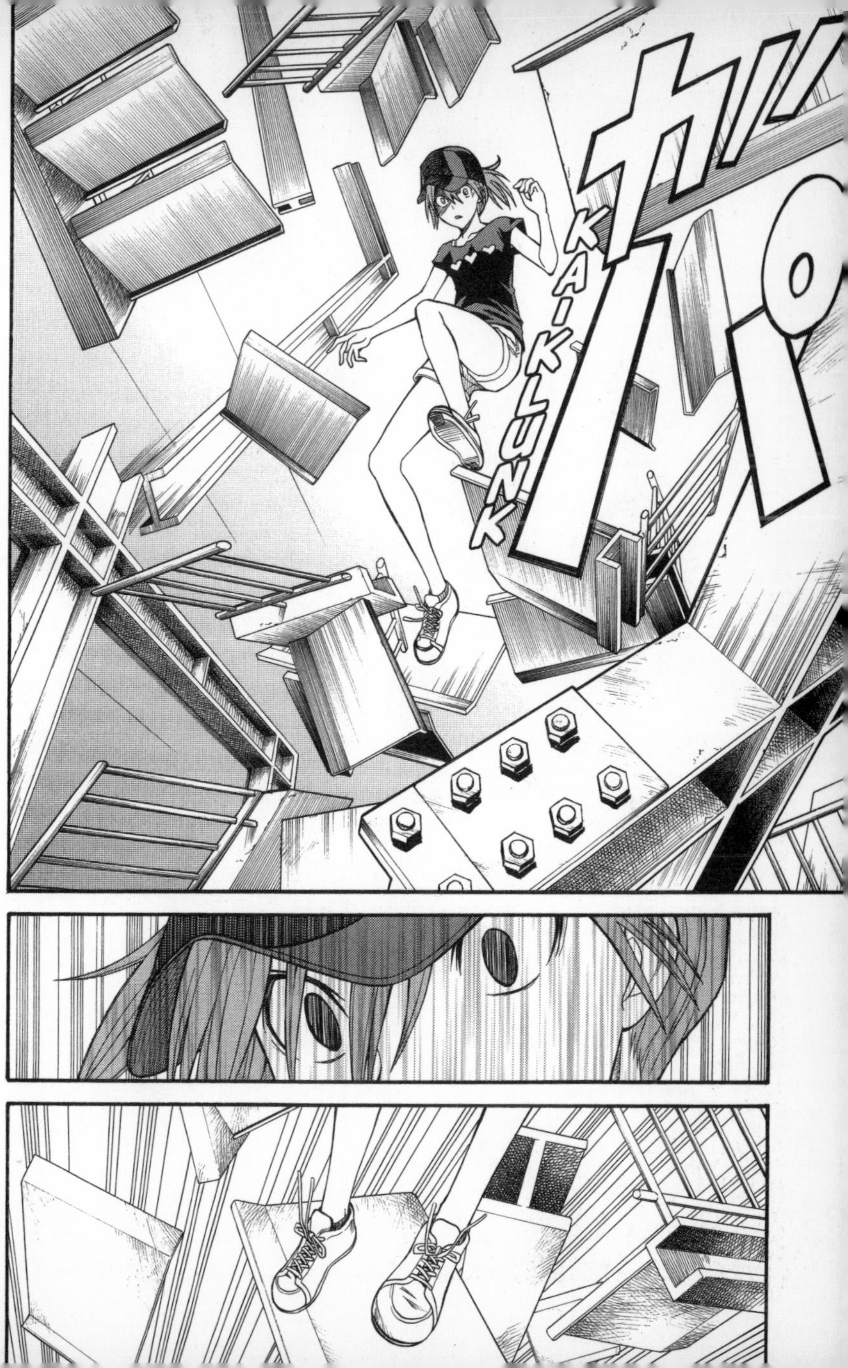
KAIKLUNK

HEE HEE HEE. ♪

IF SHE LANDS BADLY FROM THIS HEIGHT--

BAM BAM BAM BAM BAM BAM BAM
BAM BAM

HUH ...?

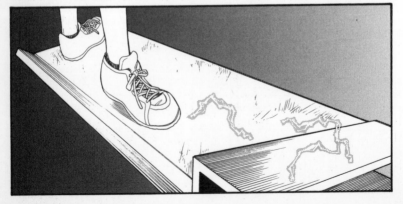

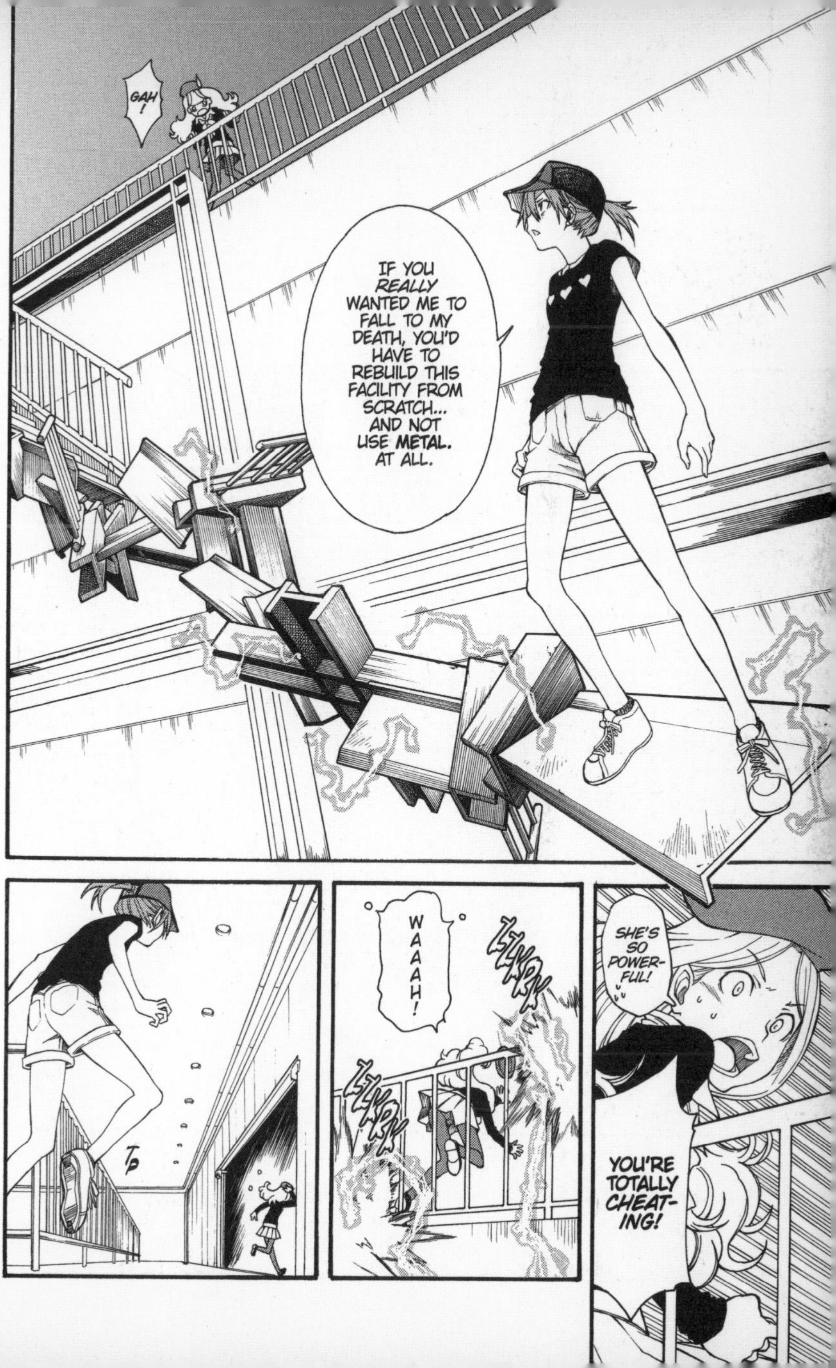
GAH!
IF YOU *REALLY* WANTED ME TO FALL TO MY DEATH, YOU'D HAVE TO REBUILD THIS FACILITY FROM SCRATCH... AND NOT USE **METAL**. AT ALL.
SHE'S SO POWER-FUL!
YOU'RE TOTALLY CHEAT-ING!
WAAAAH!
TP

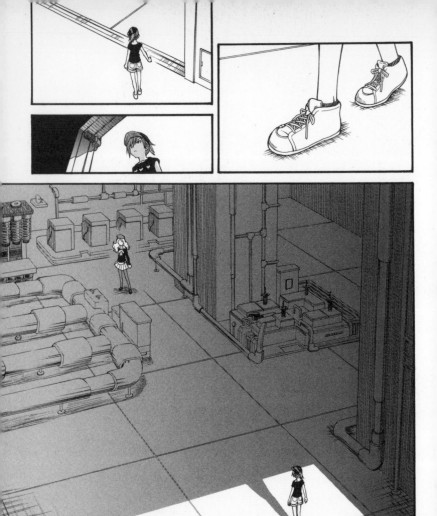

DEAD END, HUH?

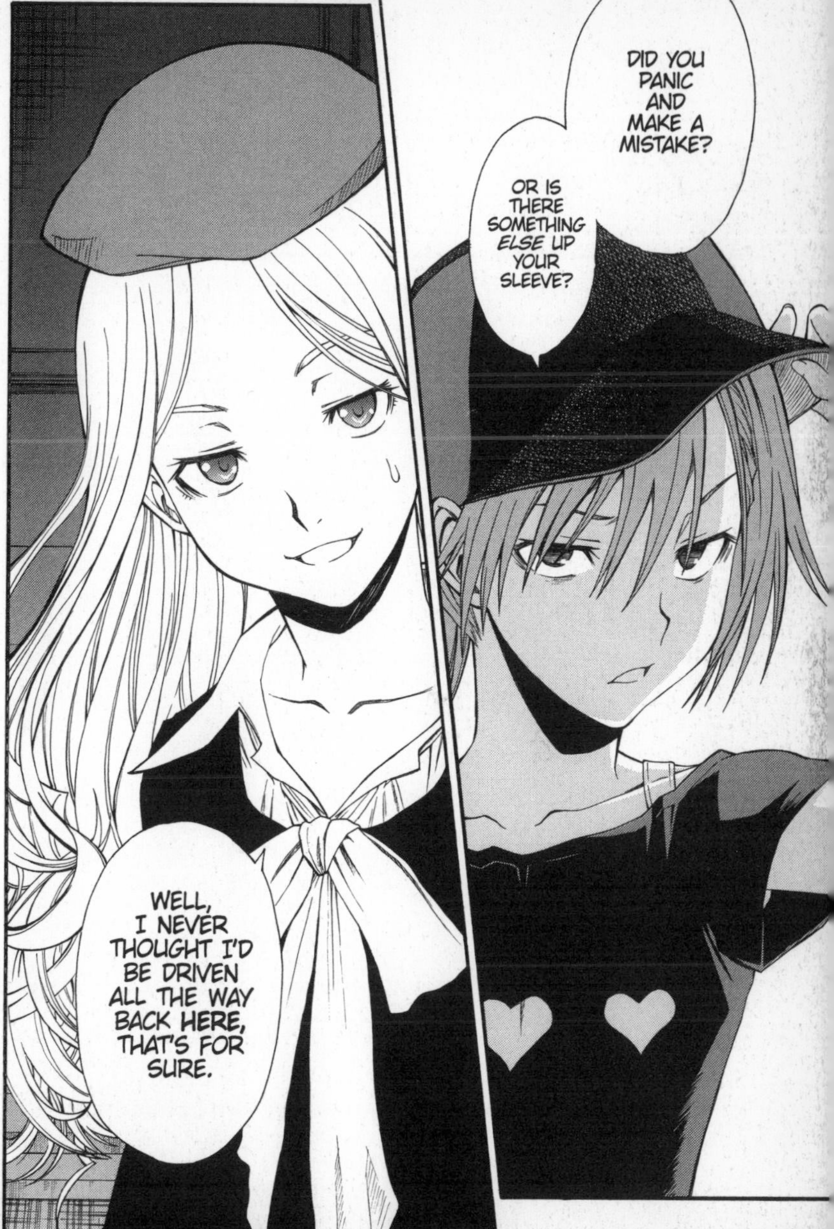
DID YOU PANIC AND MAKE A MISTAKE?
OR IS THERE SOMETHING *ELSE* UP YOUR SLEEVE?
WELL, I NEVER THOUGHT I'D BE DRIVEN ALL THE WAY BACK HERE, THAT'S FOR SURE.

A Certain SCIENTIFIC Railgun

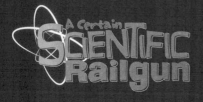

A Certain Trick's Death Flag

BOOM
BOOM
EXPLO-SIVES HIDDEN IN STUFFED ANIMALS ?!
BOOM
OH MY GOSH!
GEKOTA!
KABOOM
ドン
!
AAAAH!! HOW COULD YOOOUUU ?!!
KRKL KRKL KRKL KRKL KRKL
WHOA!
WHY'D SHE SUD-DENLY GET MADDER ?!

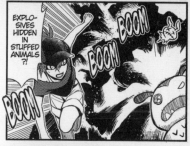

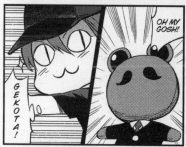

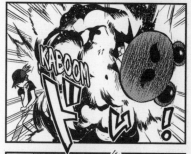

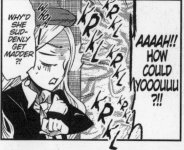

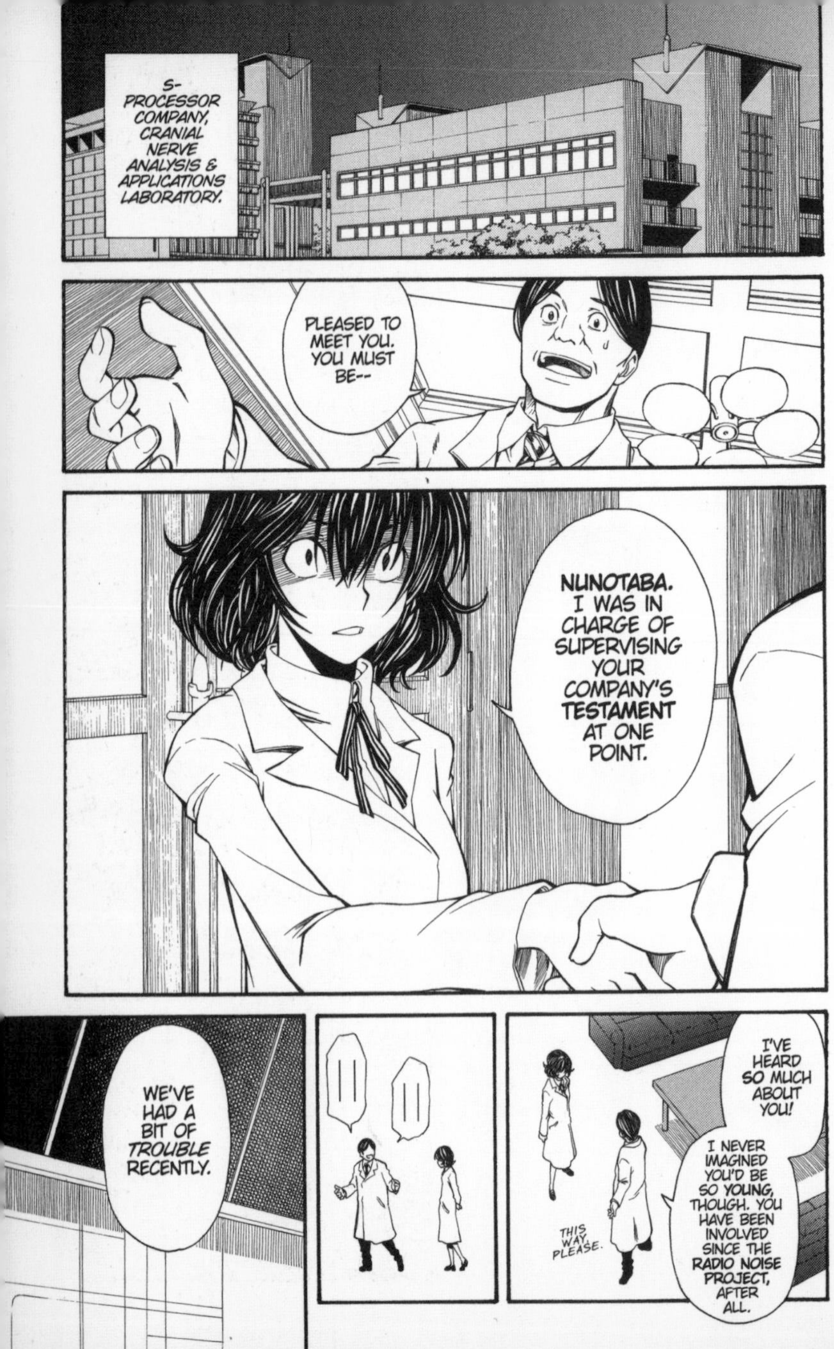
S-PROCESSOR COMPANY, CRANIAL NERVE ANALYSIS & APPLICATIONS LABORATORY.
PLEASED TO MEET YOU. YOU MUST BE--
NUNOTABA. I WAS IN CHARGE OF SUPERVISING YOUR COMPANY'S TESTAMENT AT ONE POINT.
I'VE HEARD SO MUCH ABOUT YOU!
I NEVER IMAGINED YOU'D BE SO YOUNG, THOUGH. YOU HAVE BEEN INVOLVED SINCE THE RADIO NOISE PROJECT, AFTER ALL.
THIS WAY PLEASE.
WE'VE HAD A BIT OF TROUBLE RECENTLY.

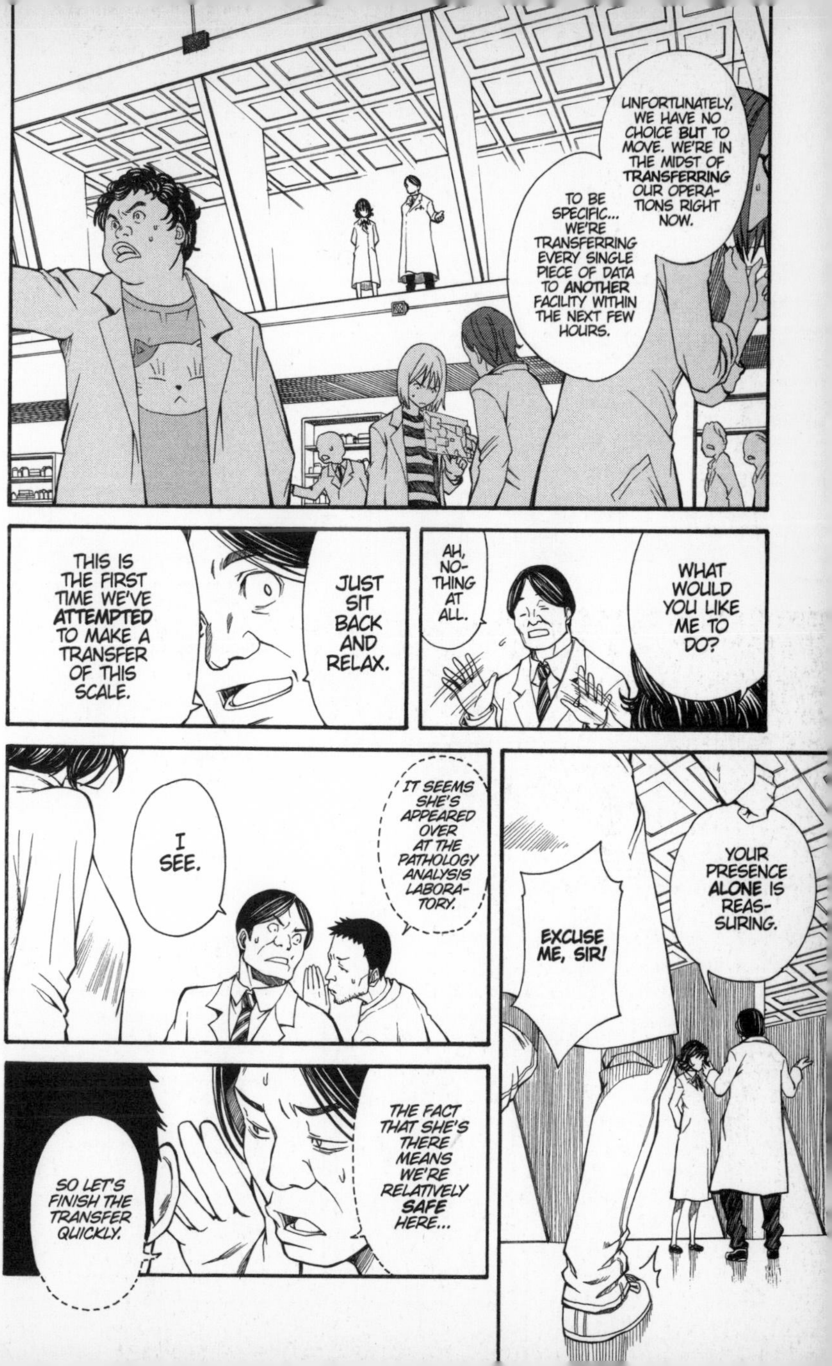
UNFORTUNATELY, WE HAVE NO CHOICE BUT TO MOVE. WE'RE IN THE MIDST OF TRANSFERRING OUR OPERATIONS RIGHT NOW.
TO BE SPECIFIC... WE'RE TRANSFERRING EVERY SINGLE PIECE OF DATA TO ANOTHER FACILITY WITHIN THE NEXT FEW HOURS.
WHAT WOULD YOU LIKE ME TO DO?
AH, NOTHING AT ALL.
JUST SIT BACK AND RELAX.
THIS IS THE FIRST TIME WE'VE ATTEMPTED TO MAKE A TRANSFER OF THIS SCALE.
YOUR PRESENCE ALONE IS REASSURING.
EXCUSE ME, SIR!
IT SEEMS SHE'S APPEARED OVER AT THE PATHOLOGY ANALYSIS LABORATORY.
I SEE.
THE FACT THAT SHE'S THERE MEANS WE'RE RELATIVELY SAFE HERE...
SO LET'S FINISH THE TRANSFER QUICKLY.

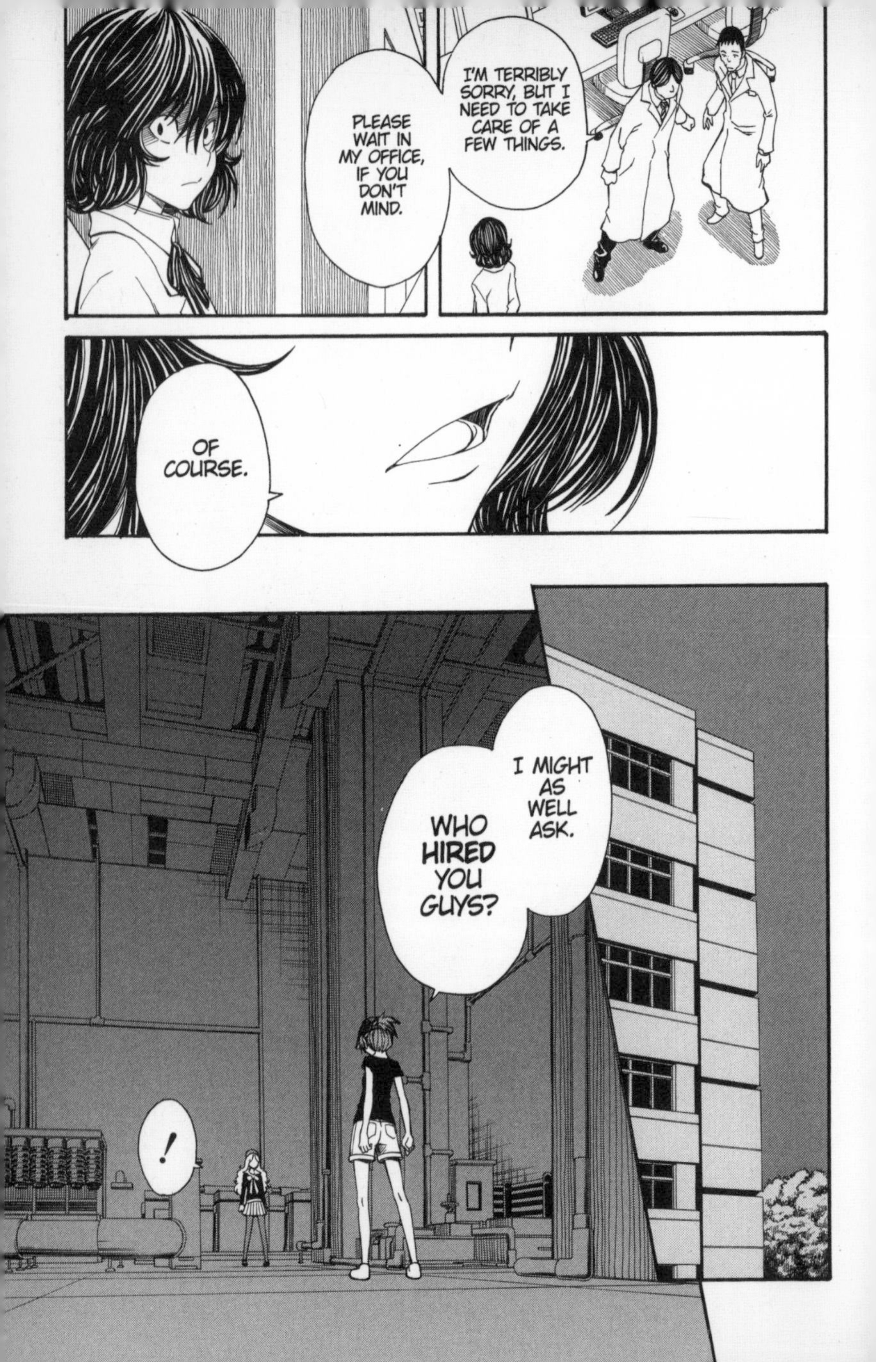
I'M TERRIBLY SORRY, BUT I NEED TO TAKE CARE OF A FEW THINGS.
PLEASE WAIT IN MY OFFICE, IF YOU DON'T MIND.
OF COURSE.
I MIGHT AS WELL ASK.
WHO HIRED YOU GUYS?
!

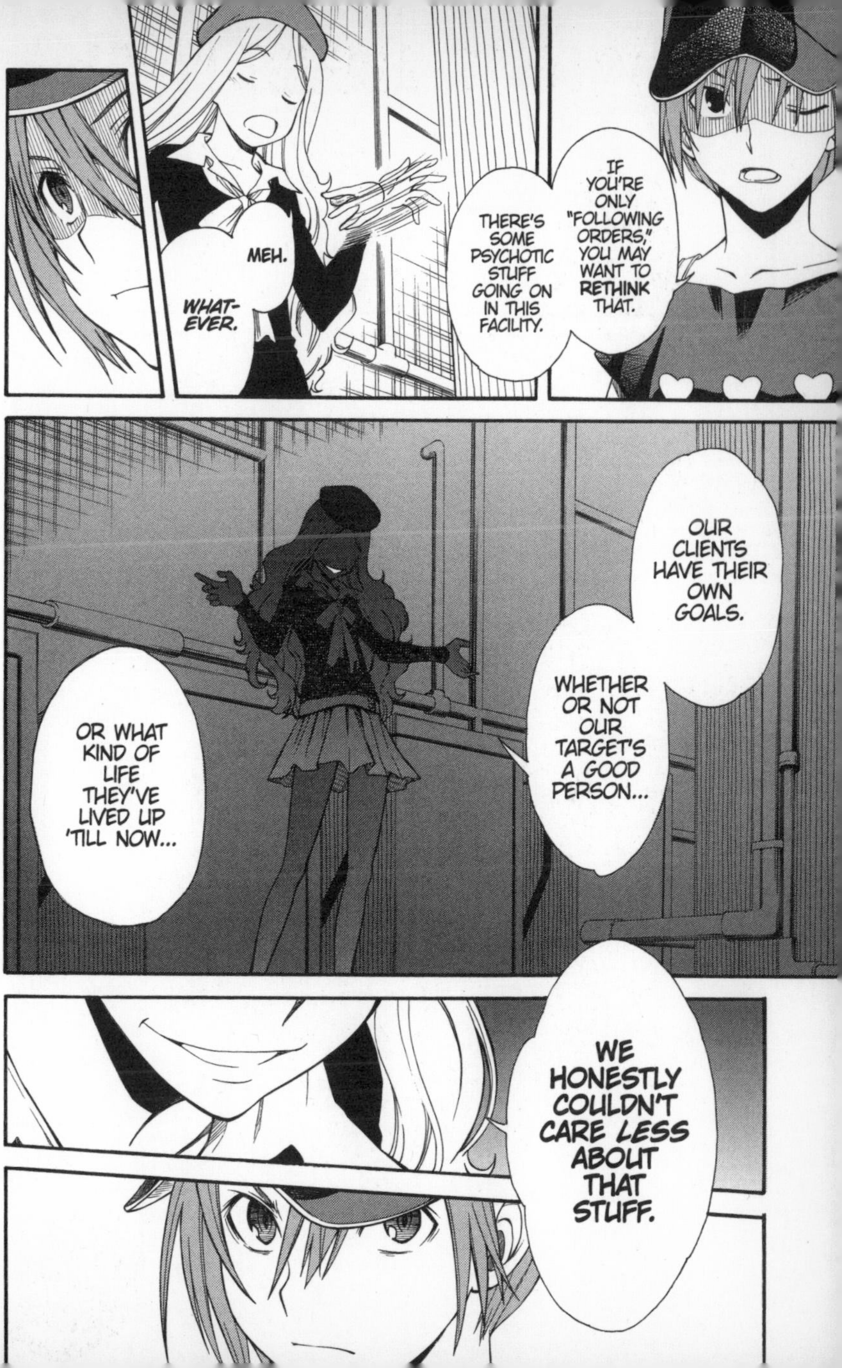
IF YOU'RE ONLY "FOLLOWING ORDERS," YOU MAY WANT TO RETHINK THAT.
THERE'S SOME PSYCHOTIC STUFF GOING ON IN THIS FACILITY.
MEH.
WHATEVER.
OUR CLIENTS HAVE THEIR OWN GOALS.
WHETHER OR NOT OUR TARGET'S A GOOD PERSON...
OR WHAT KIND OF LIFE THEY'VE LIVED UP 'TILL NOW...
WE HONESTLY COULDN'T CARE *LESS* ABOUT THAT STUFF.

CHAPTER 27: AUGUST 19 (2)

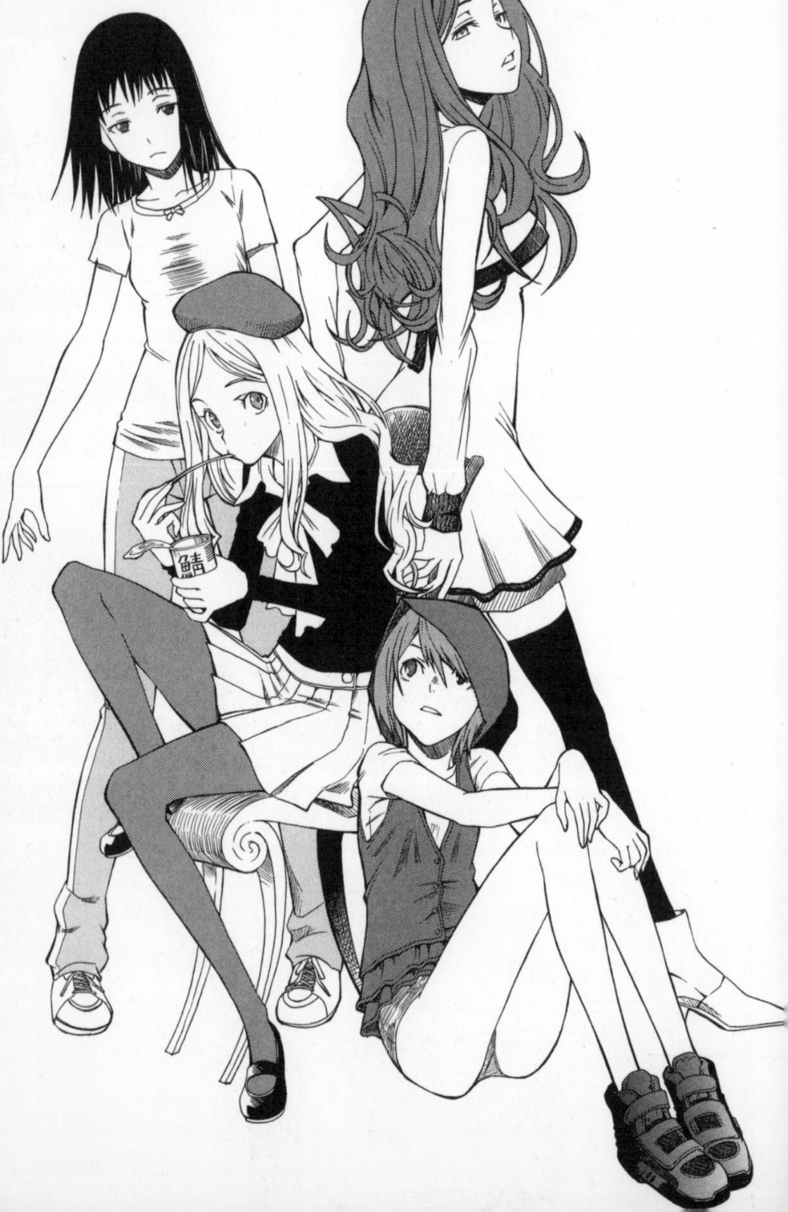
鯖

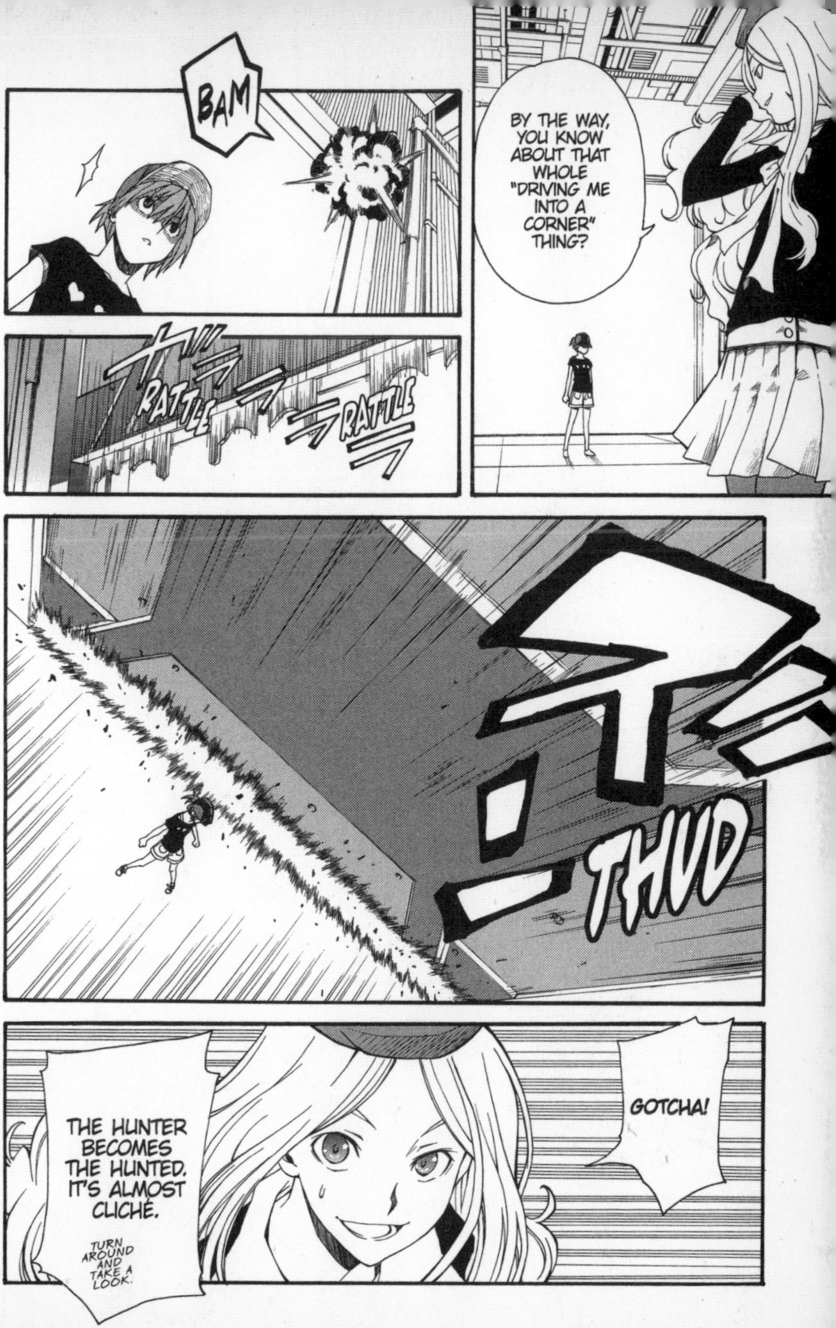
BY THE WAY, YOU KNOW ABOUT THAT WHOLE "DRIVING ME INTO A CORNER" THING?
BAM
RATTLE
RATTLE
THUD
GOTCHA!
THE HUNTER BECOMES THE HUNTED. IT'S ALMOST CLICHÉ.
TURN AROUND AND TAKE A LOOK.

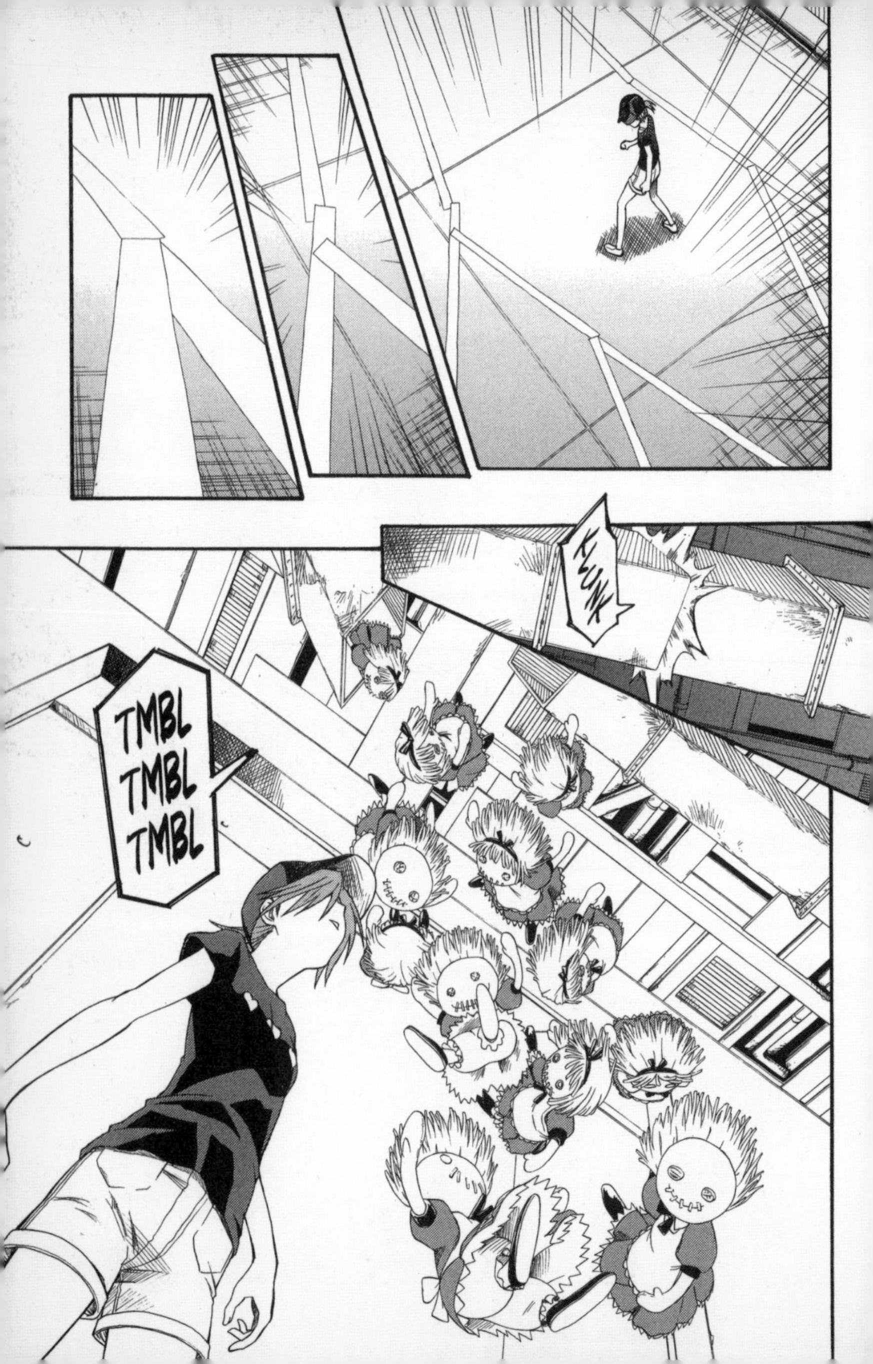
KLUNK
TMBL
TMBL
TMBL

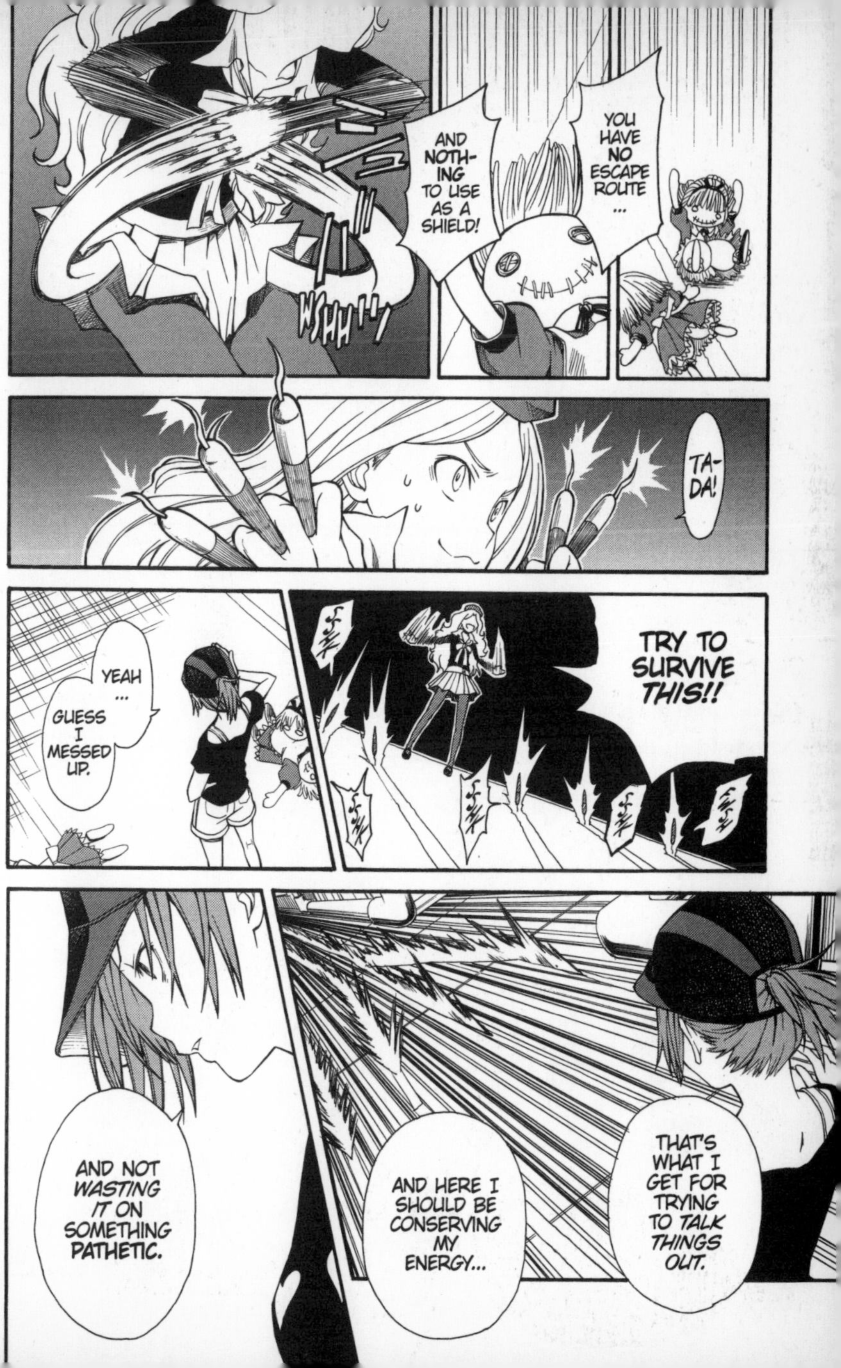
YOU HAVE NO ESCAPE ROUTE ...
AND NOTHING TO USE AS A SHIELD!
WSHH
TA-DA!
TRY TO SURVIVE THIS!!
FWSH
YEAH ... GUESS I MESSED UP.
THAT'S WHAT I GET FOR TRYING TO TALK THINGS OUT.
AND HERE I SHOULD BE CONSERVING MY ENERGY...
AND NOT WASTING IT ON SOMETHING PATHETIC.

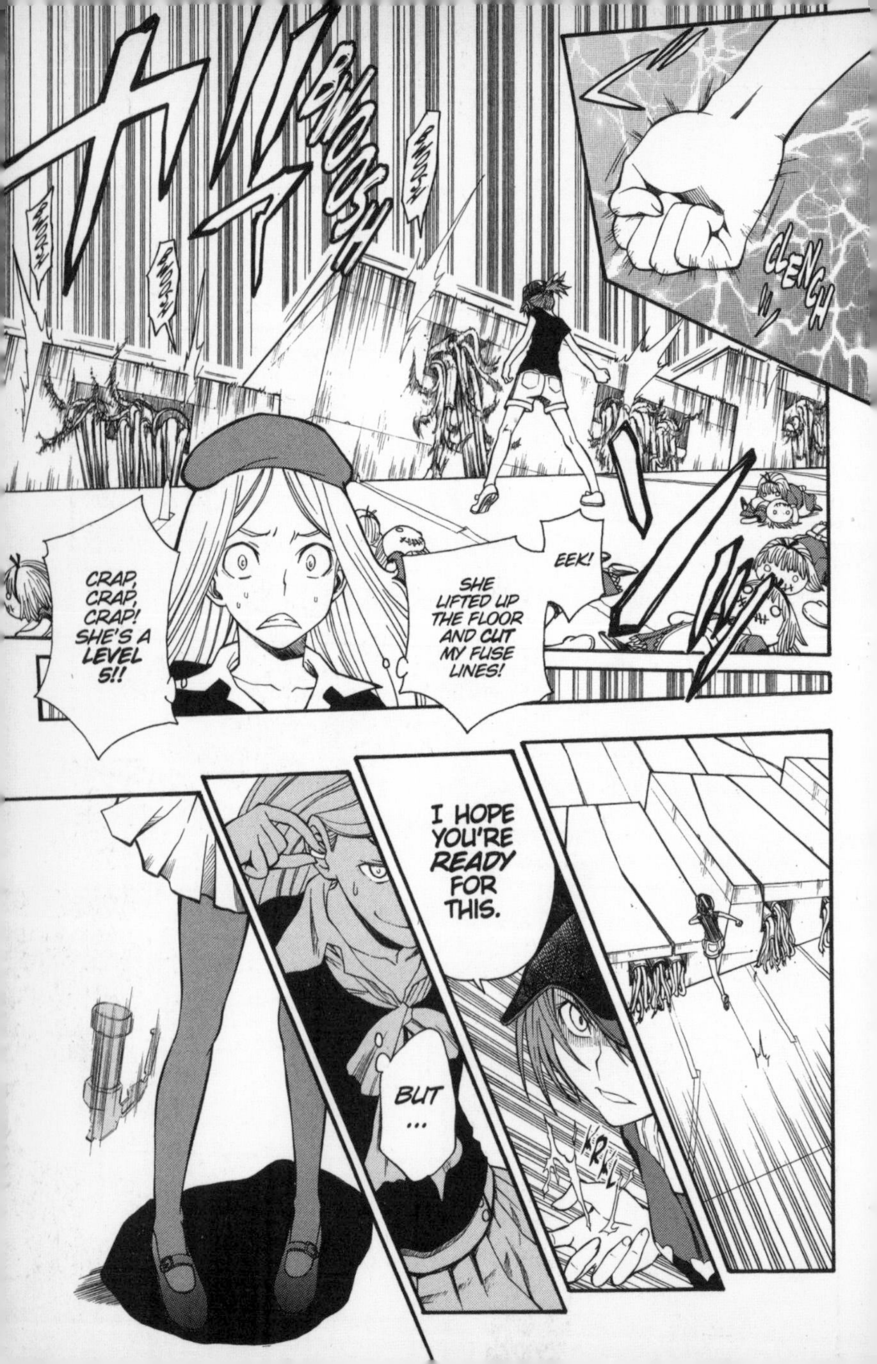
CLENCH
WHOOOSH
WHOOSH
WHOOSH
WHOOSH
EEK!
SHE LIFTED UP THE FLOOR AND CUT MY FUSE LINES!
CRAP, CRAP, CRAP! SHE'S A LEVEL 5!!
I HOPE YOU'RE READY FOR THIS.
BUT ...

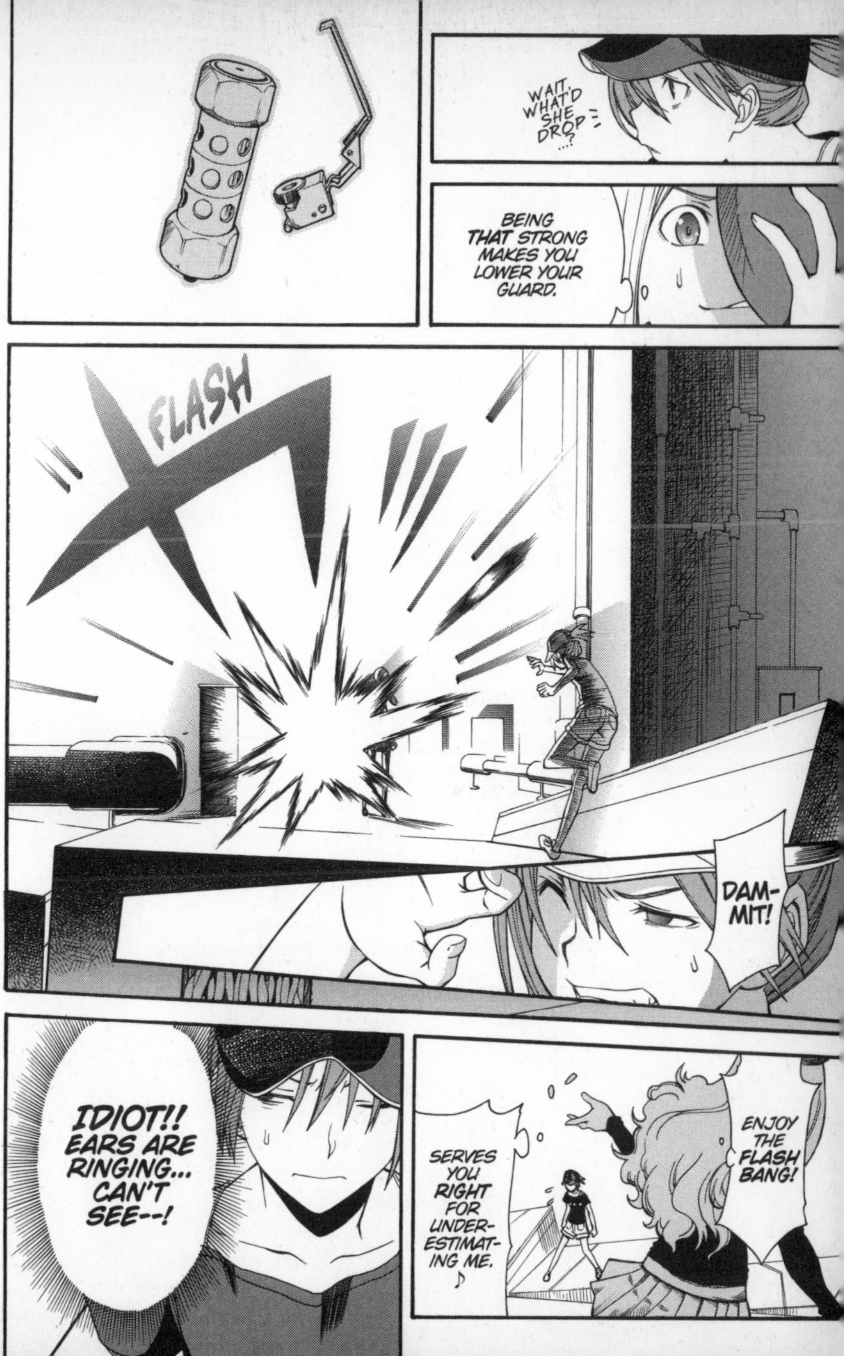
WAIT, WHAT'D SHE DROP ...?
BEING THAT STRONG MAKES YOU LOWER YOUR GUARD.
FLASH
DAM-MIT!
ENJOY THE FLASH BANG!
SERVES YOU RIGHT FOR UNDER-ESTIMAT-ING ME. ♪
IDIOT!! EARS ARE RINGING... CAN'T SEE--!

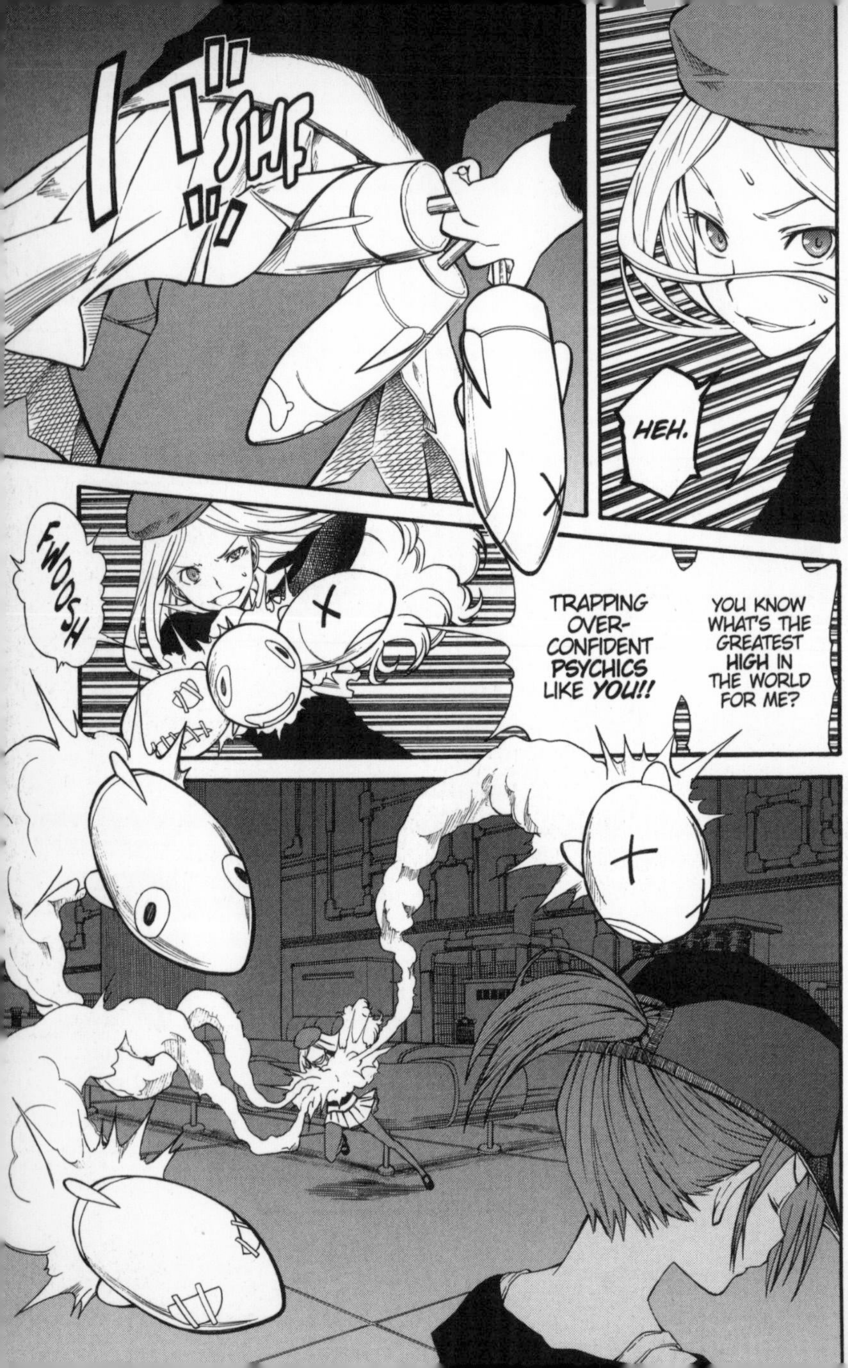
HEH.
SHF
YOU KNOW WHAT'S THE GREATEST HIGH IN THE WORLD FOR ME?
TRAPPING OVER-CONFIDENT PSYCHICS LIKE YOU!!
FWOOSH

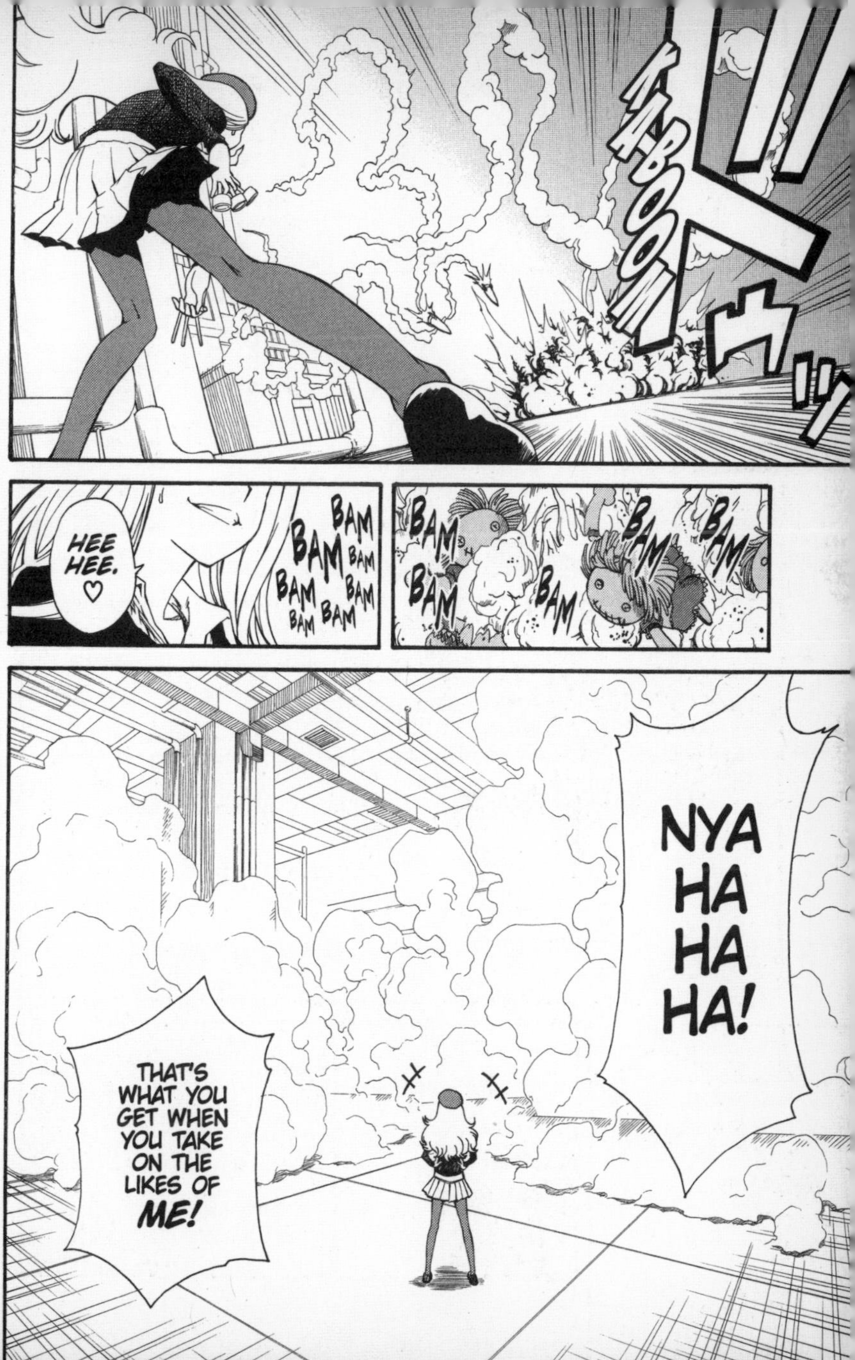
KABOOOM
ドウッ
BAM BAM BAM BAM BAM BAM
BAM BAM BAM BAM BAM BAM BAM BAM
HEE HEE. ♡
NYA HA HA HA!
THAT'S WHAT YOU GET WHEN YOU TAKE ON THE LIKES OF ME!

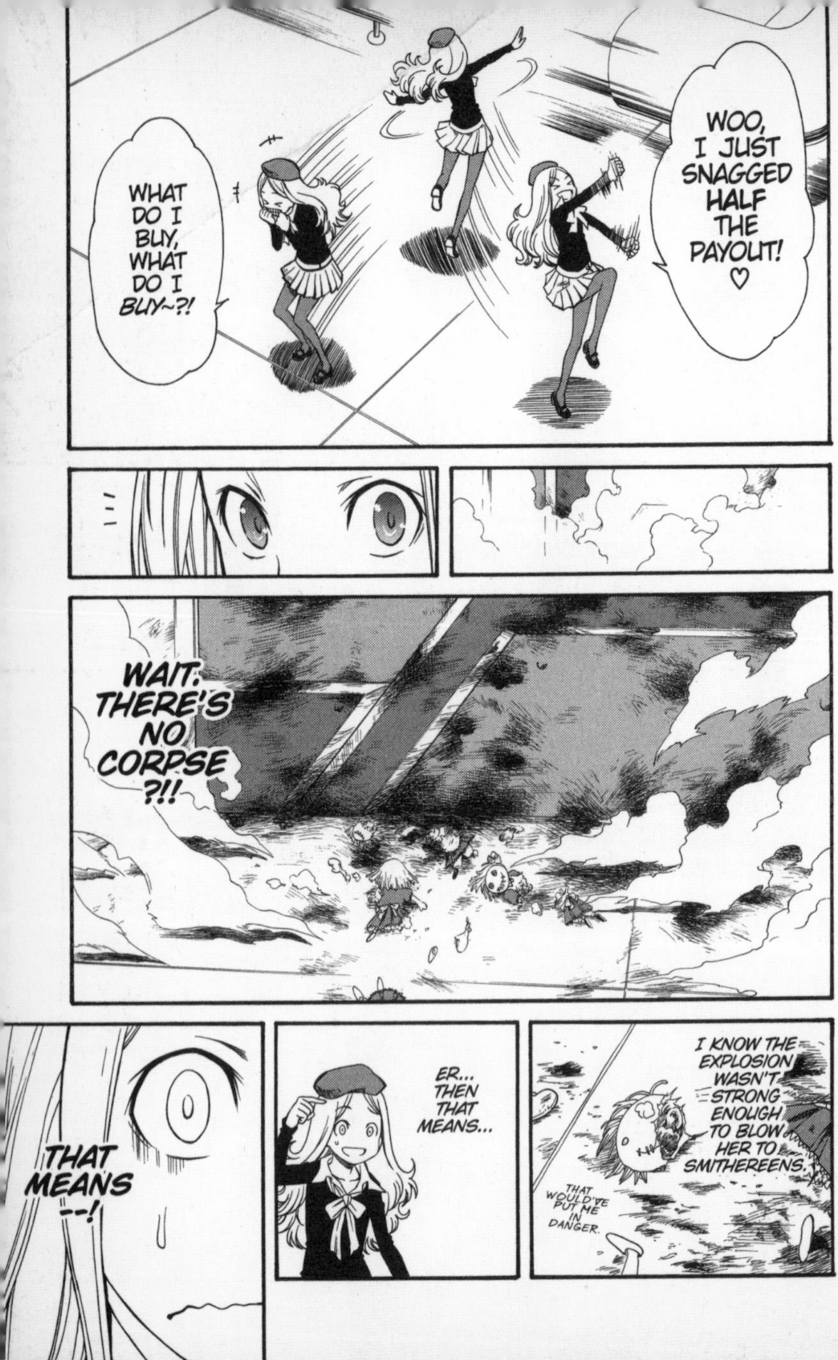
WOO, I JUST SNAGGED HALF THE PAYOUT! ♡
WHAT DO I BUY, WHAT DO I BUY~?!
WAIT. THERE'S NO CORPSE ?!!
I KNOW THE EXPLOSION WASN'T STRONG ENOUGH TO BLOW HER TO SMITHEREENS.
THAT WOULD'VE PUT ME IN DANGER.
ER... THEN THAT MEANS...
THAT MEANS --!

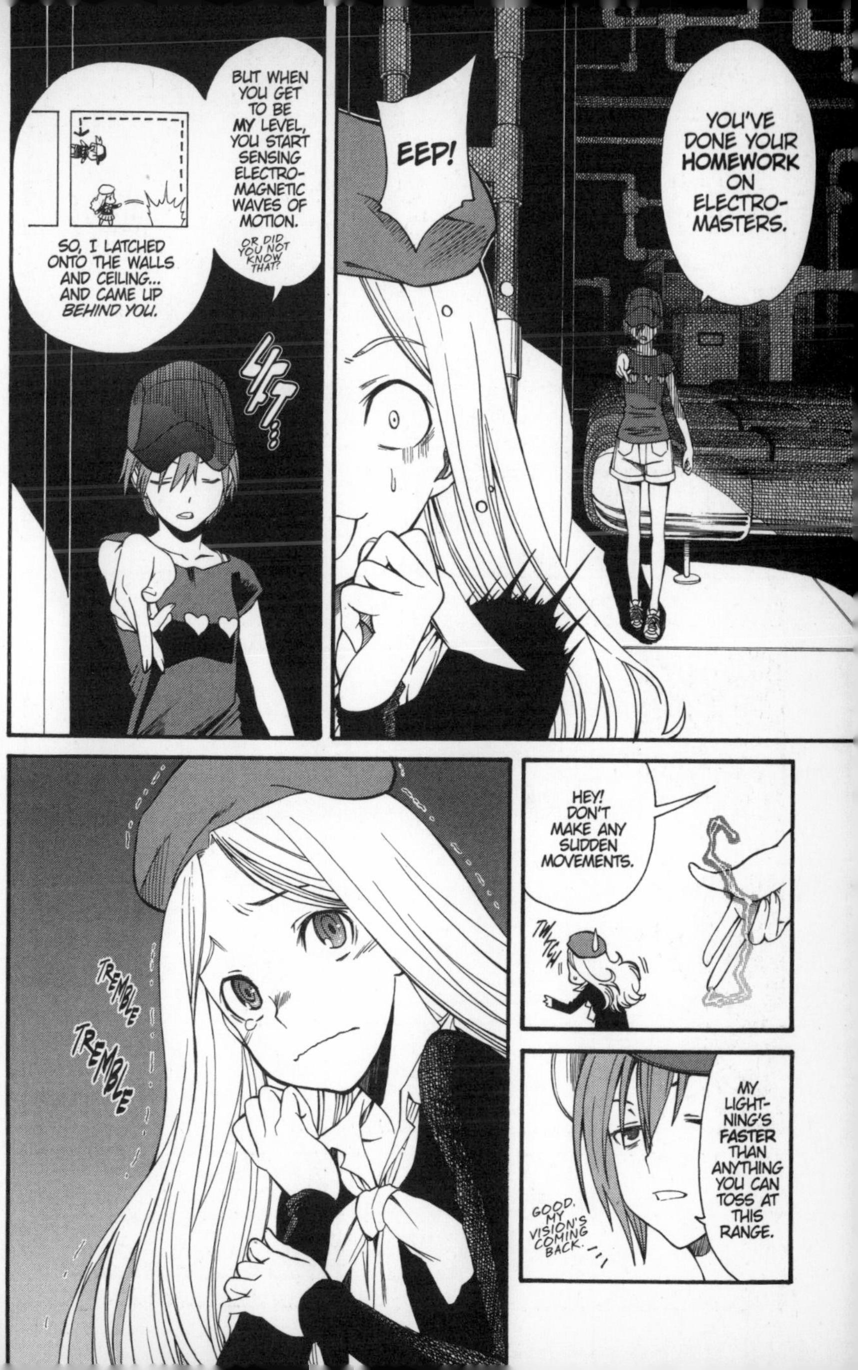
YOU'VE DONE YOUR HOMEWORK ON ELECTRO-MASTERS.
EEP!
BUT WHEN YOU GET TO BE MY LEVEL, YOU START SENSING ELECTRO-MAGNETIC WAVES OF MOTION.
OR DID YOU NOT KNOW THAT?
SO, I LATCHED ONTO THE WALLS AND CEILING... AND CAME UP *BEHIND YOU.*
HEY! DON'T MAKE ANY SUDDEN MOVEMENTS.
TWITCH
MY LIGHTNING'S FASTER THAN ANYTHING YOU CAN TOSS AT THIS RANGE.
GOOD, MY VISION'S COMING BACK.
TREMBLE
TREMBLE

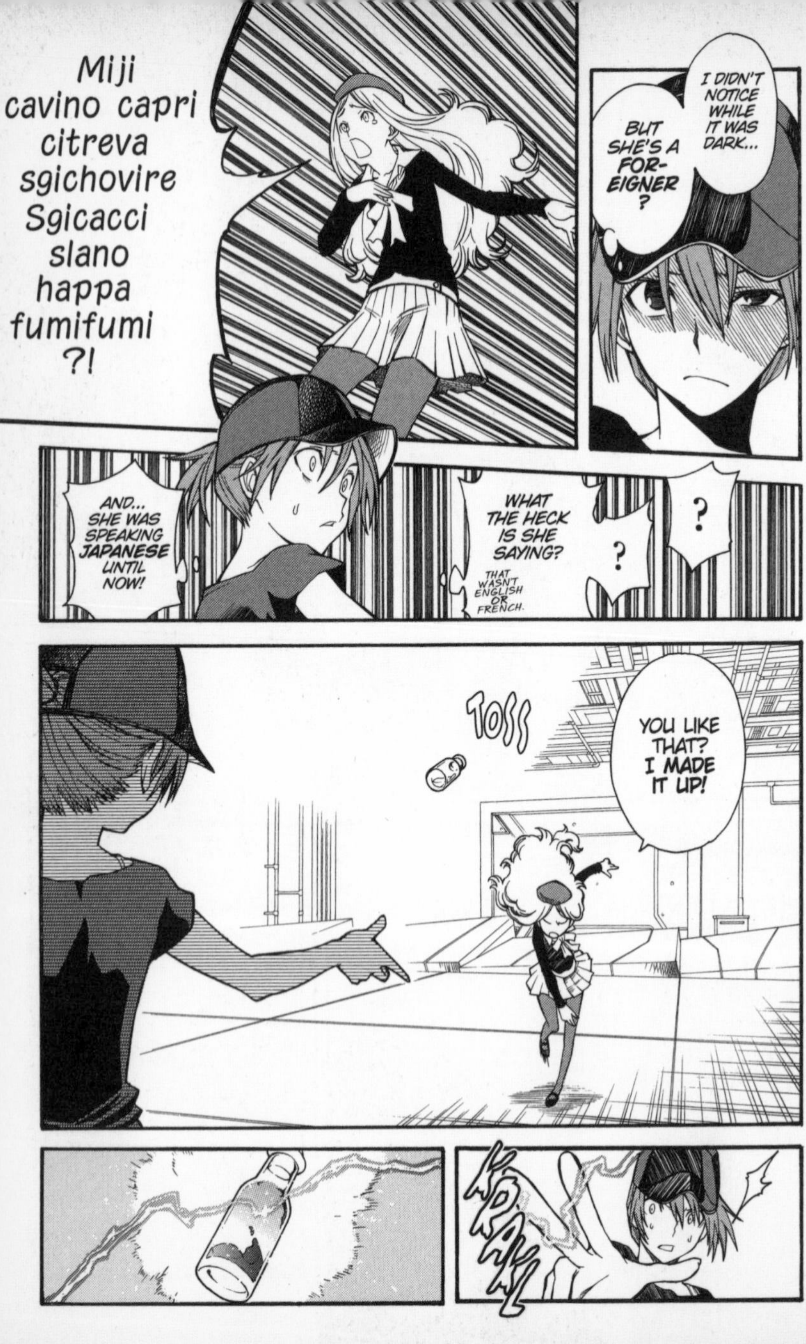
I DIDN'T NOTICE WHILE IT WAS DARK...
BUT SHE'S A FOR-EIGNER?
Miji cavino capri citreva sgichovire Sgicacci slano happa fumifumi ?!
?
?
WHAT THE HECK IS SHE SAYING?
THAT WASN'T ENGLISH OR FRENCH.
AND... SHE WAS SPEAKING JAPANESE UNTIL NOW!
YOU LIKE THAT? I MADE IT UP!
TOSS

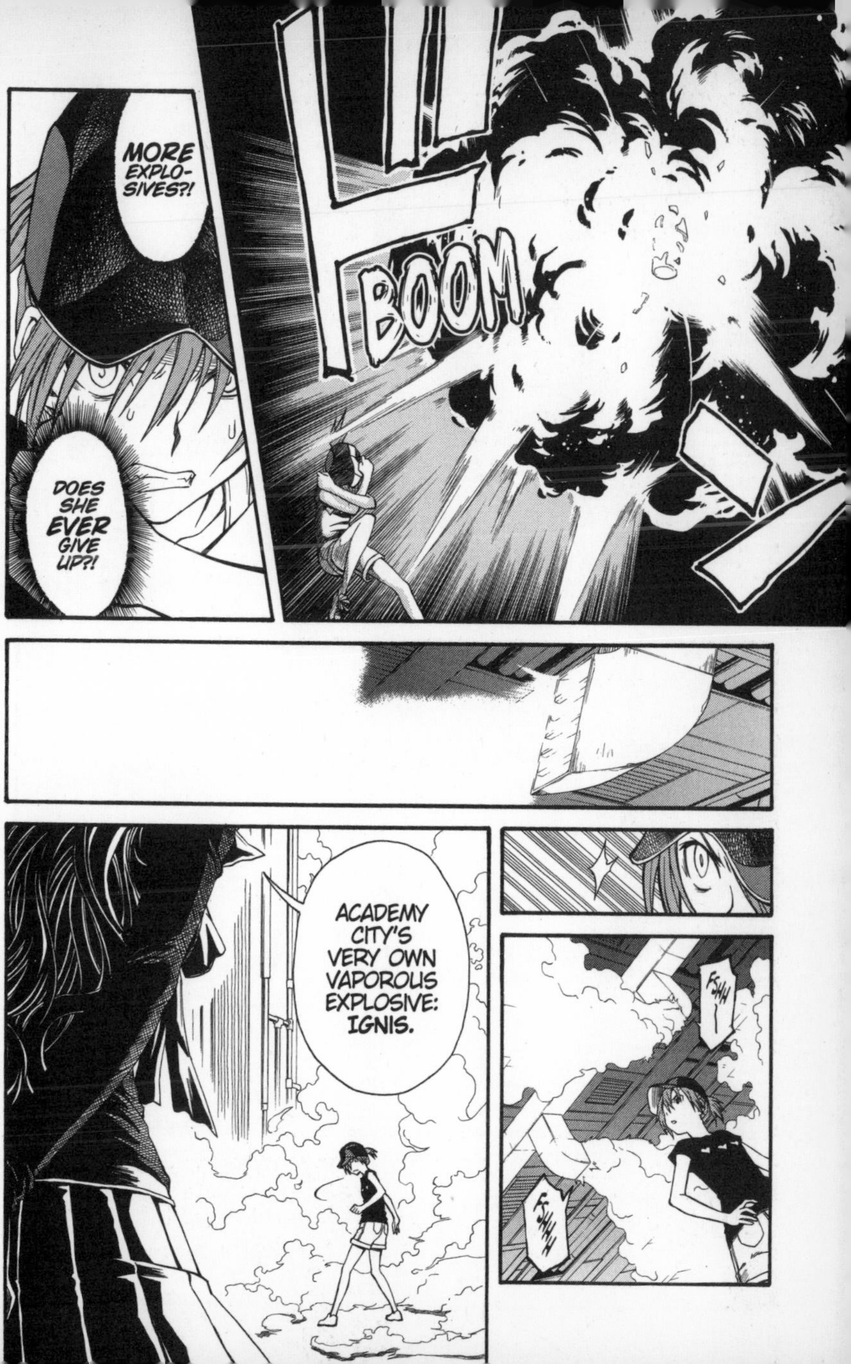
BOOM
MORE EXPLOSIVES?!
DOES SHE EVER GIVE UP?!
FSHH
FSHH
ACADEMY CITY'S VERY OWN VAPOROUS EXPLOSIVE: IGNIS.

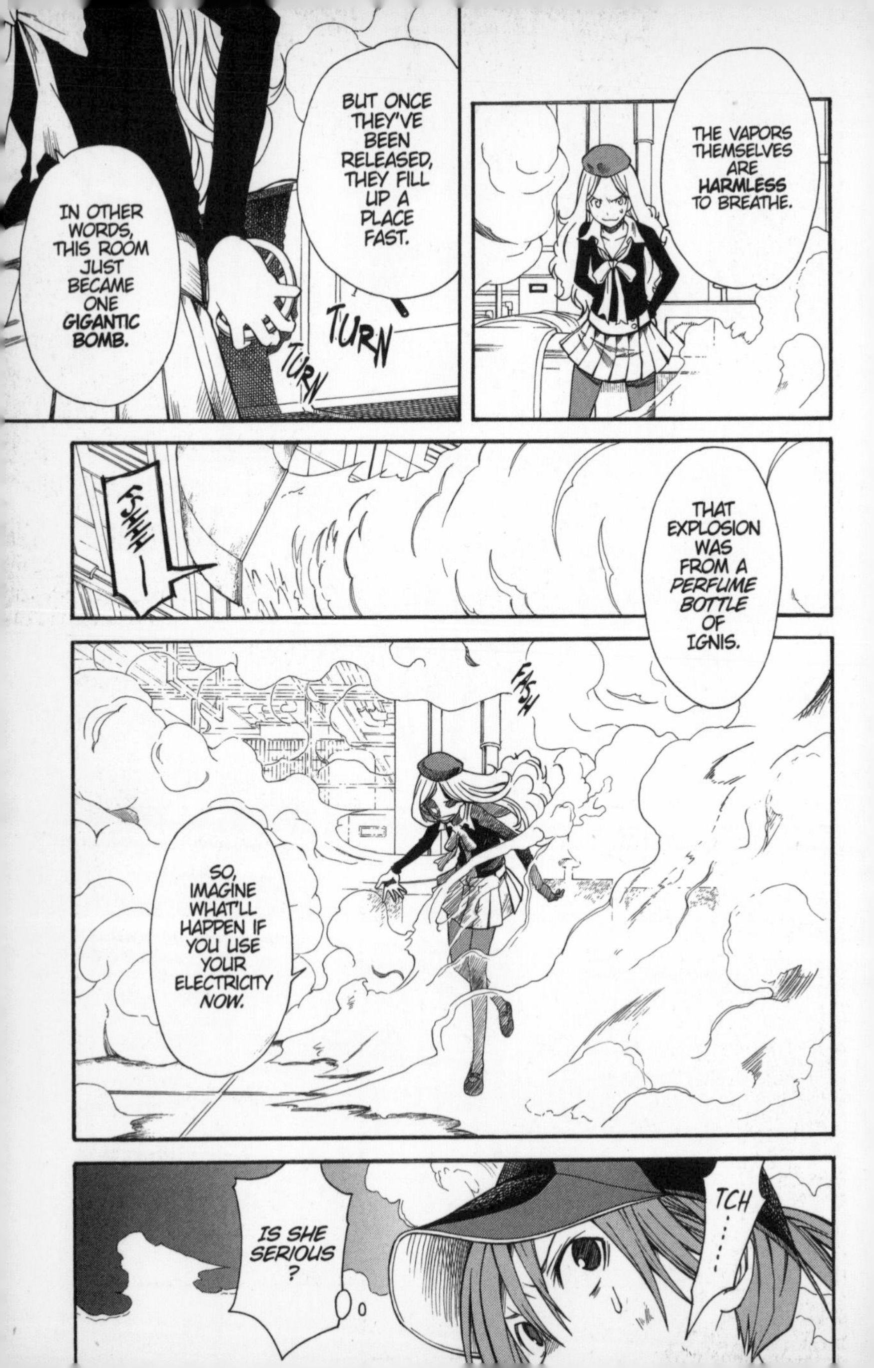
THE VAPORS THEMSELVES ARE HARMLESS TO BREATHE.
BUT ONCE THEY'VE BEEN RELEASED, THEY FILL UP A PLACE FAST.
TURN
TURN
IN OTHER WORDS, THIS ROOM JUST BECAME ONE GIGANTIC BOMB.
THAT EXPLOSION WAS FROM A PERFUME BOTTLE OF IGNIS.
FSHHH—
FASH
SO, IMAGINE WHAT'LL HAPPEN IF YOU USE YOUR ELECTRICITY NOW.
TCH......
IS SHE SERIOUS?

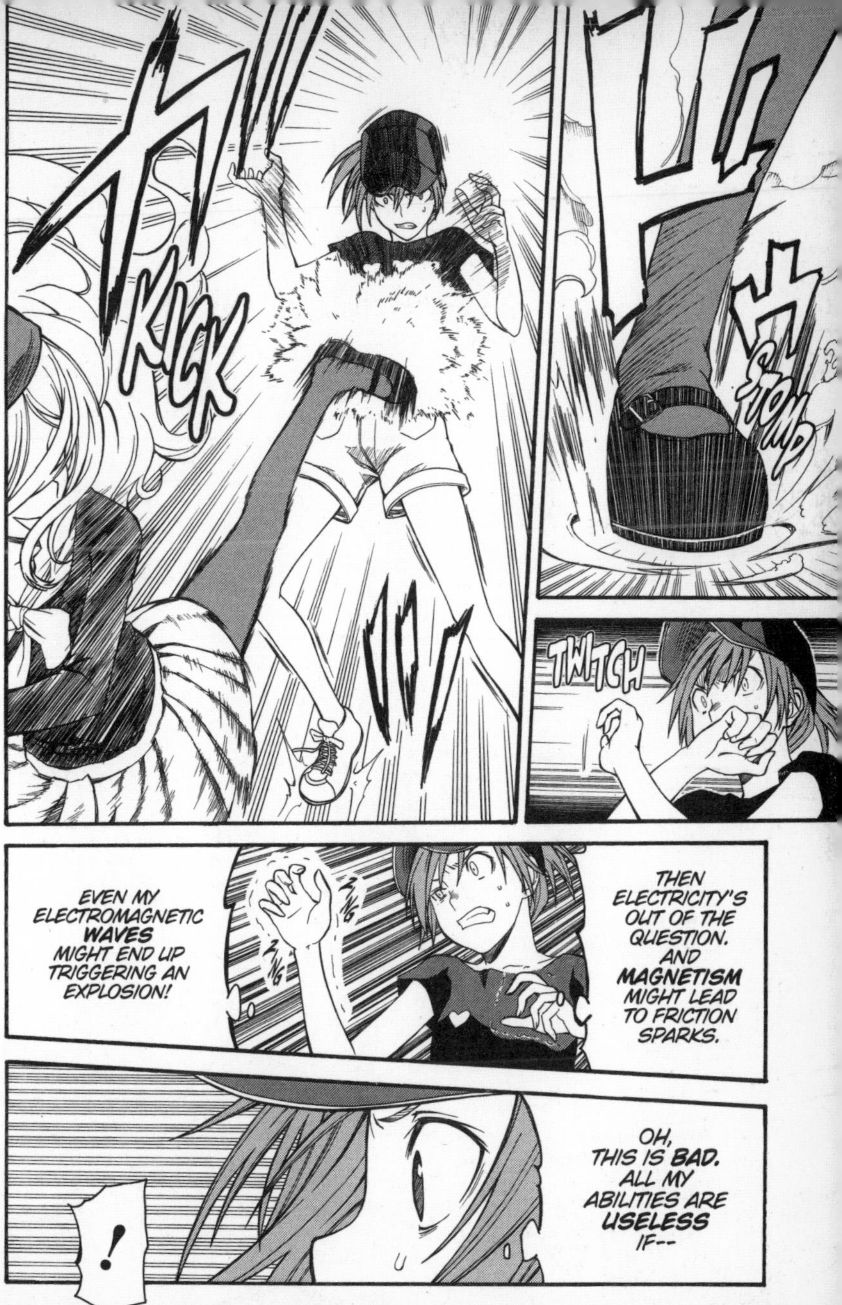
STOMP
TWITCH
KICK
THEN ELECTRICITY'S OUT OF THE QUESTION. AND MAGNETISM MIGHT LEAD TO FRICTION SPARKS.
EVEN MY ELECTROMAGNETIC WAVES MIGHT END UP TRIGGERING AN EXPLOSION!
ZING
ZING
OH, THIS IS BAD. ALL MY ABILITIES ARE USELESS IF--
!

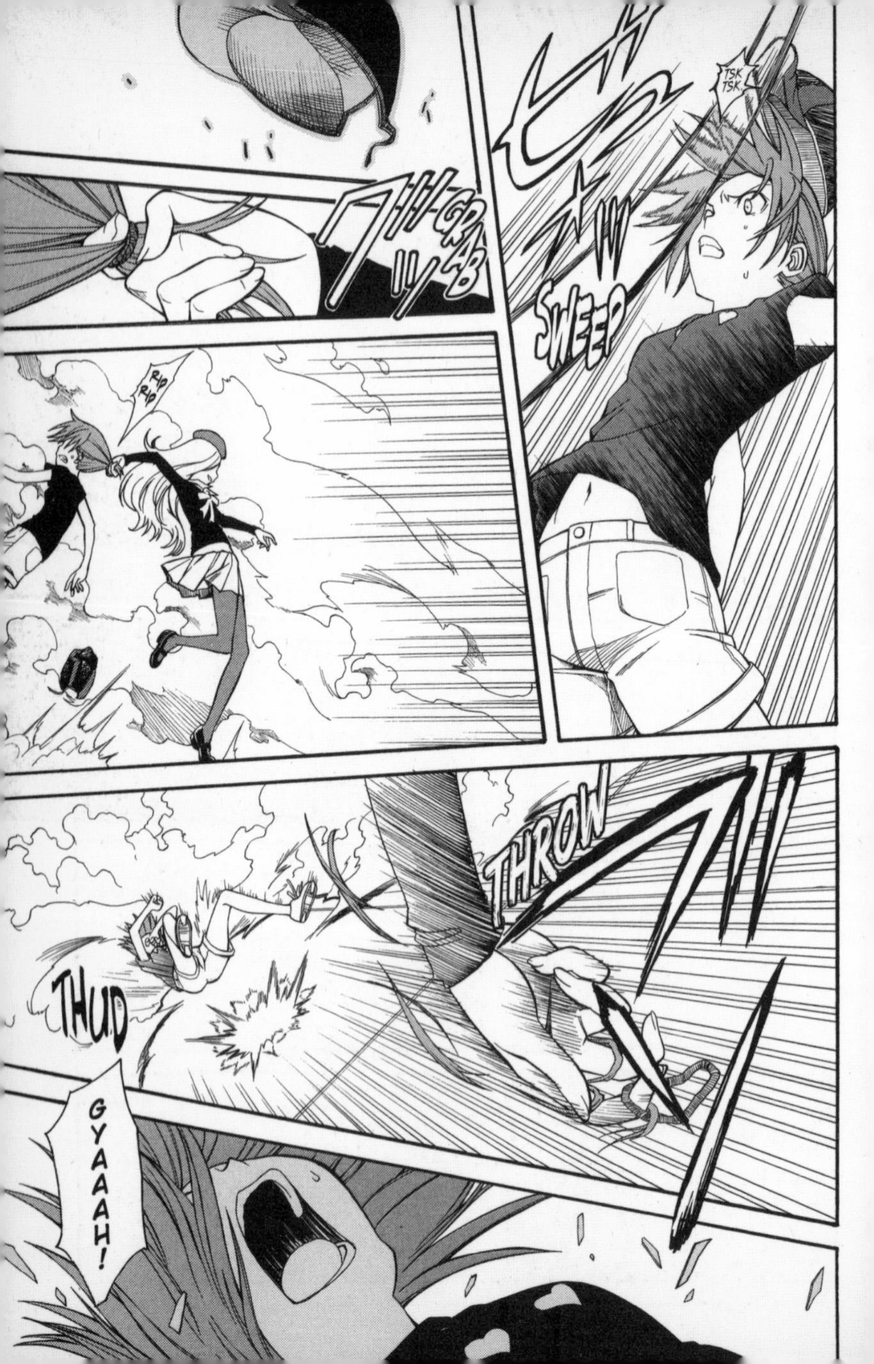
TSK TSK
SWEEP
GRAB
RIP RIP
THROW
THUD
GYAAAH!

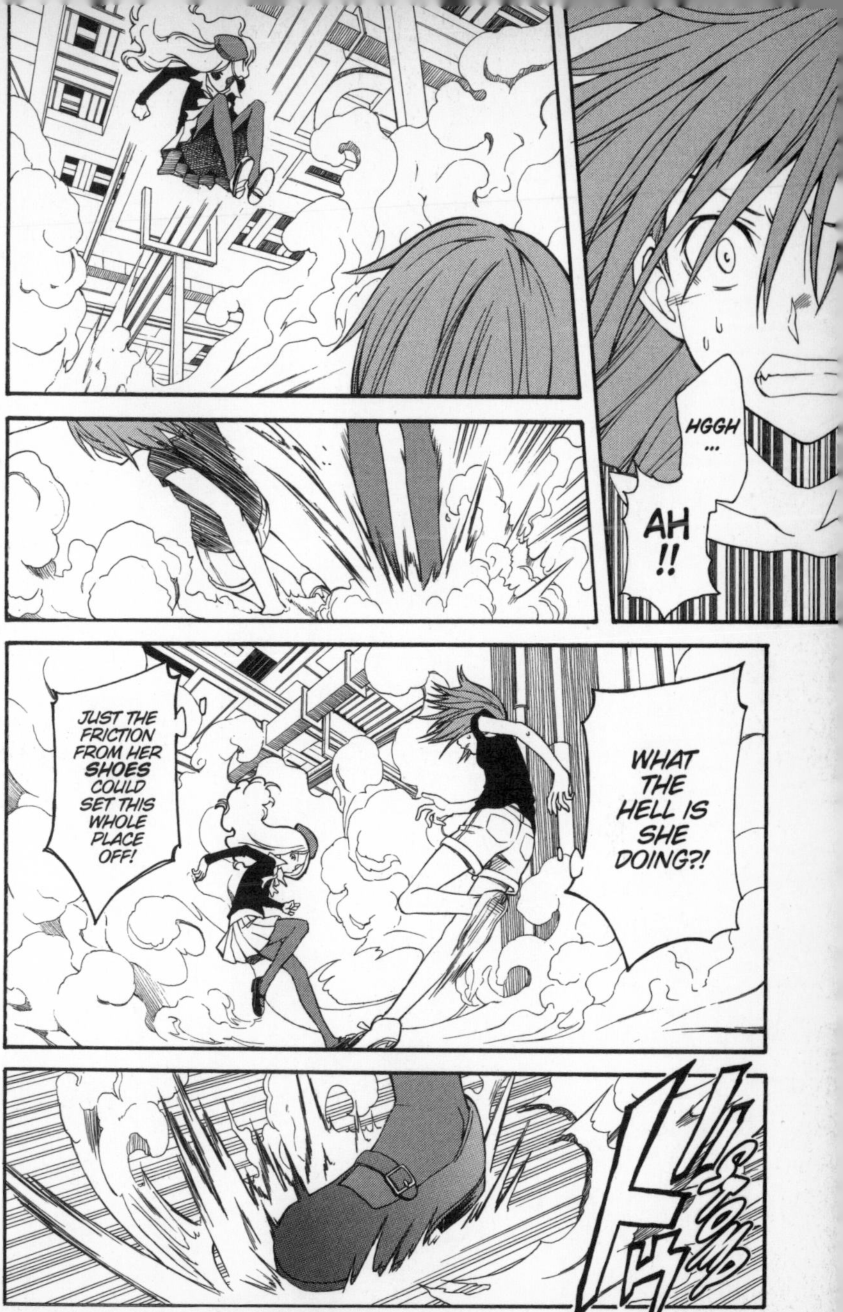
HGGH ...
AH !!
WHAT THE HELL IS SHE DOING?!
JUST THE FRICTION FROM HER SHOES COULD SET THIS WHOLE PLACE OFF!

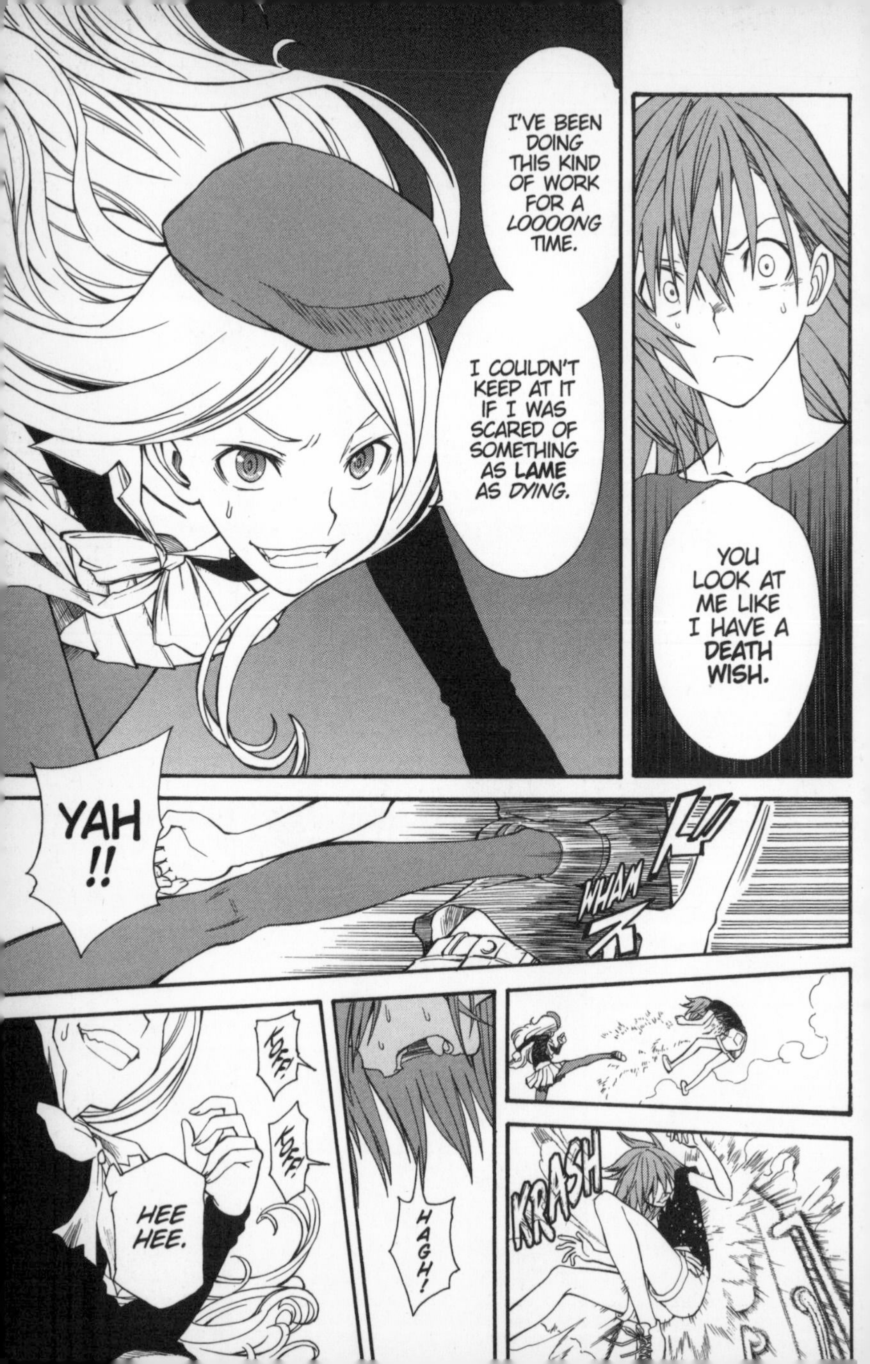
YOU LOOK AT ME LIKE I HAVE A DEATH WISH.
I'VE BEEN DOING THIS KIND OF WORK FOR A *LOOOONG* TIME.
I COULDN'T KEEP AT IT IF I WAS SCARED OF SOMETHING AS **LAME** AS *DYING*.
YAH!!
WHAM
KRASH
HAGH!
KOFF!
KOFF!
HEE HEE.

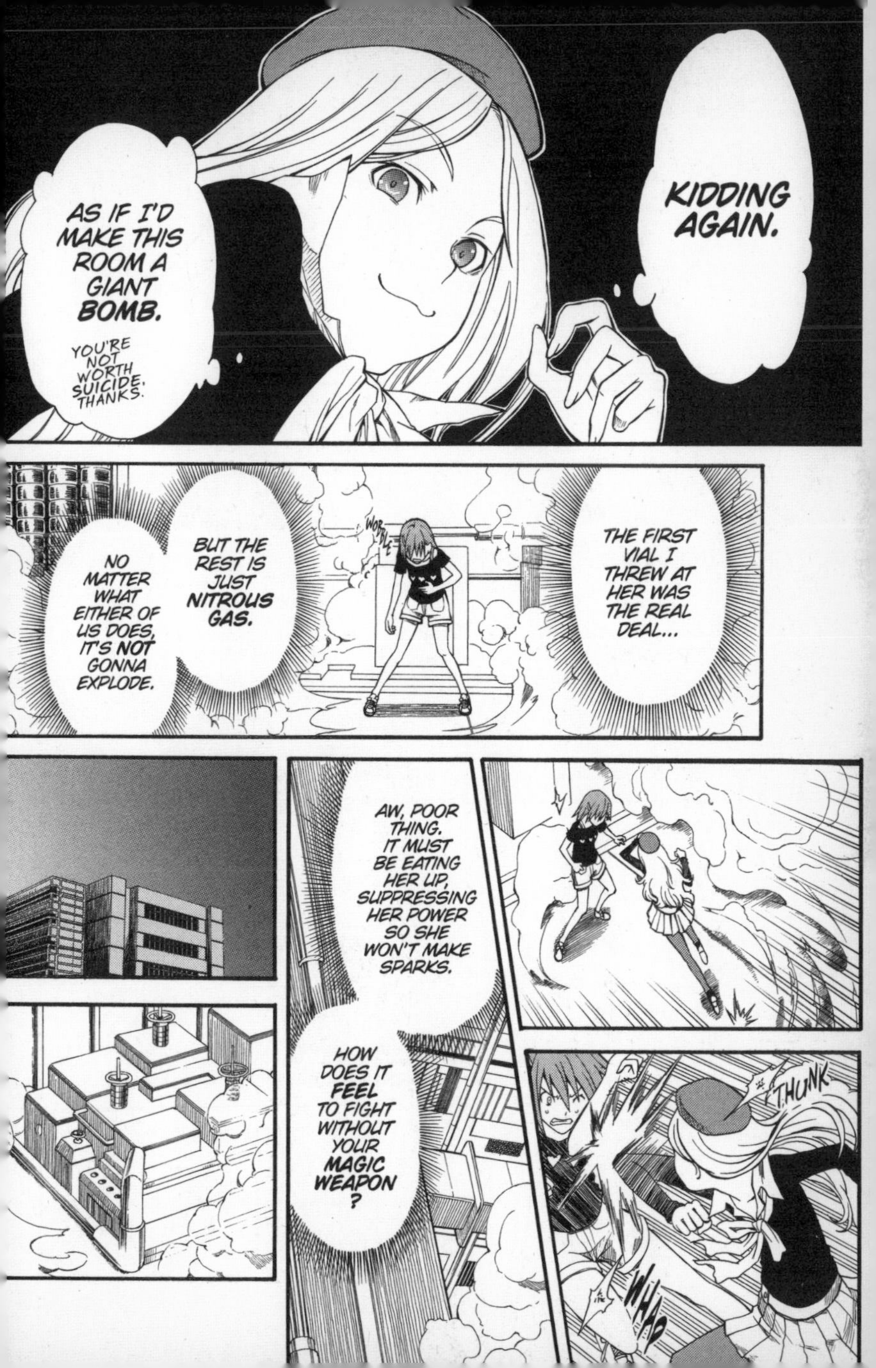
KIDDING AGAIN.
AS IF I'D MAKE THIS ROOM A GIANT BOMB.
YOU'RE NOT WORTH SUICIDE, THANKS.
THE FIRST VIAL I THREW AT HER WAS THE REAL DEAL...
BUT THE REST IS JUST NITROUS GAS.
NO MATTER WHAT EITHER OF US DOES, IT'S NOT GONNA EXPLODE.
THUNK
WHAP
AW, POOR THING. IT MUST BE EATING HER UP, SUPPRESSING HER POWER SO SHE WON'T MAKE SPARKS.
HOW DOES IT FEEL TO FIGHT WITHOUT YOUR MAGIC WEAPON?

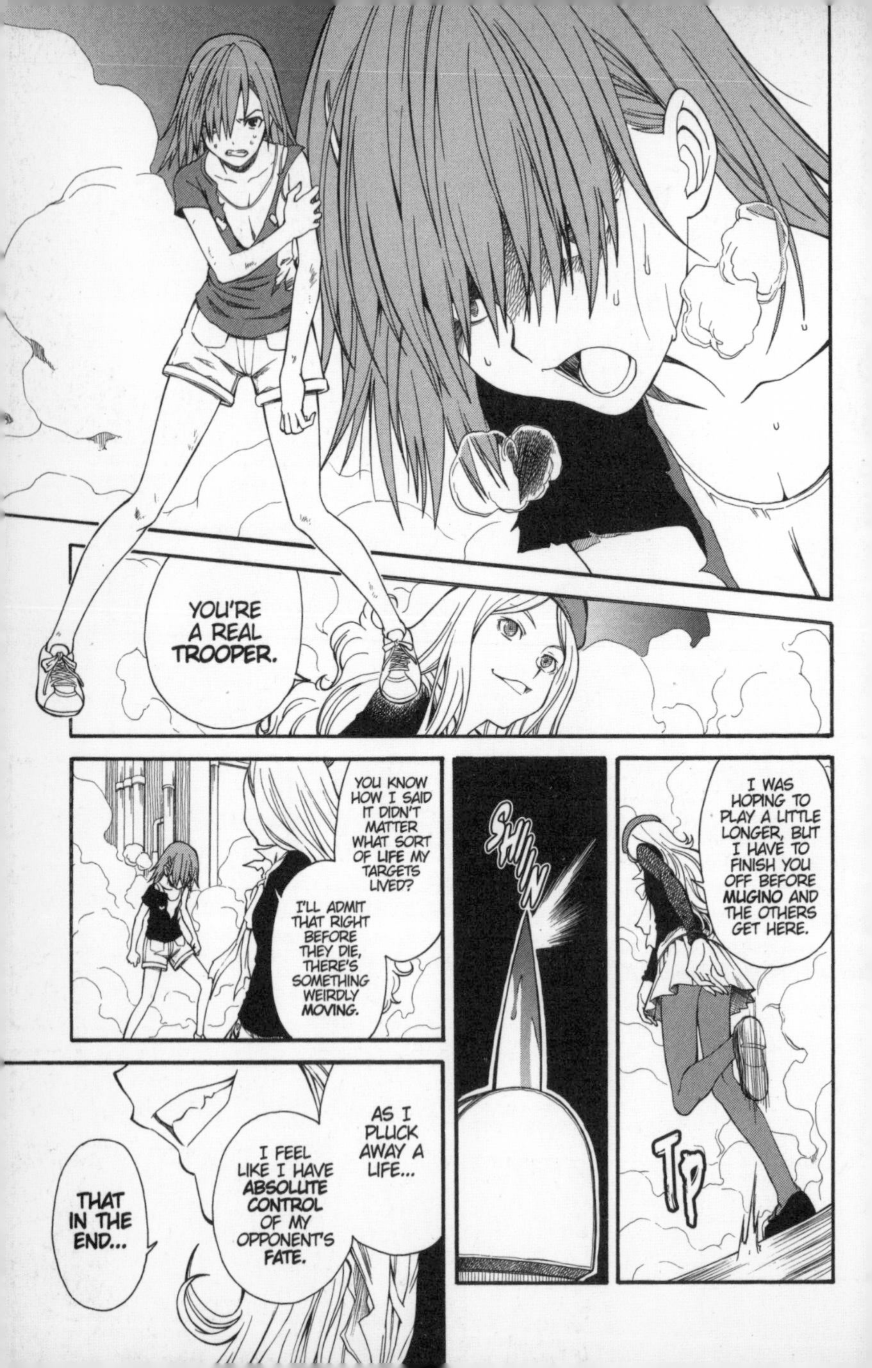
YOU'RE A REAL TROOPER.
I WAS HOPING TO PLAY A LITTLE LONGER, BUT I HAVE TO FINISH YOU OFF BEFORE MUGINO AND THE OTHERS GET HERE.
Tp
SHHIN
YOU KNOW HOW I SAID IT DIDN'T MATTER WHAT SORT OF LIFE MY TARGETS LIVED?
I'LL ADMIT THAT RIGHT BEFORE THEY DIE, THERE'S SOMETHING WEIRDLY MOVING.
AS I PLUCK AWAY A LIFE...
I FEEL LIKE I HAVE ABSOLUTE CONTROL OF MY OPPONENT'S FATE.
THAT IN THE END...

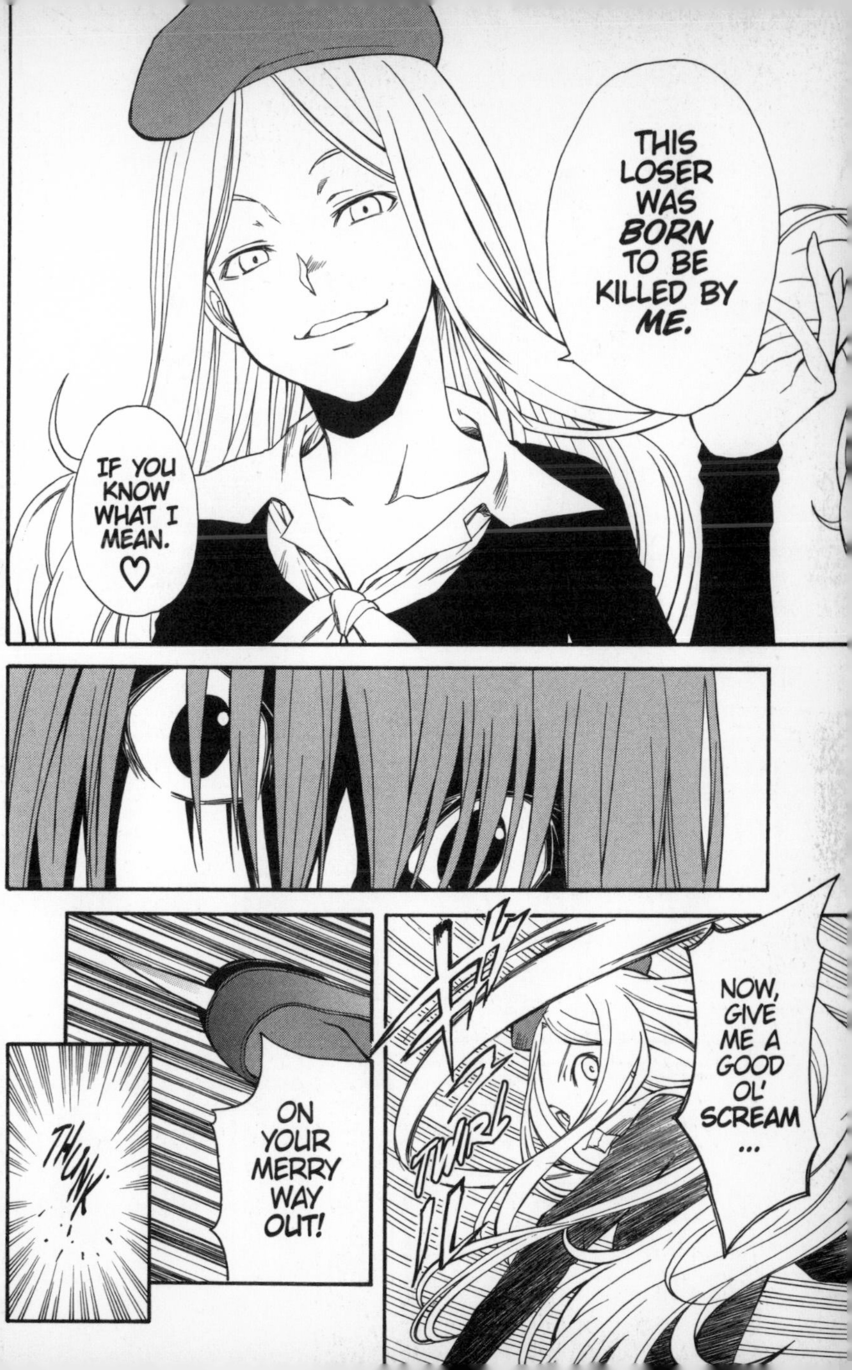
THIS LOSER WAS BORN TO BE KILLED BY ME.
IF YOU KNOW WHAT I MEAN. ♡
TWIRL
NOW, GIVE ME A GOOD OL' SCREAM ...
ON YOUR MERRY WAY OUT!
THUNK

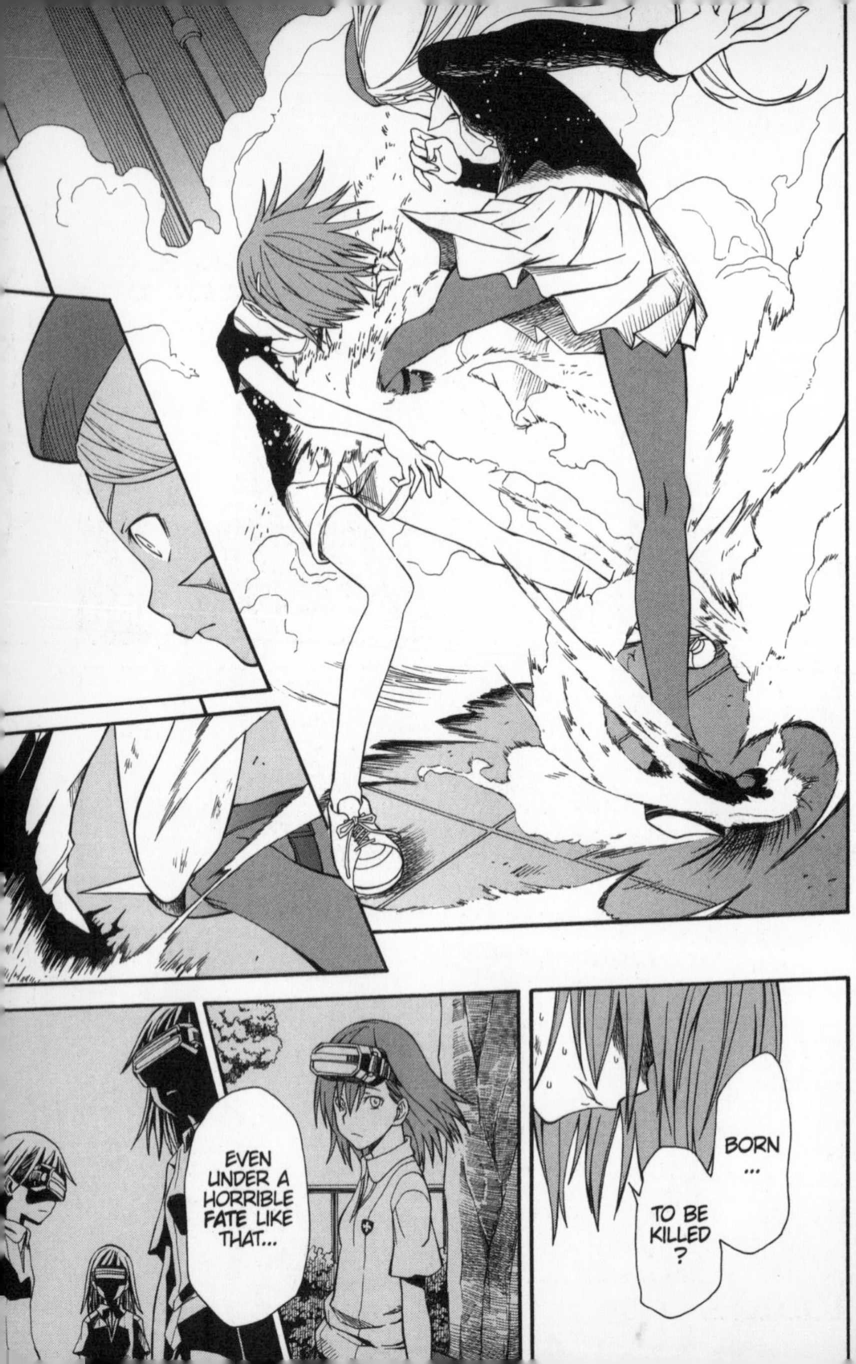
BORN ...
TO BE KILLED ?
EVEN UNDER A HORRIBLE FATE LIKE THAT...

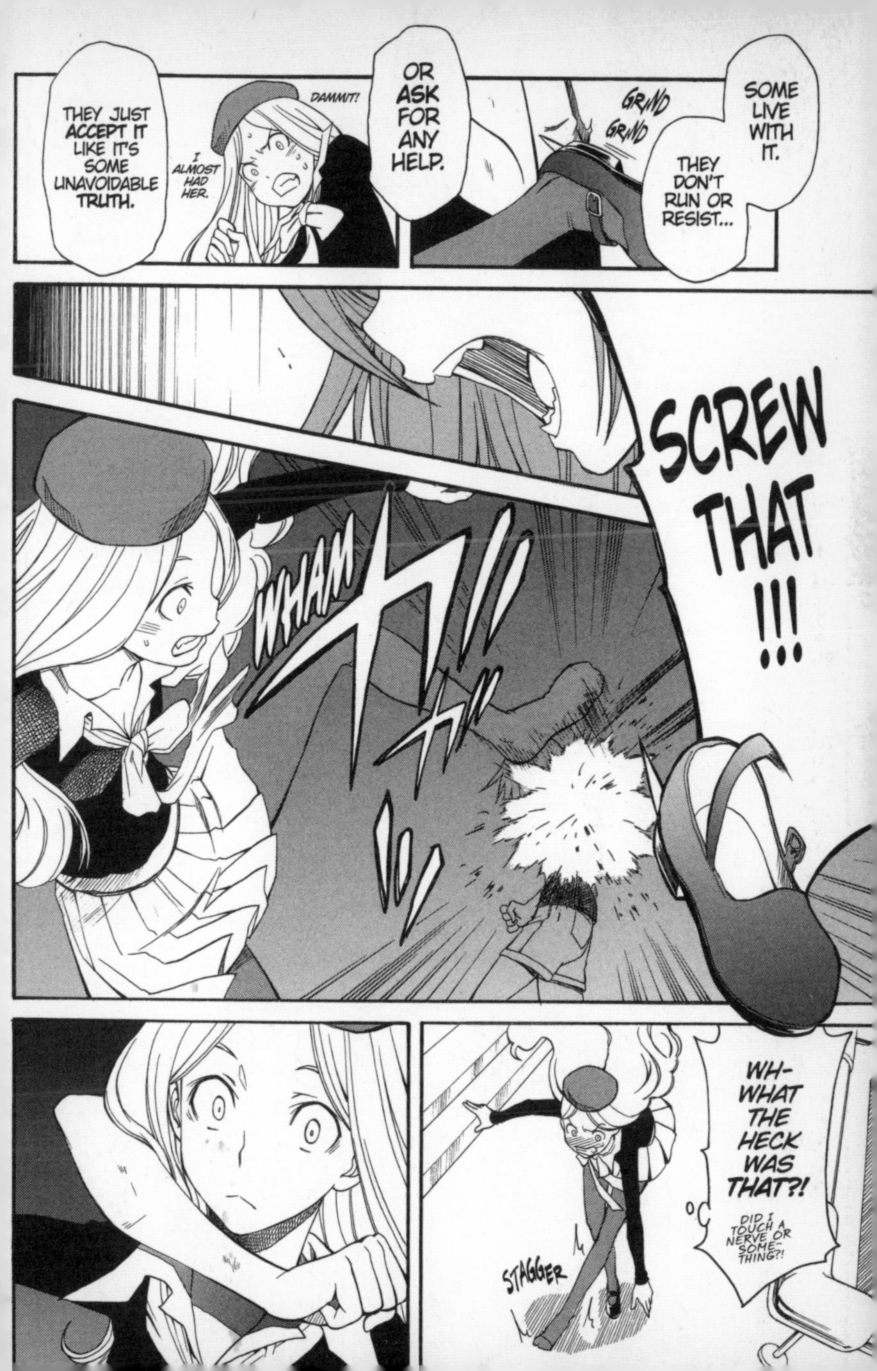
SOME LIVE WITH IT.
THEY DON'T RUN OR RESIST...
GRIND GRIND
OR ASK FOR ANY HELP.
DAMMIT!
I ALMOST HAD HER.
THEY JUST ACCEPT IT LIKE IT'S SOME UNAVOIDABLE TRUTH.
SCREW THAT!!!
WHAM
WH-WHAT THE HECK WAS THAT?!
DID I TOUCH A NERVE OR SOME-THING?!
STAGGER

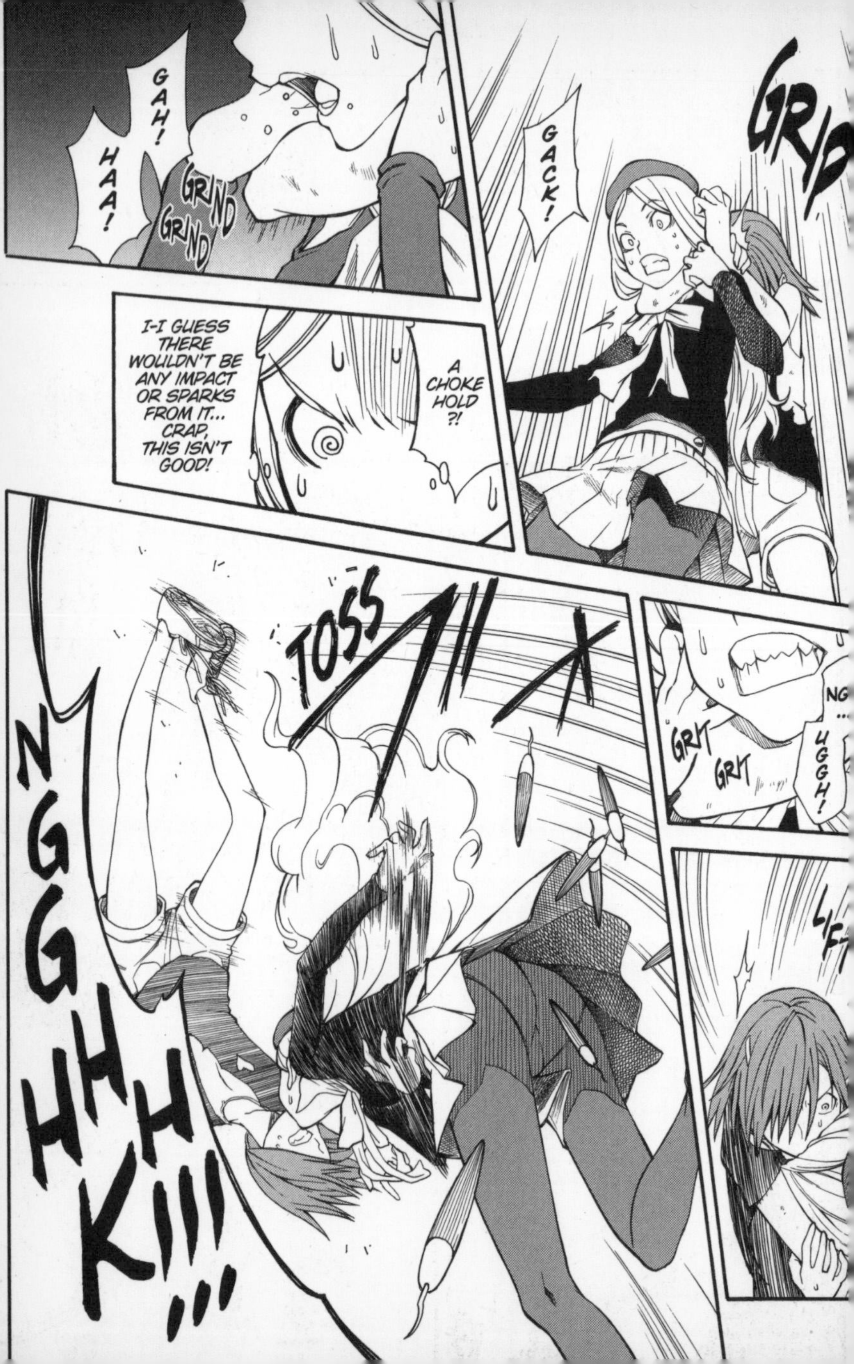
GRIP
GACK!
GRIND GRIND
GAH! HAA!
A CHOKE HOLD ?!
I-I GUESS THERE WOULDN'T BE ANY IMPACT OR SPARKS FROM IT... CRAP, THIS ISN'T GOOD!
NG ... UGGH!
GRIT GRIT
LIFT
TOSS
NGGHHHHK!!!

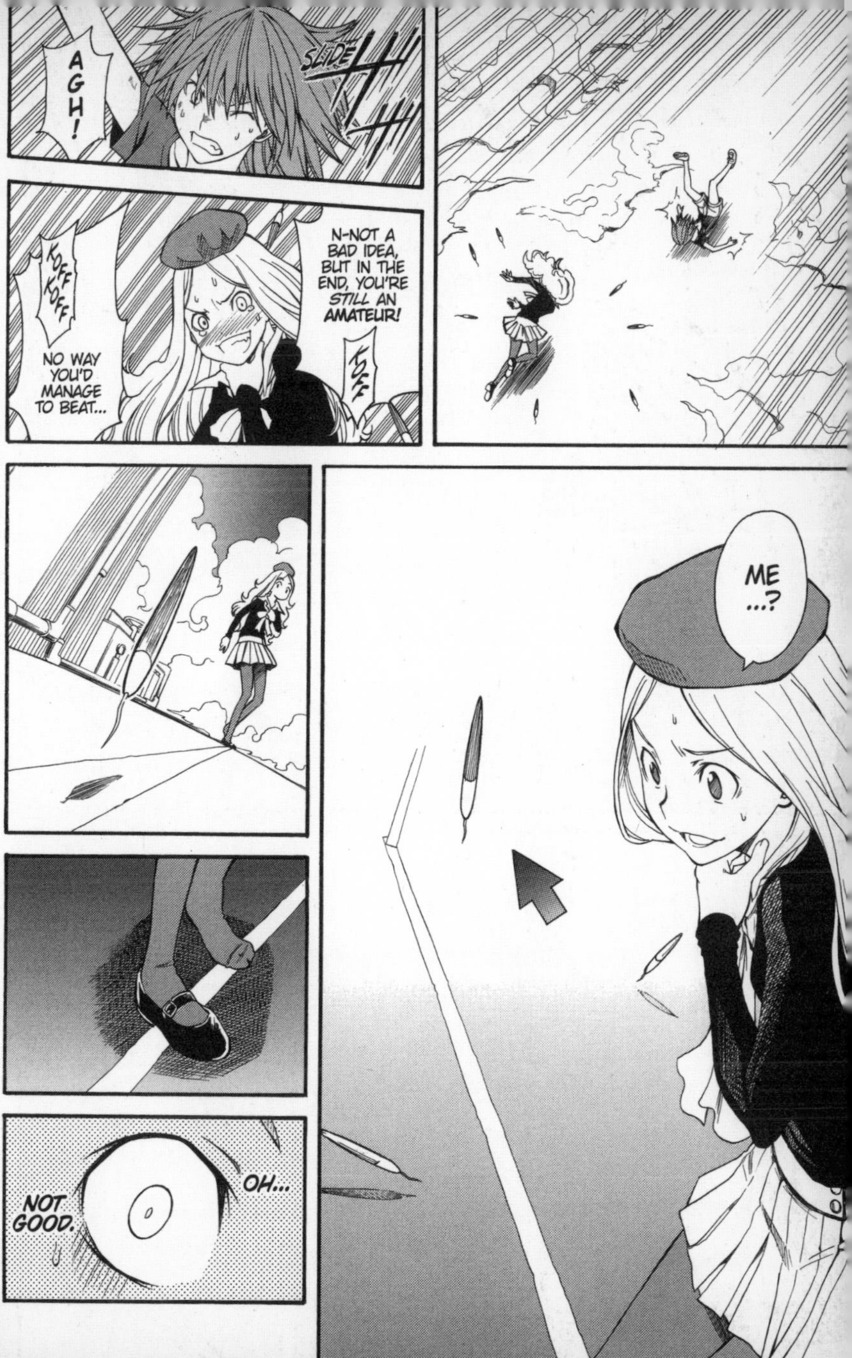
SLIDE
AGH!
N-NOT A BAD IDEA, BUT IN THE END, YOU'RE *STILL* AN **AMATEUR!**
KOFF KOFF
KOFF
NO WAY YOU'D MANAGE TO BEAT...
ME ...?
OH...
NOT GOOD.

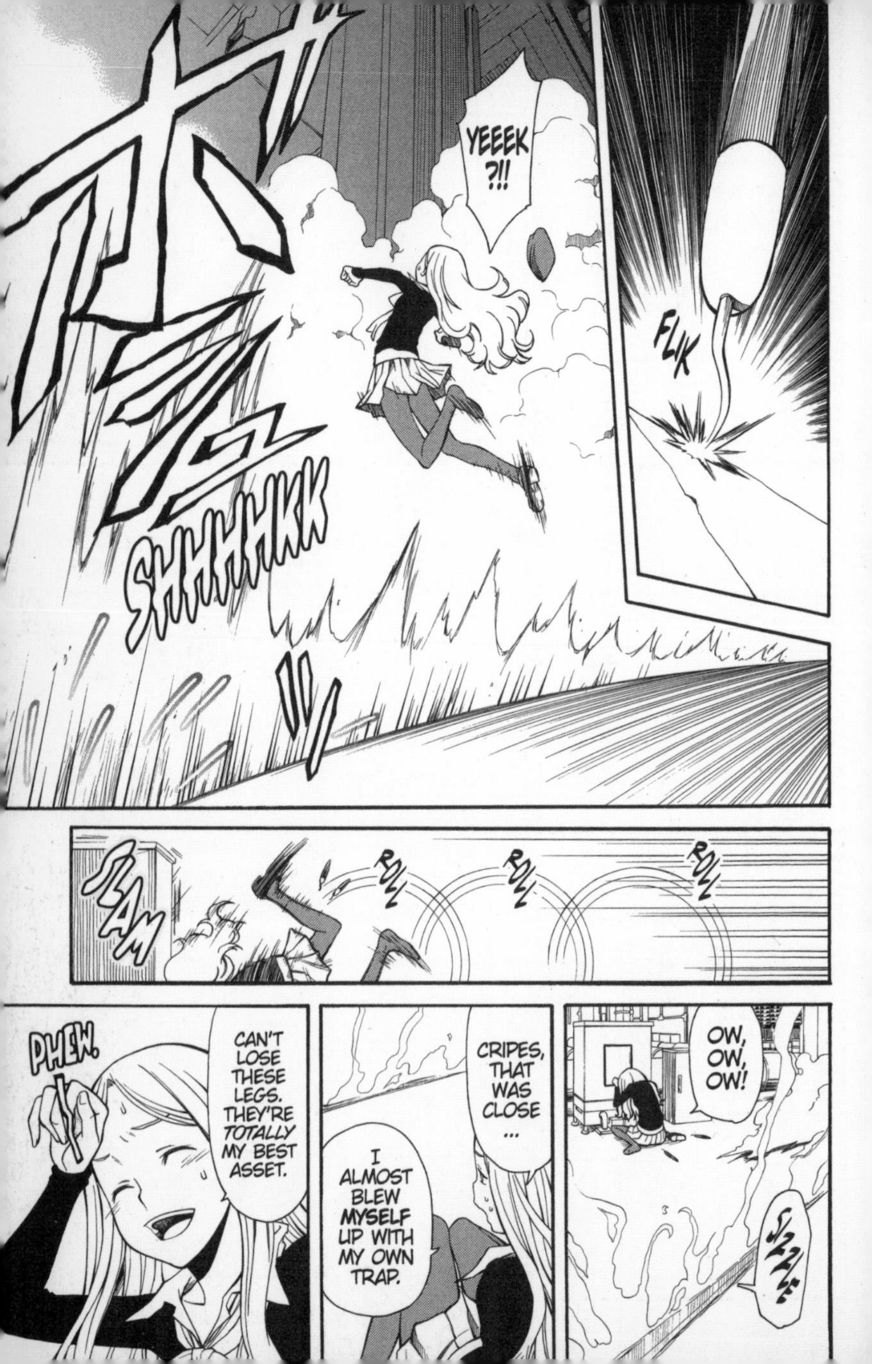
FLIK
YEEEK ?!!
SHHHHKK
ROLL
ROLL
ROLL
SLAM
OW, OW, OW!
SIZZLE
CRIPES, THAT WAS CLOSE ...
I ALMOST BLEW MYSELF UP WITH MY OWN TRAP.
PHEW.
CAN'T LOSE THESE LEGS. THEY'RE TOTALLY MY BEST ASSET.

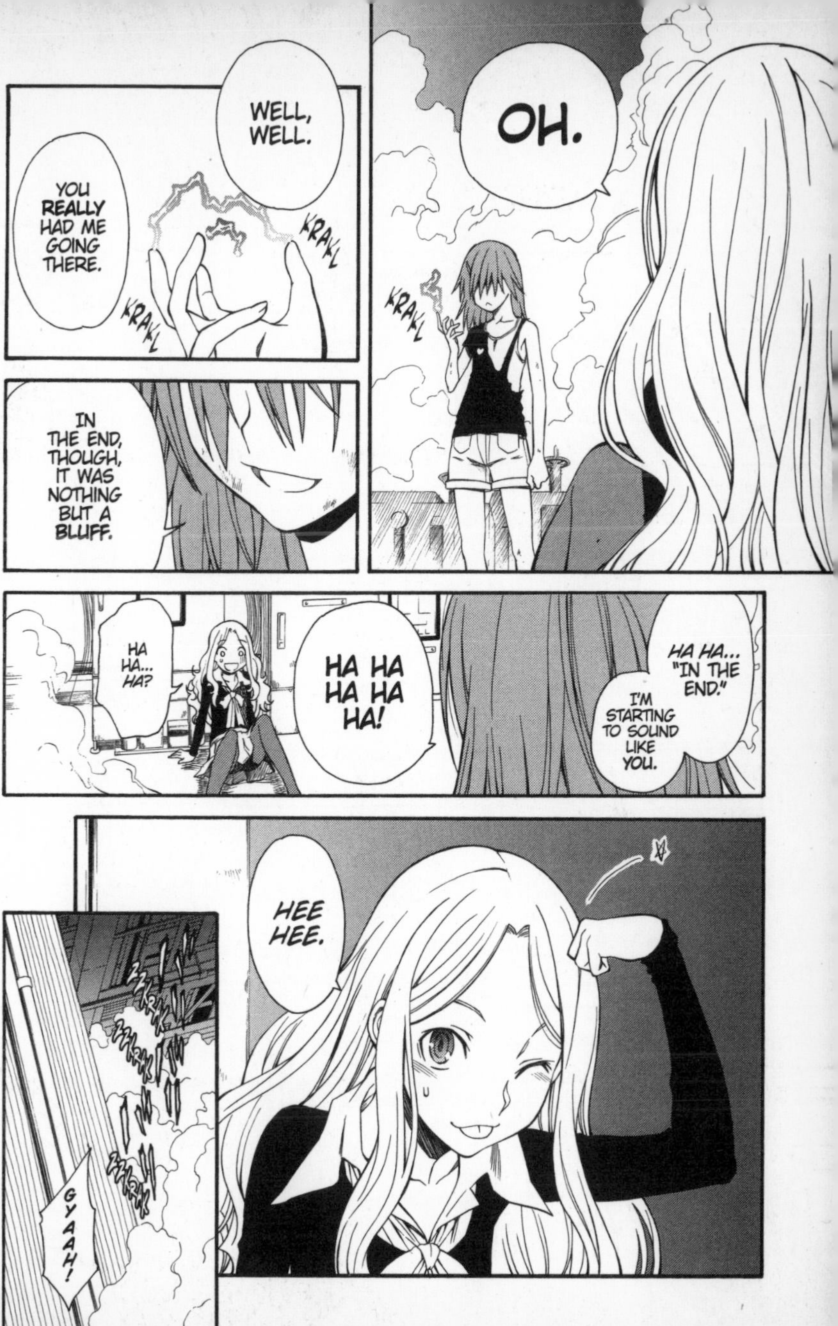
OH.
KRAKL
WELL, WELL.
YOU REALLY HAD ME GOING THERE.
KRAKL
KRAKL
IN THE END, THOUGH, IT WAS NOTHING BUT A BLUFF.
HA HA... "IN THE END."
I'M STARTING TO SOUND LIKE YOU.
HA HA HA HA HA!
HA HA... HA?
HEE HEE.
GYAAH!

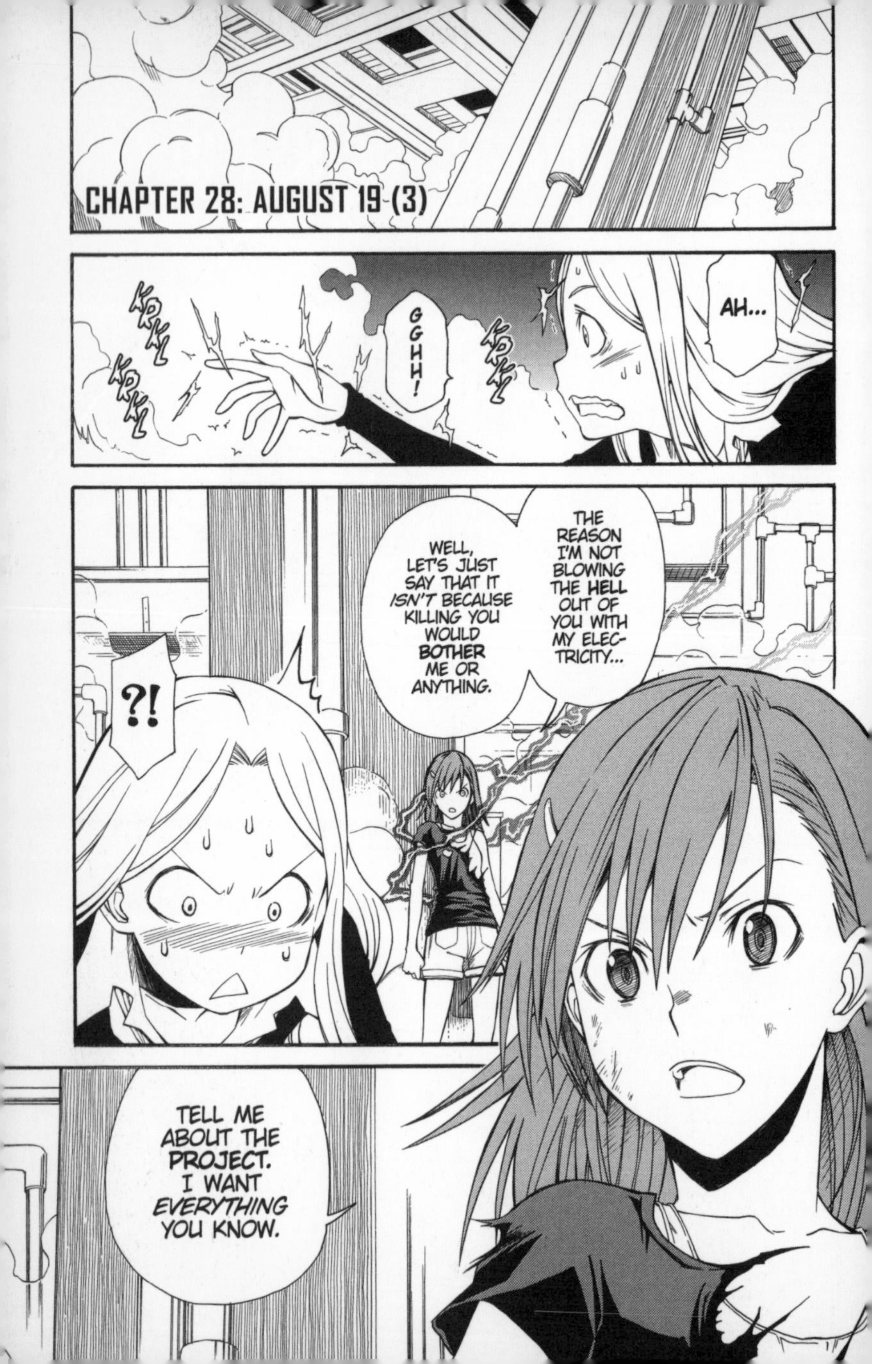
CHAPTER 28: AUGUST 19 (3)
AH...
KRKL
GGHH!
KRKL KRKL
THE REASON I'M NOT BLOWING THE HELL OUT OF YOU WITH MY ELEC-TRICITY...
WELL, LET'S JUST SAY THAT IT ISN'T BECAUSE KILLING YOU WOULD BOTHER ME OR ANYTHING.
?!
TELL ME ABOUT THE PROJECT. I WANT EVERYTHING YOU KNOW.

CHAPTER 28: AUGUST 19 (3)

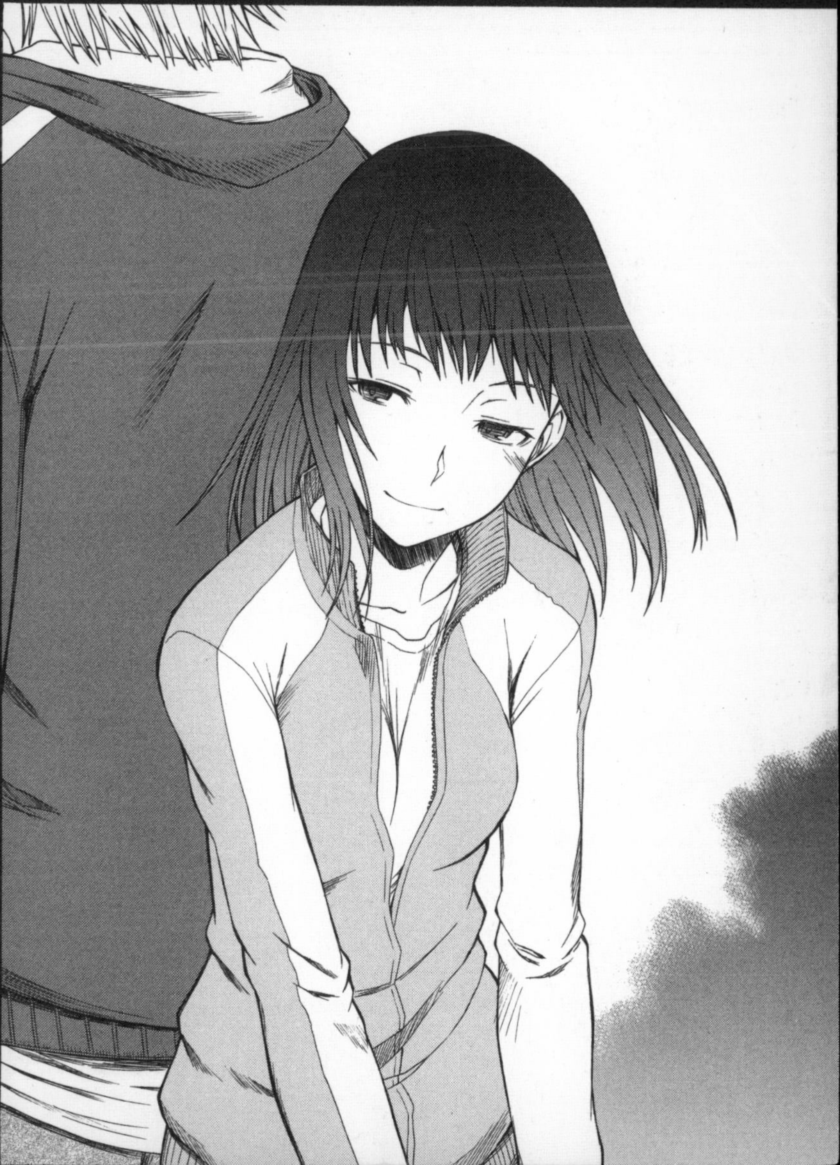

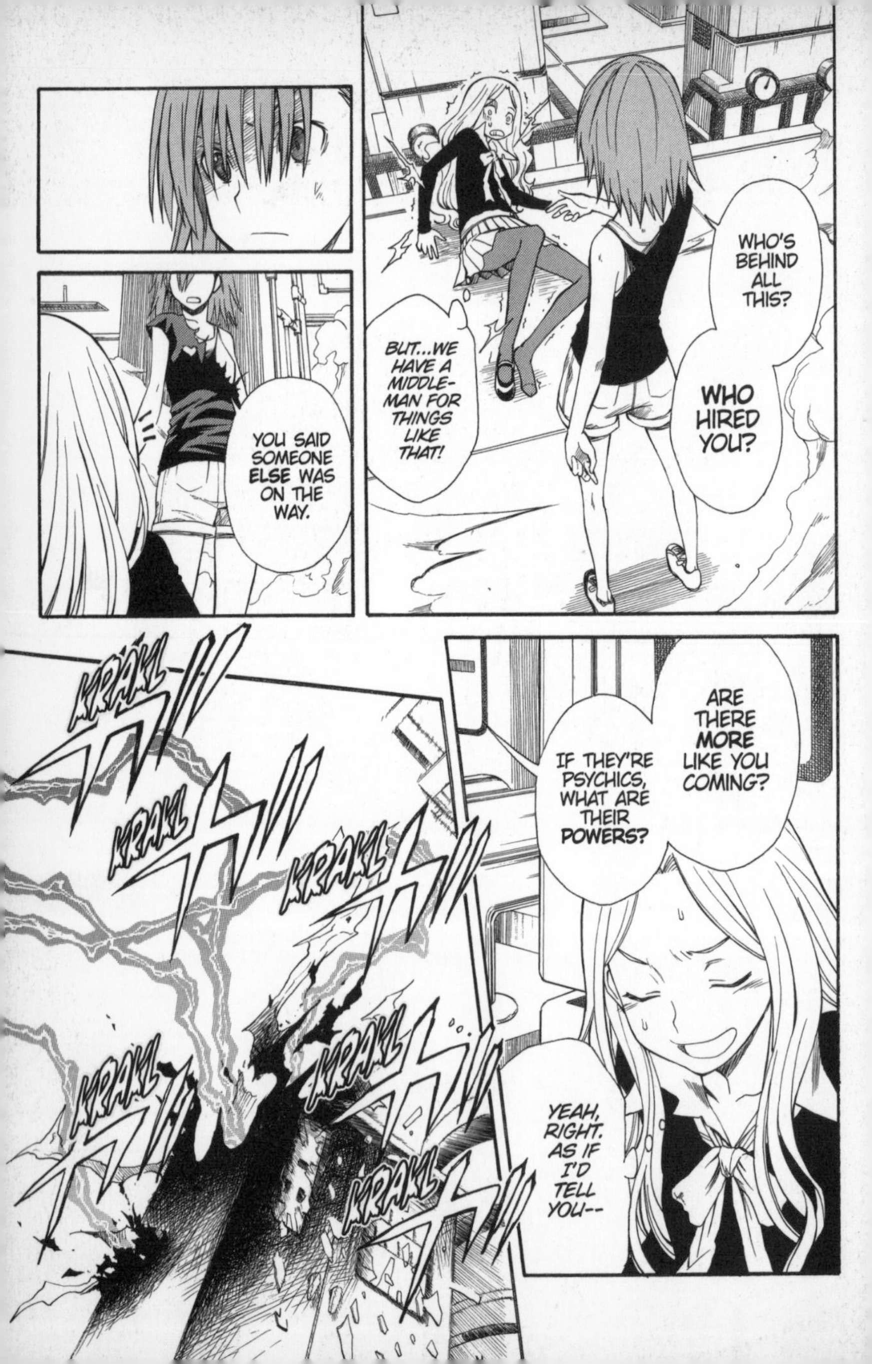
WHO'S BEHIND ALL THIS?
WHO HIRED YOU?
BUT...WE HAVE A MIDDLE-MAN FOR THINGS LIKE THAT!
YOU SAID SOMEONE ELSE WAS ON THE WAY.
ARE THERE MORE LIKE YOU COMING?
IF THEY'RE PSYCHICS, WHAT ARE THEIR POWERS?
YEAH, RIGHT. AS IF I'D TELL YOU--
KRAKL
KRAKL
KRAKL
KRAKL
KRAKL

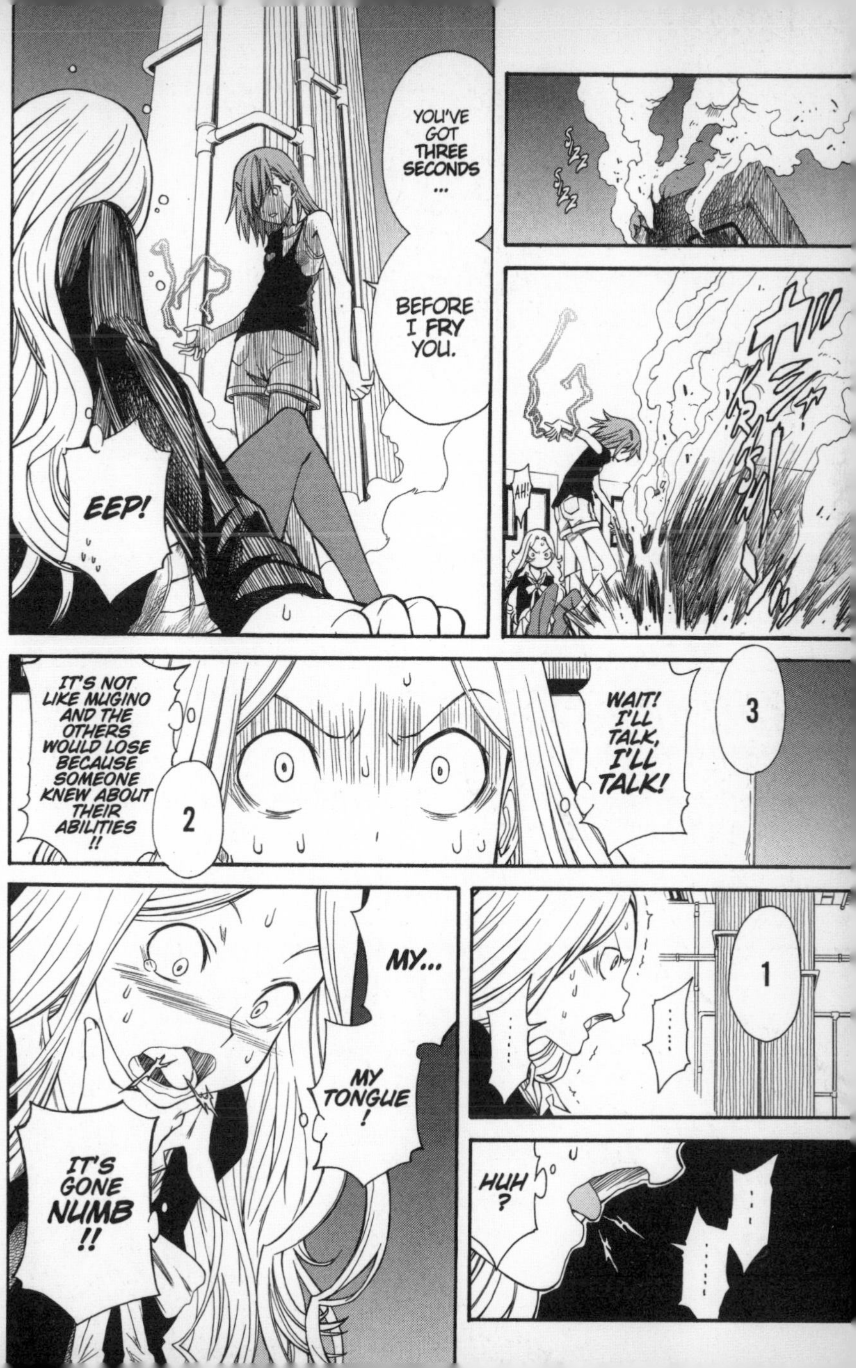
SIZZ
SIZZ
AH!
YOU'VE GOT THREE SECONDS ...
BEFORE I FRY YOU.
EEP!
3
WAIT! I'LL TALK, I'LL TALK!
2
IT'S NOT LIKE MUGINO AND THE OTHERS WOULD LOSE BECAUSE SOMEONE KNEW ABOUT THEIR ABILITIES !!
1
......
......
HUH ?
......
......
MY...
MY TONGUE !
IT'S GONE NUMB !!

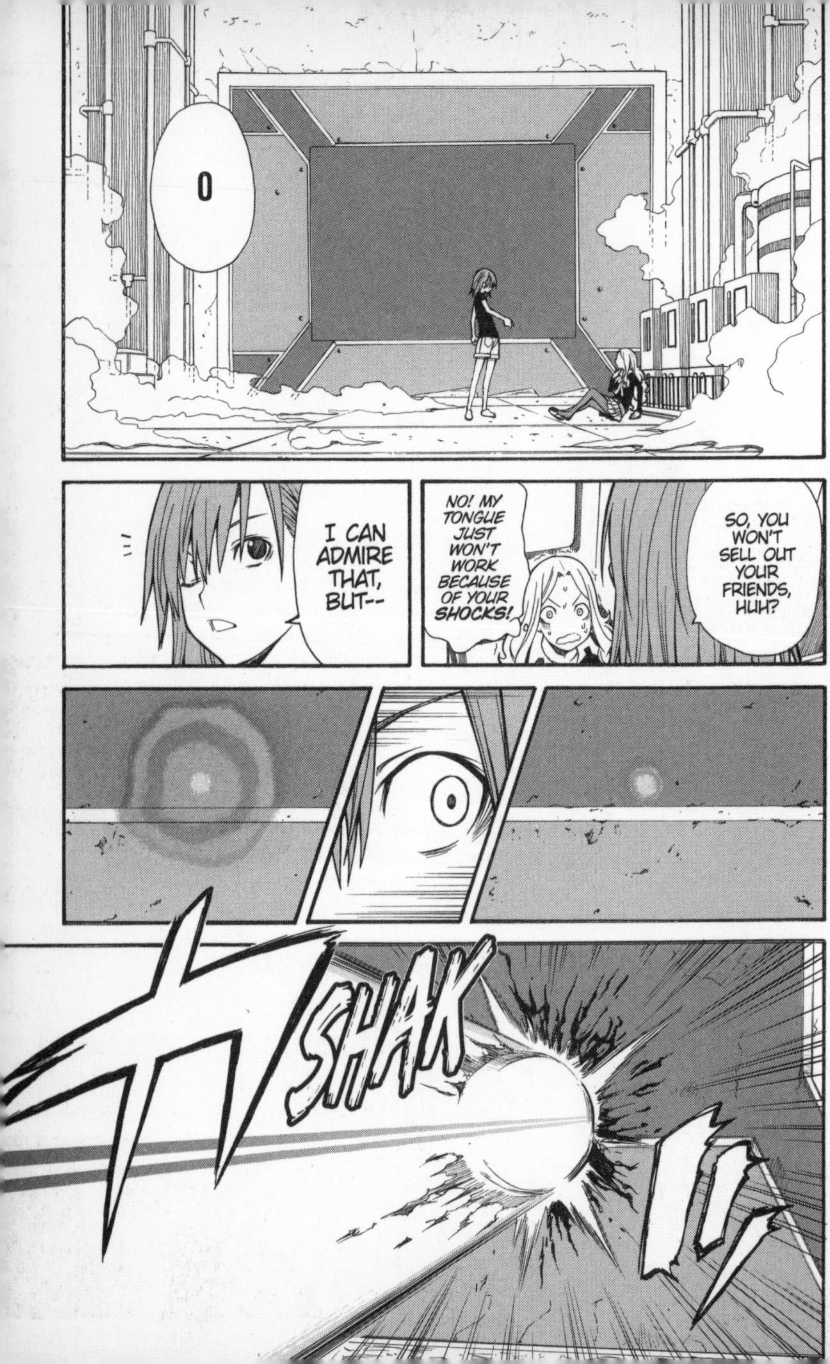
0
SO, YOU WON'T SELL OUT YOUR FRIENDS, HUH?
NO! MY TONGUE JUST WON'T WORK BECAUSE OF YOUR SHOCKS!
I CAN ADMIRE THAT, BUT--
SHAK

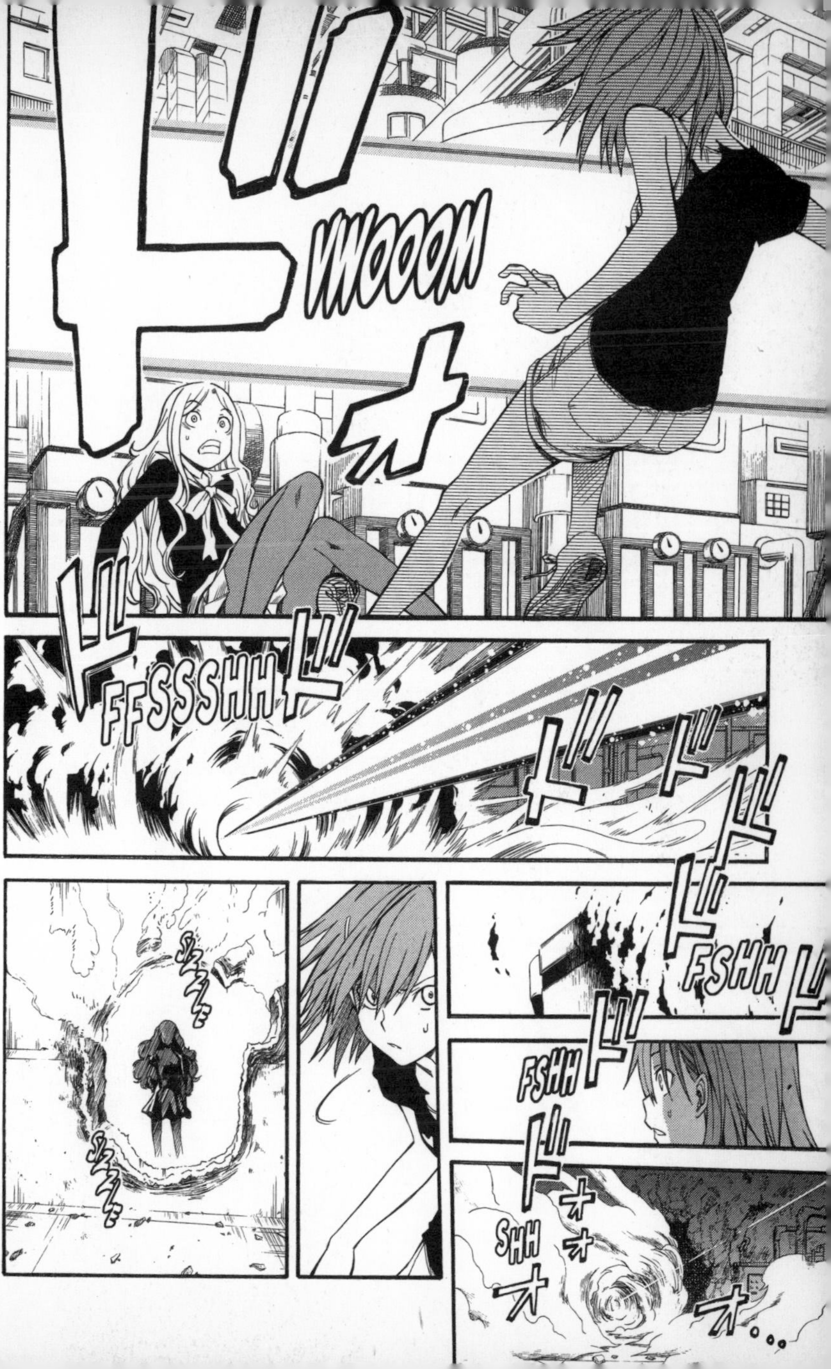
VWOOOM
FFSSSHH
FSHH
FSHH
SHH
SIZZLE
SIZZLE

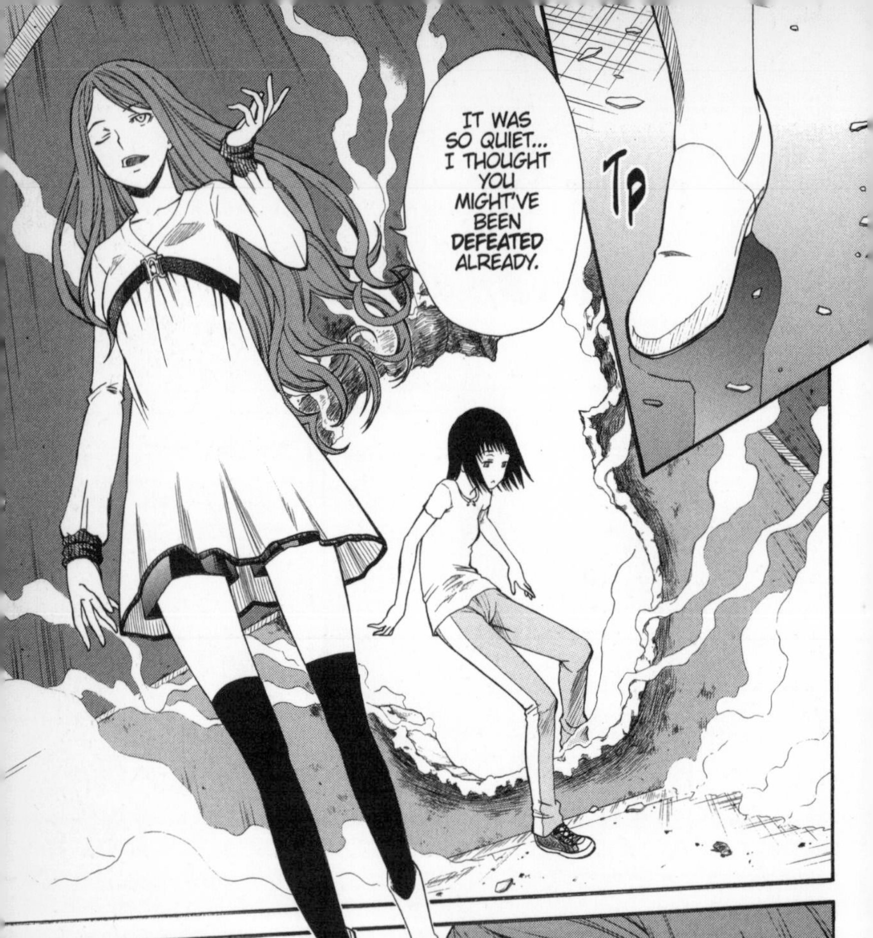
Tp
IT WAS SO QUIET... I THOUGHT YOU MIGHT'VE BEEN DEFEATED ALREADY.
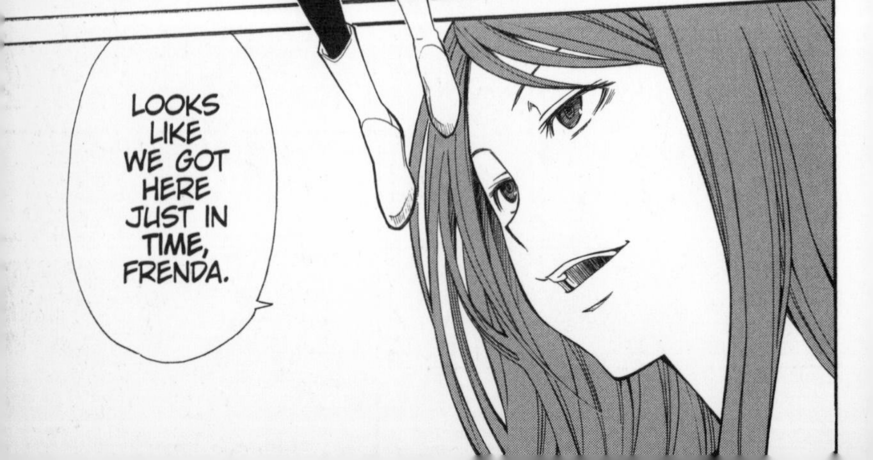
LOOKS LIKE WE GOT HERE JUST IN TIME, FRENDA.

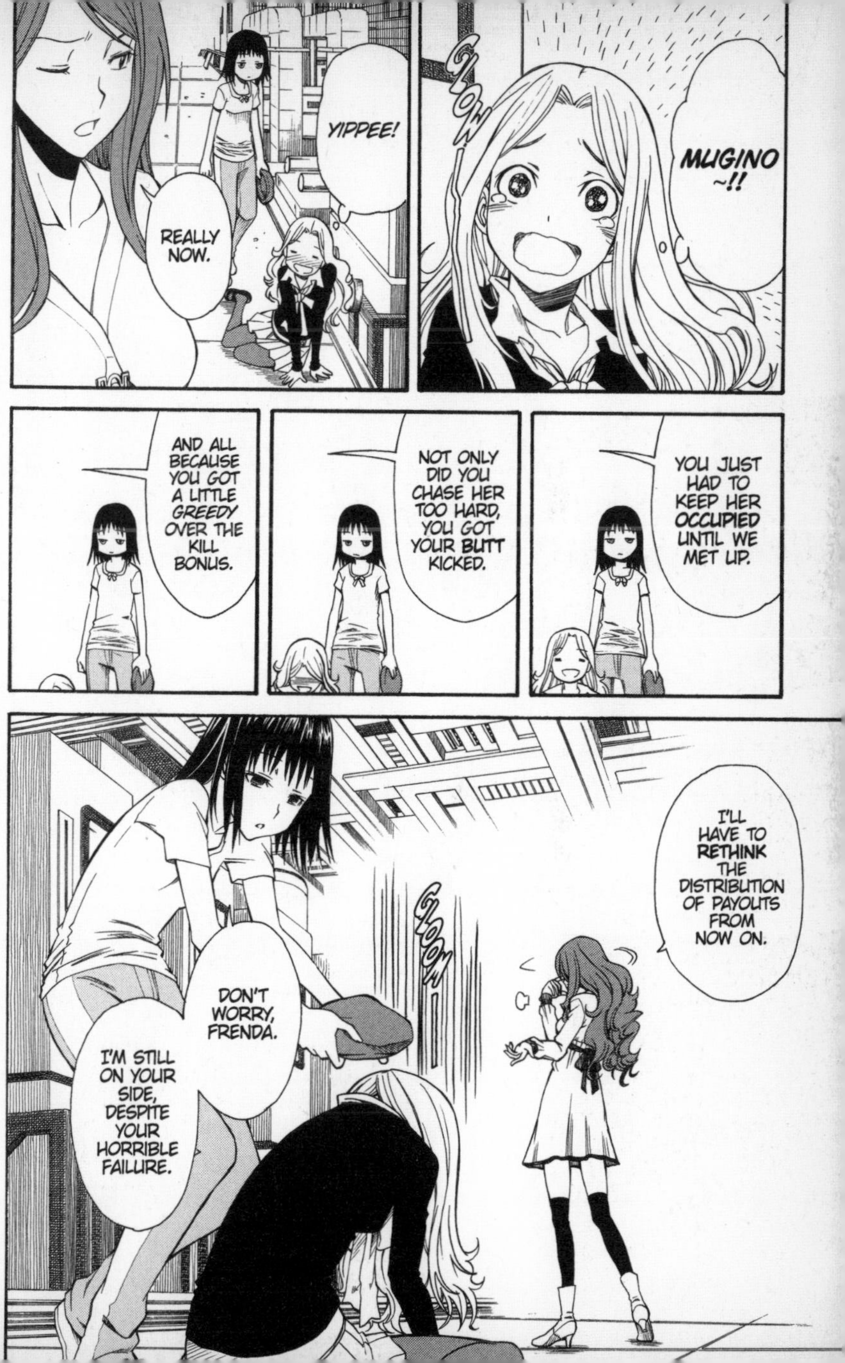
GLOW
MUGINO ~!!
YIPPEE!
REALLY NOW.
YOU JUST HAD TO KEEP HER OCCUPIED UNTIL WE MET UP.
NOT ONLY DID YOU CHASE HER TOO HARD, YOU GOT YOUR BUTT KICKED.
AND ALL BECAUSE YOU GOT A LITTLE GREEDY OVER THE KILL BONUS.
I'LL HAVE TO RETHINK THE DISTRIBUTION OF PAYOUTS FROM NOW ON.
GLOOM
DON'T WORRY, FRENDA.
I'M STILL ON YOUR SIDE, DESPITE YOUR HORRIBLE FAILURE.

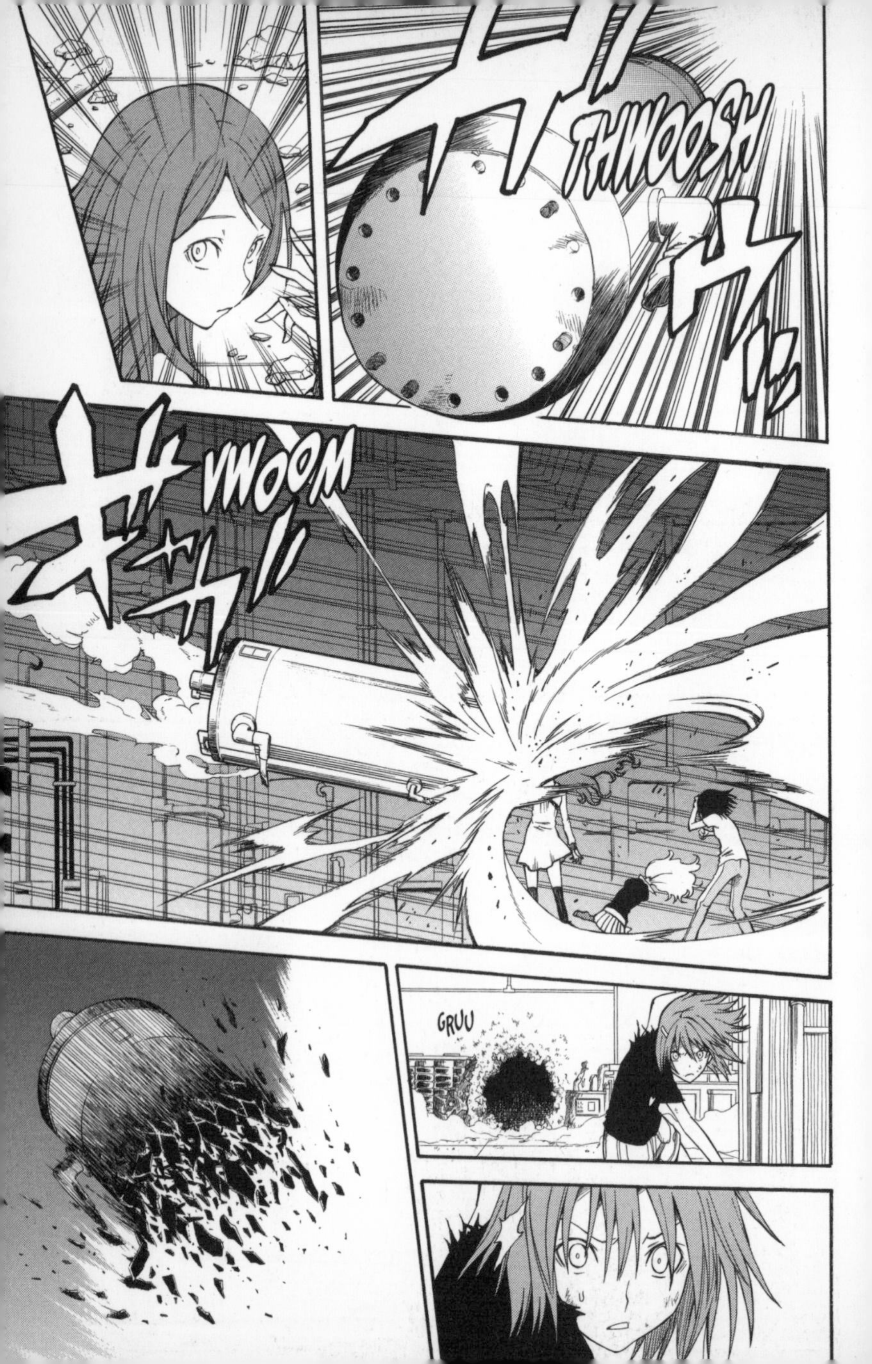
THWOOSH
VWOOM
GRUU

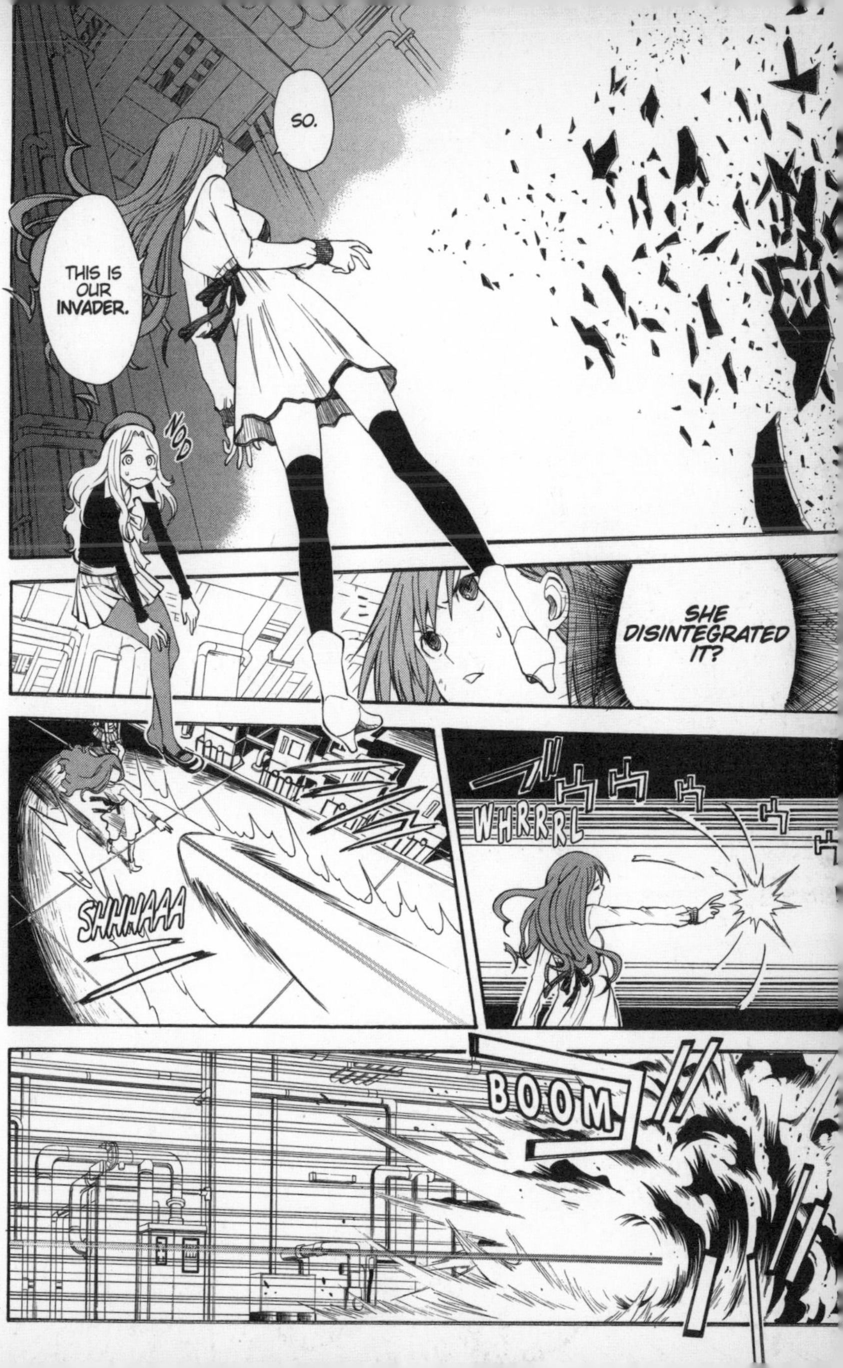
SO.
THIS IS OUR INVADER.
NOD
SHE DISINTEGRATED IT?
WHRRRL
SHHHAAA
BOOM

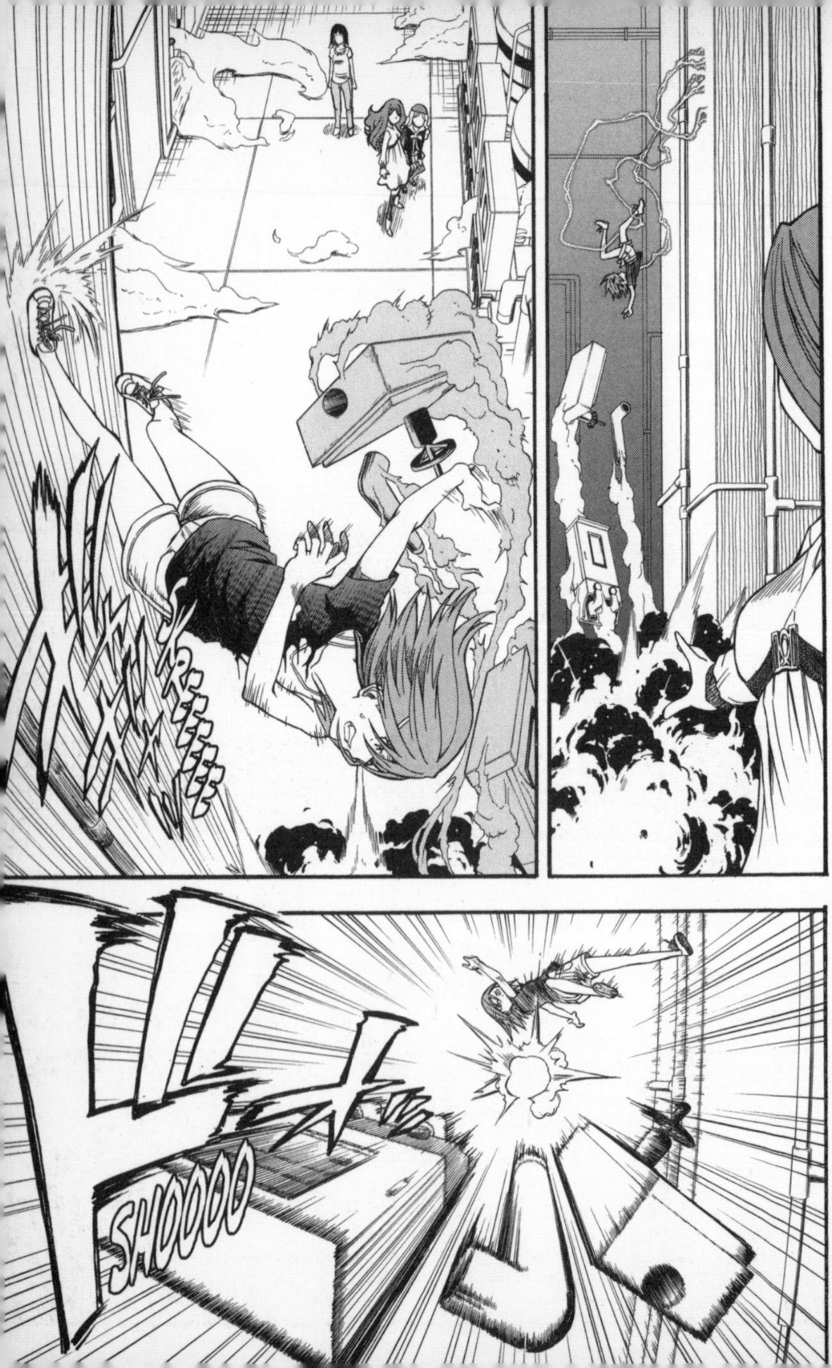
SKREEEEE
SHOOOO

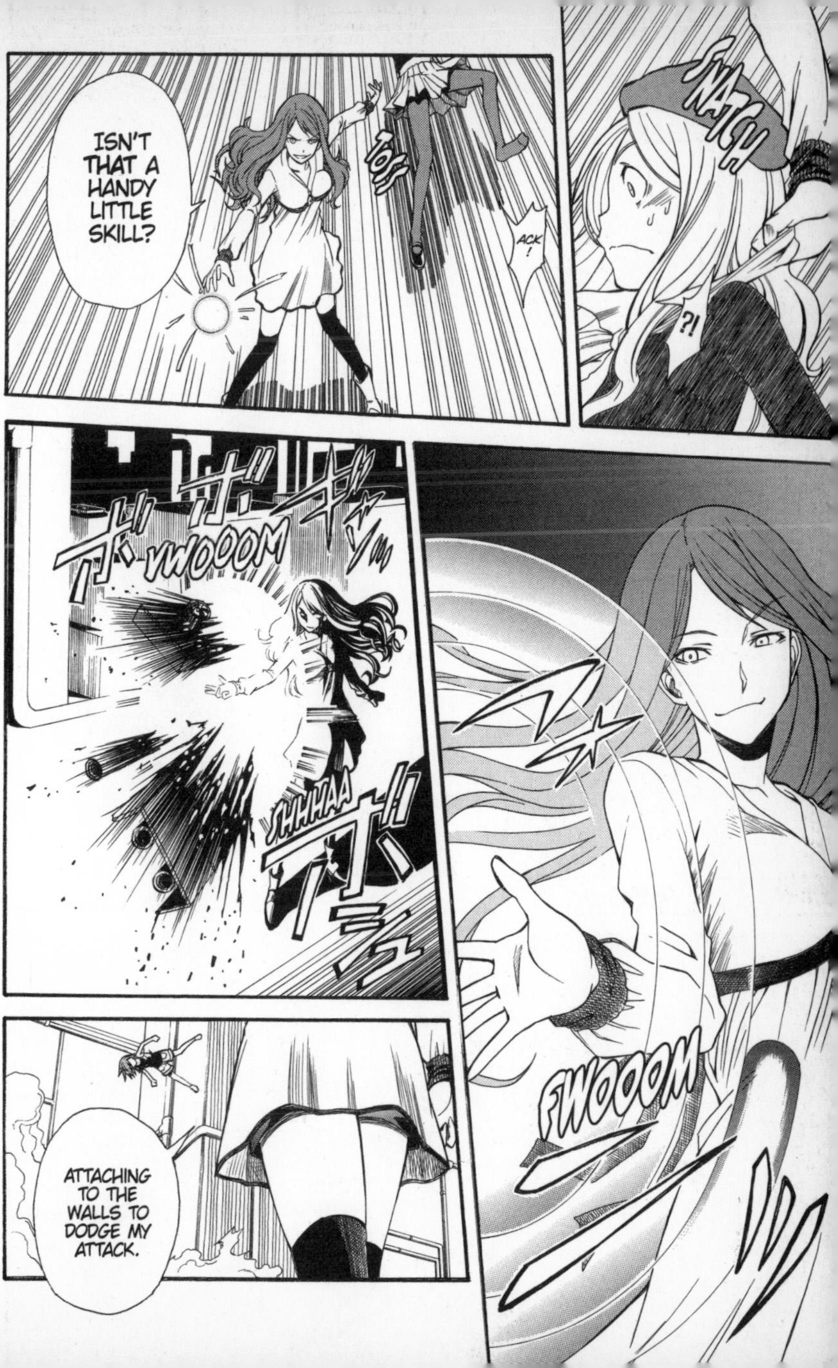
SNATCH
ACK!
?!
ISN'T THAT A HANDY LITTLE SKILL?
TOSS
FWOOOM
VWOOOM
SHHHAA
ATTACHING TO THE WALLS TO DODGE MY ATTACK.

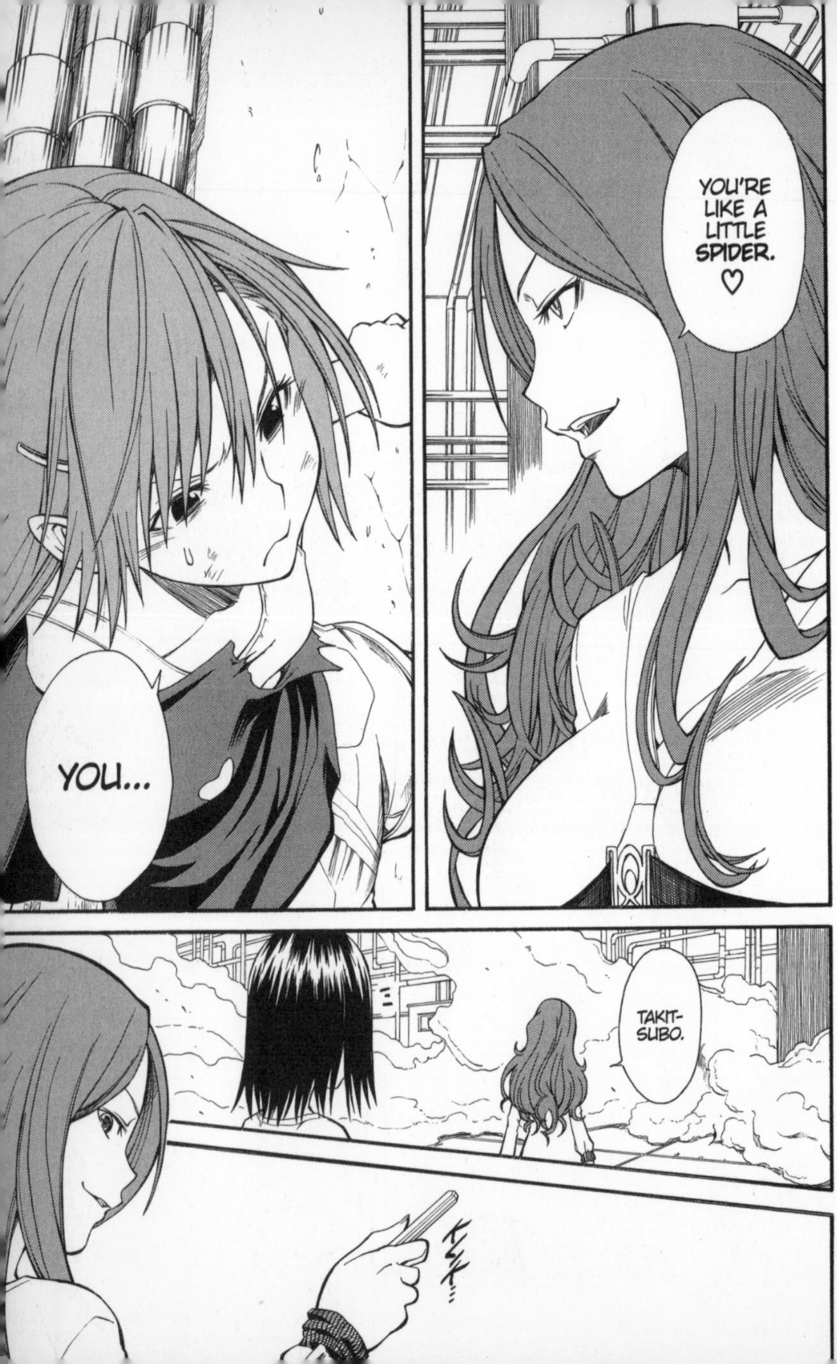
YOU'RE LIKE A LITTLE SPIDER. ♡
YOU...
TAKIT-SUBO.

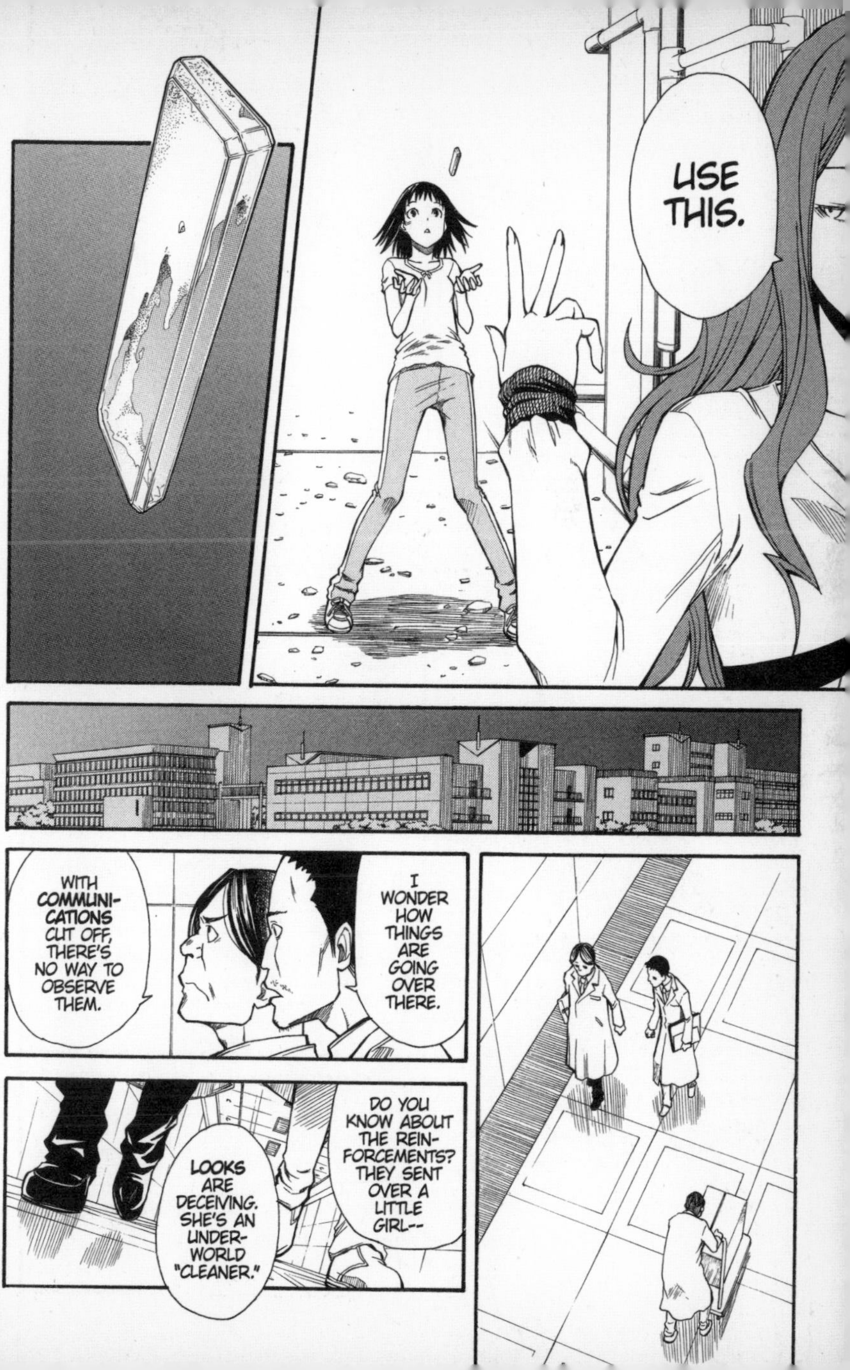
USE THIS.
I WONDER HOW THINGS ARE GOING OVER THERE.
WITH COMMUNI-CATIONS CUT OFF, THERE'S NO WAY TO OBSERVE THEM.
DO YOU KNOW ABOUT THE REIN-FORCEMENTS? THEY SENT OVER A LITTLE GIRL--
LOOKS ARE DECEIVING. SHE'S AN UNDER-WORLD "CLEANER."

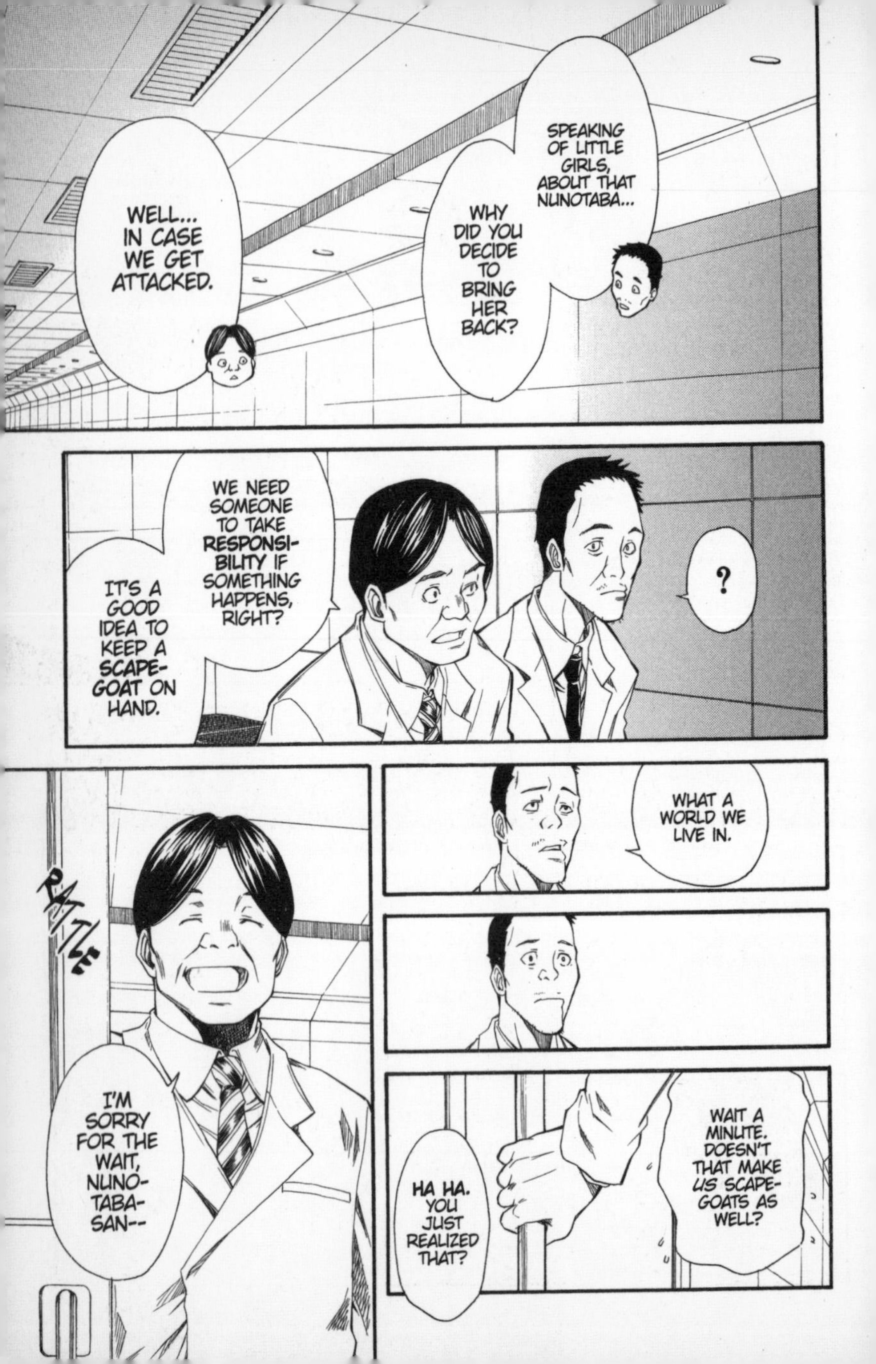
SPEAKING OF LITTLE GIRLS, ABOUT THAT NUNOTABA...
WHY DID YOU DECIDE TO BRING HER BACK?
WELL... IN CASE WE GET ATTACKED.
?
WE NEED SOMEONE TO TAKE RESPONSIBILITY IF SOMETHING HAPPENS, RIGHT?
IT'S A GOOD IDEA TO KEEP A SCAPEGOAT ON HAND.
WHAT A WORLD WE LIVE IN.
WAIT A MINUTE. DOESN'T THAT MAKE US SCAPEGOATS AS WELL?
HA HA. YOU JUST REALIZED THAT?
RATTLE
I'M SORRY FOR THE WAIT, NUNOTABA-SAN--

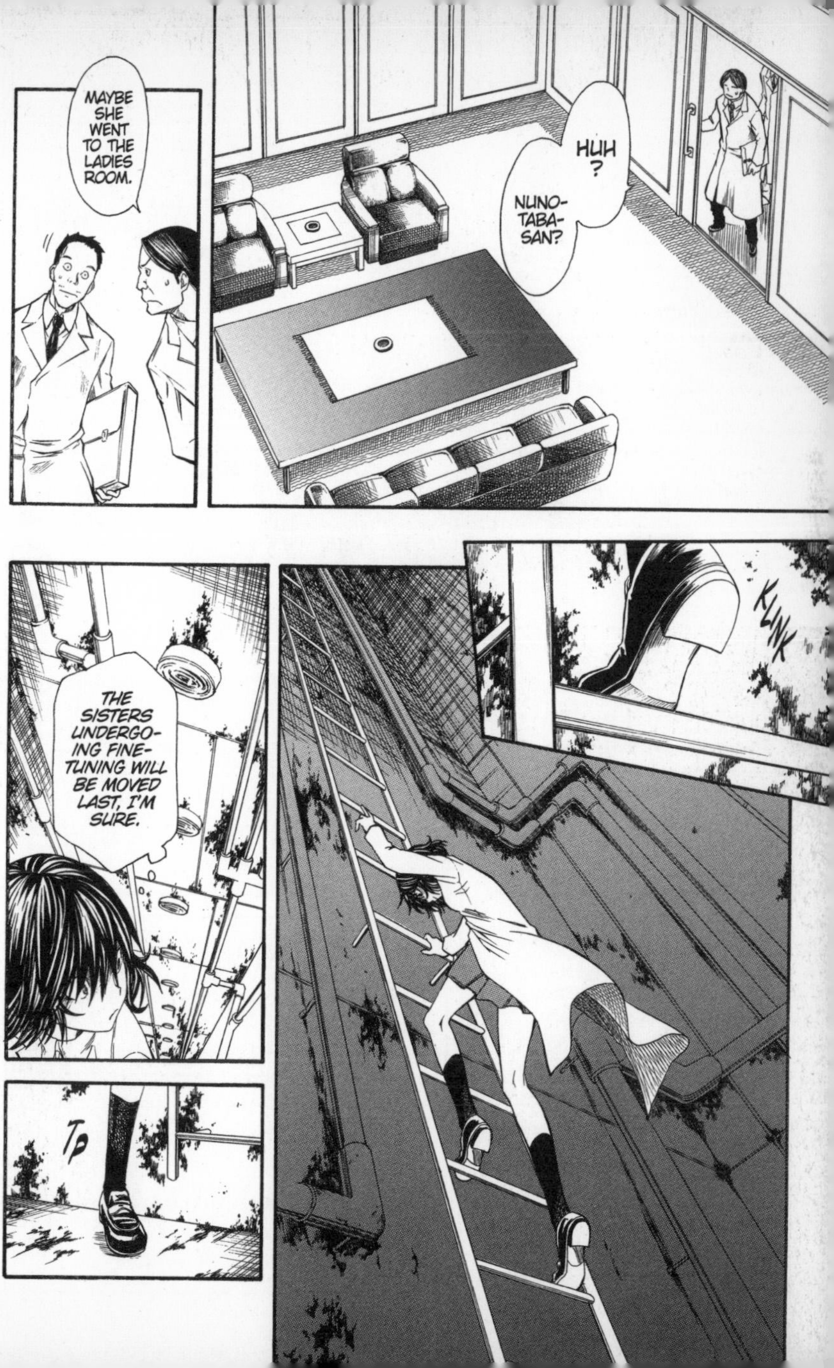
HUH?
NUNO-TABA-SAN?
MAYBE SHE WENT TO THE LADIES ROOM.
KLINK
THE SISTERS UNDERGOING FINE-TUNING WILL BE MOVED LAST, I'M SURE.
Tp

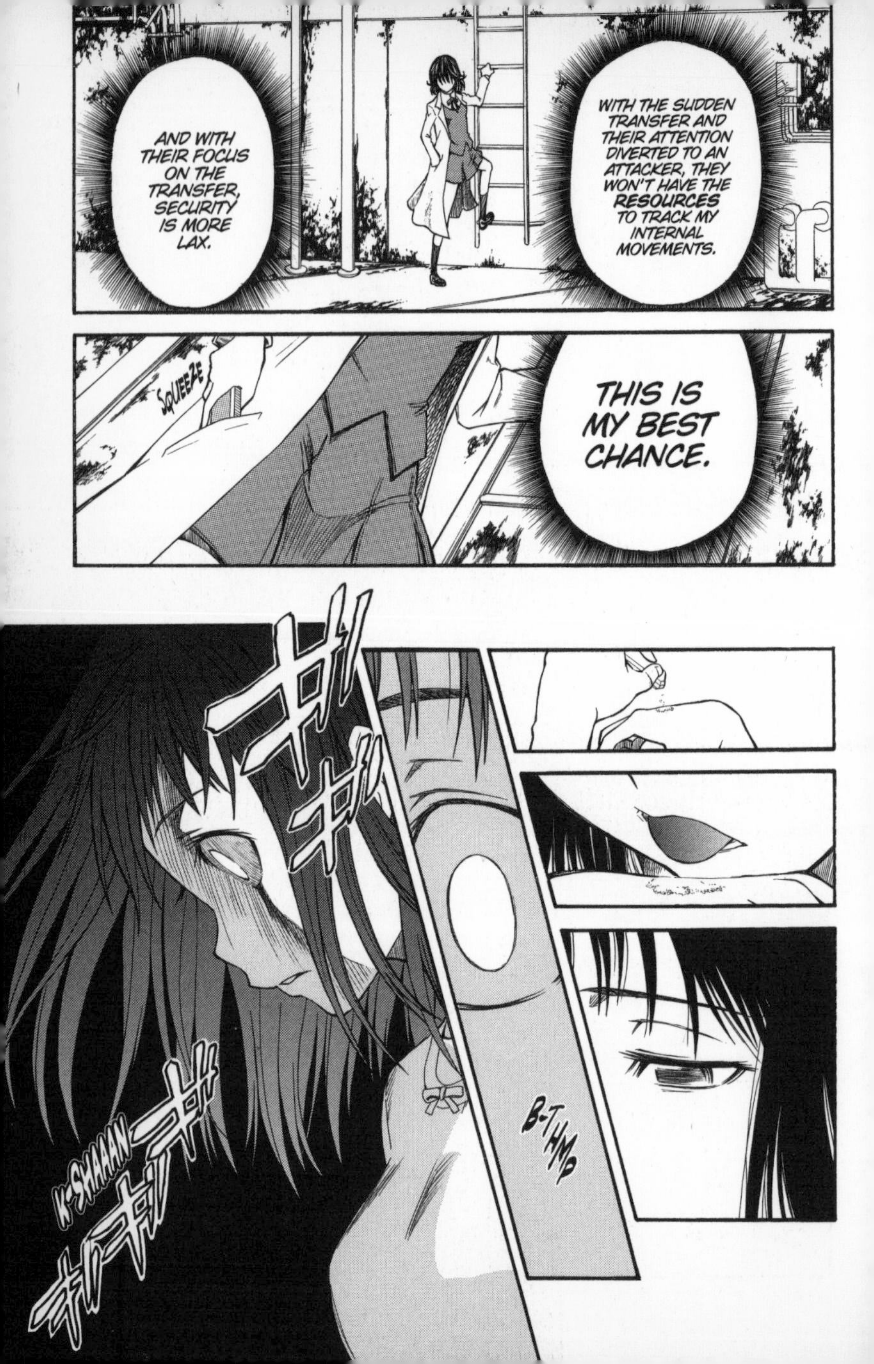
WITH THE SUDDEN TRANSFER AND THEIR ATTENTION DIVERTED TO AN ATTACKER, THEY WON'T HAVE THE RESOURCES TO TRACK MY INTERNAL MOVEMENTS.
AND WITH THEIR FOCUS ON THE TRANSFER, SECURITY IS MORE LAX.
THIS IS MY BEST CHANCE.
SQUEEZE
B-THMP
K-SHAAAN

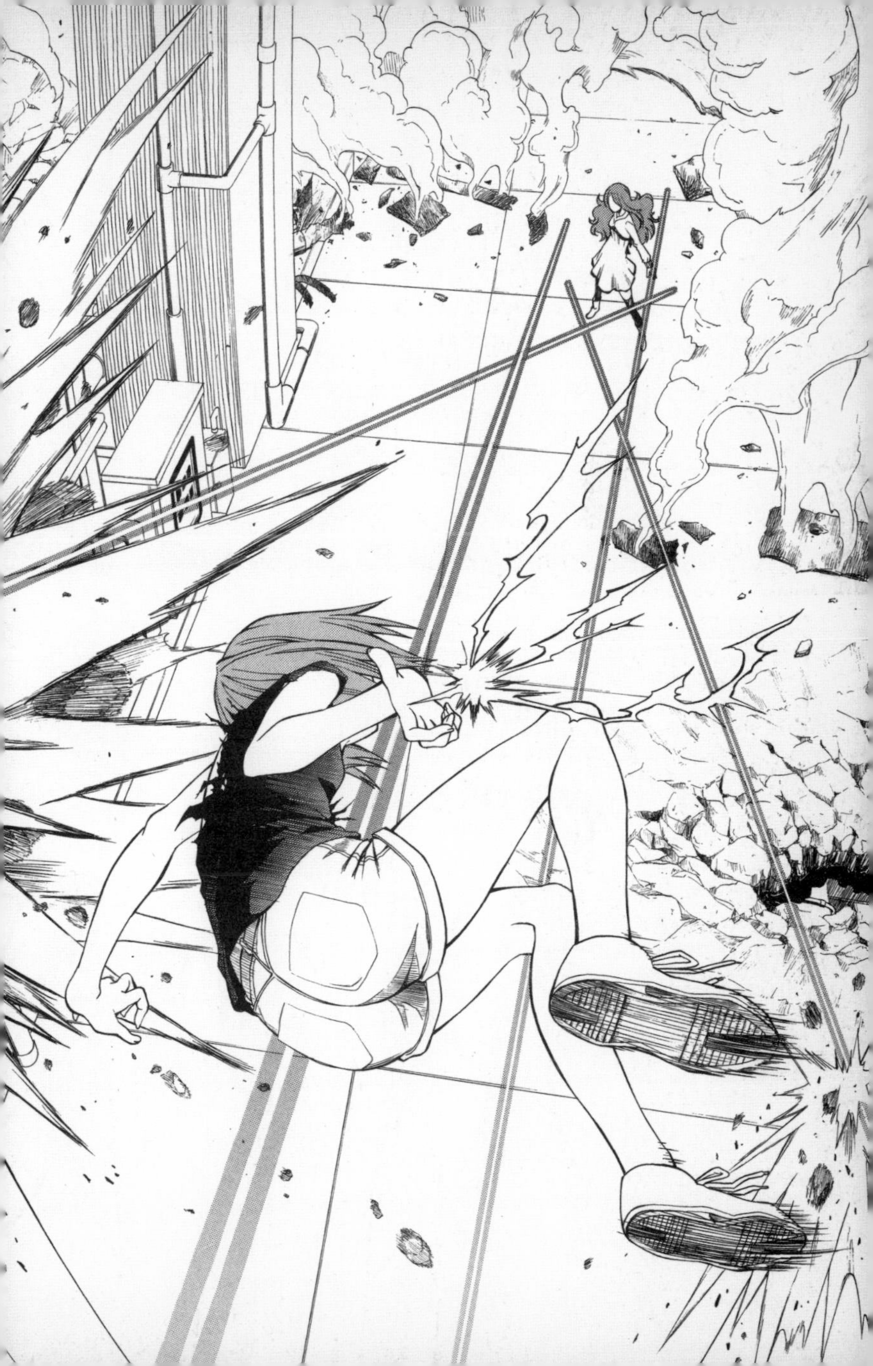

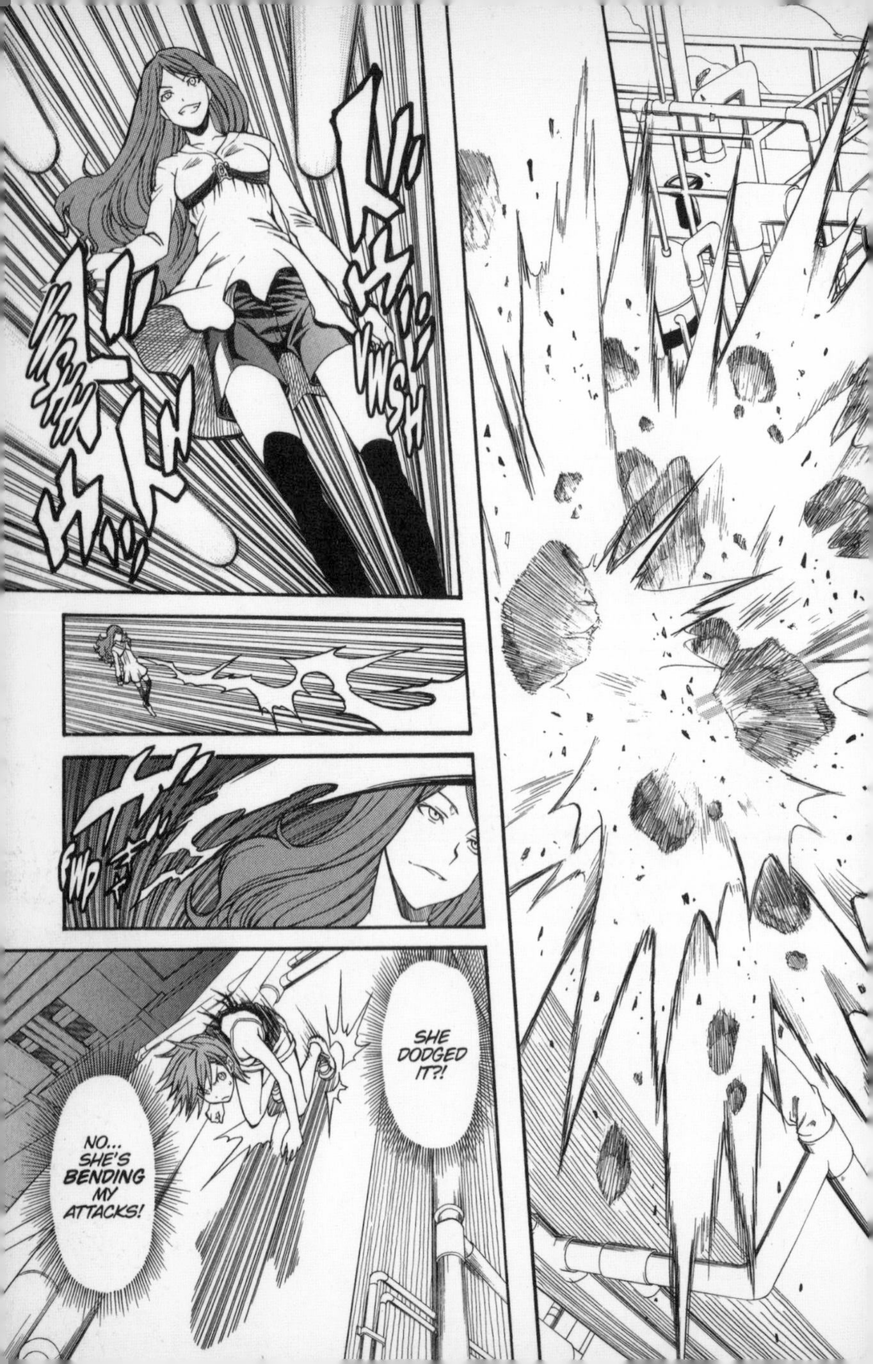
VWSH
FWP
SHE DODGED IT?!
NO... SHE'S BENDING MY ATTACKS!

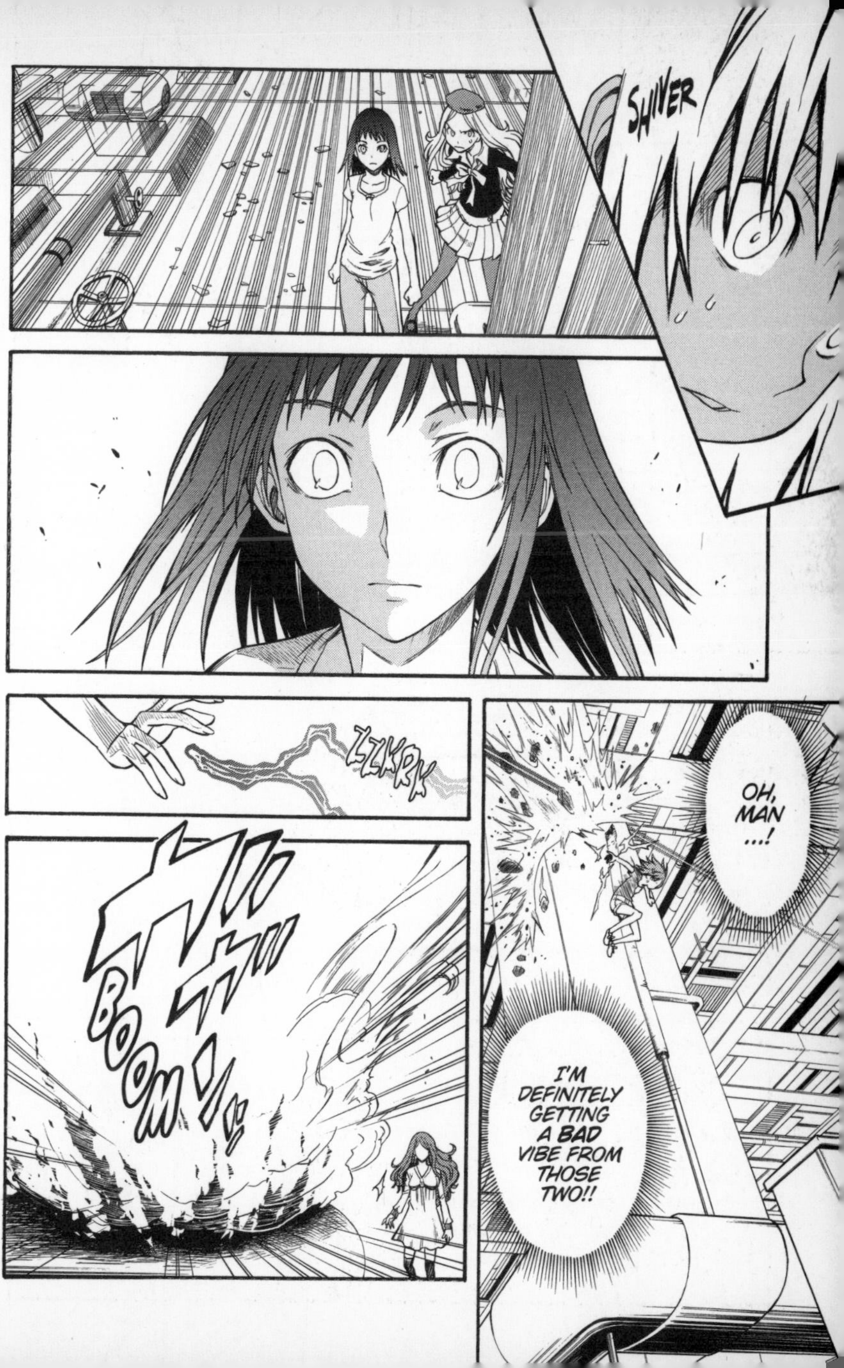
SHIVER
OH, MAN ...!
I'M DEFINITELY GETTING A BAD VIBE FROM THOSE TWO!!
ZZKRK
BOOM!!

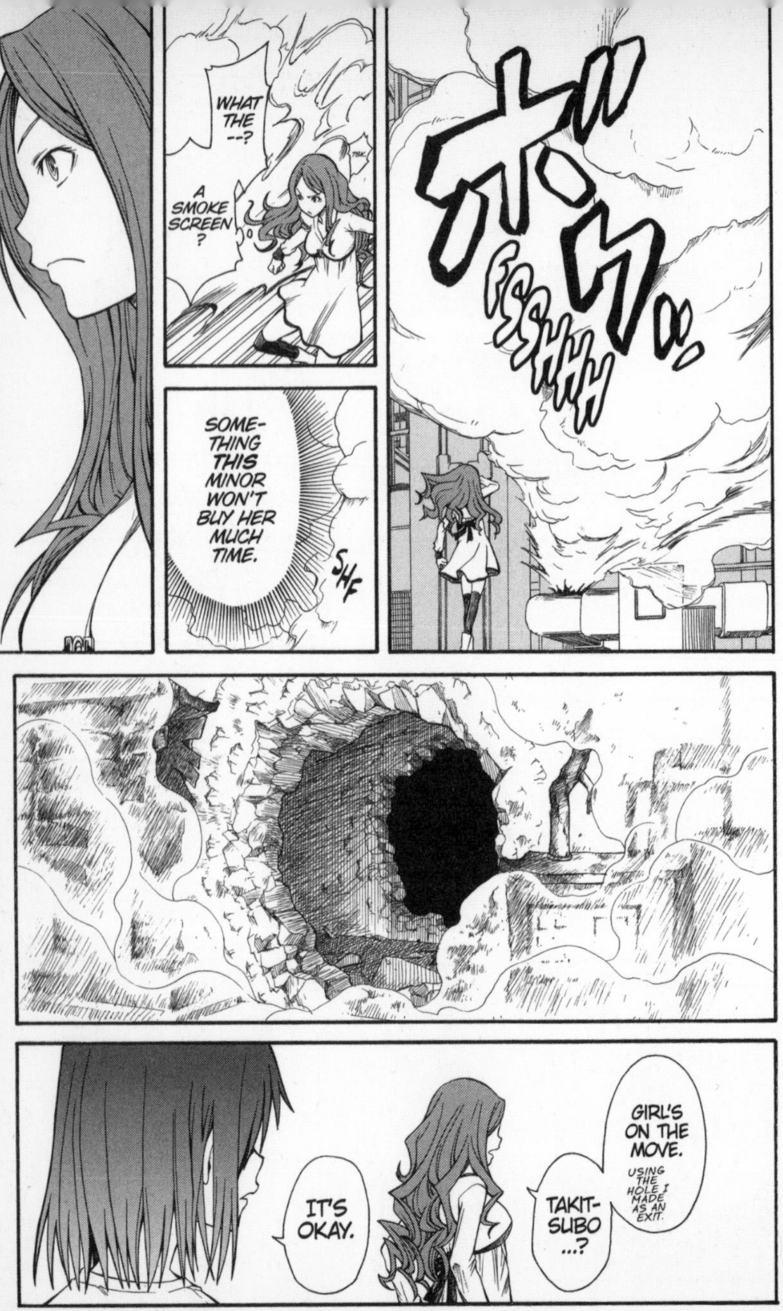
FSSHHH
WHAT THE --?
TSK.
A SMOKE SCREEN ?
SOMETHING THIS MINOR WON'T BUY HER MUCH TIME.
SHF
GIRL'S ON THE MOVE.
USING THE HOLE I MADE AS AN EXIT.
TAKIT-SUBO ...?
IT'S OKAY.

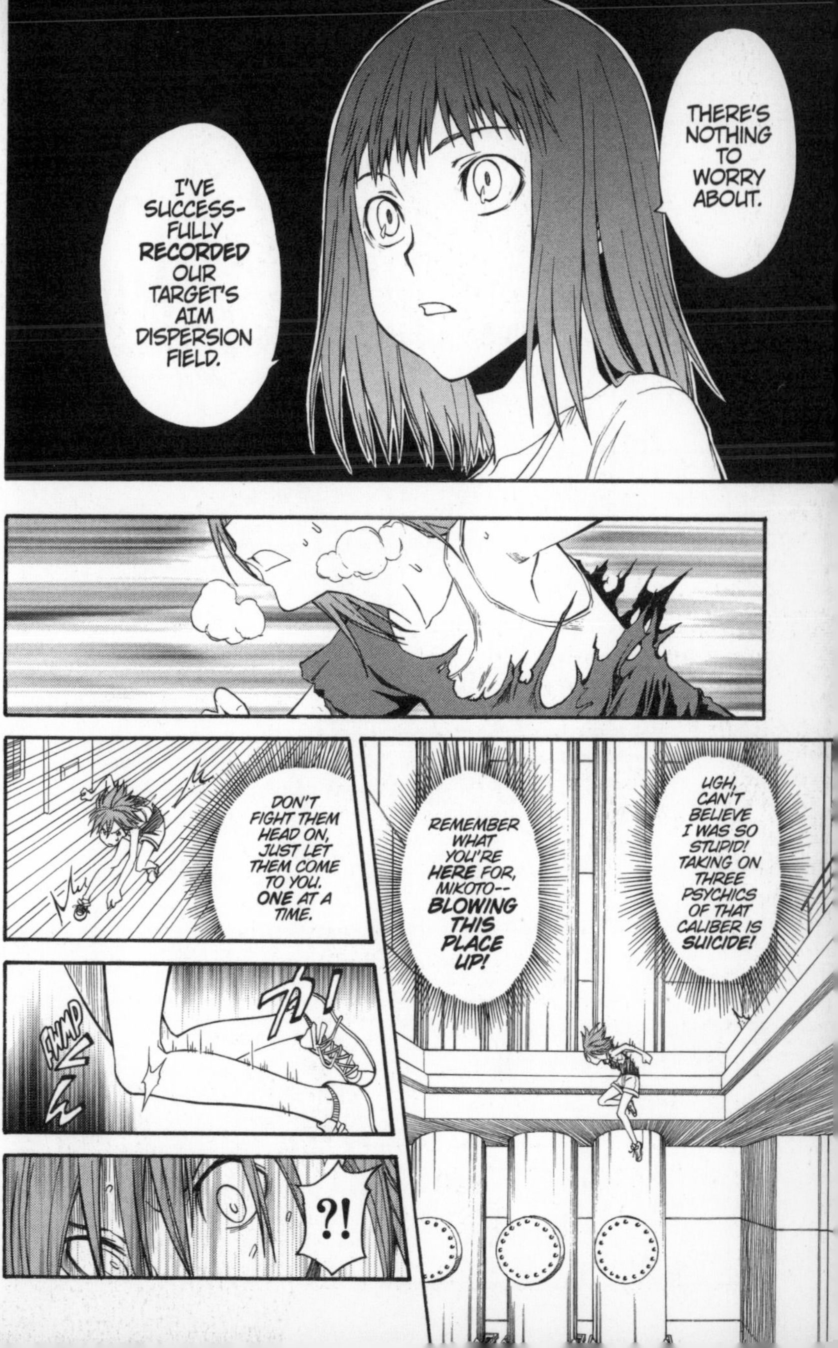
THERE'S NOTHING TO WORRY ABOUT.
I'VE SUCCESS-FULLY RECORDED OUR TARGET'S AIM DISPERSION FIELD.
UGH, CAN'T BELIEVE I WAS SO STUPID! TAKING ON THREE PSYCHICS OF THAT CALIBER IS SUICIDE!
REMEMBER WHAT YOU'RE HERE FOR, MIKOTO-- BLOWING THIS PLACE UP!
DON'T FIGHT THEM HEAD ON, JUST LET THEM COME TO YOU. ONE AT A TIME.
FWMP
?!

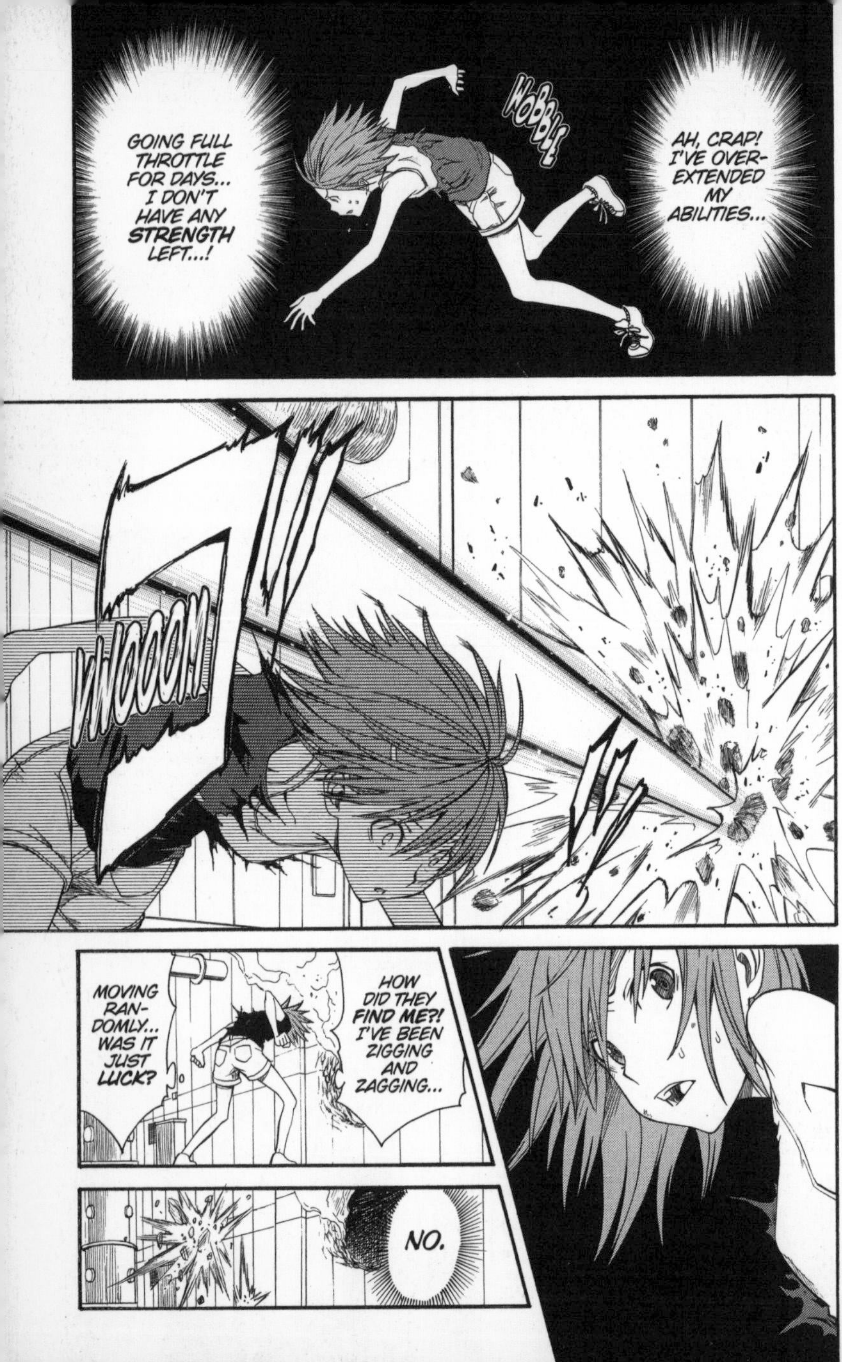
AH, CRAP! I'VE OVER-EXTENDED MY ABILITIES...
WOBBLE
GOING FULL THROTTLE FOR DAYS... I DON'T HAVE ANY STRENGTH LEFT...!
WHOOOM
HOW DID THEY FIND ME?! I'VE BEEN ZIGGING AND ZAGGING...
MOVING RAN-DOMLY... WAS IT JUST LUCK?
NO.

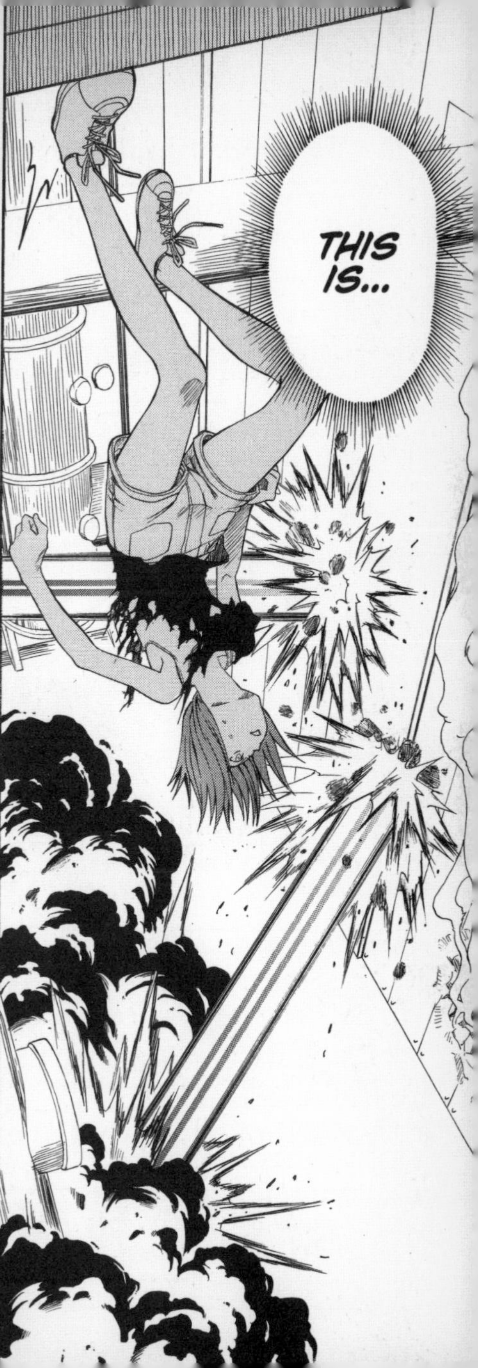
THIS IS...
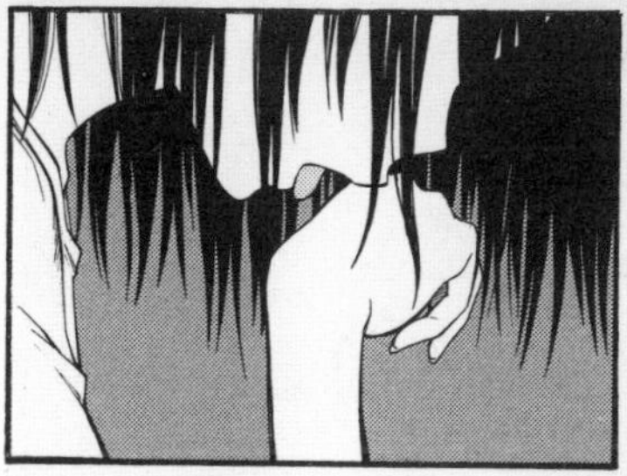
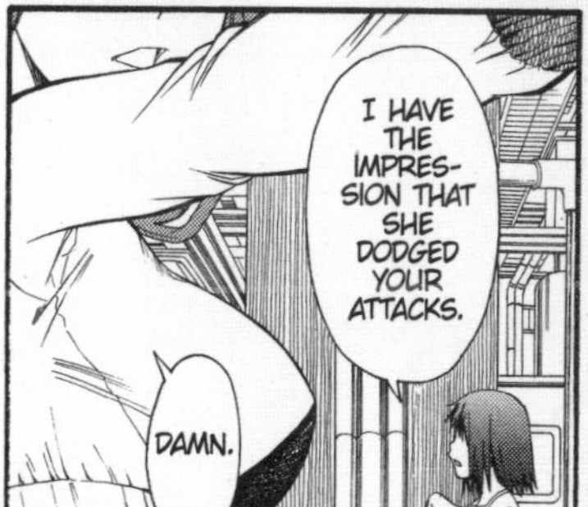
I HAVE THE IMPRESSION THAT SHE DODGED YOUR ATTACKS.
DAMN.
I WONDER IF SHE'S IN THE RAFTERS. IT'S ANNOYING TO DEAL WITH AN EXTRA PLANE.
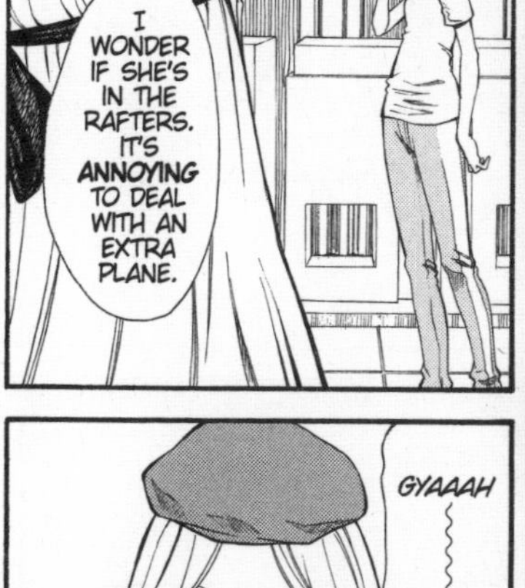
GYAAAH~~~~!

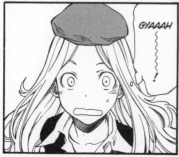

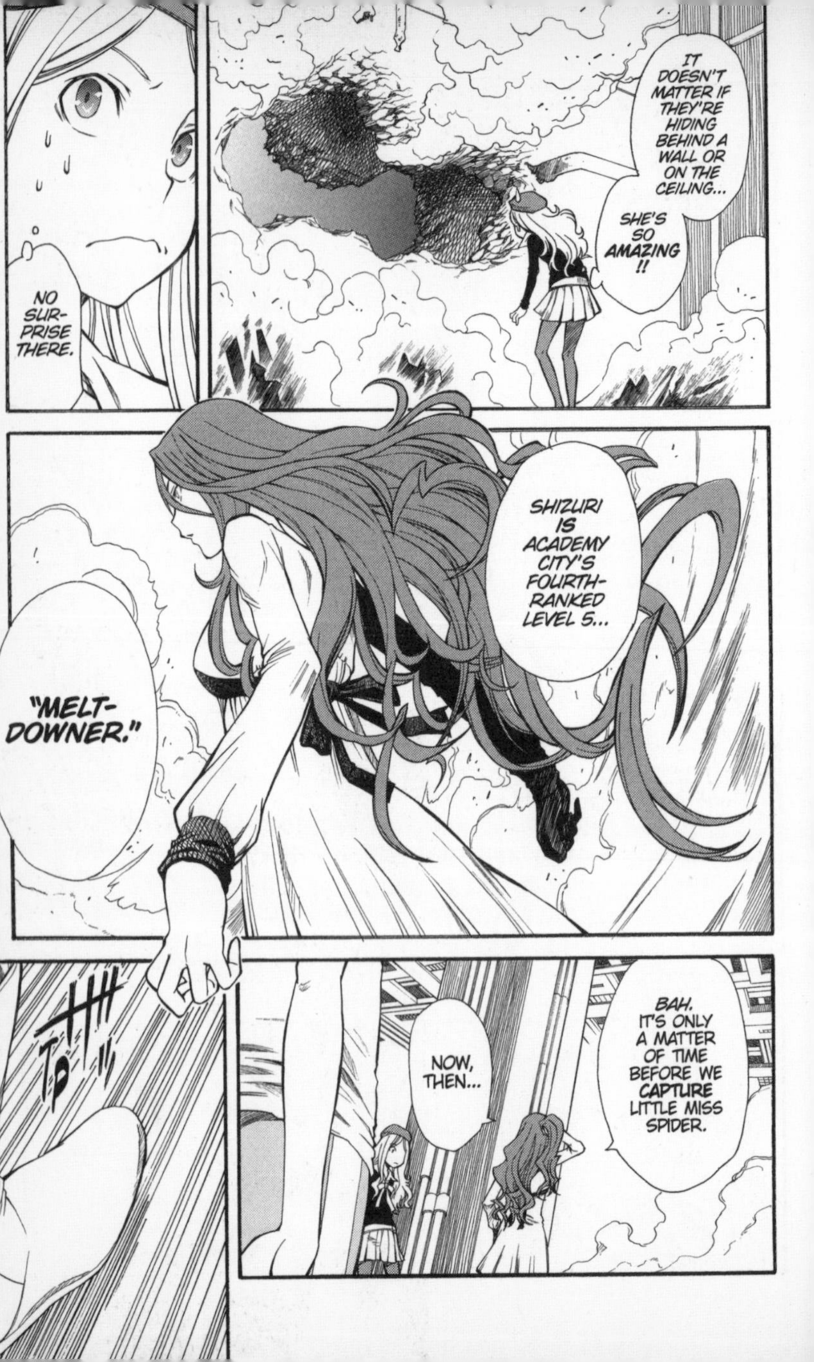
IT DOESN'T MATTER IF THEY'RE HIDING BEHIND A WALL OR ON THE CEILING...
SHE'S SO AMAZING!!
NO SURPRISE THERE.
SHIZURI IS ACADEMY CITY'S FOURTH-RANKED LEVEL 5...
"MELT-DOWNER."
BAH. IT'S ONLY A MATTER OF TIME BEFORE WE CAPTURE LITTLE MISS SPIDER.
NOW, THEN...

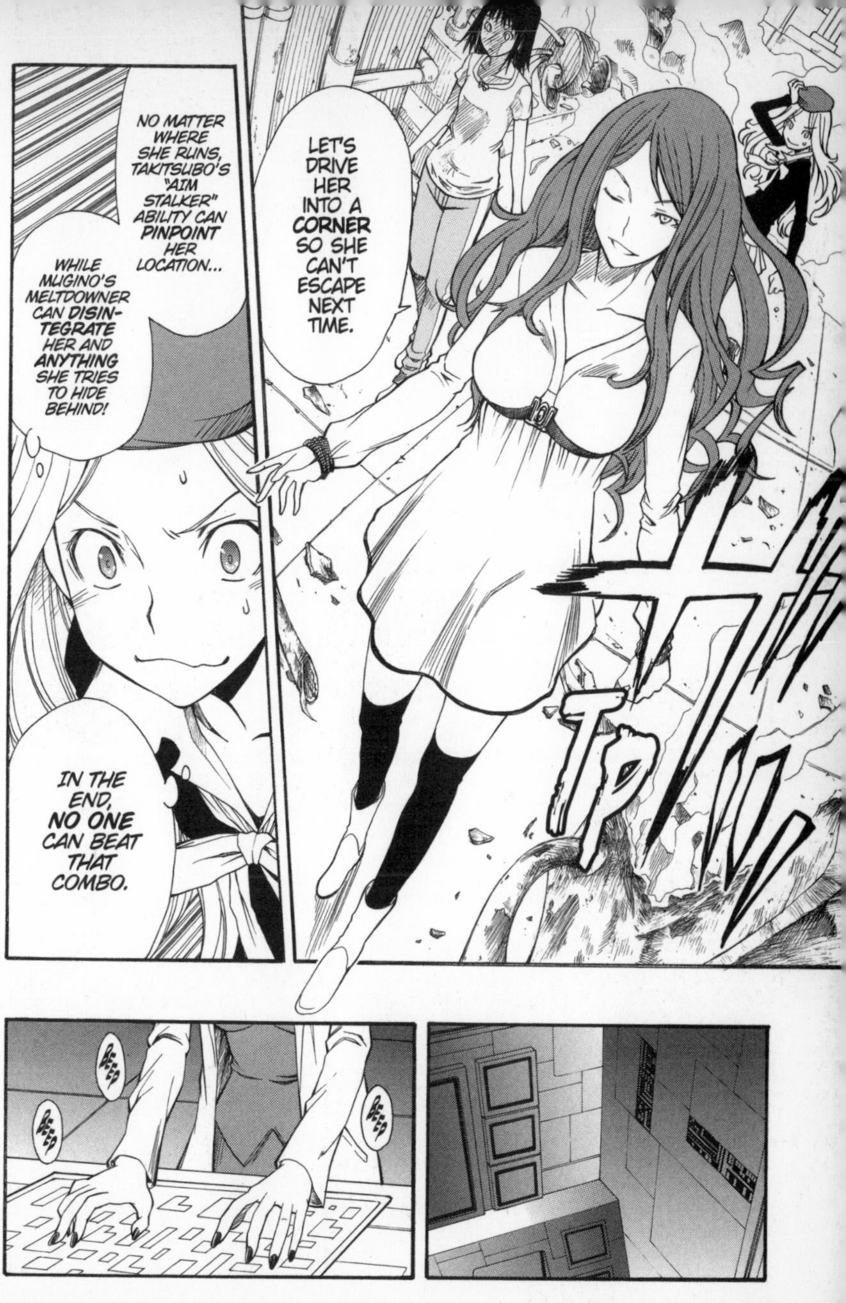
LET'S DRIVE HER INTO A CORNER SO SHE CAN'T ESCAPE NEXT TIME.
NO MATTER WHERE SHE RUNS, TAKITSUBO'S "AIM STALKER" ABILITY CAN PINPOINT HER LOCATION...
WHILE MUGINO'S MELTDOWNER CAN DISIN-TEGRATE HER AND ANYTHING SHE TRIES TO HIDE BEHIND!
IN THE END, NO ONE CAN BEAT THAT COMBO.
BEEP
BEEP
BEEP

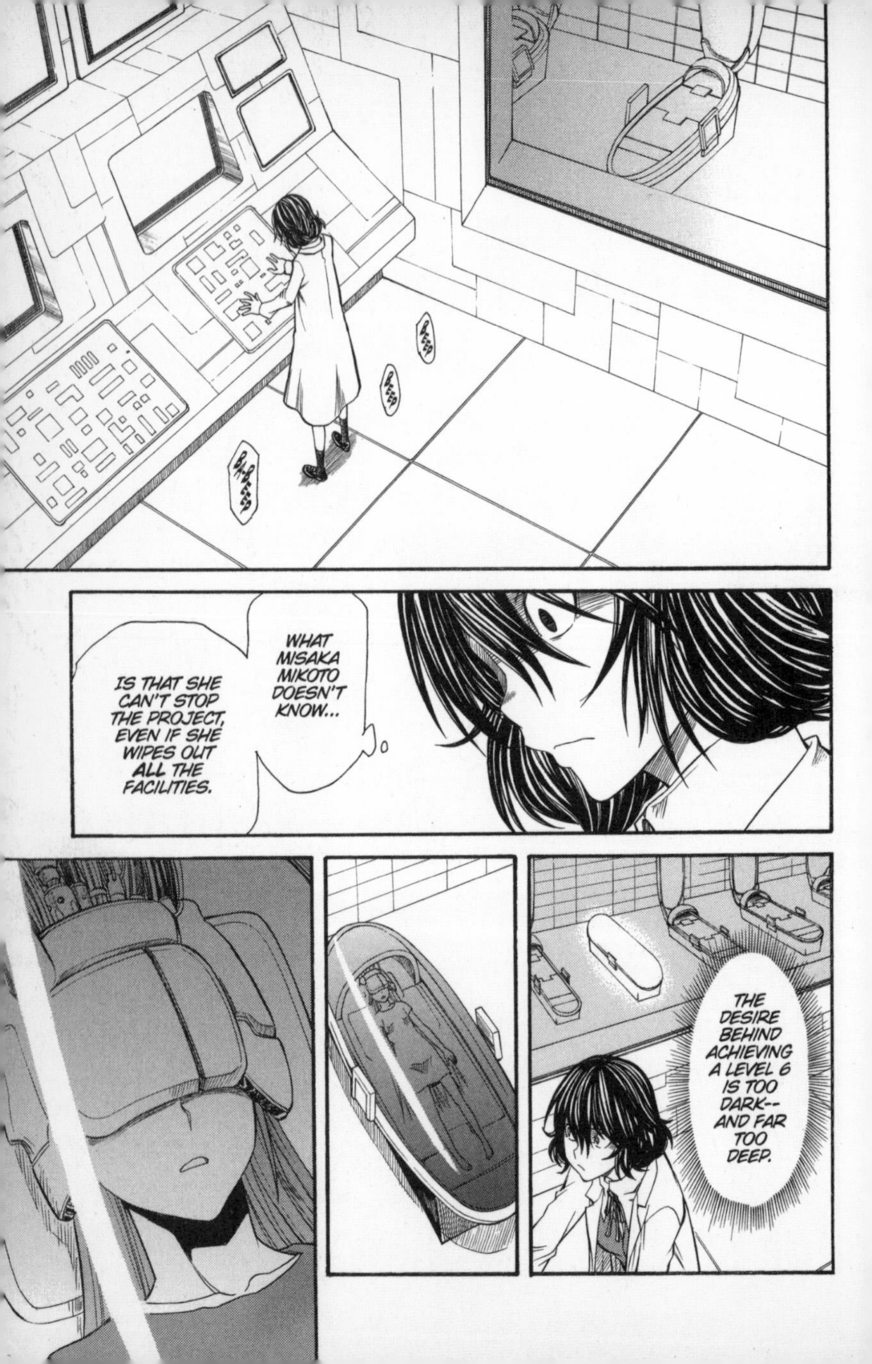
BEEP
BEEP
BA-BEEP
WHAT MISAKA MIKOTO DOESN'T KNOW...
IS THAT SHE CAN'T STOP THE PROJECT, EVEN IF SHE WIPES OUT ALL THE FACILITIES.
THE DESIRE BEHIND ACHIEVING A LEVEL 6 IS TOO DARK-- AND FAR TOO DEEP.

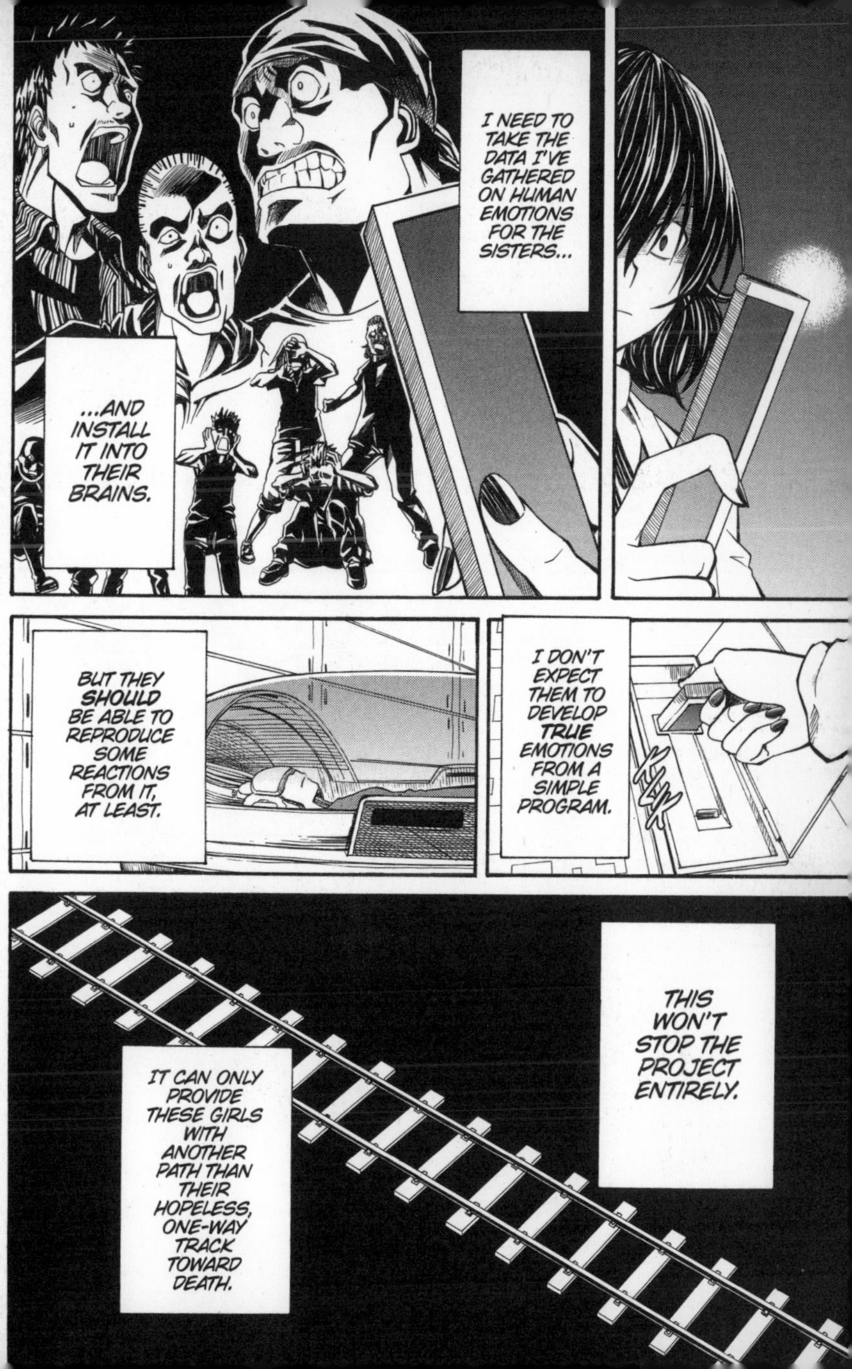
I NEED TO TAKE THE DATA I'VE GATHERED ON HUMAN EMOTIONS FOR THE SISTERS...
...AND INSTALL IT INTO THEIR BRAINS.
I DON'T EXPECT THEM TO DEVELOP **TRUE** EMOTIONS FROM A SIMPLE PROGRAM.
BUT THEY **SHOULD** BE ABLE TO REPRODUCE SOME REACTIONS FROM IT, AT LEAST.
THIS WON'T STOP THE PROJECT ENTIRELY.
IT CAN ONLY PROVIDE THESE GIRLS WITH ANOTHER PATH THAN THEIR HOPELESS, ONE-WAY TRACK TOWARD DEATH.

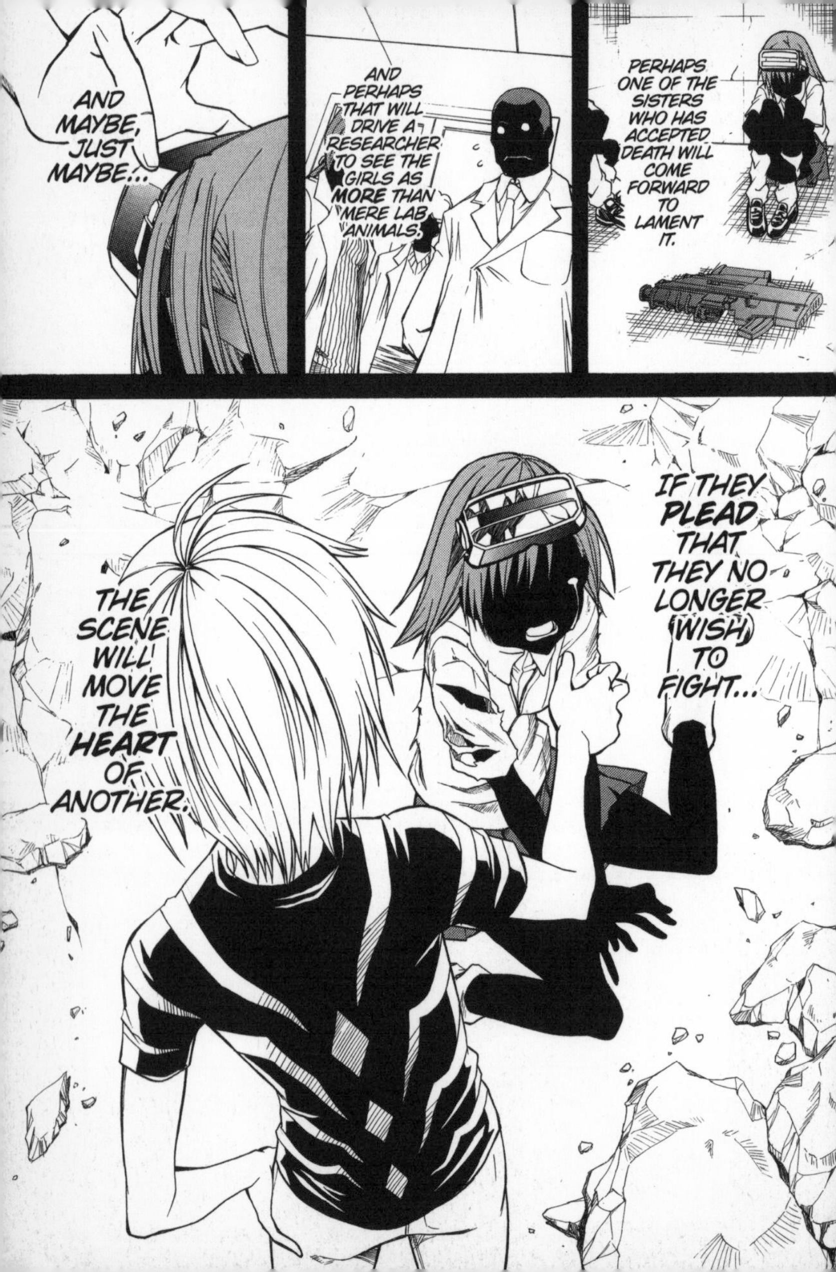
PERHAPS ONE OF THE SISTERS WHO HAS ACCEPTED DEATH WILL COME FORWARD TO LAMENT IT.
AND PERHAPS THAT WILL DRIVE A RESEARCHER TO SEE THE GIRLS AS MORE THAN MERE LAB ANIMALS.
AND MAYBE, JUST MAYBE...
IF THEY PLEAD THAT THEY NO LONGER WISH TO FIGHT...
THE SCENE WILL MOVE THE HEART OF ANOTHER.

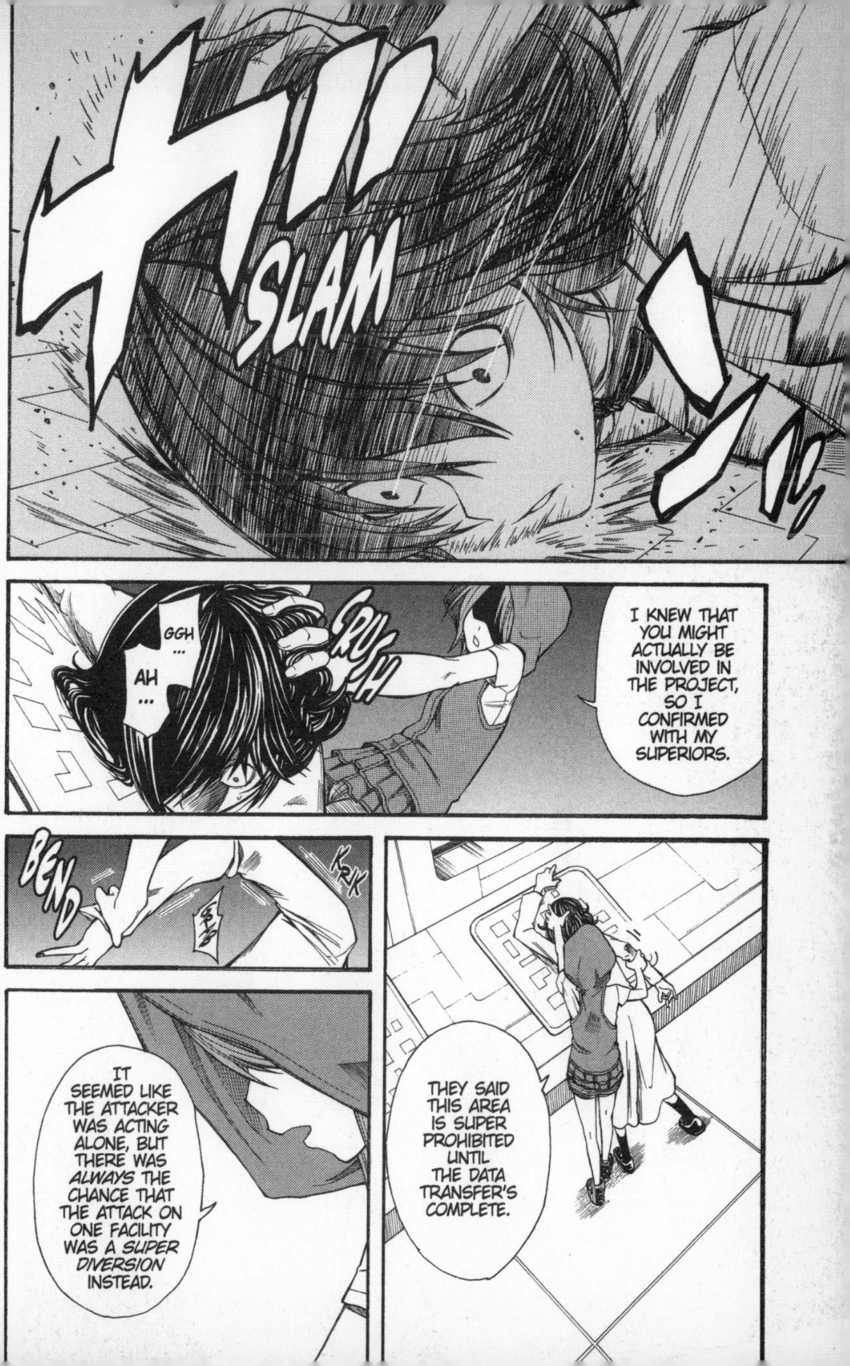
SLAM
I KNEW THAT YOU MIGHT ACTUALLY BE INVOLVED IN THE PROJECT, SO I CONFIRMED WITH MY SUPERIORS.
CRUSH
GGH ... AH ...
THEY SAID THIS AREA IS SUPER PROHIBITED UNTIL THE DATA TRANSFER'S COMPLETE.
KRIK
BEND
IT SEEMED LIKE THE ATTACKER WAS ACTING ALONE, BUT THERE WAS *ALWAYS* THE CHANCE THAT THE ATTACK ON ONE FACILITY WAS A *SUPER DIVERSION* INSTEAD.

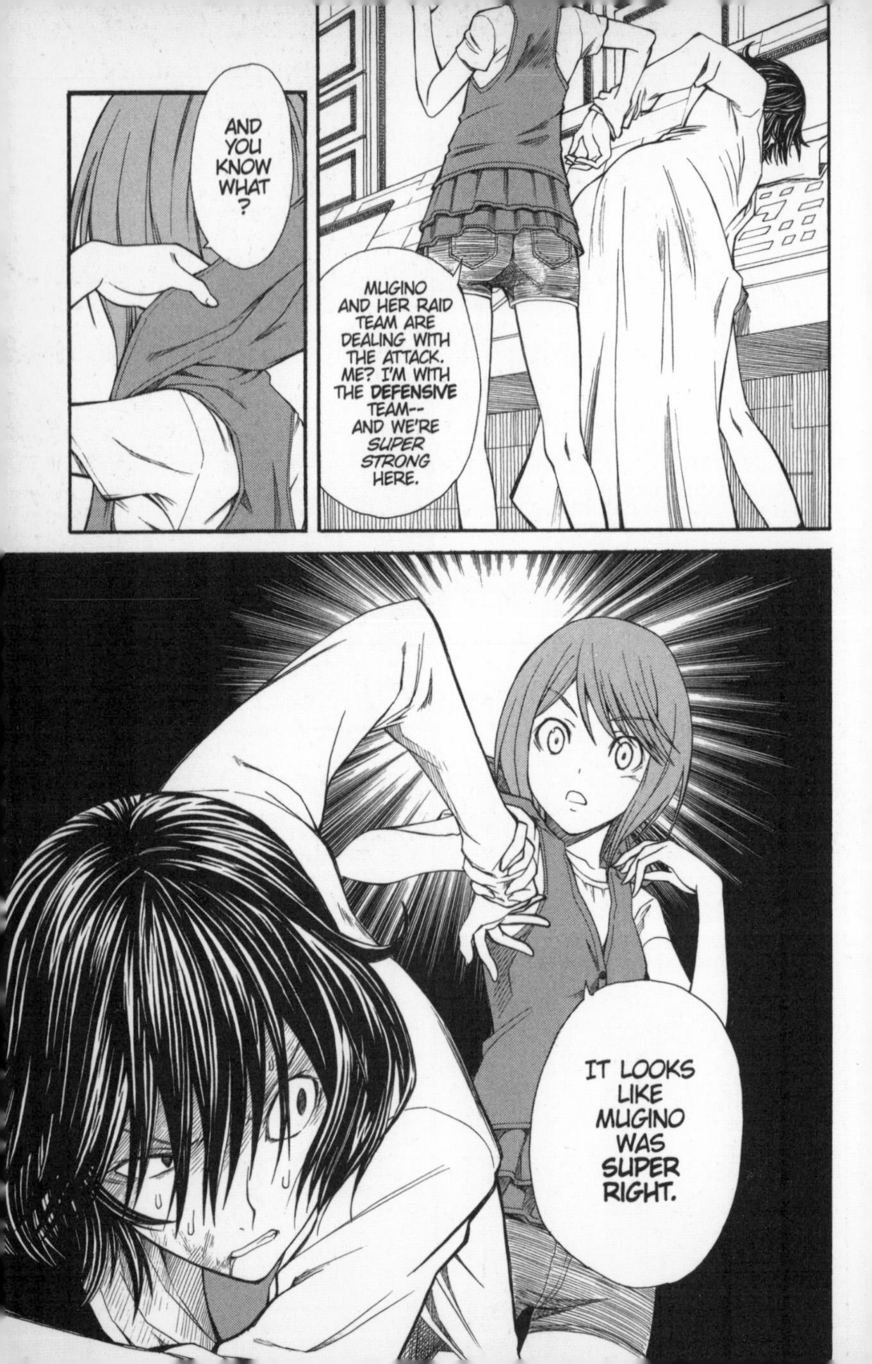
MUGINO AND HER RAID TEAM ARE DEALING WITH THE ATTACK. ME? I'M WITH THE **DEFENSIVE** TEAM-- AND WE'RE *SUPER STRONG* HERE.
AND YOU KNOW WHAT?
IT LOOKS LIKE MUGINO WAS **SUPER** RIGHT.

A Certain Fine Powder and Gianism*

TAKIT-SUBO.
USE THIS.
O...
TOSS
KAY?
SUPER SPICY CHILI PEPPER
DOOOOM
BUT, MU-GINO--
NO, NO. PLEASE. ♪
BUT THIS ISN'T--
IT'S FINE. USE THE WHOLE THING.♡ LICK IT UP IN ONE GO!
UGH.
GO ON!
WRONG BOTTLE.
UGGHH...
HERE GOES.
SNOOORT
@*%#!!!
LEVEL 5.
HO HO HO HO!
KOFF
KOFF

*Gianism refers to Doraemon's horrible bully "Giant," aka "Jaian."

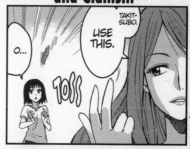

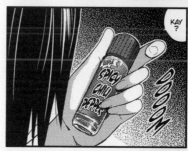

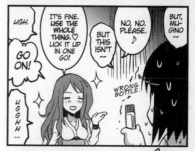

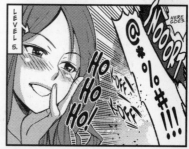

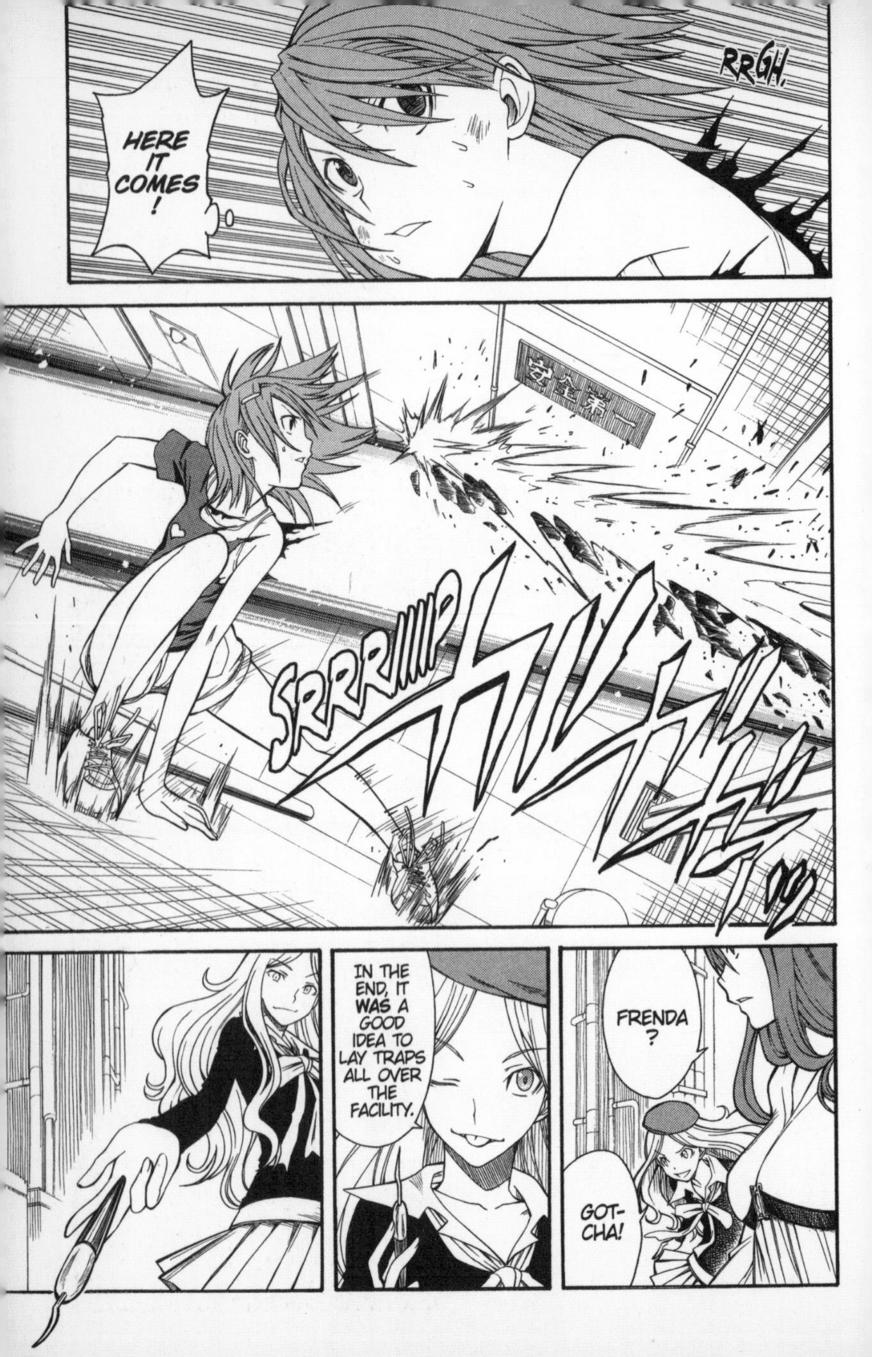
RRGH.
HERE IT COMES!
安全第一
SRRIIIIP
FRENDA?
GOT-CHA!
IN THE END, IT WAS A GOOD IDEA TO LAY TRAPS ALL OVER THE FACILITY.

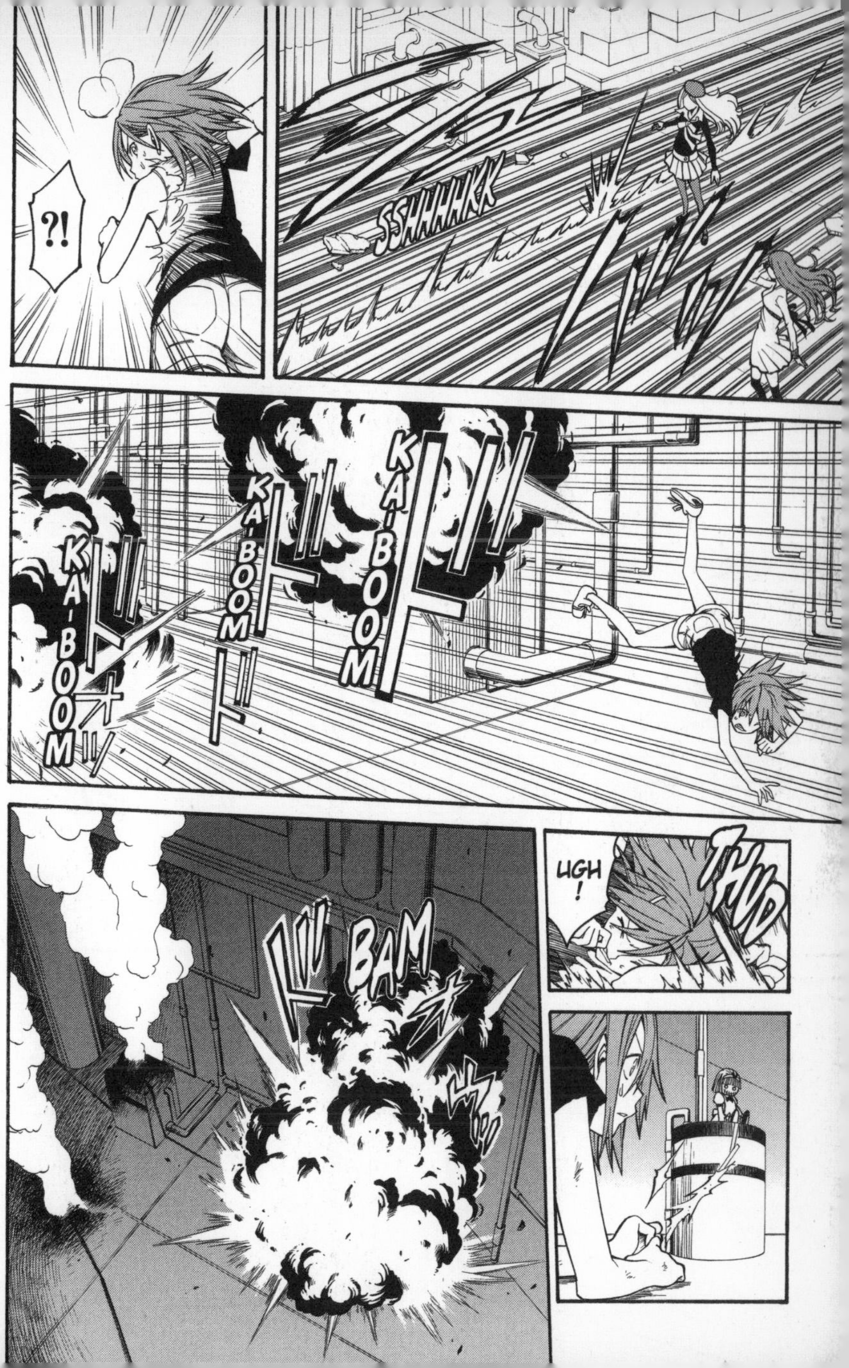
SSHHHKK
?!
KA-BOOM
KA-BOOM
KA-BOOM
UGH!
THUD
BAM

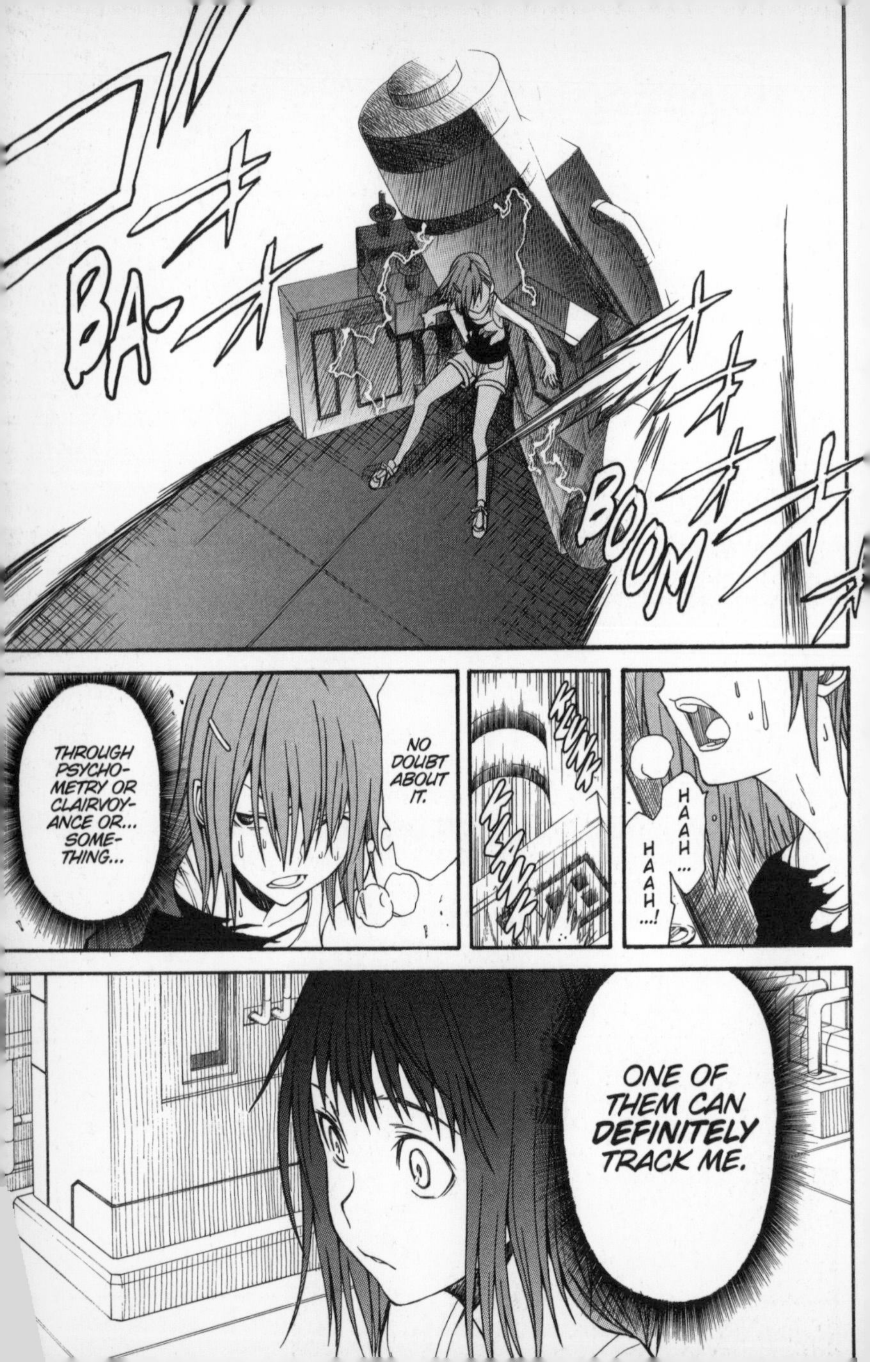
BA-
BOOM
HAAH... HAAH...!
KLUNK
KLANK
NO DOUBT ABOUT IT.
THROUGH PSYCHOMETRY OR CLAIRVOYANCE OR... SOMETHING...
ONE OF THEM CAN DEFINITELY TRACK ME.

CHAPTER 29: AUGUST 19 (4)

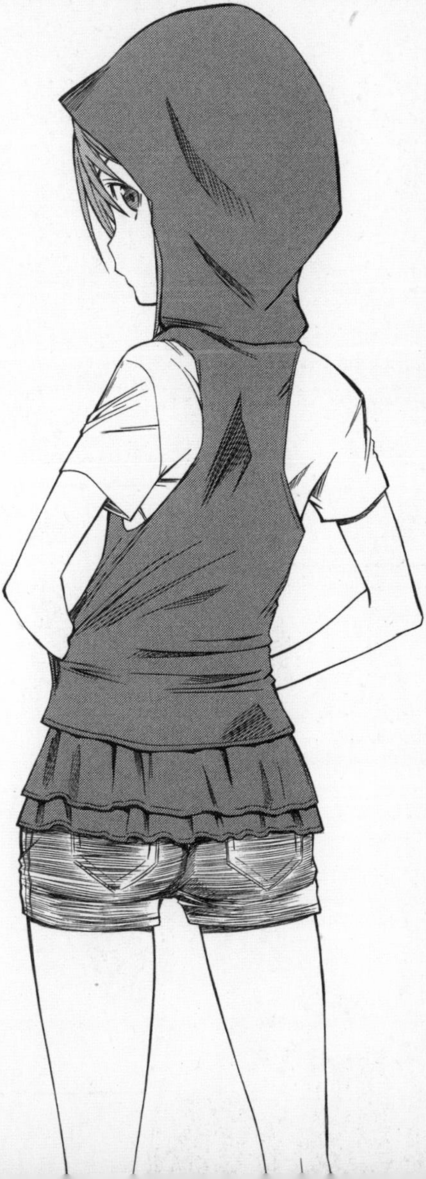

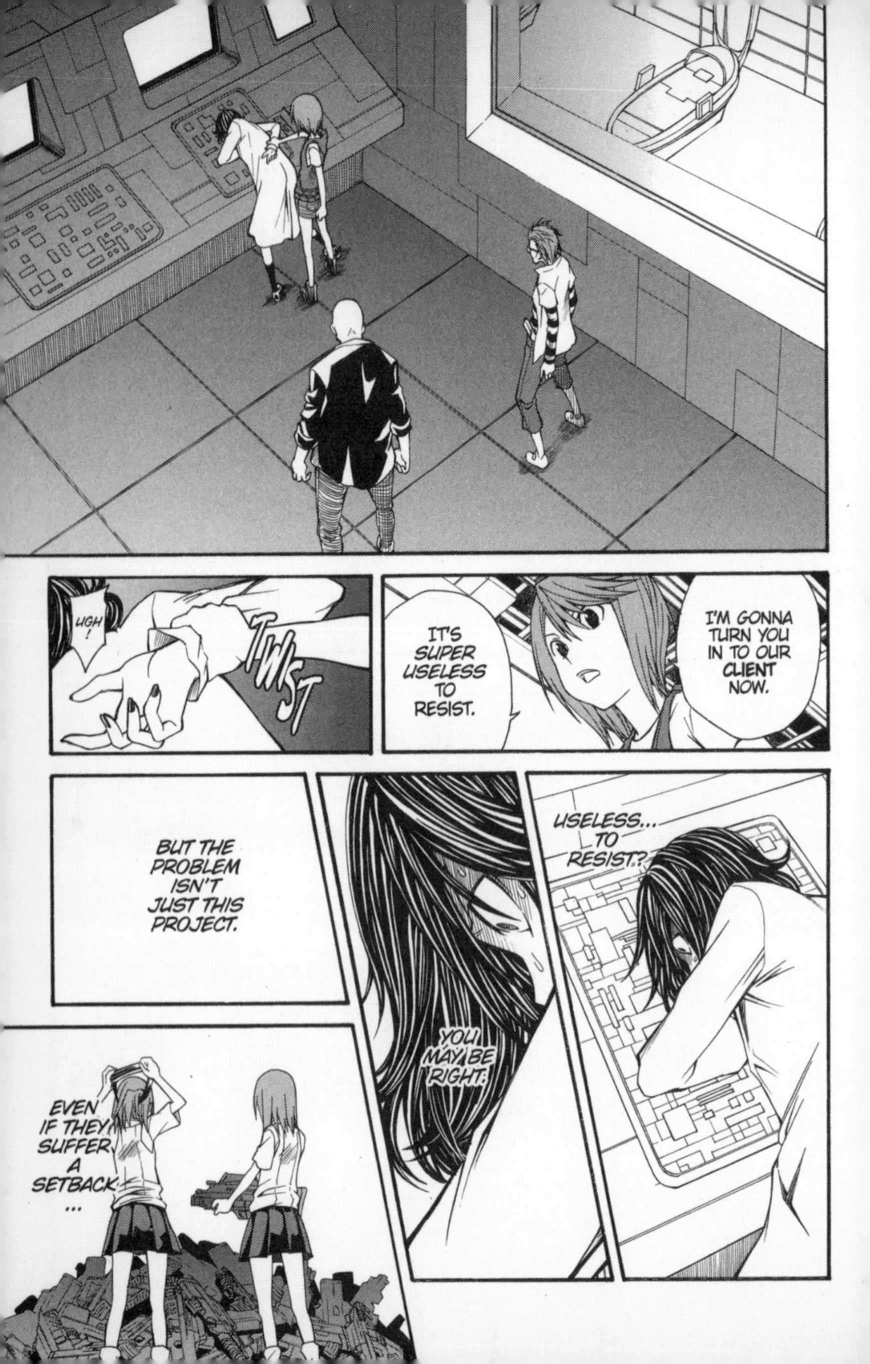
I'M GONNA TURN YOU IN TO OUR CLIENT NOW.
IT'S SUPER USELESS TO RESIST.
UGH!
TWIST
USELESS... TO RESIST?
YOU MAY BE RIGHT.
BUT THE PROBLEM ISN'T JUST THIS PROJECT.
EVEN IF THEY SUFFER A SETBACK...

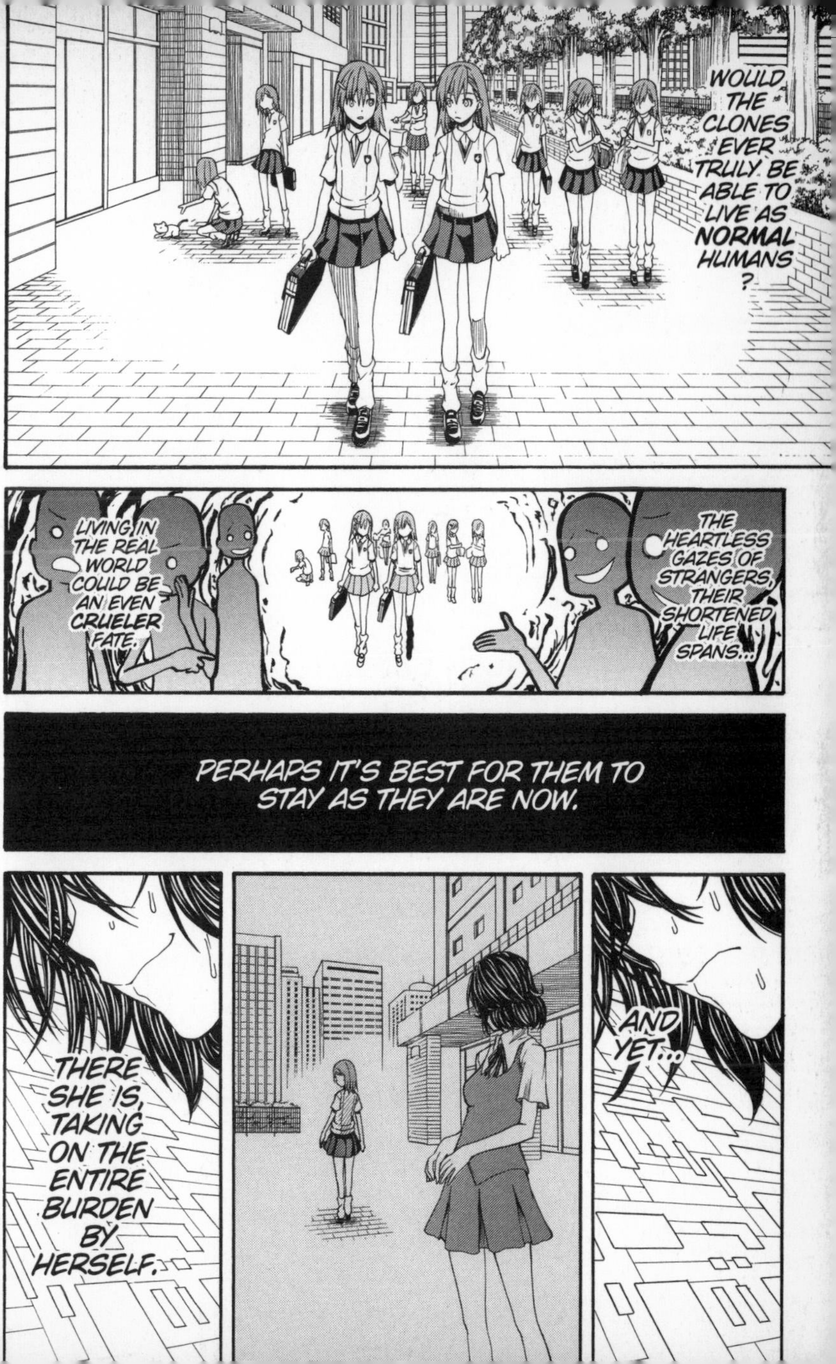
WOULD THE CLONES EVER TRULY BE ABLE TO LIVE AS NORMAL HUMANS?
THE HEARTLESS GAZES OF STRANGERS, THEIR SHORTENED LIFE SPANS...
LIVING IN THE REAL WORLD COULD BE AN EVEN CRUELER FATE.
PERHAPS IT'S BEST FOR THEM TO STAY AS THEY ARE NOW.
AND YET...
THERE SHE IS, TAKING ON THE ENTIRE BURDEN BY HERSELF.

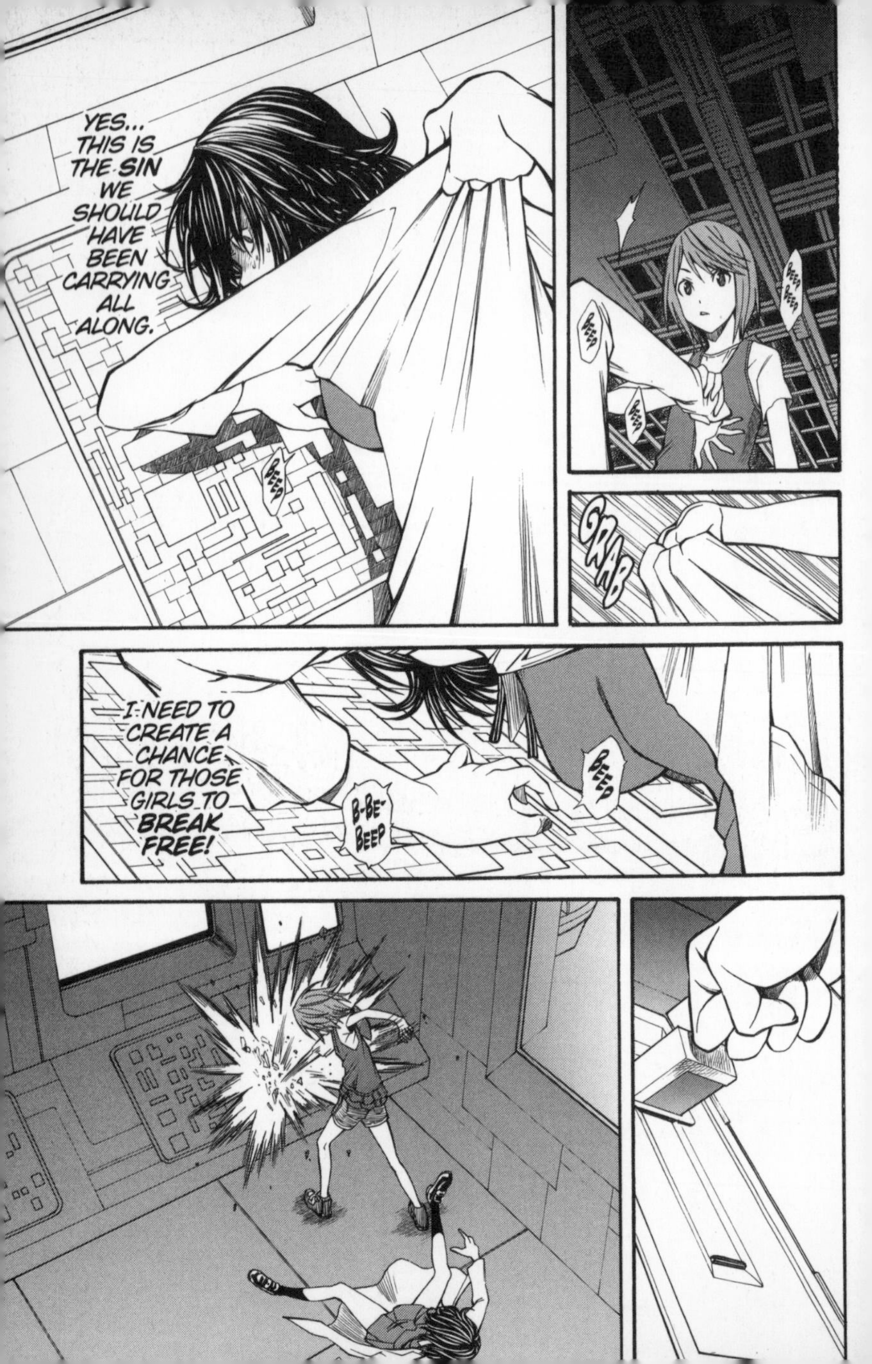
BEEP BEEP
BEEP
BEEP
GRAB
YES... THIS IS THE SIN WE SHOULD HAVE BEEN CARRYING ALL ALONG.
BEEP
I NEED TO CREATE A CHANCE FOR THOSE GIRLS TO **BREAK FREE!**
BEEP
B-BE-BEEP

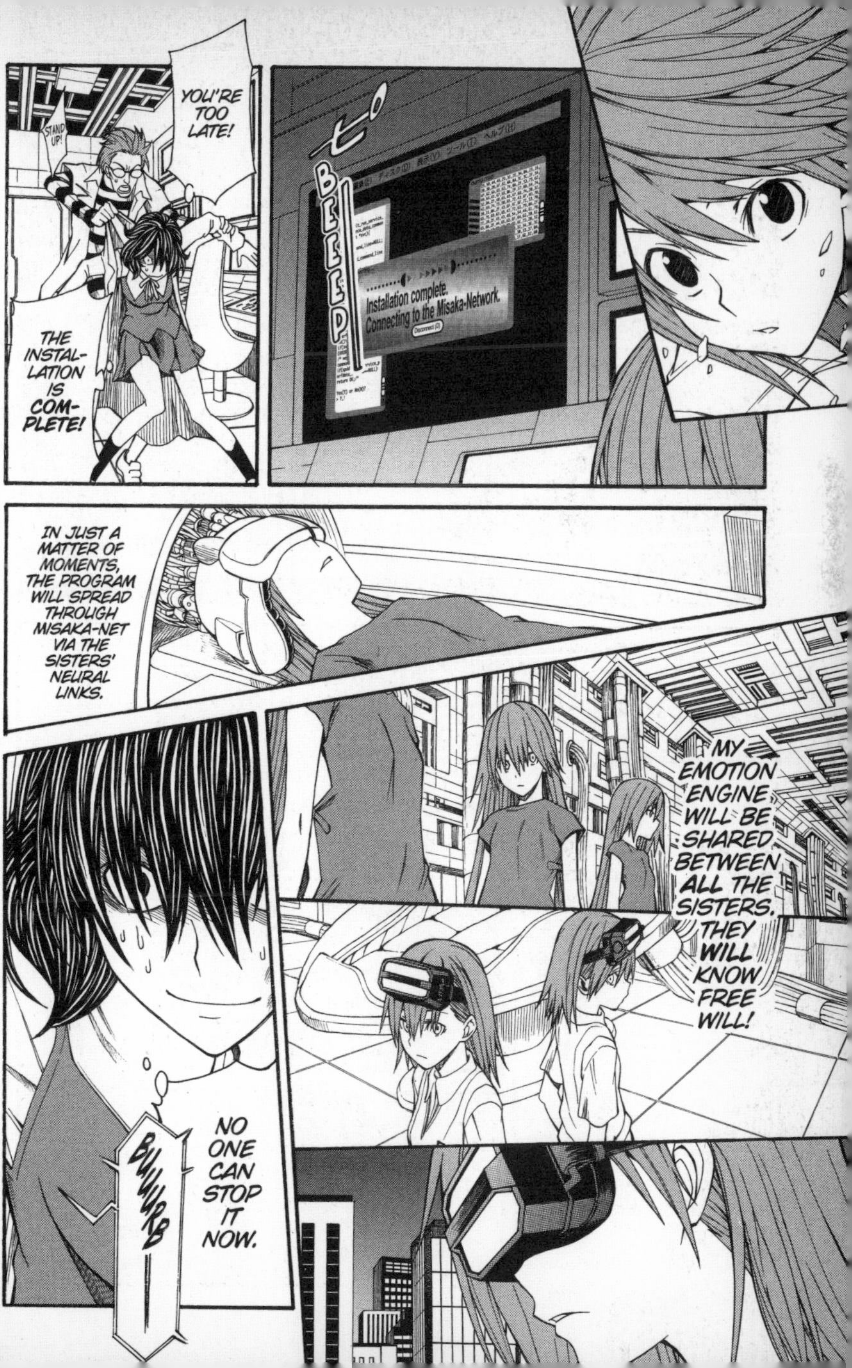
ピ
BEEEP
Installation complete.
Connecting to the Misaka-Network.
Disconnect (D)
YOU'RE TOO LATE!
STAND UP!
THE INSTALLATION IS COMPLETE!
IN JUST A MATTER OF MOMENTS, THE PROGRAM WILL SPREAD THROUGH MISAKA-NET VIA THE SISTERS' NEURAL LINKS.
MY EMOTION ENGINE WILL BE SHARED BETWEEN ALL THE SISTERS.
THEY WILL KNOW FREE WILL!
NO ONE CAN STOP IT NOW.
BUUURB

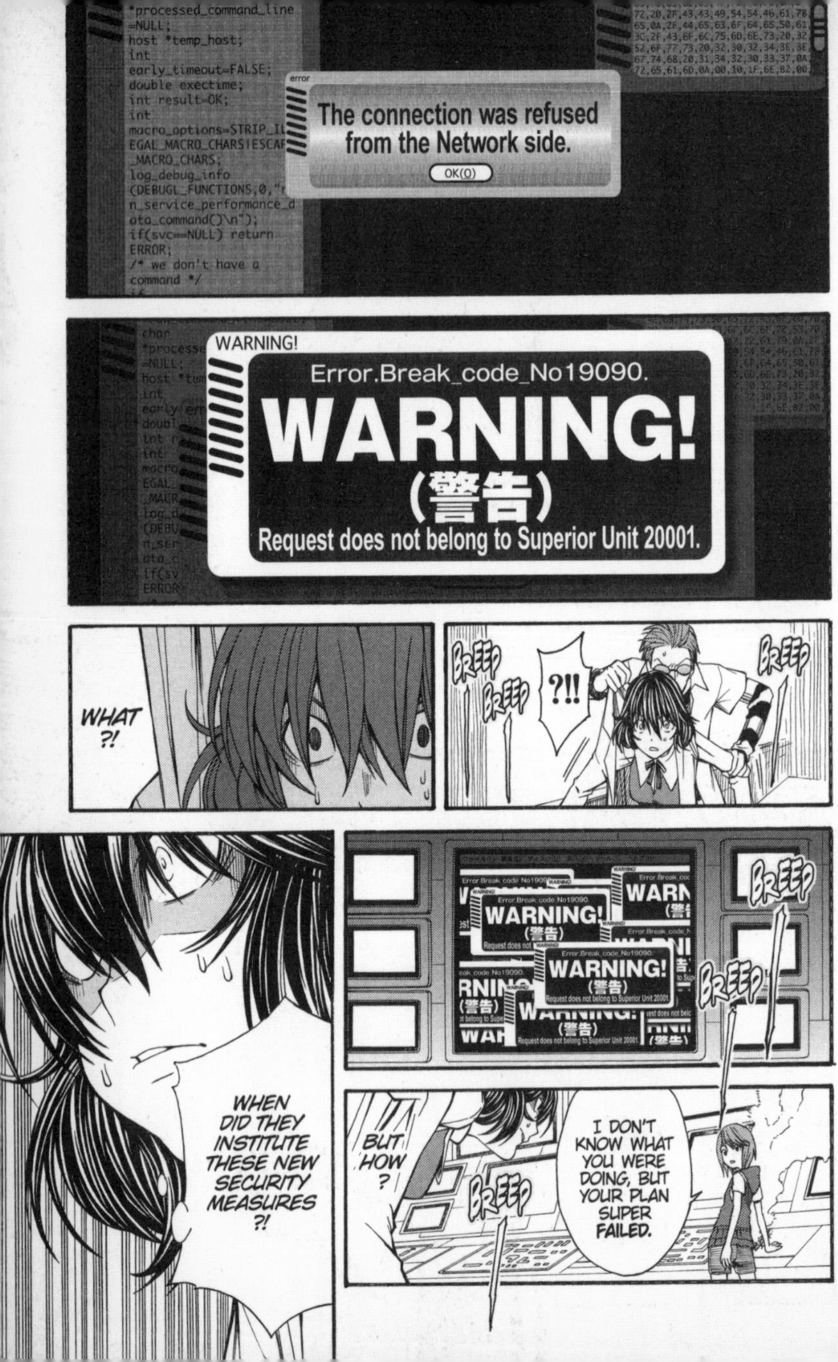
error
The connection was refused from the Network side.
OK(O)
WARNING!
Error.Break_code_No19090.
WARNING!
(警告)
Request does not belong to Superior Unit 20001.
BREEP
BREEP
?!!
BREEP
WHAT ?!
BREEP
BREEP
I DON'T KNOW WHAT YOU WERE DOING, BUT YOUR PLAN SUPER FAILED.
BUT HOW?
BREEP
WHEN DID THEY INSTITUTE THESE NEW SECURITY MEASURES ?!

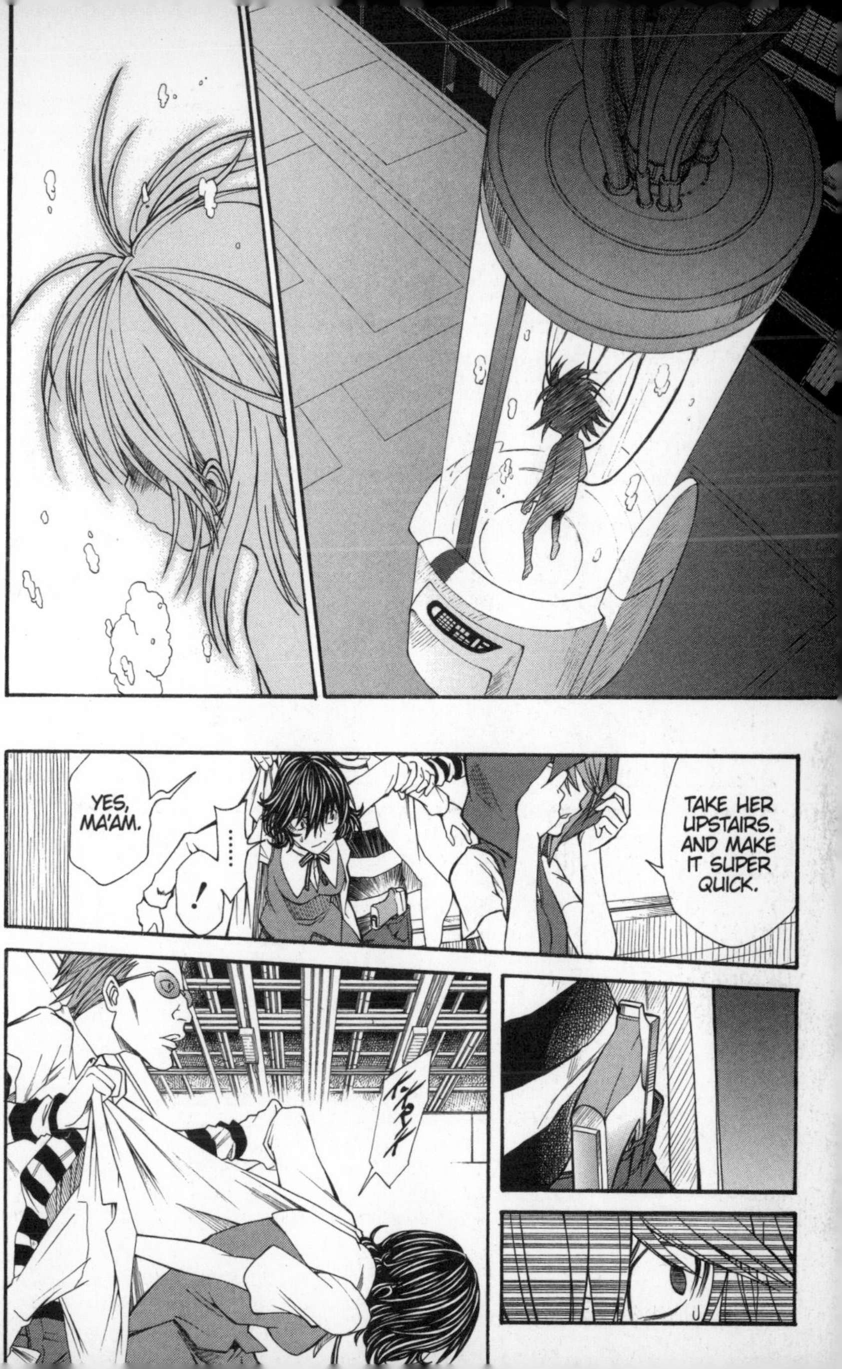
TAKE HER UPSTAIRS. AND MAKE IT SUPER QUICK.
YES, MA'AM.
......
!

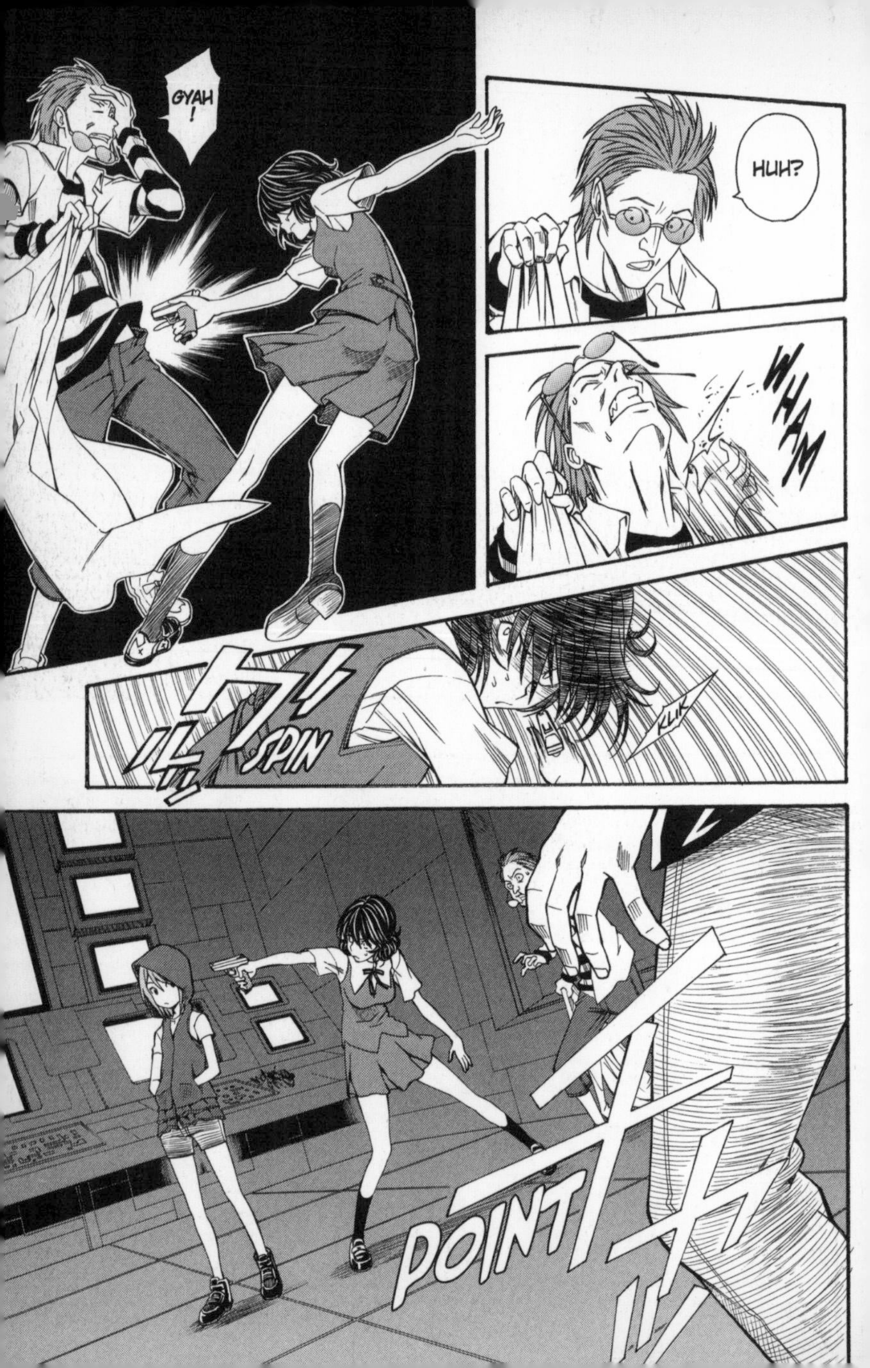
HUH?
WHAM
GYAH!
KLIK
SPIN
POINT

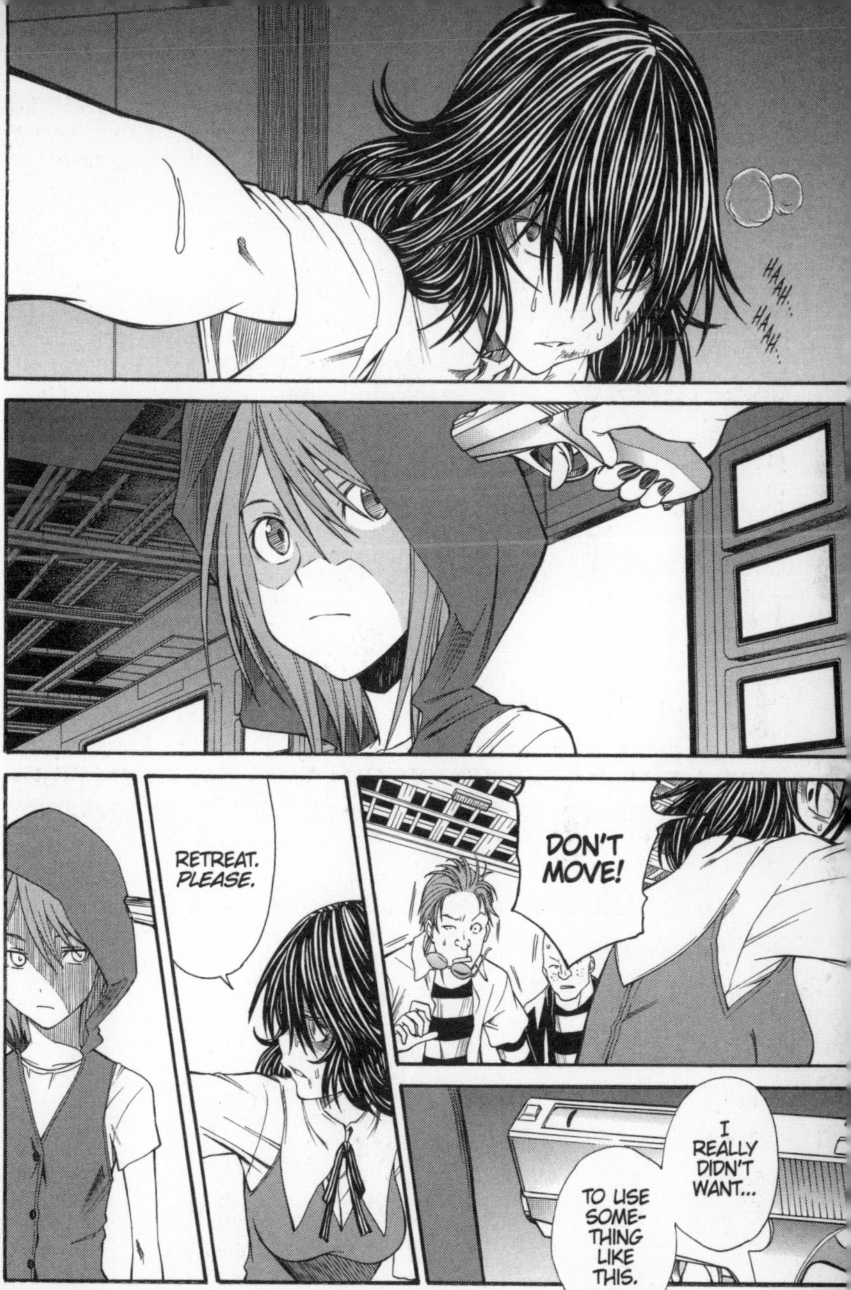
HAAH... HAAH...
DON'T MOVE!
I REALLY DIDN'T WANT...
TO USE SOME-THING LIKE THIS.
RETREAT. *PLEASE.*

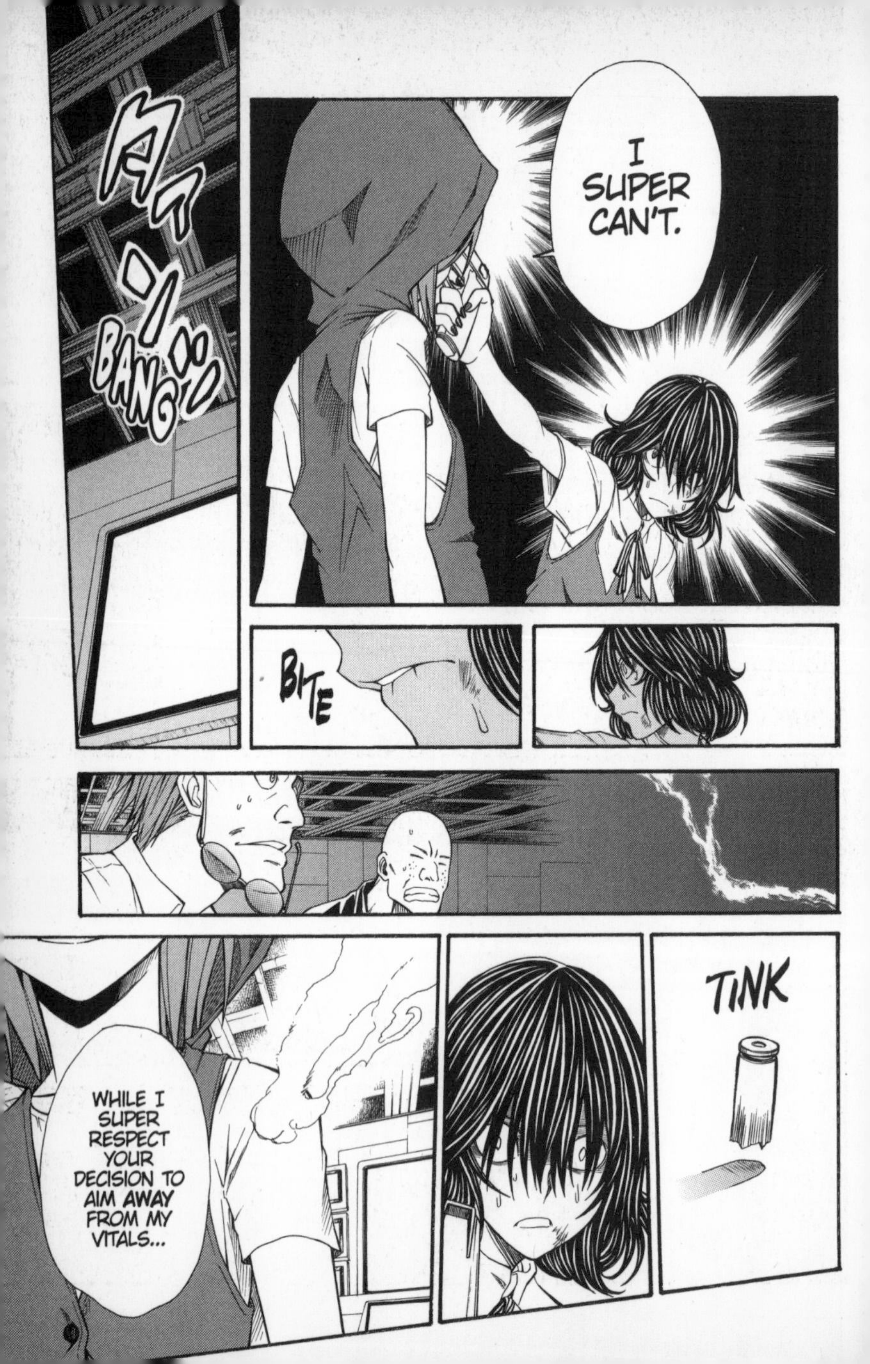
I SUPER CAN'T.
BITE
BANG!!
TINK
WHILE I SUPER RESPECT YOUR DECISION TO AIM AWAY FROM MY VITALS...

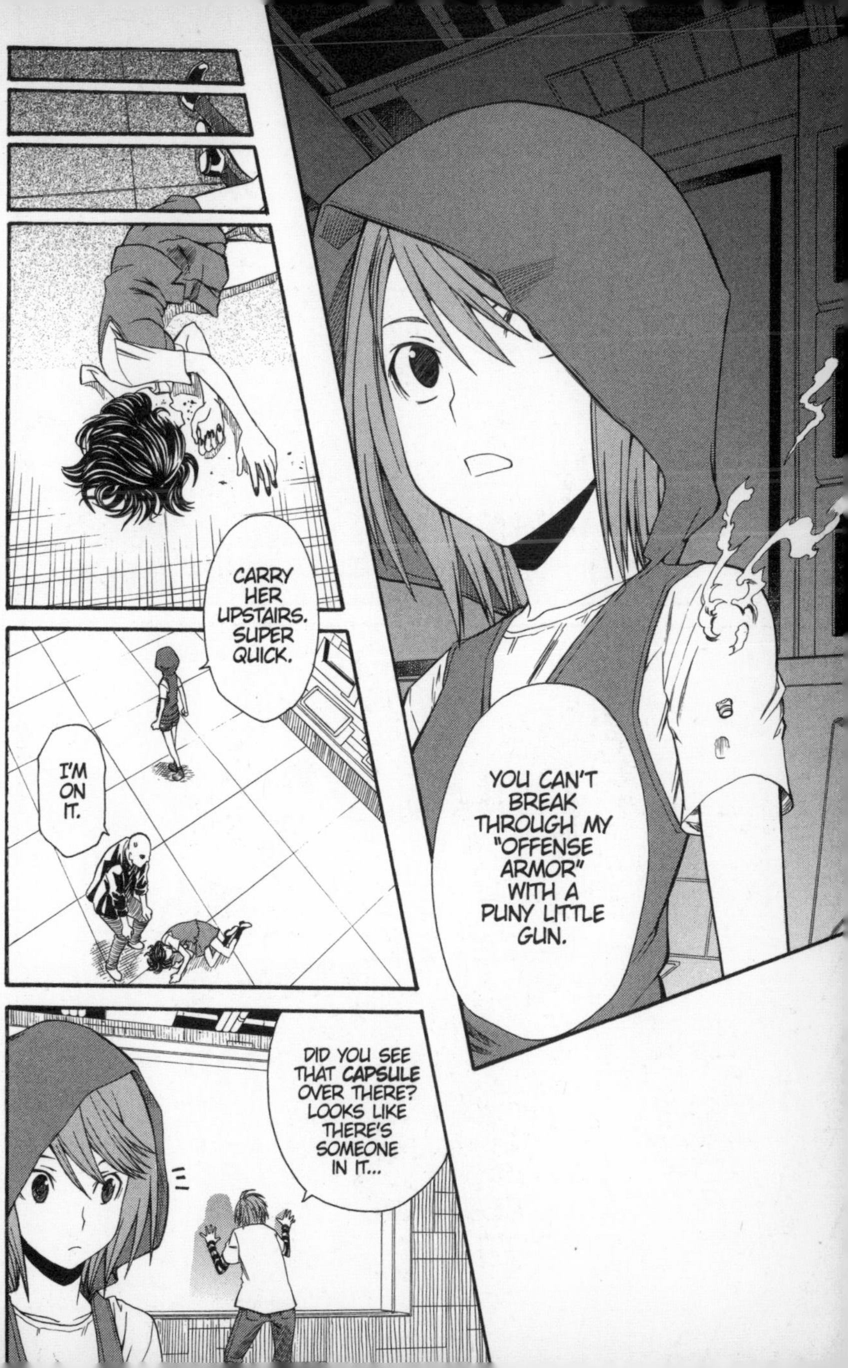
YOU CAN'T BREAK THROUGH MY "OFFENSE ARMOR" WITH A PUNY LITTLE GUN.
CARRY HER UPSTAIRS. SUPER QUICK.
I'M ON IT.
DID YOU SEE THAT CAPSULE OVER THERE? LOOKS LIKE THERE'S SOMEONE IN IT...

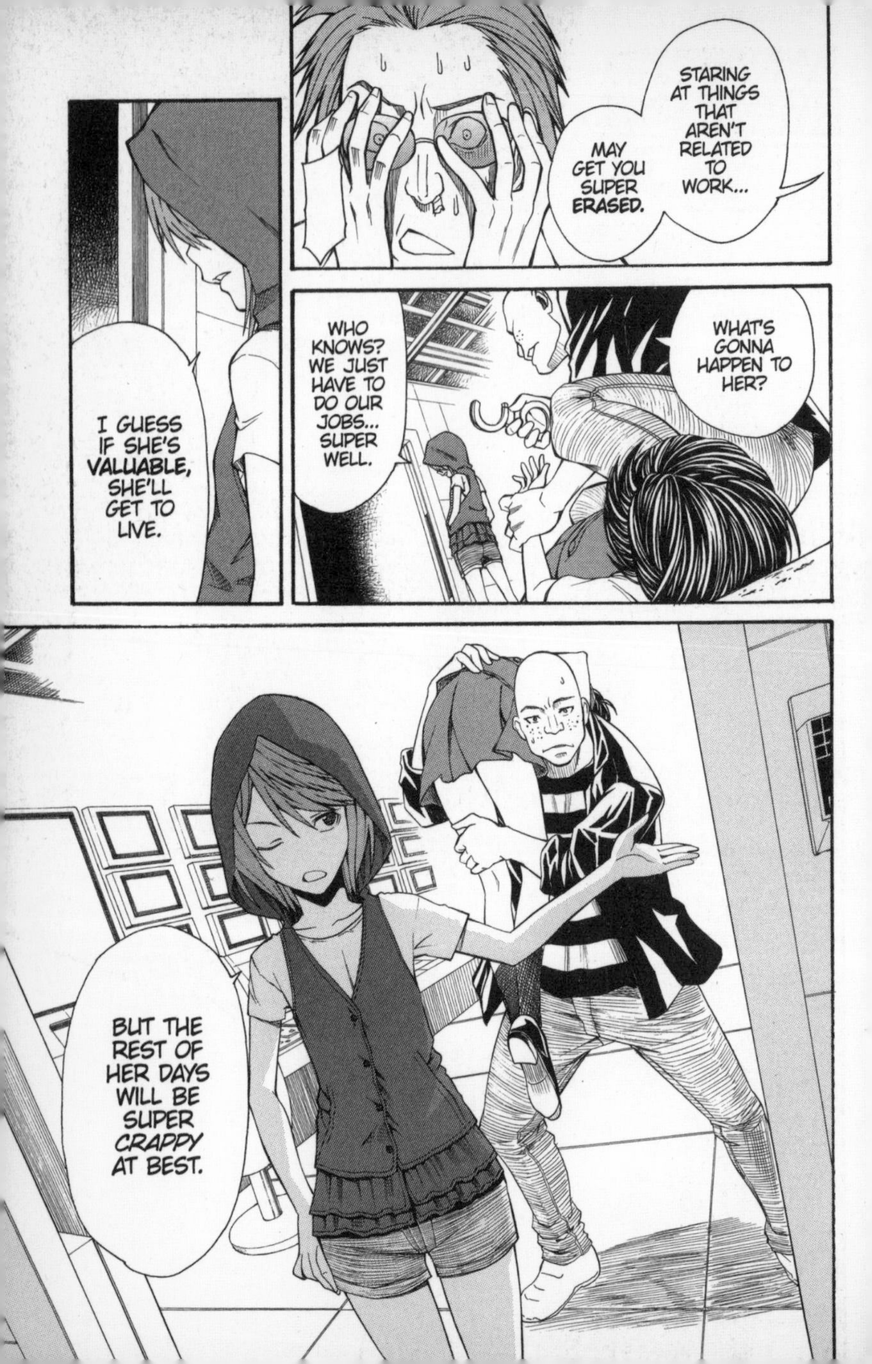
STARING AT THINGS THAT AREN'T RELATED TO WORK...
MAY GET YOU SUPER ERASED.
WHAT'S GONNA HAPPEN TO HER?
WHO KNOWS? WE JUST HAVE TO DO OUR JOBS... SUPER WELL.
I GUESS IF SHE'S VALUABLE, SHE'LL GET TO LIVE.
BUT THE REST OF HER DAYS WILL BE SUPER CRAPPY AT BEST.

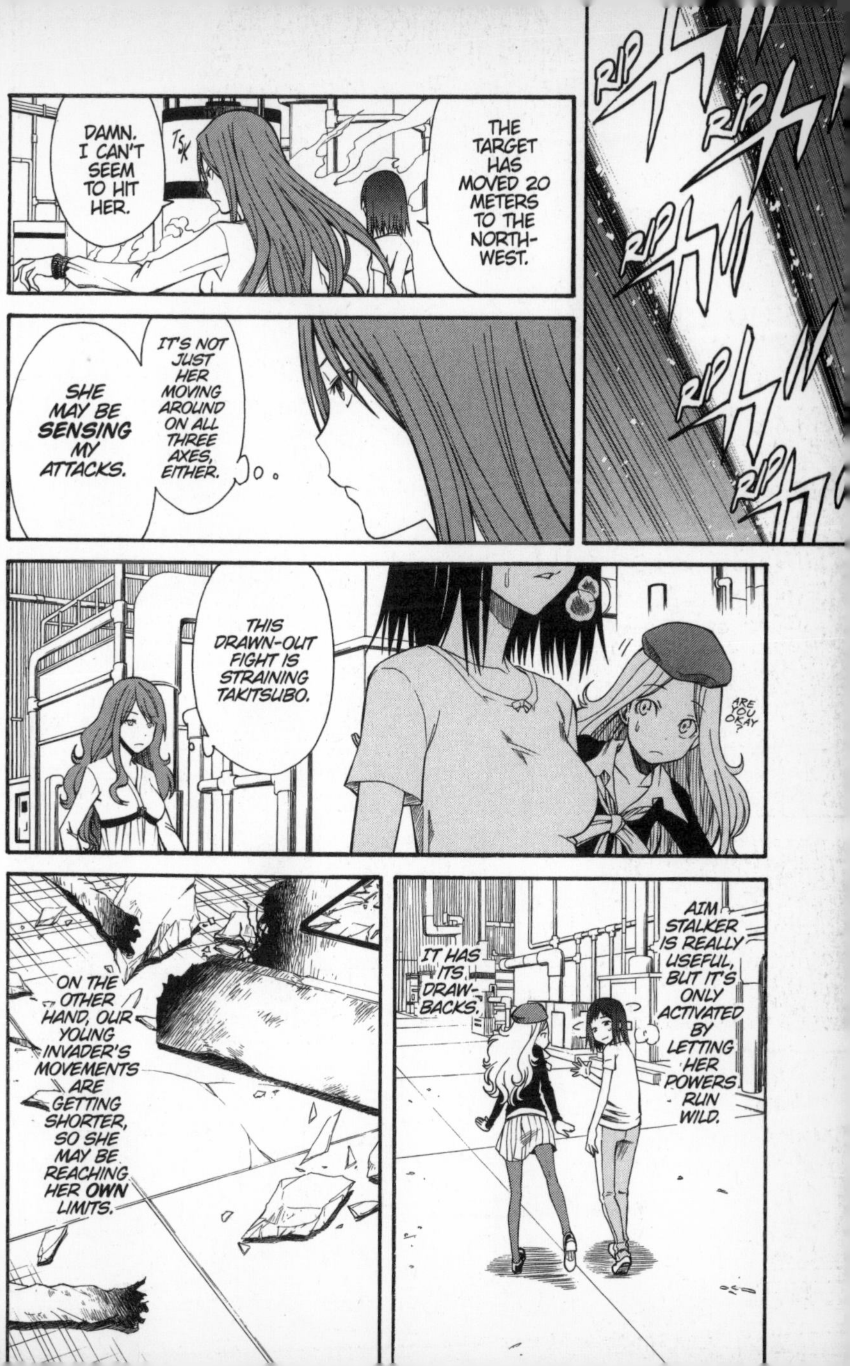
RIP RIP RIP RIP RIP
THE TARGET HAS MOVED 20 METERS TO THE NORTH-WEST.
TSK
DAMN. I CAN'T SEEM TO HIT HER.
IT'S NOT JUST HER MOVING AROUND ON ALL THREE AXES, EITHER.
SHE MAY BE SENSING MY ATTACKS.
ARE YOU OKAY?
THIS DRAWN-OUT FIGHT IS STRAINING TAKITSUBO.
AIM STALKER IS REALLY USEFUL, BUT IT'S ONLY ACTIVATED BY LETTING HER POWERS RUN WILD.
IT HAS ITS DRAW-BACKS.
ON THE OTHER HAND, OUR YOUNG INVADER'S MOVEMENTS ARE GETTING SHORTER, SO SHE MAY BE REACHING HER OWN LIMITS.

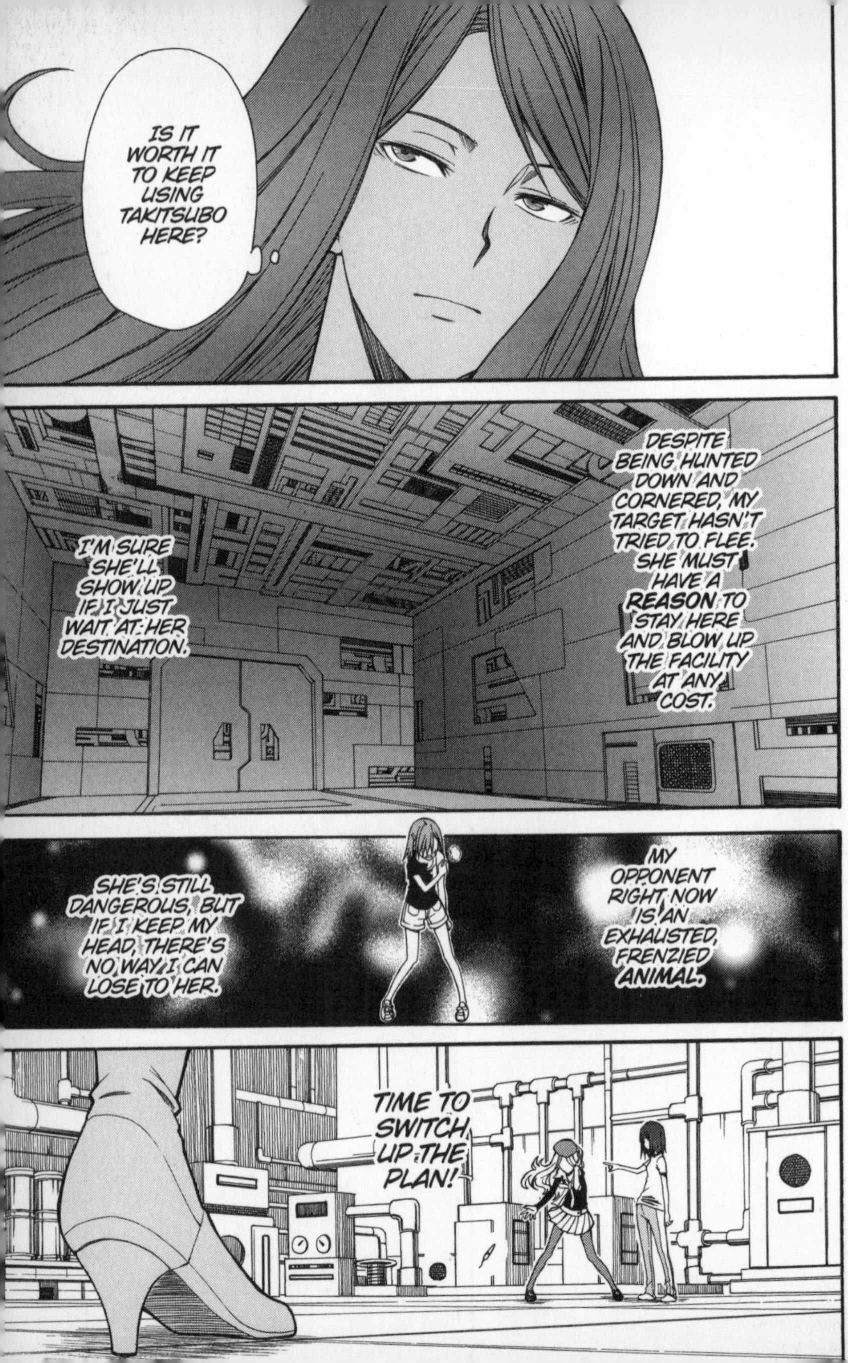
IS IT WORTH IT TO KEEP USING TAKITSUBO HERE?
DESPITE BEING HUNTED DOWN AND CORNERED, MY TARGET HASN'T TRIED TO FLEE. SHE MUST HAVE A **REASON** TO STAY HERE AND BLOW UP THE FACILITY AT ANY COST.
I'M SURE SHE'LL SHOW UP IF I JUST WAIT AT HER DESTINATION.
MY OPPONENT RIGHT NOW IS AN EXHAUSTED, FRENZIED **ANIMAL.**
SHE'S STILL DANGEROUS, BUT IF I KEEP MY HEAD, THERE'S NO WAY I CAN LOSE TO HER.
TIME TO SWITCH UP THE PLAN!

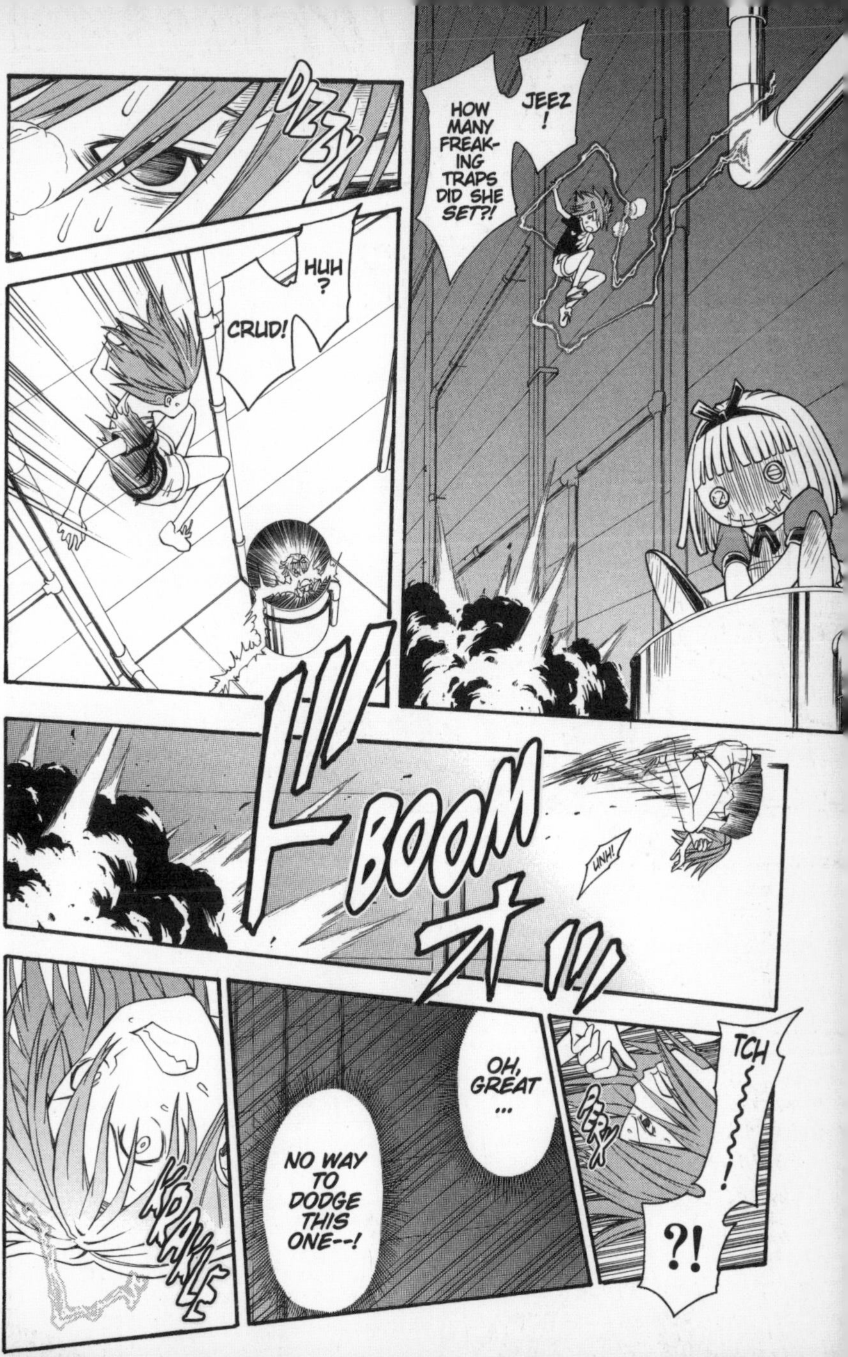
JEEZ!
HOW MANY FREAKING TRAPS DID SHE SET?!
DIZZY
HUH?
CRUD!
UNH!
BOOM
TCH~~~!
PERK
?!
OH, GREAT...
NO WAY TO DODGE THIS ONE--!
KRAKLE

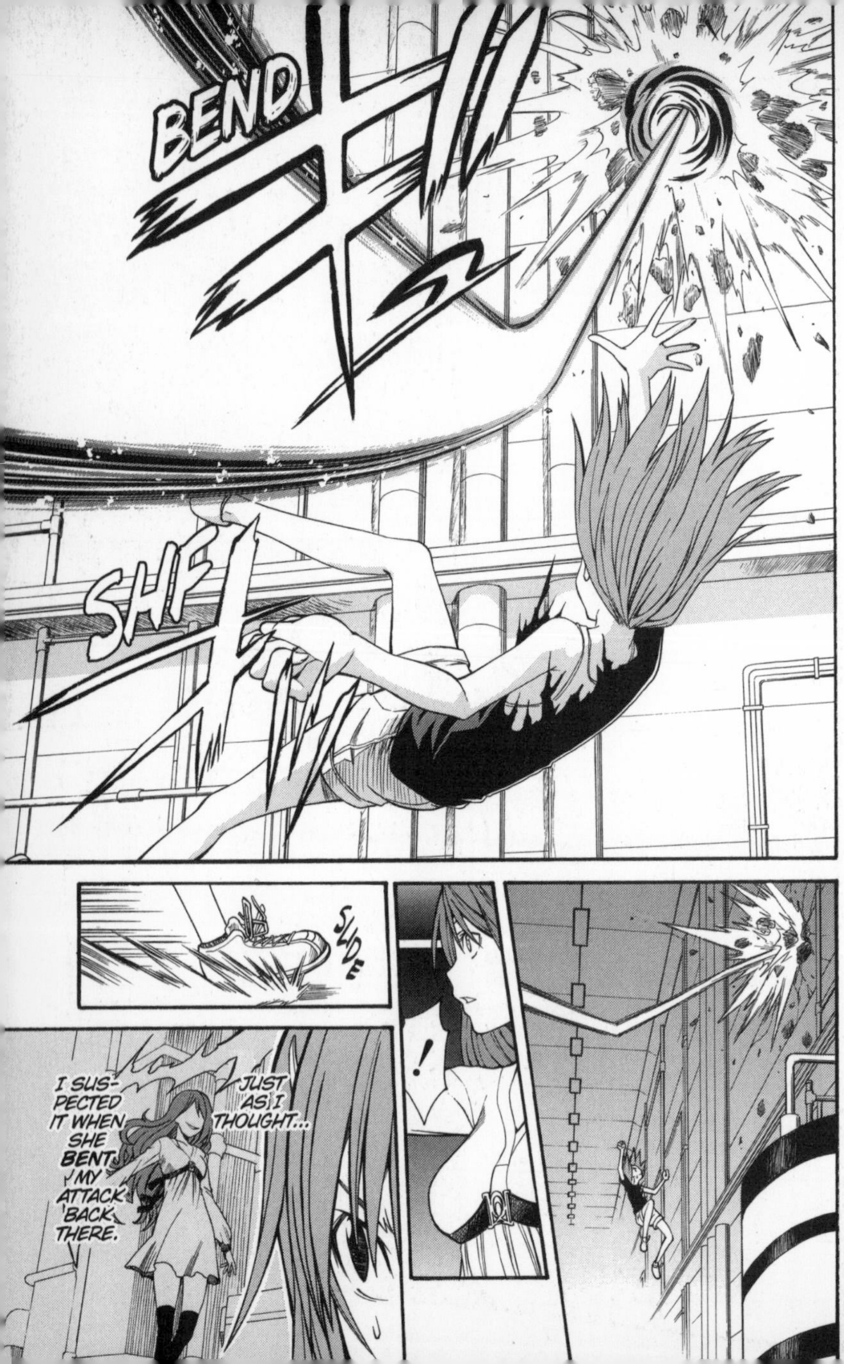
BEND
SHF
!
SLIDE
JUST AS I THOUGHT...
I SUSPECTED IT WHEN SHE BENT MY ATTACK BACK THERE.

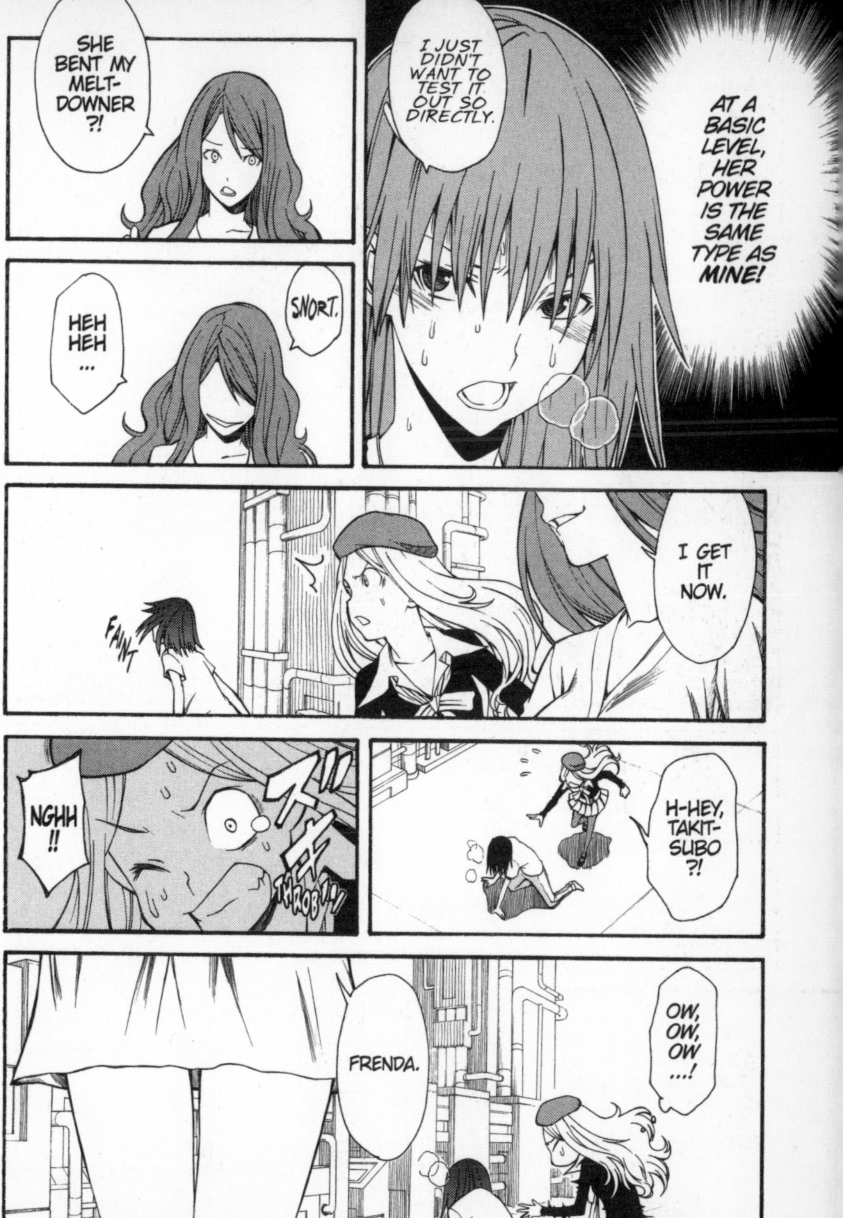
I JUST DIDN'T WANT TO TEST IT OUT SO DIRECTLY.
AT A BASIC LEVEL, HER POWER IS THE SAME TYPE AS MINE!
SHE BENT MY MELT-DOWNER ?!
SNORT.
HEH HEH ...
I GET IT NOW.
FAINT
H-HEY, TAKIT-SUBO ?!
NGHH !!
THROB
OW, OW, OW ...!
FRENDA.

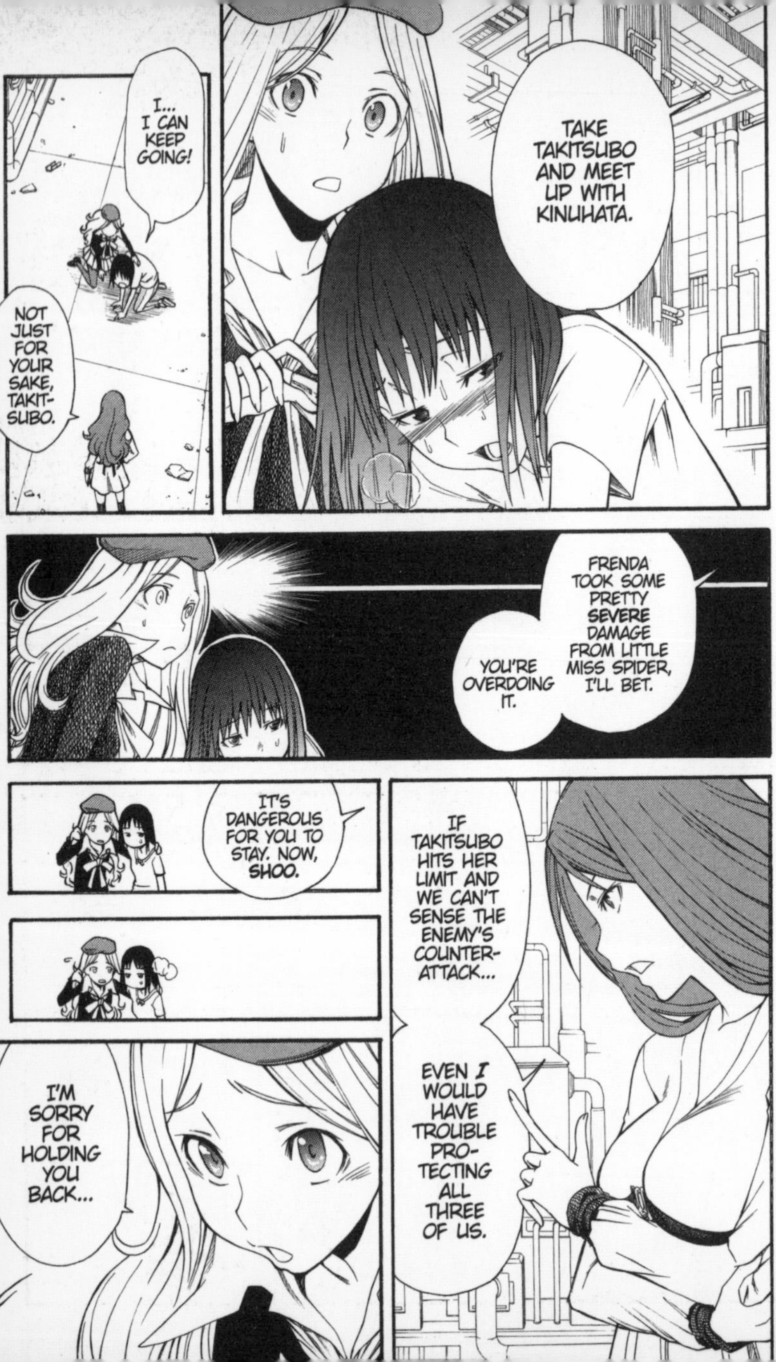
TAKE TAKITSUBO AND MEET UP WITH KINUHATA.
I... I CAN KEEP GOING!
NOT JUST FOR YOUR SAKE, TAKIT-SUBO.
FRENDA TOOK SOME PRETTY SEVERE DAMAGE FROM LITTLE MISS SPIDER, I'LL BET.
YOU'RE OVERDOING IT.
IF TAKITSUBO HITS HER LIMIT AND WE CAN'T SENSE THE ENEMY'S COUNTER-ATTACK...
EVEN *I* WOULD HAVE TROUBLE PRO-TECTING ALL THREE OF US.
IT'S DANGEROUS FOR YOU TO STAY. NOW, SHOO.
I'M SORRY FOR HOLDING YOU BACK...

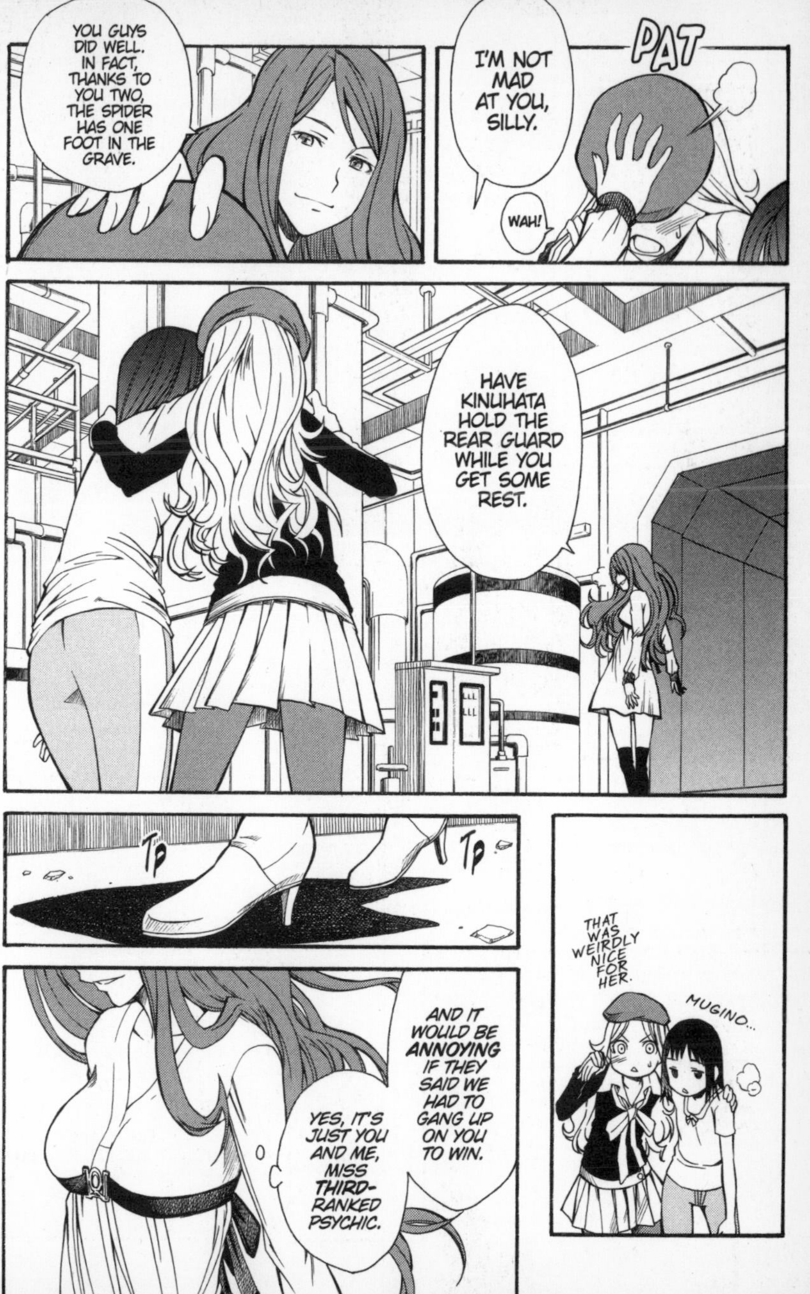
PAT
I'M NOT MAD AT YOU, SILLY.
WAH!
YOU GUYS DID WELL. IN FACT, THANKS TO YOU TWO, THE SPIDER HAS ONE FOOT IN THE GRAVE.
HAVE KINUHATA HOLD THE REAR GUARD WHILE YOU GET SOME REST.
THAT WAS WEIRDLY NICE FOR HER.
MUGINO...
Tp
Tp
AND IT WOULD BE **ANNOYING** IF THEY SAID WE HAD TO GANG UP ON YOU TO WIN.
YES, IT'S JUST YOU AND ME, MISS **THIRD-RANKED PSYCHIC.**

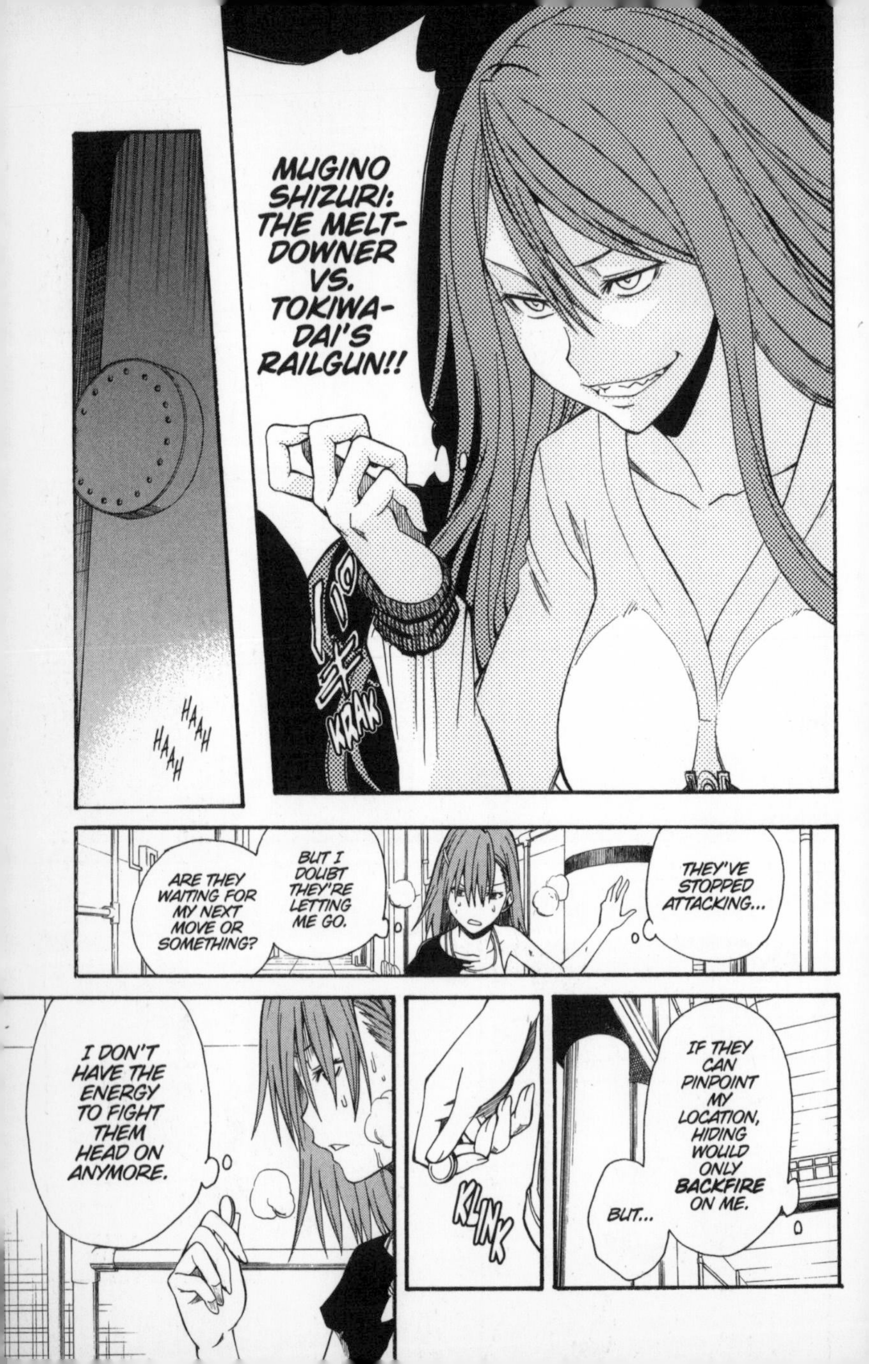

MUGINO SHIZURI: THE MELT-DOWNER VS. TOKIWA-DAI'S RAILGUN!!
KRAK
HAAH HAAH
THEY'VE STOPPED ATTACKING...
BUT I DOUBT THEY'RE LETTING ME GO.
ARE THEY WAITING FOR MY NEXT MOVE OR SOMETHING?
IF THEY CAN PINPOINT MY LOCATION, HIDING WOULD ONLY BACKFIRE ON ME.
BUT...
KLINK
I DON'T HAVE THE ENERGY TO FIGHT THEM HEAD ON ANYMORE.

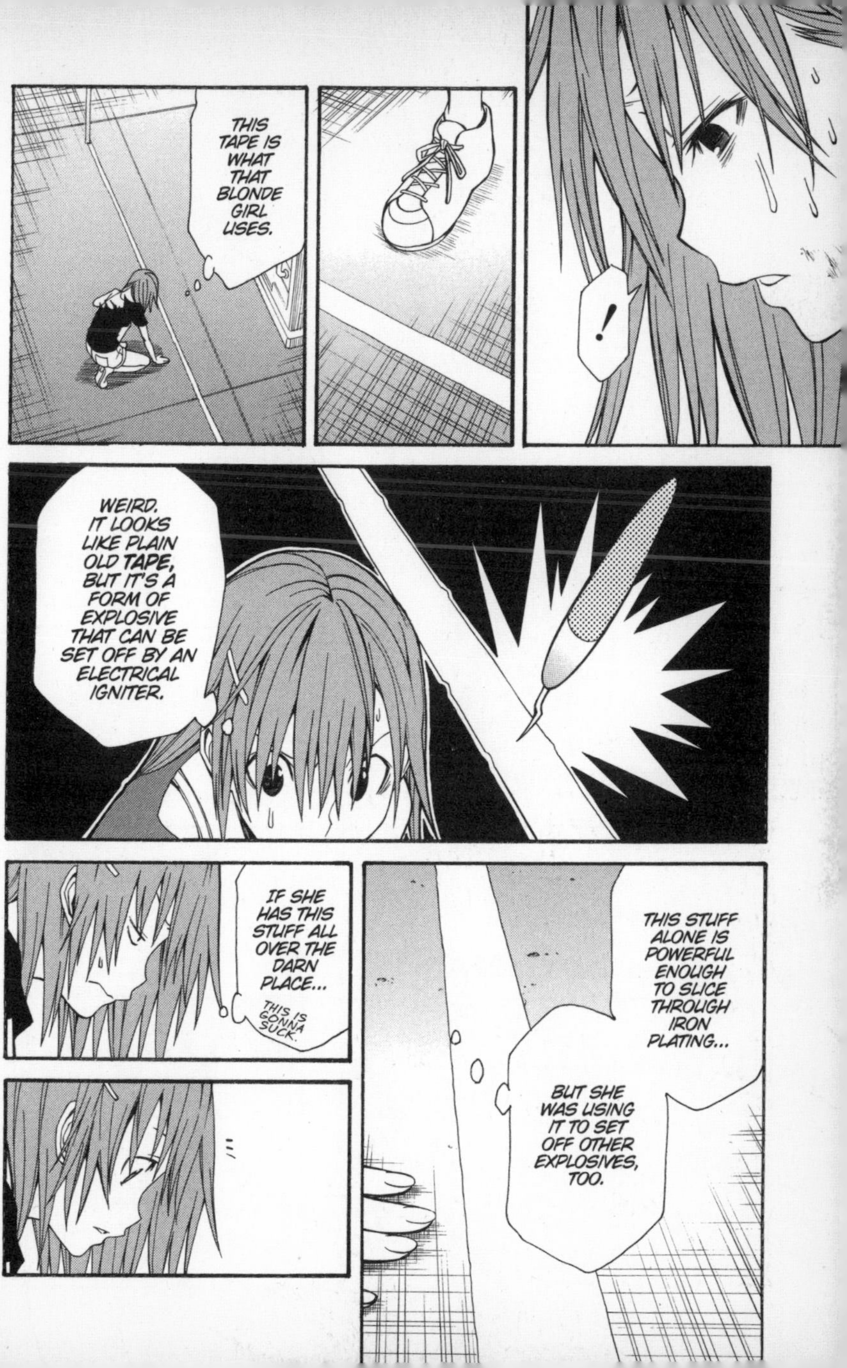
!
THIS TAPE IS WHAT THAT BLONDE GIRL USES.
WEIRD. IT LOOKS LIKE PLAIN OLD TAPE, BUT IT'S A FORM OF EXPLOSIVE THAT CAN BE SET OFF BY AN ELECTRICAL IGNITER.
THIS STUFF ALONE IS POWERFUL ENOUGH TO SLICE THROUGH IRON PLATING...
BUT SHE WAS USING IT TO SET OFF OTHER EXPLOSIVES, TOO.
IF SHE HAS THIS STUFF ALL OVER THE DARN PLACE...
THIS IS GONNA SUCK.
...

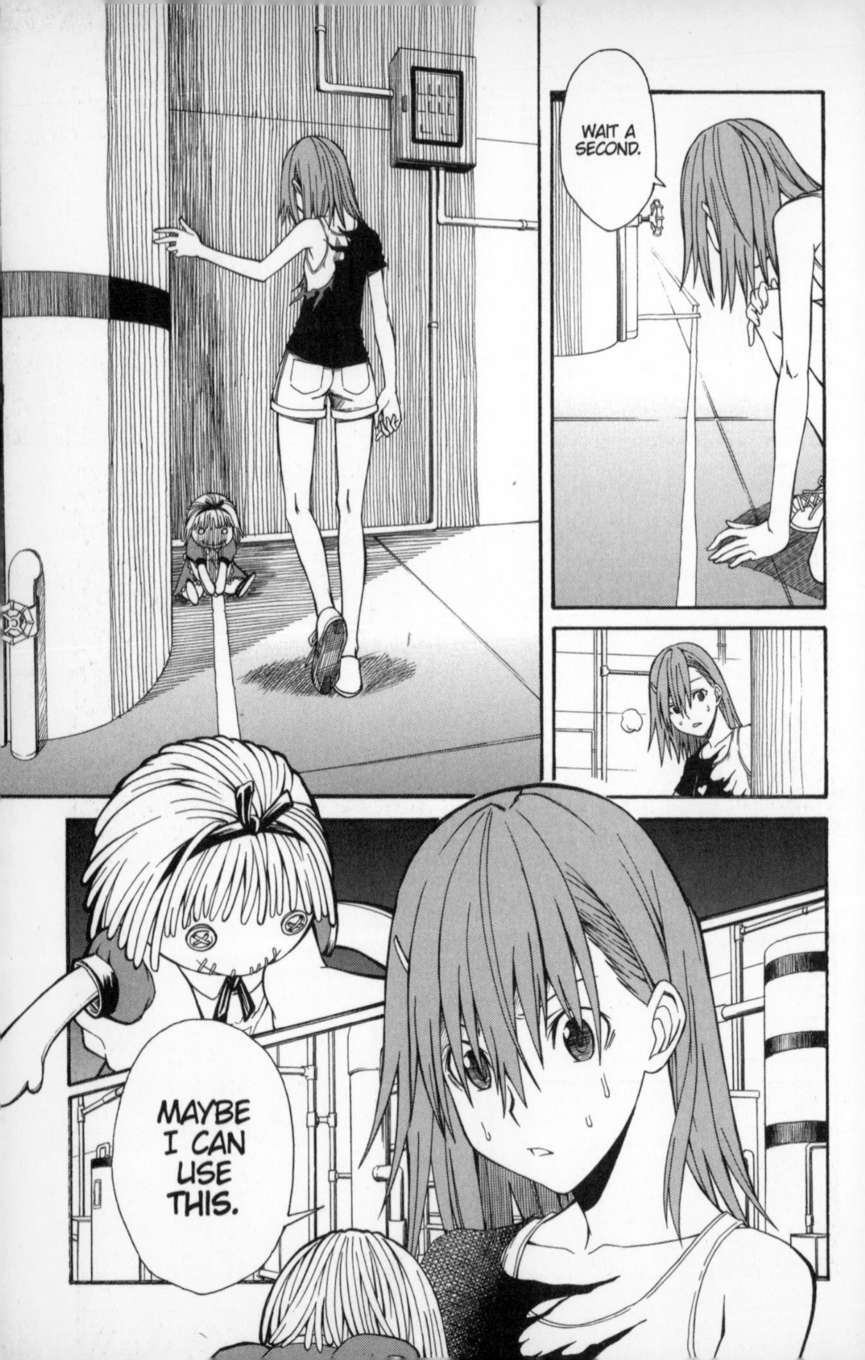
WAIT A SECOND.
MAYBE I CAN USE THIS.

A Certain Saiai's Offense Armor

BANG
TINK
WHAT?!
FSSSHHHHHH
WHILE I SUPER RESPECT YOUR DECISION TO AIM AWAY FROM MY VITALS...
YOU CAN'T BREAK THROUGH MY "OFFENSE ARMOR" WITH A PUNY LITTLE GUN...
UGH
BUT IT STILL HURTS, THOUGH.

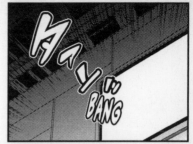

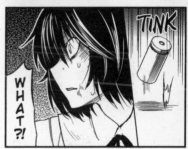

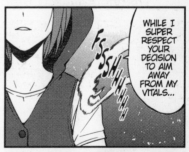

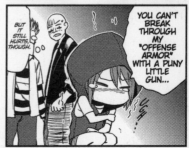

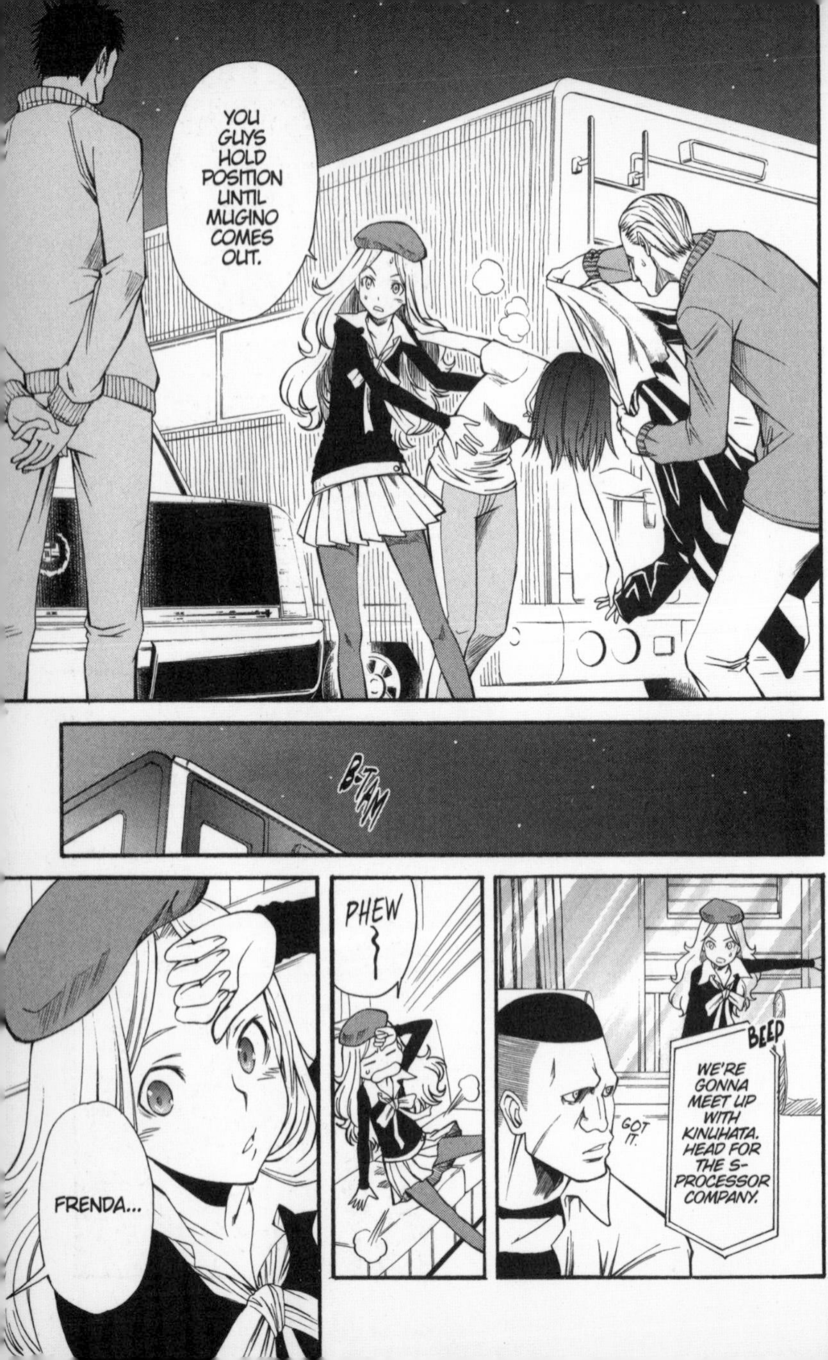
YOU GUYS HOLD POSITION UNTIL MUGINO COMES OUT.
B-TAM
BEEP
WE'RE GONNA MEET UP WITH KINUHATA. HEAD FOR THE S-PROCESSOR COMPANY.
GOT IT.
PHEW
FRENDA...

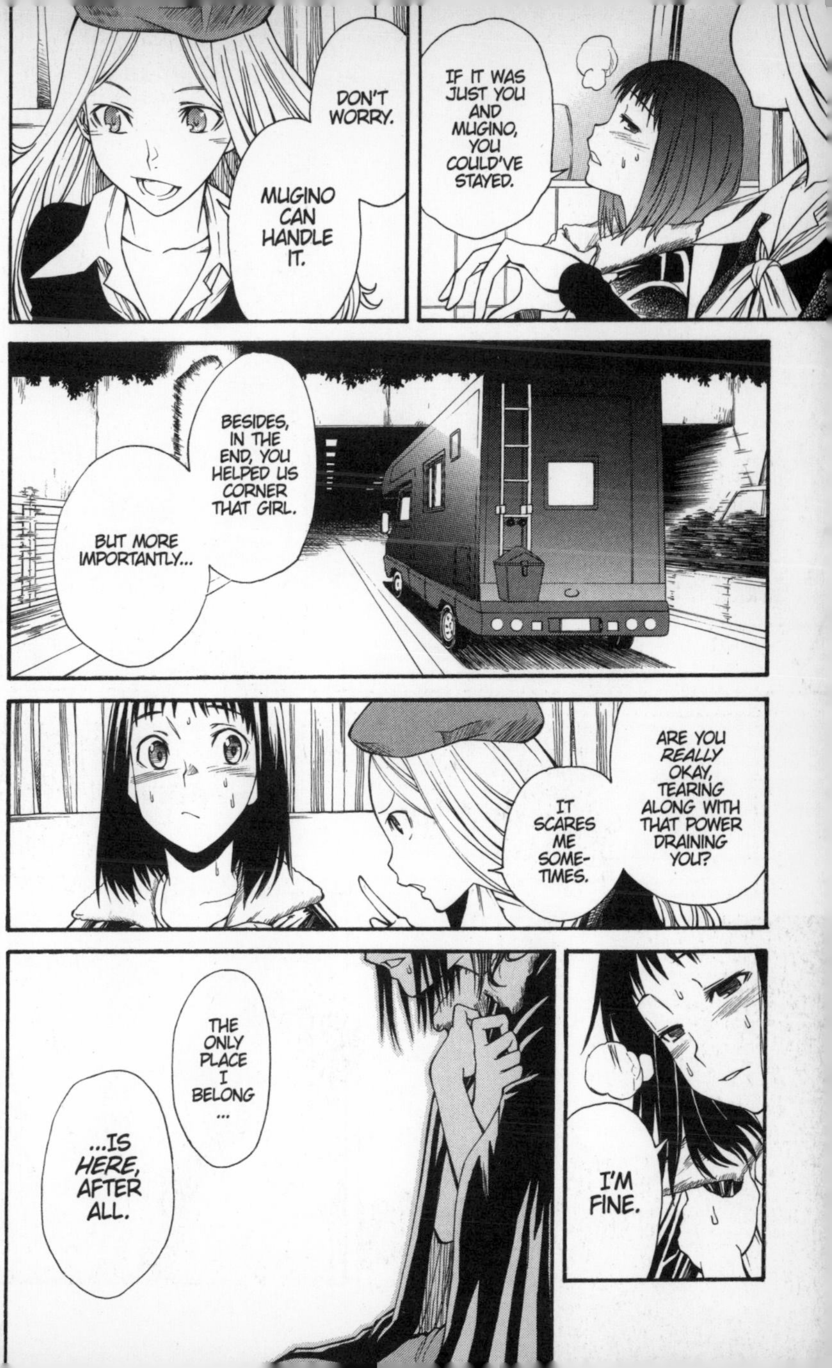
IF IT WAS JUST YOU AND MUGINO, YOU COULD'VE STAYED.
DON'T WORRY.
MUGINO CAN HANDLE IT.
BESIDES, IN THE END, YOU HELPED US CORNER THAT GIRL.
BUT MORE IMPORTANTLY...
ARE YOU *REALLY* OKAY, TEARING ALONG WITH THAT POWER DRAINING YOU?
IT SCARES ME SOME-TIMES.
I'M FINE.
THE ONLY PLACE I BELONG...
...IS *HERE*, AFTER ALL.

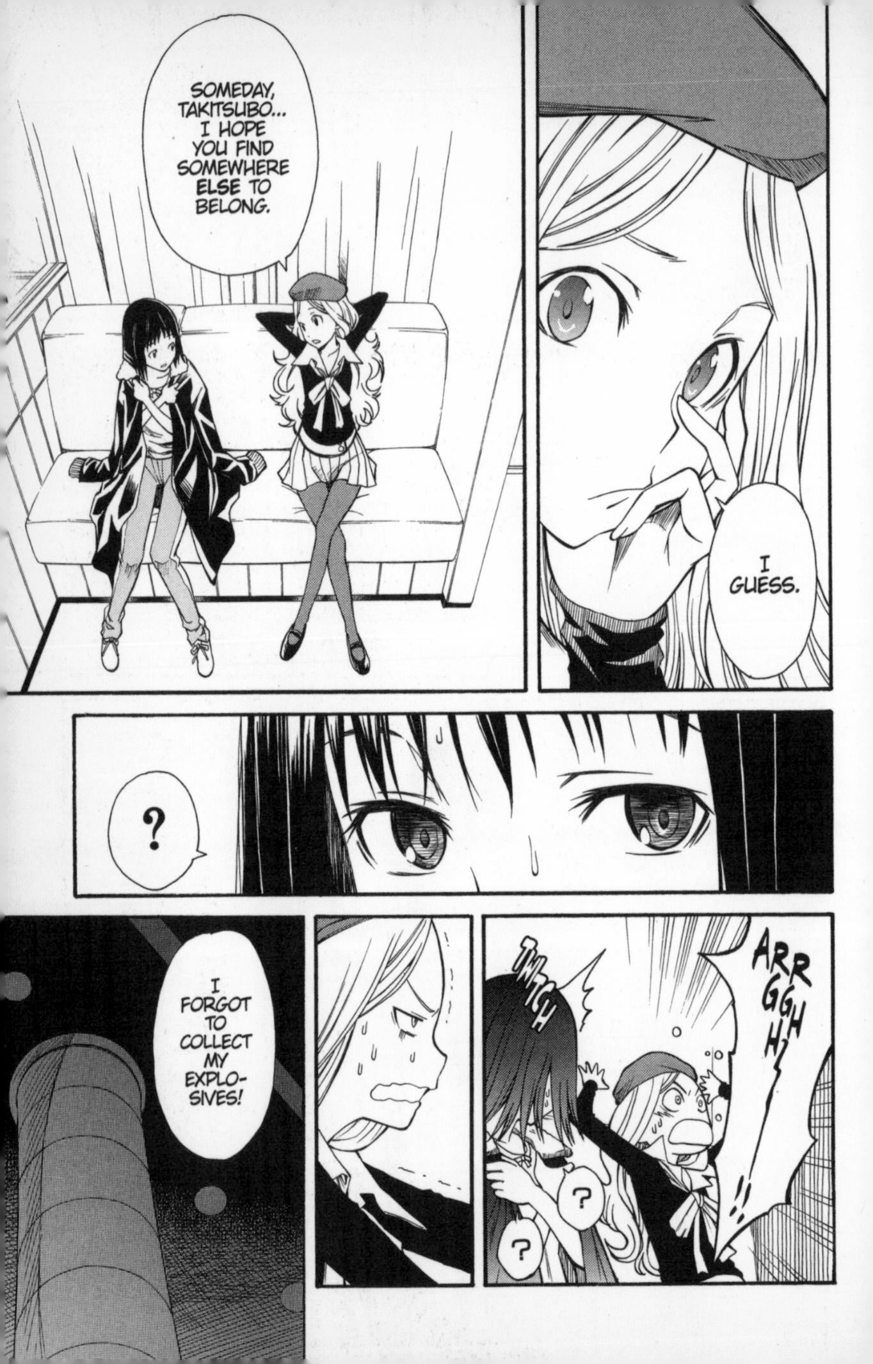
I GUESS.
SOMEDAY, TAKITSUBO... I HOPE YOU FIND SOMEWHERE ELSE TO BELONG.
?
ARRGGHH!
TWITCH
?
?
I FORGOT TO COLLECT MY EXPLOSIVES!

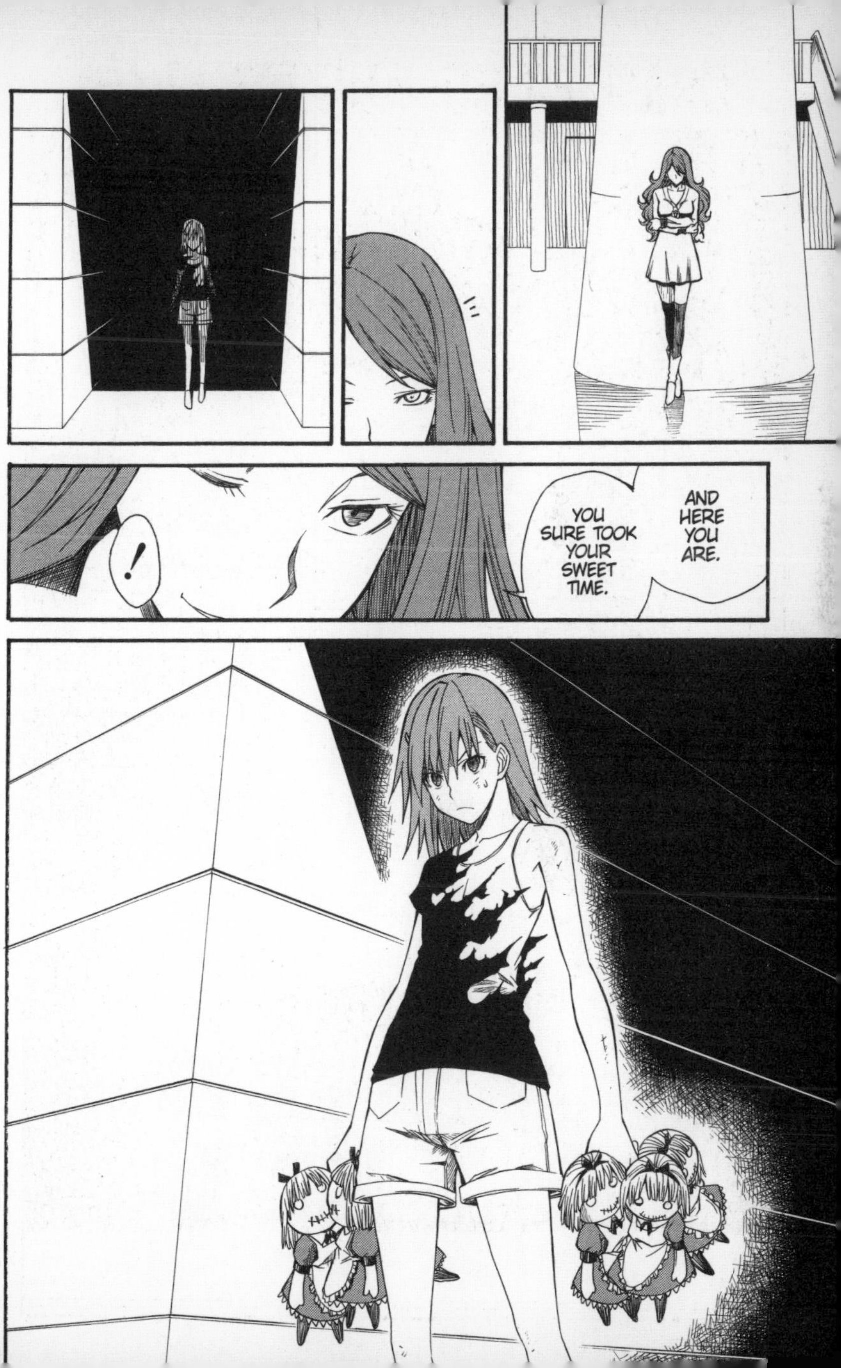
AND HERE YOU ARE.
YOU SURE TOOK YOUR SWEET TIME.
!

CHAPTER 30: AUGUST 19 (5)

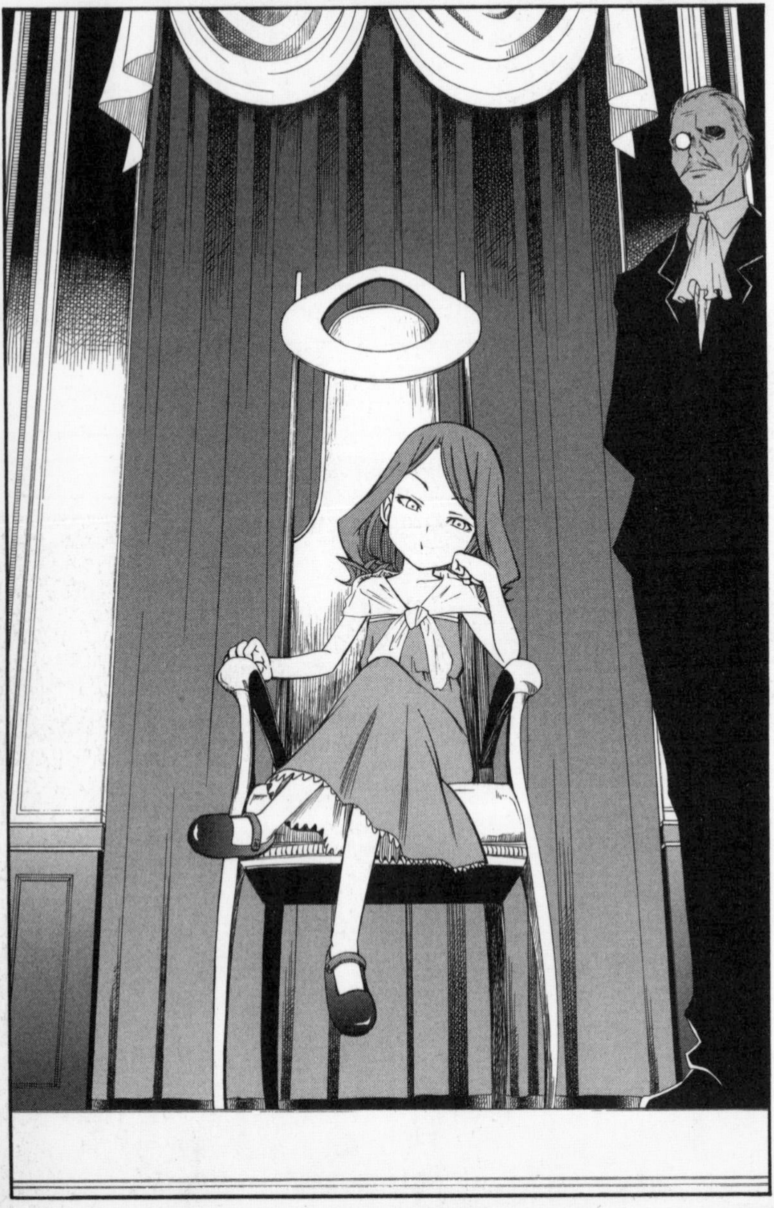

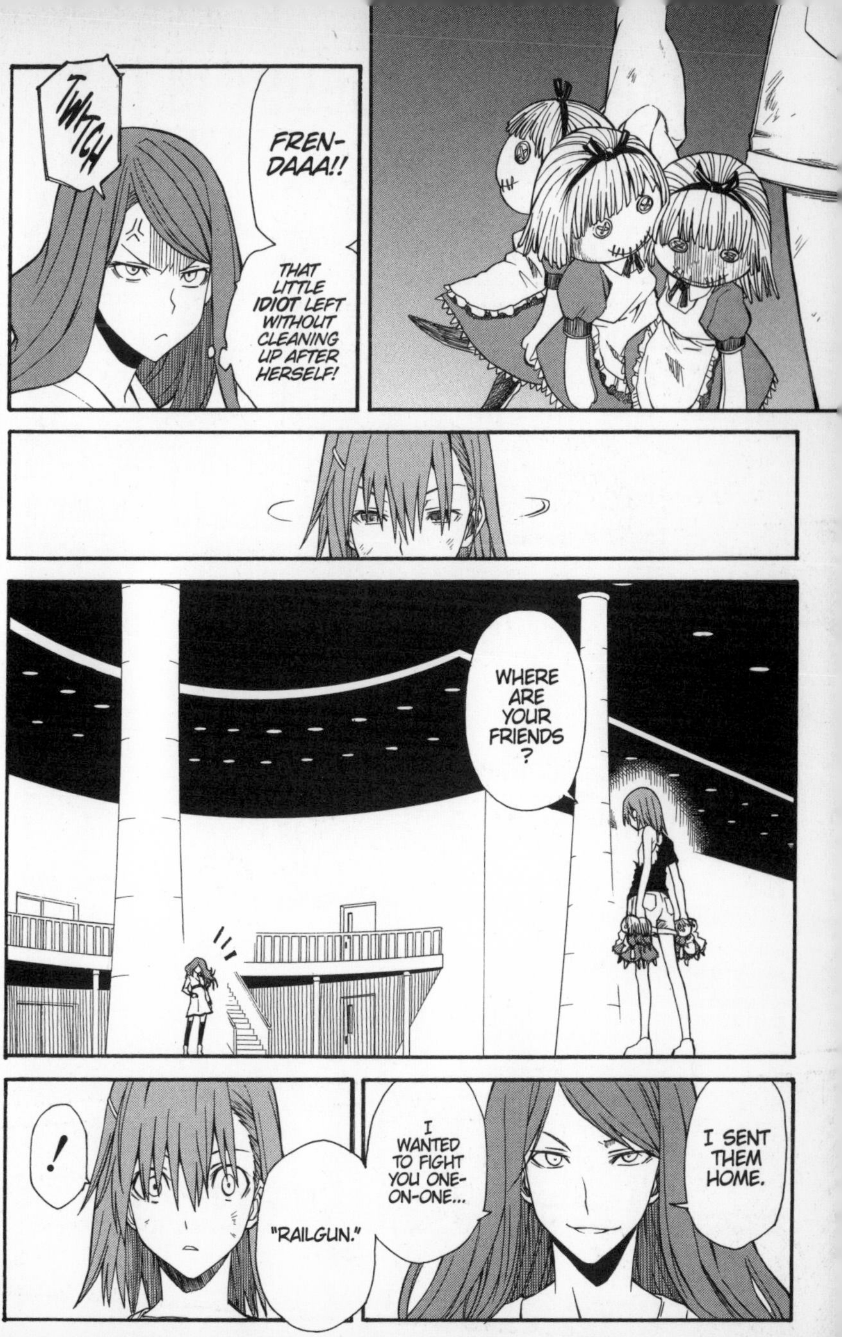
FREN-DAAA!!
TWITCH
THAT LITTLE IDIOT LEFT WITHOUT CLEANING UP AFTER HERSELF!
WHERE ARE YOUR FRIENDS?
I SENT THEM HOME.
I WANTED TO FIGHT YOU ONE-ON-ONE...
"RAILGUN."
!

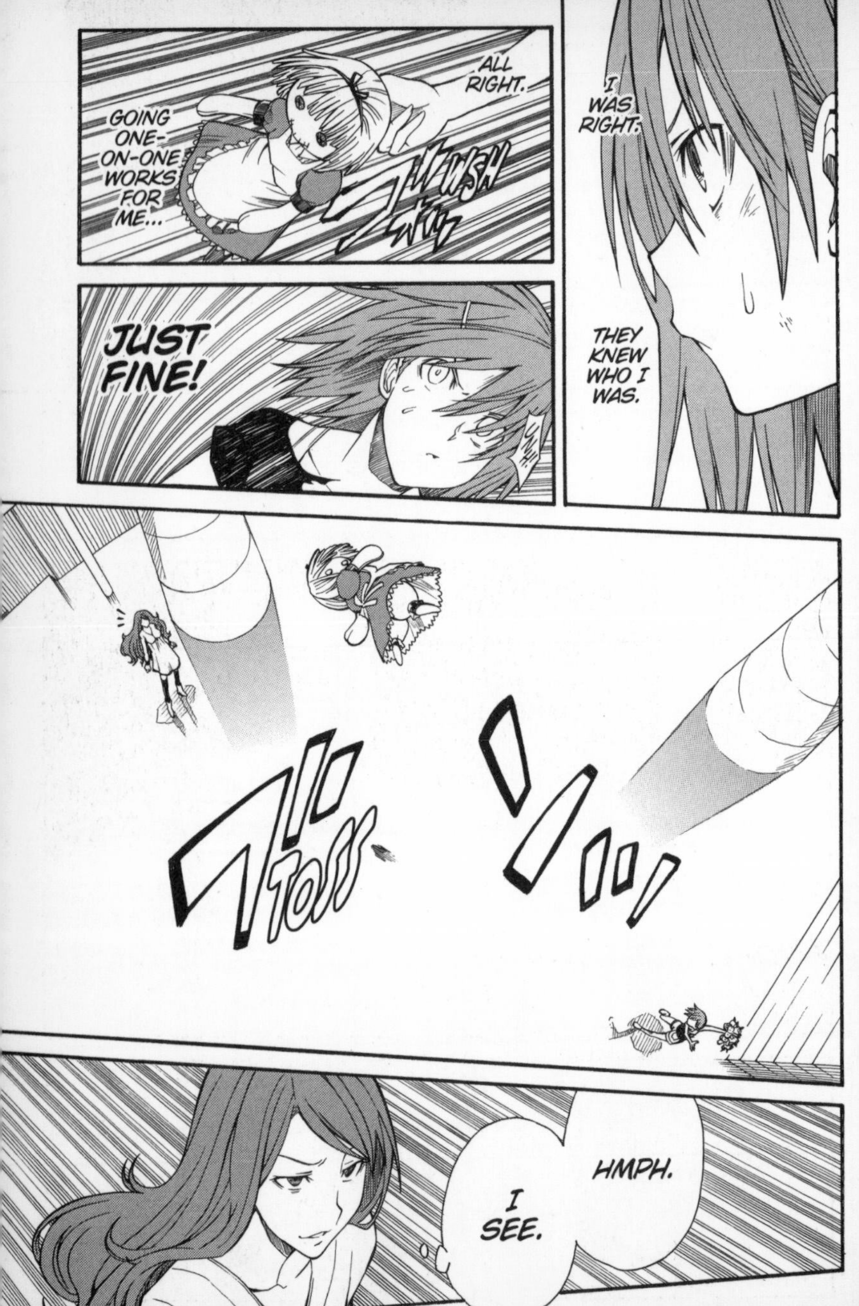
I WAS RIGHT.
THEY KNEW WHO I WAS.
ALL RIGHT.
GOING ONE-ON-ONE WORKS FOR ME...
WHSH
JUST FINE!
TOSS
HMPH.
I SEE.

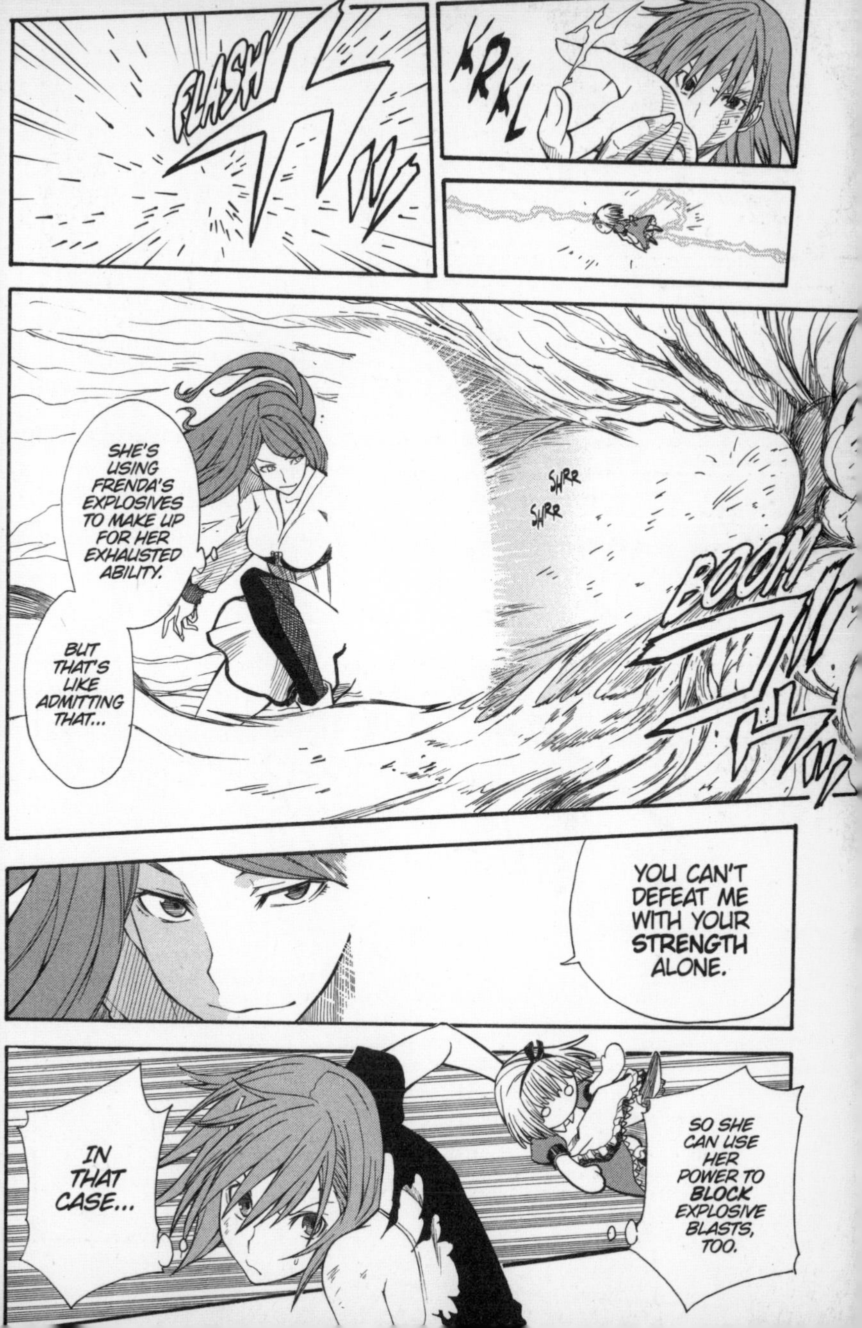
KRKL
FLASH
BOOM
SHRR
SHRR
SHE'S USING FRENDA'S EXPLOSIVES TO MAKE UP FOR HER EXHAUSTED ABILITY.
BUT THAT'S LIKE ADMITTING THAT...
YOU CAN'T DEFEAT ME WITH YOUR STRENGTH ALONE.
SO SHE CAN USE HER POWER TO BLOCK EXPLOSIVE BLASTS, TOO.
IN THAT CASE...

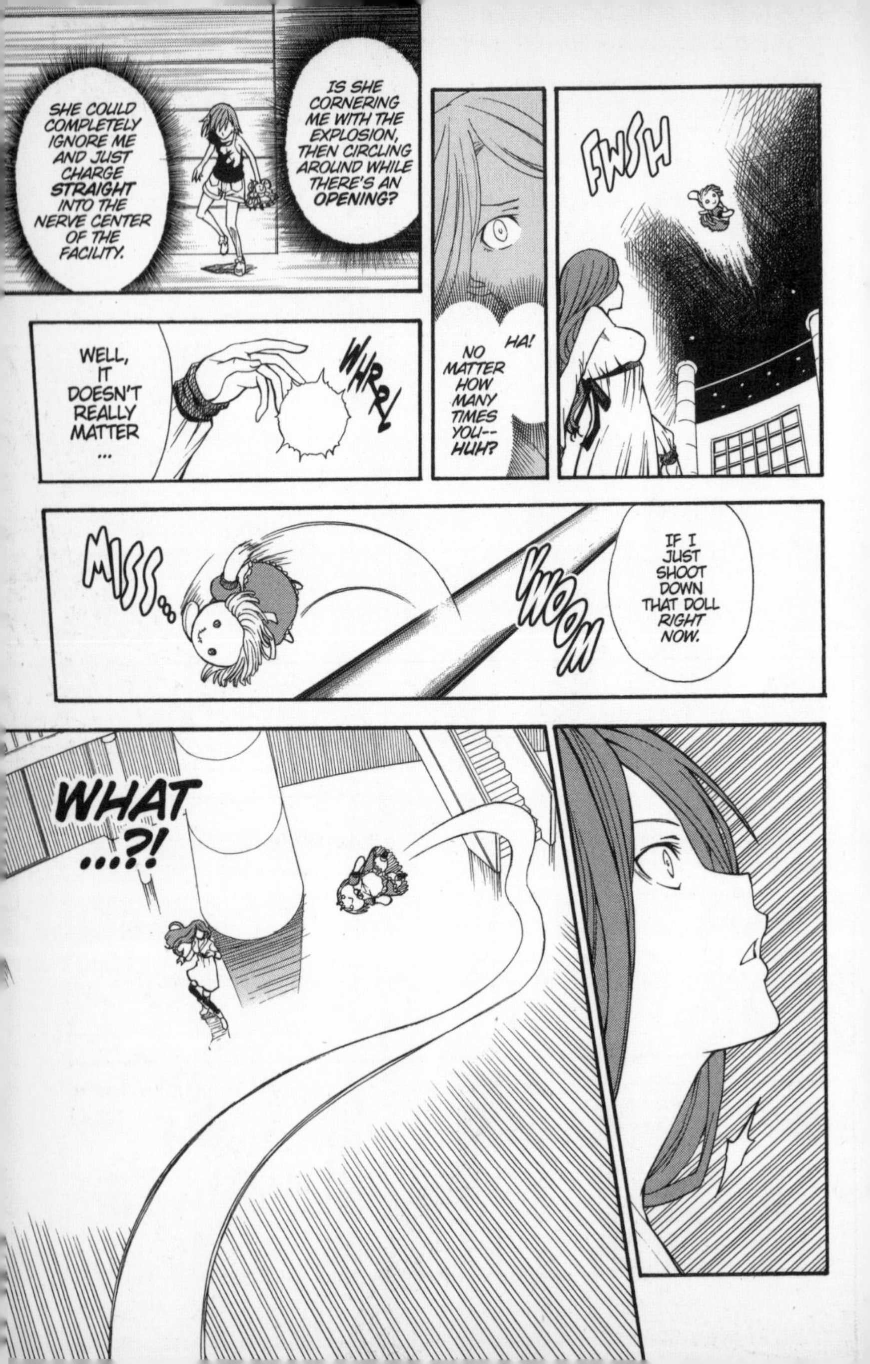
FWSH
HA!
NO MATTER HOW MANY TIMES YOU-- HUH?
IS SHE CORNERING ME WITH THE EXPLOSION, THEN CIRCLING AROUND WHILE THERE'S AN OPENING?
SHE COULD COMPLETELY IGNORE ME AND JUST CHARGE STRAIGHT INTO THE NERVE CENTER OF THE FACILITY.
WHRRL
WELL, IT DOESN'T REALLY MATTER ...
IF I JUST SHOOT DOWN THAT DOLL RIGHT NOW.
VWOOM
MISS...
WHAT ...?!

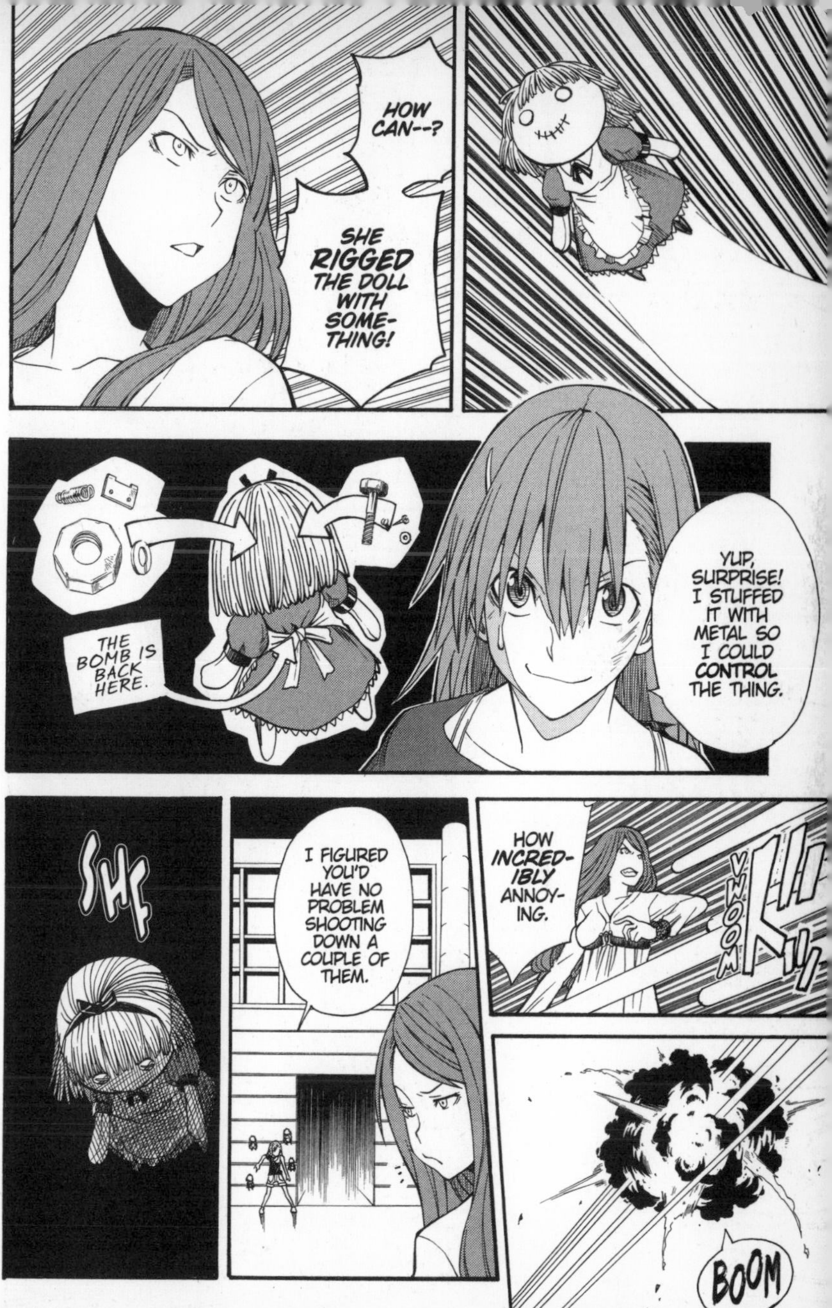
HOW CAN--?
SHE RIGGED THE DOLL WITH SOME-THING!
YUP, SURPRISE! I STUFFED IT WITH METAL SO I COULD CONTROL THE THING.
THE BOMB IS BACK HERE.
HOW INCRED-IBLY ANNOY-ING.
VWOOM
BOOM
I FIGURED YOU'D HAVE NO PROBLEM SHOOTING DOWN A COUPLE OF THEM.

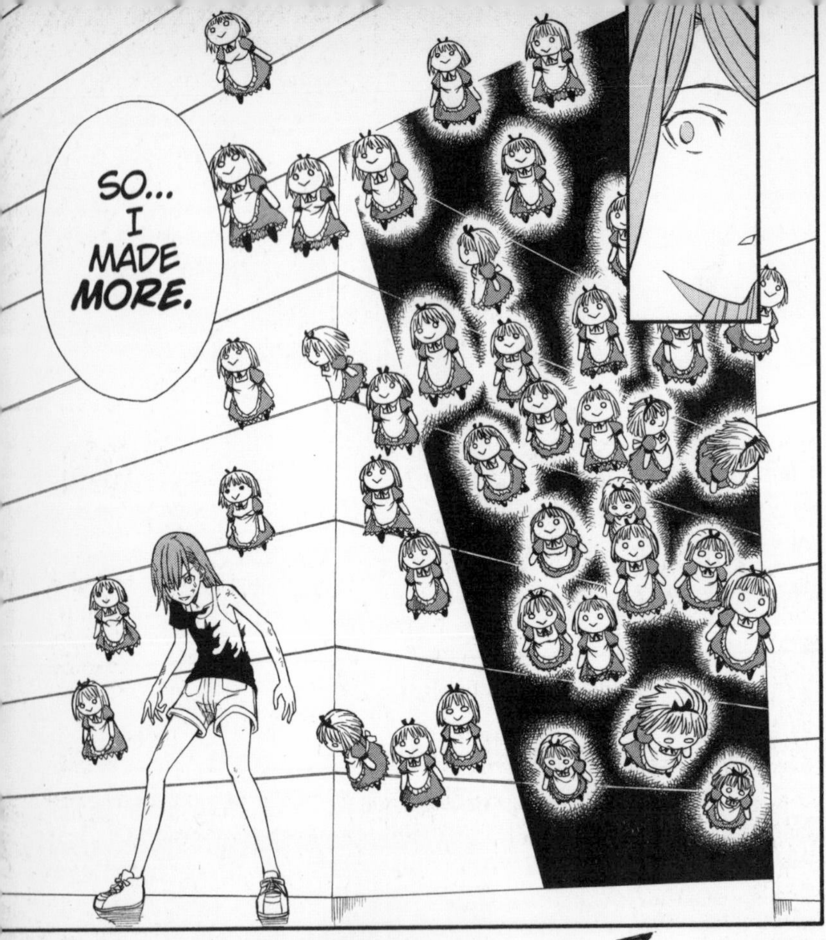
SO... I MADE MORE.
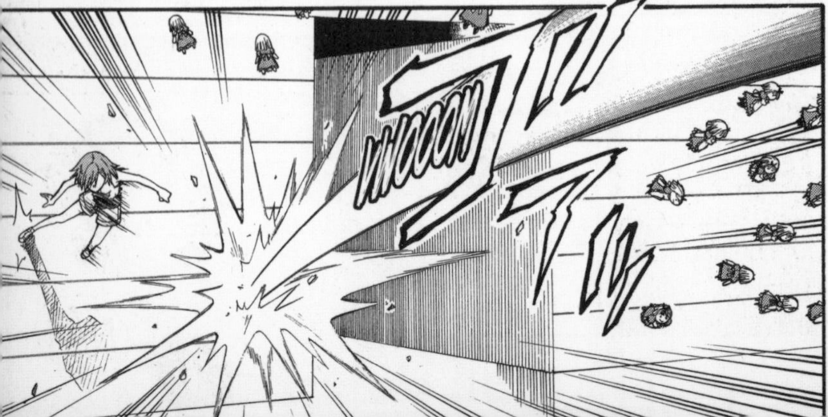
WHOOOM

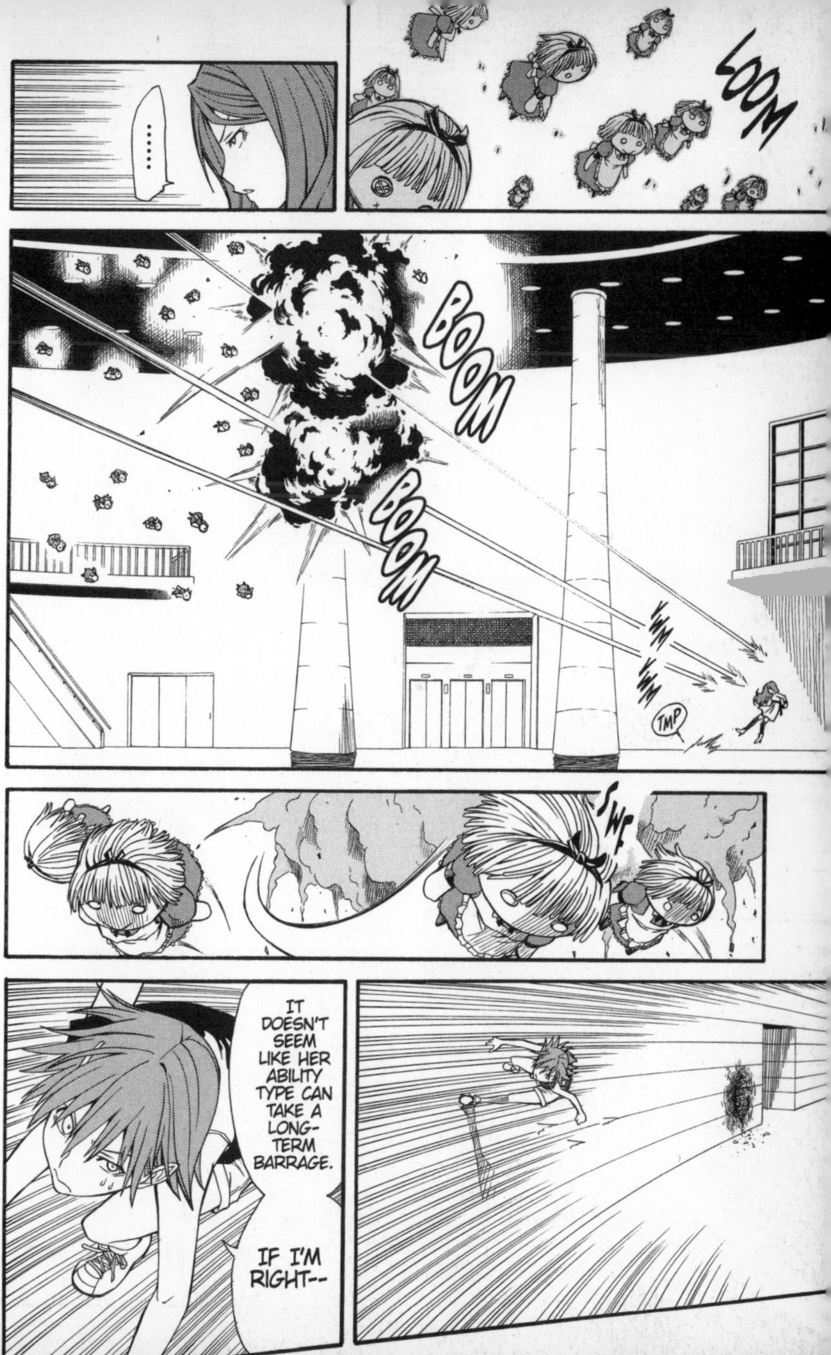
LOOM
......
BOOM
BOOM
VWM
VWM
TMP
SWF
IT DOESN'T SEEM LIKE HER ABILITY TYPE CAN TAKE A LONG-TERM BARRAGE.
IF I'M RIGHT--

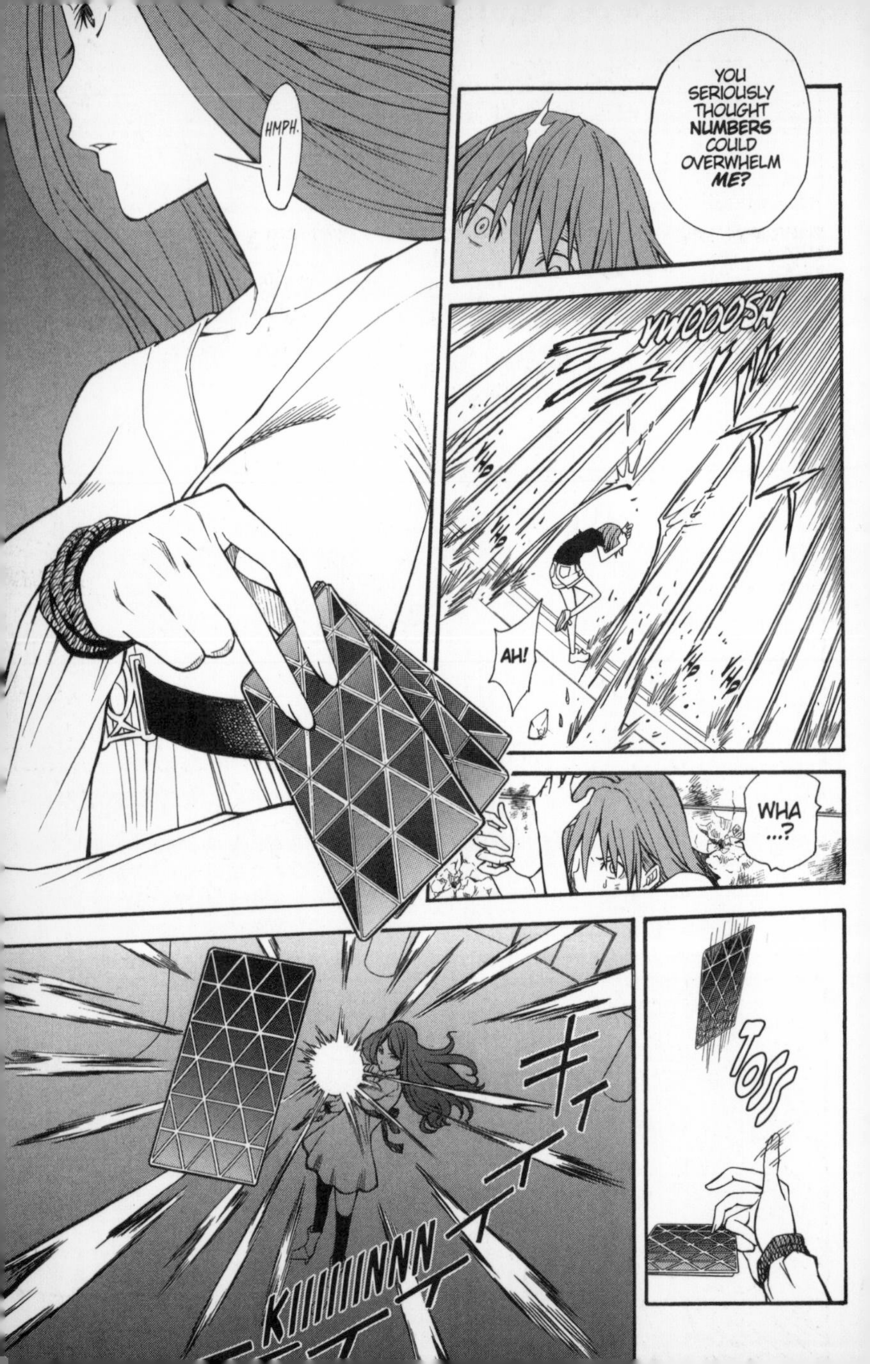
YOU SERIOUSLY THOUGHT NUMBERS COULD OVERWHELM ME?
VWOOOSH
AH!
WHA ...?
HMPH.
TOSS
KIIIIIINNN

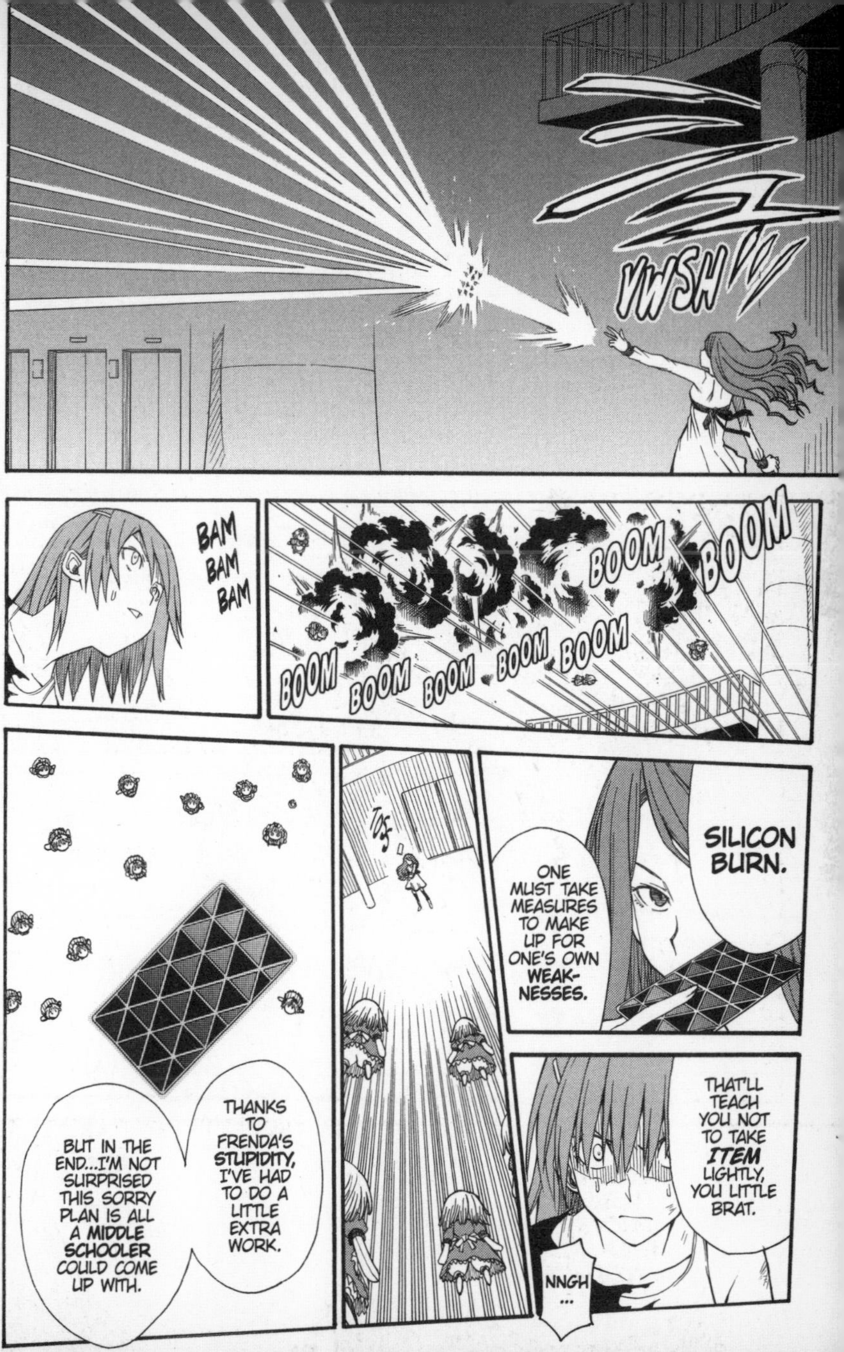
VWSH
BOOM BOOM BOOM BOOM BOOM BOOM BOOM
BAM BAM BAM
SILICON BURN.
ONE MUST TAKE MEASURES TO MAKE UP FOR ONE'S OWN WEAK-NESSES.
THAT'LL TEACH YOU NOT TO TAKE ITEM LIGHTLY, YOU LITTLE BRAT.
NNGH ...
TOF
THANKS TO FRENDA'S STUPIDITY, I'VE HAD TO DO A LITTLE EXTRA WORK.
BUT IN THE END...I'M NOT SURPRISED THIS SORRY PLAN IS ALL A MIDDLE SCHOOLER COULD COME UP WITH.

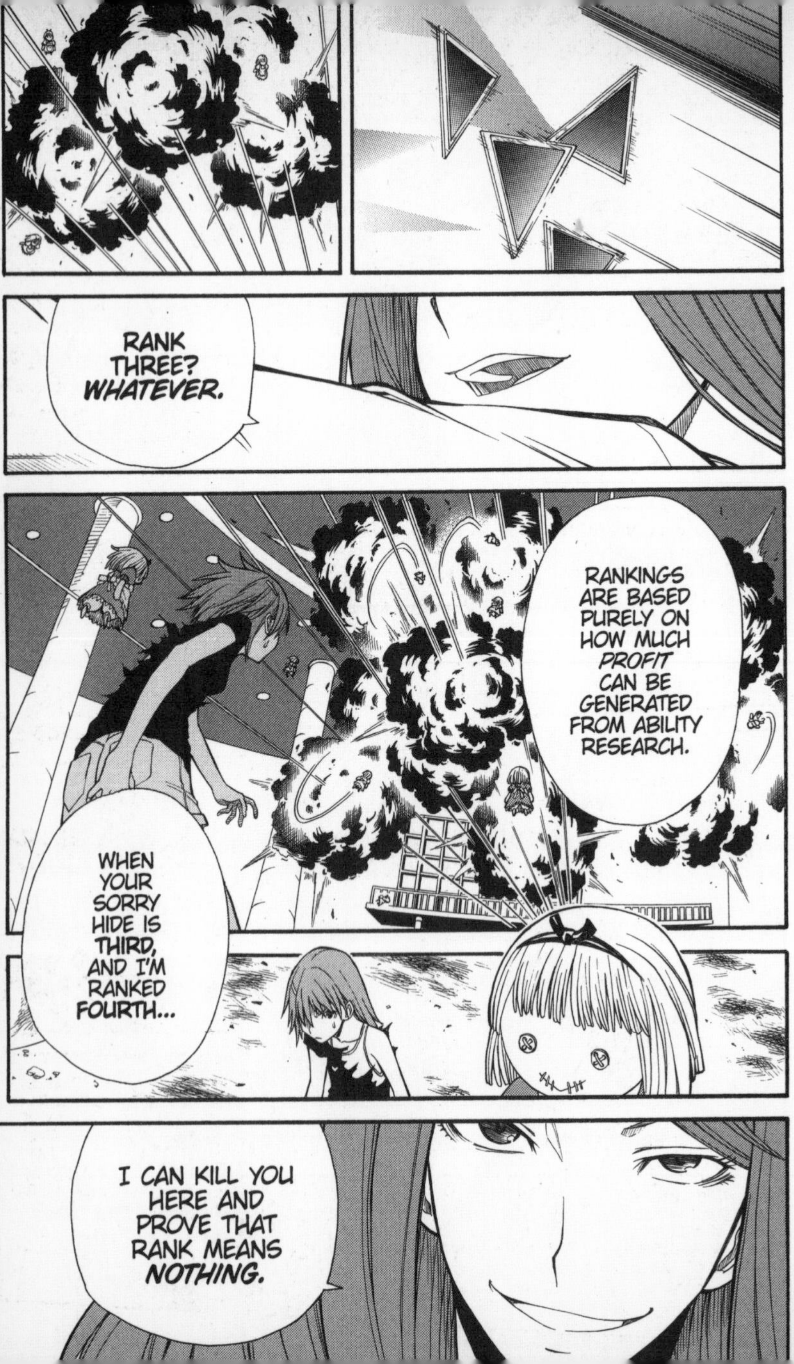
RANK THREE? WHATEVER.
RANKINGS ARE BASED PURELY ON HOW MUCH PROFIT CAN BE GENERATED FROM ABILITY RESEARCH.
WHEN YOUR SORRY HIDE IS THIRD, AND I'M RANKED FOURTH...
I CAN KILL YOU HERE AND PROVE THAT RANK MEANS NOTHING.

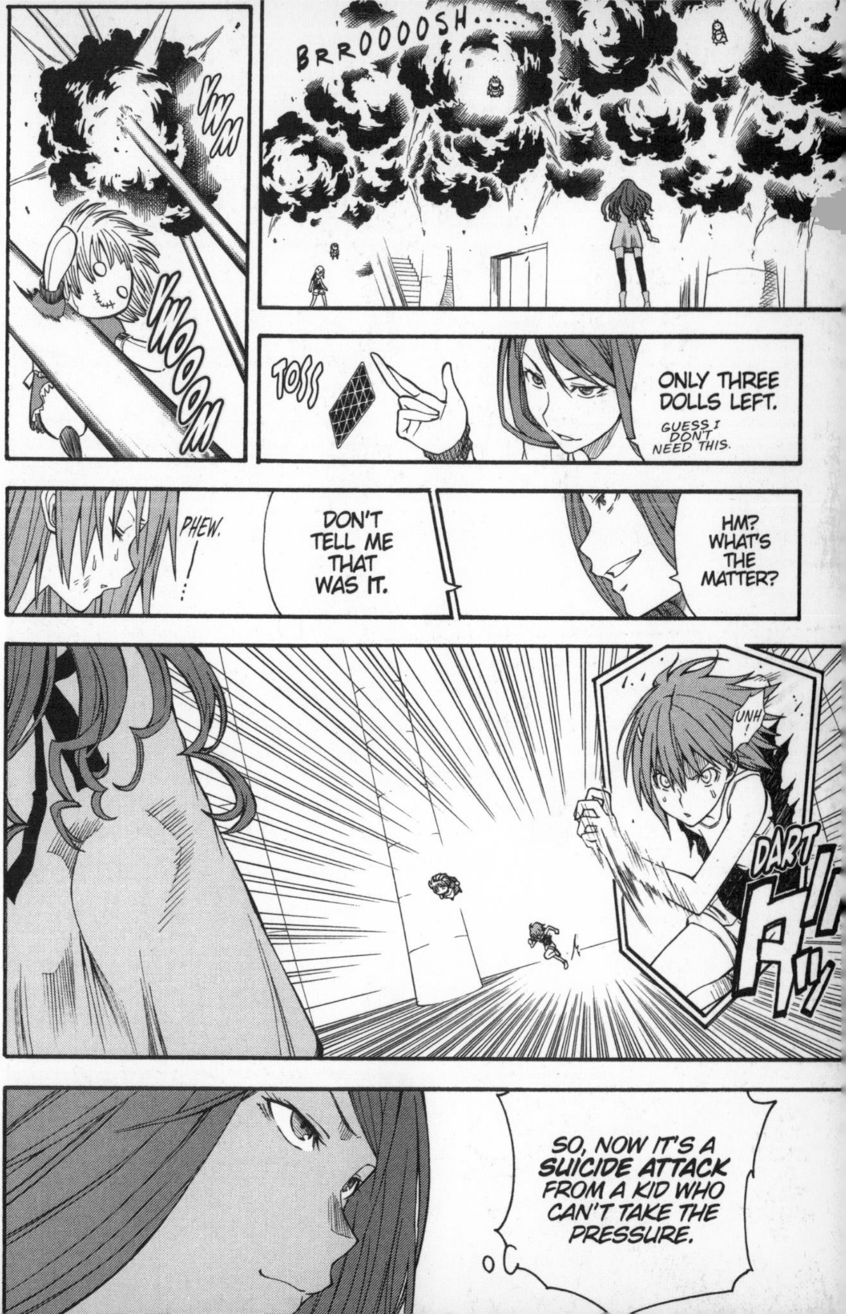
BRROOOOSH.....
TOSS
ONLY THREE DOLLS LEFT.
GUESS I DON'T NEED THIS.
VWM
VWOOOOM
HM? WHAT'S THE MATTER?
DON'T TELL ME THAT WAS IT.
PHEW.
UNH
DART
SO, NOW IT'S A SUICIDE ATTACK FROM A KID WHO CAN'T TAKE THE PRESSURE.

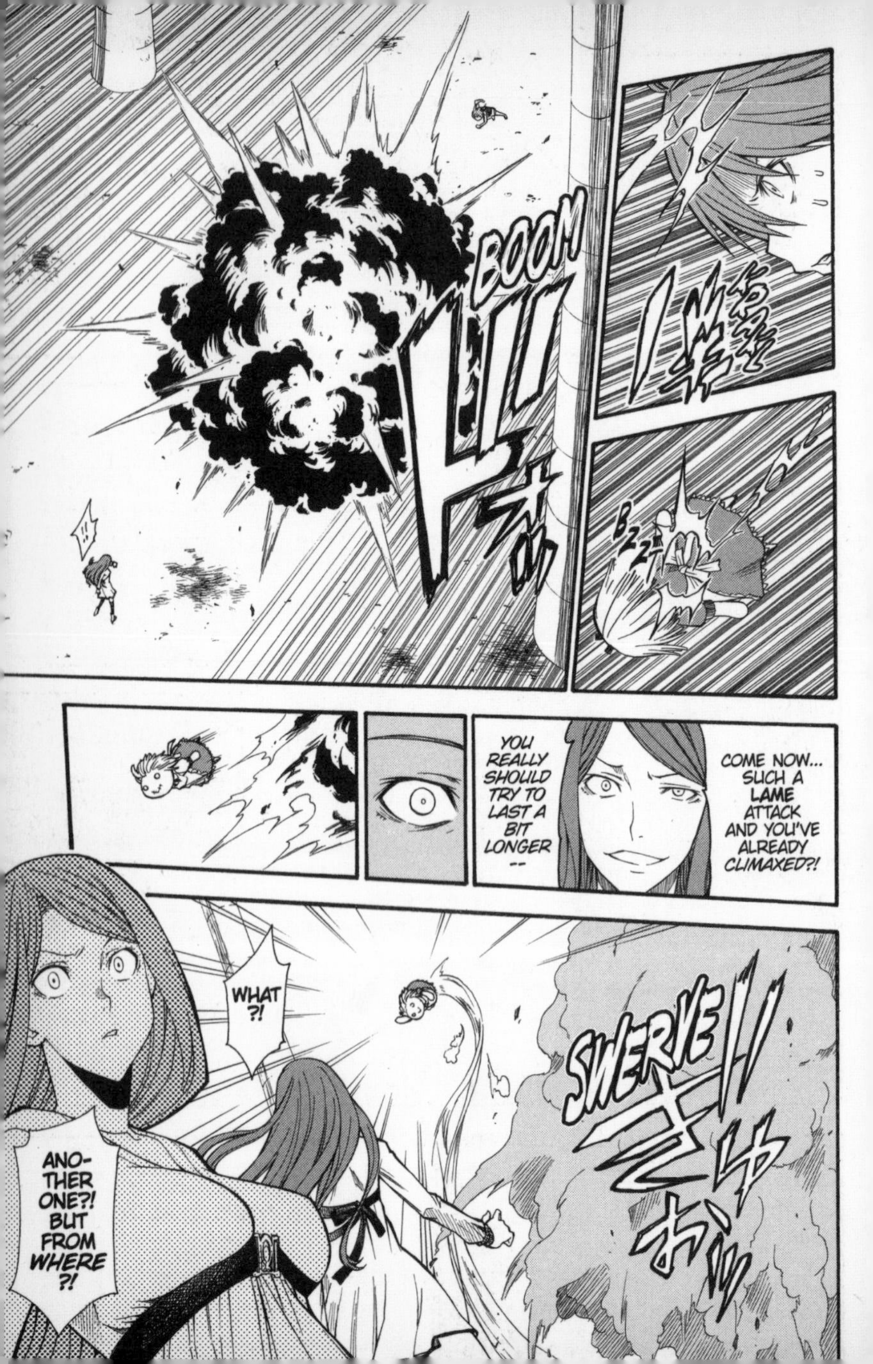
BZZ
BOOM
!!
COME NOW... SUCH A LAME ATTACK AND YOU'VE ALREADY CLIMAXED?!
YOU REALLY SHOULD TRY TO LAST A BIT LONGER --
SWERVE!!
WHAT?!
ANO-THER ONE?! BUT FROM WHERE?!

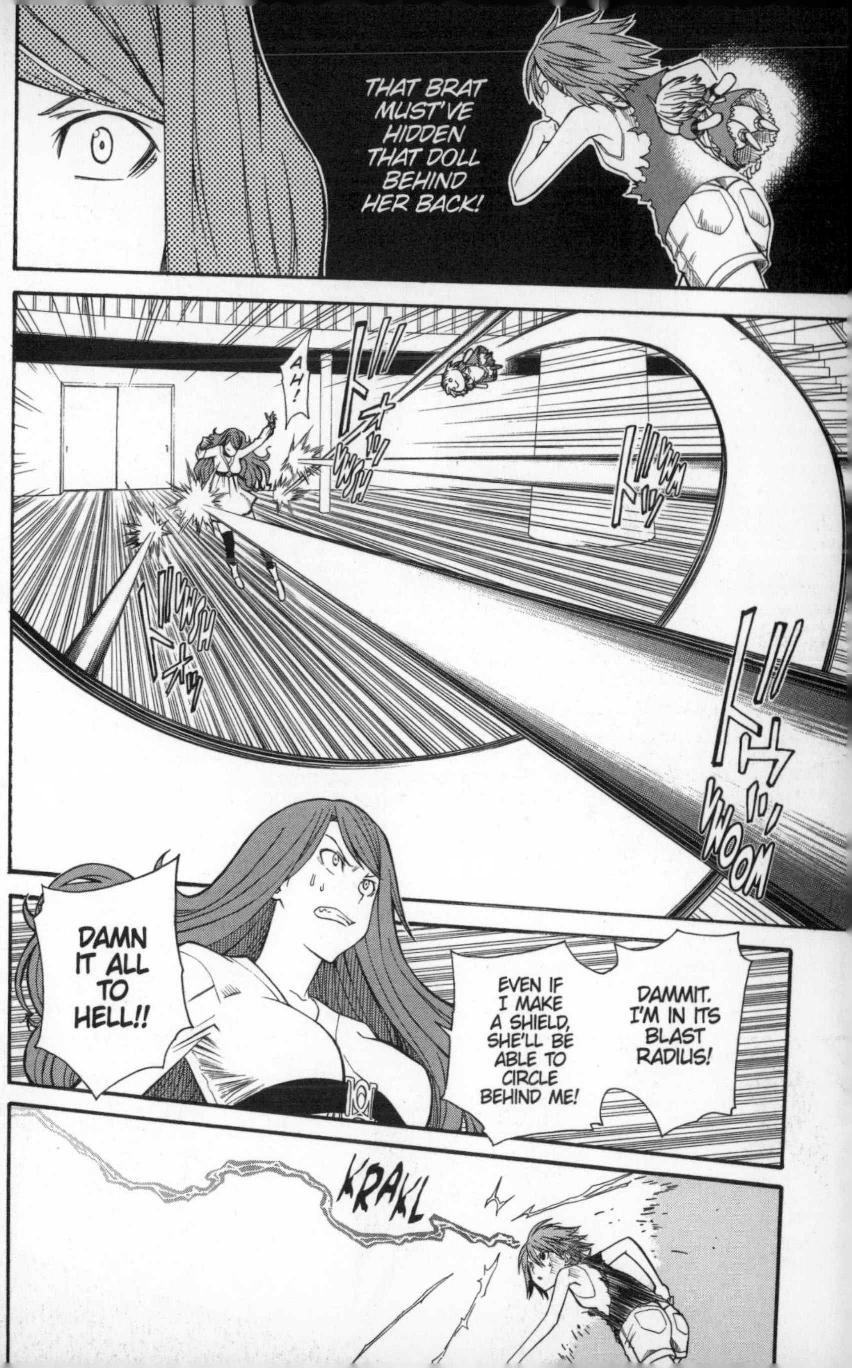
THAT BRAT MUST'VE HIDDEN THAT DOLL BEHIND HER BACK!
VWHM
VWSH
AH!
VHOOM
DAMMIT. I'M IN ITS BLAST RADIUS!
EVEN IF I MAKE A SHIELD, SHE'LL BE ABLE TO CIRCLE BEHIND ME!
DAMN IT ALL TO HELL!!
KRAKL

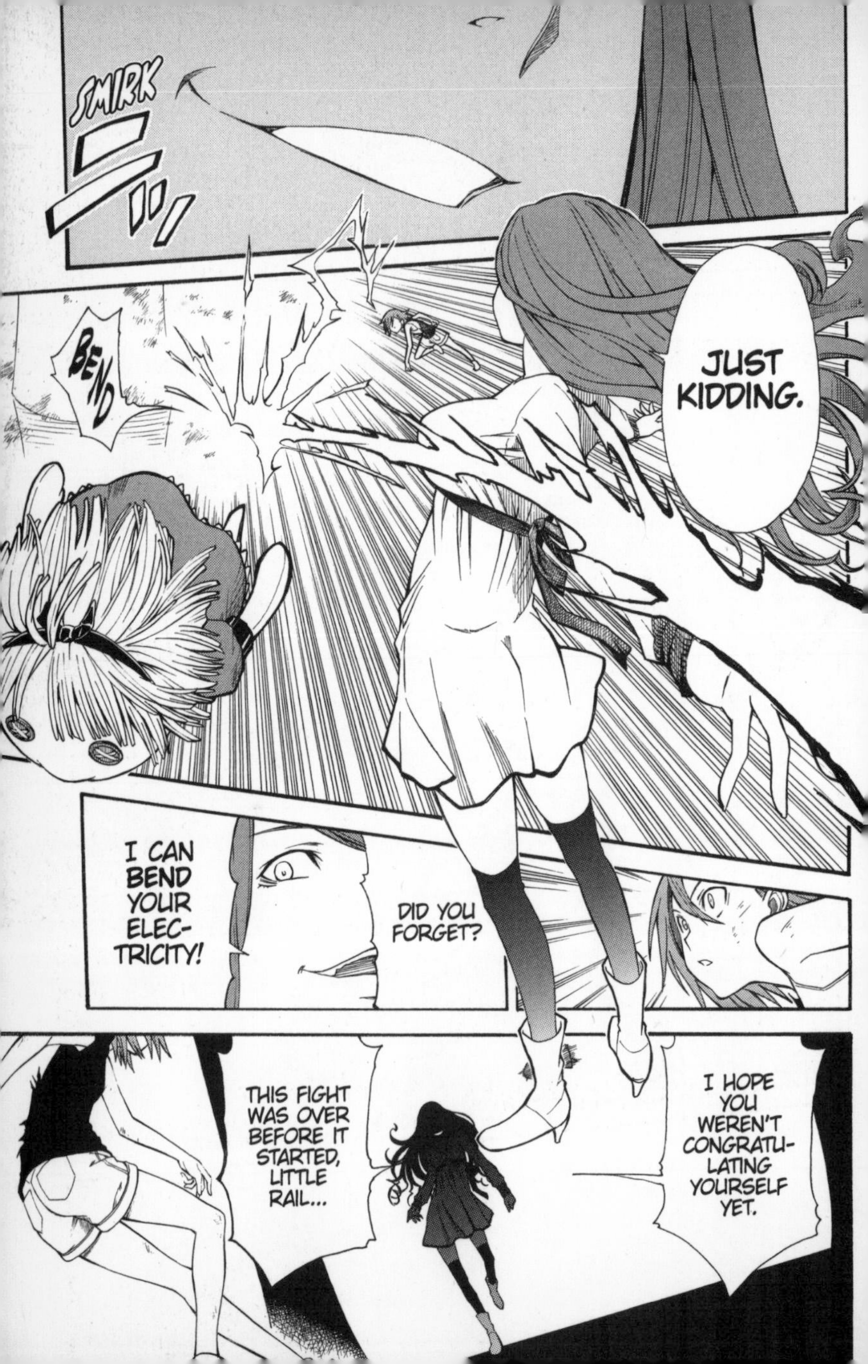
SMIRK
JUST KIDDING.
BEND
DID YOU FORGET?
I CAN BEND YOUR ELEC-TRICITY!
I HOPE YOU WEREN'T CONGRATU-LATING YOURSELF YET.
THIS FIGHT WAS OVER BEFORE IT STARTED, LITTLE RAIL...

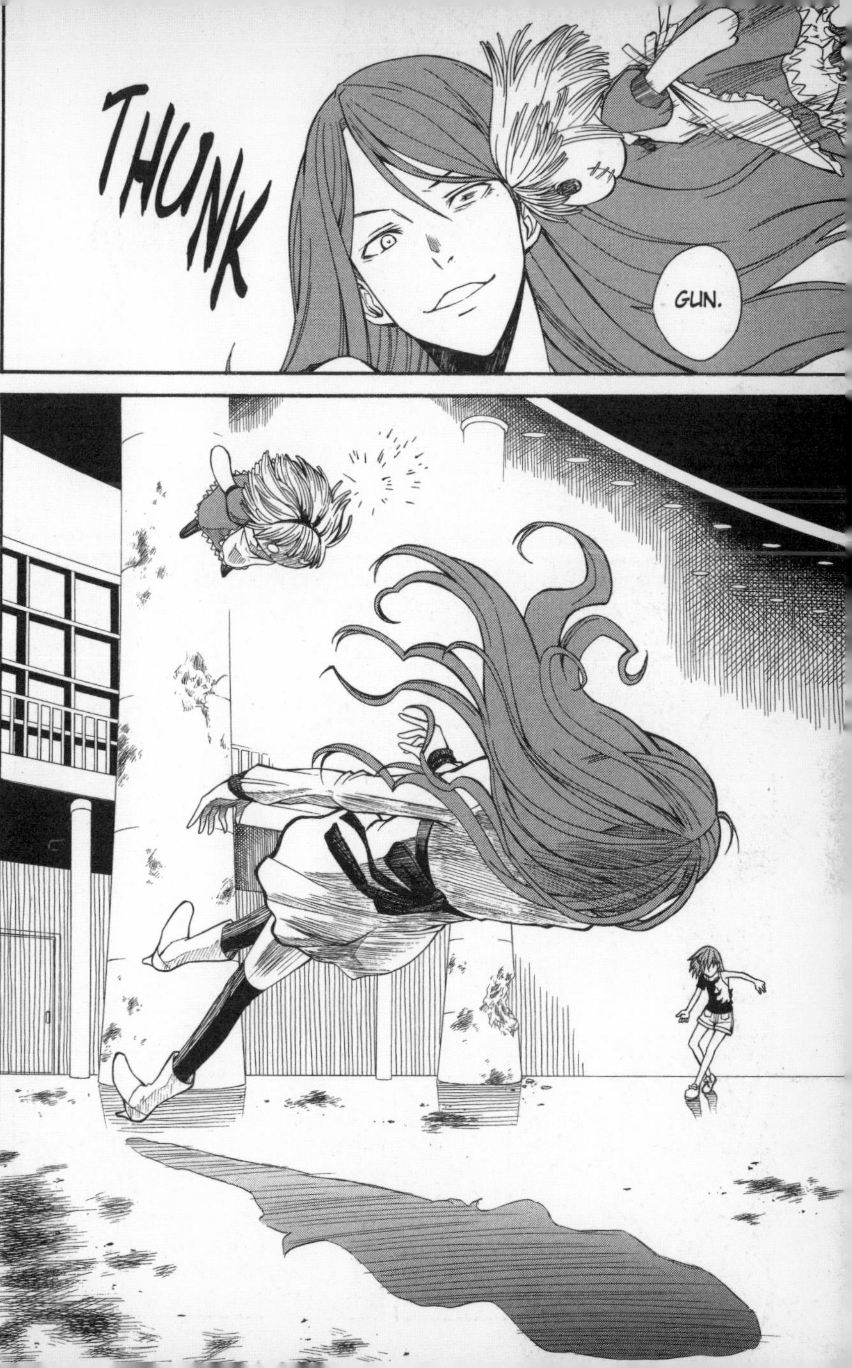
THUNK
GUN.

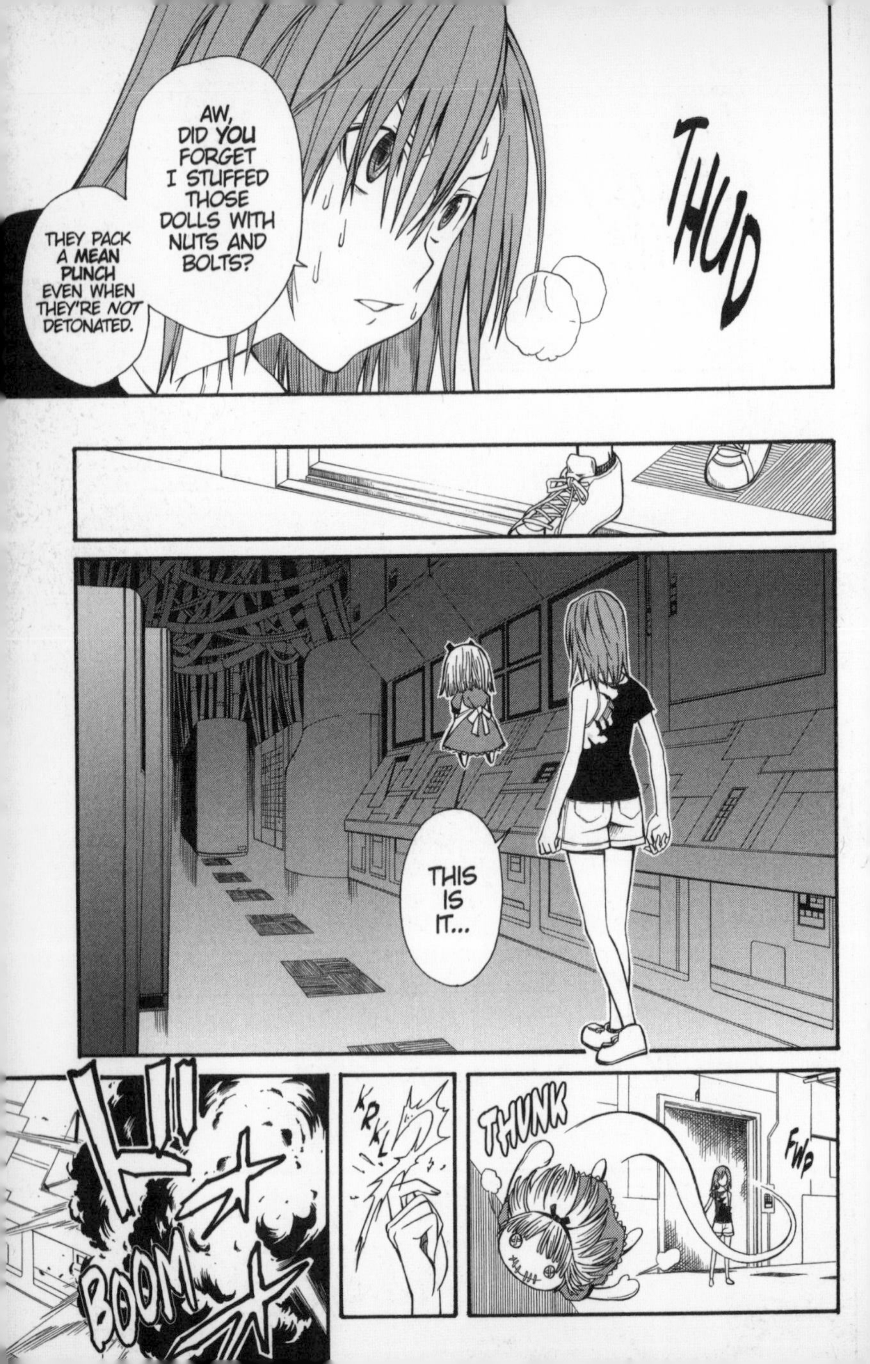
THUD
AW, DID YOU FORGET I STUFFED THOSE DOLLS WITH NUTS AND BOLTS?
THEY PACK A MEAN PUNCH EVEN WHEN THEY'RE *NOT* DETONATED.
THIS IS IT...
THUNK
FWP
KRKL
BOOM

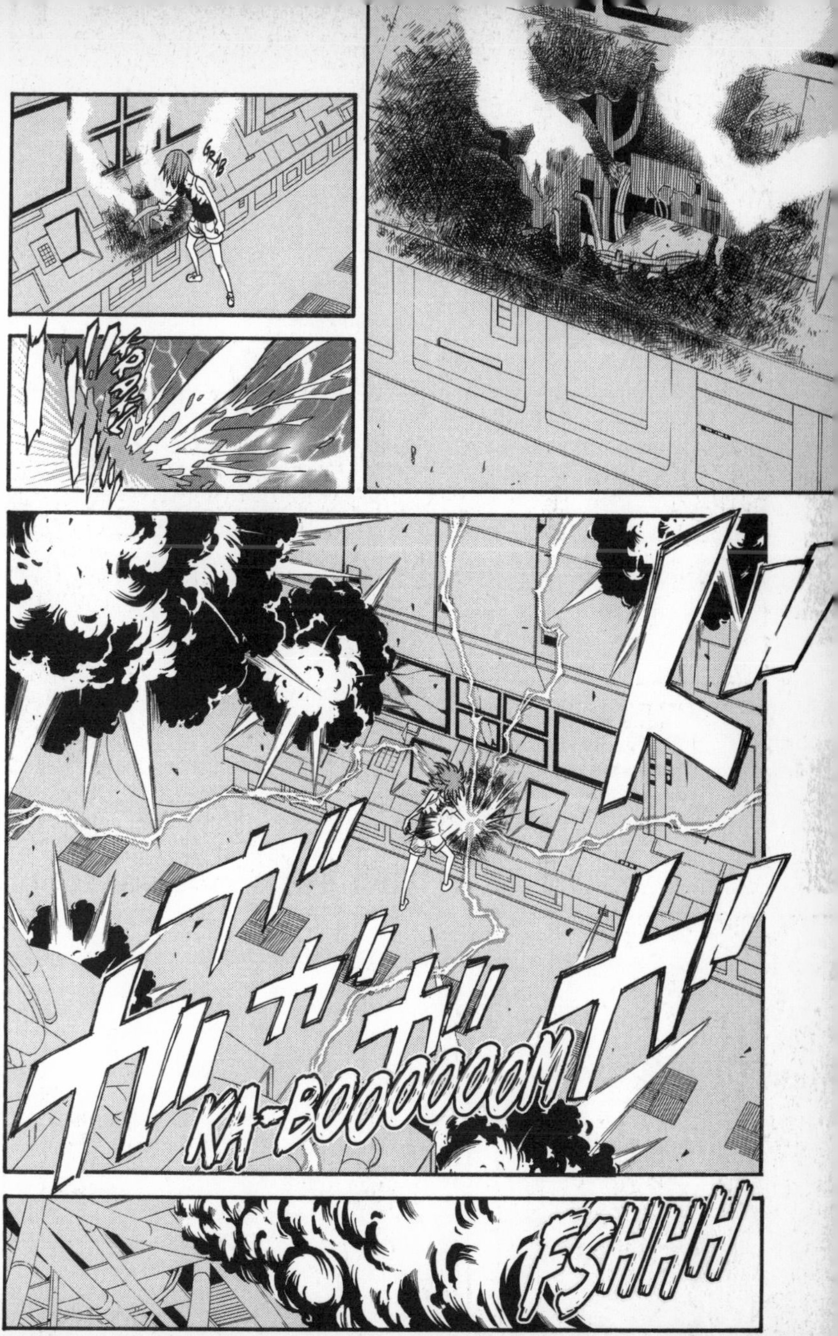
GRAB
KA-BOOOOOOM
FSHHH

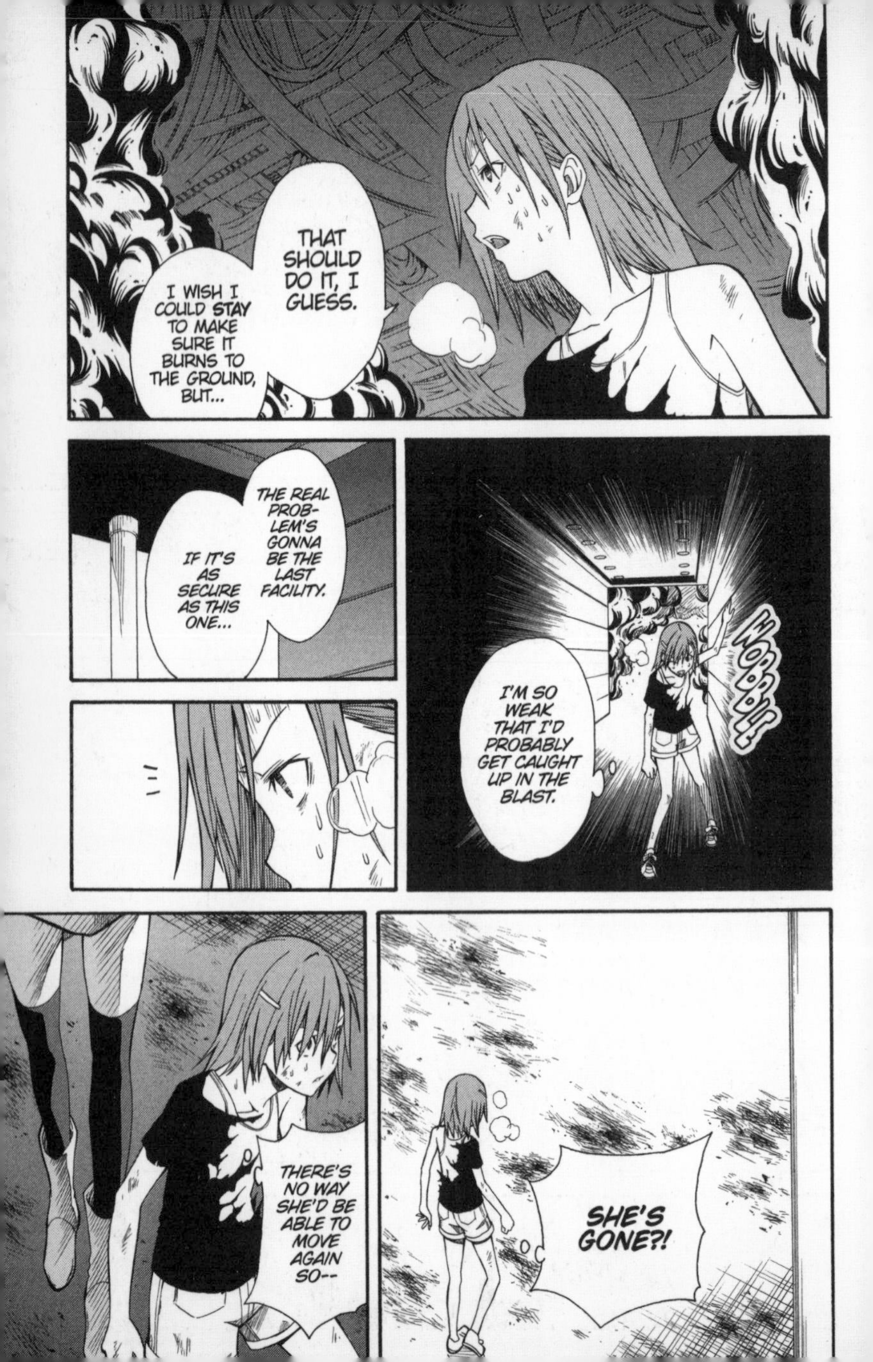
THAT SHOULD DO IT, I GUESS.
I WISH I COULD STAY TO MAKE SURE IT BURNS TO THE GROUND, BUT...
WOBBLE
I'M SO WEAK THAT I'D PROBABLY GET CAUGHT UP IN THE BLAST.
THE REAL PROB-LEM'S GONNA BE THE LAST FACILITY.
IF IT'S AS SECURE AS THIS ONE...
SHE'S GONE?!
THERE'S NO WAY SHE'D BE ABLE TO MOVE AGAIN SO--

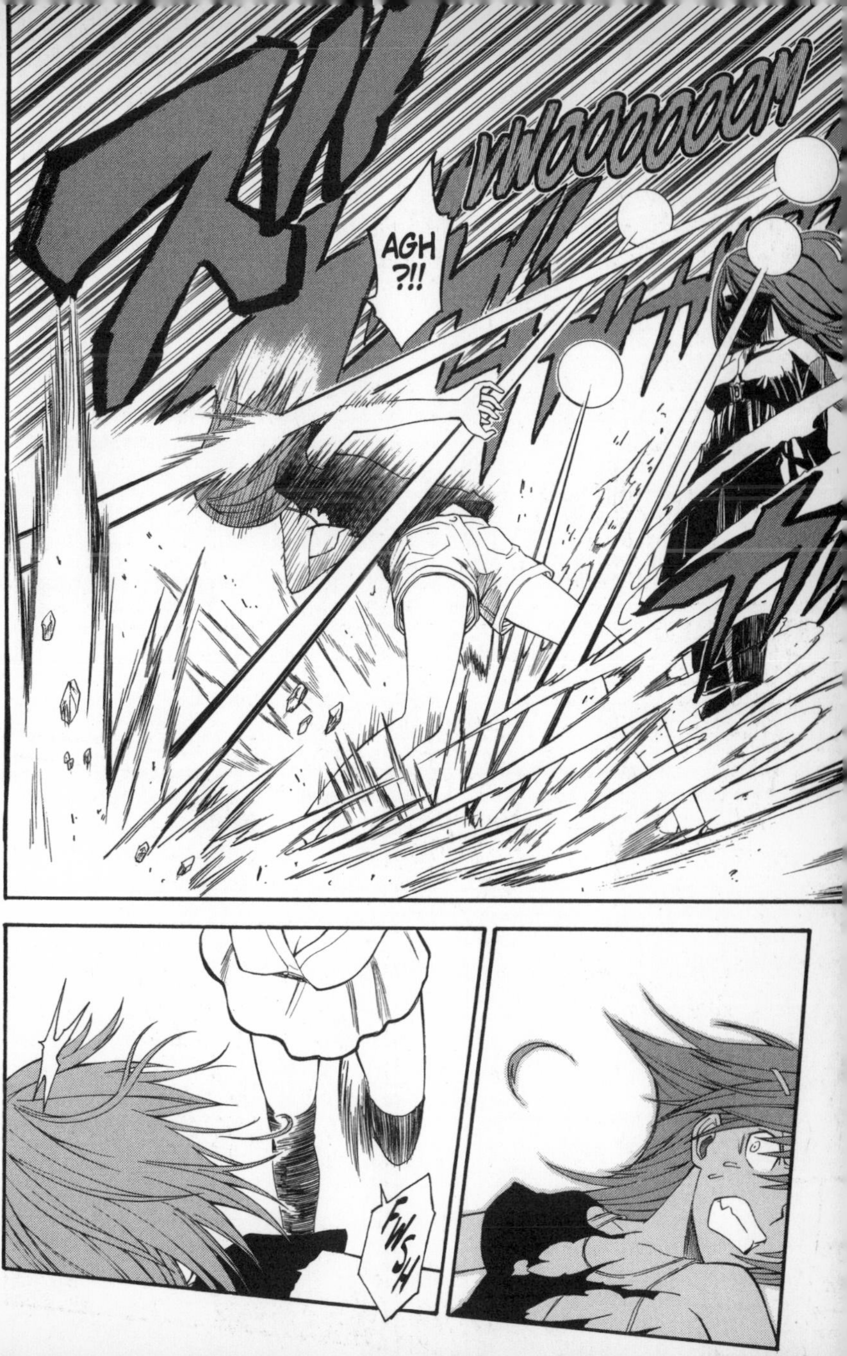
VWOOOOOOM
AGH ?!!
FWSH

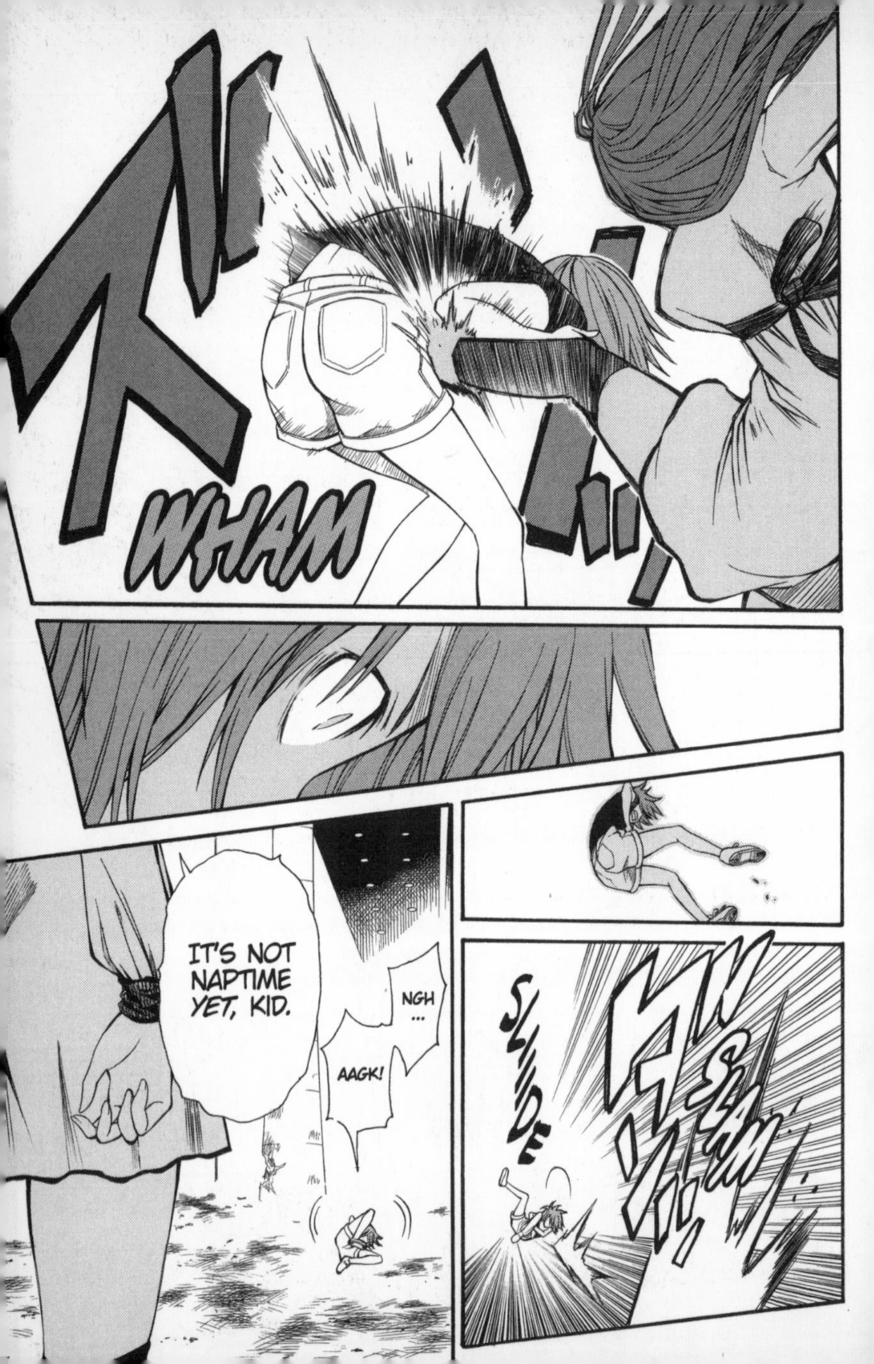
WHAM
SLIIIDE
SLAM
NGH ...
AAGK!
IT'S NOT NAPTIME YET, KID.

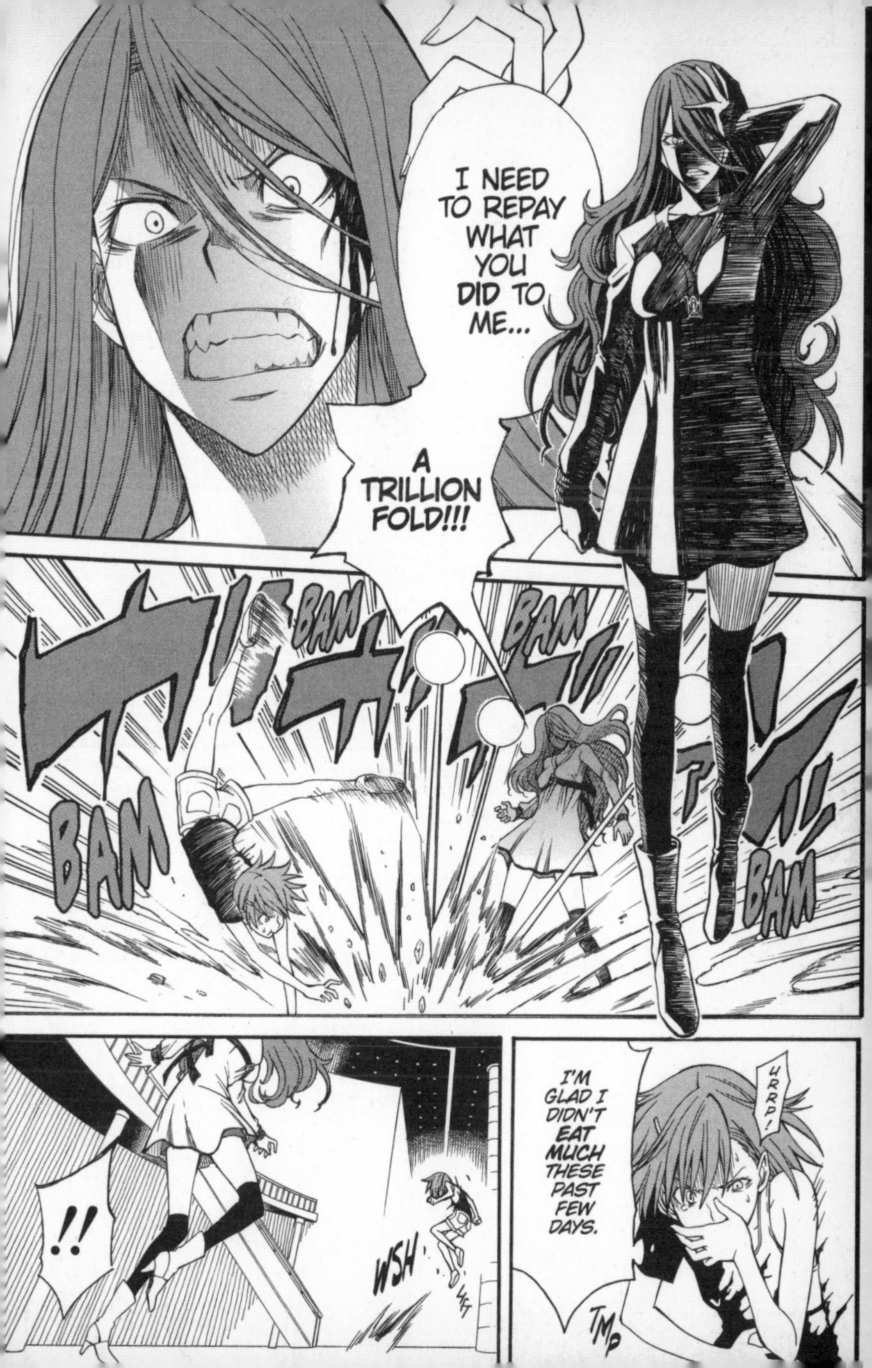
I NEED TO REPAY WHAT YOU DID TO ME...
A TRILLION FOLD!!!
BAM
BAM
BAM
BAM
BAM
URRP!
I'M GLAD I DIDN'T EAT MUCH THESE PAST FEW DAYS.
TMP
LKT
WSH
!!

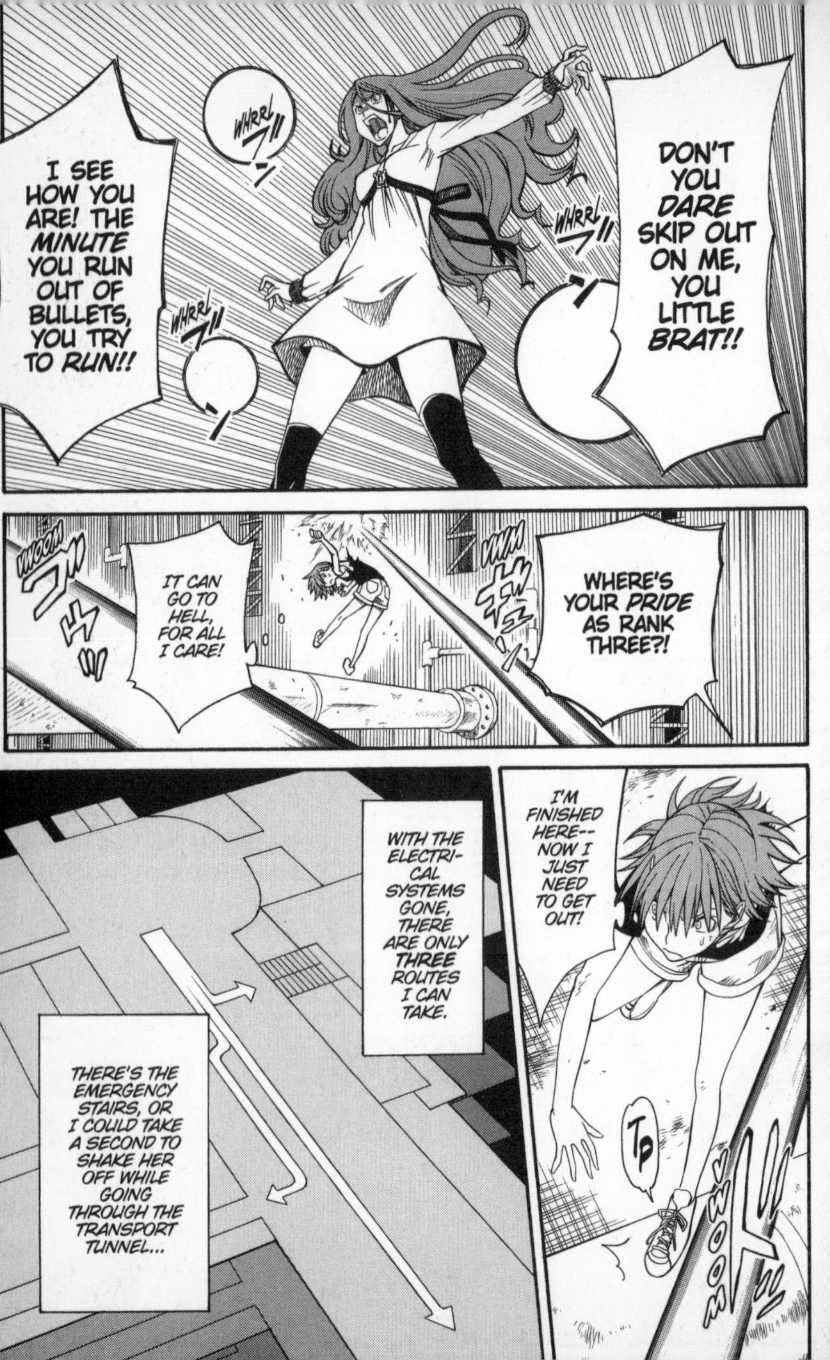
DON'T YOU DARE SKIP OUT ON ME, YOU LITTLE BRAT!!
WHRRL
WHRRL
WHRRL
I SEE HOW YOU ARE! THE MINUTE YOU RUN OUT OF BULLETS, YOU TRY TO RUN!!
WHERE'S YOUR PRIDE AS RANK THREE?!
VWM
IT CAN GO TO HELL, FOR ALL I CARE!
VWOOM
I'M FINISHED HERE-- NOW I JUST NEED TO GET OUT!
TP
VWOOM
WITH THE ELECTRI-CAL SYSTEMS GONE, THERE ARE ONLY THREE ROUTES I CAN TAKE.
THERE'S THE EMERGENCY STAIRS, OR I COULD TAKE A SECOND TO SHAKE HER OFF WHILE GOING THROUGH THE TRANSPORT TUNNEL...

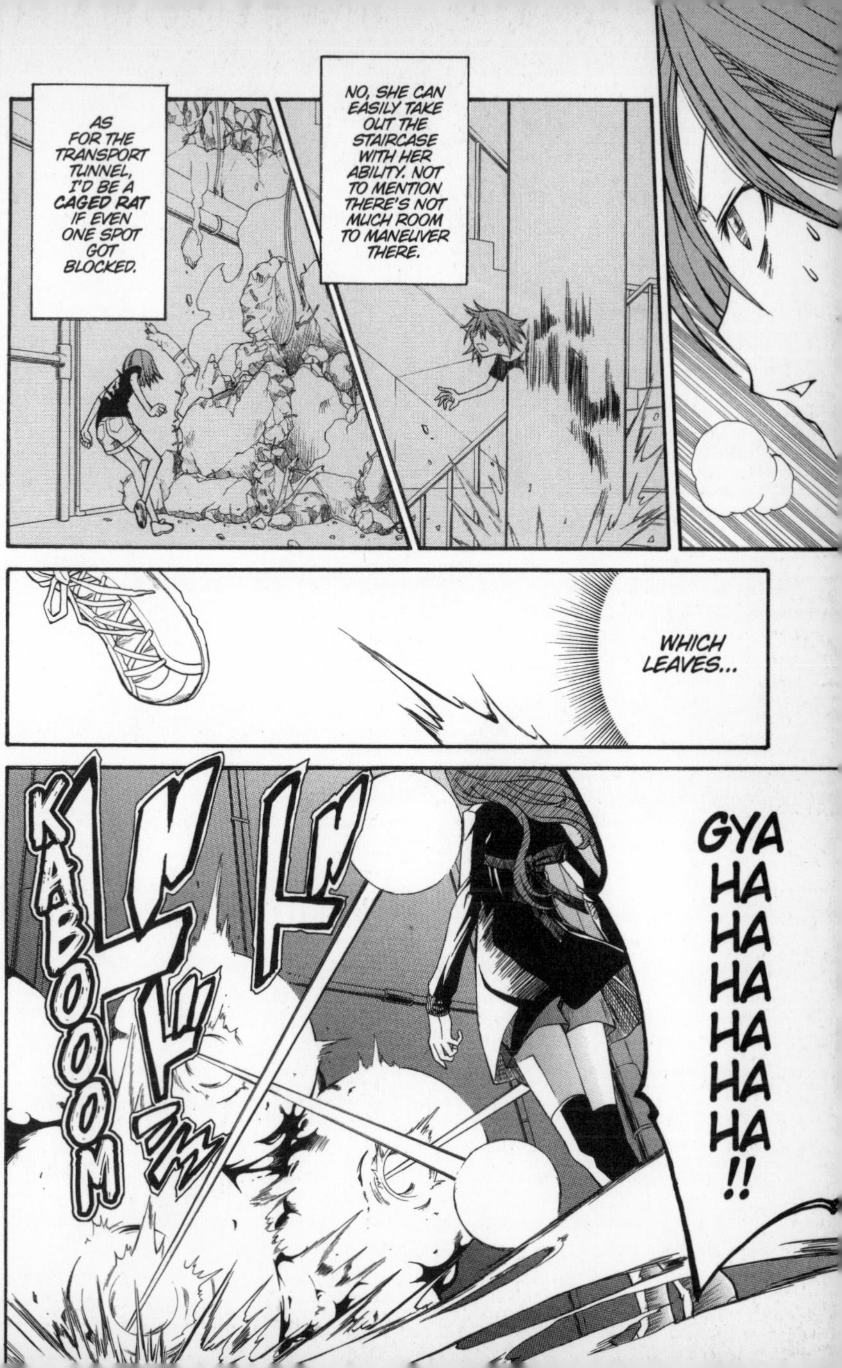
NO, SHE CAN EASILY TAKE OUT THE STAIRCASE WITH HER ABILITY. NOT TO MENTION THERE'S NOT MUCH ROOM TO MANEUVER THERE.
AS FOR THE TRANSPORT TUNNEL, I'D BE A CAGED RAT IF EVEN ONE SPOT GOT BLOCKED.
WHICH LEAVES...
GYA HA HA HA HA HA HA HA!!
KABOOOM

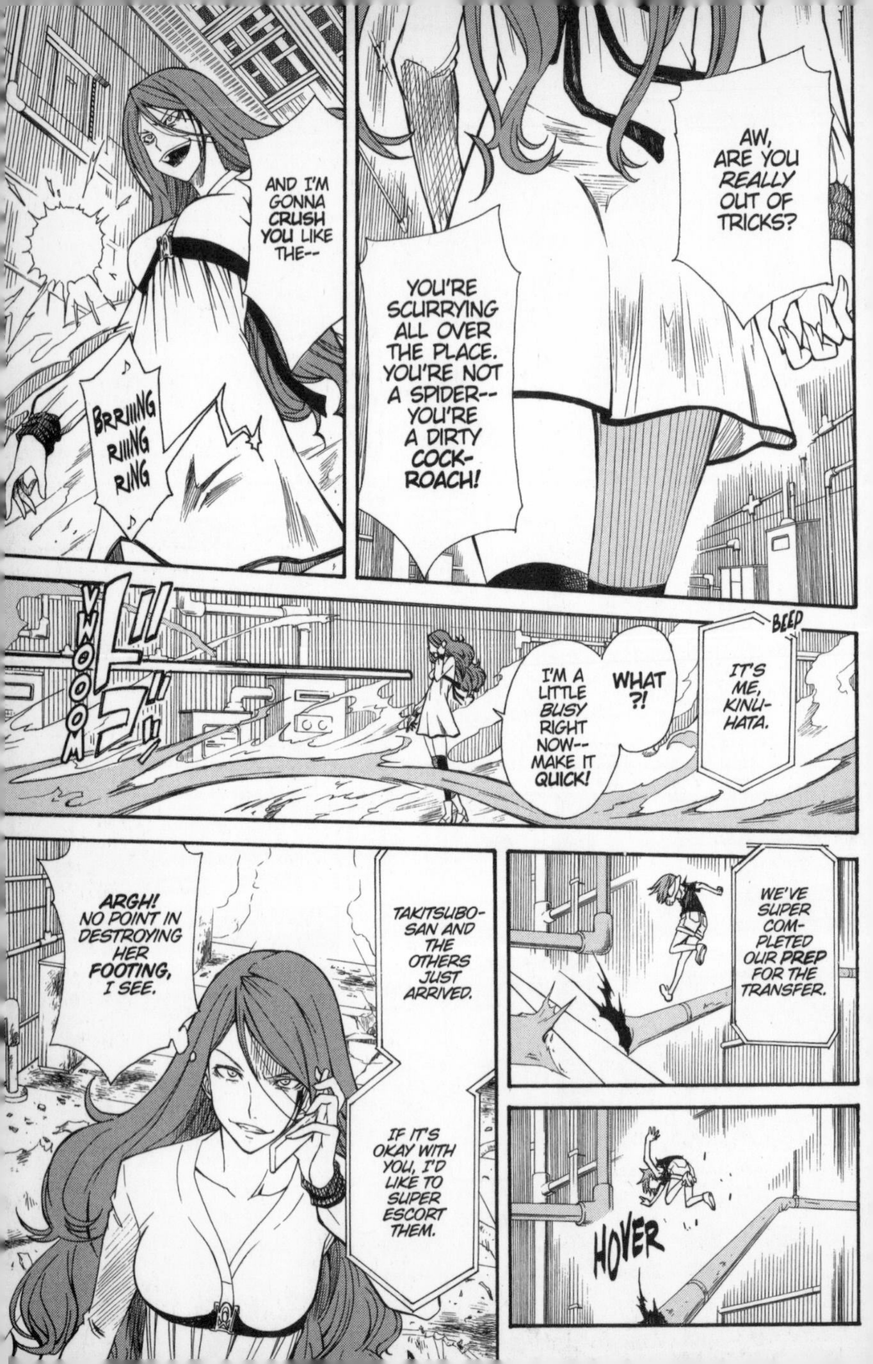
AW, ARE YOU REALLY OUT OF TRICKS?
YOU'RE SCURRYING ALL OVER THE PLACE. YOU'RE NOT A SPIDER-- YOU'RE A DIRTY COCK-ROACH!
AND I'M GONNA CRUSH YOU LIKE THE--
BRRIIING RIIING RING
BEEP
IT'S ME, KINU-HATA.
WHAT?!
I'M A LITTLE BUSY RIGHT NOW-- MAKE IT QUICK!
VWOOOOM
WE'VE SUPER COM-PLETED OUR PREP FOR THE TRANSFER.
HOVER
TAKITSUBO-SAN AND THE OTHERS JUST ARRIVED.
IF IT'S OKAY WITH YOU, I'D LIKE TO SUPER ESCORT THEM.
ARGH! NO POINT IN DESTROYING HER FOOTING, I SEE.

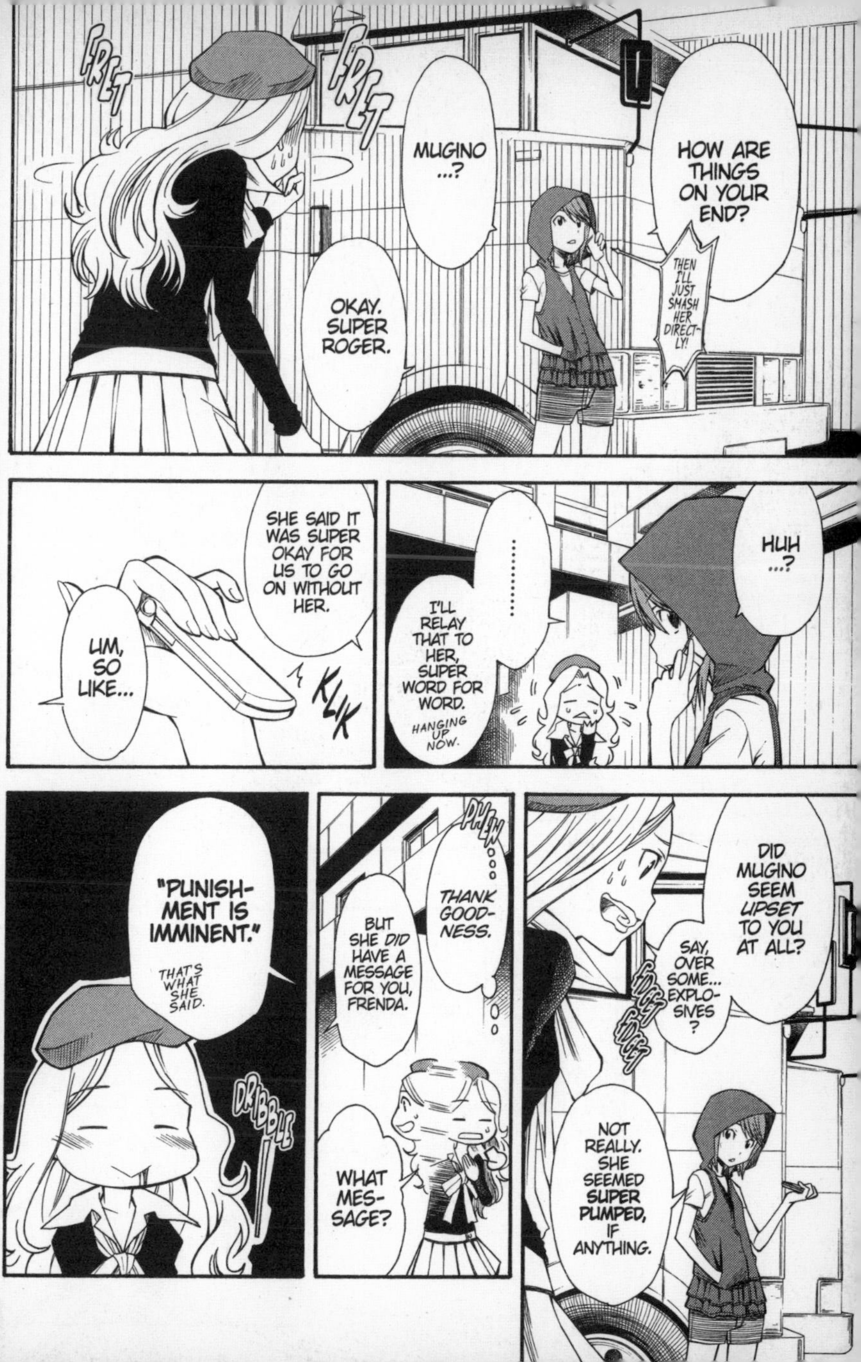
HOW ARE THINGS ON YOUR END?
THEN I'LL JUST SMASH HER DIRECTLY!
FRET
FRET
MUGINO ...?
OKAY. SUPER ROGER.
HUH ...?
......
I'LL RELAY THAT TO HER, SUPER WORD FOR WORD.
HANGING UP NOW.
SHE SAID IT WAS SUPER OKAY FOR US TO GO ON WITHOUT HER.
KLIK
UM, SO LIKE...
DID MUGINO SEEM UPSET TO YOU AT ALL?
SAY, OVER SOME... EXPLOSIVES?
NOT REALLY. SHE SEEMED SUPER PUMPED, IF ANYTHING.
PHEW
THANK GOODNESS.
BUT SHE DID HAVE A MESSAGE FOR YOU, FRENDA.
WHAT MESSAGE?
"PUNISHMENT IS IMMINENT."
THAT'S WHAT SHE SAID.
DRIBBLE

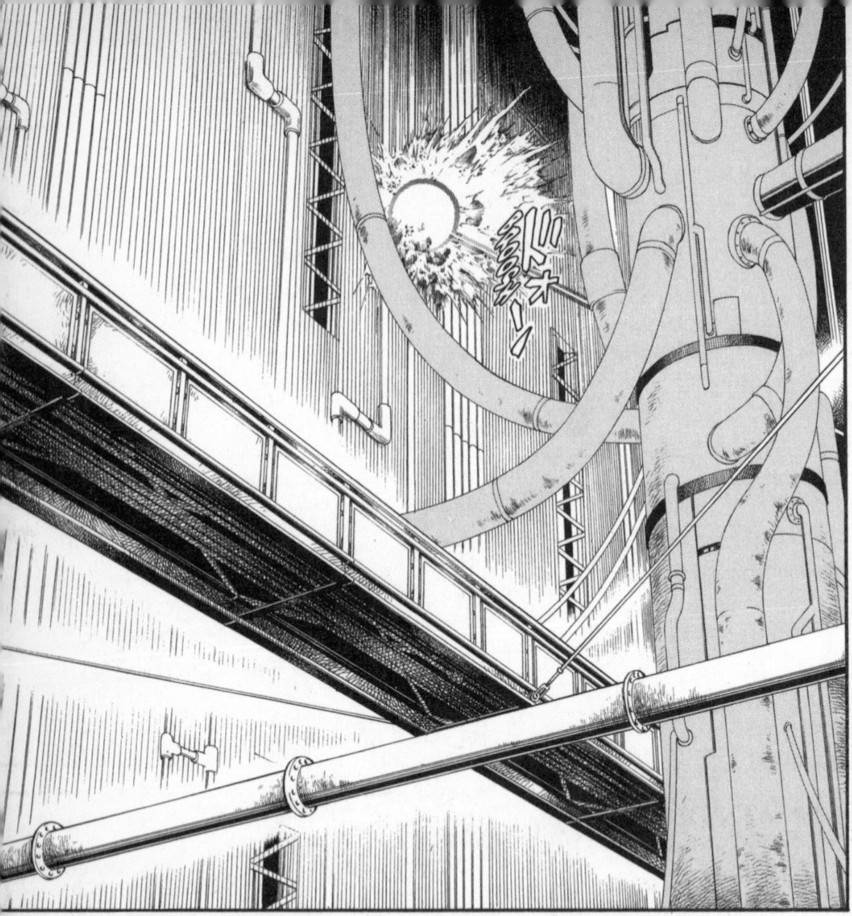
ドオーン!
BOOOOM

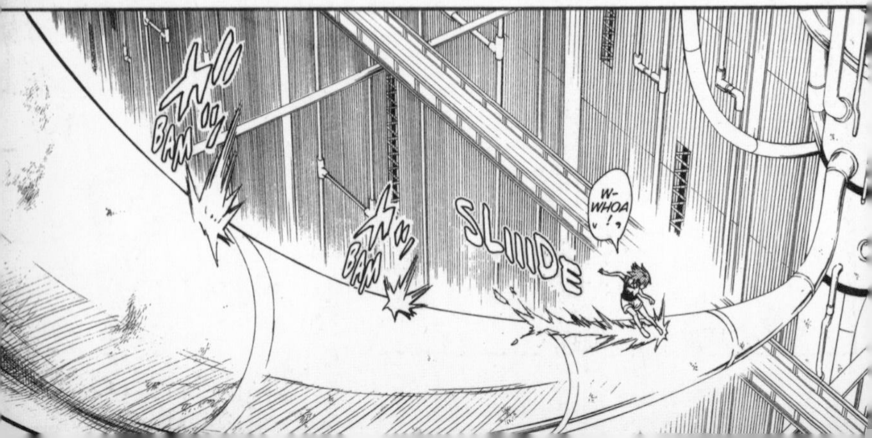
W-WHOA!
SLIIIDE
ガッ
BAM
ガッ
BAM

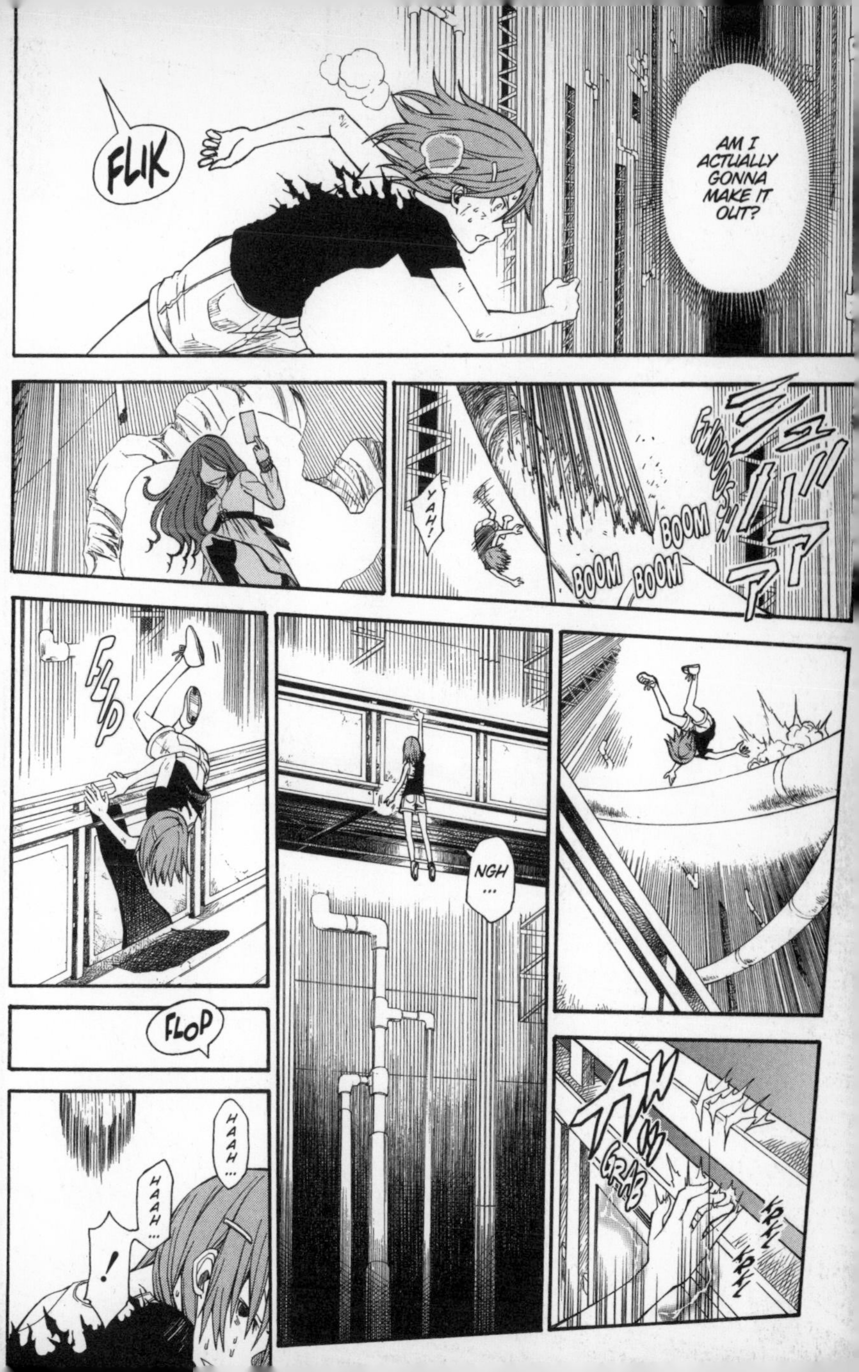
AM I ACTUALLY GONNA MAKE IT OUT?
FLIK
FWOOOSH
BOOM
BOOM
BOOM
YAH!
GRAB
KRKL
KRKL
KRKL
NGH...
FLIP
FLOP
HAAH...
HAAH...
!

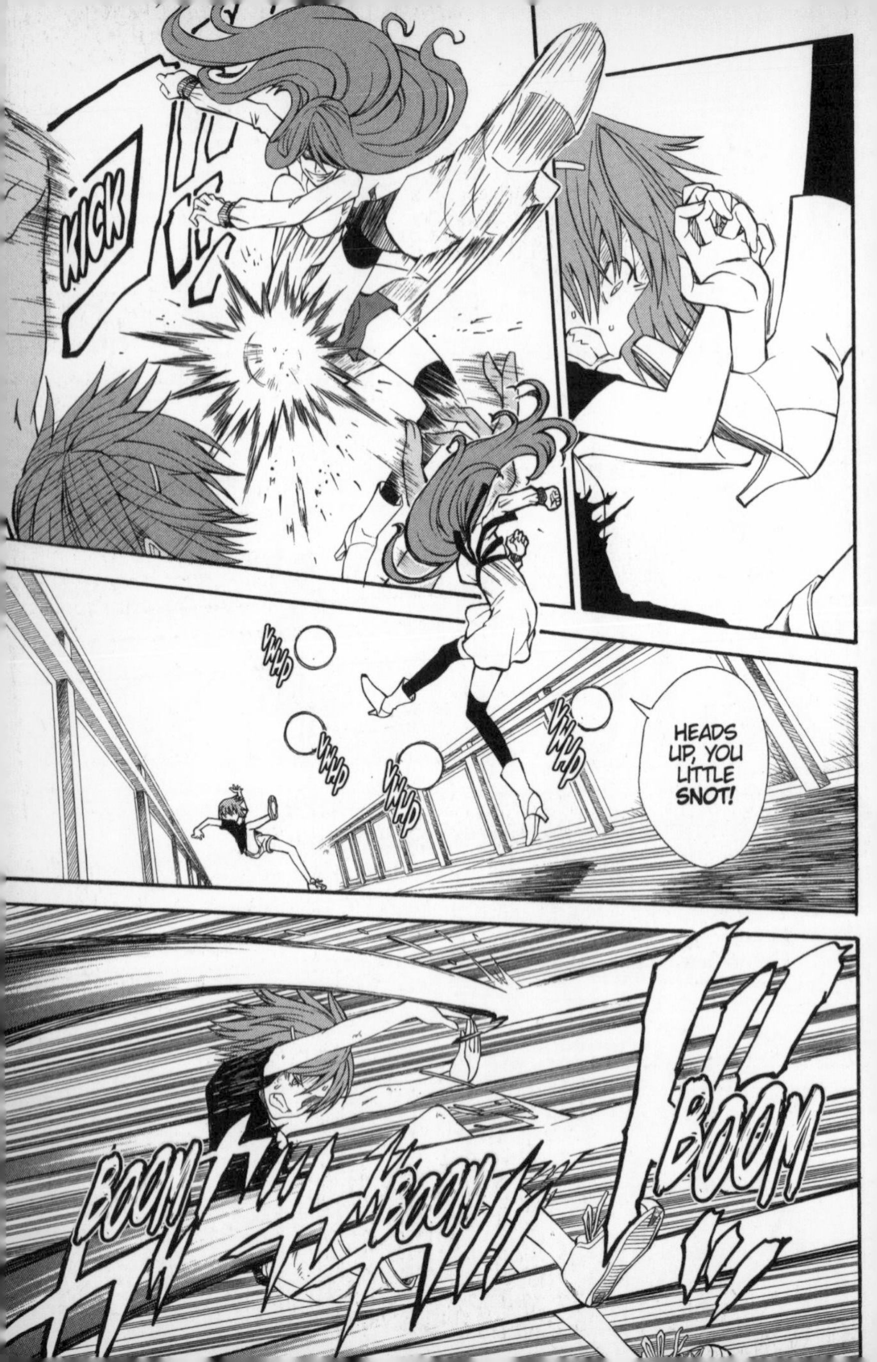
KICK
VWHP
VWHP
VWHP
VWHP
HEADS UP, YOU LITTLE SNOT!
BOOM
BOOM
BOOM

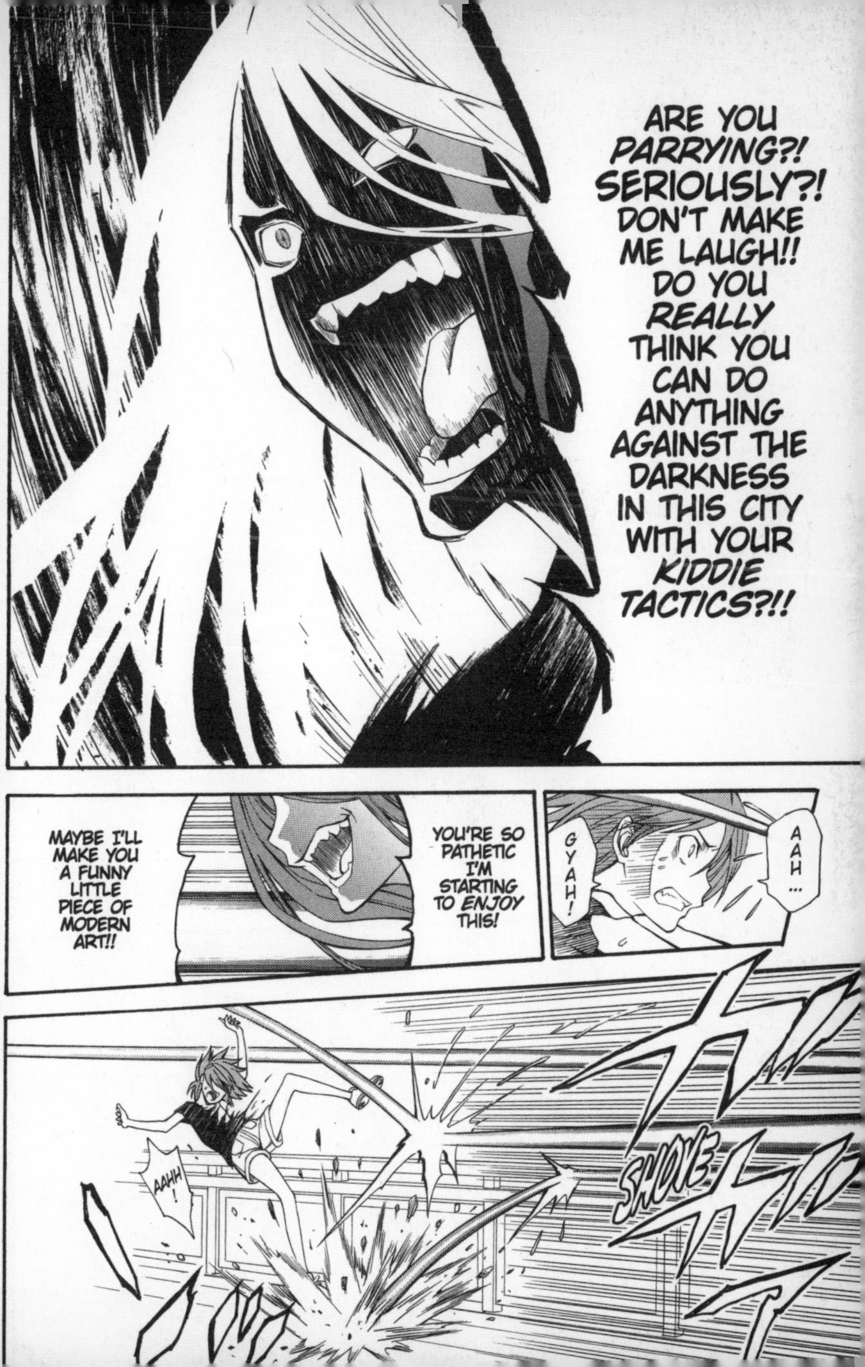
ARE YOU PARRYING?! SERIOUSLY?! DON'T MAKE ME LAUGH!! DO YOU REALLY THINK YOU CAN DO ANYTHING AGAINST THE DARKNESS IN THIS CITY WITH YOUR KIDDIE TACTICS?!!
AAH...
GYAH!
YOU'RE SO PATHETIC I'M STARTING TO ENJOY THIS!
MAYBE I'LL MAKE YOU A FUNNY LITTLE PIECE OF MODERN ART!!
SHOVE
AAHH!

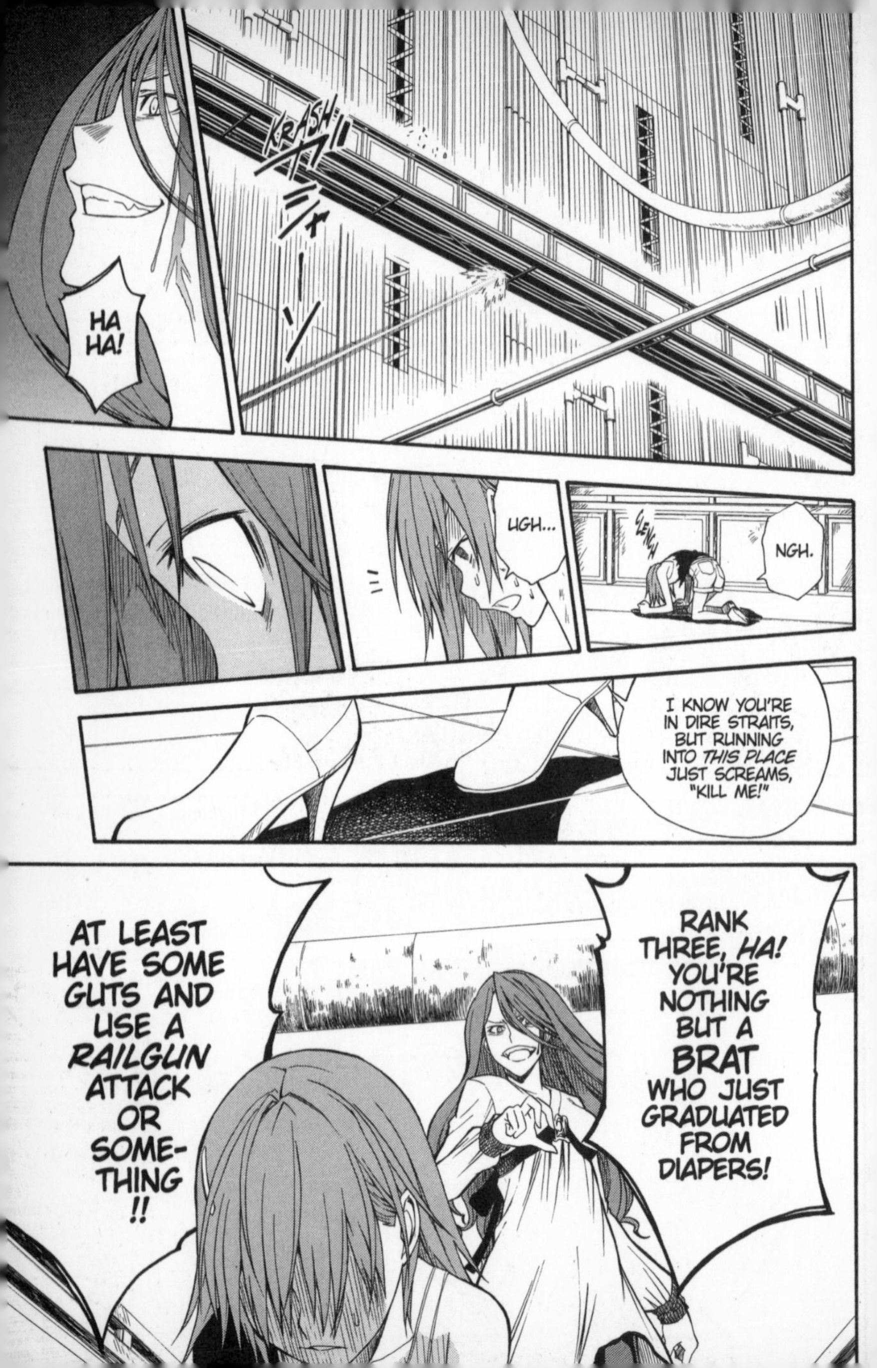

KRASH
HA HA!
CLENCH
NGH.
UGH...
I KNOW YOU'RE IN DIRE STRAITS, BUT RUNNING INTO *THIS PLACE* JUST SCREAMS, "KILL ME!"
RANK THREE, *HA!* YOU'RE NOTHING BUT A BRAT WHO JUST GRADUATED FROM DIAPERS!
AT LEAST HAVE SOME GUTS AND USE A *RAILGUN* ATTACK OR SOME-THING!!

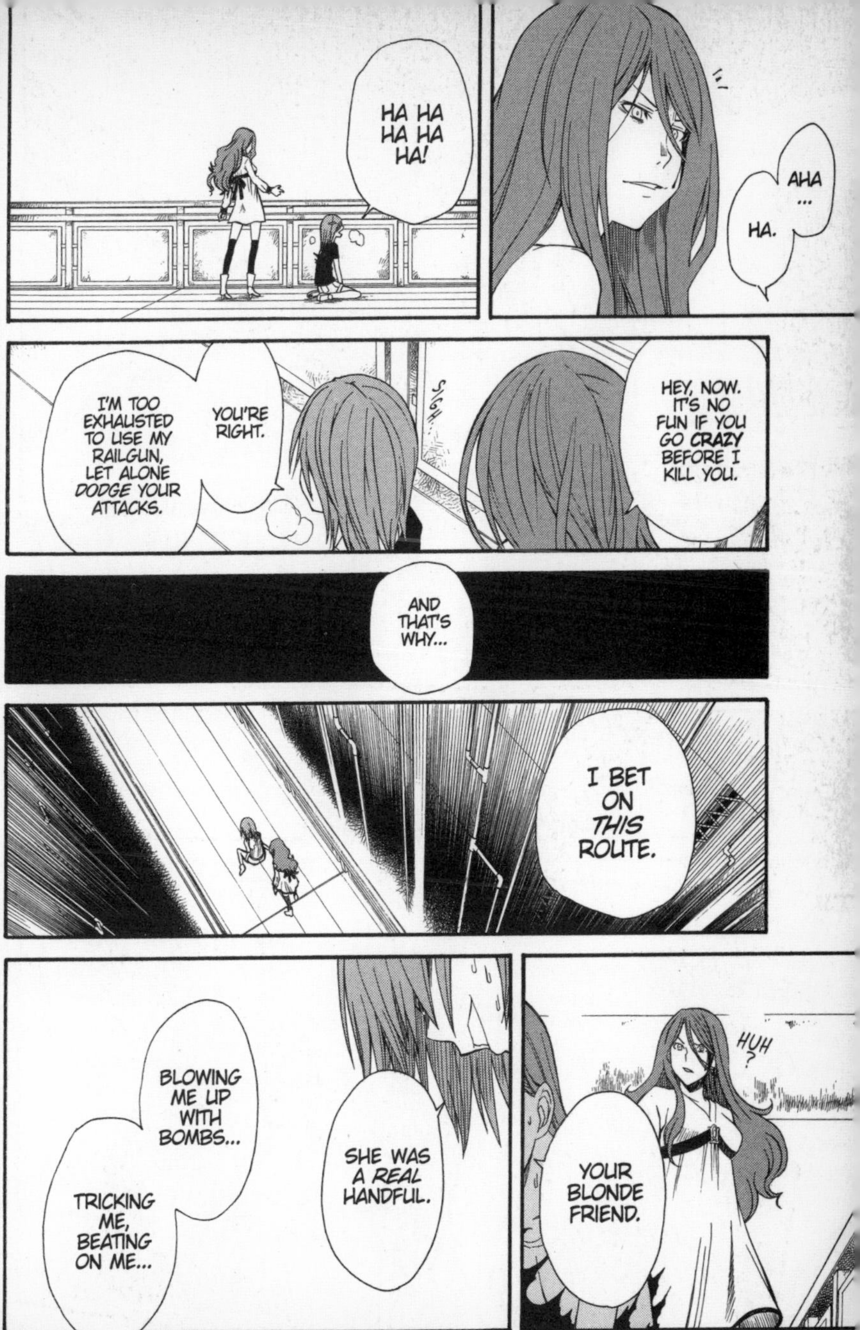
AHA ... HA.
HA HA HA HA HA!
HEY, NOW. IT'S NO FUN IF YOU GO **CRAZY** BEFORE I KILL YOU.
SIGH
YOU'RE RIGHT.
I'M TOO EXHAUSTED TO USE MY RAILGUN, LET ALONE *DODGE* YOUR ATTACKS.
AND THAT'S WHY...
I BET ON *THIS* ROUTE.
HUH?
YOUR BLONDE FRIEND.
SHE WAS A *REAL* HANDFUL.
BLOWING ME UP WITH BOMBS...
TRICKING ME, BEATING ON ME...

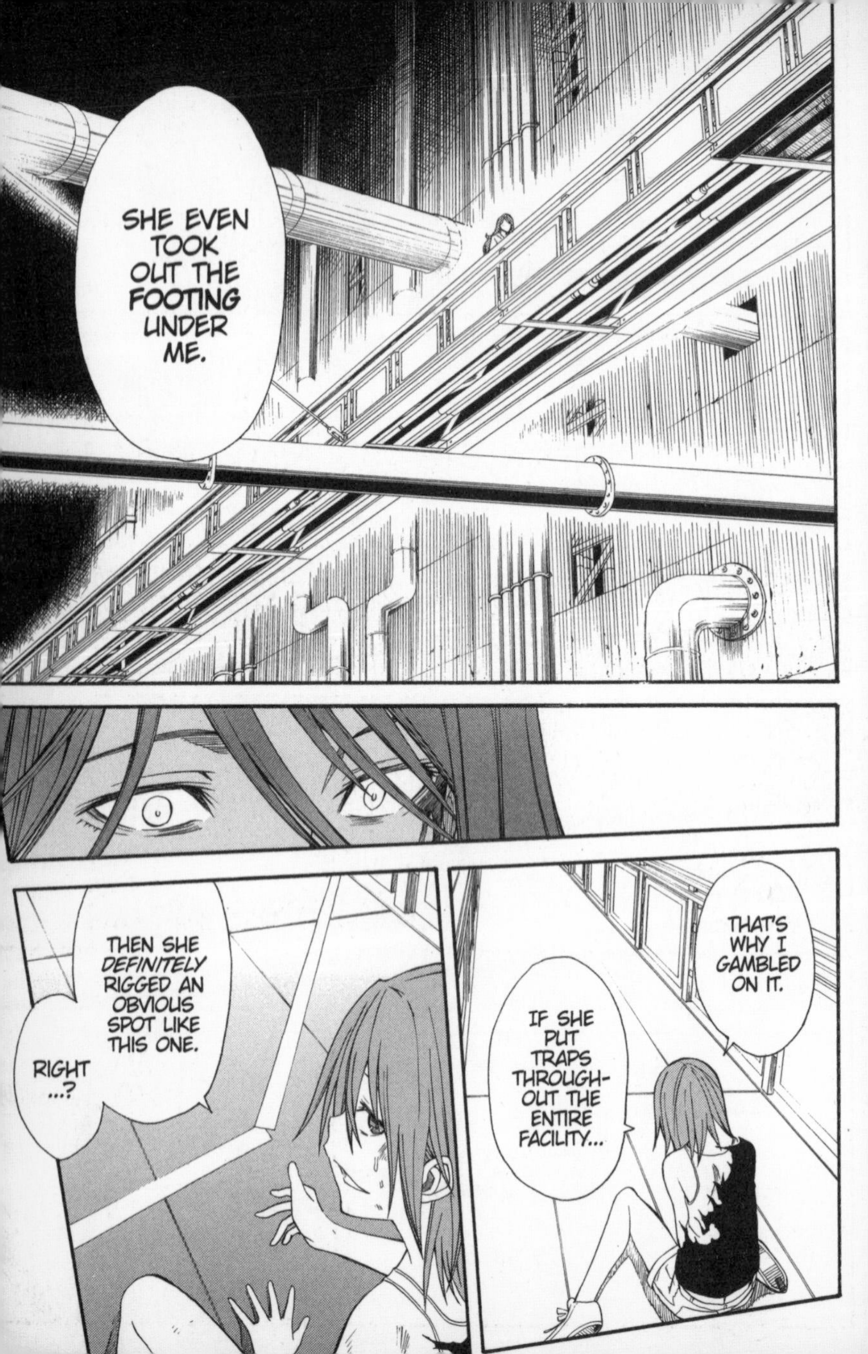
SHE EVEN TOOK OUT THE FOOTING UNDER ME.
THAT'S WHY I GAMBLED ON IT.
IF SHE PUT TRAPS THROUGH-OUT THE ENTIRE FACILITY...
THEN SHE *DEFINITELY* RIGGED AN OBVIOUS SPOT LIKE THIS ONE.
RIGHT ...?

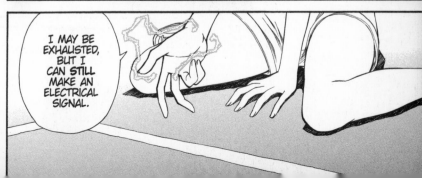

I MAY BE EXHAUSTED, BUT I CAN STILL MAKE AN ELECTRICAL SIGNAL.

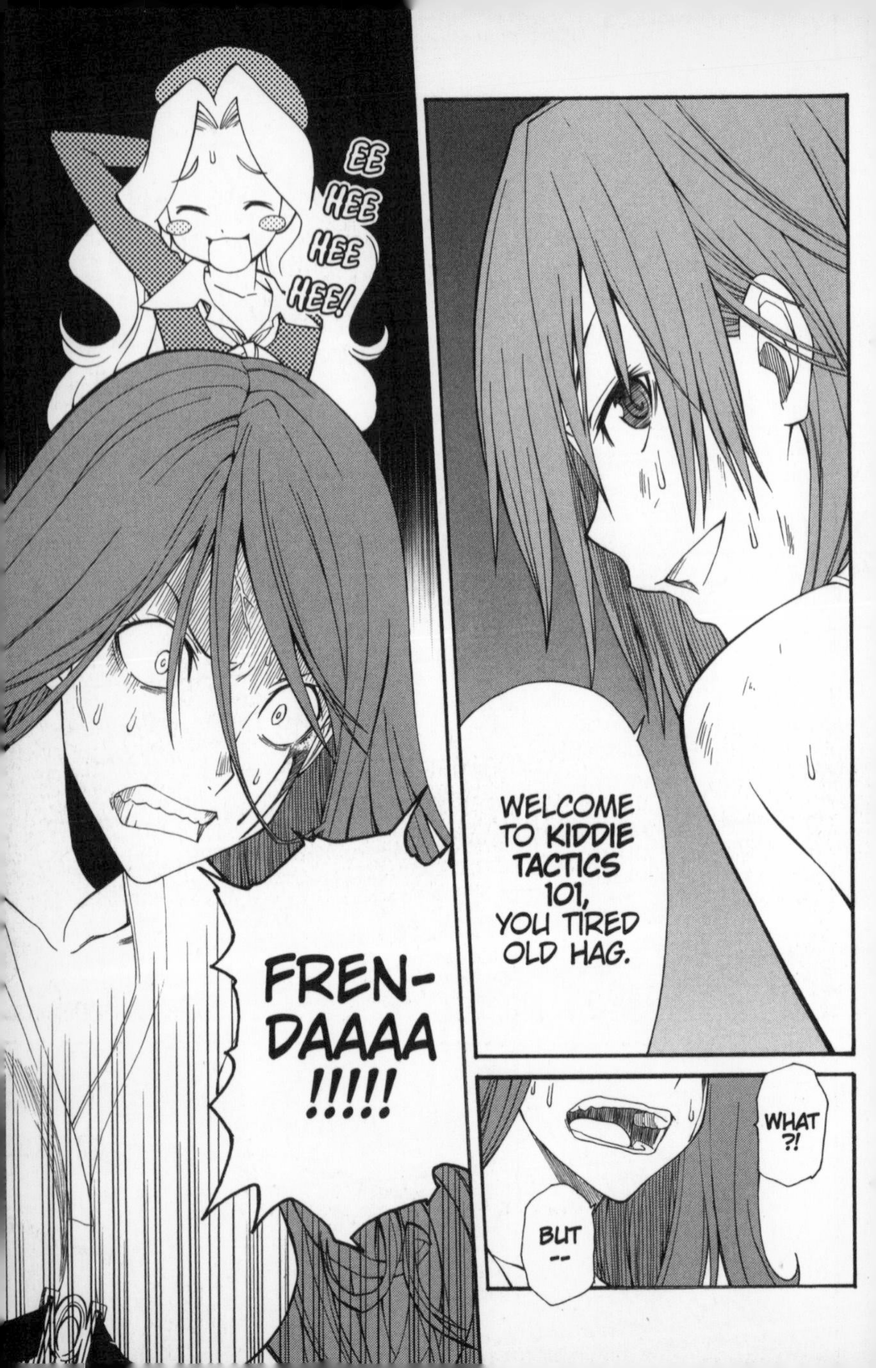
WELCOME TO KIDDIE TACTICS 101, YOU TIRED OLD HAG.
WHAT?!
BUT --
EE HEE HEE HEE!
FREN- DAAAA !!!!!

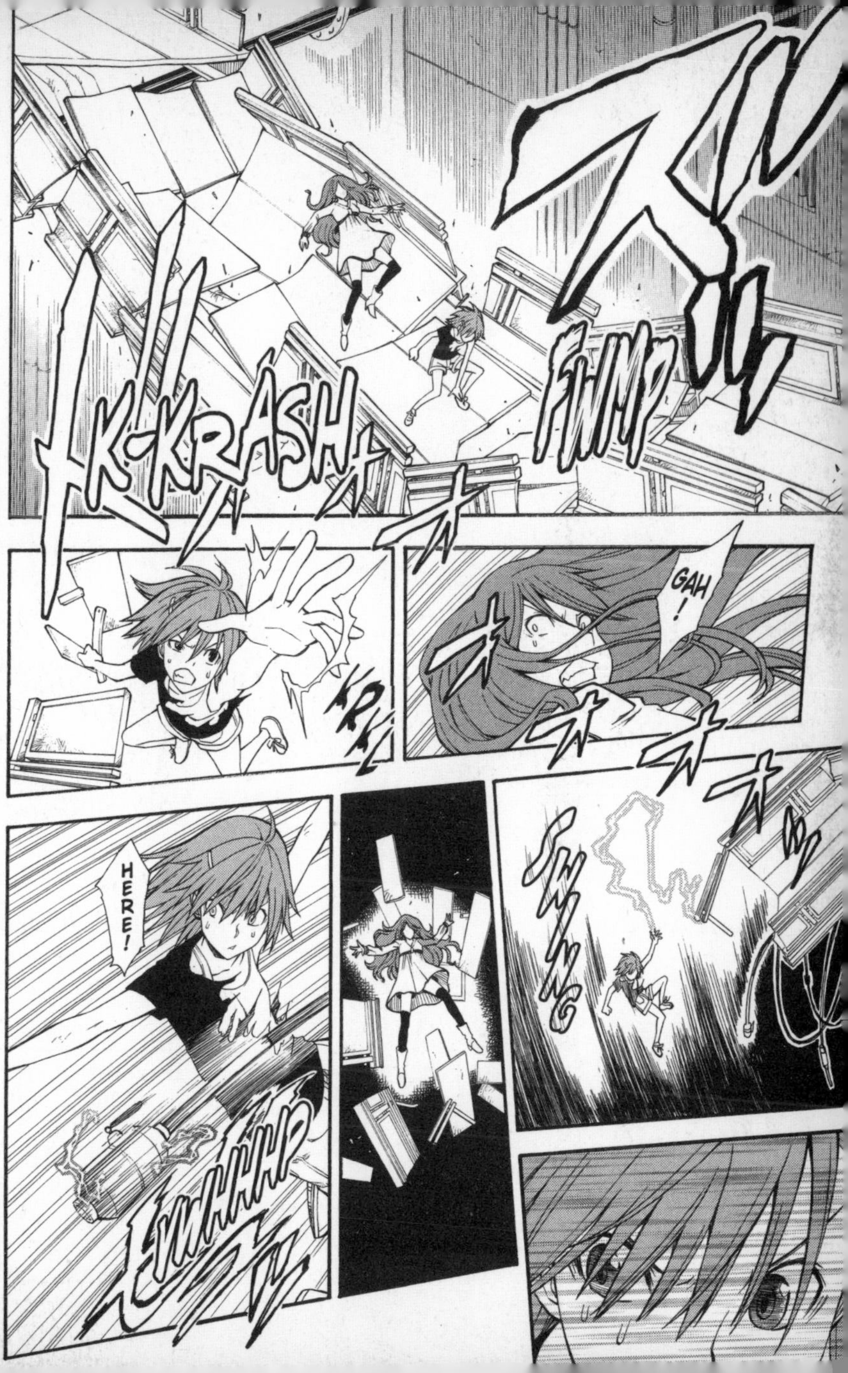
FWMP
K-KRASH
GAH!
KRK
SHWING
HERE!
FWHHHD

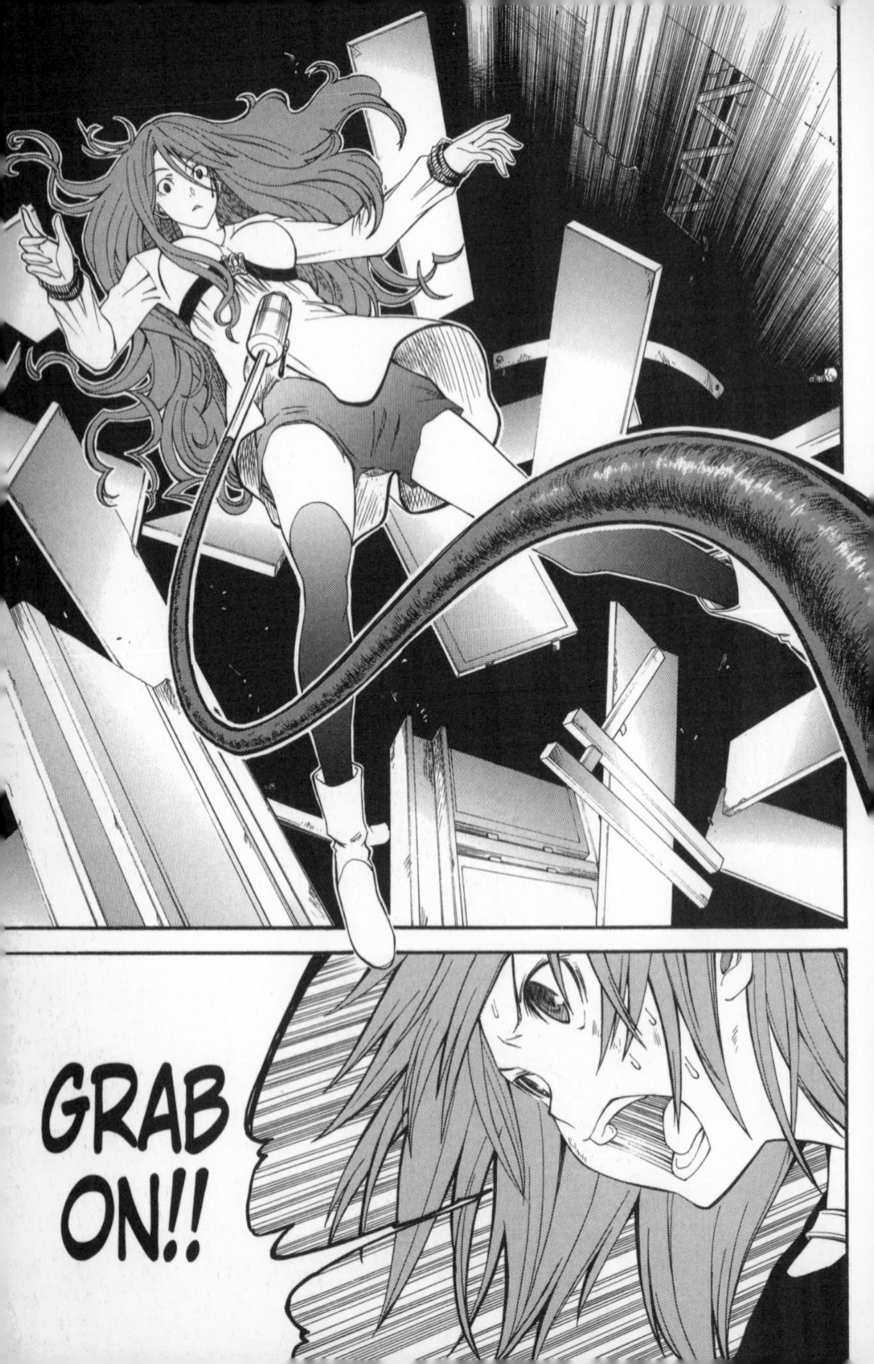
GRAB ON!!

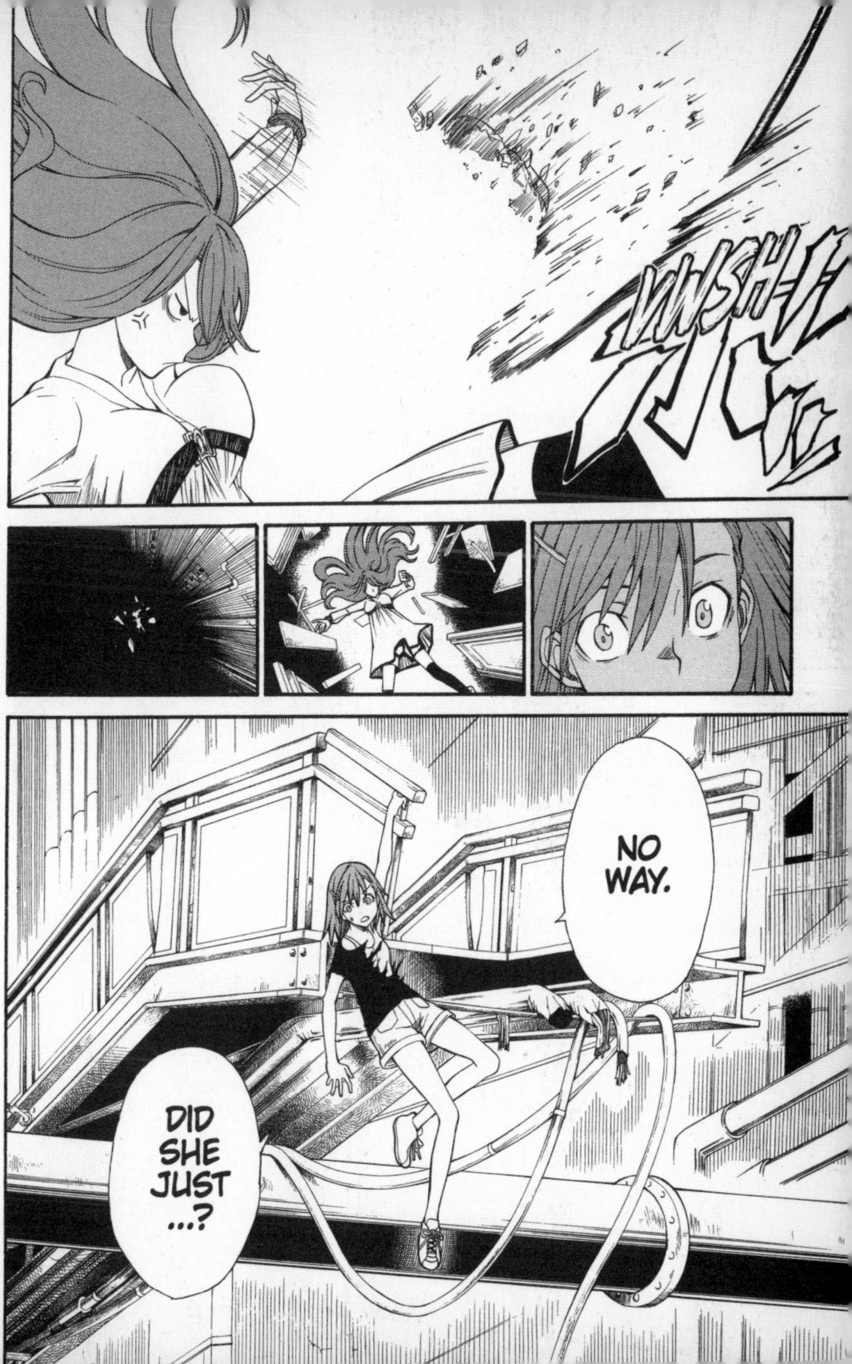
VWSH
NO WAY.
DID SHE JUST ...?

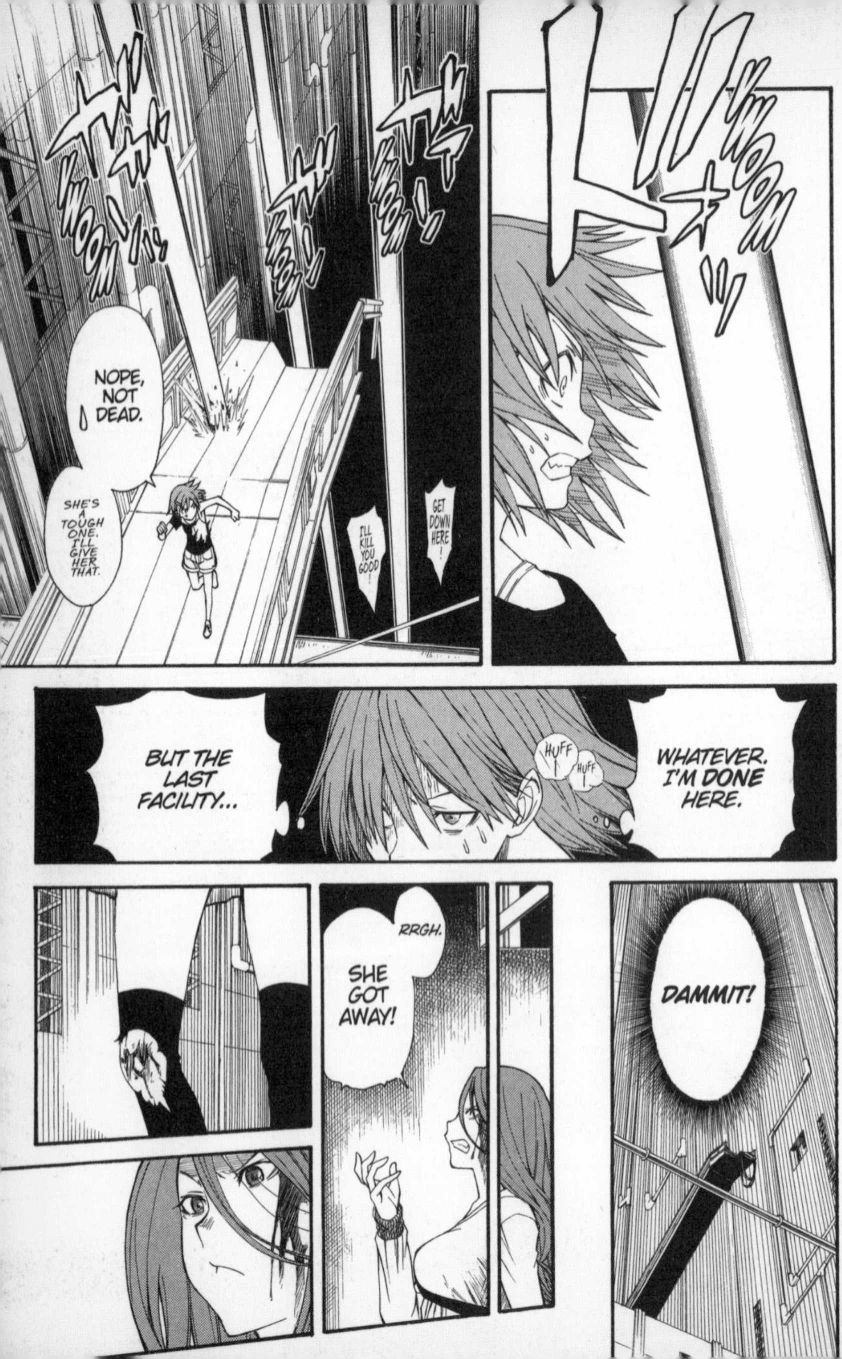
THWOOOM
VWOOOM
VWOOM
VWOOOM
GET DOWN HERE!
I'LL KILL YOU GOOD!
NOPE, NOT DEAD.
SHE'S A TOUGH ONE. I'LL GIVE HER THAT.
WHATEVER. I'M DONE HERE.
HUFF
HUFF
BUT THE LAST FACILITY...
DAMMIT!
RRGH.
SHE GOT AWAY!

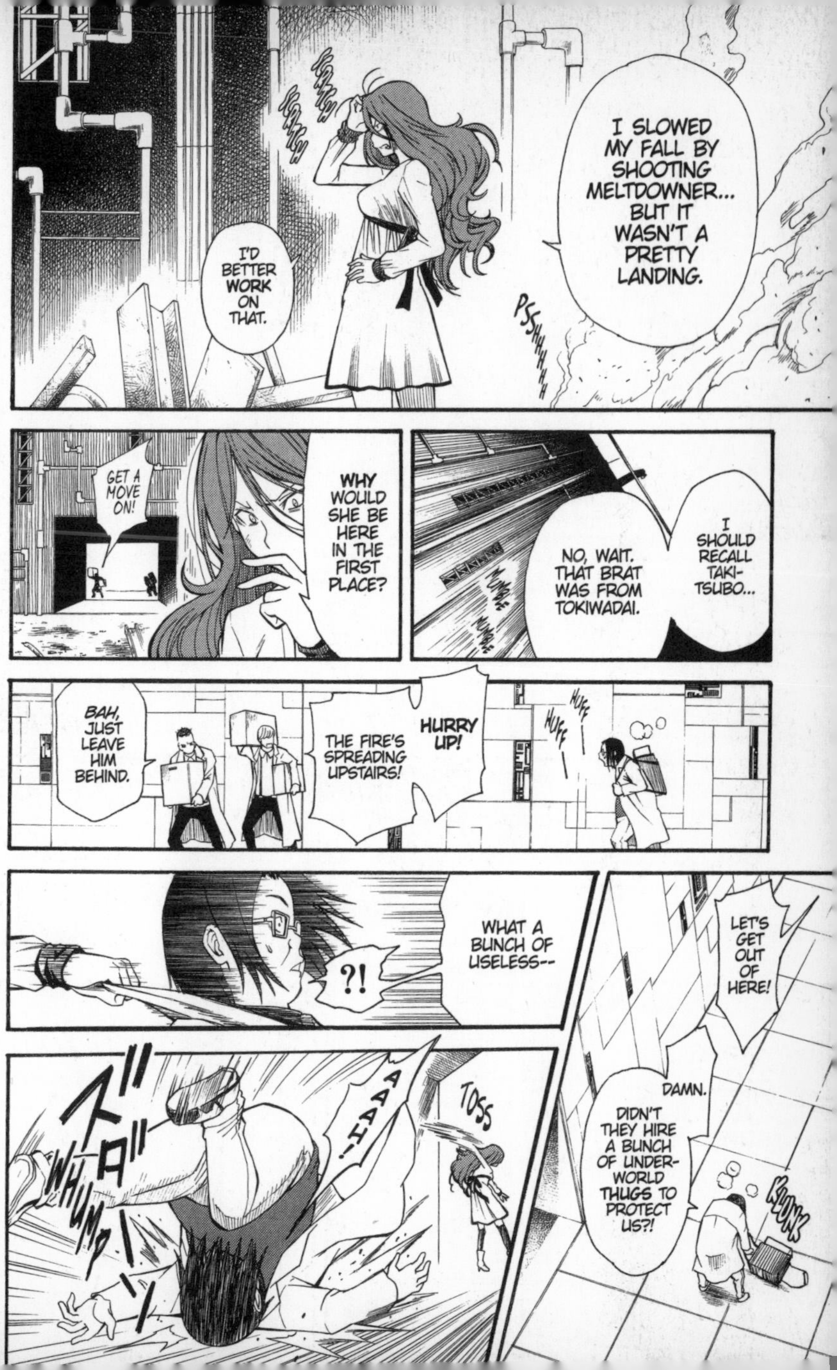
I SLOWED MY FALL BY SHOOTING MELTDOWNER... BUT IT WASN'T A PRETTY LANDING.
PSSHHHHHH
I'D BETTER WORK ON THAT.
I SHOULD RECALL TAKI-TSUBO...
NO, WAIT. THAT BRAT WAS FROM TOKIWADAI.
WHY WOULD SHE BE HERE IN THE FIRST PLACE?
GET A MOVE ON!
HUFF
HUFF
HURRY UP!
THE FIRE'S SPREADING UPSTAIRS!
BAH, JUST LEAVE HIM BEHIND.
LET'S GET OUT OF HERE!
DAMN.
DIDN'T THEY HIRE A BUNCH OF UNDER-WORLD THUGS TO PROTECT US?!
KLONK
WHAT A BUNCH OF USELESS--
?!
TOSS
AAAAH!
WHUMP

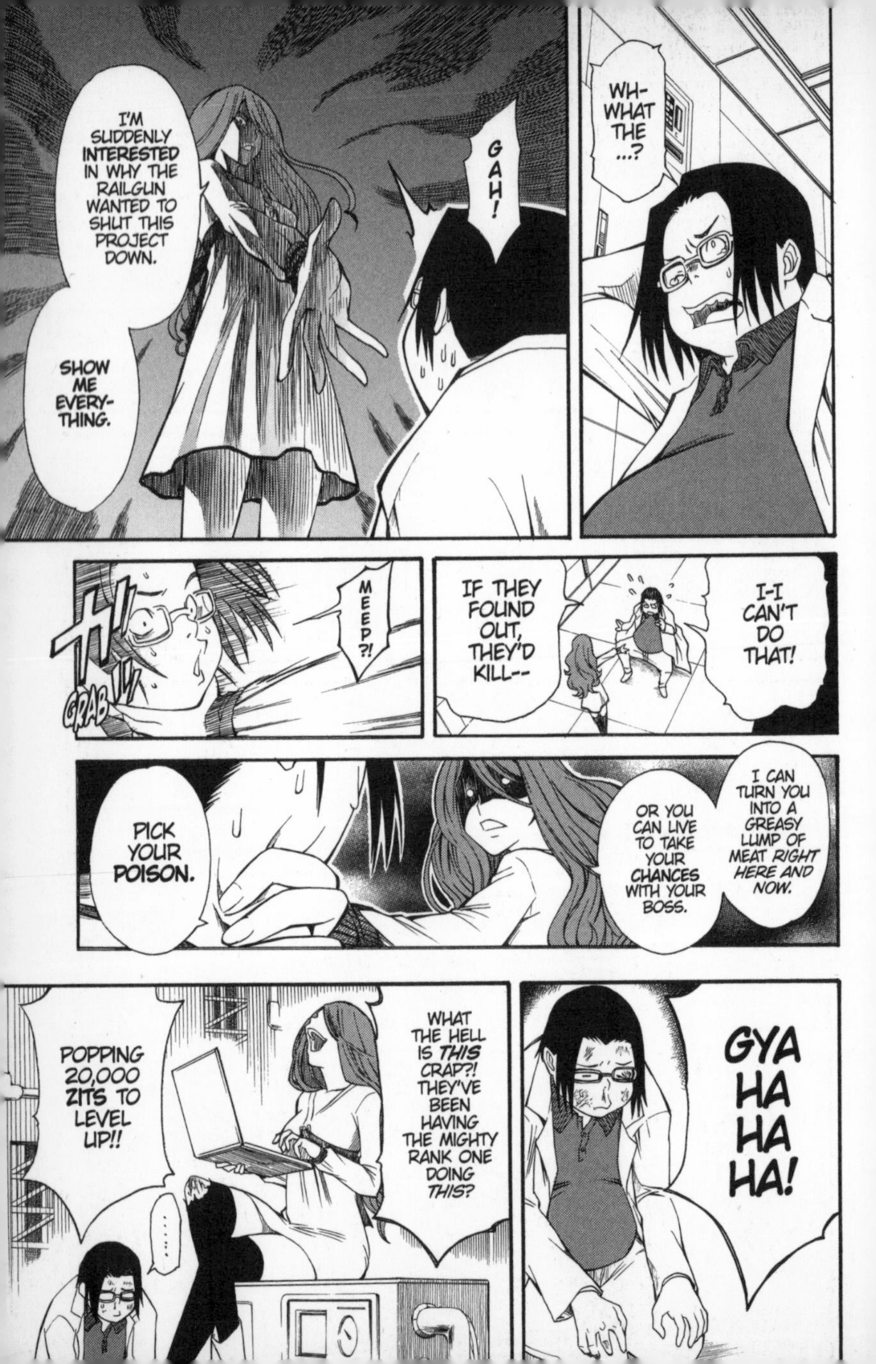
WH- WHAT THE ...?
GAH!
I'M SUDDENLY INTERESTED IN WHY THE RAILGUN WANTED TO SHUT THIS PROJECT DOWN.
SHOW ME EVERY-THING.
I-I CAN'T DO THAT!
IF THEY FOUND OUT, THEY'D KILL--
MEEP?!
GRAB
I CAN TURN YOU INTO A GREASY LUMP OF MEAT *RIGHT HERE AND NOW.*
OR YOU CAN LIVE TO TAKE YOUR CHANCES WITH YOUR BOSS.
PICK YOUR POISON.
GYA HA HA HA!
WHAT THE HELL IS *THIS* CRAP?! THEY'VE BEEN HAVING THE MIGHTY RANK ONE DOING *THIS?*
POPPING 20,000 ZITS TO LEVEL UP!!
......

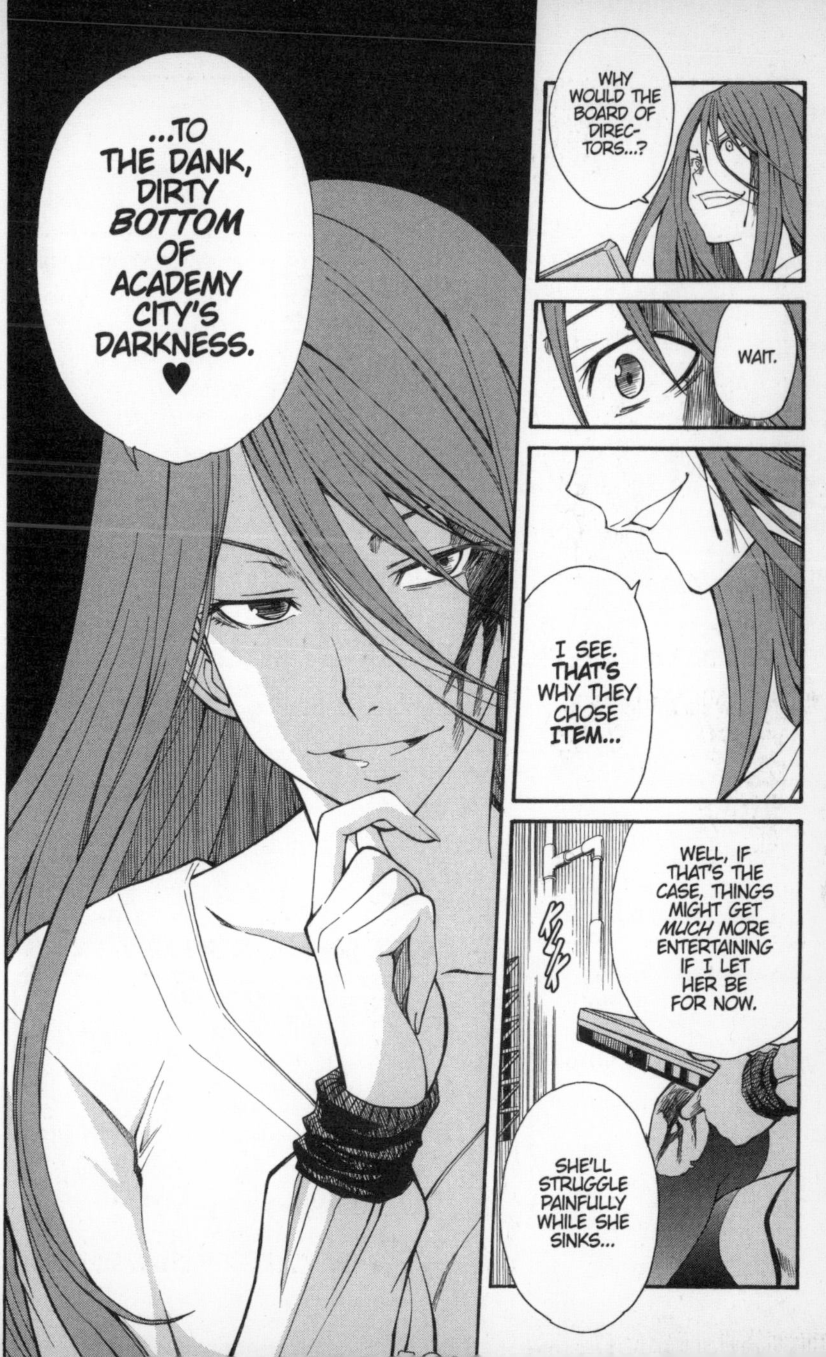
WHY WOULD THE BOARD OF DIRECTORS...?
WAIT.
I SEE. THAT'S WHY THEY CHOSE ITEM...
WELL, IF THAT'S THE CASE, THINGS MIGHT GET *MUCH* MORE ENTERTAINING IF I LET HER BE FOR NOW.
SHE'LL STRUGGLE PAINFULLY WHILE SHE SINKS...
...TO THE DANK, DIRTY *BOTTOM* OF ACADEMY CITY'S DARKNESS. ♥

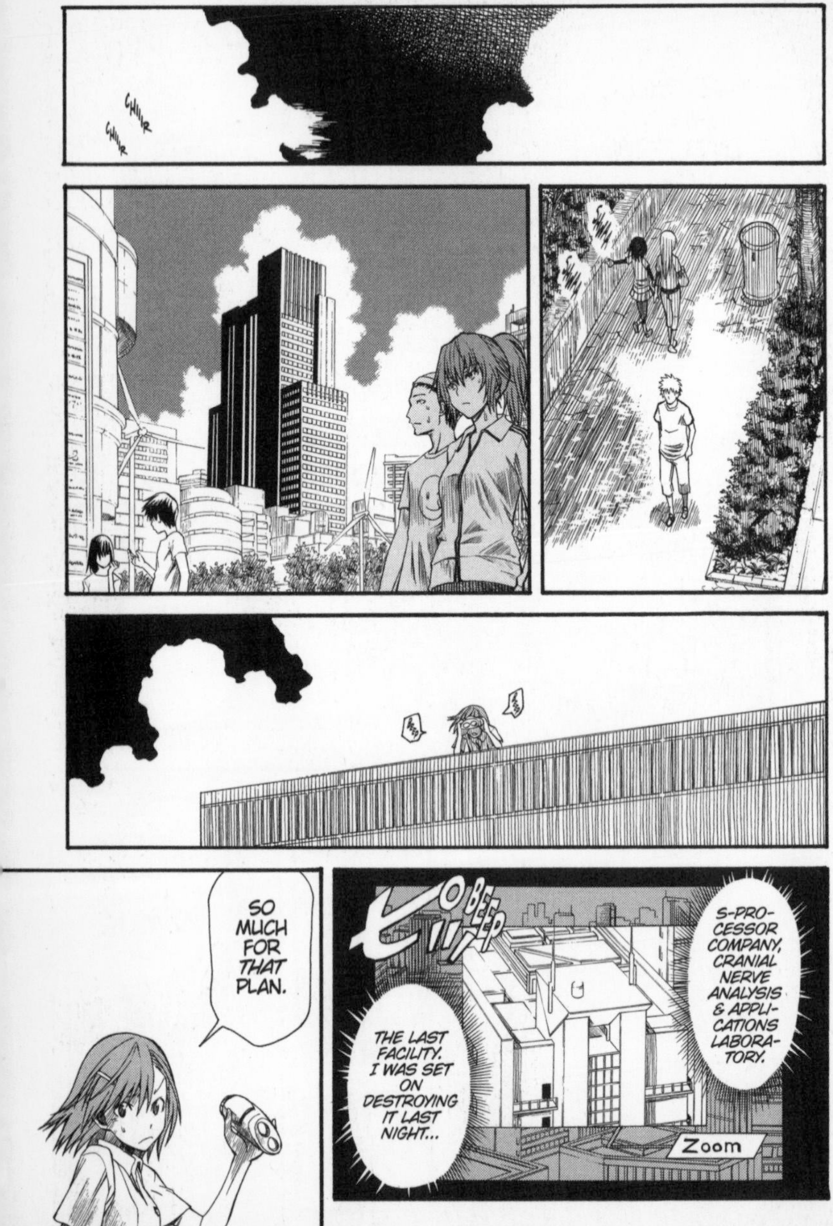
CHIIIR
CHIIIR
BEEP
BEEP
S-PROCESSOR COMPANY, CRANIAL NERVE ANALYSIS & APPLICATIONS LABORATORY.
THE LAST FACILITY. I WAS SET ON DESTROYING IT LAST NIGHT...
Zoom
SO MUCH FOR THAT PLAN.

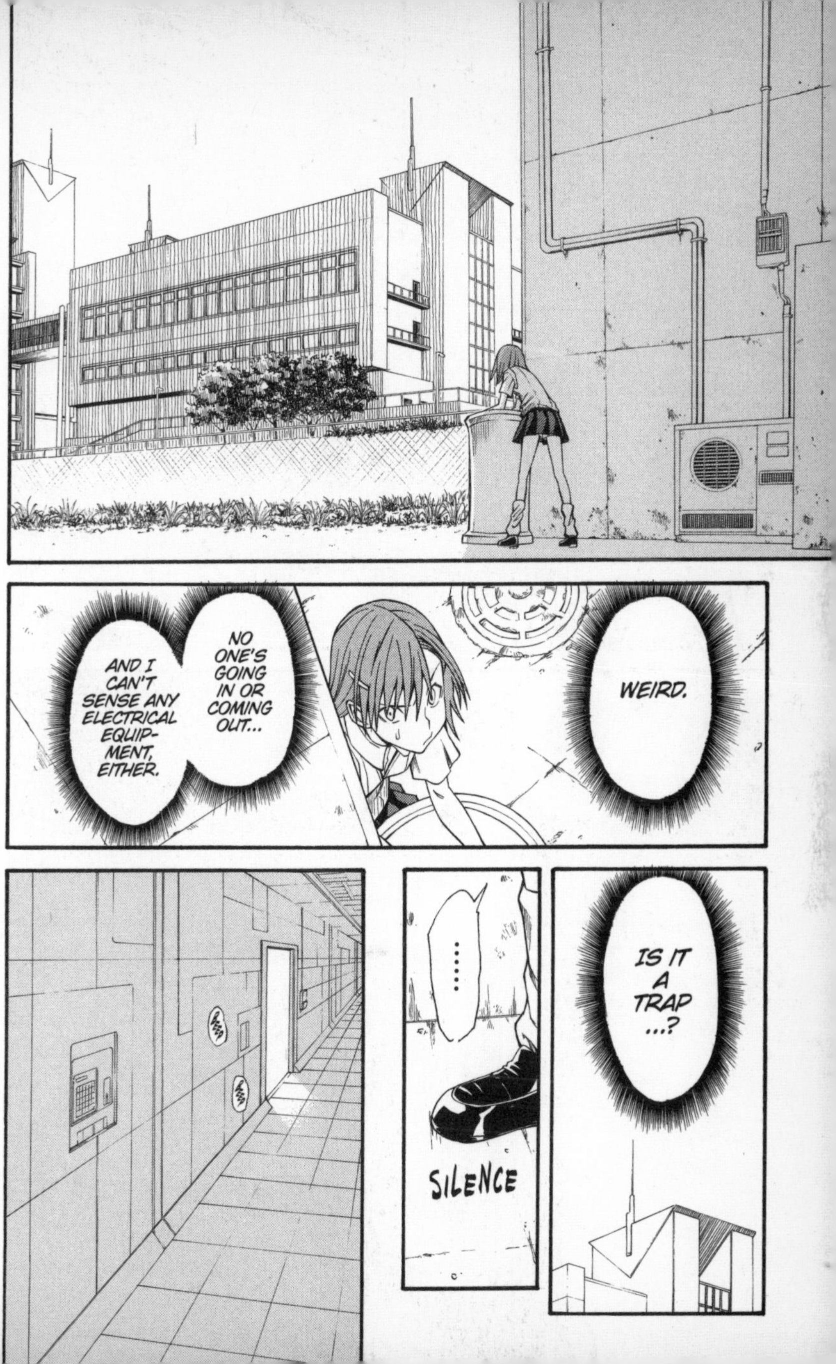
WEIRD.
NO ONE'S GOING IN OR COMING OUT...
AND I CAN'T SENSE ANY ELECTRICAL EQUIPMENT, EITHER.
IS IT A TRAP ...?
......
SILENCE

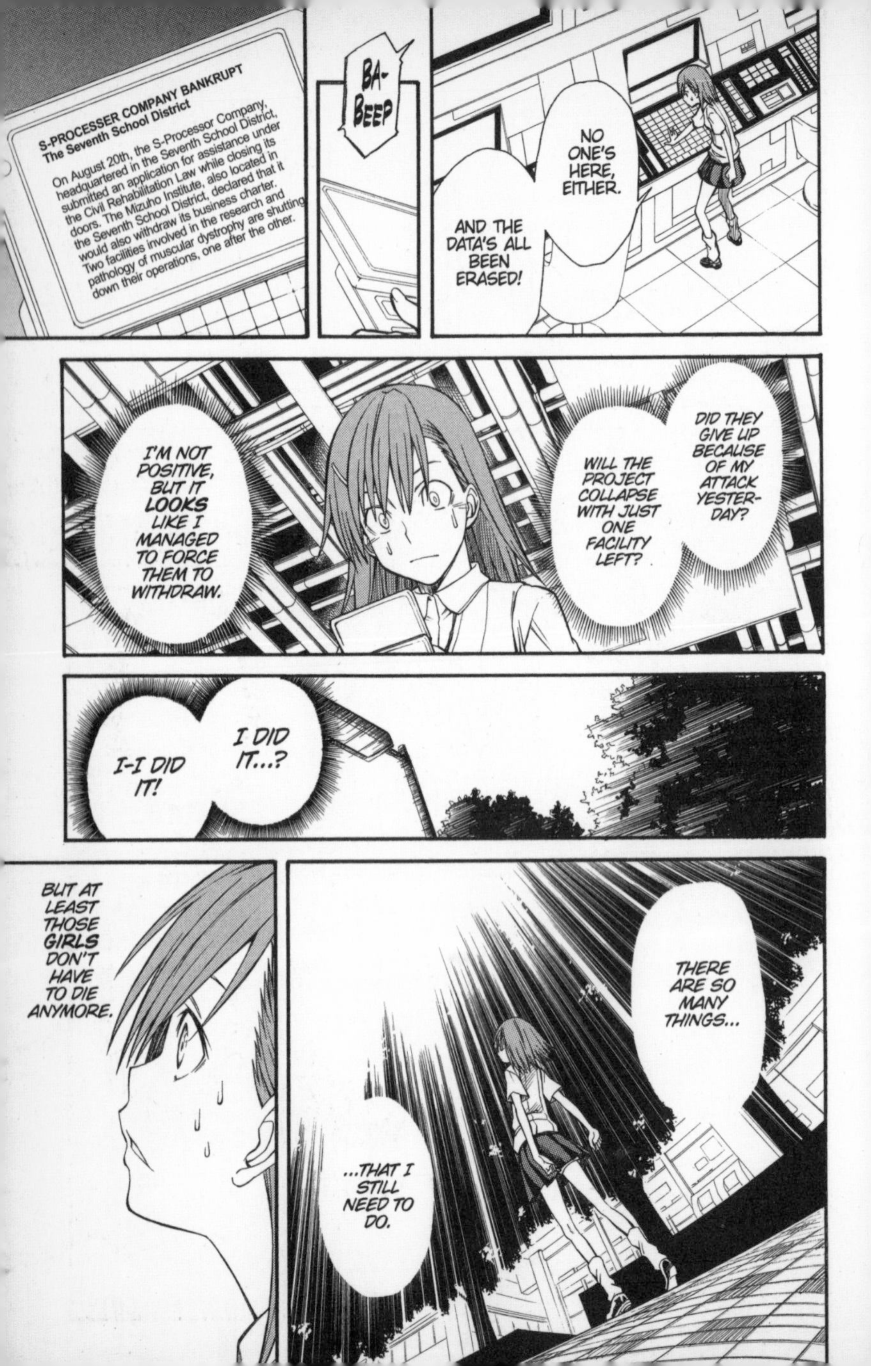
NO ONE'S HERE, EITHER.
AND THE DATA'S ALL BEEN ERASED!
BA-BEEP
S-PROCESSER COMPANY BANKRUPT
The Seventh School District
On August 20th, the S-Processor Company, headquartered in the Seventh School District, submitted an application for assistance under the Civil Rehabilitation Law while closing its doors. The Mizuho Institute, also located in the Seventh School District, declared that it would also withdraw its business charter. Two facilities involved in the research and pathology of muscular dystrophy are shutting down their operations, one after the other.
DID THEY GIVE UP BECAUSE OF MY ATTACK YESTERDAY?
WILL THE PROJECT COLLAPSE WITH JUST ONE FACILITY LEFT?
I'M NOT POSITIVE, BUT IT LOOKS LIKE I MANAGED TO FORCE THEM TO WITHDRAW.
I DID IT...?
I-I DID IT!
THERE ARE SO MANY THINGS...
...THAT I STILL NEED TO DO.
BUT AT LEAST THOSE GIRLS DON'T HAVE TO DIE ANYMORE.

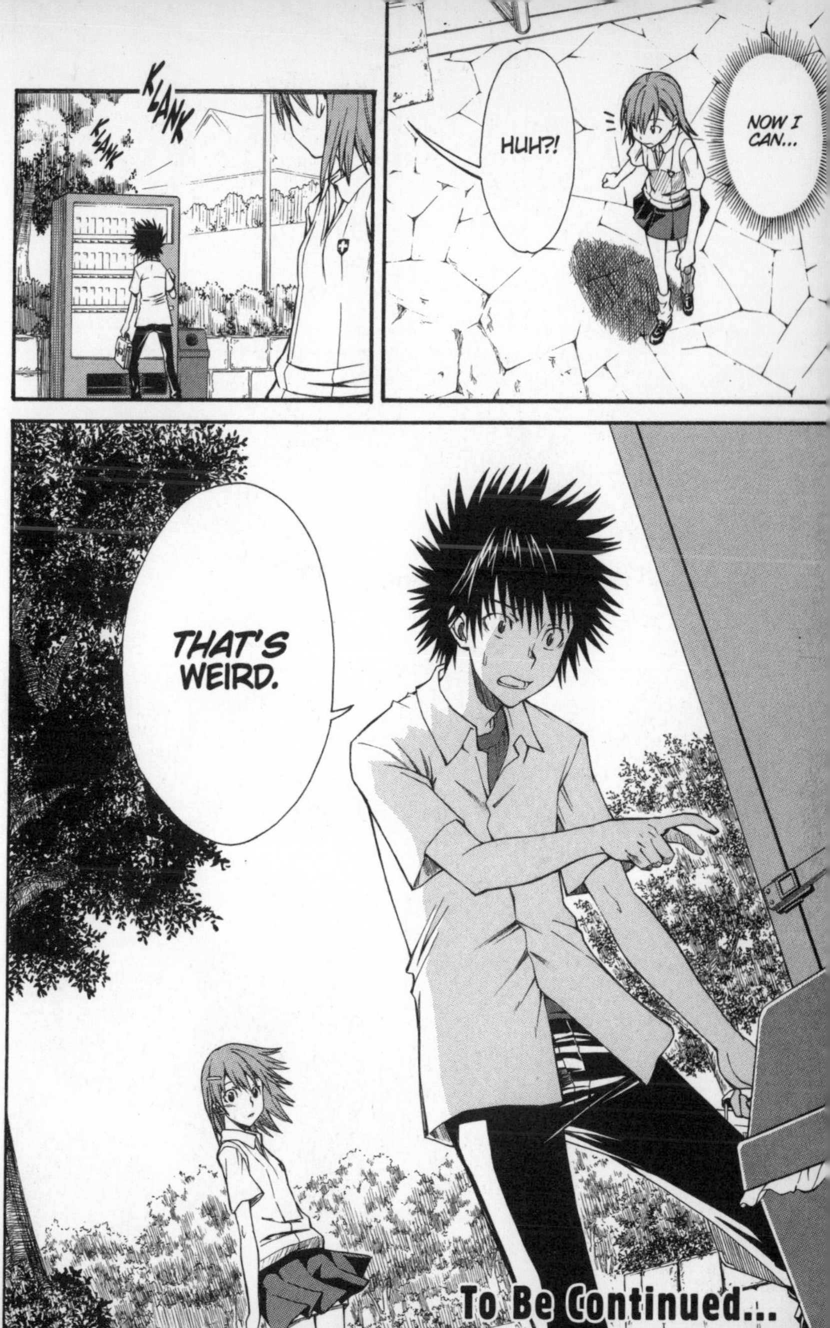
NOW I CAN...
HUH?!
KLANK
KLANK
THAT'S WEIRD.
To Be Continued...

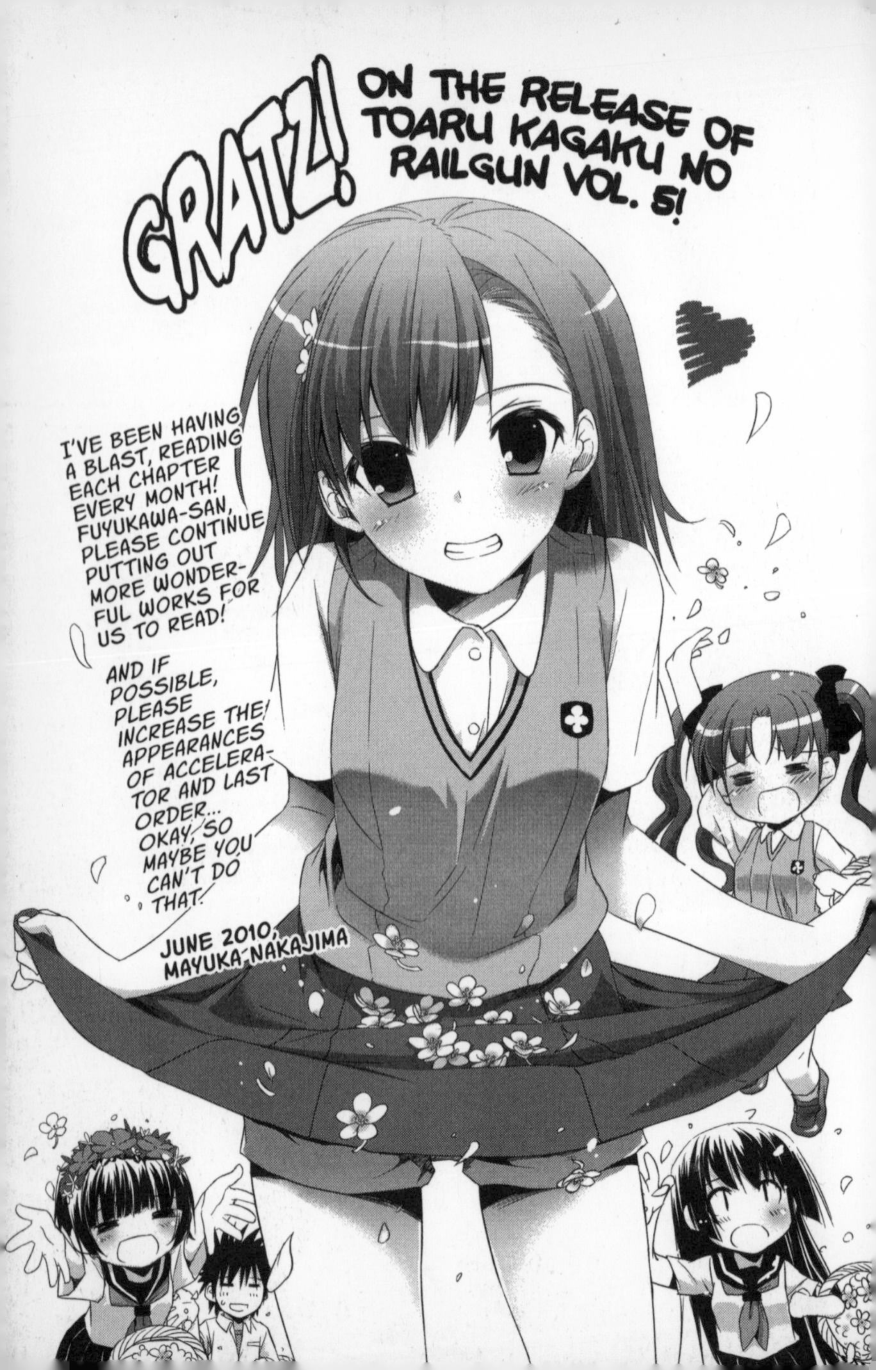
GRATZ!
ON THE RELEASE OF TOARU KAGAKU NO RAILGUN VOL. 5!
I'VE BEEN HAVING A BLAST, READING EACH CHAPTER EVERY MONTH! FUYUKAWA-SAN, PLEASE CONTINUE PUTTING OUT MORE WONDERFUL WORKS FOR US TO READ!
AND IF POSSIBLE, PLEASE INCREASE THE APPEARANCES OF ACCELERATOR AND LAST ORDER... OKAY, SO MAYBE YOU CAN'T DO THAT.
JUNE 2010, MAYUKA NAKAJIMA

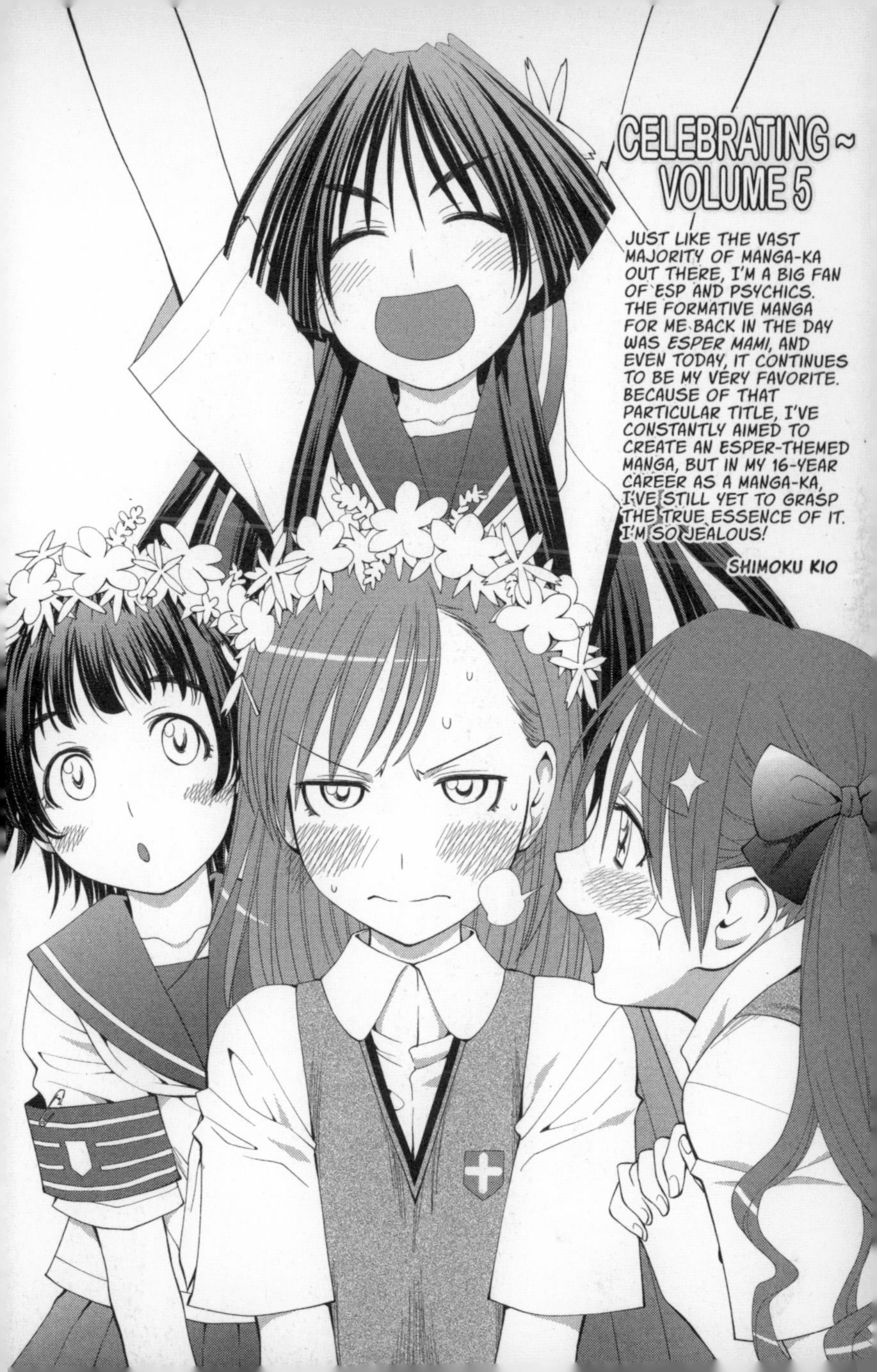
CELEBRATING ~ VOLUME 5
JUST LIKE THE VAST MAJORITY OF MANGA-KA OUT THERE, I'M A BIG FAN OF ESP AND PSYCHICS. THE FORMATIVE MANGA FOR ME BACK IN THE DAY WAS *ESPER MAMI*, AND EVEN TODAY, IT CONTINUES TO BE MY VERY FAVORITE. BECAUSE OF THAT PARTICULAR TITLE, I'VE CONSTANTLY AIMED TO CREATE AN ESPER-THEMED MANGA, BUT IN MY 16-YEAR CAREER AS A MANGA-KA, I'VE STILL YET TO GRASP THE TRUE ESSENCE OF IT. I'M SO JEALOUS!
SHIMOKU KIO

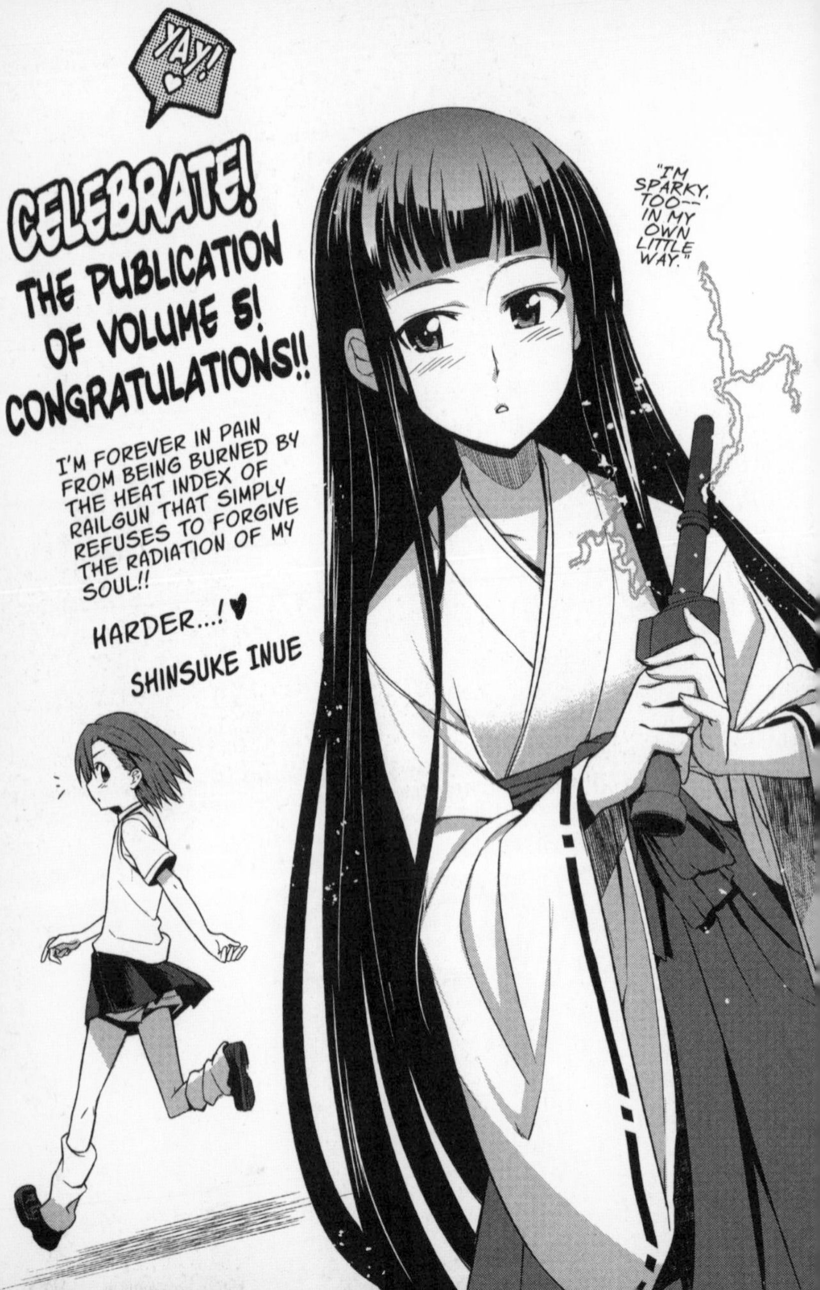
YAY! ♥
CELEBRATE!
THE PUBLICATION OF VOLUME 5! CONGRATULATIONS!!
I'M FOREVER IN PAIN FROM BEING BURNED BY THE HEAT INDEX OF THE RAILGUN THAT SIMPLY REFUSES TO FORGIVE THE RADIATION OF MY SOUL!!
HARDER...! ♥
SHINSUKE INUE
"I'M SPARKY, TOO-- IN MY OWN LITTLE WAY."

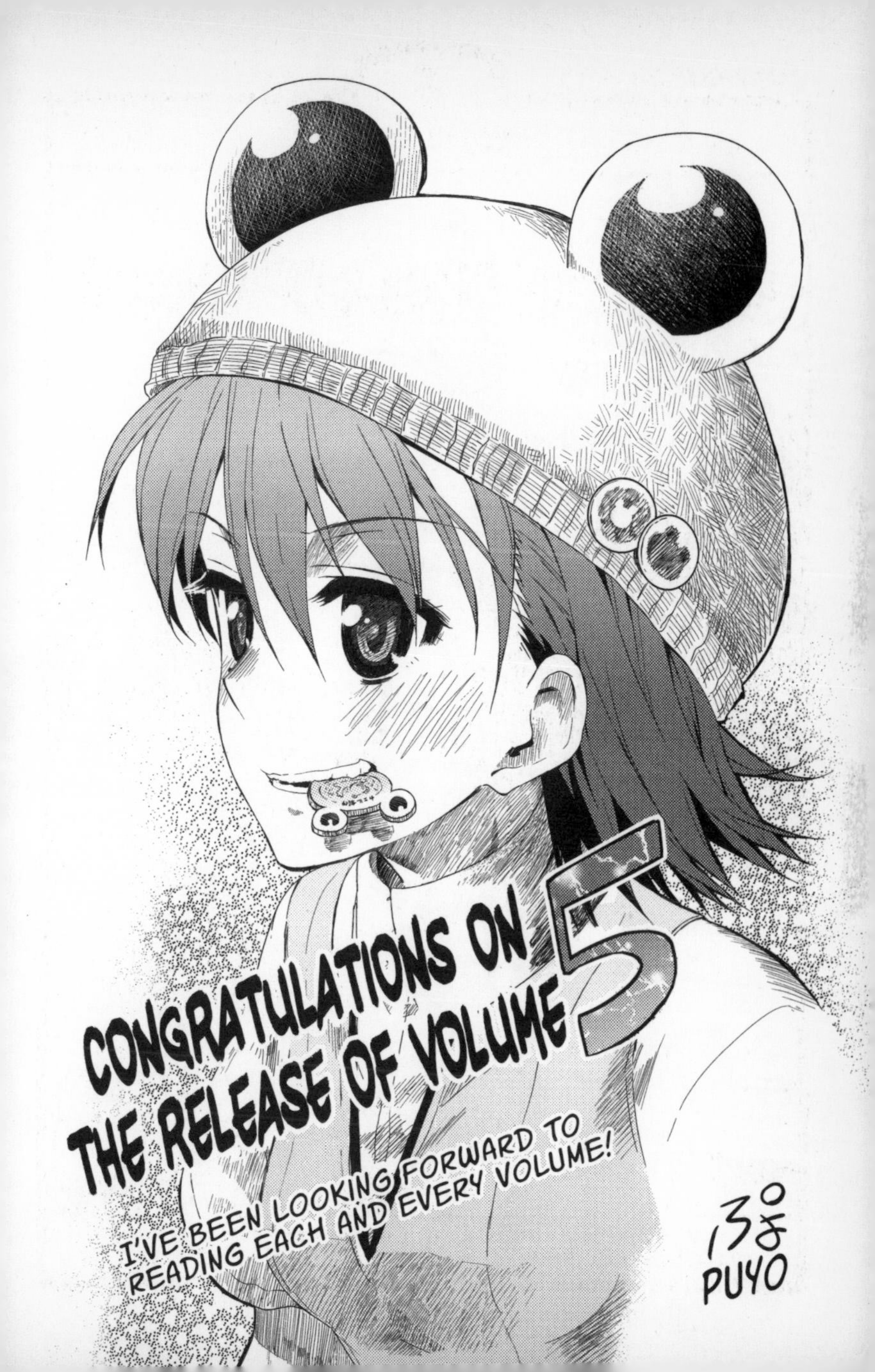
CONGRATULATIONS ON THE RELEASE OF VOLUME 5
I'VE BEEN LOOKING FORWARD TO READING EACH AND EVERY VOLUME!
ぷよ
PUYO

DENGEKI BOOKS

HERE LIE THE ORIGINS OF RAILGUN!
A CERTAIN MAGICAL INDEX

KAZUMA KAMACHI
ILLUSTRATIONS/ HAIMURA KIYOTAKA
① ~ ⑳ + SS ① ②

BIRI

LET'S FIGHT!

BIRI

TOUMA~!
I'M
HUNGRY~!!

TWITCH

Clash of the Empresses

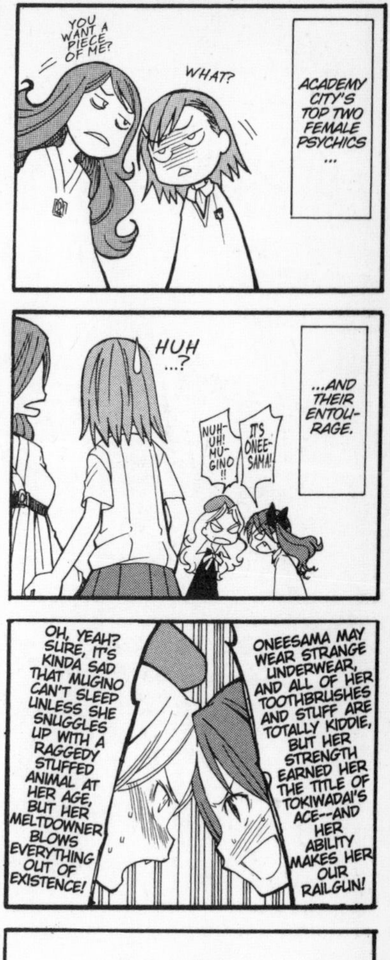
ACADEMY CITY'S TOP TWO FEMALE PSYCHICS ...
WHAT?
YOU WANT A PIECE OF ME?
...AND THEIR ENTOURAGE.
IT'S ONEESAMA!
NUH-UH! MUGINO!!
HUH ...?
ONEESAMA MAY WEAR STRANGE UNDERWEAR, AND ALL OF HER TOOTHBRUSHES AND STUFF ARE TOTALLY KIDDIE, BUT HER STRENGTH EARNED HER THE TITLE OF TOKIWADAI'S ACE--AND HER ABILITY MAKES HER OUR RAILGUN!
OH, YEAH? SURE, IT'S KINDA SAD THAT MUGINO CAN'T SLEEP UNLESS SHE SNUGGLES UP WITH A RAGGEDY STUFFED ANIMAL AT HER AGE, BUT HER MELTDOWNER BLOWS EVERYTHING OUT OF EXISTENCE!

Chest Armor

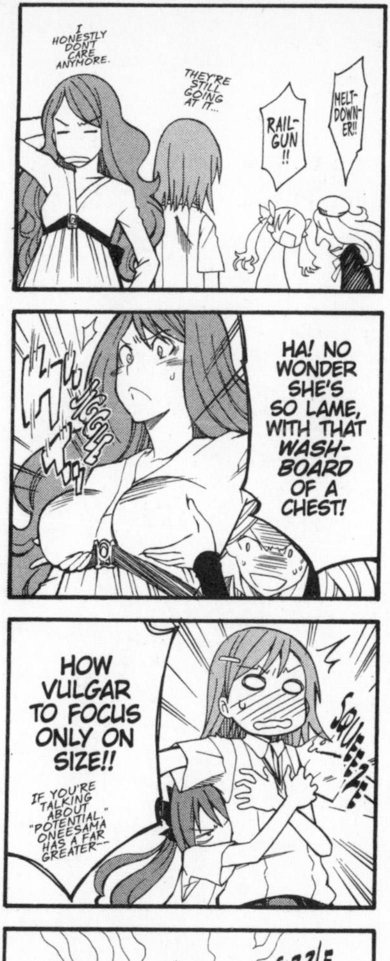
MELT-DOWN-ER!!
RAIL-GUN!!
THEY'RE STILL GOING AT IT...
I HONESTLY DON'T CARE ANYMORE.
HA! NO WONDER SHE'S SO LAME, WITH THAT WASHBOARD OF A CHEST!
SQUEEZE
HOW VULGAR TO FOCUS ONLY ON SIZE!!
IF YOU'RE TALKING ABOUT "POTENTIAL," ONEESAMA HAS A FAR GREATER--
SIZZLE

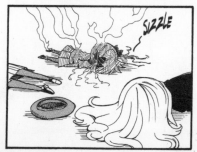

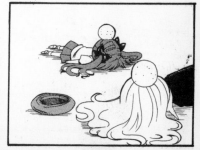

Double Stalking?

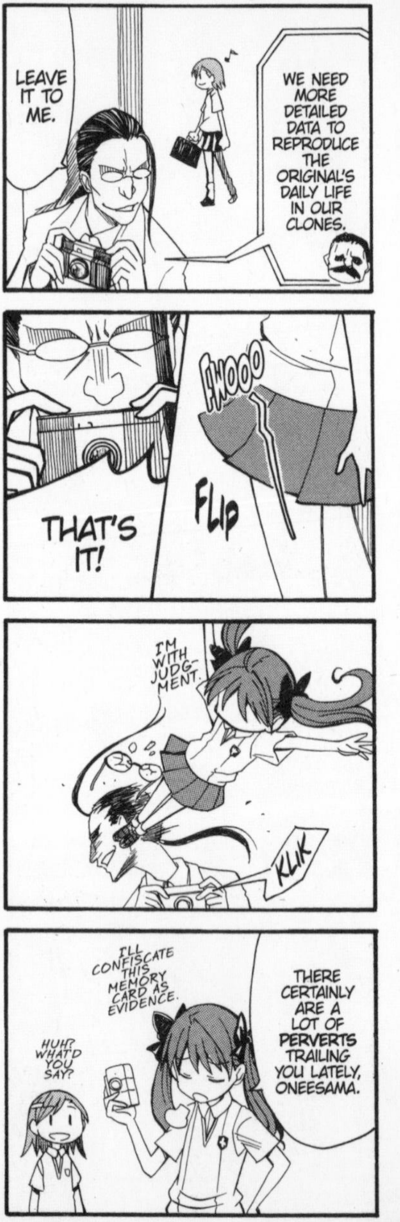
WE NEED MORE DETAILED DATA TO REPRODUCE THE ORIGINAL'S DAILY LIFE IN OUR CLONES.
LEAVE IT TO ME.
FWOOO
FLIP
THAT'S IT!
I'M WITH JUDGMENT.
KLIK
THERE CERTAINLY ARE A LOT OF PERVERTS TRAILING YOU LATELY, ONEESAMA.
I'LL CONFISCATE THIS MEMORY CARD AS EVIDENCE.
HUH? WHAT'D YOU SAY?

Make Sure to Disinfect the Filth

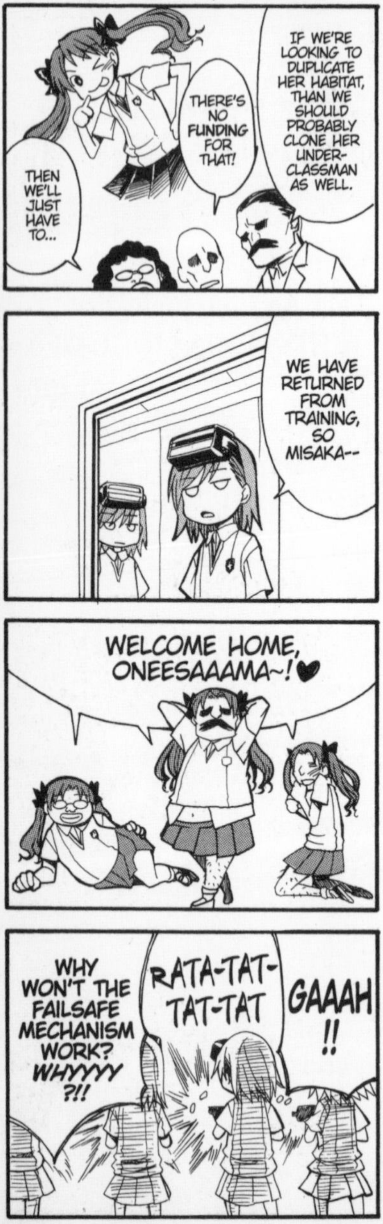
IF WE'RE LOOKING TO DUPLICATE HER HABITAT, THAN WE SHOULD PROBABLY CLONE HER UNDER-CLASSMAN AS WELL.
THERE'S NO FUNDING FOR THAT!
THEN WE'LL JUST HAVE TO...
WE HAVE RETURNED FROM TRAINING, SO MISAKA--
WELCOME HOME, ONEESAAAMA~!♥
GAAAH !!
RATA-TAT-TAT-TAT
WHY WON'T THE FAILSAFE MECHANISM WORK? WHYYYY ?!!

A Certain SCIENTIFIC Railgun

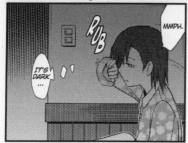

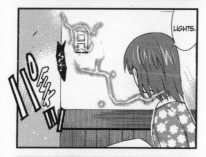

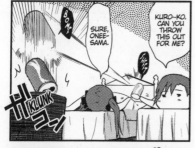

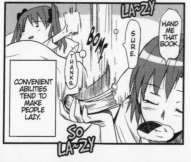

OMAKE THEATRE
CHIKI CHIKI JUDGMENT

ART: SHINSUKE INUE

A Certain Lazy Level 4 and 5

MMPH.
RUB
IT'S DARK...
LIGHTS.
FLIK
KURO~KO. CAN YOU THROW THIS OUT FOR ME?
SURE, ONEE-SAMA.
BOMF
KLUNK
LA~ZY
HAND ME THAT BOOK.
SURE.
BOMF
THANKS.
CONVENIENT ABILITIES TEND TO MAKE PEOPLE LAZY.
SO LA~ZY

A Certain Beloved Mascot

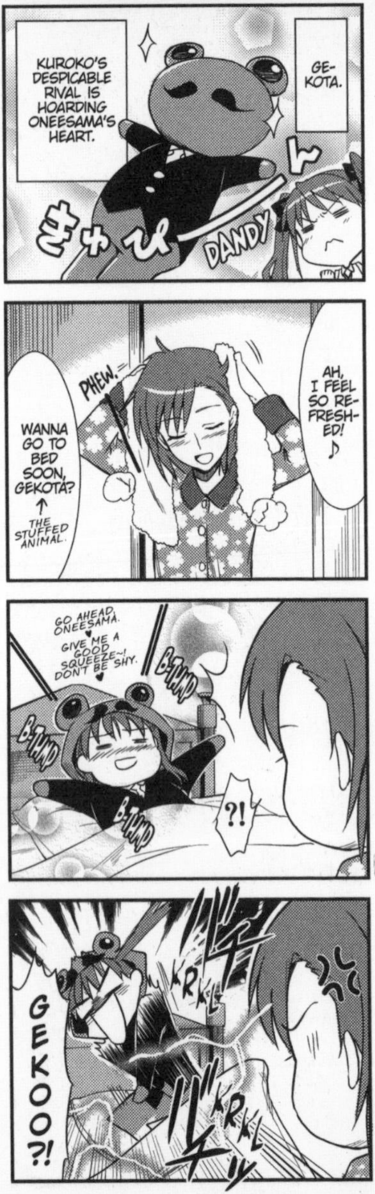
GE-KOTA.
KUROKO'S DESPICABLE RIVAL IS HOARDING ONEESAMA'S HEART.
きゅぴ
DANDY
AH, I FEEL SO REFRESHED! ♪
PHEW.
WANNA GO TO BED SOON, GEKOTA?
↑ THE STUFFED ANIMAL.
?!
B-THMP
GO AHEAD, ONEESAMA. GIVE ME A GOOD SQUEEZE~! DON'T BE SHY. ♥
B-THMP
B-THMP
KRKL
GEKOOO?!
KRKL

A Certain Duo's Hard Work

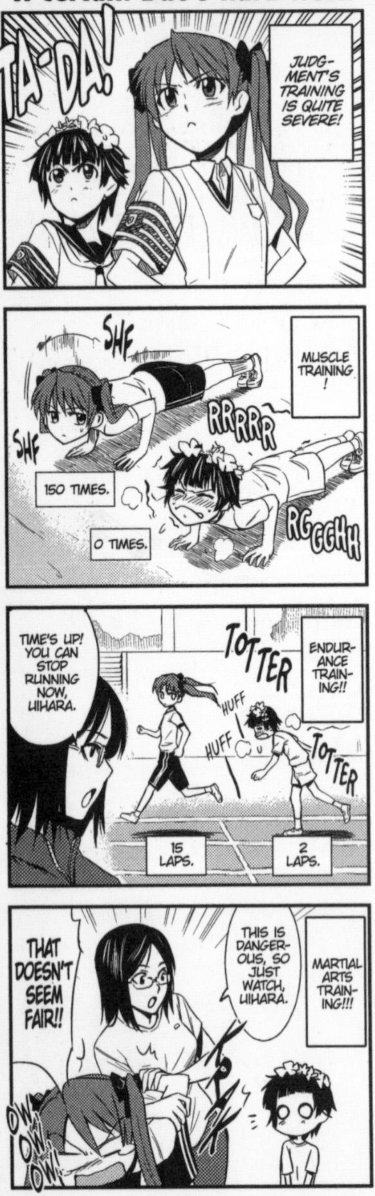
JUDGMENT'S TRAINING IS QUITE SEVERE!
TA-DA!
MUSCLE TRAINING!
SHF
RRRRR
SHF
150 TIMES.
RGGGHH
0 TIMES.
ENDURANCE TRAINING!!
TOTTER
TIME'S UP! YOU CAN STOP RUNNING NOW, UIHARA.
HUFF
HUFF
TOTTER
15 LAPS.
2 LAPS.
MARTIAL ARTS TRAINING!!!
THIS IS DANGEROUS, SO JUST WATCH, UIHARA.
THAT DOESN'T SEEM FAIR!!
OW OW OW OW!

A Certain PC's Search History

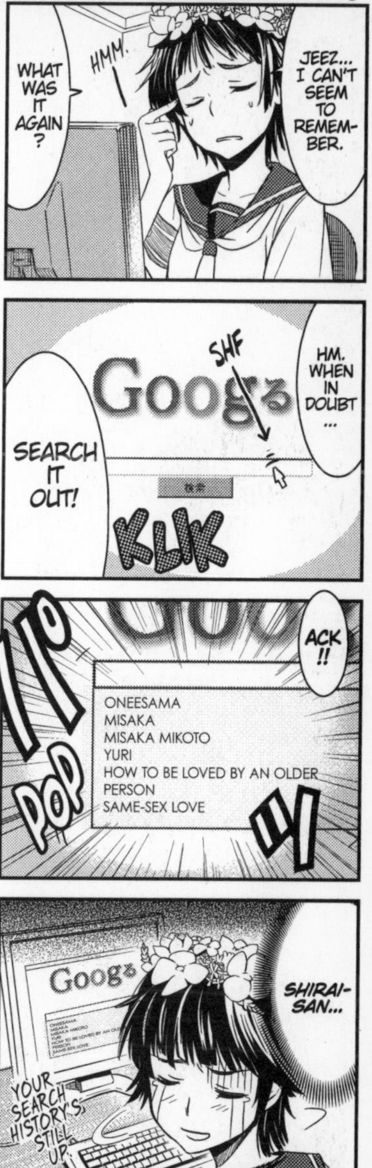
JEEZ... I CAN'T SEEM TO REMEMBER.
HMM.
WHAT WAS IT AGAIN?
HM. WHEN IN DOUBT...
SHF
Googる
検索
SEARCH IT OUT!
KLIK
ACK!!
ONEESAMA
MISAKA
MISAKA MIKOTO
YURI
HOW TO BE LOVED BY AN OLDER PERSON
SAME-SEX LOVE
POP
SHIRAI-SAN...
Googる
YOUR SEARCH HISTORY'S STILL UP.

A Certain Kuroko's OneesaMAP

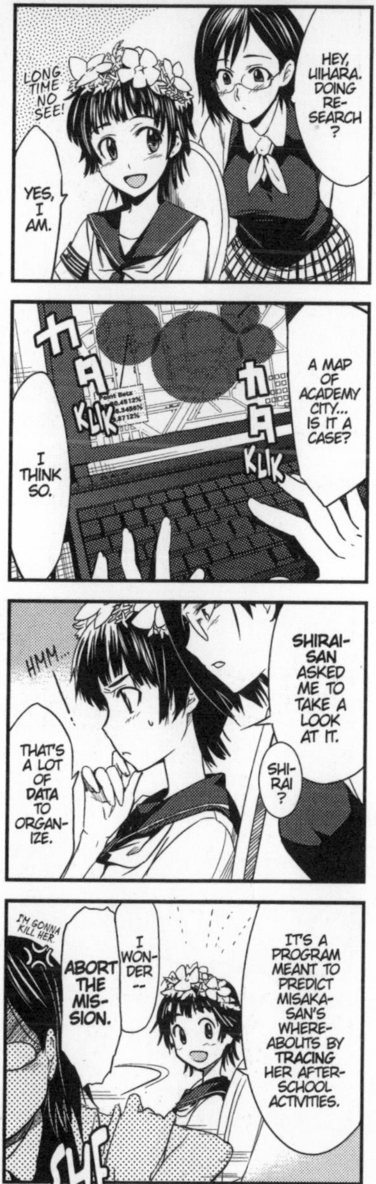
HEY, UIHARA. DOING RE-SEARCH?
LONG TIME NO SEE!
YES, I AM.
A MAP OF ACADEMY CITY... IS IT A CASE?
カタ
KLIK
カター
KLIK
I THINK SO.
SHIRAI-SAN ASKED ME TO TAKE A LOOK AT IT.
SHI-RAI?
HMM...
THAT'S A LOT OF DATA TO ORGAN-IZE.
IT'S A PROGRAM MEANT TO PREDICT MISAKA-SAN'S WHERE-ABOUTS BY TRACING HER AFTER-SCHOOL ACTIVITIES.
I WONDER--
ABORT THE MIS-SION.
I'M GONNA KILL HER.
SHF

A Certain Kazari's Raison d'Etre

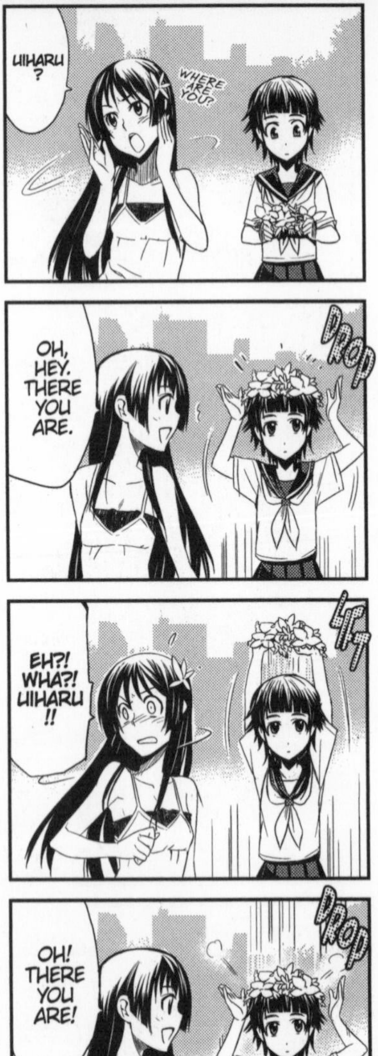
UIHARU?
WHERE ARE YOU?
DROP
OH, HEY. THERE YOU ARE.
LIFT
EH?! WHA?! UIHARU!!
DROP
OH! THERE YOU ARE!

A Certain Early Fall Image Change

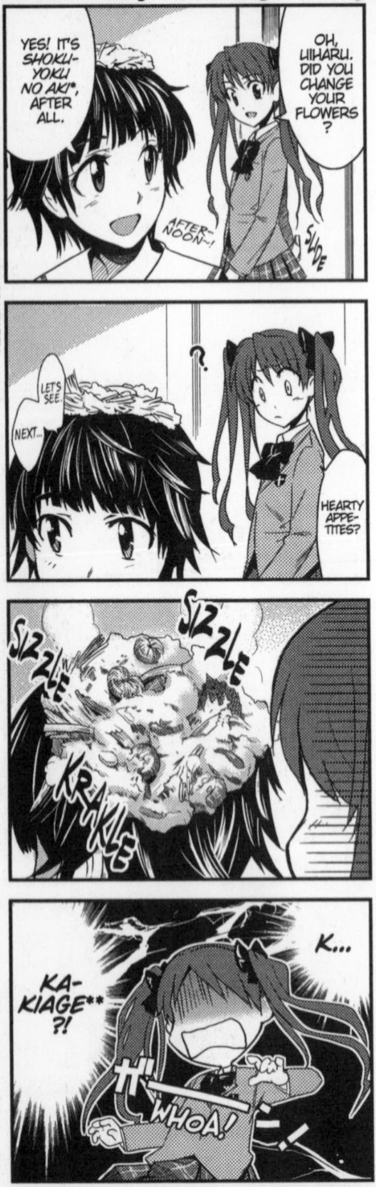
OH, UIHARU. DID YOU CHANGE YOUR FLOWERS?
YES! IT'S SHOKUYOKU NO AKI*, AFTER ALL.
AFTER-NOON~!
SLIDE
?
LET'S SEE. NEXT...
HEARTY APPE-TITES?
SIZZLE
SIZZLE
KRAKLE
K...
KA-KIAGE**?!
WHOA!

*SHOKUYOKU NO AKI, LITERALLY THE SEASON OF HEARTY APPETITES. MANY FOODS ARE AT THEIR PRIME IN FALL.

**KAKIAGE IS A MIXED VEGETABLE AND SEAFOOD TEMPURA FRIED TOGETHER IN A ROUND FRITTER.

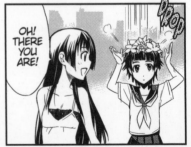

A Certain Boys' Judgment

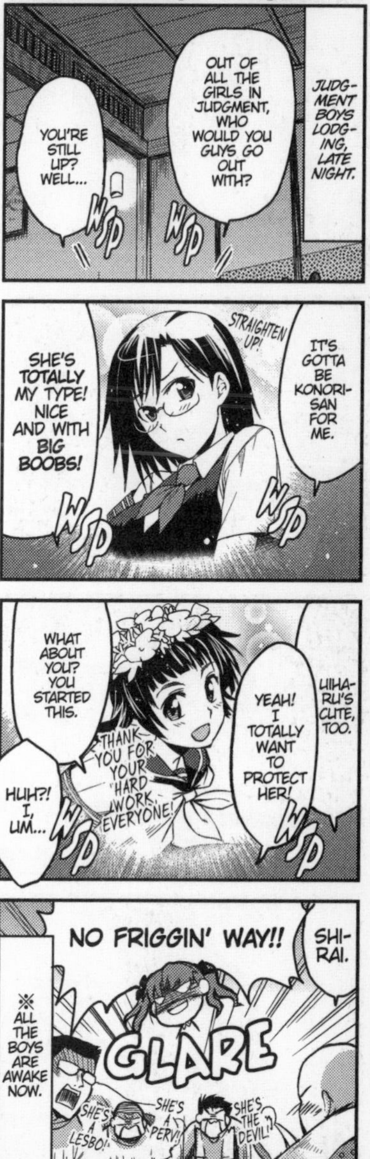
JUDGMENT BOYS LODGING, LATE NIGHT.
OUT OF ALL THE GIRLS IN JUDGMENT, WHO WOULD YOU GUYS GO OUT WITH?
YOU'RE STILL UP? WELL...
WSP
WSP
IT'S GOTTA BE KONORI-SAN FOR ME.
STRAIGHTEN UP!
SHE'S TOTALLY MY TYPE! NICE AND WITH BIG BOOBS!
WSP
WSP
UIHARU'S CUTE, TOO.
YEAH! I TOTALLY WANT TO PROTECT HER!
WHAT ABOUT YOU? YOU STARTED THIS.
THANK YOU FOR YOUR HARD WORK, EVERYONE!
HUH?! I, UM...
WSP
WSP
SHI-RAI.
NO FRIGGIN' WAY!!
※ ALL THE BOYS ARE AWAKE NOW.
GLARE
SHE'S THE DEVIL!
SHE'S A PERV!!
SHE'S A LESBO!

A Certain Mastermind's Guideline

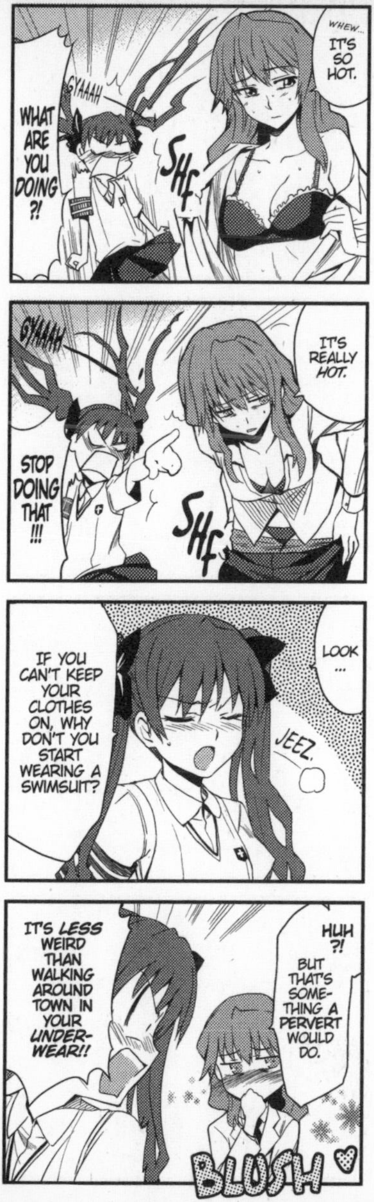
WHEW... IT'S SO HOT.
GYAAAH
SHF
WHAT ARE YOU DOING?!
IT'S REALLY HOT.
GYAAAH
SHF
STOP DOING THAT!!!
LOOK...
IF YOU CAN'T KEEP YOUR CLOTHES ON, WHY DON'T YOU START WEARING A SWIMSUIT?
JEEZ.
HUH?!
BUT THAT'S SOME-THING A PERVERT WOULD DO.
IT'S LESS WEIRD THAN WALKING AROUND TOWN IN YOUR UNDER-WEAR!!
BLUSH

A Certain Institute's Artist

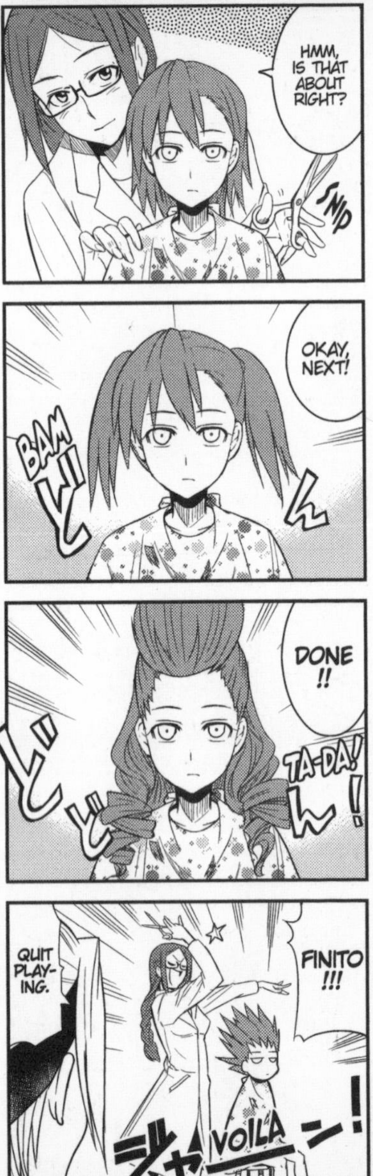
HMM, IS THAT ABOUT RIGHT?
SNIP
OKAY, NEXT!
BAM
DONE !!
TA-DA!
FINITO !!!
QUIT PLAYING.
VOILA

A Certain Misakas' Special Skill

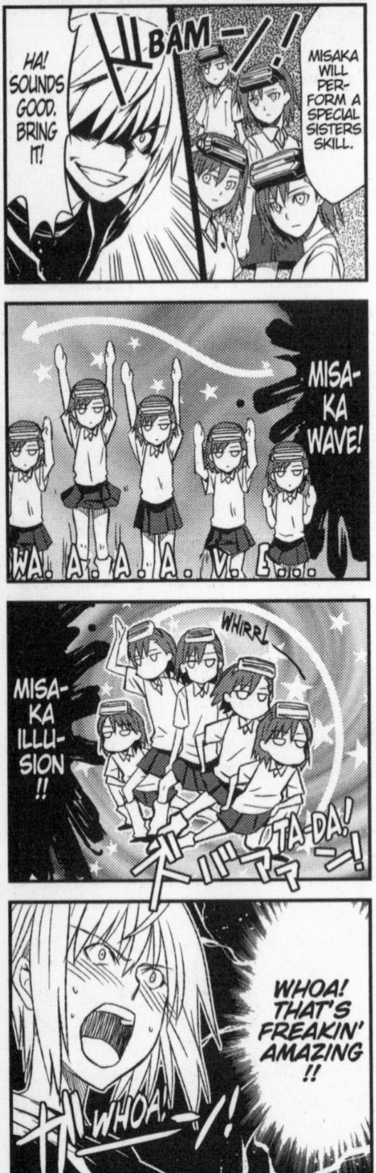
BAM —/!
MISAKA WILL PERFORM A SPECIAL SISTERS SKILL.
HA! SOUNDS GOOD. BRING IT!
MISA-KA WAVE!
WA. A. A. A. V. E...
WHIRRL
MISA-KA ILLU-SION !!
TA-DA!
WHOA! THAT'S FREAKIN' AMAZING !!
WHOA—/!

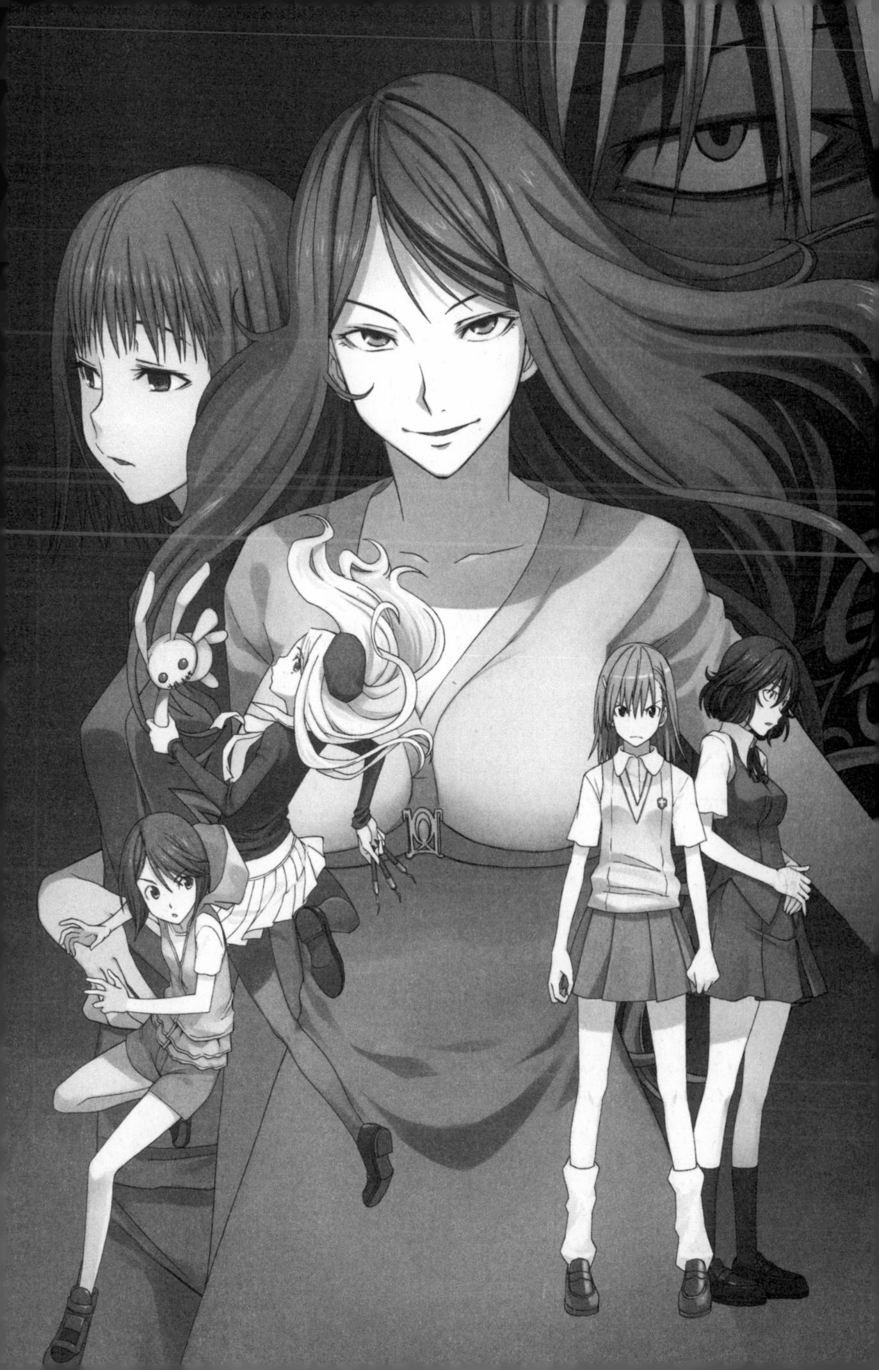

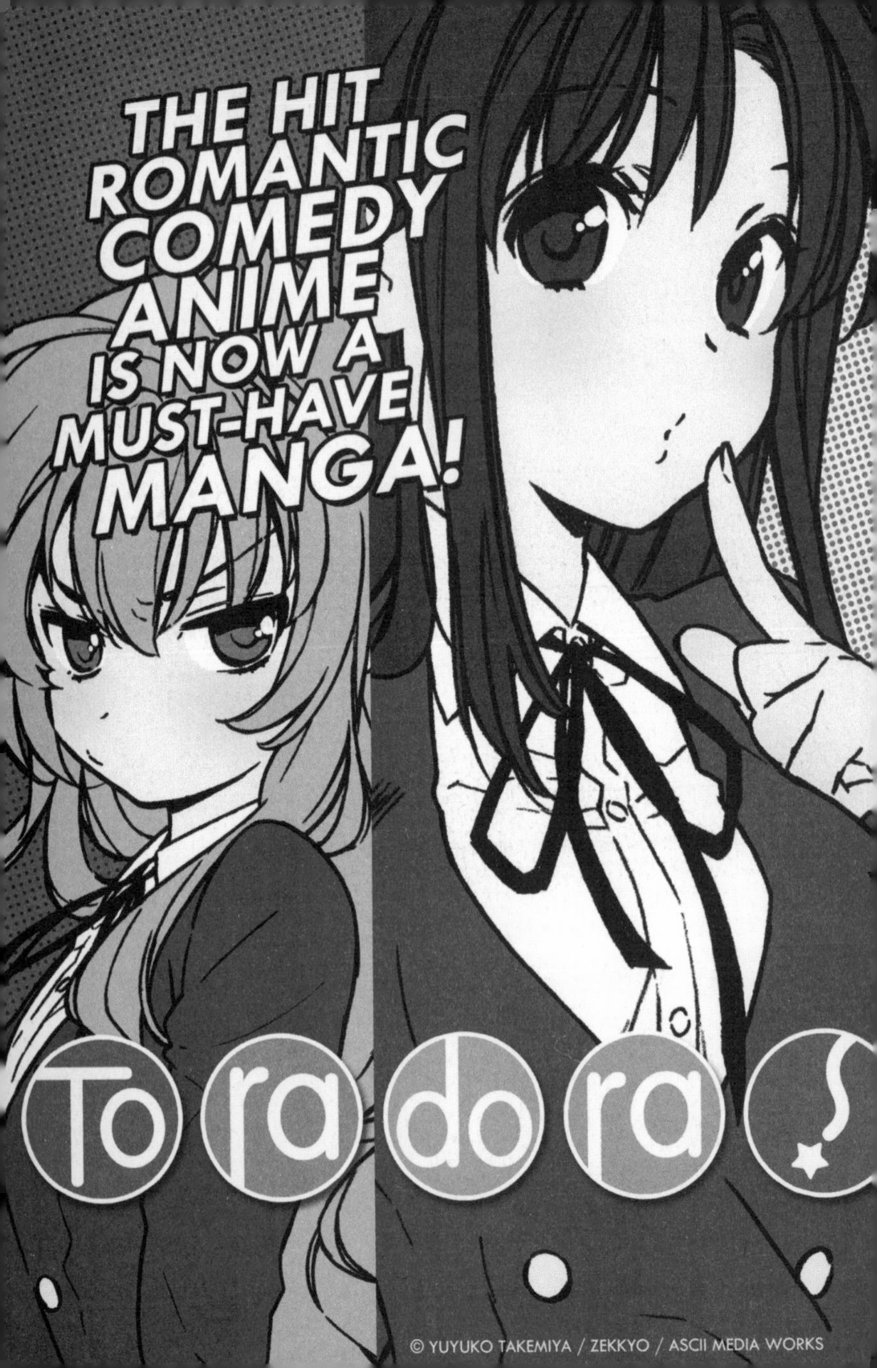
THE HIT ROMANTIC COMEDY ANIME IS NOW A MUST-HAVE MANGA!
Toradora!
© YUYUKO TAKEMIYA / ZEKKYO / ASCII MEDIA WORKS

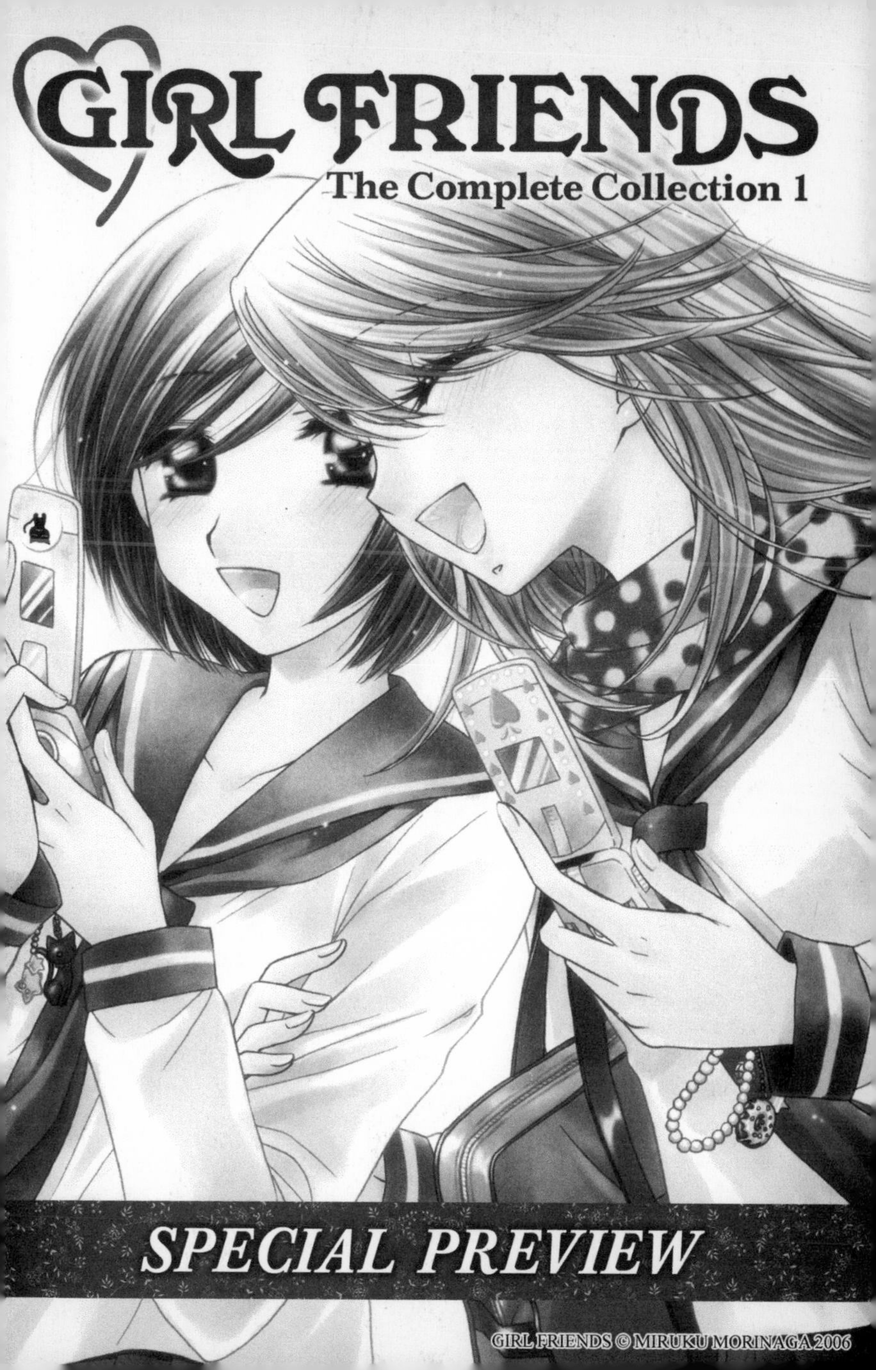
GIRL FRIENDS
The Complete Collection 1
SPECIAL PREVIEW

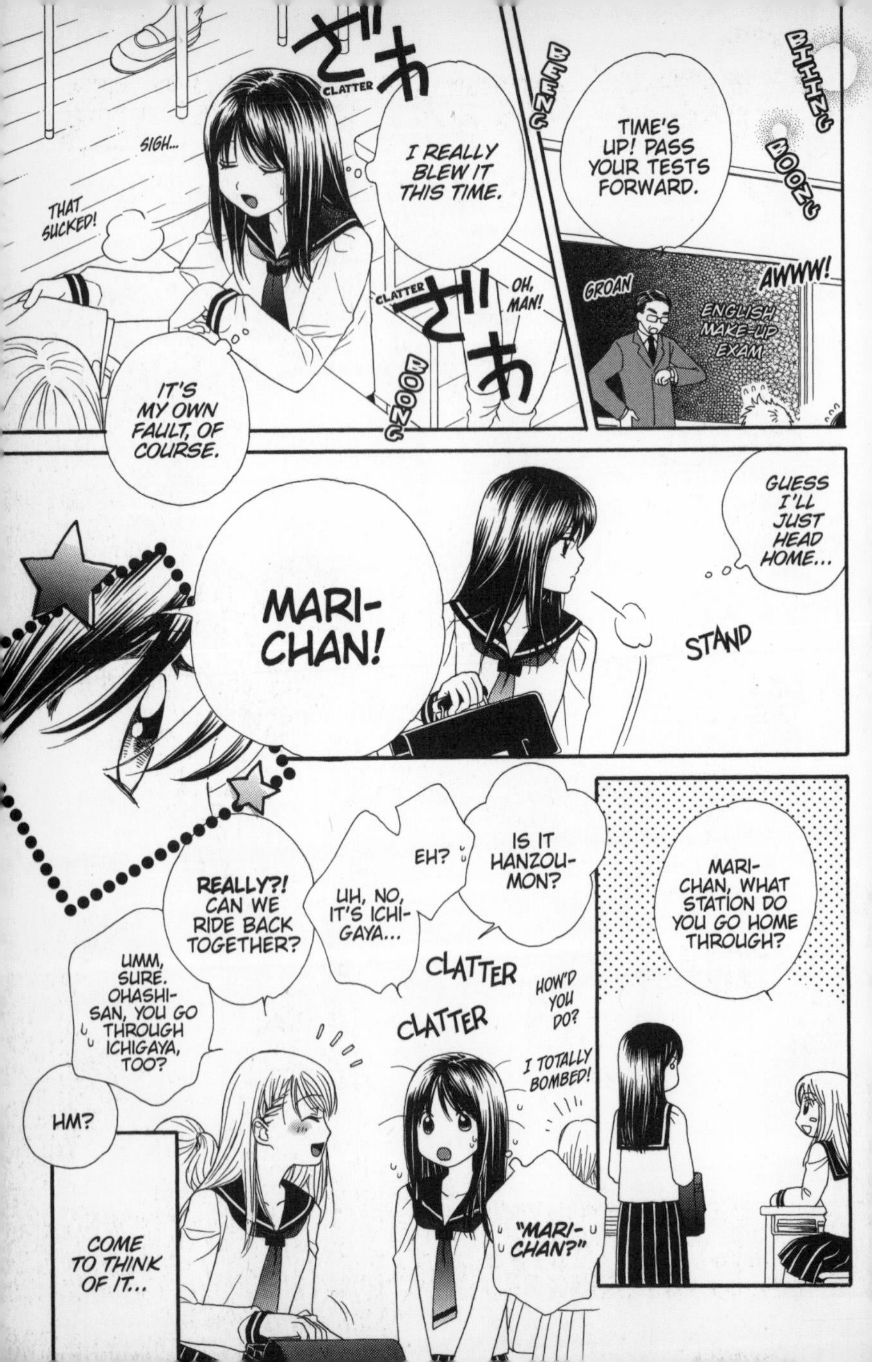
BIIING
BOONG
TIME'S UP! PASS YOUR TESTS FORWARD.
BEEENG
AWWW!
GROAN
ENGLISH MAKE-UP EXAM
ざわ
CLATTER
I REALLY BLEW IT THIS TIME.
OH, MAN!
CLATTER
ざわ
BOONG
SIGH...
THAT SUCKED!
IT'S MY OWN FAULT, OF COURSE.
GUESS I'LL JUST HEAD HOME...
STAND
MARI-CHAN!
MARI-CHAN, WHAT STATION DO YOU GO HOME THROUGH?
IS IT HANZOU-MON?
EH?
UH, NO, IT'S ICHI-GAYA...
REALLY?! CAN WE RIDE BACK TOGETHER?
CLATTER
CLATTER
HOW'D YOU DO?
I TOTALLY BOMBED!
UMM, SURE. OHASHI-SAN, YOU GO THROUGH ICHIGAYA, TOO?
HM?
"MARI-CHAN?"
COME TO THINK OF IT...

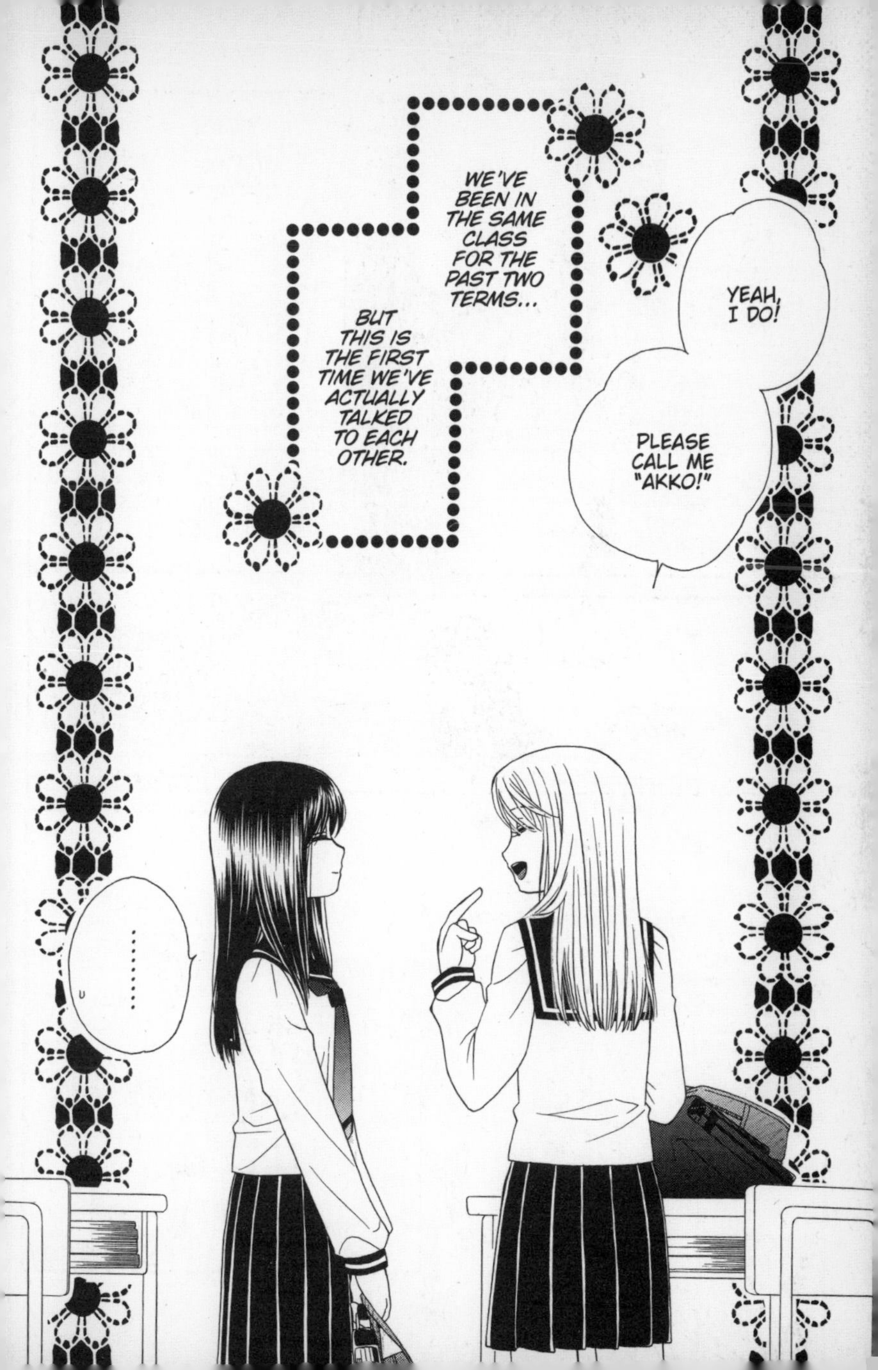
YEAH, I DO!
PLEASE CALL ME "AKKO!"
WE'VE BEEN IN THE SAME CLASS FOR THE PAST TWO TERMS...
BUT THIS IS THE FIRST TIME WE'VE ACTUALLY TALKED TO EACH OTHER.
......

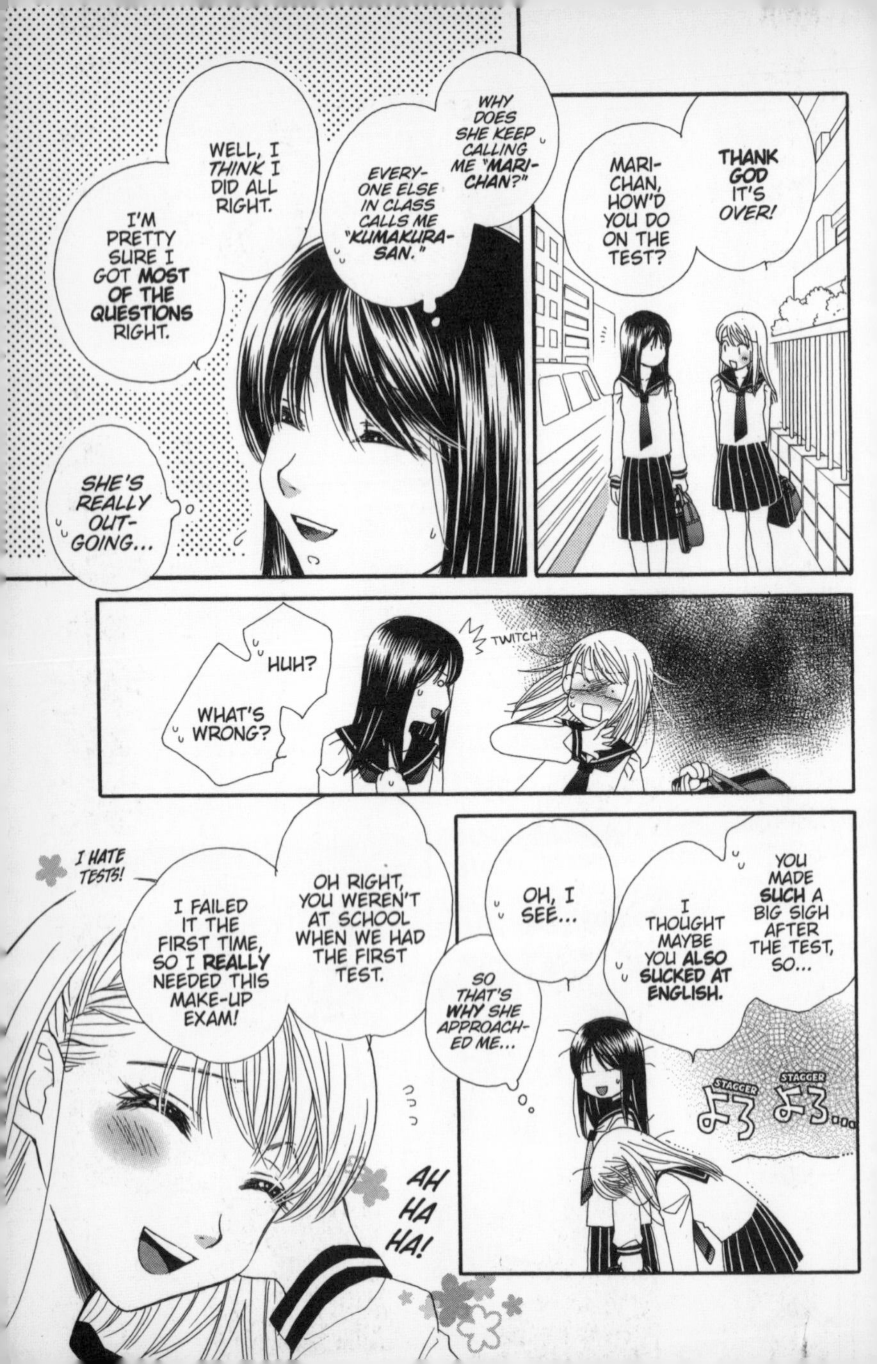
THANK GOD IT'S OVER!
MARI-CHAN, HOW'D YOU DO ON THE TEST?
WHY DOES SHE KEEP CALLING ME "MARI-CHAN?"
EVERY-ONE ELSE IN CLASS CALLS ME "KUMAKURA-SAN."
WELL, I THINK I DID ALL RIGHT.
I'M PRETTY SURE I GOT MOST OF THE QUESTIONS RIGHT.
SHE'S REALLY OUT-GOING...
TWITCH
HUH?
WHAT'S WRONG?
YOU MADE SUCH A BIG SIGH AFTER THE TEST, SO...
I THOUGHT MAYBE YOU ALSO SUCKED AT ENGLISH.
STAGGER よろ
STAGGER よろ...
OH, I SEE...
SO THAT'S WHY SHE APPROACH-ED ME...
OH RIGHT, YOU WEREN'T AT SCHOOL WHEN WE HAD THE FIRST TEST.
I FAILED IT THE FIRST TIME, SO I REALLY NEEDED THIS MAKE-UP EXAM!
I HATE TESTS!
AH HA HA!

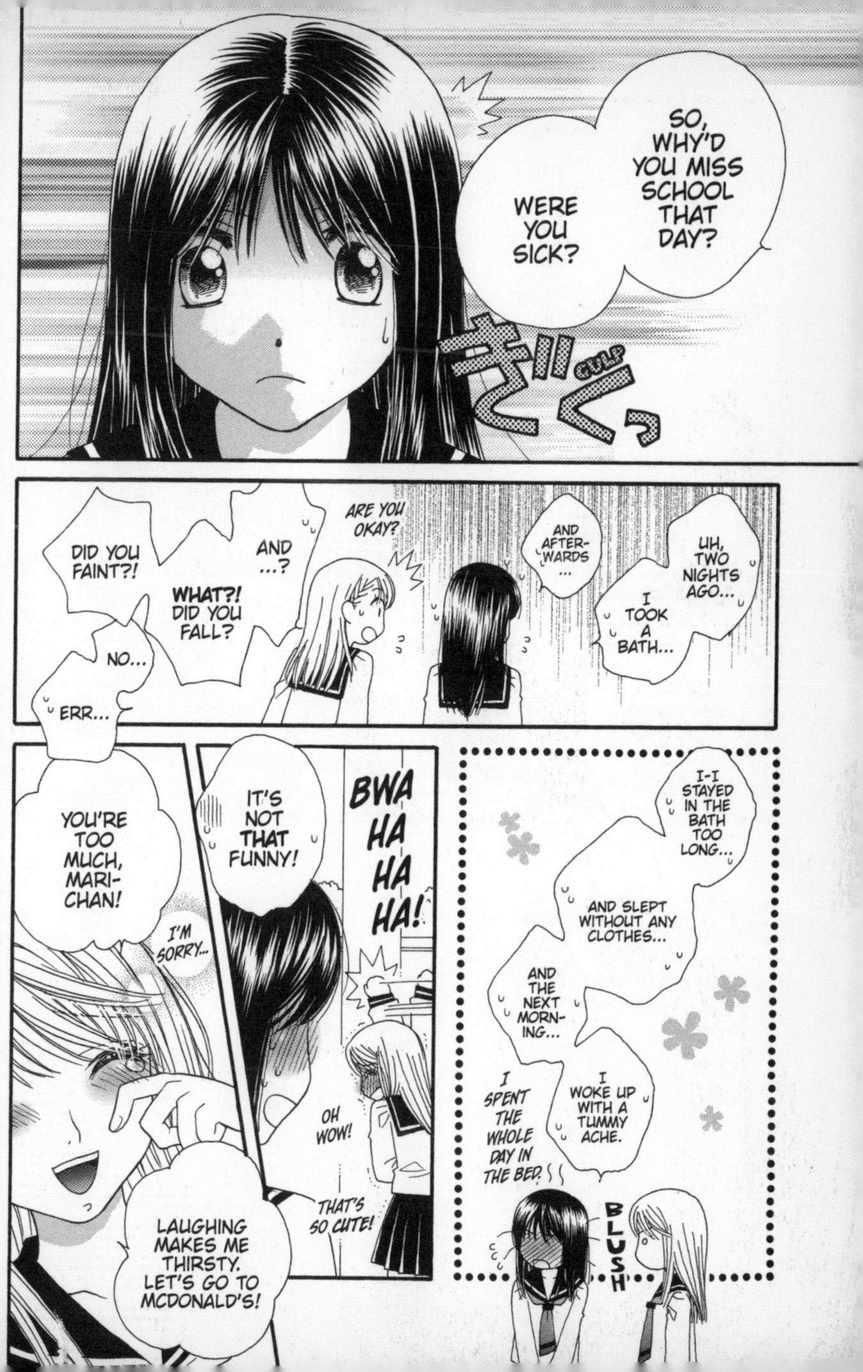
SO, WHY'D YOU MISS SCHOOL THAT DAY?
WERE YOU SICK?
ぎくっ GULP
UH, TWO NIGHTS AGO... I TOOK A BATH...
AND AFTERWARDS...
ARE YOU OKAY?
WHAT?! DID YOU FALL?
AND ...?
DID YOU FAINT?!
NO...
ERR...
I-I STAYED IN THE BATH TOO LONG...
AND SLEPT WITHOUT ANY CLOTHES...
AND THE NEXT MORNING...
I WOKE UP WITH A TUMMY ACHE.
I SPENT THE WHOLE DAY IN THE BED.
BLUSH
BWA HA HA HA!
IT'S NOT THAT FUNNY!
OH WOW!
THAT'S SO CUTE!
YOU'RE TOO MUCH, MARI-CHAN!
I'M SORRY...
LAUGHING MAKES ME THIRSTY. LET'S GO TO MCDONALD'S!

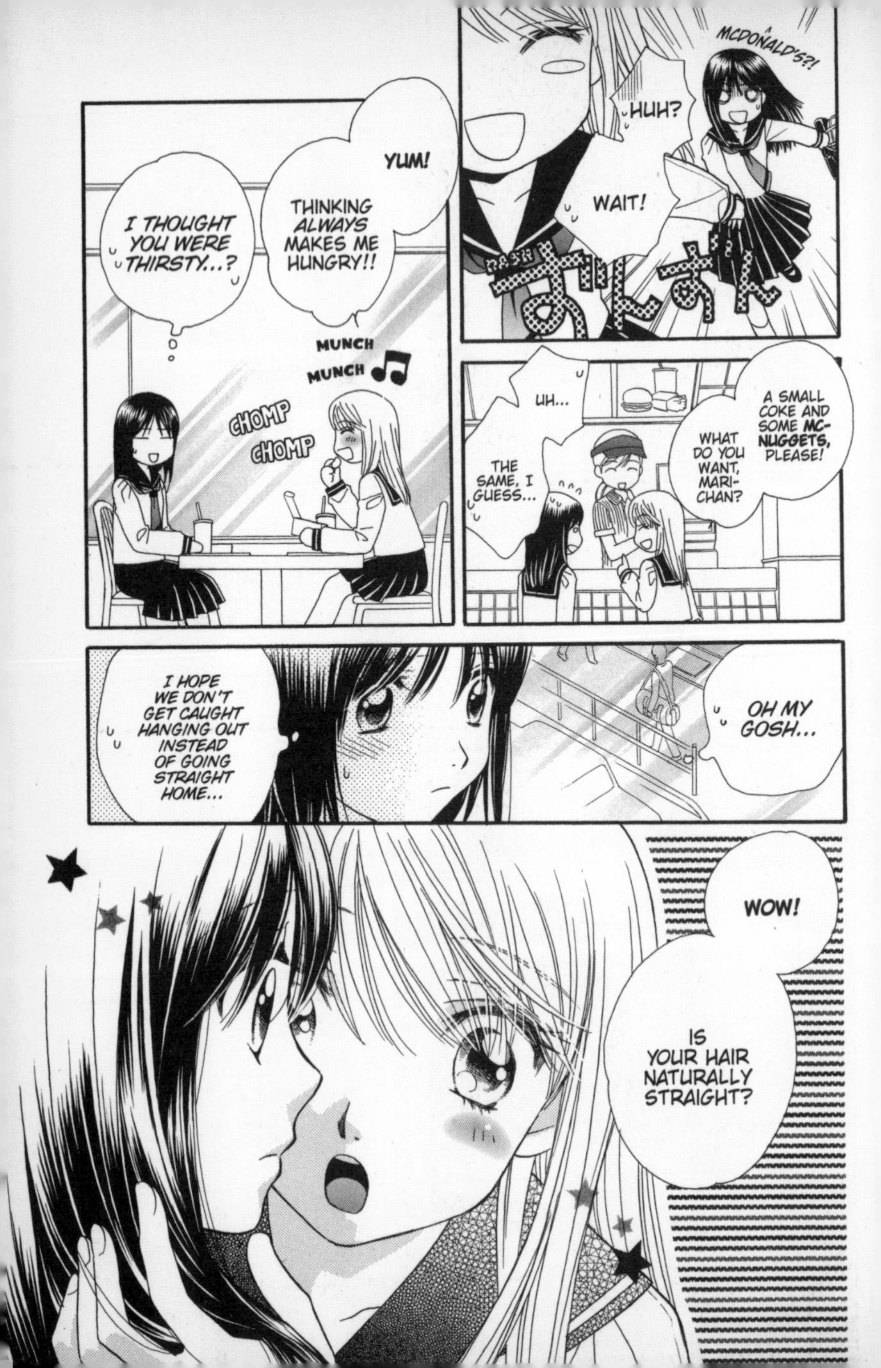
MCDONALD'S?!
HUH?
WAIT!
DASH
A SMALL COKE AND SOME MC-NUGGETS, PLEASE!
WHAT DO YOU WANT, MARI-CHAN?
UH...
THE SAME, I GUESS...
YUM!
THINKING ALWAYS MAKES ME HUNGRY!!
I THOUGHT YOU WERE THIRSTY...?
MUNCH MUNCH ♫
CHOMP CHOMP
OH MY GOSH...
I HOPE WE DON'T GET CAUGHT HANGING OUT INSTEAD OF GOING STRAIGHT HOME...
WOW!
IS YOUR HAIR NATURALLY STRAIGHT?

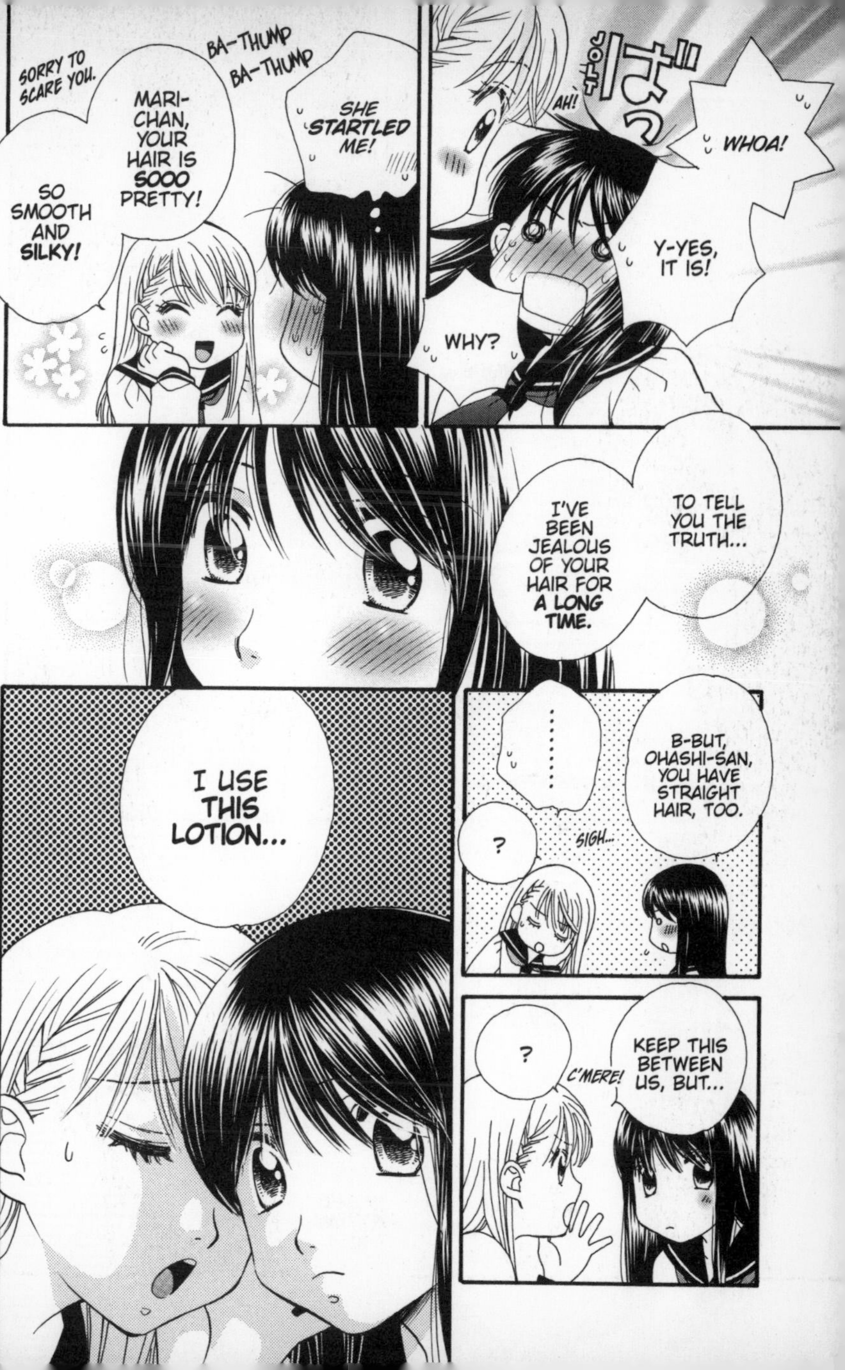
WHOA!
ぱっ
AH!
Y-YES, IT IS!
WHY?
SHE STARTLED ME!
BA-THUMP BA-THUMP
MARI-CHAN, YOUR HAIR IS SOOO PRETTY!
SORRY TO SCARE YOU.
SO SMOOTH AND SILKY!
TO TELL YOU THE TRUTH...
I'VE BEEN JEALOUS OF YOUR HAIR FOR A LONG TIME.
B-BUT, OHASHI-SAN, YOU HAVE STRAIGHT HAIR, TOO.
......
SIGH...
?
KEEP THIS BETWEEN US, BUT...
C'MERE!
?
I USE THIS LOTION...

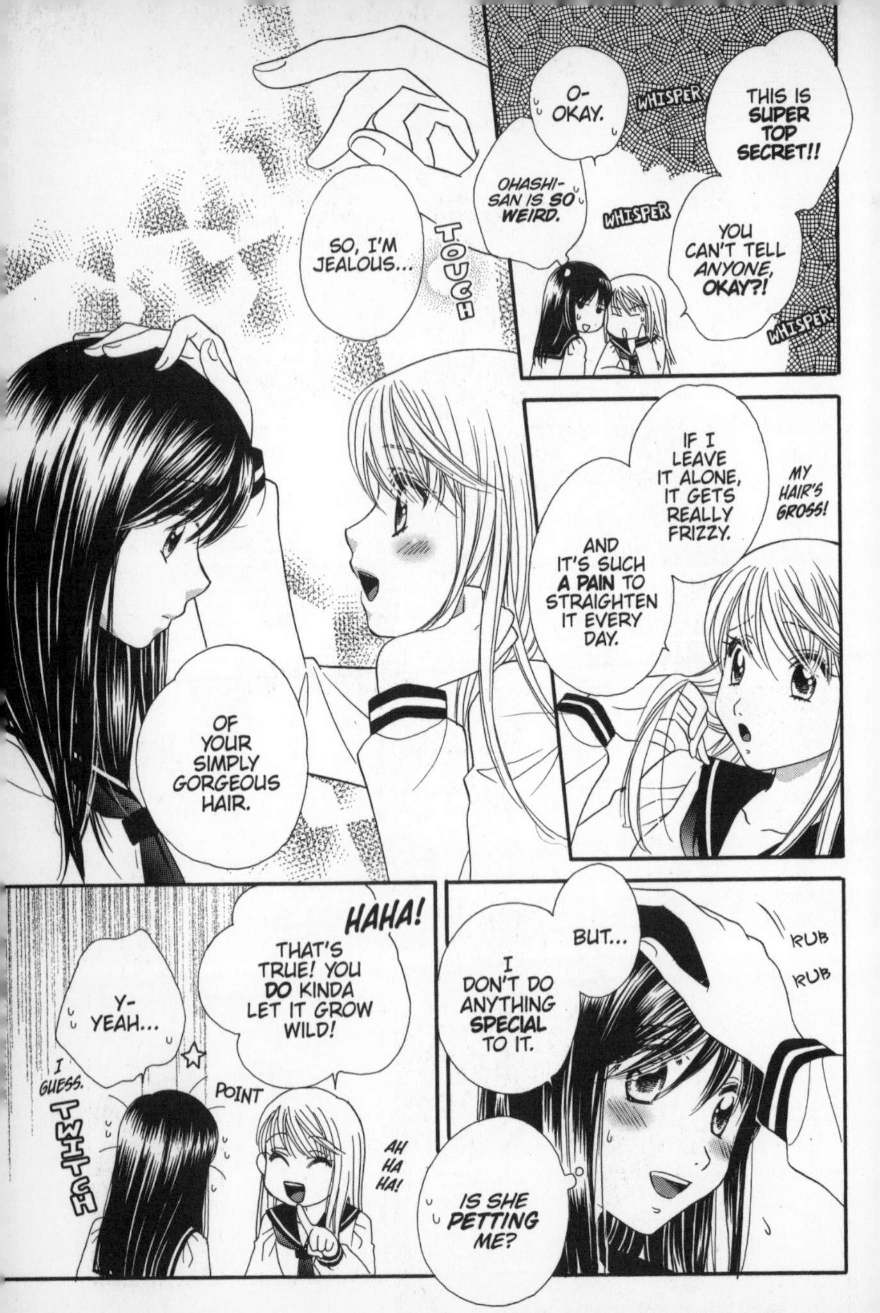
THIS IS SUPER TOP SECRET!!
WHISPER
O-OKAY.
YOU CAN'T TELL ANYONE, OKAY?!
WHISPER
OHASHI-SAN IS SO WEIRD.
WHISPER
MY HAIR'S GROSS!
IF I LEAVE IT ALONE, IT GETS REALLY FRIZZY.
AND IT'S SUCH A PAIN TO STRAIGHTEN IT EVERY DAY.
TOUCH
SO, I'M JEALOUS...
OF YOUR SIMPLY GORGEOUS HAIR.
RUB RUB
BUT...
I DON'T DO ANYTHING SPECIAL TO IT.
IS SHE PETTING ME?
HAHA!
THAT'S TRUE! YOU DO KINDA LET IT GROW WILD!
Y-YEAH...
POINT
AH HA HA!
I GUESS.
TWITCH

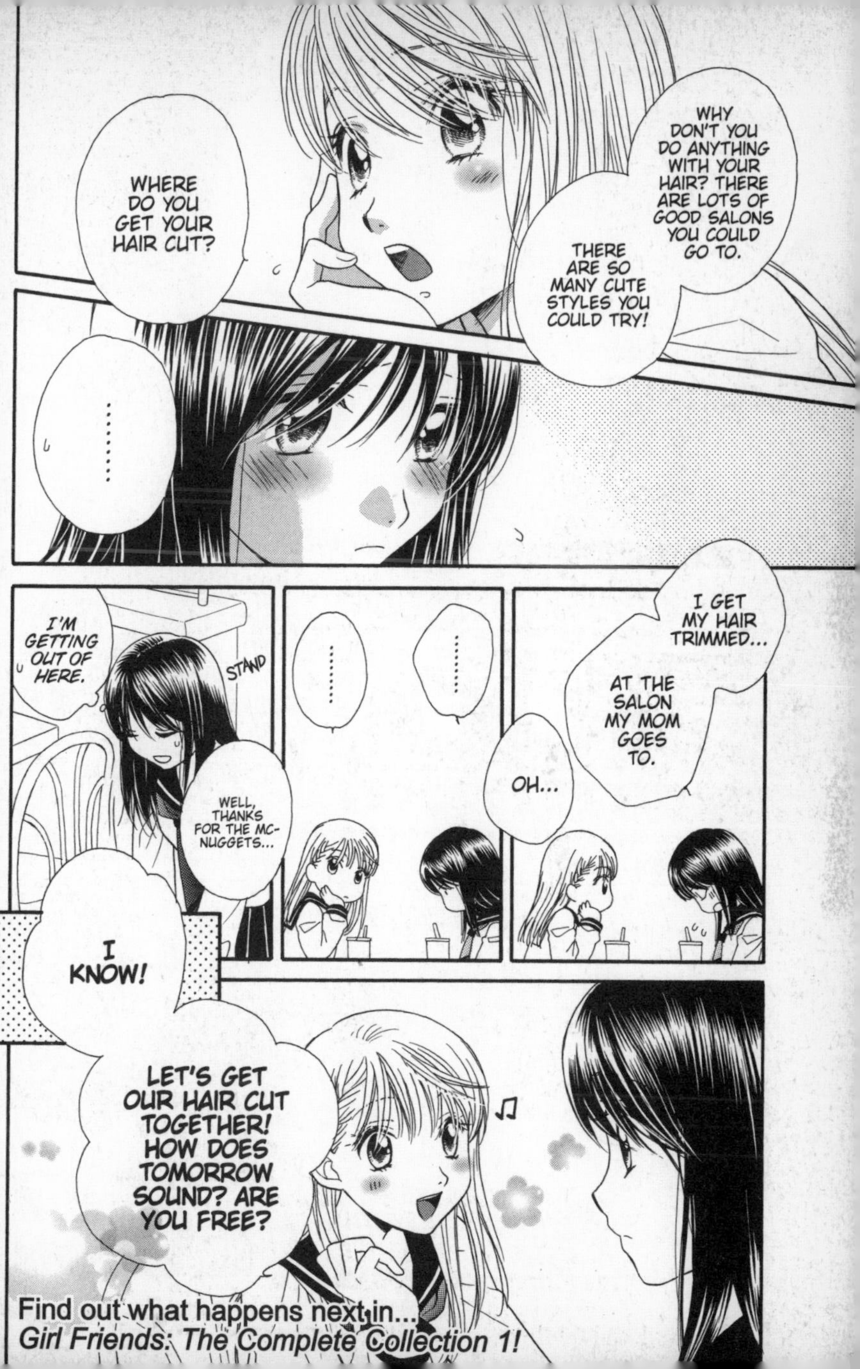
WHY DON'T YOU DO ANYTHING WITH YOUR HAIR? THERE ARE LOTS OF GOOD SALONS YOU COULD GO TO.
THERE ARE SO MANY CUTE STYLES YOU COULD TRY!
WHERE DO YOU GET YOUR HAIR CUT?
......
I GET MY HAIR TRIMMED...
AT THE SALON MY MOM GOES TO.
OH...
......
......
I'M GETTING OUT OF HERE.
STAND
WELL, THANKS FOR THE MC-NUGGETS...
I KNOW!
LET'S GET OUR HAIR CUT TOGETHER! HOW DOES TOMORROW SOUND? ARE YOU FREE?
♫

Find out what happens next in...
Girl Friends: The Complete Collection 1!

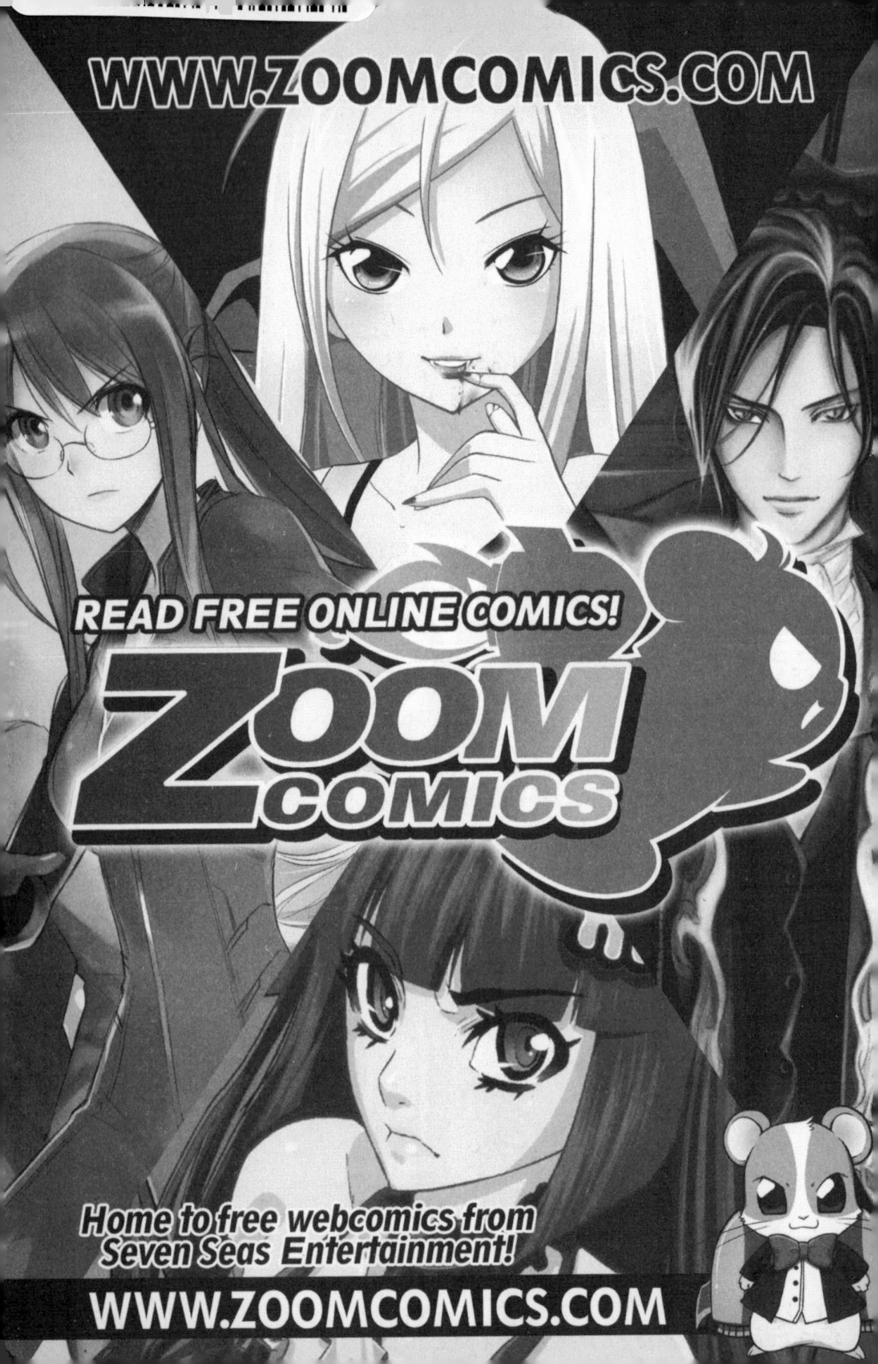
WWW.ZOOMCOMICS.COM
READ FREE ONLINE COMICS!
ZOOM COMICS
Home to free webcomics from
Seven Seas Entertainment!
WWW.ZOOMCOMICS.COM